H. IGOR ANSOFF

Critical Evaluations in Business and Management

Series editors: John C. Wood, Edith Cowan University, Australia and Michael C. Wood, Curtin University, Australia

Henri Fayol
Edited with a new introduction by John C. Wood and Michael C. Wood
2 Volume Set

F W Taylor
Edited with a new introduction by John C. Wood and Michael C. Wood
4 Volume Set

Henry Ford
Edited with a new introduction by John C. Wood and Michael C. Wood
2 Volume Set

Frank and Lillian Gilbreth
Edited with a new introduction by John C. Wood and Michael C. Wood
2 Volume Set

George Elton Mayo
Edited with a new introduction by John C. Wood and Michael C. Wood
2 Volume Set

Alfred P. Sloan
Edited with a new introduction by John C. Wood and Michael C. Wood
2 Volume Set

W. E. Deming
Edited with a new introduction by John C. Wood and Michael C. Wood
2 Volume Set

Peter F Drucker
Edited with a new introduction by John C. Wood and Michael C. Wood
1 Volume Set

Herbert A. Suma
Edited with a new introduction by John C. Wood and Michael C. Wood
3 Volume Set

Forthcoming titles in this series:

Alfred D Chandler
Edited with a new introduction by John C. Wood and Michael C. Wood
2 Volume Set

Chris Argyris
Edited with a new introduction by John C. Wood and Michael C. Wood
2 Volume Set

Henry Mintzberg
Edited with a new introduction by John C. Wood and Michael C. Wood
2 Volume Set

Tom Peters
Edited with a new introduction by John C. Wood and Michael C. Wood
2 Volume Set

Michael Porter
Edited with a new introduction by John C. Wood and Michael C. Wood
2 Volume Set

Philip Kotler
Edited with a new introduction by John C. Wood and Michael C. Wood
2 Volume Set

Rosabeth Moss Kanter
Edited with a new introduction by John C. Wood Michael C. Wood
2 Volume Set

H. IGOR ANSOFF

Critical Evaluations in Business and Management

Edited by John C. Wood and Michael C. Wood

Volume I

Routledge
Taylor & Francis Group

LONDON AND NEW YORK

First published 2007
by Routledge
2 Park Square, Milton Park, Abingdon, Oxon, OX14 4RN, UK

Simultaneously published in the USA and Canada
by Routledge
270 Madison Avenue, New York, NY 10016

Routledge is an imprint of the Taylor & Francis Group, an informa business

Typeset in 10/12pt Times by Graphicraft Limited, Hong Kong
Printed and bound in Great Britain by
MPG Books Ltd., Bodmin, Cornwall

British Library Cataloguing in Publication Data
A catalogue record for this book is available from the British Library

Library of Congress Cataloging in Publication Data
A catalog record for this book has been requested

ISBN10: 0-415-32557-9 (Set)
ISBN10: 0-415-32558-7 (Volume I)

ISBN13: 978-0-415-32557-8 (Set)
ISBN13: 978-0-415-32558-5 (Volume I)

Publisher's Note
References within each chapter are as they appear in the original complete work.

CONTENTS

CONTENTS

CONTENTS

CONTENTS

CONTENTS

CONTENTS

ACKNOWLEDGEMENTS

The editors would like to thank Dr Roberta Cowan for her indefatigable research on this and each set in this series and the editorial staff production staff and staff at Routledge who helped the volume into publication.

The editors and Dr Cowan would like to acknowledge the work of Dr Kim Benjamin and Document Delivery, Robertson Library, Curtin University of Technology for assistance with the project. Dr Cowan would like to thank the science librarians, Brown University; Mr Wim Van Hoof, Kluwer Publishing; Mr Simon Whitehouse, PE Consulting Group and Dr Rick Ansoff for assistance with tracing the publications of Igor Ansoff.

The Publishers would like to thank the following for permission to reprint their material:

Emerald Group Publishing Limited for permission to reprint Peters, J. (1993) 'On gurus. (influential theorists in the strategic management field)', *Management Decision*, 31, 6: 9–10.

The San Diego Union Tribune for permission to reprint Williams, J. (2002) 'H. Igor Ansoff, 83; educator drew worldwide acclaim', *The San Diego Union Tribune* (July 16): 16.

MIT *Sloan Management Review* for permission to reprint Mintzberg, H. and Lampel, J. (1999) 'Reflecting on the strategy process', *Sloan Management Review*, Spr: 21–30. © by Massachusetts Institute of Technology.

Reprinted by permission, Ansoff, H. I., 'A model for diversification', *Management Science*, 4, 4: 392–414 (1958) © the Institute for Operations Research and the Management Sciences (INFORMS), 7240 Parkway Drive, Suite 310, Hanover, MD 21076, USA.

Reprinted by permission, Ansoff, H. I. and Brandenberg, R. C., 'A program of research in business planning', *Management Science*, 13, 6, series B, Managerial: B219–B239 (1967) © the Institute for Operations Research and the Management Sciences (INFORMS), 7240 Parkway Drive, Suite 310, Hanover, MD 21076, USA.

Reprinted by permission, Forrester, J. W., 'Industrial dynamics – a response to Ansoff and Slevin', *Management Science*, 14, 9: 601–618 (1968) © the Institute for Operations Research and the Management Sciences (INFORMS), 7240 Parkway Drive, Suite 310, Hanover, MD 21076, USA.

Reprinted by permission, Ansoff, H. I. and Brandenberg, R. C., 'A language for organization design: part I', *Management Science*, 17, 12, Application Series: B705–B716. (1971) © the Institute for Operations Research and the Management Sciences (INFORMS), 7240 Parkway Drive, Suite 310, Hanover, MD 21076, USA.

Reprinted by permission, Ansoff, H. I. and Brandenberg, R. C., 'A language for organization design: part II', *Management Science*, 17, 12, Application Series: B717–B731 (1971) © the Institute for Operations Research and the Management Sciences (INFORMS), 7240 Parkway Drive, Suite 310, Hanover, MD 21076, USA.

Reprinted by permission, Brooker, W. M. A., 'On concepts of organizational language', *Management Science*, 19, 4, Application Series, part 1: 464–466 (1972) © the Institute for Operations Research and the Management Sciences (INFORMS), 7240 Parkway Drive, Suite 310, Hanover, MD 21076, USA.

California Management Review for permission to reprint Ansoff, I. H. (1975) 'Managing strategic surprise by response to weak signals', *California Management Review*, 18, 2: 21–33. © 1975, The Regents of the University of California.

Emerald Group Publishing Limited for permission to reprint Watts, G., Cope, J. and Hulme, M. (1998) 'Ansoff's Matrix, pain and again: Growth strategies and adaptive learning among small food producers', *International Journal of Entrepreneurial Behaviour & Research*, 4, 2: 101–111.

Elsevier for permission to reprint Nikander, I. O. and Eloranta, E. (2001) 'Project management by early warnings', *International Journal of Project Management*, 19, 7: 385–399.

John Wiley & Sons, Ltd for permission to reprint Mintzberg, H. (1990) 'The design school: reconsidering the basic premises of strategic management', *Strategic Management Journal*, 11, 3: 171–195. Reproduced by permission of John Wiley & Sons Limited.

John Wiley & Sons, Ltd for permission to reprint, Ansoff, H. I. (1991) 'Critique of Henry Mintzberg's "The design school: reconsidering the basic premises of strategic management"', *Strategic Management Journal*, 12, 6: 449–461. Reproduced by permission of John Wiley & Sons Limited.

John Wiley & Sons, Ltd for permission to reprint Mintzberg, H. (1991) 'Learning 1, planning 0: reply to Igor Ansoff', *Strategic Management*

Journal, 12, 6: 463–466. Reproduced by permission of John Wiley & Sons Limited.

American Society for Quality for permission to reprint Osburn, T. P. and Klimaszewski, D. L. (2005) 'The future of quality in Indianapolis', *Quality Progress*, 38, 10: 39–44.

John Wiley & Sons, Ltd for permission to reprint Yip, G. S. (1982) 'Diversification entry: internal development versus acquisition', *Strategic Management Journal*, 3, 4: 331–345. Reproduced by permission of John Wiley & Sons Limited.

John Wiley & Sons, Ltd for permission to reprint Rumelt, R. P., Schendel, D. and Teece, D. J. (1991) 'Strategic management and economics', *Strategic Management Journal*, 12, Special Issue: Fundamental Research Issues in Strategy and Economics: 5–29. Reproduced by permission of John Wiley & Sons Limited.

John Wiley & Sons, Ltd for permission to reprint Porter, M. E. (1991) 'Towards a dynamic theory of strategy', *Strategic Management Journal*, 12, Special Issue: Fundamental Research Issues in Strategy and Economics: 95–117. Reproduced by permission of John Wiley & Sons Limited.

Harvard Business School Publications for permission to reprint Porter, M. (1996) 'What is strategy?' *Harvard Business Review*, 74, 6: 61–78.

Disclaimer

The publishers have made every effort to contact authors/copyright holders of works reprinted in *H. Igor Ansoff: Critical Evaluations*. This has not been possible in every case, however, and we would welcome correspondence from those individuals/companies whom we have been unable to trace.

Chronological table of reprinted articles and chapters

Date	Author	Title	Source	Vol.	Chap.
1958	H. I. Ansoff	A model for diversification	*Management Science* 4(4): 392–414	I	4
1967	Russell L. Ackoff	Management misinformation systems	*Management Science* 14(4): B147–B156	II	37
1967	H. Igor Ansoff and Richard C. Brandenburg	A program of research in business planning	*Management Science* 13(6), series B, Managerial: B219–B239	I	5
1968	Jay W. Forrester	Industrial dynamics – a response to Ansoff and Slevin	*Management Science* 14(9): 601–18	I	6
1971	H. I. Ansoff and R. G. Brandenburg	A language for organization design: part I	*Management Science* 17(12), Application series: B705–B716	I	7
1971	H. I. Ansoff and R. G. Brandenburg	A language for organization design: part II	*Management Science* 17(12), Application series: B717–B731	I	8
1971	Henry Mintzberg	Managerial work: analysis from observation	*Management Science* 18(2), Application series: B79–B110	II	23
1972	W. M. A. Brooker	On concepts of organizational language	*Management Science* 19(4), Application series, part I: 464–6	I	9
1973	H. Igor Ansoff	Management in transition	T. C. Board (ed.) *Challenge to Leadership: Managing in a Changing World*, New York: The Free Press, pp. 22–63	I	10
1975	H. Igor Ansoff	Managing strategic surprise by response to weak signals	*California Management Review* 18(2): 21–33	I	11
1978	Henry Mintzberg	Patterns in strategy formation	*Management Science* 24(9): 934–48	II	24
1980	J. G. Wissema, H. W. van der Pol and H. M. Messer	Strategic management archetypes	*Strategic Management Journal* 1(1): 37–47	II	33
1981	H. Kurt Christensen and Cynthia A. Montgomery	Corporate economic performance: diversification strategy versus market structure	*Strategic Management Journal* 2(4): 327–43	II	39

Chronological Table continued

Date	Author	Title	Source	Vol.	Chap.
1981	Liam Fahey	On strategic management decision processes	*Strategic Management Journal* 2(1): 43–60	II	40
1982	Francisco J. Arcelus and Norbert V. Schaefer	Social demands as strategic issues: some conceptual problems	*Strategic Management Journal* 3(4): 347–57	II	50
1982	V. K. Narayanan and Liam Fahey	The micro-politics of strategy formulation	*Academy of Management Review* 7(1): 25–34	II	31
1982	George S. Yip	Diversification entry: internal development versus acquisition	*Strategic Management Journal* 3(4): 331–45	I	19
1985	Ellen Earle Chaffee	Three models of strategy	*Academy of Management Review* 10(1): 89–98	II	35
1985	Paul Miesing and Joseph Wolfe	The art and science of planning at the business unit level	*Management Science* 31(6): 773–81	II	28
1986	Richard Reed and George A. Luffman	Diversification: the growing confusion	*Strategic Management Journal* 7(1): 29–35	II	51
1987	Jane E. Dutton and Robert B. Duncan	The creation of momentum for change through the process of strategic issue diagnosis	*Strategic Management Journal* 8(3): 279–95	II	32
1987	David B. Jemison	Risk and the relationship among strategy, organizational processes, and performance	*Management Science* 33(9): 1087–101	II	41
1987	Henry Mintzberg	Crafting strategy	*Harvard Business Review* 65(4): 66–75	II	25
1987	Eli Segev	Strategy, strategy making, and performance – an empirical investigation	*Management Science* 33(2): 258–69	II	42
1988	Ari Ginsberg	Measuring and modelling changes in strategy: theoretical foundations and empirical directions	*Strategic Management Journal* 9(6): 559–75	II	52
1989	Gary Hamel and C. K. Prahalad	Strategic intent	*Harvard Business Review* 67(3): 63–76	II	43
1989	Carl Shapiro	The theory of business strategy	*RAND Journal of Economics* 20(1): 125–37	II	36
1990	Edward H. Bowman	Strategy changes: possible worlds and actual minds	J. W. Frederickson (ed.) *Perspectives on Strategic Management*, New York: Harper Business, pp. 9–37	II	47

Chronological Table continued

Date	Author	Title	Source	Vol.	Chap.
1990	Donald C. Hambrick	The adolescence of strategic management, 1980–1985: critical perceptions and reality	J. W. Frederickson (ed.) *Perspectives on Strategic Management*, New York: Harper Business, pp. 237–53	II	48
1990	Henry Mintzberg	The design school: reconsidering the basic premises of strategic management	*Strategic Management Journal* 11(3): 171–95	I	15
1991	H. Igor Ansoff	Critique of Henry Mintzberg's 'The design school: reconsidering the basic premises of strategic management'	*Strategic Management Journal* 12(6): 449–61	I	16
1991	John C. Camillus and Deepak K. Datta	Managing strategic issues in a turbulent environment	*Long Range Planning* 24(2): 67–74	II	29
1991	Henry Mintzberg	Learning 1, planning 0: reply to Igor Ansoff	*Strategic Management Journal* 12(6): 463–6	I	17
1991	Michael E. Porter	Towards a dynamic theory of strategy	*Strategic Management Journal* 12, Special Issue: Fundamental Research Issues in Strategy and Economics: 95–117	I	21
1991	Richard P. Rumelt, Dan Schendel and David J. Teece	Strategic management and economics	*Strategic Management Journal* 12, Special Issue: Fundamental Research Issues in Strategy and Economics: 5–29	I	20
1992	Michael Goold	Design, learning and planning: a further observation on the design school debate	*Strategic Management Journal* 13(2): 169–70	II	44
1992	J. I. Moore	H. Igor Ansoff	J. I. Moore, *Writers on Strategy and Strategic Management: the Theory of Strategy and the Practice of Strategic Management at Enterprise, Corporate, Business and Functional Levels*, Harmondsworth: Penguin, pp. 15–33	I	12
1992	George Stalk, Philip Evans and Lawrence E. Shulman	Competing on capabilities: the new rules of corporate strategy	*Harvard Business Review* 70(2): 57–69	II	45
1993	Henry Mintzberg	Twenty-five years later . . . the illusive strategy	A. G. Bedeian (ed.) *Management Laureates: Collection of Autobiographical Essays*, Stamford, Conn.: JAI Press, vol. 2, pp. 323–74	II	26

Chronological Table continued

Date	Author	Title	Source	Vol.	Chap.
1993	John Peters	On gurus	*Management Decision* 31(6): 9–10	I	1
1994	Henry Mintzberg	The fall and rise of strategic planning	*Harvard Business Review* 72(1): 107–14	II	27
1994	Alan E. Singer	Strategy as moral philosophy	*Strategic Management Journal* 15(3): 191–213	II	53
1996	William P. Barnett and Robert A. Burgelman	Evolutionary perspectives on strategy	*Strategic Management Journal* 17: 5–19	II	30
1996	Gary Hamel	Strategy as revolution	*Harvard Business Review* 74(4): 69–82	II	54
1996	Henry Mintzberg	Musings on management	*Harvard Business Review* 74(4): 61–7	II	55
1996	Sonny Nwankwo and Bill Richardson	Quality management through visionary leadership	*Managing Service Quality* 6(4): 44–7	II	46
1996	Michael E. Porter	What is strategy?	*Harvard Business Review* 74(6): 61–78	I	22
1998	Gerald Watts, Jason Cope and Michael Hulme	Ansoff's matrix, pain and gain: growth strategies and adaptive learning among small food producers	*International Journal of Entrepreneurial Behaviour & Research* 4(2): 101–11	I	13
1999	Henry Mintzberg and Joseph Lampel	Reflecting on the strategy process	*Sloan Management Review*, Spring: 21–30	I	3
1999	Peter J. Williamson	Strategy as options on the future	*Sloan Management Review*, Spring: 117–26	II	34
2001	Bruce E. Kaufman	The theory and practice of strategic HRM and participative management: antecedents in early industrial relations	*Human Resource Management Review* 11(4): 505–33	II	49
2001	Ilmari O. Nikander and Eero Eloranta	Project management by early warnings	*International Journal of Project Management* 19(7): 385–99	I	14
2002	Jack Williams	H. Igor Ansoff, 83; educator drew worldwide acclaim	*The San Diego Union Tribune*, July 16: 16	I	2
2004	Peter H. Antoniou and H. Igor Ansoff	Strategic management of technology	*Technology Analysis & Strategic Management* 16(2): 275–91	II	38
2005	Raymond Caldwell	Things fall apart? Discourses on agency and change in organizations	*Human Relations* 58(1): 83–114	II	56
2005	Terence P. Osburn and Deborah L. Klimaszewski	The future of quality in Indianapolis	*Quality Progress* 38(10): 39–44	I	18

INTRODUCTION

John C. Wood, IBT Education Ltd, Churchlords,
Western Australia and
Michael C. Wood, Curtin Business School, Curtin University
of Technology, Perth, Western Australia

Ansoff's life and times

H. Igor Ansoff was born in Vladivostock, Russia, in 1918. In 1935, at the age of 17, he moved to the United States, with very little knowledge of English. Despite this, he graduated at the top of his class at New York's elite Stuyvesant High School in 1937. Subsequently he received his master's degree in Mathematics and Physics and in general engineering at the Stephen's Institute of Technology in New Jersey, a significant educational institution at the time.

During the Second World War and into 1946 Ansoff was a member of the US Naval Reserve and served as a liaison with the Russian Navy as well as an instructor in physics at the US Naval Academy. In 1948 he joined RAND Corporation just after receiving a doctorate in applied mathematics (Ansoff 1948) from Brown University (Providence, Rhode Island). After eight years he joined Lockheed Aircraft Corporation where an early assignment was to detail a plan to enable the organisation to diversify its business. This was a relatively new idea and there were no detailed guidelines on how to undertake and achieve such a strategy. During this time Ansoff worked for Lockheed's diversification task force and developed the basis for what became his first book, *Corporate Strategy* (1965, 1968), which resulted in significant recognition (Antoniou 1998, 2000).

In 1963 Ansoff joined the Graduate School of Industrial Administration at Carnegie Mellon University (Philadelphia, Pa.) where he researched with such luminaries as Herbert Simon, Richard Cyert and Hal Leavitt. In 1969 Ansoff took up the position of Founding Dean at the Graduate School of Management, Vanderbilt University in Nashville, Tennessee. In 1973 the Management School was launched at Vanderbilt and Ansoff became the Justin Potter Professor of Free American Enterprise, a position he held until 1976. In 1973 Ansoff also accepted a joint appointment as Professor at the European Institute for Advanced Studies in Management in Brussels and at the Stockholm School of Economics. It was from these positions that he established a European network of researchers in strategic and corporate

1

management. From 1976 to 1983 he held a Professorship at the European Institute for Advanced Studies in Management.

Ansoff returned to the United States in 1983 as a Distinguished Professor at the United States International University in San Diego, California, where he remained until 2000, two years before his death in Escondido (north of San Diego) in July 2002 (Williams 2002).

Throughout his academic career he operated a private consulting firm, Ansoff Associates, and advised major companies including General Electric, IBM, Gulf Oil, General Foods and Westinghouse.

Ansoff's major works

Ansoff was a prodigious author who produced hundred of papers and ten key books, many of which were translated into the romance languages, the Slavic language groups, Russian, Finnish and the Asian language groups (Cowan 2007). Moreover, many of his works were written in cooperation with others and indicate his breadth and depth of thinking on management issues and in particular on corporate strategies.

In *Corporate Strategy* (1965, 1968) Ansoff pioneered a systematic outline for formulating a firm's future strategic activities. It was based on his work within organisations and set in the context of the economic development of the United States. His contention was that a successful organisation operated in tune with its broader environment, while at the same time fulfilling its business intentions and serving and contributing to the social and political environment. By contrast, an organisation that focused singularly on its business needs would ultimately loose direction.

Two others books, *Strategic Management* (1979, 1982) and *Implanting Strategic Management* (1984), are considered to be Ansoff's most important contributions. Indeed *Strategic Management* widened strategic planning into an interdisciplinary and multidisciplinary process by adding individual and group behaviour dynamics, organisational culture and political activities as key ingredients that determine strategic behaviour and firm success.

These works were the basis for Henry Mintzburg's comment that Ansoff was the father of strategic management' (Williams 2002). Ansoff's book, *New Corporate Strategy* (1987), argued that financial performance of the firm was maximised whenever both the strategy and management capability matched the turbulence of the firm's environment. He further proposed an approach to accommodate what he called five turbulence levels in the business environment which ranged from placid and predictable to highly changeable and unpredictable.

Ansoff had a keen sense of history and its relevance to the development of business strategies. In reviewing the American business experience he divided the years from 1820 to the late twentieth century into three periods: mass production, mass marketing and post-industrial, the last a term that he adopted from Daniel Bell (1974) in preference to Drucker's 'age of discontinuity' (1969, as quoted in Moore 1992).

Ansoff's major contributions

Unquestionably, Ansoff's most popular work, *Corporate Strategy* (1965, 1968), was also the most significant for it provided the basis of his subsequent books and numerous articles. He focused on four basic types of decision: strategy, policy, programme and standard operating procedure. To Ansoff, policy, programme and standard operating procedures all recurred (e.g. preparation for bad weather, need to organise overtime). Once these were established, there should be no requirement for decision making on the same issue, i.e. they were, as Ansoff called them, 'economics of management' and should be delegated to people throughout the organisation. Accordingly, the mathematician Ansoff was able to argue that because these activities recurred one could assign probabilities to them and group them under conditions, alternatives and probabilities. By contrast strategic decisions were quite different because they were likely to be made in conditions of minimal information far more frequently than recurring activities. Moreover, he argued that the term strategic meant relating to the firm's particular match to its own environment (Moore 1992).

In order to further analyse and understand strategy in this context, Ansoff developed a model of the business environment with five turbulence levels which ranged from placid and predictable to highly changeable and unpredictable. To match each level of turbulence he considered different behaviours which optimised the profitability of the firm (Ansoff 1979, 1982). Indeed, Ansoff was one of the first authors to argue that a firm had to balance strategic and operational issues and needed to review both internal and external environments and achieve alignment in both. In essence, a firm had to be acutely aware of its external environment as a major factor in determining strategic directions (Antoniou 1998, 2000).

Another important contribution in *Corporate Strategy* was Ansoff's distinction between objective and strategy. Essentially, he argued that an objective was an end while strategy was a means to that end (Moore 1992). More importantly, he considered that objectives and strategies acted upon each other and therefore constituted appropriate screening devices when evaluating particular strategic options. In seeking to define various components of strategy, Ansoff was both conventional and extraordinarily innovative in his thinking.

In one of his last major works, *Implanting Strategic Management* (1984), Ansoff synthesised many of his previous writings and stressed how rapidly the corporate world and its environment was changing and that unpredictability was far more acute than in previous times. Moreover, with years of observations and research, Ansoff was more aware of the difficulty of managing people within organisations. Accordingly, he redefined strategic management as a systematic approach for managing strategic change comprising three key elements – positioning the firm through strategy and capability planning; a real time strategic response through issues management; and strategic management and resistance during strategic implementation (Moore 1992).

Ansoff was always building upon his thinking. He used his model of turbulence to construct a theoretical strategic success paradigm based upon three critical variables: the turbulence level in the firm's environment; the aggressiveness of the firm's strategic behaviour in the environment; and the responsiveness of the firm's management to changes in the environment (Antoniou 1998, 2000). He realised that, since it was possible for a firm to be successful in one period and unsuccessful in another, it was vital for a firm's strategy to be aligned with the level of turbulence that it was actually experiencing. He therefore developed 'the contingent strategic success paradigm' which sought to demonstrate the link between environment, strategy and organisational capability. In 1993, Ansoff and colleagues undertook an exhaustive survey of around 1,000 strategic business units, in twelve industry sectors and eight countries (around the world) to actually validate the contingent success paradigm (Ansoff and Sullivan 1993; Antoniou 1998, 2000).

Importantly, Ansoff was always searching to ensure that his writings were relevant for business leaders and managers within organisations, and he built upon his ideas and innovations. This is evident in his later work on real-time strategic management characteristics which was based upon the contingent success paradigm and was intended to help businesses succeed within turbulent and unpredictable environments.

Ansoff considered real-time strategic management to have seven distinctive characteristics:

1   The application of the contingent strategic success paradigm to diagnose the firm's preparedness to succeed in the future.
2   Urgent attention given to ensuring that the thinking of key managers as well as the firm culture is responsive to the future turbulence level in the environment.
3   Awareness that any strategic transformation within the firm will inevitably encounter resistance to change as well as early efforts that are required to convert the resistance into organisational acceptance and support for change.
4   Realisation of the inherent unpredictability of change, particularly entering the twenty-first century, and assistance for managers in estimating the risks that surround each of their major strategic decisions.
5   A marrying of entrepreneurial strategic planning which seeks to address future success with real-time response to anticipate sudden threats and opportunities.

6 The appropriate introduction of real-time strategic control systems in the firm.
7 In turbulent environments even the most appropriately analysed strategies have a high probability of future failure (Ansoff and Sullivan 1993).

The collection and critical assessments

The collection is arranged as follows:

- Ansoff: the man
- Strategic management: schools of thought
- Strategy reflecting the organisation
- Strategy and information
- Case studies
- Strategic thinking: the past
- Strategic management: the future considered.

References

Ansoff, H. I. (1948) *The Forming of a Plastic Sheet Between Fixed Cylindrical Guides with Coulomb Friction*, Brown University: [Providence, RI].
—— (1965, 1968) *Corporate Strategy: an Analytical Approach to Business Policy for Growth and Expansion*, New York: McGraw-Hill Book Co.
—— (1979, 1982) *Strategic Management*, London: Macmillan.
—— (1984) *Implanting Strategic Management*, Englewood Cliffs, NJ: Prentice Hall Inc.
—— (1987) *New Corporate Strategy* (rev. edn), New York: Wiley.
—— and Sullivan, P. A. (1993) 'Empirical support for a paradigmatic theory of strategic success behaviours of environment-serving organizations', *International Review of Strategic Management* 4: 173–203.
Antoniou, P. H. (1998, 2000) 'Ansoff, H. Igor', in M. Warner (ed.) *The IEBM Handbook of Management Thinking*, London: International Thomson Business Press, pp. 13–17.
Bell, D. (1974) *The Coming of Post-industrial Society: a Venture in Social Forecasting*, London: Heinemann Educational.
Cowan, R. A. (2007) 'An annotated bibliography, in J. C. Wood and M. C. Wood (eds) *H. Igor Ansoff*, London: Routledge, pp. 6–26.
Drucker, P. F. (1969, 1978) *Age of Discontinuity: Guidelines to our Changing Society*, New York: Harper & Row.
Moore, J. I. (1992) *Writers on Strategy and Strategic Management: the Theory of Strategy and the Practice of Strategic Management at Enterprise, Corporate, Business and Functional Levels*, Harmondsworth: Pengiun Books.
Williams, J. (2002) 'H. Igor Ansoff, 83; educator drew worldwide acclaim', *The San Diego Union Tribune* (July 16): 16.

H. IGOR ANSOFF 1918–2002: AN ANNOTATED BIBLIOGRAPHY

Dr Roberta A. Cowan, Research Fellow, Curtin Business School, Curtin University of Technology

Two bibliographies of works of H. Igor Ansoff have appeared in print (Ansoff 1992; Hussey 1999). The latter attempted to provide additional information to some entries from the former and did not include other entries, without explanation of their omission. The items below may not represent a complete reconstruction of the literature published by Igor Ansoff since much of his work appears to have been in the form of reports and working papers. Henry Mintzberg is reported as having described Ansoff as the 'father of strategic management' (Williams 2002) and stated that 'Igor's real contribution to the literature . . . is not prescriptive but descriptive, in the concepts he provided to us' (Mintzberg 1991: 464). For these reasons it is important to record Ansoff's published works accurately.

The sources for literature are the online catalogues called WorldCat (libraries within the Online Computer Library Center Inc. (OCLC) consortium), COPAC (libraries within the academic consortium, UK), the British Library (BL), the Library of Congress (LC) and other national libraries. The search for journal articles was undertaken using the databases available at the universities in Perth, Western Australia. No non-paper media have been included in this bibliography.

Format

The bibliography is divided into four sections. The first section provides a small number of citations about Igor Ansoff. The second section provides the references which were listed in either Ansoff (1992) or Hussey (1999), listed in chronological order, grouped under topic headings that reflect the major chronological events in the autobiographical essay 'A profile of intellectual growth' (Ansoff 1992). In this section annotations have been added to most of the citations. The third section provides references that do not appear in either published bibliography. In this section are not only a number of journal articles and reports that have not been represented in either of the official bibliographies but also a number of translations of Ansoff's works. Hussey (1999: 391) indicated that Ansoff (1965) was translated into French in 1968, and Ansoff and McDonnell (1990) was translated into Korean. The author has not been able to find evidence of either of these translations in the world's library catalogues. All other translations listed in Hussey (1999) have been included in this bibliography. The fourth section is a list of references cited in the annotations to the citations. The annotations provide information regarding availability of items via the major world libraries as of 2006, journal title information where this is warranted and other information believed by the author to be important. In some citations multiple dates are given, separated by commas. This indicates the reprinting of an edition. Different editions are treated as separate citations.

1 H. Igor Ansoff

The Vanderbilt University Archives, Heard Library Annex, lists a Biographical sketch dated 1969 among the Graduate School of Management, Record Group 570 archive. The archive collection at Carnegie Mellon University was not available for online searching in 2006. No other institutional repository appears to have archival information on Igor Ansoff. This does not mean it does not exist. Ansoff Associates International (www.ansoff.com) has a short biography on the website.

Portraits of Ansoff appear in Ansoff (1964) and Ansoff (1992).

Ansoff, H. I. (1992) 'A profile of intellectual growth', in A. G. Bedeian (ed.) *Management Laureates: a Collection of Autobiographical Essays*, vol. 1, Greenwich, Conn.: JAI Press, pp. portrait, 3–39.
(As of 2006 available via WorldCat.)
'Obituary: Igor Ansoff, the father of strategic management' (2002) *Strategic Change* 11, 8: 437–8.
Williams, J. (2002) 'H. Igor Ansoff, 83; educator drew worldwide acclaim', *The San Diego Union Tribune* (July 16): 16.

2 H. Igor Ansoff: works listed in published bibliographies

H. Igor Ansoff: early scientific research

Ansoff, H. I. (1948) *The Forming of a Plastic Sheet Between Fixed Cylindrical Guides With Coulomb Friction*, PhD thesis, Brown University: [Providence, RI].
(As of 2006 available via WorldCat.)
—— and Krumhansl, J. A. (1948) 'A general stability criterion for linear oscillating systems with constant time lag', *Quarterly of Applied Mathematics* VI, 3: 337–41.

Cited in Ansoff (1992: 32) without co-author or reference to where the article appeared in the journal.[1]
—— (1949) 'Stability of linear oscillating systems with constant time lag', *Journal of Applied Mechanics* 16: 158–64, 418–20.
Cited in Ansoff (1992: 32) as No 48 A-22. Note year cited incorrectly.

H. Igor Ansoff: early research work on planning

Ansoff, H. I. (1957) 'Strategies for diversification', *Harvard Business Review* 35, 5: 113–24.
According to Hussey (1999) reprinted in Ewing, D. (ed.) (1958) *Long Range Planning for Management*, New York: Harper & Brother (rev. edition 1964, 1965, 3rd edition 1972)–the author cannot confirm the inclusion of the Ansoff article in the revised editions. (As of 2006 book available via WorldCat.)
According to Hussey (1999) reprinted in Bursk, E. and Chapman, J. (eds) (1963) *New Decision Making Tools for Managers: Mathematical Programing as an Aid in the Solving of Business Problems*, Cambridge, Mass.: Harvard University Press. (As of 2006 book available via WorldCat. Also published by New American Library: New York in 1965. Translated into Japanese in 1963 and 1966 and into French in 1970).
—— (1958) 'A model for diversification', *Management Science* 4, 4: 392–414.
According to Hussey (1999) reprinted in Berg, T. L. and Shuschman A. (eds) (1963) *Product Strategy and Management*, Holt, Reinhart and Winston, Inc., New York. (As of 2006 book available via WorldCat and BL.)
According to Hussey (1999) reprinted in Studivant, F. (ed.) (1971) *Managerial Economics*, Glenview, Ill.: Scott Foresman Co. (Book not found in WorldCat or other world repository databases.)
According to Hussey (1999) reprinted in Luck, D. (1972) *Product Management*, New York: Prentice-Hall. (Book not found in WorldCat or other world repository databases.)
Andersen, T., Ansoff, H. I., Norton, F. and Weston, J. F. (1959) 'Planning for diversification through merger', *California Management Review* 1, 4: 24–36.
Reprinted in Ansoff (1969, 1972, 1977: 290–309).
Ansoff, H. I. (1959) *A Quasi-analytic Method for Long Range Planning*, Chicago, Ill.: Institute of Management Sciences, College on Planning.
Pre-publication draft available via WorldCat. Presented at the first Symposium on Corporate Long-Range Planning, the Institute of Management Sciences, College on Planning, Chicago, Illinois, June 6, 1959.
According to Hussey (1999) reprinted in Alexis M. and Wilson C. (eds) (1967) *Organizational Decision Making*, Englewood Cliffs, NJ: Prentice-Hall. (As of 2006 book available via WorldCat and BL). Note: Ansoff (1992: 33) gave the date as 1962, but BL and WorldCat confirm that 1967 is correct for this edited collection.
—— (1962a) 'Company objectives: blueprint-or-blue sky', *Management Review* 51, 9: pp. unknown.
Reprinted in Schlender, W. E., Scott, W. G. and Filley, A. C. (eds) (1965) *Management in Perspective*, Boston Mass.: Houghton Mifflin, pp. 85–91. (As of 2006 book available via WorldCat.)
—— (1962b) 'Evaluation of applied research in business firms', in J. R. Bright (ed.) *Proceedings on the Conference on Technological Planning on the Corporate Level*,

Boston, Mass.: Harvard University, Graduate School of Business Administration, pp. unknown.
Proceedings of a conference sponsored by the Associates of the Harvard Business School, September 8 and 9, 1961. (As of 2006 proceedings available via WorldCat.)
Note: Hussey (1999) following Ansoff (1992) cites this reference as 1964 and yet WorldCat indicates 1962. James Bright did publish another book in 1964 titled *Research, Development and Technological Innovation: an Introduction*, Homewood, Ill.: R. D. Irwin.
—— and Weston, J. F. (1962) 'Merger objectives and organization structure', *Quarterly Review of Economics and Business* 2, 3: 49–58.
Reprinted in Schlender, W. E., Scott, W. G. and Filley, A. C. (eds) (1965) *Management in Perspective*, Boston Mass.: Houghton Mifflin, pp. unknown. (As of 2006 book available via WorldCat.)
—— (1963) 'Management participation in diversification', in Stanford Research Institute Client Conference (ed.) *Corporate Development Through Diversification, Proceedings*, Menlo Park, Calif.: Stanford Research Institute, Long Range Planning Service, pp. unknown.
According to WorldCat the conference was held Sept. 25–27, 1963. (As of 2006 book available via WorldCat.)
—— (1964a) 'Planning as a practical management tool', *Financial Executive* 32: 34–7.
Note p. 34 has a contemporary portrait of Ansoff.
Reprinted in Needles, B. and Skousen, K. F. (eds) (1973) *Contemporary Thought in Accounting and Organizational Control*, Encino, Calif.: Dickenson Publishing.
According to Hussey (1999) the book was published in 1965 I have found no evidence of earlier publication. (As of 2006 book available via WorldCat.)
According to Hussey (1999) reprinted in Wadia, M. S. (ed.) (1966) *The Nature and Scope of Management*, Chicago, Ill.: Scott Foreman. (As of 2006 book available via WorldCat.)
—— (1964b) 'A quasi-analytic approach to the business policy problem', *Management Technology*[2] IV, 1: 67–77.

H. Igor Ansoff: the Carnegie-Vanderbilt years 1963–73

Ansoff, H. I. (1965a) *Corporate Strategy: an Analytical Approach to Business Policy for Growth and Expansion*, New York: McGraw-Hill Book Co.
—— (1965b) 'The firm of the future', *Harvard Business Review* 43, 5: 162–78.
Reprinted in Ansoff (1969, 1972, 1977: 107–21).
—— (1967a) 'A program of research in business planning', *Management Science* 13, 6, series B, Managerial: B219–B239.
—— (1967b) 'Research and development planning', in H. B. Maynard (ed.) *Handbook of Business Administration*, New York: McGraw-Hill, pp. unknown.
The Handbook was also published in [Hong Kong?] in 1968. (As of 2006 book available via WorldCat.)
—— and Stewart, J. M. (1967) 'Strategies for technology-based business', *Harvard Business Review* 45, 6: 71–83.
This article was incorrectly cited by Ansoff (1992: 38) as having been reprinted in 1986.

Reprinted in *The Management of Technological Innovation* (1982), [Boston, Mass.]: Harvard Business Review [Reprint Dept.]. Note: not to be confused with the publication Davis, D. D. (ed.) (1986) *The Management of Technological Innovation*, San Francisco, Calif.: Jossey-Bass. (Both books are available via WorldCat, 2006.)

—— (1968a) *Corporate Strategy: an Analytical Approach to Business Policy for Growth and Expansion*, Harmondsworth, Middlesex: Penguin Books.

A part of the Pelican library of business and management series. Pelican books no. A.932.

—— (1968b) 'The innovative firm', *Long Range Planning* 1, 2: 26–7.

Note Ansoff (1992: 34) dated this item as 1969 and as having appeared in the *Journal of the PE Consulting Group*. According to Hussey (1999) the item was originally published in an 'inhouse' newsletter for the P E Consulting Group (London) and was subsequently published in *Long Range Planning*.

The original publication has not been traced. P E Consulting Group (London) is not the same as PE Consulting Group operating worldwide (but originally based in Germany) at the beginning of the twenty-first century.

—— (1968c) *Strategia Aziendale* (trans. G. Panati), Milano, Italy: ETAS Kompass.

Italian translation of Ansoff (1965) *Corporate Strategy*. A second edition of this translation was published in 1974 by Etas Libri of Milan. (As of 2006 both editions were available in Europe via Biblioteca nazionale centrale di Roma (National Central Library of Rome), Rome.)

—— (1968d) 'Vers une théorie stratégique des entreprises', *Économies et Sociétés* 2, 3: pp. unknown.

In French, translated into English (Ansoff 1969, 1972, 1977: 11–40).

—— and Slevin, D. P. (1968) 'An appreciation of industrial dynamics', *Management Science* 14, 7: 383–97.

Note Ansoff (1992: 34) dated this paper as 1967.

—— (1969a) *Kigyo senryakuron* (trans. H. Toshiaki), Tokyo: Sangyo Noritsu Tanki Daigaku Shuppanbu.

Japanese translation of Ansoff (1965) *Corporate Strategy*. (As of 2006 still available via WorldCat. Available in Japan via National Diet Library, Tokyo. Note: the latter indicates the translator as Hirota, 寿Akira.)

—— (1969b) 'Issues in national policy on growth of firms', in J. F. Weston and S. Peltzman (eds) *Public Policy Towards Mergers*, Pacific Palisades, Calif.: Goodyear Publishing Co, pp. unknown.

Public Policy Towards Mergers resulted from an Antitrust Policy Seminar conducted at the University of California at Los Angeles in 1968. (As of 2006 book available via WorldCat.)

—— (1969c) 'Managerial problem solving', in J. Blood (ed.) *Management Science in Planning and Control*, New York: Technical Association of the Pulp and Paper Industry, pp. unknown.

The publication was sponsored by the Technical Association of the Pulp and Paper Industry and was a project of the Operations Research Committee. The publication was the result of papers which were presented at the 1966 symposium as part of operations research and design of management of the information systems section. (As of 2006 book available via WorldCat.)

According to Ansoff (1992: 34) this item was reprinted in the *Journal of Business Policy*,[3] 1971, volume 2 issue 1. This could not be confirmed.

—— (ed.) (1969, 1972, 1977) *Business Strategy: Selected Readings*, Harmondsworth: Penguin.

Contains two sole author and one multiple author contribution from Ansoff with sixteen other papers or contributions chosen by Ansoff. The contributions are from John Kenneth Galbraith, Herbert Simon and Friedrich August von Hayek and illustrate objectives of a business.

This book contains the first English translation of Ansoff (1968). It is a little difficult to track this paper since the article is described as "H. I. Ansoff 'Toward a strategic theory of the firm', *Économie Appliquée*, in press" (p. 11).

—— and Brandenberg, R. G. (1969a) 'The general manager of the future', *California Management Review* 11, 3: 61–72.

Note: Ansoff (1992: 34) dated this item as 1967. According to Hussey (1999: 389) it was originally delivered at an Alumni Conference, Carnegie Institute of Technology, April 1967. Reprinted in House, W. C. (ed.) (1971) *The Impact of Information Technology on Management Operation*, Princeton, NJ: Auerbach, pp. unknown (book available via WorldCat 2006); also reprinted in Turner, J. H., Filley, A. C. and House, R. (eds) (1971) *Readings in Managerial Process and Organizational Behavior*, Glenview, Ill.: Scott-Foresman, pp. unknown (book not available via WorldCat 2006).

——, —— (1969b) 'A language for organization design', in E. Jantsch (ed.) *Perspectives of Planning*, Paris: OECD, pp. 349–93.

Note: Ansoff (1992: 34) dated this item as 1968. *Perspectives of Planning* is the published proceedings of an OECD Working Symposium on Long Range Forecasting and Planning held at Bellagio, Italy, between October 27 and November 2, 1968. Reprinted as Ansoff and Brandenburg (1971a, b). (As of 2006 book available via WorldCat.)

—— (1970) 'Review of the *Study of Policy Formation*', *Journal of Business* 43, 4: 490–3.

Review of the book–Bauer, R. A. and Gergen, K. J. (1968) *Study of Policy Formation*, New York: Free Press.

——, Avner, J., Brandenburg, R. G., Portner, F. E. and Radosevich, R. (1970) 'Does planning pay? The effect of planning on success of acquisitions in American firms', *Long Range Planning* 3, 2: 2–7.

—— (1971a) *Corporate strategy*. Paper presented at the *Preparing for Tomorrow: Management Plans for Action*, First European Management Symposium, Davos, Switzerland.

Cited by Ansoff (1992: 35) but not confirmed. The symposium is listed in the International Federation for Documentation (1969), *Yearbook of International Congress Proceedings*, The Hague: Union of International Associations but a resulting proceedings is not listed on WorldCat or COPAC.

—— (1971b) *Praktisk företagsstrategi: taktik för tillväxt och expansion* (trans. S.-E. Sjöstrand), Stockholm: Wahlström & Widstrand.

Swedish translation of Ansoff (1965) *Corporate Strategy*. (Available in 2006 from Kungl. Biblioteket (National Library of Sweden), Stockholm.)

—— (1971c) 'Strategy as a tool for coping with change', *Journal of Business Policy*[3] 1, 4: pp. unknown.

—— and Lebell, D. (1971) 'Institutional factors in strategic management', *Journal of Business Policy*[3] 1, 3: pp. unknown.

The exact authorship of this paper has not been checked for this bibliography.

——, Portner, F. E. and Radosevich, H. R. (1971) *Acquisition Behavior of U.S. Manufacturing Firms, 1946–1965*, Nashville, Tenn.: Vanderbilt University Press. This book is an expansion of Ansoff *et al.* (1970). The book was subsequently published in the UK the following year as Ansoff *et al.* (1972) but with a change of title to *Twenty Years of Acquisition Behavior in America: a Comparative Study of Mergers and Acquisitions of U.S. Manufacturing Firms 1946–1965.*

—— (1972a) 'Corporate structure, present, and future', in Affiliation of Planning Societies (ed.) *Critical Managerial Issues in a Changing World. Proceedings of the International Conference on Corporate Planning*, Montreal, Canada: published by the Conference Planning Group, for the Affiliation of Planning Societies.

Ansoff (1992: 35) cited this item as being in the *Proceedings of the International Conference on Corporate Planning* (1971) held in Brussels. WorldCat (OCLC: 63512098) lists only one conference, held in Montreal in 1971. There is no indication that this is the third international conference.

—— (1972b) 'Dolgosrochnoe planirovanie v perspective', in G. K. Popov (ed.) *Sovremennye Tendentsii v Upravlenii v Kapitalisticheskikh Stranakh*, Moskva: Izdatelstvo Progress, pp. 51–72G.

Ansoff (1992: 35) cited this item. (In Russian. As of 2006 book available via WorldCat.)

—— (1972c) *Företagsstrategi i teori och praktik* (trans. S. Sundell), Stockholm: Prisma. Swedish translation of Ansoff (1969) *Business Strategy*. (Available in 2006 from Kungl. Biblioteket (National Library of Sweden), Stockholm).

—— (1972d) *Strategisk planlægning*, (trans. E. Bang-Nielsen), København: Branner og Korch.

Danish translation of Ansoff (1965) *Corporate Strategy*. (Available in 2006 from Det Kongelige Bibliotek, Nationalbibliotek og Københavns (The Royal Library, the National Library and Copenhagen University Library), Copenhagen and Nasjonalbiblioteket (The National Library of Norway), Oslo.)

——, Brandenburg, R. G., Portner, F. E. and Radosevich, H. R. (1972) 'The concept of strategic management', *Journal of Business Policy*[3] 2, 4: pp. unknown.

Ansoff (1992: 35) indicated that this article is multi-authored, yet citations of it in Hussey (1999: 389) and other Ansoff papers have only one author.

Europe 1973–82

Ansoff, H. I. (1973a) 'Corporate structure, present, and future', in *Proceedings of the Third International Conference on Corporate Planning*, Brussels: European Society of Corporate and Strategic Planners, pp. unknown.

The conference was held in Brussels Sept 17–19, 1973. Conference proceedings have not been found in WorldCat or COPAC but were listed in the *Yearbook of Published Conference Proceedings* published by the International Federation of Documentation.

—— (1973b) 'Management in transition', in E. C. Bursk (ed.) *Challenge to Leadership: Managing in a Changing World*, New York: The Free Press, pp. 22–63.

A compilation published for The Conference Board. Note: not cited in Ansoff (1992), cited in Hussey (1999: 389) but with the title *Management on the Threshold of the Post-industrial Era*. (As of 2006 book available via WorldCat.)

—— (1973c) 'The next twenty years in management education', *The Library Quarterly* 43, 4: 293–328.

—— (1973d) *Ondernemingsstrategie: Analyse van het Ondernemingsbeleid, Gericht op Groei en Expansie*, Alphen aan den Rijn: Samsom.

Dutch translation of Ansoff (1965) *Corporate Strategy*. (As of 2006 available in the USA via WorldCat. Available in Europe via Koninklijke Bibliotheek (National Library of the Netherlands), The Hague.)

—— (1974a) *Functions of the Executive Office in a Large Conglomerate*, Working Paper 74–42, Brussels, Belgium: European Institute for Advanced Studies in Management.

(As of 2006 available via WorldCat.)

—— (1974b) *Strategia Aziendale* (trans. G. Panati), Milano, Italy: Etas Libri.

Italian translation of Ansoff (1965) *Corporate Strategy*. This is the second edition of this translation published in Milan. The first was in 1968 by ETAS Kompass. (As of 2006 both editions were available in Europe via Biblioteca nazionale centrale di Roma (National Central Library of Rome), Rome.)

—— (ed.) (1974c) *La Strategia d'impressa* (trans. M. Vitta and E. Facchini), Milan: Franco Angeli.

Italian translation of Ansoff (1969, 1972) *Business Strategy*. In some catalogues may appear to be authored by T. Andersen due to the Anglo-American misinterpretation of Italian cataloguing rules. (As of 2006 still available via WorldCat. Available in Europe via Biblioteca nazionale centrale di Roma (National Central Library of Rome), Rome.)

—— (1974d) 'Management en advieswerk: de derde generatie', *Tijdschrift voor Efficiënt Directiebeleid*[4] 44: pp. unknown.

Article in Dutch.

—— (1975a) *An Applied Managerial Theory of Strategic Behaviour*, Working Paper 75–12, Brussels: European Institute for Advanced Studies in Management.

(As of 2006 available via WorldCat and BL.)

—— (1975b) 'The knowledge professional in the post-industrial era', *Bedrijfskunde*[5] 47: 88–?

—— (1975c) 'La structure de l'entreprise aujourd'hui et demain (première partie)', *Chefs, Revue Suisse du management*[6] 2: pp. unknown

—— (1975d) 'Le concept de gestion stratégique. La résolution des problèmes de management', *Cahiers Africains d'administration Publique*[7] 15: pp. unknown.

—— (1975e) 'Management under discontinuity', in H. I. Ansoff (ed.) *Proceedings at a Conference at INSEAD*, Fontainbleau, France: INSEAD, pp. unknown.

This chapter was cited in Ansoff (1992: 36) but not by Hussey (1999). The proceedings do not appear in WorldCat or COPAC.

—— (1975f) 'Managing strategic surprise by response to weak signals', *California Management Review* 18, 2: 21–33.

Ansoff (1992: 36) dated this article as 1976.

—— (1975g) *The State of Practice in Management Systems*, Working Paper 75–11, Brussels, Belgium: European Institute for Advanced Studies in Management.

(As of 2006 available via BL.)

—— (1975, 1980) 'From strategic planning to strategic management', in D. Hahn and B. Taylor (eds) *Strategische Unternehmungsplanung: Stand und Entwicklungstendenzen*, Wien, Austria: Physica-Verlag, pp. unknown.

This chapter is cited in Ansoff (1992: 32) and dated 1972 as part of the *Proceedings of the International Conference on Strategic Management*. The proceedings were published as Ansoff *et al.* (1976).

—— (1976a) 'The changing manager', in H. I. Ansoff, R. P. Declerck and R. L. Hayes (eds) *From Strategic Planning to Strategic Management*, London: John Wiley & Sons, pp. 181–97.

—— (1976b) *La Estrategia de la Empresa*, Pamplona: Ediciones Universidad de Navarra. Spanish translation of Ansoff (1965) *Corporate Strategy*. (As of 2006 available via WorldCat. Available in Europe via Biblioteca Nacional de Español (National Library of Spain), Madrid; in Mexico from Universidad Panamericana, Mexico City.)

——, Declerck, R. P. and Hayes, R. L. (eds) (1976) *From Strategic Planning to Strategic Management*, London: John Wiley & Sons.

This is the published proceedings of the First International Conference on Strategic Management held in 1973 at Vanderbilt University. It is a Wiley-Interscience publication.

—— and Leontiades, J. C. (1976) 'Strategic portfolio management', *Journal of General Management* 4, 1: 13–29.

Ansoff (1992: 36) dated this article as 1978.

—— (1977a) *Estratégia empresarial* (trans. A. Z. Sanvicente), São Paulo, Brasil: McGraw-Hill do Brasil.

Portuguese translation of Ansoff (1965) *Corporate Strategy*. (As of 2006 available in Europe via Biblioteca Nacional de Portugal (National Library of Portugal), Lisbon.)

—— (1977b) 'The state of practice in planning systems', *Sloan Management Review* 18, 2: pp. unknown.

Reprinted in Kraegel, J. M. (1983) *Planning, Strategies for Nurse Managers*, Rockville, Md.: Aspen Systems Corp, pp. unknown. (As of 2006 book available via WorldCat.)

—— (1978a) *Corporate Capability for Managing Change*, Menlo Park, Calif.: SRI International Business Intelligence Program.

Stanford Research Institute (SRI) International, Business Intelligence Program Research Report 610. (As of 2006 report available via WorldCat.)

—— (1978b) 'Planned management of turbulent change', in L. R. Bittel and M. A. Bittel (eds) *Encyclopedia of Professional Management*, New York: McGraw-Hill, pp. unknown.

Ansoff (1992: 37) dated this article as 1979. This encyclopedia also published by Grolier International out of Danbury, UK, as a two-volume set.

——, Anders and Hedlund, G. (1978) *Proposal for Research on Future Legitimacy (Role) of the Business Firm in Europe*, Working Paper 78–45, Brussels: European Institute for Advanced Studies in Management.

This item was cited in Ansoff (1992: 37) dated incorrectly as 1979. Not found in WorldCat or other world repository databases.

—— and Thanheiser, H. T. (1978) *Corporate Planning: a Comparative View of the Evolution and Current Practice in the United States and Western Europe*, Working Paper 78–10, Brussels, Belgium: European Institute for Advanced Studies in Management.

(As of 2006 available via WorldCat.)

—— (1979a) *ABC of Strategic Management*, Working Paper 79–25, Brussels, Belgium: European Institute for Advanced Studies in Management.
This item was cited in Ansoff (1992: 37) and Hussey (1999: 390). Not found in WorldCat or other world repository databases.

—— (1979b) *Aspirations and Culture in Strategic Behavior*, Working Paper 79–12, Brussels, Belgium: European Institute for Advanced Studies in Management.
This item was cited in Ansoff (1992: 37) and Hussey (1999: 390). Not found in WorldCat or other world repository databases.

—— (1979c) 'The changing shape of the strategic problem', *Journal of General Management*[3] 4, 4: 42–58.

—— (1979d) *Societal Strategy for the Business Firm*, Working Paper 79–24, Brussels, Belgium: European Institute for Advanced Studies in Management.
This item was cited in Ansoff (1992: 37). Not found in WorldCat or other world repository databases.

—— (1979e) 'Strategic business areas', *Tehokas yritys johtamistoimen ammattilehti*,[8] pp. unknown.
This item was cited in Ansoff (1992: 37).

—— (1979f) *Strategic Management*, New York: Wiley.

—— (1979, 1982) *Strategic Management*, London: Macmillan.
This edition was published in 1979 simultaneously in London and New York by Macmillan.

—— (1980a) *Managing the Process of Discontinuous Change. Part I. Behavioral Resistance*, Working Paper 80–26, Brussels, Belgium: European Institute for Advanced Studies in Management.
(As of 2006 available via BL.)

—— (1980b) *Managing the Process of Discontinuous Change. Part II. Systematic Resistance*, Working Paper 80–36, Brussels, Belgium: European Institute for Advanced Studies in Management.
(As of 2006 available via BL.)

—— (1980c) *Managing the Process of Discontinuous Change. Part III. Alternative Approaches*, Working Paper 80–37, Brussels, Belgium: European Institute for Advanced Studies in Management.
(As of 2006 available via BL.)

—— (1980d) *Managing the Process of Discontinuous Change. Part IV. The Learning Action Approach*, Working Paper 80–38, Brussels, Belgium: European Institute for Advanced Studies in Management.
(As of 2006 available via BL.)

—— (1980e) 'Strategic issue management', *Strategic Management Journal* 1, 2: 131–48.

—— (1980f) *Senryaku keieiron* (trans. G. Nakamura), Tokyo: Sangyonoritsudaigakushuppanbu.
Japanese translation of Ansoff (1979) *Strategic Management*. (As of 2006 available via WorldCat.) This work was updated by a new publisher in 1993 (see entry below).

——, Kirsch, W. and Roventa, P. (1980) *Dispersed Positioning in Strategic Portfolio Analysis*, Working Paper 80–12, Brussels, Belgium: European Institute for Advanced Studies in Management.
(As of 2006 available via WorldCat. Available in Europe via BL.)

15

United States International University: 1982 to retirement

Ansoff, H. I., Bosman, A. and Storm, P. M. (1982) *Understanding and Managing Strategic Change: Contributions to the Theory and Practice of General Management*, Amsterdam: Elsevier Science Pub. Co.
Includes two chapters 'Managing discontinuous strategic change' and 'Societal strategy for the business firm' by Ansoff. The work is dedicated to Jan Joele. The book is widely available in national libraries. North-Holland Pub. Co., New York was the distributor for the USA and Canada.

Achleitner, P. and Ansoff, H. I. (1983) 'Die bedeutung soziopolitischer strategien', *Harvard Business Manager*[9] 4, IV: pp. unknown.

——, —— and Haskins, G. (1983) 'The firm: meeting the legitimacy challenge', *European Management Journal* 2, 1: 19–27.

Ansoff, H. I. (1983a) 'Methoden zur verwirklichung strategischer Anderungen in der Unter Nehmung', in *Strategishes Management*, Teil 1, Wiesbaden, Germany: Gabler. This item was cited by Ansoff (1992: 38) but was dated incorrectly as 1984. The book consists of two papers: the first, by Ansoff, a paper in German on managing discontinuous strategic change and the second paper titled 'Strategische Planung im Konzern' by Hans Eberhard Scheffler. This book is number 30 in the series 'Schriften zur Unternehmensführung'. (As of 2006 available via Deutsche Nationalbibliothek (German National Library).)

—— (1983b) 'Societal strategy for the business firm', in R. Lamb (ed.) *Advances in Strategic Management: a Research Annual*, vol. 1, Greenwich, Conn.: JAI Press, pp. unknown.
(As of 2006 book available via WorldCat.)

——, Hayes, R. L. and Declerck, R. P. (eds) (1983) *El Planteamiento estratégico: nueva tendencia de la administración*, la edn, México: Trillas.
Spanish translation of Ansoff *et al.* (1976) *From Strategic Planning to Strategic Management*. (As of 2006 available via WorldCat.) This publisher reprinted the translation in the following year.
• 1991 2a edn (As of 2006 available in Mexico from Universidad Panamericana, Mexico City.)

—— (1984) *Implanting Strategic Management*, Englewood Cliffs, NJ: Prentice Hall Inc.

—— (1985a) 'Conceptual underpinnings of systematic strategic management', *European Journal of Operational Research* 19, 1: 2–19.

—— (1985b) 'La perspectiva cambinante del problema estrategico', *Sinergia*[10] 1, 3?: pp. unknown.

—— (1986?) 'Bases conceptuales de la administracion estrategica sistematica', *Sinergia*[10] 1: pp. unknown.

—— (1986a) 'Competitive strategy analysis on the personal computer', *Journal of Business Strategy* 6, 3: 28–37.

—— (1986b) 'Competitive strategy analysis on the personal computer', *International Management Development Review*[11] 2: pp. unknown.

—— (1986c) *Corporate Strategy*, London: Sidgwick & Jackson.
This apparent reprinting of Ansoff (1965) *Corporate Strategy* and the revised editions published in the following year (Ansoff 1987a, c) all have a new introduction by Sir John Harvey-Jones. It is not clear whether the text has been changed;

the pagination is different but then new typesetting would account for some of these differences.

—— (1986d) *The Firm: Meeting the Legitimacy Challenge*, Brussels: European Institute for Advanced Studies in Management and European Foundation for Management Development.
This item was cited in Ansoff (1992: 38). Not found in WorldCat or other world repository databases.

—— (1986, 1987) 'The pathology of applied research in social science', in F. Heller (ed.) *The Use and Abuse of Social Science*, Beverley Hills, Calif.: Sage, pp. unknown.
(As of 2006 available via WorldCat.)

—— and Baker, T. E. (1986) 'Is corporate culture the ultimate answer?' in R. Lamb and P. Shrivastava (eds) *Advances in Strategic Management: a Research Annual*, vol. 4, Greenwich, Conn.: JAI Press, pp. unknown.
(As of 2006 book available via WorldCat.)

—— (1987a) *Corporate Strategy* (rev. edn), Harmondsworth, Middlesex, England: Penguin.
This is a revised edition of Ansoff (1965) *Corporate Strategy*. Ansoff was assisted by Edward J. McDonnell. In the USA the title was *New Corporate Strategy*.

—— (1987b) 'The emerging paradigm of strategic behavior', *Strategic Management Journal* 8, 6: 501–15.

—— (1987c) *New Corporate Strategy* (rev. edn), New York: Wiley.
This is a revised edition of Ansoff (1965) *Corporate Strategy*. Ansoff was assisted by Edward J. McDonnell. In the UK the title was *Corporate Strategy*.

—— (1987d) 'Strategic management of technology', *Journal of Business Strategy* 7, 3: 28–39.

——, Declerck, R. P. and Hayes, R. L. (eds) (1987, 1990) *Do Planejamento Estratégico à Administração Estratégica*, São Paulo, Brasil: Editora Atlas.
Portuguese translation of Ansoff *et al.* (1976) *From Strategic Planning to Strategic Management*. (As of 2006 available via Biblioteca Nacional de Portugal (National Library of Portugal), Lisbon.)

—— (1988) *The New Corporate Strategy*, New York: McGraw-Hill Book Co.
See also Ansoff (1987 a, c).

—— (1990) *Saishin senryaku keiei: senryaku sakusei jikko no tenkai to purosesu* (trans. G. Nakamura and T. Kuroda), Tokyo: Sannodaigakushuppanbu.
Japanese translation of either Ansoff (1987b or 1988) *New Corporate Strategy*. (As of 2006 available via WorldCat. Available in Japan via National Diet Library, Tokyo.)

—— and McDonnell, E. J. (1990a) *Implanting Strategic Management* (2nd edn), Hemel Hempstead, Hertfordshire: Prentice Hall International (UK).

——, —— (1990b) *Implanting Strategic Management* (2nd edn), Englewood Cliffs, NJ: Prentice Hall Inc.

—— (1991a) 'Critique of Henry Mintzberg's "The design school: reconsidering the basic premises of strategic management"', *Strategic Management Journal* 12, 6: 449–61.

—— (1991b) 'Strategic management in a historical perspective', *International Review of Strategic Management*[12] 2: 3–69.

This item may often be cited as Ansoff, H. I. (1991) 'Strategic management in a historical perspective', in D. E. Hussey (ed.) *International Review of Strategic Management*, vol. 2, Chichester, West Sussex: John Wiley & Sons, pp. 3–69.

—— and Sullivan, P. A. (1991) 'Strategic responses to environmental turbulence', in R. H. Kilmann and I. Kilmann (eds) *Making Organizations Competitive: Enhancing Networks and Relationships Across Traditional Boundaries*, San Fransisco, Calif.: Jossey Bass, pp. unknown.

This item was cited in Ansoff (1992: 39) but with the editor of the book as Gillman. (As of 2006 book available via WorldCat.)

—— (1993) 'Empirical support for a paradigmatic theory of strategic success behaviours of environment-serving organizations', *International Review of Strategic Management*[12] 4: 173–203.

This item may often be cited as Ansoff, H. I. (1993) 'Empirical support for a paradigmatic theory of strategic success behaviours of environment-serving organizations', in D. E. Hussey (ed.) *International Review of Strategic Management*, vol. 4, Chichester, West Sussex: John Wiley & Sons, pp. 173–203.

This item was cited in Ansoff (1992: 39) dated 1992 with the title '*Empirical proof of paradigmic theory of strategic success behaviors if* [sic] *environment serving organizations*'.

—— and Sullivan, P. A. (1993) 'Optimizing profitability in turbulent environments: a formula for strategic success', *Long Range Planning* 26, 5: 11–23.

—— and McDonnell, E. J. (1994) *Senryaku keiei no jissen genri: nijuisseiki kigyo no keiei baiburu* (trans. G. Nakamura, T. Kuroda and D. Che), Tokyo: Daiyamondo Sha.

Japanese translation of Ansoff (1990) *Implanting Strategic Management*. (As of 2006 available via WorldCat. Available in Japan via National Diet Library, Tokyo.)

Unmatched citations from previous bibliographies

Ansoff, H. I. (1966) 'Planning at the level of and enterprise in the USA [sic]', in *Proceedings of the Conference*

There is obviously very little information in this citation from Ansoff (1992: 34) but if we assume that Ansoff was working for Stanford Research Institute (SRI) then may be a possible source for this item the conference, held Oct. 16–18, 1967, San Francisco, available on WorldCat and consisting of photocopies of papers collected and bound locally. If so the citation should read: Ansoff, H. I. (1967?) 'Planning at the level of and enterprise in the USA', in Stanford Research Institute Client Conference (ed.) *R&D and Corporate Growth*, Menlo Park, Calif.: Stanford Research Institute, Long Range Planning Service, pp. unknown.

—— (1967a) 'The evolution of corporate planning', in *Report of the SRI Long Range Planning Service*, Palo Alto, Calif.: Stanford University, pp. unknown?

This item was cited in Ansoff (1992: 34) but has not been confirmed. Although the series *Report of the SRI Long Range Planning Service* appears in World Cat a report for 1967 does not.

—— (1967b) 'The expanding role of the computer in managerial decision-making', *Informatic*: pp. unknown.

This item was cited in Ansoff (1992: 34) but has not been confirmed. I cannot find reference to a journal with this title being published during the 1960s. A search of

WorldCat did reveal that the associated research (Johnson 1967) was occurring at Menlo Park at the same time Ansoff was working for SRI.

—— (1976) 'The future of corporate structure', *Journal of General Management*[3] 4, 1: ?–30–?

This article was cited by both Ansoff (1992: 36) and Hussey (1999: 389) but have looked through Vols 1–5 of the journal and was unable to find this article. The only other citation appears in the ISI Social Science Citation Index but only from self-citation by Ansoff.

—— (1978) 'Management in unpredictable environments', *The Intercontinental Advanced Management Report*, 1, 7: pp. unknown.

This item was cited in Ansoff (1992: 36) but has not been confirmed. There appears to be no record of this journal in WorldCat or other databases used.

—— (1985) *La Estrategia de la Empresa*, New York, McGraw-Hill.

This item was cited in Ansoff (1992: 38) but has not been confirmed. There appears to be no record of a book with this title by this publisher in WorldCat or other databases used. Note: the national library databases of Brazil, Spain and Portugal were searched for this title in 2006.

—— (1987) 'Que es la estrategia de la empressa?' in *Enciclopedia De Direccion Y Administracion De La Empresa*, s.l.: s.n.

This item was cited in Ansoff (1992: 38) but has not been confirmed.

There appears to be no record of such an encyclopaedia in WorldCat or other databases used. Note: the national library databases of Brazil, Spain and Portugal were searched for this reference book in 2006.

—— and Brandenburg, R. G. (1967) 'Design of optimal business planning system: a study proposal', *Journal for Cybernetics of Planning and Organization*: pp. unknown.

This item was cited in Ansoff (1992: 34) but has not been confirmed and I cannot find reference to this journal. The American Society for Cybernetics (ASC) met regularly in Washington, DC, USA, during 1964–74 and held five large conferences during this period. One conference in 1967 on 'Purposive Systems' and one in 1968 on 'Cybernetics and the Management of Large Systems' would have been perfect for the subject of this paper. The ASC also started a journal in 1968 but it was given the title *ASC Communications*. The society commenced publishing the *Journal of Cybernetics* in 1971.

——, Eppink, J. and Gomer, H. (1978) 'Management of strategic surprise and discontinuity: improving managerial decisiveness', *Marknads Vetande: Utgiven av Sveriges Marknadsforbund* 4/78, 9: pp. unknown.

This item was cited in Ansoff (1992: 36). This journal was not found in WorldCat or COPAC or in the Kungl Biblioteket (National Library of Sweden), Stockholm. Note that the references of Ansoff *et al.* (1982) indicate that the journal is *Marknads-Vetande* and that the volume is 4/79.

——, Kirsch, W. and Roventa, P. (1983) 'Bausteine eines stratesischen managements', in *Unscharfenpositionierung in der Strategischen Portfolio-Analyse*, New York: Walter de Gruyter, pp. unknown.

This item was cited in Ansoff (1992: 37) but has not been confirmed. The book was not found on the German National library database or any other national library catalogue. It does not appear in the de Gruyter catalogue.

3 H. Igor Ansoff: works not listed in published bibliographies

Matched citations from catalogues and other sources

Ansoff, H. I. (1957) *Some Considerations of the Role of the U.S. Air Force in Limited War*, Santa Monica, Calif.: Rand Corporation.
Not cited in Ansoff (1992). U.S. Air Force Project, RAND Report: AD 123 527 dated 16 January 1957. (As of 2006 book available via WorldCat.)
—— (1966) *Management-strategie* (trans. H. Folchert), München: verlag moderne industrie.
German translation of Ansoff (1965) *Corporate Strategy*. (As of 2006 book available via WorldCat. Available in Europe via Willkommen bei der Deutschen Nationalbibliothek, Berlin).
—— and Brandenburg, R. G. (1967) *A Program of Research in Business Planning*, Pittsburgh, Pa.: Carnegie Institute of Technology.
Graduate School of Industrial Administration, Carnegie-Mellon, reprint no. 301. (As of 2006 reprint/pamphlet available via WorldCat.)
—— and Slevin, D. P. (1968) 'Comment on Professor Forrester's "Industrial dynamics–after the first decade"', *Management Science*[2] 14, 9: 600.
—— (1970) *Stratégie du développement de l'entreprise. Analyse d'une politique de croissance et d'expansion* (trans. M. Perineau), [Puteaux]: Éditions Hommes et techniques.
French translation of Ansoff (1965) *Corporate Strategy*. (As of 2006 still available via WorldCat. Available in Europe via Bibliothèque nationale de France (National Library of France), Paris.)
There appears to be a 1968 edition of this translation by this publisher but I cannot find a major library that holds the item. This publisher reprinted the translation in the following years
• 1974, 3e éd, Paris (As of 2006 still available via WorldCat. Available in Europe via Bibliothèque nationale de France, Paris.)
• 1976, 4e éd, Suresnes, France (As of 2006 still available via WorldCat. Available in Europe via Bibliothèque nationale de France, Paris.)
• 1981, Boulogne, France (As of 2006 still available via Biblioteca Nacional de Portugal (National Library of Portugal), Lisbon.)
• 1984, Paris (As of 2006 still available via WorldCat.)
Matsuda T. and Hosoya, Y. (eds) (1970) *Hendo ni chosen suru keiei*, Tokyo: Nihon Seisansei Honbum.
In November 1969 Ansoff, Herbert Simon and Rensis Likert attended a seminar in Tokyo sponsored by the Japanese Management Association. The three seminars were published by the Japan Productivity Council as a 254-page book *The Challenge of Change to Management*. The author is unable to find the title of Ansoff's contribution. (In Japanese. As of 2006 available via National Diet Library, Tokyo.)
Ansoff, H. I. and Brandenburg, R. G. (1971a) 'A language for organization design: part I', *Management Science*[2] 17, 12, Application Series: B705–B716.
——, —— (1971b) 'A language for organization design: part II', *Management Science*[2] 17, 12, Application Series: B717–B731.
Note these two papers were originally published as Ansoff and Brandenburg (1969).

—— (1972) 企業の多角化戰略，產業能率短期大学出版部，In Japanese. A translation by Hirota, 寿Akira to produce a 246-page book on corporate diversification strategy, published by Sangyo Noritsu Tanki Daigaku Shuppanbu, Tokyo. The author cannot locate the original English text. (As of 2006 available via National Diet Library, Tokyo.)

—— (1974) *Corporate Structure Present and Future*, Working Paper 74-4, Brussels, Belgium: European Institute for Advanced Studies in Management. (As of 2006 available via WorldCat.)

—— (1975a) *The Knowledge Professional in the Post-industrial Era*, Working Paper 75-9, Brussels: European Institute for Advanced Studies in Management. (As of 2006 available via BL.)

—— (1975b) *Managing Surprise and Discontinuity: Strategic Response to Weak Signals*, Working Paper 75-21, Brussels, Belgium: European Institute for Advanced Studies in Management. (As of 2006 available via WorldCat.)

—— (1975c) 'La structure de l'entreprise aujourd'hui et demain', *Enseignement et Gestion*,[13] [1975]: pp. unknown.

——, Eppink, J. and Gomer, H. (1975) *Management of Strategic Surprise and Discontinuity: Problem of Managerial Decisiveness*, Working paper 75-29, Brussels, Belgium: European Institute for Advanced Studies in Management. This item is cited in Ansoff and Leontiades (1976). Not found in WorldCat or other world repository databases.

—— (1977) *The Changing Shape of the Strategic Problem*, Working Paper 77-12, Brussels, Belgium: European Institute for Advanced Studies in Management. (As of 2006 available via WorldCat.)

—— (1978a) *Planned Management of Turbulent Change*, Working Paper 78-3, Brussels, Belgium: European Institute for Advanced Studies in Management. (As of 2006 available via WorldCat.)

—— (1978b) *Strategisk företagsledning* (trans. J. Larsson), Stockholm: LiberFörlag. Swedish translation of Ansoff (1979) *Strategic Management*. It is interesting to note that the translation was published before the English version. This publisher reprinted the translation in the following years
- 1979, 2. tr.
- 1982, 3. tr.

Available from Kungl Biblioteket (National Library of Sweden), Stockholm (all years) and Eesti Rahvusraamatukogu (National Library of Estonia), Talinn (1979)

——, Declerck, R. P. and Hayes, R. L. (eds) (1978) *Strategisch management: recente ontwikkelingen in ondernemingsstrategie*, Alphen aan den Rijn etc.: Samsom. Dutch translation of Ansoff *et al.* (1976) *From Strategic Planning to Strategic Management*. (As of 2006 available via WorldCat. Available in Europe via Koninklijke Bibliotheek (The National Library of The Netherlands), The Hague.)

—— (1979) 'Le projet européen sur la stratégie sociétale (E.I.A.S.M. Bruxelles), en coopération avec la Fondation européenne pour le développement du management (E.F.M.D.)', *Économies et Sociétés*, [1979], N° 1 Série SG: pp. unknown. This item was not cited by Ansoff (1992) or Hussey (1999) but the citation is found on the Institut des Sciences Mathématiques et Économiques Appliquées

website (www. ismea.org) *Économies et Sociétés*, Présentation de la série Sciences et Gestion, Dossiers Les Équipes de Recherche en Sciences de Gestion, Numéro 1 (Avril–Juin 1979).
——, Eppink, J. and Gomer, H. (1979) 'Management of strategic surprise and discontinuity: problem of managerial decisiveness', *Économies et Sociétés*, [1979], Nº 1 Série SG: pp. unknown.
This item was not cited by Ansoff (1992) or Hussey (1999) but the citation is found on the Institut des Sciences Mathématiques et Économiques Appliquées website (www.ismea.org) *Économies et Sociétés*, Présentation de la série Sciences et Gestion, Management Strategique, Numéro 1 (Avril–Juin 1979).
—— (1981a) *Strateginen Johtaminen* (trans. P. Rajala), Espoo, Finland: Weilin + Göös. Finnish translation of Ansoff (1979) *Strategic Management*. (As of 2006 available via WorldCat.)
—— (1981b) *Strategisk ledelse*, s.l.: Bedriftsøkonomens forlag.
Norwegian translation of Ansoff (1979) *Strategic Management*. (As of 2006 available via Nasjonalbiblioteket (The Norwegian National Library), Oslo.)
—— (1982a) *Strategic Dimensions of Internationalization*, Working Paper 82–37, Brussels, Belgium: European Institute for Advanced Studies in Management. (As of 2006 available via WorldCat. Available in Europe via BL.)
—— (1982b) *Strategic Response in Turbulent Environments*, Working Paper 82–35, Brussels, Belgium: European Institute for Advanced Studies in Management.
(As of 2006 available via WorldCat. Available in Europe via BL.)
——, Kirsch, W. and Roventa, P. (1982) 'Dispersed positioning in strategic portfolio analysis', *Industrial Marketing Management* 11, 4: 237–52.
—— (1983a) *Administração estratégica*, São Paulo, Brasil: Atlas.
Portuguese translation of Ansoff (1979, 1982) *Strategic Management*. (As of 2006 available via Biblioteca Nacional de Portugal (National Library of Portugal), Lisbon.)
—— (1983b) *Ce lue guan li, you ming, Chuang xin jing ying ce lue gui hua* (trans. X. Shixiang and L. Xiuxiong) (Xiu ding 2 ban. edn), Taibei Shi: Qian cheng qi ye guan li gong si.
Chinese translation of Ansoff (1979, 1982) *Strategic Management*. (As of 2006 available via WorldCat.)
—— (1984) *Strateginen Johtaminen käsikirja* (trans. M. Lainema), Helsingissä [Helsinki] Hki, Finland: Otava.
Finnish translation of Ansoff (1984) *Implanting Strategic Management*. (As of 2006 available via WorldCat. Available in Europe via Kansalliskirjasto (The National Library of Finland), Helsingin Yliopisto.)
—— (1985, 1997) *La dirección y su actitud ante el entorno* (trans. J. Aspiunza), Bilbao: Deusto.
Spanish translation of Ansoff (1979, 1982) *Strategic Management*. (As of 2006 both printings available via Biblioteca Nacional de Español (National Library of Spain), Madrid. WorldCat has 1985 printing only.)
—— (1985, 1986) *La Estrategia de la Empresa*, Barcelona, Spain: Orbis, D. L.
Spanish translation of Ansoff (1965) *Corporate Strategy*.
(As of 2006 the 1985 printing available via WorldCat, both printings available via Biblioteca Nacional de Español (National Library of Spain), Madrid.)

—— (1985) *Zarzadzanie strategiczne* (trans. K. Oblój and J. N. Sajkiewicz), Warszawa: Panstwowe Wydaw. Ekonomiczne.
Polish translation of Ansoff (1979, 1982) *Strategic Management*. (As of 2006 available via WorldCat. Available in Europe via Biblioteka Narodowa (National Library of Poland), Warsaw.)
—— (1986) *La Estrategia de la Empresa*, 2ª ed, Barcelona, Spain: Orbis, D. L.
Spanish translation of Ansoff (1987a, b) *Corporate Strategy*. This publisher reprinted the translation in the following year
• 1987, 3a ed
(As of 2006 available from WorldCat. Available via Biblioteca Nacional de Español (National Library of Spain), Madrid.)
—— (1987) *Organizzazione Innovativa* (trans. L. Di Stasi and P. Pieraccini), [Milano, Italy]: IPSOA scuola d'impresa.
Italian translation of Ansoff (1984) *Implanting Strategic Management*. (As of 2006 available in Europe via Biblioteca nazionale centrale di Roma (National Central Library of Rome), Rome.)
—— (1989a) *Stratégie du développement de l'entreprise: une approche méthodologique du management stratégique dans le dernier quart du XXe siècle* (trans. B. Hou) (Ed. Nouv. éd. Mise à jour et rèv.), Paris: Ed. d'Organisation.
French translation of Ansoff (1987a) *Corporate Strategy*. There appear to be two publishers, Nouveaux Horizons and Ed. d'Organisation, both of Paris, publishing the same series 'Les Classiques EO'. (As of 2006 still available via WorldCat. Available in Europe via Bibliothèque nationale de France (The National Library of France), Paris.)
—— (1989b) *Strategicheskoe upravlenie* (trans. L. I. Evenko), Moskva: Ekonomika.
Russian translation of Ansoff (1984) *Implanting Strategic Management*. (As of 2006 available via WorldCat. Unable to confirm presence in Russian libraries.)
—— (1989c) *Strategia 2000* (trans. A. Vakkuri), [Helsinki] Hki, Finland: Rastor-julkaisut (Gummerus).
Finnish translation of Ansoff (1987b) *New Corporate Strategy*. (As of 2006 available via WorldCat.)
—— (1990) *A nova estratégia empresarial*, São Paulo, Brasil: Editora Atlas.
Portuguese translation of Ansoff (1987b) *New Corporate Strategy*. (As of 2006 available in Europe via Biblioteca Nacional de Portugal (National Library of Portugal), Lisbon.)
—— (1992) *Introduction au management stratégique* (trans. H. Allaigre), Paris: CSP.
This is a book of 126 pages. The original English version is not known. (As of 2006 still available via WorldCat. Available in Europe via Bibliothèque nationale de France (National Library of France), Paris.)
Moore, J. I. (1992) 'H. Igor Ansoff', in *Writers on Strategy and Strategic Management: the Theory of Strategy and the Practice of Strategic Management at Enterprise, Corporate, Business and Functional Levels*, Harmondsworth: Penguin Books, pp. 15–33.
(As of 2006 available via WorldCat.)
Ansoff, H. I. (1993) *Senryaku keiei* (trans. G. Nakamura), dailkan, Tokyo: Toshi Bunkasha.
Japanese translation of Ansoff (1979, 1982) *Strategic Management*. (As of 2006 available via WorldCat. Available in Japan via National Diet Library, Tokyo.)

—— and McDonnell, E. J. (1993) *Implantando a administração estratégica* (trans. A. Z. Sanvicente and G. A. Plonsky) (2. edn), São Paulo: Atlas.
Portuguese translation of Ansoff and McDonnell (1990) *Implanting Strategic Management*. (As of 2006 available via WorldCat.)

—— (1994) 'Comment on Henry Mintzberg's rethinking strategic planning', *Long Range Planning* 27, 3: 31–2.

—— and McDonnell, E. J. (1997) *La dirección estratégica en la práctica empresarial* (trans. M. A. S. Carrión) (2a edn), Wilmington, Del.: Addison-Wesley Interamericana.
Spanish translation of Ansoff (1990) *Implanting Strategic Management*. In 1998 the same publisher published a version in Mexico. (As of 2006 both versions available via WorldCat. The Mexican publication available from Universidad Panamericana, Mexico City.)

Lombriser, R. and Ansoff, H. I. (1997) 'How successful top intrapreneurs pilot [sic] firms through the turbulent 1990s', in D. E. Hussey (ed.) *The Innovation Challenge*, Chichester, West Sussex: Wiley, pp. 93–112.
(As of 2006 available via WorldCat.)

van der Velten, T. and Ansoff, H. I. (1998) 'Managing business portfolios in German companies', *Long Range Planning* 31, 6: 879–85.

Ansoff, H. I. and Antoniou, P. H. (2003) *Bian ge guo jia zhong gong si fa zhan zhan lüe*, (trans. Z. Liyun and A. Yanzhen) (Di 1 ban. edn), Beijing: Zhongguo ren min da xue chu ban she.
The publisher is the People's University Press, Beijing. It is not clear which of Ansoff's publication this is a translation of. (As of 2006 available via WorldCat.)

Antoniou, P. H. and Ansoff, H. I. (2004) 'Strategic management of technology', *Technology Analysis and Strategic Management* 16, 2: 275–91.

Unmatched citations from other sources

Ansoff, H. I. and Antoniou, P. H. (1998) *Turbulence Concept: Strategic Management for Difficult Times*, s.l.: John Wiley & Sons.
This citation can be found on the WWW and comes complete with an ISBN of 0-471-97491-9 but the item does not appear in WorldCat, LC or BL. It appears that this book was not produced by Wiley.

——, Antoniou, P. H. and Lewis, A. (2003) *Optimizing Profitability During the 21st Century*, Ann Arbor, Mich.: Xanedu Original Works.
This citation can be found on the WWW but the item does not appear in WorldCat, LC or BL. The book is published by a print-on-demand publisher and has not been placed in LC as part of legal deposit.

—— (2004) *Strategic Management: Introduction to the Ansoffian Approach*, Ann Arbor, Mich.: Xanedu Original Works.
This citation can be found on the WWW but the item does not appear in WorldCat, LC or BL. The book is published by a print-on-demand publisher and has not been placed in LC as part of legal deposit.

—— and Antoniou, P. H. (2005?) *The Secrets of Strategic Management: the Ansoffian Approach*, s.l.: Booksurge Llc.
This citation can be found on the WWW and comes complete with an ISBN of 1-419-61178-X but the item does not appear in WorldCat, LC or BL. There are

variations on the date of publication for this book between 2005 and 2006. It appears that this book has yet to be published.

4 References

Ansoff, H. I. (1964) 'Planning as a practical management tool', *Financial Executive* 32: 34–7.

—— (1965) *Corporate Strategy: an Analytical Approach to Business Policy for Growth and Expansion*, New York: McGraw-Hill Book Co.

—— (1968) 'Vers une théorie stratégique des entreprises [Towards a strategic theory of the firm]', *Économies et Sociétés* 2, 3: pp. unknown.

—— (ed.) (1969, 1972, 1977) *Business Strategy: Selected Readings*, Harmondsworth: Penguin.

—— (1979, 1982) *Strategic Management*, London: Macmillan.

—— (1984) *Implanting Strategic Management*, Englewood Cliffs, NJ: Prentice Hall Inc.

—— (1987a) *Corporate strategy* (rev. edn), Harmondsworth, Middlesex, England: Penguin Books.

—— (1987b) *New Corporate Strategy* (rev. edn), New York: Wiley.

—— (1988) *The New Corporate Strategy*, New York: McGraw-Hill Book Co.

—— (1992) 'A profile of intellectual growth', in A. G. Bedeian (ed.) *Management Laureates: a Collection of Autobiographical Essays*, vol. 1, Greenwich, Conn.: JAI Press, pp. portrait, 3–39.

Ansoff, H. I., Avner, J., Brandenburg, R. G., Portner, F. E. and Radosevich, R. (1970) 'Does planning pay? The effect of planning on success of acquisitions in American firms', *Long Range Planning* 3, 2: 2–7.

Ansoff, H. I. and Brandenburg, R. G. (1969) 'A language for organization design', in E. Jantsch (ed.) *Perspectives of Planning*, Paris: OECD, pp. 349–93.

——, —— (1971a) 'A language for organization design: part I', *Management Science* 17, 12, Application Series: B705–B716.

——, —— (1971b) 'A language for organization design: part II', *Management Science* 17, 12, Application Series: B717–B731.

——, Brandenburg, R. G., Portner, F. E. and Radosevich, H. R. (1972) *Twenty Years of Acquisition Behavior in America: a Comparative Study of Mergers and Acquisitions of U.S. Manufacturing Firms 1946–1965*, London: Cassell/Associated Business Programmes.

——, Declerck, R. P. and Hayes, R. L. (eds) (1976) *From Strategic Planning to Strategic Management*, London: John Wiley & Sons.

——, Kirsch, W. and Roventa, P. (1982) 'Dispersed positioning in strategic portfolio analysis', *Industrial Marketing Management* 11, 4: 237–52.

—— and Leontiades, J. C. (1976) 'Strategic portfolio management', *Journal of General Management* 4, 1: 13–29.

—— and McDonnell, E. J. (1990) *Implanting Strategic Management* (2nd edn), Hemel Hempstead, Hertfordshire: Prentice Hall International (UK).

Hussey, D. E. (1999) 'Igor Ansoff's continuing contribution to strategic management', *Strategic Change* 8, 7: 375–92.

Johnson, R. L (1967) *Interface: Some Thoughts on the Impact of Computerized Management Information Systems on Corporate Management-staff Relationships* Menlo Park, Calif.: Stanford Research Institute.

Mintzberg, H. (1991) 'Learning 1, planning 0: Reply to Igor Ansoff', *Strategic Management Journal* 12, 6: 463–6.

Williams, J. (2002) 'H. Igor Ansoff, 83; educator drew worldwide acclaim', *The San Diego Union Tribune* (July 16): 16.

Notes

1 The librarians at Brown University, Rhode Island, USA, were extremely helpful in finding the correct bibliographic citation of this article for me.

2 *Management Technology* (ISSN 0542-4917) was published from 1960–64 before being absorbed into *Management Science* (ISSN 0025-1909). The journal is available via JStor.

3 The *Journal of Business Policy* ran from the northern Autumn, 1970 to 1973 (ISSN 0021 9479) and was subsumed into the *Journal of General Management* (ISSN 0306 3070) from late 1973.

4 *Tijdschrift voor Efficiënt Directiebeleid* (ISSN unknown) published by the Netherlands Institute for Efficiency, The Hague, is available in the USA via WorldCat, its longest run from Michigan State University, and can also be accessed in The Netherlands and South Africa

5 *Bedrijfskunde* (ISSN 0165 0971) is available for 1975 from the Library of Congress, Washington DC. It has not been published since the second issue 2003.

6 There are two journals with the same name published in French, one from Lausanne by the Centre romand de Promotion du Management (ISSN 0009-2177) which ran from 1939 to 1982 and the other published in Genève by the Association d'Organisation Scientifique du Travail which ran from 1947 to 1982, ISSN unknown. The former journal is available in part via WorldCat from Montreal, the latter from Northern Illinois University and is also available from the Bibliothèque nationale de France.

7 *Cahiers Africains d'administration Publique* or *African Administrative Studies* (ISSN 0007-9588) is published twice yearly.

8 *Tehokas yritys johtamistoimen ammattilehti* (ISSN 0356-5327) was a monthly periodical which ran from 1975 to 1980. It is available via Worldcat and Kansalliskirjasto (The National Library of Finland), Helsingin Yliopisto.

9 *Harvard Business Manager* is a German serial publication published in Hamburg by Manager Magazine and is the German edition of *Harvard Business Review*. The preceding title of the journal was *Harvard Manager*. Available via WorldCat.

10 *Sinergia* (ISSN unknown) is an irregular publication of Universidade do Rio Grande, Departmento de Ciencias Economicas, Administrativas e Contabeis, which commenced publication in 1985. According to the Biblioteca Nacional do Brasil (National Library of Brazil), Rio de Janeiro, Brazil, publication was suspended in 1986–1987 and from 1989 to 1991. Note: there is a science fiction periodical published from Buenos Aires in the 1980s also with this title.

11 *International Management Development Review* (ISSN 0266-7908) is an annual UK publication available via BL.

12 *International Review of Strategic Management* (ISSN 1047-7918) is an annual serial which ran from 1990 to 1995 published by Wiley. The individual volumes were often given titles and treated as compilations and provided with individual ISBNs.

13 *Enseignement et Gestion* was published in Paris from 1971 to 1985 for *Fondation nationale pour l'enseignement de la gestion des entreprises* as individual numbers (ISSN 0765-7579). This journal is available from the Bibliothèque nationale de France. From 1986 the journal became *Formation et Gestion* and then *Revue française de Gestion*.

Part 1

ANSOFF: THE MAN

1

ON GURUS

John Peters

Source: *Management Decision* 31(6) (1993): 9–10.

Many, many authors have contributed with value to the field of business policy. What follows is a brief round-up of six of the best, as an introduction to some of the ideas which govern both research and practice.

H. Igor Ansoff

The father of the study of strategic management, and the first of the strategy "gurus", was Professor H. Igor Ansoff, with his classic book back in the 1960s, *Corporate Strategy*[2].

Ansoff separated the decisions about a business, or *business policy*, into three areas:

1   the operational, or how to do what we do better;
2   the administrative, or how we support and organize for what we do;
3   the strategic, or what we want to be doing (see Table I).

Though the world has changed mightily since the 1960s, Ansoff's analysis and insights have hardly been bettered. Business policy is about decisions. The operational decisions of an organization require constant attention.

There is always something going wrong which needs to be fixed; always some matter which needs to be addressed. So constant is this attention, it can drive out the opportunity to reflect on the future. The urgent can easily drive out the important.

But, as Ansoff pointed out all those years ago, recurring *operational* problem solving can indicate the need for *strategic* decisions to be taken. The repeated series of customer complaints requiring attention may indicate the need for attention to be paid to the product-service package itself.

It was Ansoff who introduced the notion of the "planning horizon"; as far as you can see to predict the future with an accuracy of plus or minus

Table I Principal Decision Classes in the Firm.

	Strategic	Administrative	Operating
Problem	To select product-market mix which optimizes firm's ROI[a] potential	To structure firm's resources for optimum performance	To optimize realization of ROI potential
Nature of problem	Allocation of total resources among product-market opportunities	Organization, acquisition, and development of resources	Budgeting of resources among principal functional areas Scheduling resource application and conversion Supervision and control
Key decisions	Objectives and goals Diversification strategy Expansion strategy Administrative strategy Finance strategy Growth method Timing of growth	Organization: structure of information, authority, and responsibility flows Structure of resource-conversion: work flows, distribution system, facilities location Resource acquisition and development: financing facilities and equipment, personnel, raw materials	Operating objectives and goals Pricing and output levels. Operating levels: production schedules, inventory levels, warehousing, etc. Marketing policies and strategy R&D policies and strategy Control
Key characteristics	Decisions centralized Partial ignorance Decisions non-repetitive Decisions not self-regenerative	Conflict between strategy and operations Conflict between individual and institutional objectives Strong coupling between economic and social variables Decisions triggered by strategic and/or operating problems	Decentralized decisions Risk and uncertainty Repetitive decisions Large volume of decisions Suboptimization forced by complexity Decisions self-regenerative

[a] ROI stands for "return on investment".
Source: [2]

20 per cent. How much more useful this is as a concept than those who say plans should be five years ahead, or one year ahead, or some fixed term. Plans should be as far ahead as the horizon stretches; if the atmosphere is misty, they will have a shorter horizon than if the day is a clear one.

It was Ansoff also who introduced the idea of four strategic directional options; existing products to existing markets; existing products to new markets; new products to existing markets; and new products to new markets.

Corporate Strategy is a simple, short book. How much we have complicated this simple picture over the years.

2

H. IGOR ANSOFF, 83; EDUCATOR DREW WORLDWIDE ACCLAIM

Jack Williams

Source: *The San Diego Union Tribune*, July 16 (2002): 16.

H. Igor Ansoff, a retired educator and author whose visionary theories on strategic business management inspired worldwide acclaim, died Sunday in Escondido. He was 83.

The cause of death was complications of pneumonia, said Mink Stavenga, dean of the business college at Alliant International University.

Dr. Ansoff, who died at Silverado Senior Living, taught 17 years at U.S. International University before retiring two years ago as a distinguished professor emeritus. USIU became Alliant International University in July 2001.

An applied mathematician, Dr. Ansoff shifted his emphasis to economics in the 1950s while employed by RAND Corp., a brain trust created by the U.S. Air Force.

In 1956, he took a job as a planning specialist for Lockheed Aircraft Corp., gaining practical experience in analyzing the complexities of a business environment. It was his introduction into the "real world" of business management, he would later say.

Dr. Ansoff left Lockheed in 1963 to teach at the graduate school of Carnegie Mellon University and complete the first of five books, the ground-breaking "Corporate Strategies."

The book, which explored the need for corporate managers to prepare for the future by anticipating changes in the firm's environment, was translated into several foreign languages.

By the time he joined the USIU faculty in 1983, creating the school's strategic management program, he had been called "the father of strategic management" by Henry Mintzburg, one of the leading researchers in the field.

Yet Dr. Ansoff was probably better known in Europe and Japan than in the United States, said Stavenga and USIU graduate Peter M. Antoniou.

"He was considered way too much on the frontier in the U.S. in the 1960s and 1970s, even though a lot of European countries were applying his strategies," Antoniou said. "The U.S. considered it too complex. The more complex the business environment, the better it applies, and now U.S. companies are coming closer to what he proposed in the 1970s."

Dr. Ansoff theorized that if a company becomes purely self-serving it soon loses track of its direction and dies. He believed long-term profitability results from a commitment to understanding the political and social fabric of a community.

His strategic success hypothesis, formulated in his last book, "The New Corporate Strategy," contends that the financial performance of a firm is maximized whenever both the strategy and management capability match the turbulence of the firm's environment.

He proposed approaches to accommodate what he called five "turbulence levels" in the business environment ranging from placid and predictable to highly changeable and unpredictable.

In his book "Strategic Management," Dr. Ansoff broadened strategic planning into a multidisciplinary process, adding individual and group dynamics, political processes and organizational culture.

Stavenga said Dr. Ansoff made an immediate impact at USIU, attracting students from all over the world who have gone on to validate his theories.

"His popularity and fame are equal to that of Peter Drucker as a management guru," Stavenga said.

Through his private consulting firm, Ansoff Associates, Dr. Ansoff advised such major companies as General Electric, Philips, IBM, Gulf Oil, General Foods and Westinghouse.

Every two years, the Ansoff Strategic Management Award is presented to an individual who significantly contributes to the development of strategic thinking.

Dr. Ansoff was born in Vladivostok, Russia, and moved to the United States with his parents at 17.

Despite limited knowledge of English, he graduated at the top of his class at New York's elite Stuyvesant High School in 1937. He earned master's degrees in math and physics and in general engineering at Stevens Institute of Technology in New Jersey.

During World War II and into 1946, he was a member of the U.S. Naval Reserve. He served as a liaison with the Russian Navy and as an instructor in physics at the U.S. Naval Academy.

In 1948, before joining RAND Corp., he received a doctorate in applied mathematics at Brown University. He also was awarded five honorary doctorates over the years.

Dr. Ansoff held a joint appointment for seven years at the Stockholm School of Economics and at the European Institute for Advanced Studies in Management. Based in Brussels, Belgium, at the time, he was looking for a more moderate climate and found it in San Diego. While based at USIU, he lived in Scripps Ranch. Survivors include his wife, Skip; sons, Rick of Scripps Ranch, Chris of Memphis, Tenn., and Peter of Washington, D.C.; and two grandchildren.

A celebration of life is scheduled from 4 to 6 p.m. Aug. 3 at Scripps Ranch Library.

Donations are suggested to the Silverado Senior Living Foundation, 1500 Borden Road, Escondido, CA 92026.

Part 2

STRATEGIC MANAGEMENT

3

REFLECTING ON
THE STRATEGY PROCESS

Henry Mintzberg and Joseph Lampel

Source: *Sloan Management Review*, Spring (1999): 21–30.

Strategy has long had its historical distinctions; fortunately, it is experiencing a newfound eclecticism.

We are the blind people and strategy formation is our elephant. Each of us, in trying to cope with the mysteries of the beast, grabs hold of some part or other, and, in the words of John Godfrey Saxe's poem of the last century:

> *Rail on in utter ignorance*
> *of what each other mean,*
> *And prate about an Elephant*
> *Not one of [us] has seen!*

Consultants have been like big game hunters embarking on their safaris for tusks and trophies, while academics have preferred photo safaris — keeping a safe distance from the animals they pretend to observe.

Managers take one narrow perspective or another — the glories of planning or the wonders of learning, the demands of external competitive analyses or the imperatives of an internal "resource-based" view. Much of this writing and advising has been decidedly dysfunctional, simply because managers have no choice but to cope with the entire beast.

In the first part of this article, we review briefly the evolution of the field in terms of ten "schools."[1] We ask whether these perspectives represent fundamentally different processes of strategy making or different *parts* of the same process. In both cases, our answer is yes. We seek to show how some recent work tends to cut across these historical perspectives — in a sense, how cross-fertilization has occurred. To academics, this represents confusion and disorder, whereas to others — including ourselves — it expresses a certain welcome eclecticism, a broadening of perspectives. We discuss this in terms of another metaphor that is also popular in strategic management: the tree with its roots and branches.

Ten schools of strategy formation

In his article "The Magic Number Seven, Plus or Minus Two: Some Limits on Our Capacity for Processing Information," psychologist George Miller suggested in 1956 that the popularity of typologies using the number seven implies the number of "chunks" of information people can comfortably retain in their short-term memory.[2] We hope that people interested in strategy can function at the upper limit of this range and, indeed, a bit beyond, because our historical survey of strategy literature suggests that it has been characterized by ten major schools since its inception in the 1960s — three *prescriptive* (or "ought") and seven *descriptive* (or "is").

We assume that the reader is familiar with the literature and practice of strategic management, if not necessarily with this particular characterization of them. Accordingly, we briefly summarize the schools *(see also Table 1)*.

Design school: a process of conception

The original perspective — dating back to Selznick, followed by Chandler, and given sharper definition by Andrews — sees strategy formation as achieving the essential fit between internal strengths and weaknesses and external threats and opportunities.[3] Senior management formulates clear, simple, and unique strategies in a deliberate process of conscious thought — which is neither formally analytical nor informally intuitive — so that everyone can implement the strategies. This was the dominant view of the strategy process, at least into the 1970s, and, some might argue, to the present day, given its implicit influence on most teaching and practice. The design school did not develop, however, in the sense of giving rise to variants within its own context. Rather, it combined with other views in rather different contexts.

Planning school: a formal process

The planning school grew in parallel with the design school — indeed H. Igor Ansoff's book appeared in 1965, as did the initial Andrews text.[4] But, in sheer volume of publication, the planning school predominated by the mid-1970s, faltered in the 1980s, yet continues to be an important branch of the literature today. Ansoff's book reflects most of the design school's assumptions except a rather significant one: that the process is not just cerebral but formal, decomposable into distinct steps, delineated by

Table 1 Dimensions of the Ten Schools, Part A.

	Design	Planning	Positioning	Entrepreneurial	Cognitive
Sources	P. Selznick (and perhaps earlier work, for example, by W. H. Newman), then K. R. Andrews.[a]	H. I. Ansoff.[b]	Purdue University work (D. E. Schendel, K. J. Hatten), then notably M. E. Porter.[c]	J. A. Schumpeter, A. H. Cole, and others in economics.[d]	H. A. Simon and J. G. March.[e]
Base Discipline	None (architecture as metaphor).	Some links to urban planning, systems theory, and cybernetics.	Economics (industrial organization) and millitary history.	None (although early writings come from economists).	Psychology (cognitive).
Champions	Case study teachers (especially at or from Harvard University), leadership aficionados — especially in the United States.	"Professional" managers, MBAs, staff experts (especially in finance), consultants, and government controllers — especially in France and the United States.	As in planning school, particularly analytical staff types, consulting "boutiques," and military writers — especially in the United States.	Popular business press, individualists, small business people everywhere, but most decidedly in Latin America and among overseas Chinese.	Those with a psychological bent — pessimists in one wing, optimists in the other.
Intended Message	Fit.	Formalize.	Analyze.	Envision.	Cope or create.
Realized Message	Think (strategy making as case study).	Program (rather than formulate).	Calculate (rather than create or commit).	Centralize (then hope).	Worry (being unable to cope in either case).
School Category	Prescriptive.	Prescriptive.	Prescriptive.	Descriptive (some prescriptive).	Descriptive.
Associated Homily	"Look before you leap."	"A stitch in time saves nine."	"Nothin' but the facts, ma'am."	"Take us to your leader."	"I'll see it when I believe it."

[a] P. Selznick, *Leadership in Administration: A Sociological Interpretation* (Evanston, Illinois: Row, Peterson, 1957);
W. H. Newman. *Administrative Action. The Techniques of Organization and Management.* New Jersey: Prentice-Hall, 1951); and
E. P. Learned, C. R. Christensen, K. R. Andrews, and W. D. Guth, *Business Policy: Text and Cases* (Homewood, Illinois: Irwin, 1965).
[b] H. I. Ansoff, *Corporate Strategy* (New York: McGraw-Hill, 1965).
[c] K. J. Hatten and D. E. Schendel, "Heterogeneity within an Industry: Firm Conduct in the U. S. Brewing Industry, 1952–1971," *Journal of Industrial Economics*, volume 26, December 1977, pp. 97–113.
M. E. Porter, *Competitive Strategy* (New York: Free Press, 1980); and
M. E. Porter, *Competitive Advantage: Creating and Sustaining Superior Performance* (New York: Free Press, 1985).
[d] J. A. Schumpeter, *The Theory of Economic Development* (Cambridge, Massachusetts: Harvard University Press, 1934); and
A. H. Cole, *Business Enterprise in Its Social Setting* (Cambridge, Massachusetts: Harvard University Press, 1959).
[e] H. A. Simon, *Administrative Behavior* (New York: Macmillan, 1947); and
J. G. March and H. A. Simon, *Organizations* (New York: Wiley, 1958).

Table 1 Dimensions of the Ten Schools, Part B.

	Learning	Power	Cultural	Environmental	Configuration
Sources	C. E. Lindblom, R. M. Cyert and J. G. March, K. E. Weick, J. B. Quinn, and C. K. Prahalad and G. Hamel.[f]	G. T. Allison (micro), J. Pfeffer and G. R. Salancik, and W. G. Astley (macro).[g]	E. Rhenman and R. Normann in Sweden. No obvious source elsewhere.[h]	M. T. Hannan and J. Freeman. Contingency theorists (e.g., D. S. Pugh et al.).[i]	A. D. Chandler, McGill University group (H. Mintzberg, D. Miller, and others), R. E. Miles and C. C. Snow.[j]
Base Discipline	None (perhaps some peripheral links to learning theory in psychology and education). Chaos theory in mathematics.	Political science.	Anthropology.	Biology.	History.
Champions	People inclined to experimentation, ambiguity, adaptability — especially in Japan and Scandinavia.	People who like power, politics, and conspiracy — especially in France.	People who like the social, the spiritual, the collective — especially in Scandinavia and Japan.	Population ecologists, some organization theorists, and positivists in general — especially in the Anglo-Saxon countries.	Lumpers and integrators in general, as well as change agents. Configuration perhaps most popular in the Netherlands. Transformation most popular in the United States.
Intended Message	Learn.	Promote.	Coalesce.	React.	Integrate, transform.
Realized Message	Play (rather than pursue).	Hoard (rather than share).	Perpetuate (rather than change).	Capitulate (rather than confront).	Lump (rather than split, adapt).
School Category	Descriptive.	Descriptive.	Descriptive.	Descriptive.	Descriptive and prescriptive.
Associated Homily	"If at first you don't succeed, try, try again."	"Look out for number one."	"An apple never falls far from the tree."	"It all depends."	"To everything there is a season. . . ."

[f] D. Braybrooke and C. E. Lindblom, *A Strategy of Decision* (New York: Free Press, 1963);
R. M. Cyert and J. G. March, *A Behavioral Theory of the Firm* (Englewood Cliffs, New Jersey: Prentice-Hall, 1963);
K. E. Weick, The Social Psychology of Organizing (Reading, Massachusetts: Addison-Wesley, first edition 1969, second edition 1979);
J. B. Quinn, *Strategies for Change: Logical Incrementalism* (Homewood, Illinois: Irwin, 1980); and
G. Hamel and C. K. Prahalad, *Competing for the Future* (Boston: Harvard Business School Press, 1994);
[g] G. T. Allison, *Essence of Decision: Explaining the Cuban Missile Crisis* (Boston: Little, Brown, 1971);
J. Pfeffer and G. R. Salancik, *The External Control of Organizations. A Resource Dependence Perspective* (New York: Harper & Row, 1978); and
W. G. Astley, "Toward an Appreciation of Collective Strategy," *Academy of Management Review*, volume 9, July 1984, pp. 526–533.
[h] E. Rhenman, *Organization Theory for Long-Range Planning* (London: Wiley, 1973); and
R. Normann, *Management for Growth* (New York: Wiley, 1977).
[i] M. T. Hannan and J. Freeman, "The Population Ecology of Organizations," *American Journal of Sociology*, volume 82, March 1977, pp. 929–964; and
D. S. Pugh, D. J. Hickson, C. R. Hinings, and C. Turner, "Dimensions of Organizational Structure," *Administrative Science Quarterly*, volume 13, June 1968, pp. 65–105.
[j] A. D. Chandler, *Strategy and Structure: Chapters in the History of the Industrial Enterprise* (Cambridge, Massachusetts: MIT Press, 1962);
H. Mintzberg, *The Structuring of Organizations* (Englewood Cliffs, New Jersey, Prentice-Hall, 1979); and

checklists, and supported by techniques (especially with regard to objectives, budgets. programs, and operating plans). This means that staff planners replaced senior managers, de facto, as the key players in the process.

Positioning school: an analytical process

The third of the prescriptive schools, commonly labeled positioning, was the dominant view of strategy formation in the 1980s. It was given impetus especially by Michael Porter in 1980, following earlier work on strategic positioning in academe (notably by Hatten and Schendel) and in consulting by the Boston Consulting Group and the PIMS project — all preceded by a long literature on military strategy, dating back to Sun Tzu in 400 B.C.[5] In this view, strategy reduces to generic positions selected through formalized analyses of industry situations. Hence, the planners become analysts. This proved especially lucrative to consultants and academics alike, who could sink their teeth into hard data and promote their "scientific truths" to journals and companies. This literature grew in all directions to include strategic groups, value chains, game theories, and other ideas — but always with this analytical bent.

Entrepreneurial school: a visionary process

Meanwhile, on other fronts, mostly in trickles and streams rather than waves, wholly different approaches to strategy formation arose. Much like the design school, the entrepreneurial school centered the process on the chief executive; but unlike the design school and opposite from the planning school, it rooted that process in the mysteries of intuition. That shifted strategies from precise designs, plans. or positions to vague *visions* or broad perspectives, to be seen, in a sense, often through metaphor. This focused the process on particular contexts — start-up, niche, or private ownership, as well as "turnaround" by the forceful leader — although the case was certainly put forth that every organization needs the vision of a creative leader. In this view, however, the leader maintains such close control over *implementing* his or her *formulated* vision that the distinction central to the three prescriptive schools begins to break down.

Cognitive school: a mental process

On the academic front, the origin of strategies generated considerable interest. If strategies developed in people's minds as frames, models, maps, concepts, or schemas, what could be understood about those mental processes? Particularly in the 1980s and continuing today, research has grown steadily on cognitive biases in strategy making and on cognition as information processing, knowledge structure mapping, and concept attainment —

the latter important for strategy formation, yet on which progress has been minimal. Meanwhile, another, newer branch of this school adopted a more subjective *interpretative* or *constructivist* view of the strategy process: that cognition is used to construct strategies as creative interpretations, rather than simply to map reality in some more or less objective way, however distorted.

Learning school: an emergent process

Of all the *descriptive* schools, the learning school grew into a veritable wave and challenged the always dominant prescriptive schools. Dating back to Lindblom's early work on disjointed incrementalism and running through Quinn's logical incrementalism, Bower's and Burgelman's notions of venturing, Mintzberg *et al.*'s ideas about emergent strategy, and Weick's notion of retrospective sense making, a model of strategy making as learning developed that differed from the earlier schools.[6] In this view, strategies are emergent, strategists can be found throughout the organization, and so-called formulation and implementation intertwine.

Power school: a process of negotiation

A thin, but quite different stream in the literature has focused on strategy making rooted in power. Two separate orientations seem to exist. *Micro* power sees the development of strategies *within* the organization as essentially political — a process involving bargaining, persuasion, and confrontation among actors who divide the power. *Macro* power views the organization as an entity that uses its power over others and among its partners in alliances, joint ventures, and other network relationships to negotiate "collective" strategies in its interest.

Cultural school: a social process

Hold power up to a mirror and its reverse image is culture. Whereas the former focuses on self-interest and fragmentation, the latter focuses on common interest and integration — strategy formation as a social process rooted in culture. Again, we find a thin stream of literature, focused particularly on the influence of culture in discouraging significant strategic change. Culture became a big issue in the U.S. literature after the impact of Japanese management was fully realized in the 1980s; later, some attention to the implications for strategy formation followed. However, interesting research developed in Sweden in the 1970s with culture as a central, although hardly exclusive, theme, stimulated by the early work of Rhenman and Normann, and carried out by people such as Hedberg and Jonsson, and others.[7]

Environmental school: a reactive process

Perhaps not strictly strategic management, if one defines the term as being concerned with how organizations use degrees of freedom to maneuver through their environments, the environmental school nevertheless deserves some attention for illuminating the demands of environment. In this category, we include so-called "contingency theory" that considers which responses are expected of organizations facing particular environmental conditions and "population ecology" writings that claim severe limits to strategic choice. "Institutional theory," which is concerned with the institutional pressures faced by organizations, is perhaps a hybrid of the power and cognitive schools.

Configuration school: a process of transformation

Finally, we come to a more extensive and integrative literature and practice. One side of this school, more academic and descriptive, sees organization as configuration — coherent clusters of characteristics and behaviors — and integrates the claims of the other schools — each configuration, in effect, in its own place. Planning, for example, prevails in machine-type organizations under conditions of relative stability, while entrepreneurship can be found under more dynamic configurations of start-up and turnaround. But if organizations can be described by such *states*, change must be described as rather dramatic *transformation* — the leap from one state to another. And so, a literature and practice of transformation — more prescriptive and practitioner oriented (and consultant promoted) — developed. These two different literatures and practices nevertheless complement one another and so, in our opinion, belong to the same school.

Prating about strategic management

During the nineteenth century, numerous explorers went in search of the source of the Nile. In time, it became increasingly evident that the source was not definitive. This was not something the expedition backers or the public wanted to hear. After some debate, the explorers announced their discovery: the source of the Nile was Lake Victoria! This is a verdict generally rejected by contemporary geographers, who believe the headstreams of the Kagera River in the highland of Burundi is a better answer. Different views may prevail in the future: the source of a river, after all, is a matter of interpretation, not a fact waiting to be discovered.

Strategic management has suffered from the problem that bedeviled the Victorian explorers. We, too, are a community of explorers, competing for discoveries, with backers eager for results and a public that demands answers.

43

Some explorers searching for the source of strategy have found "first principles" that explain the nature of the process. These have usually been rooted in basic disciplines, such as economics, sociology, or biology. Others have invoked a central concept, such as organization culture, to explain why some strategies succeed and others do not. The consequence has been to grasp one part of the strategic management elephant and prate about it as though none other exists. Or to acknowledge that other parts exist, but dismiss them as irrelevant. Consider Michael Porter's article "What Is Strategy?" which depicts the strategy process as deliberate and deductive.[8] Porter does not dismiss strategic learning so much as deny its very existence:

"If strategy is stretched to include employees and organizational arrangements, it becomes virtually everything a company does or consists of. Not only does this complicate matters, but it obscures the chain of causality that runs from competitive environment to position to activities to employee skills and organization."[9]

But why can't strategy be "everything a company does or consists of"? Is that not strategy as perspective — in contrast to position? And why must there be such a chain of causality, let alone one that runs in a single direction?

Porter's view of the strategy process leads him to the surprising conclusion that Japanese companies "rarely have strategies" and that they "will have to learn strategy."[10] Were this true, and given the performance of so many Japanese companies, strategy would hardly seem to be a necessary condition for corporate success. In our opinion, however, this is not the case. (Bear in mind that current problems in the Japanese economy or in its banking systems have not rendered many Japanese companies any less effective in their managerial practices.) Rather than having to learn about strategy, the Japanese might better teach Michael Porter about strategic learning.

Of course, in the affairs of writing and consulting, to succeed and to sell, champions must defend their positions, erecting borders around their views while dismissing or denying others. Or, to return to our metaphor, like butchers (we include ourselves in this group), they chop up reality for their own convenience, just as poachers grab the tusks of the elephant and leave the carcass to rot.

To repeat a key issue, such behavior ultimately does not serve the practicing manager. These people, as noted, have to deal with the entire beast of strategy formation, not only to keep it alive but to help sustain some real life energy. True, they can use it in various ways — just as an elephant can be a beast of burden or a symbol of ceremony — but only if it remains intact as a living being. The greatest failings of strategic management have occurred when managers took one point of view too seriously. This field had its obsession with planning, then generic positions based on careful calculations, and now learning.

Table 2 Blending of the Strategy Formation Schools.

Approach	Schools
Dynamic capabilities	Design, Learning
Resource-based theory	Cultural, Learning
Soft techniques (e.g., scenario analysis and stakeholder analysis)	Planning, Learning or Power
Constructionism	Cognitive, Cultural
Chaos and evolutionary theory	Learning, Environmental
Institutional theory	Environmental, Power or Cognitive
Intrapreneurship (venturing)	Environmental, Entrepreneurial
Revolutionary change	Configuration, Entrepreneurial
Negotiated strategy	Power, Positioning
Strategic maneuvering	Positioning, Power

Opening up the schools

Hence, we take pleasure in noting that some of the more recent approaches to strategy formation cut across these ten schools in eclectic and interesting ways. This suggests a broadening of the literature. (*See Table 2*, for a list of these across-school approaches.) For example, research on stakeholder analysis links the planning and positioning schools, whereas the work of Porter and others on what can be called strategic maneuvering (first-mover advantage, use of feints, etc.) connect the positioning to the power school.

Particularly popular are recent variants that blend the learning school with insights from other schools. Chaos theory, as applied to strategic management, might be seen as a hybrid of the learning and environmental schools. Perhaps best known is the "dynamic capabilities" approach of Prahalad and Hamel. We see their notions of core competence, strategic intent, and stretch — reminiscent of Itami's earlier work — as a hybrid of the learning and design schools: strong leadership to encourage continuous strategic learning.[11] "Resource-based theory," which seems similar, in fact, appears more like a hybrid of the learning and cultural schools. These two new views differ in orientation, if not content — the former more prescriptive and practitioner-focused, the latter more descriptive and research-focused. Leadership (as favored in the design school) is not a central concern to resource-based theorists. Instead they focus on competencies rooted in the essence of an organization (namely, its culture).[12]

One process or different approaches

As distinct as the schools may be, one issue about them is not clear. Do they represent different processes, that is, different approaches to strategy formation, or different parts of the same process? We have been ambiguous on

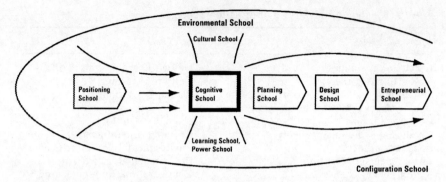

Figure 1 Strategy Formation as a Single Process.

this point, and we prefer to remain so, because we find either answer too constraining.

Some of the schools clearly are stages or aspects of the strategy formation process *(see Figure 1):*

- The cognitive school resides in the mind of the strategist located at the *center.*
- The positioning school looks *behind* at established data that is analyzed and fed into the black box of strategy making.
- The planning school looks slightly *ahead*, to program the strategies created in other ways.
- The design school looks farther *ahead* to a strategic perspective.
- The entrepreneurial school looks *beyond* to a unique vision of the future.
- The learning and power schools look *below*, enmeshed in details. Learning looks into the grass roots, whereas power looks under the rocks — to places that organizations may not want to expose.
- The cultural school looks *down*, enshrouded in clouds of beliefs.
- Above the cultural school, the environmental school looks *on*, so to speak.
- The configuration school, looks *at* the process, or, we might say, *all around* it, in contrast to the cognitive school that tries to look *inside* the process.

Dealing with all this complexity in one process may seem overwhelming. But that is the nature of the beast, for the fault lies neither in the stars nor in ourselves, but in the process itself. Strategy formation *is* judgmental designing, intuitive visioning, and emergent learning; it is about transformation as well as perpetuation; it must involve individual cognition and social interaction, cooperative as well as conflictive; it has to include analyzing before and programming after as well as negotiating during; and all this must be in response to what may be a demanding environment. Try to omit any of this, and watch what happens!

Yet, just as clearly, the process can tilt toward the attributes of one school or another: toward the entrepreneurial school during start-up or when there is the need for a dramatic turnaround, toward the learning school under dynamic conditions when prediction is well nigh impossible, and so on. Sometimes the process has to be more individually cognitive than socially interactive (in small business, for example). Some strategies seem to be more rationally deliberate (especially in mature mass-production industries and government), whereas others tend to be more adaptively emergent (as in dynamic, high-technology industries). The environment can sometimes be highly demanding (during social upheaval), yet at other times (or even at the same times) entrepreneurial leaders are able to maneuver through it with ease. There are, after all, identifiable stages and periods in strategy making, not in any absolute sense but as recognizable tendencies.

The inclination has been to favor the interpretation that the schools represent fundamentally different processes. (*Figure 2* plots the schools along two dimensions: states of the internal process and states of the external world. The schools scatter across the plot, implying that they represent different processes.) This may not be so bad if practitioners can at least pick and choose among the various processes (or combine them when appropriate) — as long as any one is not pushed to its illogical extreme *(see Table 3)*.

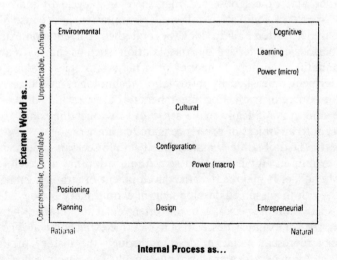

Figure 2 Strategy Formation as Many Processes.

Table 3 Going Over the Edge in Strategy Formation.

School	Illogical Extreme
Design	Fixation
Planning	Ritual
Positioning	Fortification
Entrepreneurial	Idolatry
Cognitive	Fantasy
Learning	Drift
Power	Intrigue
Cultural	Eccentricity
Environmental	Conformity
Configuration	Degeneration

Evolution of strategy?

Safari may be a single idea, but it is many experiences. As noted at the outset, there are safaris at ground level, whether of big game hunters or of tourists snapping pictures. There are also safaris from the air, which take a bird's eye view of different species as they hunt and rest. All reveal important truths. The problem for the thoughtful observer is to balance and combine these short- and long-term views. One way is to take an evolutionary perspective: strategy evolves, not passively but creatively, and so unpredictably, simply because organizations seek to be unique. The ingenuity of those who practice strategy should, therefore, constantly surprise those who study it.

Chandler and others observed that there is a cycle of innovation in strategy: spurts of innovation followed by imitation and consolidation.[13] Yet researchers often fail to look beyond their current contexts. Some studied periods characterized by consolidation, such as the 1970s and early 1980s, and then developed theories of generic strategies. Others observe today's ferment unleashed by information technologies and declare chaos theory the source of truth. For researchers to observe what some organizations do and systematically make sense of it is one thing, but to turn a generality into an object of reverence is quite another.

Hence, the field of strategy management should seek an understanding of its own evolution. But it must do so without adopting a pseudoscientific theory of change. It may be that the development of strategic management is at odds with the assumed development in evolutionary biology. This presumes a succession of species, with one often replacing another — the zebra and the horse, for example, descending from some extinct animal. The schools of strategy represent a line of descent through the history of the field, but this may not be a descent by replacement. The design school may be an ancestor of the positioning school, but it is not extinct. Older schools contribute to newer ones in complicated and often subterranean ways. They continue to live in practice, infiltrating newer frameworks under various guises.

The evolution of strategic management obeys different principles because it is driven by ideas and practices that originate from qualitatively different sources. We note four:

- New kinds of strategies emerge from *collaborative contacts* between organizations. Firms cannot avoid learning and borrowing when they trade and work together.
- The evolution of strategy is also pushed along by *competition and confrontation*. In strategy, as in other areas, necessity is the mother of invention, and, as elsewhere, new ideas and practices arise when managers try to outwit or beat back powerful rivals.
- New strategies are often a *recasting of the old*. In a sense, old strategic ideas never disappear entirely. They go underground and infiltrate new practices covertly. Not so much old wines in new bottles, but more like the blending of old and new malt whiskies.
- Finally, strategy is pushed along by the *sheer creativity* of managers, because they explore new ways of doing things.

Biologists often use the tree as a device for illustrating the relationship between species. Here, for us, the roots are the basic disciplines — economics, psychology, sociology, anthropology, political science, biology, and so on — that nourish and so exert a powerful influence over growth. The branches are our two types of schools. On the right side are the prescriptive schools: design, planning, positioning, and (partly perhaps) entrepreneurial. These are relatively well defined — carefully trimmed, if you like. On the left are the more descriptive schools, especially cultural, learning, cognitive, power, and environmental. These schools may have grown as relatively distinct and coherent, but they have become intertwined. In fact, as noted earlier, we find a general blurring of the boundaries here — or, if you like, tangling of the branches. The descriptive schools stray into each other's space, over time increasingly borrowing from each other.

The contrast between the prescriptive and descriptive schools is to some extent due to a fundamentally different attitude toward how research and knowledge should be developed. The proponents of the prescriptive schools tend to adopt a "managed growth" approach to knowledge: they fertilize and trim carefully to curb disruptive influence. In contrast, the descriptive schools prefer a more "natural growth," although they do graft to see what results.

There are obvious advantages and dangers to both approaches. The prescriptive schools are clear and consistent. This makes discussion and transmission of ideas easier, but it can also foster sterility in thinking and application. The descriptive schools tend to be fuller and richer, allowing for more experimentation and innovation. At the same time, they can end up in tangled confusion, generating many contingencies and multiple perspectives that stymie application.

In the end, the tree may be a more suitable image for the growth and development of strategy formation than Darwinian evolution because it does not favor a progression of what is newer and more elaborate. In a tree, the branches are no more or less important than the roots, and the branches on either side cannot be cut off without putting the tree out of balance. The structure seems untidy, but it is actually quite attractive. And it has and will continue to bear fruit!

In search of strategic management

Scholars and consultants should certainly continue to probe the important elements of each school. But, more importantly, we have to get beyond the narrowness of each school: we need to know how strategy formation, which combines all these schools and more, really works.

We need to ask better questions and generate fewer hypotheses — to allow ourselves to be pulled by real-life concerns rather than being pushed by reified concepts. We need better practice, not neater theory. So we must concern ourselves with process and content, statics and dynamics, constraint and inspiration. the cognitive and the collective, the planned and the learned, the economic and the political. In other words, we must give more attention to the entire elephant — to strategy formation as a whole. We may never see it fully, but we can certainly see it better.

References

1 H. Mintzberg, B. Ahlstrand, and J. Lampel, *Strategy Safari: A Guided Tour through the Wilds of Strategic Management* (New York: Free Press, 1998); see also:
   H. Mintzberg, "Strategy Formation: School of Thought," in J. Frederickson, ed., *Perspectives on Strategic Management* (New York: HarperCollins, 1990); and
   H. Mintzberg, *The Rise and Fall of Strategic Planning* (New York: Free Press. 1994).
2 G. A. Miller, "The Magic Number Seven Plus or Minus Two: Some Limits on Our Capacity for Processing Information," *Psychology Review*, volume 63, March 1956, pp. 81–97.
3 P. Selznick, *Leadership in Administration: A Sociological Interpretation* (Evanston, Illinois: Row, Peterson, 1957);
   A. D. Chandler, *Strategy and Structure: Chapters in the History of the Industrial Enterprise* (Cambridge, Massachusetts: MIT Press, 1962); and
   E. P. Learned, C. R. Christensen, K. R. Andrews, and W. D. Guth, *Business Policy: Text and Cases* (Homewood, Illinois: Irwin, 1965).

4 H. I. Ansoff, *Corporate Strategy* (New York: McGraw-Hill, 1965).

5 M. E. Porter, *Competitive Strategy: Techniques for Analyzing Industries and Competitors* (New York: Free Press, 1980);

K. J. Hatten and D. E. Schendel, "Heterogeneity within an Industry: Firm Conduct in the U. S. Brewing Industry, 1952–1971," *Journal of Industrial Economics*, Volume 26, December 1977, pp. 97–113;

B. D. Henderson, *Henderson on Corporate Strategy* (Cambridge, Massachusetts: Abt Books, 1979);

S. Schoeffler, R. D. Buzzell, and D. F. Heany, "Impact of Strategic Planning on Profit Performance," *Harvard Business Review*, volume 54, March–April 1974, pp. 137–145; and

Sun Tzu, *The Art of War* (New York: Oxford University Press, 1971).

6 D. Braybrooke and C. E. Lindblom, *A Strategy of Decision* (New York: Free Press, 1963);

J. B. Quinn, *Strategies for Change: Logical Incrementalism* (Homewood, Illinois: Irwin, 1980);

J. L. Bower, *Managing the Resource Allocation Process: A Study of Planning and Investment* (Boston: Harvard University Business School, 1970);

R. A. Burgelman, "A Process Model of Internal Corporate Venturing in the Diversified Major Firm," *Administrative Science Quarterly*, volume 28, June 1983, pp. 223–244;

H. Mintzberg, "Patterns in Strategy Formation," *Management Science*, volume 24, number 9, May 1978, pp. 934–948;

H. Mintzberg and A. McHugh, "Strategy Formation in an Adhocracy," *Administrative Science Quarterly*, volume 30, June 1985, pp. 160–197;

H. Mintzberg and J. A. Waters, "Of Strategies, Deliberate and Emergent." *Strategic Management Journal*, volume 6, July–September 1985, pp. 257–272; and

K. E. Weick, *The Social Psychology of Organizing* (Reading, Massachusetts: Addison Wesley, 1979).

7 E. Rhenman, *Organization Theory for Long-Range Planning* (London: Wiley, 1973); R. Normann, *Management for Growth* (New York: Wiley, 1977); and

B. Hedberg and S. A. Jonsson, "Strategy Formulation as a Discontinuous Process," *International Studies of Management and Organization*, volume 7, Summer 1977, pp. 88–109.

8 M. E. Porter, "What Is Strategy?," *Harvard Business Review*, volume 74, November–December 1996, pp. 61–78.

9 "What Is Strategy?," *Harvard Business Review*, volume 75, March–April 1997, p. 162 (letter to the editor).

10 Ibid., p. 63.

11 C. K. Prahalad and G. Hamel, "The Core Competence of the Corporation," *Harvard Business Review*, volume 68, May–June 1990, pp. 79–91; and H. Itami and T. W. Roehl, *Mobilizing Invisible Assets* (Cambridge, Massachusetts: Harvard University Press, 1987).

12 See, especially:

J. B. Barney, "Organizational Culture: Can It Be a Source of Sustained Competitive Advantage?," *Academy of Management Review*, volume 11, July 1986, pp. 656–665.

13 Chandler (1962).

4

A MODEL FOR DIVERSIFICATION

H. I. Ansoff

Source: *Management Science* 4(4) (1958): 392–414.

During the past few years, many interesting papers have been written on the subject of product-market diversification. A majority of the writers have dealt with either case histories of successful diversification or with qualitative checkoff lists to be used in analyzing specific diversification opportunities. A much smaller group of papers has been devoted to formulation of a systematic approach which a company can use to compare alternative diversification decisions.

This paper falls in the latter category. As a first step, diversification is defined and distinguished from other company growth alternatives. Typical growth perspectives are described which may motivate a company to diversify. Diversification objectives are established and related to the company's long-range objectives.

A two-step evaluation scheme is proposed for selection of the preferred diversification strategy. The first is a qualitative step, which narrows a wide field of diversification opportunities to a selected few which are consistent with the company's diversification objectives and long-range policy. In the second step, a quantitative procedure is outlined for evaluating the relative profit potential of the selected alternatives. Finally, limitations of the present method are discussed.

1. Purpose of the paper

The purpose of this paper is to construct a model describing a business phenomenon commonly known as diversification. It is generally recognized that a variety of very different models can be constructed to describe any given real-life situation. The models will differ depending on the skill and knowledge of the analyst, as well as on the particular purpose of the analysis. A recent paper by J. Sayer Minas (Ref. 1) describes an inherent conflict between comprehensiveness and accuracy with which the real-life situation is covered on one hand and the precision and mathematical completeness of the model on the other. The resolution of this conflict can be likened to a kind of "Heisenberg principle": The closer a model is made to mirror reality, the lower the precision of measurements which can be made with the aid of the model.

The model presented in this paper is oriented toward the specific purpose of providing top management of a large corporation with a tool for making intelligent diversification decisions. Our purpose will be to make it a reasonably comprehensive and accurate mirror of reality without attempting, for the time being, to provide an algorithm for selection of "optimum strategies." The purpose will be to identify the variables which have a first-order influence on diversification decisions and to identify important structural relations among them. In the language of classical physics we appear to be dealing with a step which is intermediate between a "description" and a "model." If this effort is successful, the results should provide management with a means for making informed diversification decisions through a combination of computation and judgment.

2. Product-market strategies

Many different definitions can be found for the term "diversification." For the purpose of this paper we will define it in terms of a particular kind of change in the product-market makeup of a company.

Let the *product line* of a manufacturing company be described by two sets of statements:

(a) Statement of the physical characteristics of the individual products (for example, size, weight, materials, tolerances, etc.) which is sufficiently complete for the purpose of setting up a manufacturing operation;
(b) The performance characteristics of the products (for example, in the case of an airplane, its performance in terms of speed, range, altitude, payload, etc.) which endow them with competitive characteristics on the markets on which they are sold.

For a definition of the "market" we can borrow a concept commonly used by the military—the concept of a mission. Let a *product mission* be a description of the job which the product is intended to perform[1].

To borrow another example from the airplane industry, one of the missions to which Lockheed Aircraft Corporation caters is commercial air transportation of passengers; another is provision of airborne early warning for the Air Defense Command; a third is performance of air-to-air combat.

In each of these examples the mission can be described in specific quantitative terms and performance of competing products can be evaluated quantitatively. In many other types of business which have less well defined product missions, such as "cleansing of the teeth and prevention of tooth

53

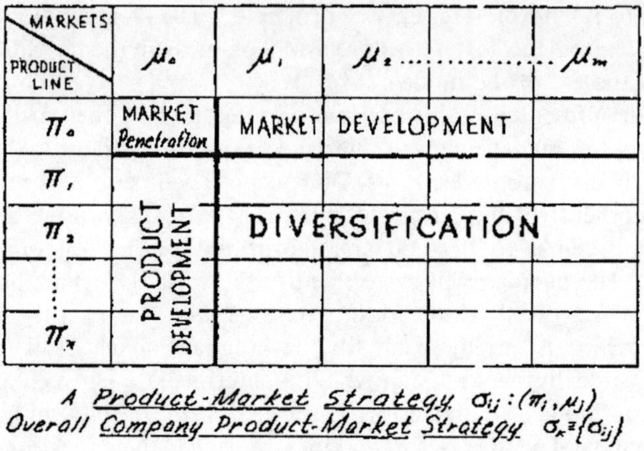

MARKETS / PRODUCT LINE	μ_o	μ_1	μ_2 .... μ_m		
π_o	MARKET Penetration	MARKET DEVELOPMENT			
π_1					
π_2	PRODUCT DEVELOPMENT	DIVERSIFICATION			
$\vdots$					
π_x					

A Product-Market Strategy $\sigma_{ij} : (\pi_i, \mu_j)$
Overall Company Product-Market Strategy $\sigma_r = \{\sigma_{ij}\}$

Figure 1

decay," job specification and hence measurement of competitive performance is a great deal more difficult[2].

Using the concepts of product line and product mission, we can now define a *product-market strategy* as a joint statement of a product line and the corresponding set of missions which the products are designed to fulfill. Thus, if we let π_i represent the product line and μ_j the corresponding set of missions, then the pair $\sigma_{ij} : (\pi_i, \mu_j)$ is a product-market strategy.

Four commonly recognized business growth alternatives can now be identified as different product-market strategies. Thus, *market penetration* (See Fig. 1) is an effort to increase company sales without departing from an original product-market strategy. The company seeks to improve business performance either by increasing the volume of sales to its present customers or by finding new customers who have mission requirement μ_0. *Market development* can be identified as a strategy in which the company attempts to adapt its present product line (generally with some modification in the product characteristics) to new missions. For example, an airplane company which adapts and sells its passenger transport for the mission of cargo transportation engages in market development.

A *product development* strategy, on the other hand, retains the present mission and pursues development of products with new and different characteristics which will improve the performance of the mission. *Diversification* is the final alternative. It calls for a simultaneous departure from the present product line and the present market structure.

Each of the above strategies describes a distinct path which a business can take toward future growth. In most actual situations a business will simultaneously follow several of these paths. As a matter of fact, a simultaneous pursuit of market penetration, product development, and market development is usually recognized as a sign of a progressive, well-run business.

Pursuit of all three of these strategies is essential to survival in the face of economic competition.

The diversification strategy stands apart from the other three. While the latter are usually pursued with the same technical, financial, and merchandising resources which are used for the original product line, pursuit of diversification generally requires new skills, new techniques, and new facilities. As a result, diversification almost invariably leads to physical and organizational changes in the structure of the business which represent a distinct break with past business experience. In view of these differences, it is logical to inquire into the conditions under which pursuit of a diversification strategy becomes necessary or desirable for a company.

The question can be put in the following form. We can think of market penetration, market development, and product development as component strategies of the *overall company product strategy* and ask whether this overall strategy should be broadened to include diversification.

3. Why companies diversify

A study of business literature and of company histories reveals many different reasons for diversification. Companies diversify to compensate for technological obsolescence, to distribute risk, to utilize excess productive capacity, to re-invest earnings, to obtain top management, etc., etc. One study of diversification (Ref. 2) lists a total of 43 reasons for diversification. Fortunately, all of these reasons can be interpreted in terms of a relatively small number of typical expected patterns of business activity for a given company.

A standard method used to analyze future company growth prospects is through the means of long range sales forecasts. Preparation of such forecasts involves simultaneous consideration of world-wide business trends alongside the trends in the particular industry to which the company belongs. Among the major factors considered are:

(a) General economic trends.
(b) Political and international trends.
(c) Trends peculiar to the industry. (For example, forecasts prepared in the airplane industry must take account of the following major prospects:

    i.   A changeover, which is taking place within the military establishment, from manned aircraft to missiles.
    ii. Trends in government expenditures for the military establishment.
    iii. Trends in demand for commercial air transportation.
    iv. Prospective changes in the government "mobilization base" concept and consequent changes toward the aircraft industry.
    v. Rising expenditures required for research and development.)

(d) Estimates of the company's competitive strength as compared to other members of the industry.
(e) Estimates of improvements in company performance which can be achieved through market penetration, product development, and market development.
(f) Trends in the manufacturing costs.

Such forecasts usually assume that company management will be aggressive and that management policies will be such as to take full advantage of the opportunities offered by the environmental trends. Thus, a long range forecast of this type can be taken as an estimate of the best possible results the business can hope to achieve short of diversification.

The results fall into three typical trends which are illustrated in Fig. 2. These trends are compared to a growth curve for the national economy (GNP), as well as to a hypothetical growth curve for the industry to which the company belongs.

One of the curves illustrates a sales forecast which declines with time. This may be the result of an expected contraction of demand, obsolescence of manufacturing techniques, emergence of new products better suited to the mission to which the company caters, etc. Another typical pattern is one of cyclic sales activity. One common cause of this is seasonal variations of demand. Less apparent, but more important, are slower cyclic changes, such as, for example, peace-war variation in demand in the aircraft industry.

If the most optimistic sales estimates (which can be attained short of diversification) fall in either of the preceding cases, diversification is strongly indicated. However, a company may choose to diversify even if its prospects may, on the whole, appear favorable. This is illustrated by the "slow growth curve." As drawn in Fig. 2, the curve indicates rising sales which, in fact, grow faster than the economy as a whole. Nevertheless, the particular company may belong to one of the so-called "growth industries" which as a whole is surging ahead. A company may diversify because it feels that its prospective growth rate is not satisfactory by comparison to the industry.

Preparation of trend forecasts is far from a precise science. There is always uncertainty about the likelihood of the basic environmental trends, as well as about the effect of these trends on the industry. Furthermore, there is additional uncertainty about the ability of a particular business organization to perform in the new environment. Consequently, any realistic company forecast would include several different trend forecasts, each with an (explicitly or implicitly) assigned probability. As an alternative, the trend forecast may be represented by a widening spread between two extremes, similar to that shown for GNP in Fig. 2.

In addition to trends, long range plans must also take account of another class of events. These are certain environmental conditions which, if they occurred, would have a recognizable effect on sales; however, their

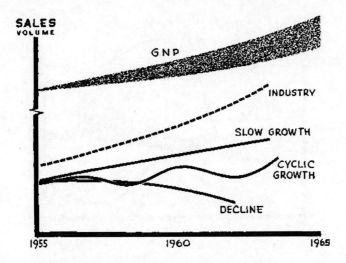

Figure 2

occurrence cannot be predicted with certainty—they may be called *contingent* (or catastrophic) events.

For example, in the aircraft industry catastrophic forecasts may be based on the following environmental discontinuities:

(a) A major technological discontinuity (popularly described as a "breakthrough") whose characteristics can be foreseen, but timing cannot at present be determined. This would occur, for example, if a new manufacturing process were discovered for manufacture of high strength, thermally resistant aircraft bodies.
(b) An economic recession which would lead to loss of orders for commercial aircraft and would change the pattern of spending for military aircraft.
(c) A limited war which would sharply increase the demand for goods produced by the air industry.
(d) Sudden cessation of cold war (which was a subject of considerable interest a year ago).
(e) A major economic depression.

The two types of sales forecast are illustrated on Fig. 3 for a hypothetical company. Sales curves S_1 and S_2 represent a spread of trend forecasts and S_3 and S_4, two contingent forecasts. The difference between the two types lies in the degree of uncertainty associated with each.

In the case of trend forecasts we can trace a crude time history of sales based on events which we fully expect to happen. Our uncertainty arises from not knowing when they will take place and the way they will interact with the business activity. In the case of contingency forecasts we can again trace a crude time history. However, our uncertainty is greater. We lack

57

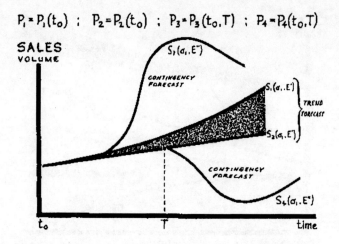

$$P_1 = P_1(t_0) \quad ; \quad P_2 = P_2(t_0) \quad ; \quad P_3 = P_3(t_0,T) \quad ; \quad P_4 = P_4(t_0,T)$$

Figure 3

precise knowledge of not only *when* they will occur, but also of *whether* they will occur. In describing trend forecasts, we can assign to each a probability $p = p(t_0)$, whereas for contingency forecasts, the best we can do is to express its probability with $p = p(t_0, T)$, where T is the time at which the catastrophic event occurs. In going from a trend to a contingency forecast we advance, so to speak, one notch up the scale of ignorance.

In considering the relative weight which should be given to contingent events in diversification planning, it is necessary to take account not only of the magnitude of the effect it would produce on sales, but also the relative probability of its occurrence. For example, if a deep economic depression were to occur, its effect on many industries would be devastating. However, many companies feel safe in neglecting it in their planning because it is generally felt that the likelihood of a deep depression is very small, at least for the near future.

It appears to be a common business practice to put primary emphasis on trend forecasts. In fact, in many cases long range planning is devoted exclusively to this. Potential corporate instability in the light of contingency is frequently viewed either as "something one cannot plan for" or as a second-order correction to be applied only after the trends have been taken into account. The emphasis is on "planning for growth" and planning for contingencies is viewed as an "insurance policy" against reversals.

People familiar with planning problems in the military establishment will note here an interesting difference between the military and the business attitudes. While business planning emphasizes trends, military planning emphasizes contingencies. To use a crude analogy, a business planner is concerned with planning for continuous, successful, day-after-day operation of a supermarket. If he is progressive, he also buys an insurance policy against fire, but he spends relatively little time in planning for fires. The military is more like the fire engine company. The fire is the thing. Day-to-day operations are of interest only insofar as they can be utilized to improve readiness and fire-fighting techniques. It appears that in some important respects the business planning problem is the easier one of the two.

4. Sales objectives

Analysis of forecasts is useful, not only for determining the desirability of diversification, it also indicates two basic goals toward which diversification action should contribute. These goals may be referred to as *long range sales objectives*. They are illustrated on Fig. 4.

The solid lines describe the performance of a hypothetical company before diversification (when its overall product strategy was σ_1) under a general trend, which is represented by the sales curve market $S_1(\sigma_1, E')$, and in a contingency represented by $S_1(\sigma_1, E'')$, where E' and E'' describe the respective environmental conditions. The dashed lines show the improved performance as a result of diversification when the overall product-market strategy becomes σ_2.

The first diversification effect was to improve the growth pattern of the company. The corresponding *growth objective* can be stated in the form:[3]

$$\dot{S}_1(\sigma_2, E') - \dot{S}_1(\sigma_1, E') \geqq \delta(t)$$

The second effect desired of diversification is improvement in company stability under contingent conditions. Not only should diversification prevent

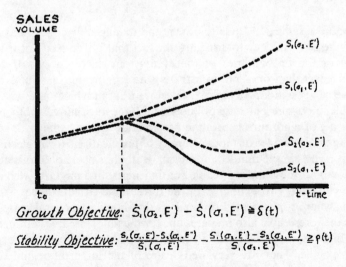

Figure 4

sales from dropping as low as they might have before diversification, but the *percentage drop* should also be lower. The second sales objective is thus a *stability objective*:

$$\frac{S_1(\sigma_1, E') - S_2(\sigma_1, E'')}{S_1(\sigma_1, E'')} - \frac{S_1(\sigma_2, E') - S_2(\sigma_2, E'')}{S_1(\sigma_2, E')} \geqq \rho(t)$$

As will be seen later, the two sales objectives can be viewed as constraints on the choice of the preferred diversification strategy.

5. Unforeseeable contingencies

So far our discussion has dealt with reasons and objectives for diversification which can be inferred from market forecasts. These objectives are based on what may be called *foreseeable* market conditions—conditions which can be interpreted in terms of time-phased sales curves. We have dealt with forecasts on two levels of ignorance: trend forecasts for which complete time histories can be traced and contingent forecasts, the occurrence of which is described by probability distribution. In problems dealing with planning under uncertainty, it is often assumed that trends and contingencies, taken together, exhaust all possible alternatives. In other words, if $p_0 \ldots p_n$ are the respective probabilities of occurrence assigned to the respective alternatives, the assumption is made that

$$\sum_{i=0}^{n} p_i = 1$$

Since this assumption leads to a neat and manageable conceptual framework, there is a tendency to disregard the fact that it is indeed not true, that the sum of the probabilities of the events for which we can draw time histories is less than one, and that there is a recognizable class of events to which we can assign a probability of occurrence, but which otherwise is not specifiable in our present state of knowledge. One must move another notch up the scale of ignorance before the possibilities can be exhausted.

Among analysts one runs into a variety of justifications for neglecting this last step. One simple-minded argument is that, since no information is available about these unforeseeable contingencies, one might as well devote his time and energy to planning for the foreseeable circumstances. Another somewhat more sophisticated rationale is that in a very general sense, planning for the foreseeable also prepares one for the unforeseeable contingencies.

One finds a very different attitude among experienced military and business people. They are very well aware of the importance and relative probability of unforeseeable events. They point to this fact and ask why one

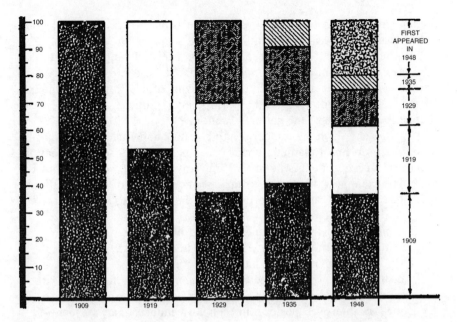

Figure 5

should go through an elaborate mockery of specific planning steps for the foreseeable events while neglecting the really important possibilities. Their substitute for such planning is contained in practical maxims for conducting one's business—be solvent, be light on your feet, be flexible. Unfortunately, it is not always clear (even to the people who preach it) what this flexibility means.

An example of the importance of the unforeseeable class of events to business can be found in a very interesting study by the Brookings Institution (Ref. 3). A part of this study examined the historical ranking of 100 largest ranking corporations over the period of the last 50 years. An example of the mobility among the 100 largest is given in Fig. 5. It is seen that of the 100 on the 1909 list, only 36 were among the 100 largest in 1948. A majority of the giants of yesteryear have dropped behind in a relatively short span of time.

The lesson to be drawn from this illustration is that if most of the companies which dropped from the 1909 list had made forecasts of the foreseeable type at that time (some of them undoubtedly did so), they would have very likely found the future growth prospects to be excellent. A majority of the events that hurt them could not at the time be specifically foreseen. Railroads, which loomed as the primary means of transportation, have given way to the automobile and the airplane. The textile industry, which appeared to have a built-in demand in an expanding world population, was challenged and

61

dominated by synthetics. Radio, radar, television created means of communication unforeseeable in significance and scope in 1909.

But the lessons of the past 50 years appear fully applicable today. The pace of economic and technological change is so rapid as to make it virtually certain that major breakthroughs comparable to those of the last 50 years, and yet not foreseeable in scope and character, will profoundly change the structure of the national economy.

This problem which, by comparison to planning under uncertainty, may be called the problem of planning under ignorance, deserves serious attention. A natural question at this point is, "Can any lessons be drawn from the preceding example with respect to the specific problem of diversification?" An indication of the answer is provided by the Brookings study:

> The majority of the companies included among the 100 largest of our day have attained their positions within the last two decades. They are companies that have started new industries or have transformed old ones to create or meet consumer preferences. The companies that have not only grown in absolute terms but have gained an improved position in their own industry may be identified as companies that are notable for drastic changes made in their product mix and methods, generating or responding to new competition. There are two outstanding cases in which the industry leader of 1909 had by 1948 risen in position relative to its own industry group and also in rank among the 100 largest—one in chemicals and the other in electrical equipment. These two (General Electric and DuPont) are hardly recognizable as the same companies they were in 1909 except for retention of the name; for in each case the product mix of 1948 is vastly different from what it was in the earlier year, and the markets in which the companies meet competition are incomparably broader than those that accounted for their earlier place at the top of their industries. They exemplify the flux in the market positions of the most successful industrial giants during the past four decades and a general growth rather than a consolidation of supremacy in a circumscribed line.

This suggests that existence of specific undesirable trends is a sufficient, but not a necessary, condition in order to commend diversification to a company. An examination of the foreseeable alternatives should be accompanied by an analysis of how well the overall company product-market strategy covers the so-called growth areas of technology—areas which appear fraught with potential discoveries. If such analysis shows that the company's product line is too narrow and that its chances of taking advantage of important discoveries are limited, such company is well advised to diversify, even if its definable horizons appear bright.

6. Diversification objectives

As formulated in Section 4, long range objectives have the advantage of generality; they serve as a common yardstick to any new product-market strategy which a company may contemplate. The price for this generality is a lack of specificity; the objectives provide no indication of where a company should look for diversification opportunities in the broad product-market field of the national economy. Nor do they provide a means for a final evaluation of the respective merits of different opportunities which compete for company attention. The objectives are mainly useful as minimal goals which must be attained in order to give a company desirable growth characteristics. As we shall see later, they operate as constraints in the final evaluation processes: only strategies which meet the long range sales objectives are admitted to the final test of the probable business success of the competing diversification strategies.

To complete the formulation of our problem, it remains to specify two things: a means of reducing a very large field of possibilities to a particular set of diversification strategies which deserve close scrutiny by a diversifying company, and a means for evaluating the merits of the respective strategies within this set.

Business literature employs a variety of terms to describe alternative directions which a diversification program can follow. A commonly encountered breakdown is into vertical, horizontal, and lateral diversification directions.

Each product manufactured by a company is made up of functional components, parts, and basic materials which go into the final assembly. It is usual for a manufacturing concern to buy a large fraction of these from outside suppliers. One way to diversify is to branch out into production of components, parts, and materials. This is commonly known as *vertical diversification* (or sometimes as vertical integration). Perhaps the most outstanding example of vertical diversification is afforded by the Ford empire in the days of Henry Ford, Sr.[4]

Horizontal diversification can be described as introduction of new products which, while they do not contribute to the present product line in any way, cater to missions which lie within the industry of which the company is a member. The term "industry" is taken here to mean an area of economic activity to which the present activities of the company have a substantial carry-over of know-how and experience by virtue of its past experience in technical, financial, and marketing areas.[5]

Lateral diversification can be described as a move beyond the confines of the industry to which a company belongs. This obviously opens a great many possibilities, from operating banana boats to building atomic reactors. It can be seen that while definitions of vertical and horizontal diversification are restrictive, in the sense that they de-limit the field of interest, lateral diversification is permissive. Adoption of a lateral diversification policy is merely an announcement of intent of the company to range far afield from its present market structure.

How does a company choose among these diversification directions? In part the answer depends on the reasons which prompt diversification action. If a company is diversifying because its sales trend shows a declining volume of demand, it would be unwise to consider vertical diversification, since this would be at best a temporary device to stave off an eventual decline of business. On the other hand, if the trend forecast indicates "slow growth" in an otherwise healthy and growing industry, then both vertical and horizontal diversification would be desirable for strengthening the position of the company in a field in which its knowledge and experience are concentrated.

If the major concern is with stability under a contingent forecast, chances are that both horizontal and vertical diversification could not provide a sufficient stabilizing influence and that lateral action is indicated. Finally, if the concern is with the narrowness of the technological base in the face of what we have called unforeseeable contingencies, then lateral diversification into new areas of technology would be clearly called for.

An analysis of the sales trends impelling diversification can thus be used to formulate conditions which diversification possibilities must meet in order to fit the company requirements. These conditions can be termed as *diversification objectives*. In contrast to sales objectives which set forth general growth requirements, diversification objectives specify types of diversification strategies which will improve the product-market balance of the company.

For example, in the light of the trends described for the aircraft industry, an aircraft company may formulate the following diversification objectives:

In order to meet long range sales objectives through diversification the company needs the following moves:

(a) a vertical diversification move to contribute to the technological progress of the present product line;
(b) a horizontal move to improve the coverage of the military market;
(c) a horizontal move to increase the percentage of commercial sales in the overall sales program;
(d) a lateral move to stabilize sales against a recession.
(e) a lateral move to broaden company's technological base.

Some of the diversification objectives apply to characteristics of the product, some to those of the product missions. Each objective is designed to improve some aspect of the balance between the overall product-market strategy and the expected environment. Thus, objectives (a), (b), and (c) are designed to improve the balance under the trend conditions, objectives (c) and (d) under foreseeable contingencies, and objective (e) to strengthen the company against unforeseeable contingencies.

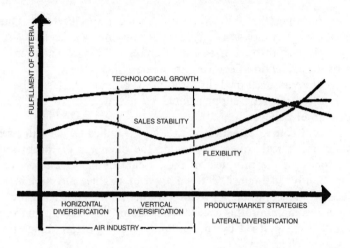

Figure 6

It is apparent that a diversification strategy which is highly desirable for one of the objectives is likely to be less desirable for others. A schematic graphical illustration of this is presented in Fig. 6. The horizontal axis represents alternative diversification strategies in a decreasing order of affinity with respect to the present market structure (including both technological and business characteristics). In the air industry, which is going through a period of rapid technological change, the best promise for taking advantage of the growth trend seems to lie in the fields of vertical diversification into major system components or lateral diversification in adjacent areas of technology, such as electronics. The problem of sales stability could probably be best met through lateral diversification. However, horizontal diversification into new types of new products for the air industry is also desirable for this purpose. Finally, if its participation in the technological growth of the national economy is confined to one major area, an airframe company is well adivsed to diversify laterally as a means of acquiring a flexibility for unforeseen contingencies.

Diversification objectives are useful for determining merits of individual cases. However, they do not provide a central orienting theme which can give shape and a sense of direction to the diversification program. Such theme must be sought in the long range objectives of the company.

7. Long range company objectives

So long as a company confines its growth to changes other than diversification, statement of long range company objectives can frequently be confined to generalities: "growth," "flexibility," "financial stability," etc. However, when a break is contemplated with the past pattern of business, it becomes necessary to reduce the objectives to much more specific form. Questions, such as where the company is going, what unifying characteristics it should preserve as it goes through a period of change, should be answered before intelligent diversification decisions are made.

Sales objectives described in Section 4 provide part of the answer. However, these must be supplemented by a statement of the long range product-market policy.

A consistent course of action is to adopt a policy which will preserve a kind of technological coherence among the members of the product line with the focus on the products of the parent company. Thus, a company which is mainly distinguished for a type of engineering and production excellence would continue to select product-market entries which would strengthen and maintain this excellence. Perhaps the best known example of such policy is exemplified by the DuPont slogan, "Better things for better living through chemistry."

Another approach is to set long term growth policy in terms of the breadth of market which the company intends to cover. It may choose to confine its diversification to the vertical or horizontal direction, or it may select a type of lateral diversification which is circumscribed by the characteristics of the missions to which the company intends to cater. For example, a company which has its origins in the field of air transportation may expand its interest to all forms of transportation of people and cargo. "Better transportation for better living through advanced engineering," while a borrowed slogan, might be descriptive of such long range policy.

A greatly different policy is to place a primary emphasis on the financial characteristics of the corporation. This method of diversification generally places no limits on engineering and manufacturing characteristics of new products (although in practice, competence and interests of the corporate management will usually provide some orientation for diversification moves). The decisions regarding the desirability of new acquisitions are made exclusively on the basis of financial considerations. Rather than a manufacturing entity, the corporate character is now one of a "holding company." The top management delegates a large share of its product planning and administrative functions to the divisions and concerns itself largely with coordination and financial problems of the corporation and with building up a balanced "portfolio of products" within the corporate structure.

These alternative long range policies demonstrate the extremes. Most actual diversification case histories have taken a path intermediate between them; furthermore, neither of the extremes can be claimed to offer an intrinsically more promising road to success. The choice of policy rests in large part on the preferences and objectives of the management of the diversifying company, as well as on the skills and training of its people.

The fact that there is more than one successful path to diversification is illustrated by the case of the aircraft industry. Among the major successful airframe manufacturers, Douglas and Boeing have to date limited their growth to horizontal diversification into missiles and new markets for new types of aircraft. Lockheed has carried horizontal diversification further to include aircraft maintenance, aircraft service, and production of ground handling equipment. North American Aviation, on the other hand, appears to have chosen vertical diversification through establishment of its subsidiaries in Atomics International, Autonetics, and Rocketdyne, thus providing a basis for manufacture of complete air vehicles of the future.

Bell appears to have adopted a policy of technological consistency among the members of its product line. It has diversified laterally but primarily into types of products for which it had previous know-how and experience. General Dynamics provides a further interesting contrast. It is a widely laterally diversified company and, among major manufacturers of air vehicles, appears to come closest to the "holding company" extreme. Its airplane and missile manufacturing operations in Convair are paralleled by production of submarines in the Electric Boat Division, military, industrial, and consumer electronic products in the Stromberg-Carlson Division, and electric motors in the Electro Dynamic Division.

8. Qualitative evaluation

In the preceding sections we have dealt with two basic factors which affect diversification actions. These are the long range objectives of the company and the more specific diversification objectives.

The problem now is to apply these to evaluation of diversification opportunities. Since the objectives are stated in both quantitative (sales objectives) and qualitative terms (diversification objectives and company product-market policy), it is convenient to construct a two-step evaluation process: first, application of qualitative criteria in order to narrow the field of diversification opportunities; and second, application of numerical criteria to select the preferred strategy (or strategies).

The long range product-market policy can be applied as a criterion for the first rough cut in the qualitative evaluation. It can be used to order a large field of opportunities (which each company can compile by using commonly available industrial classifications) into classes of diversification moves which are consistent with the basic character of the diversifying company. For example, a company whose policy is to remain a manufacturing concern deriving its competitive strength from technical excellence of its products would eliminate as inconsistent classes of consumer products which are sold on the strength of advertising appeal rather than superior quality.

Each individual diversification opportunity which is consistent with the long range objectives can next be examined in the light of individual diversification objectives. This process tends to eliminate opportunities which, while consistent with the desired product-market makeup, are nevertheless likely to lead to an unbalance between the company product line and the probable environment. For example, a company which wishes to preserve and expand its technical excellence in, say, design of large highly-stressed machines controlled by feedback techniques may find consistent product opportunities both inside and outside the industry to which it presently caters. If a major diversification objective of this company is to correct cyclic variations in demand characteristic of the industry, it would choose opportunities which lie outside.

The diversification opprtunities which have gone through the two screening steps can be referred to as the "admissible set." A member of the set satisfies at least one diversification objective, but very probably it will not satisfy all of them. Therefore, before subjecting them to the quantitative evaluation, it is necessary to group them into several alternative overall company product-market strategies, composed of the original strategy and one or more of the admissible diversification strategies. These alternative overall strategies should be roughly equivalent in meeting all of the diversification objectives.

At this stage it is particularly important to make allowance for the unforeseeable contingencies discussed in Section 5. Since available numerical evaluation techniques are applicable only to trends and foreseeable contingencies, it is important to make sure that the alternatives subjected to the evaluation have a comparable built-in diversified technological base. In practice this process is less formidable than it may appear. For example, a company in the aircraft industry has to take account of the areas of technology in which major discoveries are likely to affect the future of the industry. This would include atomic propulsion, certain areas of electronics, automation of complex processes, etc. In designing alternative overall strategies the company would then make sure that each contains product entries which will give the company a desirable and comparable degree of participation in these areas.

A schematic description of the preceding steps looks as follows:

$$\{\text{totality of } \sigma_{ij} \text{ available to company}\} \xrightarrow{\text{Long range}} \text{product-market policy}$$

$$\{\sigma_{ij} \text{ consistent with policy}\} \xrightarrow{\substack{\text{Individual} \\ \text{Diversification objectives}}}$$

$$\{\text{admissible } \sigma_{ij}\} \xrightarrow{\substack{\text{Diversification objectives} \\ \text{as a group} \\ \text{Balance for unforeseeable} \\ \text{contingencies}}}$$

$$\{\text{alternative overall product-market strategies } \sigma_k = \sigma_l + \sigma_{ij}\}$$

9. Quantitative evaluation

So far we have been concerned with establishing a balanced relationship between the company and its business environment. An important remaining question is: "Given such relationship will the company make money, will its profit structure be more attractive after diversification?"

The measurement we seek might be called the *profit potential* of diversification. It should accomplish two purposes. It should compare the performance of the company before and after a given diversification move; it should also compare the performances of several alternative diversification strategies. In the light of the characteristics of the diversification problem discussed in the preceding sections, the profit potential should have the following properties:

(a) Since diversification is invariably accompanied by a change in the investment structure of the business, profit potential should take account of such changes. It should take explicit account of new capital brought into the business, changes in the rate of capital formation resulting from diversification, as well as the costs of borrowed capital.

(b) Usually the combined performance of the new and the old product-market lines is not a simple sum of their separate performances (another common reason for diversification is to take advantage of this inherent characteristic—to produce a combined performance which exceeds the sum of individual performances). Profit potential should take account of this non-linear characteristic.

(c) Each diversification move is characterized by a transition period during which readjustment of the company structure to new operating conditions takes place. The benefits of a diversification move may not be realized fully for some time (in fact, one of the common purposes of diversification into so-called growth industries is to "start small and grow big"). Therefore, measurement of profit potential should span a sufficient length of time to allow for effects of the transition.

(d) Business performance will vary depending on the particular economic-political environment. Profit potential must provide an overall estimate of the probable effect of alternative environments described earlier in this paper.

(e) The statement of sales objectives in Section 4 specified the general characteristics of growth and stability which are desired. Profit potential function should be compatible with these characteristics.

Unfortunately there is no single yardstick of performance among those commonly used in business practice which possesses all of these characteristics. In fact, the techniques currently used for measurement of business performance constitute, at best, an imprecise art. It is common to measure different aspects of performance through application of different performance tests. Thus, the earning ability of the business is measured through tests of income adequacy; preparedness for contingencies, through tests of debt coverage and liquidity; attractiveness to investors through measurement of shareholders' position; efficiency in the use of money, physical assets and personnel, through tests of sales efficiency and personnel productivity. These tests employ a variety of different performance ratios, such as return on sales, return on net worth, return on assets, turnover of net worth, ratio of assets to liabilities, etc. The total number of ratios may run as high as 20 in a single case.

In the final evaluation of a diversification opportunity which immediately precedes a diversification decision, all of these tests, tempered with business judgment, would normally be applied. However, for the purpose of preliminary elimination of alternatives, it has become common to use a single test in the form of return on investment, which is a ratio between earnings and the capital invested in producing these earnings.

While the usefulness of return on investment is commonly accepted, there appears to be considerable room for argument regarding its limitations and its pratical application (See, for example, Ref. 7 and Ref. 8). Fundamentally, the difficulty with the concept seems to be that on one hand it fails to provide an absolute measure of business performance applicable to a range of very different industries, and on the other, definition of the term "investment" is subject to a variety of interpretations.

Since our aim is to use the concept as a measure of *relative* performance of different diversification strategies, we need not be concerned with its failure to provide a yardstick for comparison with other industries, nor even with other companies in the same industry as the parent company. Similarly, so long as a consistent practice is used for defining investment in alternative courses of action, our concern with proper definition of investment can be smaller than in many other cases. Nevertheless, a particular definition of what constitutes profit-producing capital cannot be given in general terms. It would have to be determined in each case in the light of particular business characteristics and practices (such as, for example, the extent of government-owned assets, depreciation practices, inflationary trends, etc.).

For the numerator of our return on investment we shall use net earnings after taxes. A going business concern has standard techniques for estimating its future earnings. These depend on the projected sales volume, tax structure, trends in material and labor costs, productivity, etc. If the diversification opportunity being considered is itself a going concern, its profit projections can be used for estimates of combined future earnings. If the opportunity is a new venture, its profit estimates should be made on the basis of the average performance for the industry.

In the light of earlier discussion, it is important for our purposes to recognize that estimated earnings depend on the overall product-market strategy, the amount of capital to be invested in diversification, the estimated sales volume, and the particular economic-political environment being studied. If we use previously employed notation and let P stand for earnings and I for the capital investment, we can recognize the determining influences on the earnings in the following *profit function*:

$$P = h(I, S, E, \sigma) \tag{1}$$

As mentioned previously, a diversification move is accompanied by a change in the investment structure of the diversifying company. The type of change used in any given case, as well as the amount of capital involved, will depend on the resources available for diversification purposes, the particular product-market strategy, as well as on the method which the diversifying company selects for expansion of its manufacturing activities. The choice of the particular method of expansion (there are four basic alternatives: use of existing facilities, expansion, acquisition of controlling interest, and merger) is a part of the larger problem of business fit (See Sec. 10). For this reason it will not be discussed in this paper. We will assume that for each product-market entry an appropriate type of expansion can be selected (See Ref. 9).

The source of investment for the new venture may be one of the following:

1. The diversifying company may be in the fortunate position of having excess capital.
2. The company may be in a position to borrow capital at attractive rates.
3. It may be in a position to exchange part of its equity for an equity in another company (for example, through an exchange of stock).
4. It may decide to withdraw some of the capital invested in the present business operation and invest it in diversification.

Let us define the following:

σ_l	Original product-market strategy of the company.
$\sigma_k = \sigma_l + \sigma_{ij}$	Overall product-market strategy resulting from the qualitative evaluation (where σ_{ij} is the diversification strategy).
$I(t)$	Total capital invested in the business in year t.
$i_1(t),\ i_2(t),\ i_3(t),\ i_4(t)$	Investments made in σ_{ij} in year t from the four respective sources enumerated above.
$r(t)$	Prevailing interest rate for capital on the open market.
$k(t)$	Dividends paid out in year t

Also let us make the following assumptions:

(a) That the diversification program may be spread over a period of time and that investments in diversification may be made yearly from time $t = 0$ up to t.

71

(b) That all four types of investment described on the preceding page may be made during this period.
(c) That if the company does not diversify, earnings of the company, in excess of paid out dividends, may be divided between additional investments in the company's product-market line and investments in outside ventures.
(d) If the company diversifies, earnings in excess of dividends are all reinvested in the business either in the original product strategy σ_l or in the diversification strategy σ_{ij}.

To simplify notation, select a particular economic-political environment, a diversification strategy, and a specified sales volume so that Expression (1) becomes

$$P = h(I, S, E, \sigma) = h(I)$$

Let $P_0 = h_0(I)$ be profit earned by σ_l before diversification.
$P_1 = h_1(I)$ be profit earned by σ_l after diversification.
$P_2 = h_2(I)$ be profit earned by σ_{ij} after diversification.
Using this notation and the preceding assumptions we can write the *present value* of return on investment in the following form:
If the company does not diversify

$$R(t) = \frac{P(t)(1 + r)^{-(t+1)}}{I_p(t)}, \tag{2}$$

where $P(t)$ represents earnings for year t

$$P(t) = h_0\left(I(t) - \sum_{\tau=0}^{t} i_1(r)\right) + r\sum_{\tau=0}^{t} i_1(r), \tag{3}$$

$I(t)$ is the total capital available to the business in year t

$$I(t) = I(0) + \sum_{\tau=1}^{t} P(r - 1)(1 - k(r)), \tag{3}$$

and $I_p(t)$ is the present value of the total capital which is in the business in year t

$$I_p(t) = I(0) + \sum_{\tau=1}^{t} P(r - 1)(1 - k(r))(1 + r)^{-r} \tag{3}$$

If the company does diversify, the present value of return on investment becomes

$$\bar{R}(t) = \frac{\bar{P}(t)(1 + r)^{-(t+1)}}{\bar{I}_p(t)}, \tag{4}$$

where $\bar{P}(t)$ represents earnings

$$\bar{P}(t) = h_1\left(\bar{I}(t) - \sum_{r=0}^{t}\sum_{j=1}^{4} i_j(r)\right) + h_2\left(\sum_{r=0}^{t}\sum_{j=1}^{4} i_j(r)\right) - r\sum_{r=0}^{t} i_2(r), \tag{5}$$

$\bar{I}(t)$ represents the capital

$$\bar{I}(t) = I(0) + \sum_{r=0}^{t} \bar{P}(r-1)(1 - k(r)) + \sum_{r=0}^{t}[i_2(r) + i_3(r)], \tag{5}$$

and $\bar{I}_p(t) = I(0) + \sum_{r=1}^{t} \bar{P}(r-1)(1 - k(r))(1 + r)^{-r} + \sum_{r=0}^{t}[i_2(r) + i_3(r)](1 + r)^{-r}$

$$\tag{5}$$

Using (2) and (4) we Using (2) and (4) we obtain the improvement in return on investment in year t which can be brought about by diversification:

$$\Delta R(t) = \bar{R}(t) - R(t) \tag{6}$$

For a selected investment policy, $i_1(t)$, $i_2(t)$, $i_3(t)$ and $i_4(t)$ specified for $r = 0 \ldots t$, ΔR can be computed for each year for which forecasted data are available employing information normally provided in such forecasts.

The next step is to consider the return on investment in a time perspective. Completion of a diversification move by a company will normally span a period of time. During this period the return on investment should be expected to vary, and even drop temporarily below pre-diversification levels. In order to assess the full effect of diversification, it is, therefore, desirable to compute an average return over a period which includes the transition to diversifying operations and which extends as far as possible into the future beyond the transition.

In principle it would be desirable to measure the effects of diversification over an indefinite future (See, for example, Ref. 10). In practice this period will be measured by the time span for which long range forecasts are available.

Let N be a period which includes transition and for which forecasted data are available. Further, recall that ΔR was computed for a particular

73

environment E and that usually several different forecasts will be available in order to take account of several probable environments. Let $E^1 \dots E^n \dots E^q$ be the environments considered by the company, each with an associated probability distribution $p^n(T)$ (See Sec. 3).

Then the expected average improvement in return to be derived from the diversified operations can be written in the form

$$(\Delta R)_e = \frac{1}{N} \sum_{n=1}^{s} \sum_{t=0}^{N} \sum_{r=t}^{N} \Delta R(E^n, r) p^n(r) \tag{7}$$

$(\Delta R)_e$ meets all of the conditions laid down for profit potential earlier in this section.

Recall that (7) is computed for a particular overall product-market strategy $\sigma_k = \sigma_l + \sigma_{ij}$, and that in the preceding section the totality of diversification possibilities was reduced to a set of such strategies, say $\{\sigma_k\}_m$.

The final step of selecting the preferred strategy through comparison of their respective prospect potentials can be stated as follows:

For a given increase in investment $\bar{I}_p$ $I(0)$ over a period from $t = 0$ to $t = N$ and an investment policy $i_1(t)$, $i_2(t)$, $i_3(t)$, $i_4(t)$ for $t = 0 \dots N$ specified for each σ_k, we can compute $(\Delta R(\sigma_k))_e$.

Recall that in Sec. 4 we stated long range sales objectives which require that certain minimum sales performance be shown for each E^n. Since (see Eq. 1 in this section) $(\Delta R)_e$ is a function of sales S, the long range sales objectives can be viewed as a constraint to be applied to $\Delta(R(\sigma_k))_e$.

Thus, the preferred overall company strategy σ_p is such that

$$[\Delta R(\sigma_p)]_e = \max_m (\Delta R(\sigma_k))_e \tag{8}$$

subject to the conditions that in the trend environment

$$\dot{S}_1(\sigma_k, E^1) - \dot{S}_l(\sigma_l, E^1) \geq \delta(t) \tag{9}$$

and for contingent environments E^n, $n = 2 \dots g$, where g is the number of distinct environments considered in the forecast,

$$\frac{S_1(\sigma_1, E^1) - S_2(\sigma_1, E^n)}{S_1(\sigma_1, E^1)} - \frac{S_1(\sigma_k, E^1) - S_2(\sigma_k, E^n)}{S_1(\sigma_k, E^1)} \geq \rho^n(t) \tag{10}$$

10. Interpretation of results

The approach used above in arriving at the desirable diversification strategies is, of course, not rigorous in the mathematical sense of the word. The conceptual model is one of successive elimination of alternatives involving either application of qualitative criteria, or straightforward numerical comparisons. Mathematical notation has served more as a shorthand language than a tool of analysis. While straightforward, the required evaluations may involve some difficult practical problems, such as computation of capital investment or assignment of earnings to the respective members of the product line. Nevertheless, all of the required basic data are normally available in long range sales and financial forecasts.

The final numerical evaluation is recognizable as a form of the problem of allocation of resources under uncertainty. While expected value is used for the payoff function, the usual danger, implicit in the expected value approach, of unbalanced preparedness for alternative environments is anticipated through the requirement of a minimum performance level in each, as expressed in the sales objectives. Incidentally, since the sales objectives can be computed independently of $(\Delta R)_e$, they are not constraints in the usual sense of the word. They can be applied to the admissible set $\{\sigma_k\}_m$ before $(\Delta R)_e$ are computed. The method for providing against what we have called unforeseeable contingencies is not as satisfactory as it should be in view of the importance of this class of futures. A rationale and an accompanying quantitative evaluation are needed and these should be used to restate the problem of allocation of resources under uncertainty.

One of the reasons why a simplified approach was possible lies in the fact that we have dealt with only a half of the diversification problem. Our concern has been with what might be called *external* aspects of diversification. We have sought to select diversification strategies in the light of the probable economic-political environments and the long range goals of the company. We have not been concerned with the influence of the internal, organizational, and business characteristics of the company on the diversification decisions.

It happens that business performance of a company is determined both by external characteristics of the product-market strategy and internal fit between the strategy and business resources. The first of these factors is what we have called *profit potential* of the product-market strategy, the second is the *business fit* of the strategy with respect to the diversifying company. Profit potential measures potential earnings as a function of the economic-political environment, characteristics of the demand, and nature of the competition under the assumption that the diversifying company is capable of offering effective competition in the new product-market area.

Business fit tests the validity of this assumption. It is a measure of the company's ability to penetrate the new market. It is determined by the particular strengths and weaknesses which the company brings to the new venture, such as the capabilities and past experience in engineering, production, finance, and merchandising.

Business fit is only one of the important internal aspects of the diversification problem. Other aspects include organization for diversification, development of new product-market ideas, methods of corporate expansion, anti-merger legislation, problems of corporate control, etc. While the external aspects generally deal with the advantages to be derived from diversification, the internal aspects deal with assessment of costs and risks. The overall diversification problem is to balance these against one another.

Unfortunately, quantitative evaluation of internal aspects is even more difficult than for the external ones. Consequently, a usual approach to this part of the problem is to derive qualitative criteria which are added to those discussed in this paper.

An interesting discussion of the internal aspects can be found in Ref. 2 and Ref. 5. It is also the subject of forthcoming Ref. 9.

Notes

1 For our purposes, the concept of a mission is more useful in describing market alternatives than would be the concept of a "customer," since a customer usually has many different missions, each requiring a different product.
2 One is tempted to enunciate an appropriate Parkinson's Law to the effect that advertising budget spent on a product is in an inverse ratio to the precision with which its mission can be specified.
3 Some companies (particularly in the growth industries) fix an annual rate of growth which they wish to attain. Every year this rate of growth is compared to the actual growth during the past year. A decision with respect to diversification action for the coming year is then based on the extent of the disparity between the objective and the actual rate of growth.
4 At first glance it would appear that vertical diversification is inconsistent with our definition of a diversification strategy (see Section 2). It should be recognized, however, that the respective missions which components, parts, and materials are designed to perform are distinct and different from the mission of the overall product. Furthermore, the technology in fabrication and manufacture of these is again likely to be very different from the technology of manufacturing the final product. Thus, vertical diversification does imply both catering to new missions and introduction of new products.
5 As is well known, the term "industry" is commonly used in several senses. Sometimes it is taken to mean a set of missions which have a basic underlying characteristic in common, such as, for example, the air industry, the automotive industry, etc. Sometimes the unifying notion is a common area of technology, such as electronics industry, chemical industry, steel industry, etc.

References

1 J. SAYER MINAS, "Formalism, Realism and Management Science," *Management Science* 3, 9–14 (1956).
2 THOMAS A. STAUDT, "Program for Product Diversification," *Harvard Business Review*, Nov–Dec. 1954.

3 A. D. H. KAPLAN, "Big Enterprise in a Competitive System," The Brookings Institution, Washington 6, D.C., 1954.
4 FEDERAL TRADE COMMISSION, "Report on Corporate Mergers and Acquisitions," Government Printing, Office, Washington, D.C., May 1955.
5 CHARLES H. KLINE, "The Strategy of Product Policy," Harvard Business Review, July–August 1955.
6 DAVID BENDEL HERT, "Operations Research in Long-Range Diversification Planning," Special Report No. 17, Operations Research Applied (New Uses and Extensions), American Management Association, 1957.
7 CHARLES R. SCHWARTZ, "The Return-on-Investment Concept as a Tool for Decision Making," General Management Series AMA Pamphlet #183, American Management Association, New York, 1956. (42–61)
8 PETER F. DRUCKER, The Practice of Management. New York, Harper & Brothers, 1954.
9 H. IGOR ANSOFF, "An Action Program for Diversification," Lockheed Aircraft Corporation, Burbank, California, 1957.
10 JOHN BURR WILLIAMS, The Theory of Investment Value, Amsterdam: North-Holland Publishing Co., Printed in the Netherlands, First printing 1938, Second printing 1956.
11 AMA CONFERENCE HANDBOOK, Mergers and Acquisitions: for Growth and Expansion, Published for distribution at the AMA Special Finance Conference, October 31-November 2, 1956, Hotel Roosevelt, New York.
12 FINANCIAL MANAGEMENT SERIES #113, "Integration Policies and Problems in Mergers and Acquisitions," American Management Association, New York, 1957.
13 FINANCIAL MANAGEMENT SERIES #114, "Legal, Financial, and Tax Aspects of Mergers and Acquisitions," American Management Association, New York, 1957.
14 FINANCIAL MANAGEMENT SERIES #115, "A Case Study in Corporate Acquisition," American Management Association, New York, 1957.
15 W. F. ROCKWELL JR., "Planned Diversification of Industrial Concerns," Advanced Management, May 1956.
16 W. E. HILL, Planned Product Diversification, William E. Hill Co., 660 Madison Ave., New York 21, N.Y.
17 WESLEY A. SONGER, "Organizing for Growth and Change," General Management Series AMA Pamphlet #171, American Management Association, New York.
18 HARRY R. LANGE, "Expansion Through Acquisition," Implementing Long-Range Company Planning, Stanford Research Institute, Menlo Park, Calif. (Speech given before Industrial Economics Conference, San Francisco, Jan. 21–22, 1957.)

5

A PROGRAM OF RESEARCH
IN BUSINESS PLANNING

H. Igor Ansoff and Richard C. Brandenburg

Source: *Management Science* 13(6), series B, Managerial (1967): B219–B239.

The purpose of this paper is to outline a program of research which is needed to improve the state of the art of business planning. We have approached this task by relating planning to management science on one hand, and to certain areas of descriptive knowledge on the other. From these relations we have constructed a comprehensive program for research on planning. Some parts of this program are being actively pursued, some are still in need of attention. It is our hope that this paper will contribute to a two-fold purpose: that it will help give the business planner a sense of unique identity, and that it will provide bim with a research program which he can pursue in strengthening this identity.

Introduction

In the light of its current popularity, it is easy to forget that formal planning is a very new management tool. A recent survey (1960) of the chemical processing industry [1] which is one of the most progressive users of modern management methods, showed, on one band, that upward of 90% of chemical firms currently engage in long-range planning, and on the other hand that practically none used formal planning so recently as 1948.

During this rapid growth of planning practice, the problems and the challenges faced by business planners have undergone a similarly accelerated change. In the early and middle fifties the challenge was to sell business on the advantages of formal planning. A small group of pioneers, spearheaded by Green, Kami, Steiner and Drucker, devoted itself to spreading the new religion. Their efforts made a significant contribution toward the current acceptance of planning by business. To be sure, today many firms still have no formal plans [2], [3], [4]. Among those which have them, there are various degrees of refinement and sophistication. Nevertheless, it is fair to

78

say that the proselyting days are over, that the near-standard speech on the hows and the whys and the wonders of planning has pretty much outlived its usefulness. It is time for planners to turn attention to new challenges.

Interesting challenges are in abundance. Adoption of planning has raised a number of pressing questions which the profession is ill-equipped to answer. How much planning is enough; what are the cost-benefit relationships in planning; what kinds of planning are appropriate to different firms, to different business conditions within firms; how should firms organize for planning; how is planning related to control; what is the role of computers in planning; how should planning practices differ among industries; how should uncertainty be handled? These and a host of other questions need to be answered if planning is to become a clearly understood and fully effective tool of management. The issues, the concepts and the techniques which underlie these answers will someday form a cohesive body of knowledge which will be called a theory of planning. In the past fifteen years the literature on planning has provided a skeleton outline for this theory. The need now is to put flesh on the skeleton. This fleshing out can come only from a considerable amount of new research into the problem of the business firm and of the planning process. Our purpose in this paper is to develop a broad framework and directions for such research.

We shall start with a broad review of human knowledge and then narrow it to areas of knowledge which are particularly relevant to business planning. This process would hopefully describe what every well-educated planner should know. It will also point to areas where there is a gap between the state of the art and the needs of business. A delineation of the most important gaps will constitute a program of research in business planning.

As a result we shall see that the gaps are many and needs for new knowledge are urgent. Thus a major challenge to planners today is to engage in active research so that, having sold the idea of planning to business, the planning profession can keep it sold and keep making it an increasingly effective management tool.

Taxonomy of science

In attempting to circumscribe knowledge which is distinctive and relevant to the job of a business planner, we must be prepared for the conclusion that there is no such distinctive body. It may be that business planning is coextensive with the field of management science. If this were the case, planning would be defined primarily as a job slot and a business process which has no specialized knowledge contents. In order to become a good planner a person would need to be a competent management scientist. To do research he would select an area of management science in which he is technically competent, and he would do this without special reference to planning.

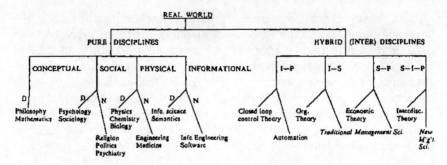

Figure 1

As one would suspect, the answer is neither black nor white. In this paper we hope to show that, while planning is not a unique and distinctive body of knowledge, neither is it coextensive with management science. A large part of knowledge relevant to planning will be seen to lie *within* management science. Another part of relevant knowledge lies outside management science in economics, organization theory, and theory of knowledge.

A broad taxonomy of human knowledge is shown on Figure 1. Distinctive areas are described by corresponding classes of real world phenomena which are related and which have similar properties. We shall call such classes *disciplines*.

(1) The *conceptual discipline* is one which is concerned with *ideas* of and about the world. Two mainstream sciences which study pure ideas are mathematics and philosophy. Both are highly relevant as inputs to both management science and planning. Mathematics provides internally consistent logic structures and appropriate calculi for transformations within the structures. Philosophy is one of two major sources of value systems which provide management analysts with criteria for choice among alternatives.

As its title implies, the conceptual discipline is the only one in our structure which is concerned exclusively with ideas and their relationship and not with empirical observations.

(2) The *social discipline* is built on an empirical foundation. It studies behavior, attitudes and motivation of human beings. In this and the remaining disciplines, science takes two complementary points of view, (a) the *descriptive* or predictive viewpoint which studies the environment "as is"— as it manifests itself to the eyes of the observer; and (b) the *prescriptive* or normative viewpoint which is concerned with the means by which desired modes of behavior can be induced.

Among major contributions of social sciences to the planning problem are: (a) Empirical data on objectives of organizations and of individuals. This is the second source of value systems; it can be used to confirm or refute the philosophical viewpoints; (b) Knowledge about structure, cohesiveness and stability of organizations. As will be seen below, this particular contribution will gain in importance, as behavior of firms becomes more dynamic.

(3) The *physical discipline* includes a long list of natural sciences of which physics, chemistry and biology are the major historical cornerstones. Their contribution to business planning is through the light they shed on the characteristics, capabilities, and limitations of the resource conversion processes in the firm.

(4) The three preceding disciplines represent the historical mainstreams of search for knowledge. During the past twenty years there has been an explosive growth of interest in another homogeneous class of real world phenomena—the *information discipline*. Although at present there is no unanimity on the point, there is a growing body of evidence that information sciences will take their place along the other mainstreams as a study of a distinctive class of real world phenomena.

The potential contribution to business from studies of information is very great. Many of the early ideas and concepts of planning have neglected the problem of information transfer. Accumulated experience suggests the very opposite: that search for information, processing of large volumes of data, and communication and acceptance of processed information, all have major influences on the success of business planning.

The above four disciplines may be called the "pure" mainstreams of search for knowledge, each concerned with a distinctive and similar group of phenomena. They may be described as "vertical" searches for knowledge which formed the core of the scientific tradition prior to the twentieth century. Since the 1900's some of the most promising expansions of knowledge have come from interdisciplinary or "horizontal" searches for knowledge. These are concerned with studies of *systems*, each of which incorporates more than one of the "pure" disciplines. Startling advances in engineering have, for example, been made through closed loop control theory which is concerned with combinations of physical and informational phenomena. A most promising viewpoint for study of combined social-physical-information systems (such as business firms, military organizations) was enunciated in 1948 by Wiener in his now famous theory of cybernetics.[1]

An exploration of the potentials of various interdisciplinary approaches to knowledge is a subject of great currency and interest. It is, however, beyond the scope of this paper. Our interest in such approaches is confined to the fact that a proper purview of management science and consequently of planning is properly describable in terms of interdisciplinary systems. One particular interdisciplinary system which made a major contribution to management science is the field of economics, which is concerned with a simultaneous study of social behavior and of conversion and distribution of physical resources in a closed society.

Using the above concepts we can now attempt to describe management science as follows.[2]

81

(1) The bulk of management science to date has been concerned with two-dimensional physical-social interdisciplinary systems. The physical element has provided the substance of the models and the social element, the decision criteria. Much of the work has been focussed on conversion and distribution of resources within the firm (e.g., inventory control, production scheduling, distribution). The criteria (measures of effectiveness) have usually been borrowed from classical economics—profit maximization in its various proxy forms.

(2) The problem of acquisition, transfer and handling information has generally been excluded from the models. On the other hand, some "pure" information models have been constructed which exclude both physical resource conversion and economic criteria.

(3) Social phenomena of human motivation (other than profit motivation) have generally been excluded from models. As a result, management science has been studying "dehumanized" business firms after the pattern of classical economists.

(4) A relatively recent but strong and significant trend has started toward a fully interdisciplinary view of business problems which includes simultaneously physical, informational, economic and noneconomic behavioral variables.

(5) A very important fact for planners is that *management science has been normative* and that its descriptive insights have been borrowed from the respective "pure" fields of knowledge. On one hand, this implies the assumption that the insights available in pure disciplines are rich enough and adequate for normative models. On the other hand, this also assumes that interdisciplinary combinations of pure knowledge are simply additive and no new descriptive insights result from study of hybrid systems. Experience has shown that neither of these assumptions is correct either for management science or for planning. Thus, for example, the work of Cyert and March [5] shows that it is not a simple matter to combine economic and social behavior. At the present time a principal need in planning is for an interdisciplinary *applied* theory of the firm which is rich enough to resemble real firms and which can provide a better foundation for normative models than the economists' theory of the firm [6].

In summary, management science can be defined as a normative study of interdisciplinary systems involving human participants. Historically this study has been heavily biased toward the physical resource conversion process in the firm.[3] The recent important and encouraging trend is toward removal of this bias and a balanced view of physical, social, and informational aspects of organizations.

Management science seeks to change and guide organizations toward attainment of some specified purpose (e.g., profit, victory, or personal goals of the participants). Planning also seeks to change and guide organizations through the specific means of strategies, policies, standing rules, plans and budgets. Therefore, the *normative* aspect of planning is a part of management science. This conclusion is neither novel, nor surprising. Two questions are of greater interest: (a) What *parts* of management science are of major interest to planners and (b) what *descriptive* knowledge should be a part of a planner's equipment? We now turn to the first of these questions.

Planning as part of the decision process

In order to place planning within the context of management science we start with the management process. The process can be described through the Management Decision Cycle shown in Figure 2. We shall break into the cycle at the left of the diagram.

1. Three time consuming management activities are (a) response to problems which are brought up by others in the organization (*problem triggers*), (b) a continuing search for opportunities which permit improvement of the firm's performance (*search for opportunities*), and (c) periodic review (*clock triggers*) of past performance.

Although by definition management science is concerned with all of the activities shown on Figure 2, it has paid little attention to the problem of search, since in most of its models the opportunities are assumed to be available at the outset of analysis [7]. Until recently, planners also have contributed little to the problem of search. The growing importance of strategic planning has brought the problem to the forefront. This is clearly an area of important research for planners.

2. The second step—*decision analysis*—has traditionally been a major focus of management science attention. A majority of the published models is concerned with analysis of consequences of *given* alternatives under *given* decision criteria.

Planners, on the other hand, have been remiss in this area. Much of the planning literature has concerned itself with programming of the firm's

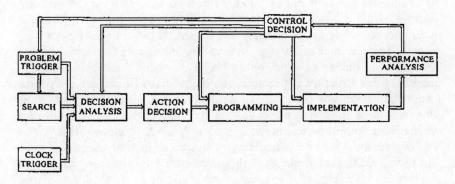

Figure 2

activities and not with the manner in which the underlying decisions are arrived at. At best, planners are offered checklists: "analyze the problem", "select the preferred course of action", etc. As a result, most planning formats make no provision for explicit recording of decision analysis. It is somehow supposed to be made on "backs of envelopes", or in the manager's head.[4]

In the area of decision analysis planners need not imitate the bulk of the management science profession and thus become developers of new decision analysis models. They would do better to rely on existing models and focus their attention on the badly needed study of relevance of theoretical models to particular practical situations. In doing this, they can help in several ways: remove a major obstacle to application of good existing models by translating them into business language, point to limitations of unrealistic models, and stimulate development of new useful models.

A major advance in this area is about to be made through introduction of computers to planning.[5] This will open new vistas for decision analysis and will enable planners to bring to the decision maker greatly improved choices of alternatives. If planners are to retain their role as useful advisers to management, they *must* do research and lead in applications of computers in this area.

Another major advance in decision analysis will lie in the emergence of interdisciplinary descriptive models of the firm in place of the currently predominant economic model. These will broaden the economic-physical resource analysis to include explicit treatment of information and of social interactions among organizational participants. Knowledge in this area is still rudimentary and much research is needed before useful normative models emerge. Planners need to keep current here. They can also make a useful contribution to original research, because they frequently have a viewpoint of the firm which is broader and better integrated than that of most management scientists.

3. We have separated the *decision* phase from decision analysis in order to distinguish the problem of building decision models from the problem of formulating decision criteria (utility functions). The aim of the former is to predict consequences of alternatives; the aim of the latter is to determine how a decision maker chooses among the alternatives, given the consequences. In much of the normative problem solving the decision analysis models which structure the relations among variables have generally been better than the accompanying utility functions. This is the reason why, in spite of a large amount of effort devoted to it, utility theory has found very little application in the making of important business decisions. It is fair to say that many otherwise potentially fruitful decision analysis models have not been used in practice because they contained poor decision criteria.

Planners have largely stayed away from study of utility theory primarily because of a frank realization that interest in decision theory can be dangerous to the professional relationship between the planner and the decision maker. Fortunately in our opinion, little has been lost to planning as a result. Again, as with model building, planners can play a useful role as interpreters by relating various decision theories to practice. They can make an original contribution through studying the dimensions of the decision maker's utility spaces and relating these dimensions to the available theories. Thus it is possible to visualize practical use of some utility functions as suboptimization criteria in a larger field of decision variables defined by planners.

4. *Programming* is a management activity which translates decisions into specific action patterns for implementation. The primary management tasks in this phase are

(a) Scheduling activities in support of decisions[6]
(b) Assignment and scheduling of resources in support of decisions (commonly referred to as budgeting)
(c) Establishing patterns of work flows in the firm
(d) Establishing patterns of authority and responsibility
(e) Establishing communication flow networks.

This area of management activity has traditionally been the focus of planners. This is where planning was born. Many planners can be found in the profession today who would argue that programming, as defined above, is the core and the substance of planning and that the major job of the planner is to serve as: (i) a catalyst in initiating activities (a) through (e) above; (ii) as an integrator of the inputs received from the rest of the organization; and (iii) as an interpreter of the results for the management.

The scope of planning is, of course, a matter of arbitrary definition. Therefore, we do not propose to argue the right of some planners to define their jobs in this narrow context. It needs to be pointed out, however, that line management is feeling increasing needs for help in the search and decision analysis phases of the decision cycle. The activities in those phases are inextricably related to programming. We would predict, therefore, that planners who refuse to take a broader view of their job are on the way to extinction.

Thanks to the concentration of effort in this area, understanding of programming is better developed than of the other parts of the planner's job. An impressive structure of formats and procedures exists in many business firms which, when properly used, can make a major contribution to the effectiveness of management.[7]

At the same time a number of important research challenges exists in this area:

(a) One of these stems from the fact that while most existing business planning systems are effective in *resource scheduling*, they are very poor in *activity scheduling*. This was graphically illustrated in the Polaris missile development when the Navy discovered that, while its contractor had one of the most progressive business planning systems, this system was unable to provide the kind of activity scheduling information which was needed for control of a very large and complex crash project.

Since then, several PERT-type project control systems have been developed and used. However, they have remained tools of management scientists used on a project by project basis and largely unintegrated into business planning systems. A major challenge to planners is to develop integrated planning systems which will combine financial and physical resource scheduling with performance scheduling.

(b) Another major challenge lies in the need to integrate decision analysis and programming. As discussed above, these two planning phases have remained separate with the former frequently being given a "lick and a promise". As a very undesirable consequence, management was left with little flexibility in making decisions. Key decisions which determined the future of the firm remained imbedded and hidden in programs and budgets. A top manager, who did not like the looks of the resulting budgets, had no facility for exploring consequences of different decisions [13].

This is another area in which the computer holds great promise. Some firms have already put their budgeting cycle on the computer with the resulting gain of flexibility in varying assumptions at little cost and loss in time. Research is needed in the following directions: (i) constructing decision analysis models, (ii) developing performance scheduling models and combining them with existing budgeting models and, (iii) programming both on the computer; and, finally, (iv) integrating decision analysis and programming into an overall planning model of the firm.

(c) A third research challenge lies in the area of organization planning described by item (4) (d), above. It had been the subject of business attention for at least as long as budgeting. However, it has generally remained dissociated, both substantively and organizationally, from the usual concerns of the business planner: The business planner and the organization planner frequently reported separately to top management and each performed his job independently of the other.

The research need is to seek an understanding of *task-oriented dynamic* organization planning which will inject business needs into organizational design. In the past students of organizations have shown little concern with design to the specifications of the job. Instead, their concern has been largely directed to describing behavior of established organizations and to studying forces which motivate individuals to participate in organizations [14], [15]. On the other hand, practitioners of organizational design within firms have somehow managed to remain aloof from the relationship between profitability of the firm and its organizational structure. Furthermore, most of their thinking about organizations has been in static rather than dynamic time-dependent terms.

The need for research in organizational design is highlighted by the new dynamics of the firm's product-market environment [16]. If one were forced to state a single central problem which will face the firm of tomorrow, it may well be the need to innovate continuously. And the organizational form is a major instrument for filling the need.

(d) A fourth research challenge is posed by item (4) (e) above. It is the need for task-oriented information system design. Unlike organization planning, information system planning is a relatively recent business activity which was brought about by the growing size and complexity of firms and made possible by the capabilities of the computer. The impetus for research in this area was provided by the large scale military warning and control systems such as SAGE. Considerable management science effort has been devoted to the military applications and, more recently, some leading firms have begun to design and install integrated information systems.

In view of considerable management science interest in this area, our recommendation to planners, unlike in organization design, is that they monitor and adapt work which is current, and which will undoubtedly expand, to the needs of the business firm. It is probable that for some time in the future business planners and information system planners will continue to work separately on their respective problems. The prospects for eventual integration of their efforts will be discussed below.

5. The fifth stage in management decision cycle, *implementation*, is probably the most time consuming management activity. It consists of

(a) Disseminating information about the plans and programs
(b) Securing their acceptance by responsible participants
(c) Triggering off organizational action
(d) Providing coordination among related activities
(e) Providing leadership and otherwise motivating the participants.

While the general manager's load is heavy in this phase, the planner's attention is confined to (a) and (b). Practical experience as well as psychological experiments have shown that the best prepared programs may be frustrated and diluted in implementation, unless their content is properly communicated to managers and workers who carry them out, and unless the managers and the workers become willing participants in the programs.

Psychological experimentation in this area has centered around the problem of participative versus authoritarian management. The experimenters have sought to measure the extent to which participation by subordinates in decision making improves both the decision making process and the subsequent implementation. While a considerable amount of research has been done here, the results are far from conclusive [17], [18], [19].

The practitioners of management have sought to resolve the same problem in practice by using participative techniques. This has led to a philosophy of *management by objectives* which has been adopted by some firms [20]. Applied to planning, it involves a programming activity which flows "from the bottom up": from the lowest levels of supervision to top management.

Neither the theoretical nor the practical issues are resolved, much research and experimentation remains to be done. Again our suggestion to planners is to do research on application of theoretical formulation and to suggest useful formulations for further theoretical explorations, rather than to engage in active original research.

6. The remaining two phases of Figure 2, Performance Analysis, and Control Decision, have traditionally lain outside the business planner's purview. Frequently the staff responsibility[8] for these functions is lodged with the controller who, in turn, is a member of the finance branch of the firm. Since business planners usually report directly to top operating management, the planning function and the control function are performed in parallel, frequently without a close coupling between them.

While there is much to be said for keeping staff planning and control responsibilities separated, important developments in the art of planning will make it necessary that the planner concern himself with some aspects of measurement and control problems.

(a) As discussed above, traditional programming has been adapted to *resource* scheduling which can be measured in terms of dollars. The use of financial measurement as the performance yardstick was the primary reason why the controller's function gravitated to the finance branch.

As *activity* scheduling and measurement is introduced, the logic of having the finance branch perform the control function will become less clear. Regardless of how organizational implications are resolved,[9] planners will have to become concerned with designing activity programs in ways which will enable and expedite effective performance measurement and control. This area of research is very much a job for the planners, since it cannot be effectively separated from the design of activity scheduling systems.

(b) The control decision box in Figure 2 shows four possible types of decision which can result from a comparison of performance to plans and programs:

(i)   To redirect implementation in a way which will result in meeting planned objectives.
(ii)   To seek for alternatives that are different from the one being implemented. This represents a recognition that the fault lies with the decision itself and not the way it was either programmed or implemented.
(iii) To reprogram the activity without changing the basic objective and nature of the activity.
(iv)   To review the decision analysis procedure. This represents recognition that the process of decision analysis needs improvement: that good

88

alternatives were available, but the one chosen was not the best one for the firm.

Of the four control feedbacks planners should have particular interest (and responsibility) for (iii)—reprogram, and (iv)—improve decision analysis. These feedbacks are to be fully expected, since no procedure can be perfect the first time, and the best way to learn how to plan effectively is to learn from experience.

As a practical matter, feedbacks of this kind do take place. (Sometimes they result in loss of jobs for unfortunate planners.) However, very little research has been done on how to design the planning system so as to assure that feedbacks take place regularly and are used for progressive improvement of planning. This is another research area in which planners should have a first-hand interest.

(c) The final research area to be discussed in connection with the management decision cycle is integration of planning and control into combined computer models. As mentioned above, traditionally the planner's job stopped with completion of the programming phase when the controller took over. As the planners become concerned with activity control (see (a) above), and as comprehensive planning models are programmed on computers, much of the logic of separation of planning from control will disappear. It will certainly disappear to the point where integrated planning *and* control models of the firm become a reality.

Therefore, planners need to do research on the total planning-control system. The first steps can start at the interface by assuring that plans provide *for* effective control within existing control systems. However, as performance scheduling becomes integrated with resource scheduling, as behavioral elements are introduced into models, a fully integrated planning-control viewpoint should become the object of planning research. In this work the planner will have to work with the controller, each retaining his primary purpose—the former of creating effective guidelines for the firm, and the latter in assuring compliance with the guidelines.

Planner as a specialist within management science

By means of the management decision cycle we have described the field of normative knowledge about interdisciplinary purposive systems (such as the business firm) which is of concern to management science. Within this field we have singled out areas of particular concern to business planners. We are now in a position to define both planning and the job of the planner.

We define planning as a process of setting formal guidelines and constraints for the behavior of the firm. This includes search for threats and opportunities, analysis of these, selecting preferred ones, scheduling their implementation and using performance feedback to improve the process.[10]

Planning is not the exclusive province of the professional planner. On one side, he reports to a line manager who is an active participant. In particular, the manager has the exclusive prerogative at the "moment of truth" when the decision is made to program and implement a particular action alternative. The planner can and should make recommendations, but he has neither responsibility nor the authority for making the final choice.

On the other side of the planner are his colleagues in management science who have a strong interest in the same phases of the management decision cycle. The planner differs from them in several important respects.

1. His interest is directed to models which are of direct relevance and usefulness to the firm. In a compromise between "formalism" and "realism", which each management scientist has to make, the planner inclines toward the latter [22].

2. The planner's job is "on line". As a part of management he is a daily "real time" participant of the ongoing management process. By contrast, many other management scientists within firms operate "off line" (in OR or management science groups) on special problems and assignments.

3. A consequence of the on line responsibility is the planner's concern with programming, again in contrast to many other management scientists who consider the problem "solved" when the preferred alternative is chosen.

4. Similarly the planner is concerned with organizational acceptance of planning, with implementation, with measurement, and feedback into the planning process.

A program of research for planners

We are now in a position to present a summary program for research in planning. In the beginning of the paper we sought research topics within a broad taxonomy of human knowledge. This provided us with areas of descriptive knowledge which are relevant to the planning process. Secondly, we focussed attention on the management decision cycle. This enabled us first to describe in detail the normative field of interdisciplinary knowledge known as management science, and then to single out within it the normative interests of the planner.

Thus both normative and descriptive research topics have been uncovered. We have further made judgment on the manner in which planners should address each topic. The judgments were based on several considerations: special relevance to planning, the importance of a practical viewpoint, urgency of the need for improvements, and the level of current research activity by other management scientists. In the following listing we shall assign each topic to one of three categories: (a) topics on which planners should do original research, (b) topics which offer opportunities for applications of research by others, (c) topics where planners should be cognizant of research by others. These categories are denoted by three, two or one asterisks, respectively.

A. Concepts and methodology

1*   The time is not far distant when every planner will need a general understanding of tools of management science. As a minimum, planners need to be cognizant of computer application, linear programming, decision theory, game theory and probability and statistics.

2***   Planners can make original contributions to developing *tests of relevance* for determining the suitability of the theoretical model to practical applications. This would include not only tests of availability of data, variability of data, and sensitivity of model results to data, all of which are fairly well understood, but also tests of alternative mathematical formulations for the accuracy with which they reflect reality.

3**   Research is needed in finding practical application for a large body of existing decision analysis models and models of utility theory.

4***   Literature is virtually barren in answer to the question "how can we tell that whether the proposed plan is a good plan?"

5***   Management science has concentrated on models of what has been called "well structured problems" [23]. As planning pervades the firm, planners will be increasingly confronted with *ill-structured problems*. Relatively few management scientists today are motivated by an interest in methodologies of ill-structured problems [24] through [28]. Planners, by virtue of their on line position and preference for realism can do useful research on a spectrum of methodologies ranging from unstructured to fully structured problems.

6**   As mentioned earlier, planners have a strong interest in computer simulations of the business firm [29], [30], [31]. Much of early research in this area has been done by people outside planning departments with a resulting lack of realism in some of the models [32].

7**   Planners have a strong interest in development of models which combine realistic decision analysis with detailed implementation scheduling and which are also *dynamic*, in the sense of being able to adjust quickly and efficiently to major changes in decisions.

8**   Planners should have a strong interest in *decision analysis models in which decision alternatives are not known in advance*, but are introduced over time [33], and in which *estimates of decision outcomes also change with time*.

9***   A related need for research deals with *models of search for information and generation of decision alternatives*. (The empirical counterpart of this problem is described below.)

10***   Turning to the realm of philosophy, research is needed to answer the questions of the role of the firm in society and to the objectives of the firm. Most of the past research in this area has been done by people outside firms. Planners can contribute useful philosophical views from the vantage point of an insider.

B. Social behavior

The expansion of planning from economic to the broader interdisciplinary viewpoint will depend on a number of important contributions from the social sciences. Planners whose technical training is in this environment can find a number of important areas for research. The following are among them [34].

1*** Theoretical studies of the firm's objectives must be backed up by empirical studies of goal structure of organizations, as well as for normative models for setting objectives [35] through [39]. A study of the dynamics of objectives formulation and change in relation to the changes of the firm is in particular need of attention.

2*** Descriptive work by Barnard [40], and Simon and March [41], made major contributions to understanding of viability and coherence of organizations. The area of *task oriented* organizational theory is in much poorer shape. Success here will mean extension of research from purely social phenomena to include the economics of physical resource conversion within the firm, as well as the communications system.

3** An area critical to success of planning is *organizational adaptability to change*. Descriptive understanding is needed of what makes some organizations responsive to change while others fail to respond. A point of departure is probably in the study of social phenomena, but again, the viewpoint will have to be enlarged to a fuller behavioral perspective before useful normative models emerge.[11]

4** Further work is needed on what determines *organizational acceptance* of plans and the effectiveness of *compliance* with plans. A better understanding is needed on effectiveness of participative management and particularly of the relative influence of its motivational and cognitive aspects.

C. Physical and information resource conversion

1* An effective business needs to have an understanding of the physical and information resource conversion processes which take place within the firm. Therefore he needs acquaintance with the structure and dynamics of primary resource conversion activities: finance, production, marketing, R and D, as well as of the information generation and use as practiced in accounting and controllership.

D. Applied theory of the firm

It is an obvious fact that a researcher who seeks ways to improve the behavior of the firm is in need of a clear understanding of how firms behave. Without this understanding he is akin to a self-made mechanic who seeks to repair an automobile without an understanding of internal combustion principles. It is an unfortunate fact that most planners and many of the management scientists have been such self-made mechanics with respect to the business firm. They have been forced into this role by the lack of an adequate theory of the firm [42].

Our examination of the taxonomy of knowledge suggests that the foundations of such theory must come from a hybrid combination ("interdiscipline") of the traditional pure disciplines. Research on such a theory is still in its incipient stages and is not widespread [43] through [49]. The need, from the planner's viewpoint, is urgent. Furthermore, a technically competent planner is uniquely qualified to do research on theory which will have a close relation to practice. For these reasons it is our recommendation that the planning profession give high priority to research on the applied theory of the firm.

1. *Comparative descriptions of the firm.* One of the major reasons why much of the economic theory of the firm is inapplicable to the real world stems from a lack of discrimination among individual firms. All firms are expected to follow, in a similar way, the same behavioral hypothesis (maximization of near term profit). In practice we find significant differences among firms both in their objectives and in the way they pursue the objectives. We need to understand the reasons for these differences.

    (a) A series of studies is needed which describes firms' behavior under different sets of circumstances.

        i.***   intra-industry studies of what makes for success and failure patterns.

        ii.***   inter-industry studies of how different external conditions and different product technologies affect behavior of firms.

        iii.***   international studies of behavior patterns in different social-economic-social environments.

        iv.***   intra-firm studies of differences between the internal functions of the firm.

    (b) i.**   A number of speculative papers [50], [51], [52] have appeared which prognosticate *what the computer is doing to the internal management* structure of the firm. These need to be extended and supported with historical data.

        ii.***   A companion perception of the influence of *trends external to the firm* on firms' behavior is in much worse shape.

Here both theoretical formulations and empirical analyses are badly needed [53].

(c)** Little has been written about the way *management attitudes* affect the firm's behavior under different conditions, or about how these attitudes are formed. We suspect that management attitude is one of the major determinants of differences in intra-industry behavior. Success here again requires a hybrid viewpoint of physical, social and informational phenomena.

2.** *Dynamic theory of the firm.* We believe that the comparative studies of the kind described above will radically change theories of the firm's overall behavior. Most current theories and models are static in the sense that the external product-market environment remains structurally unchanged. Only scalar changes in sales volume, prices, etc. are usually studied. Research is needed on how the accelerated dynamics of the environment affect both descriptive and normative theories of the firm [54], [55].

3.** The third major thrust for research in behavior of firms should be in the direction of combining economic-social and informational variables into interdisciplinary models. The need for this research has been discussed above [56].

4.*** Research is needed on the way firms relate to their environment; specifically on the manner the environment is searched for threats, opportunities and other relevant information and the manner in which it is filtered and used by the firm.

5.*** Those who have engaged in research on the business firm are aware of the fact that traditional business data collection, processing, and recording systems frequently lack information needed for constructive research. One of the most pressing and potentially most useful directions for descriptive research is in *designing and installing data gathering systems* which will permit better research on the business firm. The current trend toward automated data systems provides unusual opportunities to do this. Additional data requirements can be introduced at small additional costs—a procedure which was not feasible under manual or semi-automatic data processing.

6.*** Finally, the conceptual work on model verification described above must be matched with practice. Research is needed on planning *experimentation* which can be conducted at justifiable costs within an ongoing business process.

E. Design of the planning process

The preceding areas have dealt with a wide range of needs for research on the basic tools of the planner. The last two areas deal with the design of the planning process within the firm. Important as the tool developments are, planner's concern with his own job must take priority. Therefore, if choices are to be made, the remaining areas must be the major focus of research in planning. Many of the relevant topics have been discussed in the section on the management decision cycle. They are briefly summarized below.

1.** Research is needed on adaptation and inclusion of *decision analysis* models into business planning systems.

2.** Available *performance scheduling* and *control* models must be adapted to management use.

3.*** Several stages of model *integration* need research:

    i.   integration of performance scheduling with resource scheduling.

    ii. integration of decision analysis with programming into overall planning models.

    iii. integration of planning and control into overall planning-control model of the firm.

4.*** As discussed previously, *application of the computer* to all phases of the planning process should receive high priority.

5.*** Research is needed on making the planning process *adaptive to the resulting performance* in both the decision analysis and the programming phases.

6.*** The planning process must also be made *adaptive to the internal* and *external dynamics* of the firm.

Special needs are:

    i.   planning systems which have a sensitive perception of the changes in the external conditions of the firms.

    ii. systems capable of rapid response to drastic changes in the product-market position of the firm.

    iii. planning systems which change as the firm changes.

7.*** A major effort is needed in designing *planning systems* which can be *tailored to the needs of the firm*. This includes

    i.   development of cost-benefits relations for planning.

    ii. design of planning systems to fit the particular threats and opportunities faced by the firm and to its internal structure.

    iii. design of planning systems appropriate to different functions within the firm.

    iv. tailoring of planning systems to the size of the firm.

F. Organizational and information design

Organizational planning needs to receive the recognition it deserves as a vital part of the planning process.

1.** Some progress has been made in illuminating the relationship between strategy and organization [57]. Broader progress is needed in *task-oriented organizational design*.

2.** Procedures are needed which will *match the organization to the dynamics of the firm's environment*. Particularly needed are organizational forms which will accelerate change within the firm.

3.** Most of organization planning today is static. There is a need for formats, procedures and models for planning *dynamic time-variant organizations*.

4.*** A specific responsibility of the planner is to organize his own operation. This requires *matching the organization of the planning group to the demands of the firm's planning process*.

5.*** Design of *planning information systems* is in need of research.

6.*** Finally, a better understanding is needed of organizational and planning procedures which enhance *acceptance* of and compliance with plans.

Methodology for research on planning

A necessary point of departure for research on planning is a systematic appraisal of the current state of knowledge. Some investigations may build on already well-established conceptual and empirical foundations, while other lines of inquiry may have to begin without any appreciable base of available research findings or relevant theories. Therefore, after an area of research is selected, it is useful to map the internal structural characteristics of existing models. One way to do this is to classify models and other types of information in terms of degrees of relevance to practical uses. This would include assessment of the effectiveness with which models have been abstracted from the real situation, availability of data, computational complexity, and the problem of communicating, and implementing results obtained from the models.

One result of such appraisal might be better definition of the type of research efforts required. For example, comprehensive histories of well-understood planning phenomena may be available in a few cases. The task then is to find applications. In other cases, normative procedures may have been formulated but need testing and refinement through trial applications. Alternatively, well-specified descriptive hypotheses about organization behavior might be available but as yet untested with empirical data. In a larger number of cases, the state of knowledge will probably require formulation of meaningful hypotheses before other stages of research and development can be initiated.

A key issue in methodology for research on planning is the trade off between precise, manipulable models, versus accurate but prescriptively ambiguous models. The costs and benefits of "formalism" versus "realism" for activities of management scientists have been noted by Minas [60]. As stated previously, the business planner, more than the management scientist, should be an "on-line" participant in the management process. Therefore, the planner is particularly sensitive to constraints on resources available for his decision analyses, and the plausibility of his management process inputs to the executives who use them. It follows that research on planning must place priority on realism rather than formalism when this trade off is encountered.

Although "realism" is more appropriate to research on planning than "formalism", two qualifications must be mentioned. First, if realism is sought only through increasing model size and complexity, problems may occur in validating the model as an accurate reflection of a system or an operation. Conway has cited some of these difficulties in connection with research in computer simulation [61]. He further suggests that thorough working knowledge is needed of how individual components in a system operate, and that complex simulations are most useful in preliminary explorations. These suggestions deserve attention in efforts to gain realism through computer simulations in research on planning. Second, formal models may be useful predecessors to realistic models. A precise, highly abstract, normative model may generate hypotheses which can be measured and compared more easily than highly detailed description. Such results, plus explicit statements via the model of factors which are and are not included in the analysis, can be fed back through successive stages of model re-design to converge on relevant working techniques for the planner.

The existing state of knowledge and the difficulties inherent in assuring the relevance of research results have implications for the rate of research progress in planning. They suggest that there may be important differences between what is researchable in the form of extensions from existing information, and what is desirable in the form of solutions to the planning problems of the total business enterprise. The research program proposed here includes numerous possibilities for incremental extensions of existing boundaries of knowledge. Research undertaken in these areas can provide opportunities for development and testing of improved methodologies, and thereby can contribute to an accelerated advance toward understanding and solving the significant problems of business planning.

Notes

1 For a variety of reasons, two of which may be the fact that Wiener's theory was both too far in advance of its time, and not very clearly enunciated, cybernetics did not "take" in the U.S. Experienced observers suggest that it has provided a unifying outlook on study of management in the U.S.S.R.
2 This definition can be verified by a review of articles which appeared in *Management Science* and similar publication during the past ten years.

3 If an exact parallel is drawn with pure environments (see Figure 1), the word "science" appears inappropriate to a normative body of knowledge. A better term for management science might be "management engineering".

4 The military planners have been more progressive in the decision analysis phase through the use of the Estimate of the Situation [8].

5 For a discussion of computers in planning see [9] and [10].

6 The schedules may be time phased programs, rules for unconditional repetition of activity (standing operating procedures), rules for conditional repetition (policies), or rules for further decision making (strategies). For further discussion of different types of schedules, see Chapter 6 of [11].

7 For a discussion of this structure and its advantages and limitations, see [12].

8 The line responsibility in these areas continues, of course, to reside with the responsible line manager.

9 They may well be resolved in some firms in favor of the data systems manager assuming the control function.

10 This definition is practically synonymous with a more colorful one by Peter Drucker [21]. He defines planning as:

"a continuous process of making present entrepreneurial decisions systematically and with best possible knowledge of their futurity, organizing systematically the effort needed to carry out these decisions, and measuring the results of those decisions against expectations through organized systematic feedback."

11 For example, some organizations fail to change not because of risk preferences of the participants, but because their physical resources are highly specialized.

References

1 *Chemical Week*, June 6, 1960.
2 *Management Methods*, Vol. 13, No. 4, Jan. 1958. pp. 14–17.
3 *Business Week*, "Focusing Farther and Sharper," June 1965.
4 BERNARD H. SURD AND GLENN A. WALSH, *Business Budgeting* (Controllership Foundation, 1958), Chapter 5.
5 RICHARD M. CYERT, JAMES G. MARCE, *A Behavioral Theory of the Firm* (Prentice-Hall, Englewood Cliffs, N. J., 1963).
6 *Op. cit.* [5], Chapter 2.
7 W. BERANEK, *Analysis of Financial Decisions* (Irwin, 1963), p. 27.
8 FM 101–5, *Department of the Army Manual, Staff Officers Field Manual, Staff Organization and Procedure*, Governement Printing Office, Washington, D. C., 1954.
9 H. IGOR ANSOFF, "State of the Art in Business Planning," presented to National Association of Accountants Long Range Profit Planning Conference, Cleveland, Ohio, March 12, 1964.
10 H. IGOR ANSOFF, A. BRUCE ROZET, AND THEODORE BRAUN, "Computers in the Entrepreneurial Role"—Use of computers in land development, unpublished.
11 H. IGOR ANSOFF, *Corporate Strategy* (McGraw-Hill, 1965).
12 *Op. cit.* [9].
13 *Op. cit.* [9].

14 CHESTER I. BARNARD, *The Functions of the Executive* (Harvard University Press, Cambridge, Mass., 1940).

15 JAMES G. MARCH AND HERBERT A. SIMON, *Organizations* (Wiley, 1958).

16 H. IGOR ANSOFF, "The Firm of the Future," *Harvard Business Review*, Vol. 43, No. 5, Sept.–Oct., 1965, pp. 162–178.

17 L. COCH AND J. R. P. FRENCH, JR., "Overcoming Resistance to Change," *Human Relations*, 1948, Vol. 1, No. 4, pp. 512–532.

18 ALEX BAVELAS reporting in *Experiments in Spcial Process: A Symposium on Social Psychology* (New York: McGraw-Hill, 1950).

19 B. M. BASS AND H. J. LEAVITT, "Somer Experiments in Planning and Operating," *Management Science*, 1963, 9, pp. 574–585.

20 A. KING MCCORD, "Management by Objectives," presented at the 14th Annual Award Dinner, Duquesne University Chapter, Society for Advancement of Management, May 10, 1962.

21 P. F. DRUCKER, "Long-Range Planning—Challenge to Management Science," *Management Science*, 5 (3), April, 1959, pp. 238–249.

22 J. SAYER MINAS, "Formalism, Realism and Management Science," *Management Science*, Oct. 1956, pp. 9–14.

23 H. A. SIMON AND A. NEWELL, "Heuristic Problem-Solving: The Next Advance in Operations Research," *Operations Research*, Jan.–Feb., 1958, Vol. 6, No. 1, pp. 1–10.

24 H. A. SIMON, *New Science of Management Decision* (Harper and Row, New York, 1960).

25 H. I. ANSOFF, "Quasi-Analytic Method for Long-Range Planning," presented at the First Symposium on Corporate Long-Range Planning, TIMS College on Planning, June 6, 1959; and 6th Annual International Meeting, TIMS, Paris, France, Sept. 9, 1959.

26 H. I. ANSOFF, "A Quasi-Analytic Approach to the Business Strategy Problem," *Management Technology*, 4 (1), June 1964.

27 ALAN EAGLE, "Methodologies of Long Range Planning," Stanford Research institute, Menlo Park, Cal., March, 1965.

28 H. I. ANSOFF, *Corporate Strategy* (McGraw-Hill, 1965).

29 DAVID B. HERTZ, "Risk Analysis in Capital Investment," *Harvard Business Review*, 42 (1), Jan–Feb., 1964. pp. 95–106.

30 DAVID B. HERTZ, "The Unity of Science and Management," *Management Science*, 11 (6), April, 1965, pp. 89–97.

31 *Op. cit.* [10].

32 D. F. BOYD, "The Emerging Role of Enterprise Simulation Models," IBM Advanced Systems Division, Yorktown Heights, N. Y. Presented at the International Meeting of the Western Section of the Operations Research Society of America, Honolulu, Hawaii, Sept. 14–18, 1964.

33 GORDON M. KAUFMAN, *Statistical Decision and Related Techniques in Oil and Gas Exploration*, Ford Foundation doctoral dissertation Series 1962 award winner (Prentice-Hall, Englewood Cliffs, N. J.).

34 W. W. COOPER, H. J. LEAVITT, AND M. W. SHELLY, *New Perspectives in Organization Research* (John Wiley, New York, 1964).

35 R. M. CYERT AND J. G. MARCH, *A Behavioral Theory of the Firm* (Prentice-Hall, Englewood Cliffs, N. J., 1963).

36 PETER F. DRUCKER, "Long-Range Planning—Challenge to Management Science," *Management Science*, Vol. 5, No. 3, April 1959, pp. 238–249.

37 C. H. GRANGER, "The Hierarchy of Objectives," *Harvard Business Review* 42 (3), May–June, 1964, pp. 63–74.

38 *Op. cit.* [28], pp. 29–75.

39 HERBERT A. SIMON, "On The Concept of Organizational Goal," *Administrative Science Quarterly*, June 1964, pp. 1–22.

40 CHESTER I. BARNARD, *The Functions of the Executive* (Harvard University Press, Cambridge, Mass., 1938).

41 JAMES G. MARCH AND HERBERT A. SIMON [15] p. 26.

42 *Op. cit.* [35], Chapter 2.

43 *Op. cit.* [35], p. 28.

44 *Op. cit.* [28].

45 CHARLES P. BONINI, "Accounting Information Systems in the Firm," doctoral dissertation, Carnegie Institute of Technology, 1962.

46 *Op. cit.* [33].

47 G. P. E. CLARKSON, *Portfolio Selection: A Simulation of Trust Investment* (Prentice Hall, Englewood Cliffs, N. J., 1962). Ford Foundation doctoral dissertation Series 1961 award winner.

48 A. CHARNES AND A. C. STEDRY, "The Attainment of Organizational Goals Through Appropriate Selection of Sub-Unit Goals," ONR Research Memorandum No. 33, August 5, 1964; CIT; Pittsburgh, Pa.

49 *Op. cit.* [49].

50 HERBERT A. SIMON, "The Corporation: Will It Be Managed by Machines?" in *Management and Corporations 1985*, (McGraw-Hill, 1960) pp. 17–55.

51 HAROLD J. LEAVITT AND THOMAS L. WHISLER, "Management in the 1980's," *Harvard Business Review*, Vol. 36, No. 6, Nov.–Dec., 1958, pp. 41–48.

52 MELVIN ANSHEN, "The Manager and The Black Box," *Harvard Business Review*, Vol. 38, No. 6, Nov.–Dec., 1960, pp. 85–92.

53 *Op. cit.* [16].

54 *Op. cit.* [28].

55 ALFRED D. CHANDLER, JR., *op. cit.* (28).

56 C. P. BONINI, *op. cit.* [45].

57 ALFRED D. CHANDLER, JR., *op. cit.* (28).

58 R. F. STEWART, "The Strategic Plan," Stanford Research Institute, Menlo Park, Cal., April, 1963.

59 W. BOYD CHRISTIANSEN, "Long Range Planning As Applied to the Allstate Group Managerial Long Range Planning," George Steiner (ed.) (McGraw-Hill) 1963, pp. 98–114.

60 *Op. cit.* [22].

61 CONWAY, R. W. in Bonini, C. P., Jaedicke, R. K., and Wagner, H. M. (eds.) *Management Controls*, (McGraw-Hill, 1964). pp. 140–142.

6

INDUSTRIAL DYNAMICS –
A RESPONSE TO ANSOFF
AND SLEVIN

Jay W. Forrester

Source: *Management Science* 14(9) (1968): 601–18.

In the March, 1968, issue of *Management Science*, Ansoff and Slevin discuss industrial dynamics [2]. Although the authors acknowledge writing without having used industrial dynamics, their paper contributes by raising important questions which need discussion. The rapidly increasing domestic and international interest in industrial dynamics makes especially timely their paper and an opportunity to respond.

The authors base their viewpoint on information available from the published literature. I respond from the viewpoint of one familiar with much additional work in the field which has not yet reached the public press. This may account for some of our differences. Between glimpsing early results and seeing these in print, five or more years can elapse. The work must be consolidated and improved, articles written, and publication delays awaited. Access through publication is also impeded by proprietary restrictions placed on some of the more important and exciting applications of industrial dynamics in industry.

Although space limits discussion to those points where I differ, the authors have developed many important ideas in their paper. They have performed a valuable service for industrial dynamics. The comments that follow are grouped by subject and not in the sequence of their article.

What is industrial dynamics?

Much of the confusion surrounding industrial dynamics arises from differing perceptions of how the subject relates to the management scene. In particular, distinctions are confused between industrial dynamics, management information processing, and operations research. Admittedly, none of

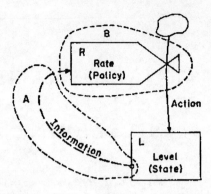

Figure 1 Management information processing and operations research in the feed-back loop setting.

these three areas has been precisely defined. There is a substantial overlap in the implicit definitions. But the following distinctions are acceptable to at least some of the practitioners in each area and may help to clarify the present discussion.

Accepting the feedback loop as the structure surrounding a decision process, we can place the central focuses of management information processing, operations research, and industrial dynamics with respect to such a loop. (Questions about appropriateness of feedback loop structure are discussed in a later section.) Figure 1 shows the simplest possible feedback loop consisting of one policy statement, the rate equation R, and one system state, the level equation L [10, p. 406].

In Figure 1, management information processing stresses the information link enclosed in the dotted area A. Operations research focuses on the decision process in area B. Industrial dynamics deals with the interactions around the loop in its entirety.

Information processing in area A gathers information from the levels (state variables) of the real system and makes the information available to control the rates (decision points as defined by policy). Information processing must be concerned with the details of how information is to be acquired, filed, transferred, and delivered. It must handle individual items of information.

Operations research tends to focus on an individual decision (in contrast to the time-varying decision stream) at area B in Figure 1. In so doing, operations research assumes a set of system states represented by the available information and arrives at a specific, isolated decision. Or, if not the single decision, an incoming information stream having certain statistical characteristics is assumed and an open-loop action stream is generated which does not itself alter the assumed input information.

But dotted areas A and B by themselves are not sufficient. To understand the system, these components should not be treated independently and without recognition of how they are linked through the feed-back loop. The structure of interconnections and the interactions are often far more important than the parts. Some approach that achieves the objectives of industrial dynamics, must examine the structure and dynamics of the entire loop before the performance specifications can be determined for the component areas A and B. With respect to area A, Ackoff in his article, "Management Misinformation Systems," stresses that a system viewpoint must be the basis for specifying components, "The moral is simple: one cannot specify what information is required for decision making until an explanatory model of a decision process and the system involved has been constructed and tested. Information systems are subsystems of control systems. They cannot be designed adequately without taking control in account" [1, p. B-150].

The industrial dynamics view of the loop components in Figure 1 is more broad-brush and aggregated than would be appropriate for either management information processing or operations research. At A, industrial dynamics would deal with what information should be available at a decision point and the consequences of defects in the information, but not with how actually to process the information. At R, industrial dynamics would design policy and its relation to information but might not say how best to implement the individual decisions.

The compartmentalization from separating system parts becomes more evident in a system of greater complexity as in Figure 2. Area A again

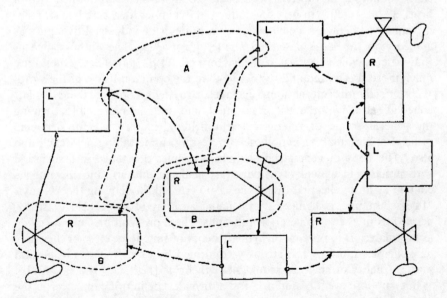

Figure 2 Management information processing and operations research treating parts of a system.

suggests the purview of management information systems and the two areas *B* the focus of decision theory or operations research. Attention on components of a system can easily lead to omission of essential components as well as omission of the interaction between components. The policy statements *R* and the information links on the bottom and righthand edges of the diagram imply loops which have major influence on the total system but have been omitted from formal treatment in areas *A* and *B*. Until the purpose of a model has been specified, proper boundaries for that purpose have been determined, and the major loop structure of the system has been identified, there is no basis for stating what should be included in areas *A* and *B*.

Ansoff[1] discusses industrial dynamics without showing a consistent image of how the subject is related to other management theory and practice. "Industrial dynamics is discussed as a simulation approach to problem solving," [2, abstract] and, "We shall start by discussing industrial dynamics as a simulation approach within the limits of the definition quoted in the last section" [2, p. 387]. But the referenced definition stresses the information-feedback characteristics of industrial activity and makes no mention of simulation as such. The phrase "problem solving" seems to focus on the individual decision-making event, rather than on policy that controls an action stream and on how the action continuously modifies the states of the system.

The issue of identifying industrial dynamics is most clearly raised when the authors question whether industrial dynamics should be considered a body of theory. "It is suggested that little evidence to date qualifies industrial dynamics to be viewed as a distinctive body of theory about behavior of firms" [2, abstract]. "In perusing industrial dynamics literature one searches in vain for statements which even begin to describe industrial dynamics as a theory in the sense described above" [2, p. 395]. The authors give us four criteria which they ask a theory to meet [2, p. 394]. These criteria are much more specialized and restrictive than the common usage of the word. Webster's Third International includes two definitions of theory: "The coherent set of hypothetical, conceptual, and pragmatic principles forming the general frame of reference for a field of inquiry (as for deducing principles, formulating hypotheses for testing, undertaking actions)," and also "The body of generalizations and principles developed in association with practice in a field of activity (as medicine, music), and forming its content as an intellectual discipline." And Russell, in defining theory, says, "In its best use, it signifies a systematic account of some field of study, derived from a set of general propositions. These propositions may be taken as postulates, as in pure mathematics (theory of functions, etc.), or they may be principles more or less strongly confirmed by experience, as in natural science (theory of heat, electromagnetic theory)" [12].

But suppose we do not ask for a broader definition and accept the authors' four criteria for what constitutes a theory. Does not industrial dynamics qualify?

They ask first that a theory "should embrace a well-defined body of observable variables" [2, p. 394]. Industrial dynamics is a theory of structure of systems and of dynamic behavior in systems, not a theory limited to the description of a single system (in fact, the name has become a misnomer as the areas of application steadily broaden). Particular applications of industrial dynamics could become theories of behavior of particular systems. A "well-defined body of observable variables" can be interpreted as the level and rate variables which are asserted to be necessary and sufficient for representing any dynamic system which can be defined in terms of lumped parameters [5, 7, 10]. (Systems having continuous space distribution of variables are approximated by lumped parameter systems when numerical solutions must be used because analytical methods fail.)

The authors ask second for "an explicitly stated set of hypotheses about these variables" [2, p. 394]. This would seem to be met by the structural relationships between levels and rates (level and rate variables must alternate along any path through a flow diagram, levels control rates and rates generate levels) and by the insistence that these level and rate variables be formed into feedback loops from which dynamic behavior will arise.

As a third requirement the authors want "a calculus, a method which, relying on the hypotheses, permits construction of statements about the variables" [2, p. 394]. This would appear to be met in two separate areas. First are the computational relationships and the specifications on the solution interval which control the simulation phase to convert the component hypotheses in the model into the behavior time sequence of variables for the system as a whole. Second, the criteria should also be met by the principles of dynamic behavior which relate structure to dynamic consequences. These principles of system behavior are now being developed. They are not adequately represented in the literature except insofar as many of them are implicit in the mathematics of feedback systems and in the literature of network behavior and signal smoothing and distortion. Principles of behavior in nonlinear systems are only now beginning to be recognized as we generalize from the behavior seen in individual models of systems. These principles that relate structure to behavior are beginning to be taught at M.I.T. but admittedly the authors had no access to such material in developing their paper.[2]

As a fourth criterion, the authors ask that a theory be a "statement of its own limitations, an implicit definition of areas of experience to which the theory does not apply" [2, p. 394]. Industrial dynamics does not apply to problems that lack systematic interrelationship. It does not apply to areas where the past does not influence the future. It does not apply to situations where changes through time are not of interest.

So even by the restrictive definitions of the authors, industrial dynamics should qualify as a body of theory. Still more easily could it be accepted by the broader and more general definitions of a theory. The authors ask that "a theory possesses an invaluable property of transferentiality of insights and predictions from one observable situation to another" [2, p. 395]. Here the authors seem to use "theory" to cover many of the ideas which Bruner includes in "structure." Bruner says:

> Grasping the structure of a subject is understanding it in a way that permits many other things to be related to it meaningfully. . . . The teaching and learning of structure, rather than simply the mastery of facts and techniques, is at the center of the classic problem of transfer. . . . Inherent in the preceding discussions are at least four general claims that can be made for teaching the fundamental structure of a subject. . . . The first is that understanding funda- mentals makes a subject more comprehensible. . . . The second point relates to human memory, perhaps the most basic thing that can be said about human memory, after a century of intensive research, is that unless detail is placed into a structured pattern, it is rapidly forgotten . . . Third, an understanding of fundamental principles and ideas as noted earlier, appears, to be the main road to ade- quate 'transfer of training.'. . . The fourth claim for emphasis on structure and principles in teaching, is that by constantly reexam- ining material taught . . . one is able to narrow the gap between 'advanced' knowledge and 'elementary' knowledge.
>
> [3, pp. 7–26]

Industrial dynamics deals with structure in the sense that the word is used by Bruner and relates structure, including parameter values, to the dynamic behavior of a system.

The authors say "Forrester remarked that he views industrial dynamics as a beginning of a 'systems theory' of the firm in much the same way in which Cybernetics is a theory of social behavior" [2, p. 395]. In this paraphrase they have narrowed the scope and changed the meaning of my commun- ication to them which said, "I would indeed assert that industrial dynamics is a general theory of systems and would like to have it compared against any other body of knowledge which asserts that it is a general theory of systems. In doing so, however, we should be careful about any claims for originality which are perhaps unjustifiably implied at one or two points in the paper. Industrial dynamics is a clarification and codification of many ideas that run through cybernetics, servomechanisms theory, psychology, and economics."

Before considering other comments by Ansoff on theory, we should recognize that industrial dynamics provides theory on two separate planes. The preceding has discussed a theory of systems in general without the theory being specialized to a particular system. But on a more specific plane, an industrial dynamics model is a theory of structure and dynamic behavior

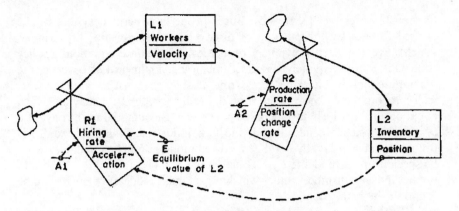

Figure 3 Systems with second-order, negative-feed back-loop structure without minor loops.

for a particular class of systems. In this sense, systems belong to the same class if they can be represented by the same structure.

To illustrate the meaning of a class of systems consider two systems belonging to the same class, having the structure of Figure 3. First imagine a simplified employment-inventory system in which the rate of hiring of workers is inversely proportional to the inventory discrepancy with respect to desired or equilibrium inventory; workers are determined by the integral of hiring rate; the rate of production for inventory is proportional to the level of workers; and inventory is the integral of net production rate minus sales. Second, consider a swinging pendulum in which the acceleration (rate of change of velocity) is inversely proportional to position discrepancy with respect to the equilibrium position; velocity is the integral of acceleration; the rate of change of position is proportional (equal) to velocity; and position is the integral of velocity. Both systems have the same structure— two integrations (or levels) in a major negative-feed-back loop without minor loops around the individual integrations. If either system is disturbed, it will exhibit sustained, undamped oscillation regardless of parameter values. Change of parameters will change only the period of oscillation. The same equation relating period to parameter values applies to both systems. Structures, including ones more complex and interesting than this, recur throughout our social systems. Once the dynamics of a structure are known, that understanding is transferable to any situation that is properly described by the same structure.

The authors fail to see the industrial dynamics model as a theory of a particular form of system with that form recurring in many places. In suggesting that industrial dynamics does not meet their four criteria for a theory, the authors say, "This definition, when satisfied, permits an analyst to make *predictions* about the relations of variables which have not been previously observed" [2, p. 395]. But a properly structured system model is used for exactly the purpose of discovering "relationships of variables which have not been previously observed." If the rate equations (policy statements) are adequately described including nonlinearities covering the maximum conceivable range of system variables (not just the range historically encountered) the model should predict modes of behavior which could occur but which have perhaps never been encountered in the past of a particular system. In addition, if the best industrial dynamics practice is followed, one will usually build generalized models of a phenomenon before he specializes the model to a particular situation. The general model should predict the circumstances under which a particular mode of behavior will be found in the real system.

As further argument for a model being a theory of a particular class of system, a model can exhibit the peculiar ensemble of data patterns that belong to a particular mode of operation and these alert the manager to the existence of the corresponding system structure and mode when it is encountered in a different situation. The authors say that a theory "also permits a *verification of validity* of the theory through comparison of relations established in theory with observable relations in the real world" [2, p. 395]. Time after time, one sees kinds of behavior in a system model the significance of which had previously gone unrecognized in the real-life situation. When, however, such behavior is recognized in the model one finds in the real-life system clear indication that the same dynamic modes exist in reality as well as in the model. As an example, see Figure 15–21 in *Industrial Dynamics* [5, pp. 180–182] where a factory capacity limit accentuates fluctuations in many of the system variables. In fact, many managers have reached their enthusiasm for industrial dynamics exactly for the reason that "relations established in theory (are) . . . observable . . . in the real world." In even the very limited number of industrial dynamics models which have been published to date, managers find reflections of and explanations of their own particular situations.

Finally, on theory, the quotation by Ansoff from *Industrial Dynamics* is out of context. "I feel we are not ready to attempt this last level of abstraction until we have achieved acknowledged success in applying art and judgment and intuition to the extraction of the decision policies themselves!" (exclamation mark added by the authors) [2, p. 395] [5, p. 101, par. 1]. In the present context his quotation applies to a supertheory. Theory has been discussed above on two planes. On the first plane we have a particular model structure which is a theory of that class of systems. On a second and more abstract plane the theory of structure specifies general characteristics about the form of an appropriate system model. But the quotation refers to a third and still more abstract plane where we do not yet have a theory that specifies the exact procedure for defining the system boundary, choosing the feedback loops, and identifying the significant levels and rates. Every theory, at some plane of greater abstraction, lacks a theory of how to apply itself.

Given the body of principles being developed within industrial dynamics, there is indeed still art and intuition at work in deciding when, how, and where to apply that body of principles. Higher planes of abstraction may progressively become understood to the point of formalization in the future, the quote discusses the present.

Areas of usefulness

Ansoff considers industrial dynamics most useful in areas which are already best structured. "One would expect that better structured functional areas would be the most likely candidates for simulation, and among those, the descending order of fit would range from production and distribution, to marketing and down to research and development. On the general management level one would expect Industrial Dynamics to be the most useful in operating problems dealing with price-quantity problems, less useful in organizational design, and least useful in studies of the firm's product-market strategy" [2, p. 392]. Here the authors are confusing usefulness with ease. Published applications of industrial dynamics have tended to deal with production and distribution because the already-structured areas are the easiest to approach first. But in managerial systems, I feel this ease is inversely related to importance. The areas which are already best structured are also the ones that are already best understood. Because industrial dynamics provides a framework that permits structuring of the more nebulous areas, it can be most effective in clarifying the least understood aspects of our social systems. Application of industrial dynamics to corporate growth, allocation of resources, relationships between company and market, effect of traditions on goal structures, and internal power relationships, will usually contribute far more to the management of a company than will a study of production and distribution [6, pp. 69–72]. Various industrial dynamics publications on product and market strategy show how advertising can cause long-period instability in a marketing system [5, Ch. 16], how forecasting can increase the instability of an industrial system [5, Appendix L], how seasonal cycles can be generated by the data analysis methods [5, Appendix N], and how some interactions producing product growth and stagnation arise out of relationships between sales practices, the market, and capital investment policy [9]. Great promise has also been shown by unpublished industrial dynamics studies in the psychology of group behavior, dynamics of conflict, epidemics, and internal medicine.

To support their case for industrial dynamics being most applicable to the well-structured areas, the authors attribute an implication to Carlson [2, p. 392] and ignore Carlson's explicit statements on the subject:

> Industrial dynamics as a discipline is increasingly concerned with more intangible aspects of industrial behavior.... Higher level

problems deal with such things as new product growth, divisional growth, or total corporate growth; in general, they are more important, have a longer range, and are more difficult to solve. Most significantly, they deal more with intangibles, and the benefits of a study are likely to come more from insights gained in making the study than from any mathematical decision rules which may emerge.... Industrial dynamics will make its major contribution by providing new insights into why things happen the way they do, especially when dealing with the more intangible problems that occur at higher management levels.

[4, p. 19]

Structure

The authors ignore the importance of the theory of structure which is a part of industrial dynamics [10, pp. 406–411]. The feedback loop structure of systems and the level and rate equation substructure are asserted in the industrial dynamics viewpoint to be conceptually sound. The claim is that natural processes and social systems are in reality constructed in a corresponding manner. The authors do not confront this claim. They seem to see the structure of industrial dynamics as happenstance and to be explained simply as conforming to the DYNAMO compiler. "One purpose of this highly stylized structure and of a comparably stylized system of notation is to make the model compatible with a special compiler called DYNAMO ..." [2, p. 386]. "One gets the suspicion of a man being driven by a computer. Behind the protestation of validity of quantification one senses the spectre of Dynamo, the investment it represents, and its appetite for data in a very particular data format" [2, p. 391]. The investment in DYNAMO is a very small fraction of the investment in industrial dynamics. The structure of industrial dynamics was determined before DYNAMO was cast in its final form. A complete redesign to produce DYNAMO II is now nearing completion including changes as major as incorporating an algebraic translator and using a different computer language, but the structure continues to conform to that which industrial dynamics asserts is a theoretically correct representation of systems.

Anyone who disagrees with these concepts of structure which are asserted to be basic and fundamental could make a valuable contribution to the discussion by pointing out particular fallacies or even equally effective alternative structures.

Three minor points about structure should be mentioned. First, the authors state that the flows in an industrial dynamics system must be incompressible [2, p. 385]. This is correct but one should at the same time remember that the levels in a system are the accumulations which allow the compression necessary for decoupling rates which are not instantaneously equal.

A level equation can be inserted where compressibility is necessary. Second, the authors speak of two separate purposes for a rate equation [2, p. 385]. Their first description is correct but they also say "In the second role, rate equations are used to determine system dynamics, such as delay in transit of a particular flow between two levels." This second role is in no sense different from or distinguishable from the first. Not the rate equations but the levels in a delay create the change in time-shape observed between the input and the output of a delay. The rate equations connected with a delay have no conceptual distinction from any other rate equations. (The confusion here may arise because the DYNAMO special function "DELAY3" is written as a rate equation but is in fact a macro program representing a group of level and rate equations.) Third is an unclear statement about delays, "The dynamic properties of the first-order delay may not be adequate to describe slower responding systems . . ." [2 p. 386]. The higher order delays are not needed for slower response if slower means a longer delay. Higher order delays tend to produce an initial inaction followed by a steeper and quicker response than seen in a first-order delay.

Feedback loops

Industrial dynamics stresses the feedback-loop structure of a system. The feedback loop is seen as the fundamental system building block [10, p. 408]. A decision is taken for the purpose of influencing the state of a system. It is the state of the system which provides the succeeding information inputs to the same decision point. Assumptions about a system which destroy the loop structure cause most of the managerial significance to be lost.

The authors seem to miss the overriding importance of feedback to system structure and behavior. To suggest that the loop structure is not general, the authors quote Holt ". . . circular causality . . . is capable of being either true or false . . . for example, a manager with a budget constraint governing several different types of expenditure" [2, p. 393]. The quotation is irrelevant. It describes a possible kind of decision policy but is silent on the structure surrounding the policy. The budget constraint referred to reflects a system state and is an input to the decision function. It is one of the determinants of how present allocations will be made out of presently available funds. The quotation does not deny that the present allocation decision may affect the availability of future funds. Almost certainly the manager is attempting to allocate now in a manner which will influence his future funds, his future constraints, and his future opportunities for allocation. If he is not trying to change the system from which his information inputs come, he serves no purpose.

The authors also quote Carlson who raises doubts about feedback relationships between company and market [2 p. 393]. In the system to which Carlson refers, dynamic considerations show that such a conclusion is premature. The system about which Carlson writes has a natural period of several years. Any conclusion about loop coupling would require several full periods for a valid observation. Carlson's article was written after observing the system for not more than a half period. Up to that time only transients associated with the policy shift from the old system to the new system would have been observable.

In discussing feedback loops the authors use several undefined phrases without showing pertinence to loop structure. "Industrial dynamics is . . . built around the concept of tight loop information feedback. . . . the appropriateness of the information feedback viewpoint should be determined on the basis of the relative influence of the feedback information on the decision in any given situation. Again this suggests production and distribution systems as the best candidates . . ." [2, p. 392]. "Tight loop" has no generally accepted meaning. Perhaps tight coupling means accurate information used within a well understood structure. If so, our studies of systems indicate that the greatest dynamic mischief often comes from loops with very long time constants and ones in which gain may be low and there are substantial defects in the information linkages—for example, the loop containing product quality, customer perception of quality, management perception of customer reaction to quality, and allocation of resources to creating quality.

Various critics have asked that the generality of feedback loop structure be proved. Such a request fails to recognize that this class of theory is not subject to positive proof. Once the theory has been stated and a range of acceptable examples are given, the only possible proof is negative. If one can show an important and purposeful decision which is not imbedded in a feedback loop structure then the generality is destroyed. At MIT we customarily assign to doubting students the problem of finding some conscious or subconscious decision which they themselves make which is not significantly imbedded in a feedback relationship. So far the challenge stands intact.

The authors recognize the importance of this negative proof because in the first draft of their paper they suggested as an example of a decision without feedback that general management would view an airplane as an open loop profit producing system. I replied to them "I find managers very aware of how their decision to buy and run an airplane will generate the profits which affect their future ability to buy and operate airplanes. Not only is this a closed-loop system but general management recognizes it as such, although they perhaps do not use the same formal systems terminology." Following my comment, the negative example was withdrawn from the paper without replacement, but inexplicably the assertion about lack of generality of feedback loop structure remained.

Quantification in models

The authors cast doubt on the desirability of a completely stated quantitative model. They suggest no alternative except the possibility of "human

112

participation in the simulation runs" [2, p. 384]. If by human participation in any particular simulation run they mean management games, the relationship between industrial dynamics and management games has been discussed elsewhere [5, Section 20.5]. Of course the investigator ordinarily does participate by changing model structure, decision functions, and parameters between successive simulation runs. The authors say "Forrester justifies this position, first, on the basis of his conviction that managers in the real world apply rather simple decision rules which lend themselves to quantification" [2, p. 384]. No source is cited and several thoughts appear to be intermixed. Simplicity is a relative matter and certain industrial dynamics rate equations would look very complex to some people. Quantification is a matter of precise (that is, unambiguous) statement rather than simplicity.

A peculiar position is taken by the authors on quantification, "What is open to question, however, is the requirement that a simulation approach *all* variables and phenomena which are relevant to the real world problem being quantified" [2, p. 390]. They use "relevant" whereas the paragraph which they immediately quote from *Industrial Dynamics* says "essential." Do the authors suggest that essential considerations be omitted? As an argument against full quantification the authors question the use of table functions to describe the relationship between two variables. "It is also perhaps very dangerous, for it encourages the inclusion of hidden, arbitrary assumptions . . ." [2, p. 391]. It is hard to see how the inclusion of an explicit table function with its stated input and its output and a graph of its functional relationship can be more hidden than an alternative like omitting the relationship and making no mention of the omission. Furthermore, a table function is usually a far clearer and less hidden representation than an algebraic equation. And rather than being an "arbitrary assumption" the table function is so conspicuous that it demands explanation and justification.

Sources of information

The article implies that Ansoff expects those who use industrial dynamics to be naive and gullible. "Forrester does not appear to see any need to make allowances for the possibility that the rules which the managers verbalize may not be the ones they actually use, nor the possibility that they will vary the rules from one set of circumstances to another" [2, p. 385]. "The manager is interrogated by a dynamicist and is made to verbalize the basis on which he makes particular decisions. He may, to please the analyst, focus on the 'hard facts' which he manipulates in making production scheduling decisions . . . but 'soft facts' may be equally influential" [2, p. 391]. A successful industrial dynamics model formulation cannot be expected of a person who lacks substantial insights into the nature and psychology of managerial practice. It seems a truism that one must understand much about the system which he is modeling. As has been suggested [5, Chapter 10] vast amounts of information exist in the minds of those participating in the particular social system. To ignore this information is to cut off our greatest source from which we may learn, but to accept everything which is said at face value would be an equal mistake. An earlier statement still fits, "perceptive observation, searching discussions with persons making the decisions, study of already existing data, and the examination of specific examples of decisions and actions will all illuminate the principal factors that influence decisions" [5, p. 103].

The literature is not sufficiently clear about the importance of perceiving the feedback loop structure of a system before model construction is undertaken. This may have misled Ansoff into saying "The verbal description of the firm is translated into a logical framework and the feedback characteristics become graphically evident via the closed loops on the flow charts" [2, p. 385]. This seems to imply that one gathers a hodgepodge of verbal statements, sets them all down in a model, then looks to see what loop structure has occurred. Many beginners do this, the results are usually futile. The capable industrial dynamicist gathers all of the information he can find—data, historical curves of performance, discussions with all levels within the company from chief executive officer to workman, rumors, opinions of customers, and opinions from competitors if available. This material is sifted and compared. Cross verification and contradictions are sought. Similarities begin to emerge between the new information and previous systems which are already understood. Whether the process is one of matching an old system structure to the new situation or whether it is the perception of a structure not previously modeled, the first major step is the sketching of the important feedback loops. This can probably be done only by a person who has knowledge of how various structures can lead to different dynamic consequences. After the feedback loops are identified, the level and rate substructure can be filled in.

The authors suggest, "As more people become competent in Industrial Dynamics and as more firms rely on EDP systems, we would expect the costs of application of this technique to be reduced" [2, p. 393]. More competent people will make a tremendous improvement in a situation where the demand now exceeds the supply by a large multiple. The kind of EDP systems now being installed may help but to a much lesser extent. Such systems are not making substantial penetration of the large mass of informal information on which a company operates. These are the very channels which make the difference between company success and failure and which must be modeled if we expect to understand the growth and stability of organizations. Probably this information will not be formalized within EDP until after system models show its importance to organizational success. Much greater than the assistance to be expected in the near future from EDP will be the help that would come from a substantial library of

114

models of typical and important industrial subsystems. Probably 20 to 30 models as illustrated by product growth and stagnation [9], production-distribution [5, Ch. 15], and the employment stability system [5, Chapters 17 and 18] would cover 90% of the system relationships with which managers contend. These generalized models of typical system relationships would include descriptions of the symptoms that develop from the system and the historical patterns which suggest the applicability of the particular model. Given this library of generalized models and trained professionals, progress will be rapid. Both are coming, but slowly.

Validity of models

Controversy about the validity of industrial dynamics models seems to arise from confusion about the nature of proof and about the avenues available for establishing confidence in a model. Two points must be recognized as a basis for discussing validity.

First, a model cannot be expected to have absolute validity. A model is constructed for a purpose. It should be valid for that purpose but may be irrelevant or wrong for some other purpose. The importance of model purpose as the cornerstone for a discussion of validity has already been stated [5, p. 122], [13, p. B-105].

A second essential point in clarifying a discussion of validity is to realize the impossibility of positive proof. The difficulty starts in selecting criteria of validity. There is no absolute proof but only a degree of hope and confidence that a particular measure is pertinent in linking together the model, the real system, and the purpose. But assuming one has a measure of validity, one probably even so cannot prove the degree to which the model need meet the measure for a specific purpose. Also, if two very different kinds of models are so measured, there is no assurance that the model that better meets the measure is the more useful model [5, p. 126]. Furthermore there is always the possibility that a model meets the measure but for wrong reasons which will invalidate the model when parameters or decisions are changed and the model is used to predict future modes of behavior rather than correspond to past modes.

Unfortunately Ansoff is not alone in seeming to want a model to pass some specific validity test, even if the test is without meaning or defense, "two average management scientists . . . would make an effort to establish an explicit test of descriptive validity. They would also establish an explicit objective function . . . they would very likely feel that a formal objective statement or a formal validity test carries with it no implication one way or the other regarding absolute accuracy" [2, p. 390], "Both will be 'right' to the extent that each, with different tests of validity, can probably show that his model describes an aspect of the real universe" [2, p. 388]. But is not the ability to meet a meaningless validity test a hollow victory?

Because there is always an underlying foundation at which validation criteria cannot themselves be validated and proven to be pertinent, no single measure of validity will be sufficient. One must use every means available which is economically acceptable in view of the particular model objectives [5, Chapter 13]. Multi-stage verification has also been discussed more recently by Naylor [11, p. B-95].

On the subject of validation there is much criticism from the sidelines. But these critics give few positive suggestions stating what tests are both possible and acceptable to them. They appear not to realize that no positive proof is conceptually possible for any theory or model which rests on experimental observation rather than on an assumed set of postulates. Very often a critic asks that a model predict future events in a system or match an ensemble of past data. But, for broad-band systems, to which class belong social systems, this has been shown to be impossible in any useful way [5, Appendix K], where it is demonstrated that even with two identical models one is not an effective predictor of the other.

The authors, as do others, imply that simulation models present uniquely difficult validation hurdles. "Industrial Dynamics shares with other simulation approaches some difficult problems of model validation" [2 p. 387]. But actually for a system description in the form of a simulation model it is far easier to develop confidence than for other forms of description as, for example, a verbal description in a management case study. A written description of a system can only be compared statement-by-statement with the actual system. This can also be done with the simulation model, but in addition the model can show that its component assumptions will interact to produce behavior of the same kind as the real system. Furthermore, as details of the model are changed, the plausibility of the resulting changes in behavior can be examined. The simulation model is unique in the extent to which "multi-stage verification" can be employed. It is therefore the form of system description which is most readily accepted if it indeed meets the available multi-stage tests. I have never personally encountered a situation where, in the context of a specific system, a particular model, and a clear purpose, there was continuing disagreement about validity. In the abstract there are no satisfying answers to the question of validity, but in the concrete situation competent and professional industrial dynamics practice responds to and answers the doubts. But when agreement is reached, we must remember that it is agreement, not proof. This rather ambiguous situation differs, if at all, only in degree, not in kind, from other professions, sciences, and theories.

The authors raise a question about nonquantitative criteria for model validation, "Having established a 'dynamic validity' principle . . . Forrester remains vague on . . . specific criteria to be applied . . . degree of correspondence to be sought. . . . Thus the validation process is not only qualitative but it is largely subjective" [2, pp. 389–390], "While the approach to validation is clear, Forrester's view to its implementation shows a curious paradox. While insisting on reduction of model *content* to fully quantitative terms, he argues that model *validation* need not meet this requirement since 'a preponderant amount of human knowledge is in nonquantitative form'" [2, p. 386]. The most "curious paradox" is the reversal in emphasis from Chapter 13 of *Industrial Dynamics* created by the authors in these quotations. The original makes the opposite point in referring to time intervals between peaks, natural periods, time-phase relationships between variables, and abruptness with which values change, "Many of the preceding behavior characteristics can be quantitatively measured. For these an objective set of criteria could be established as a basis for comparing models with data from actual systems" [5, p. 121]. Even the authors' quotation from *Industrial Dynamics* sounds different in its original context, "We sometimes encounter the attitude that model validity can be treated *only* (emphasis added) in a numerical and quantitative manner. This hardly seems justified when such a preponderant amount of human knowledge is in nonquantitative form . . . Quantitative validation of a model should be done when possible *and* (emphasis in original) when the anticipated results are expected to justify the cost and effort" [5, p. 128].

The authors reach very far for a point when they assert that wind tunnel analogies have been used to justify validity, "In defense of its validity, Industrial Dynamics simulation has been likened to wind tunnel tests in aerodynamics and to pilot plant test in chemical process design" [2, p. 387]. There follows a quote from Holt who is the only person to have juxtaposed the wind tunnel analogy and the important question to validity. By so doing he created a straw man to fight and the authors have joined the battle. The analogy does not appear in the chapter on validity in *Industrial Dynamics* [5, Chapter 13]. The discussion to which the authors refer is not the matching of a model to real life but the design of policies in a model to which the real system can then be made to conform [See 5, Section 13.6]. "Perhaps the most charitable thing which can be said about the 'wind tunnel analogy' is that it helps to explain the simulation concept" [2, p. 387]. And indeed that is all it has been used for.

On the positive side, validation should include all the steps that the application requires and justifies. There is a very wide span of multi-stage testing available. Usually no single stage is sufficient. No combination of stages of validation can offer absolute proof. It seems unlikely that one will ever be able to specify validation criteria and degree of fit without reference to the particular situation. The required amount of demonstration of validity differs with the uncertainties in the particular study. The feasibility of a measure depends on the corresponding information being available from the real system. Validation criteria drawn from the field of descriptive information are necessarily given at least implied quantitative interpretation when they are compared with the model, how much this is formalized depends on the circumstances and on who are the participants. (Regarding the dynamic behavior characteristics of a model these are quantized throughout *Industrial Dynamics* [5], see Section 18.6, for example.) Much of the information from the real system is used for a "plausibility" check [5, pp. 119–120]. A model which shows no significant inconsistency with the full range of information available from the real system has passed a powerful composite test, even if each individual test is weak. In this full range of tests, we should not omit subjecting the model to unusual or unlikely conditions; it should still behave plausibly. One category of information about the real system is its probable response to various crises and unlikely occurrences. Rather than an absence of validity tests the problem is one of being overwhelmed with opportunities, no one test being sufficient, all going far beyond economic justification. Validation is a task of selection and compromise to fit the circumstances. Those who expect the simple, universal answer will long remain disappointed. Those who move ahead and use the presently available validation opportunities will find that competent model building, not validation, is their major problem. The purposeless, ill structured, and obviously implausible models are the ones that present insurmountable questions of validation.

Time and cost

The authors show a concern about the cost of industrial dynamics. Cost must be compared to value; if small value is perceived, then small costs loom important. "'The few sensitive parameters will be identified by model tests.' Just how this is to be done in a multi-parameter system, short of laborious sensitivity studies, he does not say" [2, p. 389]. One will often be working with opportunities as great as doubling the profit rate of a company, when so, substantial labor is justified.

Ansoff suggests that an industrial dynamics application be carried only through the flow diagram stage, "a significant benefit comes before the simulation during the flow chart modeling . . . the costs are clearly an order of magnitude less than involved in a full-fledged simulation . . . perhaps an Industrial Dynamics application which stops at the flow charting stage would be preferable for some firms from the cost-benefits standpoint" [2, p. 393]. This viewpoint contains several misconceptions. Flow charting without writing equations, done by a person who is not able to write the explicit system equations, will add only little clarity and precision. It would not differ from an ordinary "systems and procedures" diagram. If the flow diagram is clear and detailed to the satisfaction of a professional in industrial dynamics, it will almost certainly be done with a parallel detailing of the equations. After arriving at this point, it is not true that "costs are clearly an order of magnitude less," quite the reverse. And to stop short of the simulation stage precludes most of the multi-stage validity checking

118

of which the authors want more, not less. Of the five major sequential stages in an industrial dynamics application to policy design—model formulation, simulation, validation, policy redesign, and implementation—theinitial simulation leadinginto validation is the least expensive. The order of increasing expense will usually be simulation, validation, policy redesign, formulation, and implementation. However, costs will be substantialy influenced by how the learning about industrial dynamics is charged. The costs of most applications to date have been multiplied several-fold because they have been first applications for the particular organization and for a fledgling industrial dynamicist so that education has cost more than the actual application.

At the end of their article, the authors quote several sentences from *Industrial Dynamics* (without disagreeing with their content!) and attribute to these the slow acceptance of industrial dynamics. But in so doing they overlook much more substantial pace setters like the long time delays that educational processes introduce. First, adequate educational materials must be generated and, although this is being done, four or five more years may pass before a complete package exists which would support the initiation of top quality industrial dynamics educational programs or individual self-learning. Even with an adequate range of materials available, those who watch while others do the pioneering will wait another decade for trained men to become available. Industrial dynamics has the scope not of a simple technique to be learned in a semester but of an entire profession. Like the recognized professions there is an underlying body of principle and theory to be learned, applications to be studied to illustrate the principles, cases to build a background on which to draw, and an internship to develop the art of applying the theory.

Notes

1 For brevity Ansoff and Slevin will be referred to either as "Ansoff" or as "the authors."
2 I have about one-third of a "Principles of Systems" book completed which deals with the relationships between structure and dynamics. As this material is developed it is being used experimentally as a theory of dynamic behavior to serve as an educational transition from the background of the average student into industrial dynamics.

References

1 ACKOFF, RUSSEL L., "Management Misinformation Systems," *Management Science*, Vol. 14, No. 4, (December 1967), pp. B-147 to B-156.
2 ANSOFF, H. IGOR, AND SLEVIN, DENNIS, "An Appreciation of Industrial Dynamics," *Management Science*, Vol. 14, No. 7, (March, 1968), pp. 383–397.
3 BRUNER, JEROME S., *The Process of Education*, Harvard University Press, Cambridge, 1963.

4 CARLSON, BRUCE R., "An Industrialist Views Industrial Dynamics," *Industrial Management Review*, Sloan School, M.I.T., Vol. 6, No. 1, (Fall 1964), pp. 15–20.

5 FORRESTER, JAY W., *Industrial Dynamics*, M.I.T. Press, 1961.

6 ——, "Common Foundations Underlying Engineering and Management," *Spectrum*, Institute of Electrical and Electronic Engineers, Vol. 1, No. 9, (September 1964), pp. 66–77.

7 ——, "The Structure Underlying Management Processes," *Proceedings of the 24th Annual Meeting*, Academy of Management, December 28–30, 1964, pp. 58–68.

8 ——, "Modeling of Market and Company Interactions," *Marketing and Economic Development, Proceedings of 1965 Fall Conference*, American Marketing Association, September 1–3, 1965, pp. 353–364.

9 ——, "Structure and Dynamics of Feedback Systems in Marketing," *Industrial Management Review*, Sloan School, M.I.T., Vol. 9, No. 2, (Winter 1967–8). Also forthcoming in *Systems Analysis: Research and Implications For Marketing*, Urbana, Illinois: Bureau of Economic and Business Research, University of Illinois, 1968.

10 ——, "Industrial Dynamics—After the First Decade," *Management Science*, Vol. 14, No. 7, (March 1968), pp. 398–415.

11 NAYLOR, THOMAS H., AND FINGER, J. M., "Verification of Computer Simulation Models, "*Management Science*, Vol. 14, No. 2, (October 1967), pp. B-92 to B-101.

12 RUSSELL, LEONARD JAMES, "Theory," *Encyclopedia Britannica*, Vol. 22, 1965, p. 69.

13 SCHRANK, WILLIAM E., AND HOLT, Charles C., "Critique of: Verification of Computer Simulation Models," *Management Science*, Vol. 14, No. 2, (October 1967), pp. B-104 to B-106.

7

A LANGUAGE FOR ORGANIZATION DESIGN: PART I

H. I. Ansoff and R. G. Brandenburg

Source: *Management Science* 17(12), Application series (1971): B705–B716.

This paper develops a language for designing the structure of a purposive organization so as to maximize organizational performance potential for achieving given objectives. Four categories of performance attributes are specified, each contributing to the particular objectives an organization pursues in seeking maximum return from the resources it employs:

> steady-state efficiency,
> operating responsiveness,
> strategic responsiveness,
> structural responsiveness.

A fifth category, decision and information quality criteria, further contributes to organizational success. These five types of criteria, combined with tests of economic and human resource feasibility, are used to select and tailor one of several basic organizational forms to meet the particular needs of a firm.

Basic organizational forms, observable in business practice, analyzed with respect to the above performance attributes, include:

> centralized functional form,
> decentralized divisional form,
> project management form,
> innovative form.

Several variations on these forms, which have been used in business, are listed along with conditions for the applicability of each, reflecting the need for individual firms to adapt basic structures to suit their distinctive requirements.

Major steps in the logic of the overall design process are specified.

Introduction

Managers need improved methods for designing organizations which are best suited to accomplish specified objectives. Several factors combine to make the problem of what the organization should be, rather than how to get the most results from an existing organization, a high priority issue for today's executive. Rapid changes in customer needs and product-process technologies require organizations that are flexible and responsive. Diversity of product lines and multinational scope of operations require organizations which are efficient in spite of their size and complexity. As the human resources of professional and managerial manpower are recognized as key corporate assets, forms which channel expert talents toward organizational goals are needed. Getting maximum payoff from the new management technology of computers and information systems requires new definitions of centralization, decentralization, and span of control. Realization of top management strategies for corporate growth and development creates organizational imperatives for setting up new businesses, divestment of old businesses, merging with other organizations, and formation of programs for new product research, development, and commercialization which cut across existing organizational boundaries.

Planners and managers constantly are changing their organizations in response to the above forces. For example, a survey of 61 companies, conducted by the National Industrial Conference Board, revealed four major trends in changing corporate structures [17].

1. greater divisionalization plus decentralization,
2. elaboration and changing rules of corporate staff,
3. emergence of group executives,
4. elaboration of the chief executive's office.

Designs for these current organization changes draw upon several areas of business theory and practice. Layouts of plants and manufacturing processes use standard industrial engineering techniques. Organization charts build upon generally aceepted principles of specialization, span of control, accountability, authority, and responsibility in the assignment and allocation of decisions. Job position descriptions are written, payroll and incentive schemes are established, and explicit styles of management are spelled out in policy statements with guidance from human relations, personnel management, and industrial relations experts. More recently, systems analysts use criteria for designing decision making, reporting, and order processing systems which take into account timeliness, accuracy, and cost of information appropriate to organizational needs.

A small body of research literature on organizational design also has emerged. See for example [6], [9], [11]. (The latter reference [11] has an extensive bibliography of published research relevant to organization design.) One line of inquiry has been to use operations research models, such as markov chains, queueing and learning theory, reliability models, and information theory concepts, to describe certain internal operating characteristics of complex organizations. Another theme has been to categorize and more rigorously define what the problems of organizational design are, using systems analysis terminology. Further, some work has been done which combines economic theory with organizational principles in the formulation of models which explain how performance of simplified organizations would respond to alternative assumptions about market structure. Still other researchers have formulated and tested explanations of why organizations use particular information processing procedures for making decisions.

Mathematical programming techniques have been suggested as organization design tools in two ways which are particularly relevant to this paper. First, Sengupta and Ackoff have addressed the problem of how to assign decision making activities and distribute constraints among various management levels in an organizational hierarchy so as to insure that outcomes of decisions made at each level are "optimum" from the viewpoint of the organization as a whole [13], [1].

Second, dynamic features of the assignment of individuals to tasks in an organization have been explored by Charnes, Cooper, and Stedry [8]. They have extended a linear programming model to situations in which an initial assignment of an organizational participant to an activity alters characteristics of the individual as well as of the job. This formulation is suggested as a way of exploring alternatives to organizational designs which assume first a set of static, predetermined activity requirements, and then the assignment of available personnel to meet the given set of requirements. Full elaboration of this design conception would encompass provisions for changing job content, supervisor subordinate relationships, setting up new jobs and eliminating existing ones; i.e., a methodology for designing internally dynamic organizations responsive to rapid changes in organizational environment and purpose.

Each of the above approaches from management practice and research is a relevant, although partial, organization design conception. Methods for synthesizing answers provided by various techniques of analysis into an overall statement of organizational form are, as yet, unavailable. A new conception which integrates physical, information, behavioral, and economic variables is needed which provides a comprehensive language to aid managers in selecting effective organization structures. Conflicts and interactions among major design variables must be recognized explicitly within a framework encompassing the organization as a whole. Evolutionary changes in organizations, while satisfactory in the past, are no longer practical.

The purpose of this paper is to formulate a practical language for organization design. Our design language will be limited to purposive organizations.

We define "purposive" to mean that there is an identifiable output which the organization seeks to produce efficiently; i.e., it seeks to maximize output over time with a given amount of resources, or to minimize the amount of resources needed to meet a specified demand for output. Thus, we assume that organizational purpose is the major determinant of structure, and purposes of individual participants are modifiers of structure. After a general organizational form is derived, the balance of inducements the organization offers against contributions by the participants is applied as secondary design consideration. Further, we shall not deal explicitly with notions of "informal" organization but shall assume that accommodations to personalities, styles, and limitations in the skills of individuals are made through adjustments in the basic form.

Working concepts and definitions

Within a business firm, logistic activities are carried out to convert physical and information resources into the end products or services the firm sells to its customers. Logistic units may be departments, divisions, functional branches, such as production, R & D laboratory, or sales, or a firm as a whole. The complete list of generic resource conversion steps contains:

R & D (which generates an output of ideas for new or improved products and processes)

Purchasing ⎫
Personnel Hiring ⎬ (acquisition of input resources)
Financing ⎭

Manufacturing (conversion of input resource and ideas into output products)

Marketing (pricing, promotion, and selling activities).

Distribution (transferring products to locations from which they are available for purchase by and delivery to customers).

While these generic steps in the logistic process typically are applicable to a manufacturing firm, they can be generalized with varying degrees of emphasis to other enterprises, including insurance companies, hotels, or department stores. Appropriately translated and interpreted, the concepts also can be used to describe logistic activities in other types of organizations, such as hospitals, schools, or government agencies.

At some level within each organization, logistic process steps are grouped into categories like those listed above. Within each group, there is further specialization of tasks, such as the distinctions between basic research, product development, and customer applications engineering groups in an industrial research laboratory. For our purposes, however, we will subdivide logistic activities only to the level of the major functional areas of R & D, manufacturing, and marketing in our example of the business firm.

Management activities

Management activities are the guidance and control processes of the organization. We shall structure these activities along two dimensions:

a. Types of problems which must be solved by managers;
b. Problem solving process used by managers.

The first type of problem faced by business managers is choosing the products, or services to make, and the customers and markets to which to sell them. This selection of what the organization's "output vector" should be is called the *strategic problem*. Second, management has to organize the firm by assigning decision making authority and responsibility among participans, establishing work flows, laying out facilities, and setting-up information and reporting systems. These requirements for grouping, configuring, and establishing relationships among logistic and management activities are called *administrative problems* of management. Third, managers must schedule manufacturing operations, set pricing policies, carry out advertising programs, undertake research projects, collect accounts receivable, etc., in order to generate the desired output vector, using the established administrative relationships. Carrying out these activities in the most efficient manner possible poses *operating problems* for managers.

Figure 1 shows eleven generic information processing steps used in managerial problem solving. In different problem situations, different groups of these steps are employed. In the practice of management, the three widely used subroutines have emerged, called planning, implementation, and control.[1]

The *implementation subroutine* recycles steps (8) and (9). The *control subroutine* uses steps (1), (2), (3), and (9) to monitor and evaluate past performance, and take corrective action on deviations from objectives. The third and most complex subroutine is planning, which uses steps (1), (2), (3), (4), (5), (6), (7), and (10) to define and elaborate future courses of organizational action.

In this paper, we will be concerned with the manner in which authority and responsibility for the three categories of problems (strategic, administrative, operating) and three types of problem solving processes which can apply to each category (implementation, control, planning) are distributed throughout the organization. Therefore, we will be concerned with designing what is usually called *line management* activities. In a later paper, we will disaggregate our analysis to the level of the above eleven individual steps in management problem solving. This will enable us to design roles for staff specialists in the overall management process.

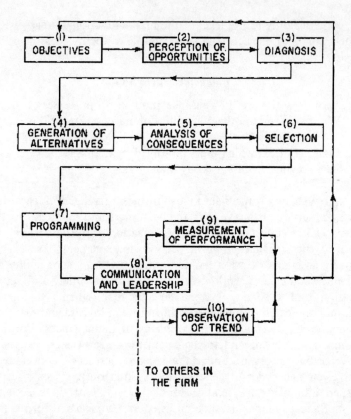

Figure 1 Management Cycle.

Objectives of organizational design

In this paper, we shall take the firm's strategy as given and shall assume that the operating style will be adjusted to the organizational structure. Thus, our problem can be stated as follows: given organizational objectives and its strategy, to design a structure which will offer the maximum performance potential for achieving the objectives.

As the objective of the organization, we choose maximization of return to the organization (from disposal of its products and services) on the resources employed in the organization. The concept of maximum return is difficult to make operational in practice, largely because of difficulties of prediction over long term horizons ([2, Chapter 4]). Therefore, we shall use three approximations:

1. An objective of maximizing near term performance (up to a *planning horizon*).

2. An objective of long term growth which will develop a posture for successful long term performance (attained, for example, by acquiring a

long-lived source of raw materials such as timber, or by doing basic research).

3. An objective of protecting the firm against catastrophic risks, such as sudden obsolescence of its technology (attained, for example, by basing the firm's position on several technologies—the maxim of keeping one's eggs in several baskets).

If our understanding of organizational design were much greater than it is at present, in particular, if we knew how to construct analytic models of organizations, the three objectives of the organization could be used also as criteria of organizational design. Alternative designs could be modeled, the outcome of each design predicted for each objective, and the design which contributes most to the objectives would be selected.

Criteria of organizational effectiveness

At the present stage of our understanding, we are forced to use process rather than outcome oriented *criteria*. We group these criteria into four categories of organizational attributes. The first is *steady-state efficiency* which measures efficiency when the levels of throughput and the nature of throughput (the products made and the customers) remain relatively stable over time.

Table I lists a number of specific criteria. Steady-state efficiency is heavily dependent on the configuration of the elements of the logistic system. The optimal structure is one which would produce a specified level of throughput at least cost. Under steady-state conditions, the design of the logistic system is amenable to quantitative analysis. Such analysis frequently can be made to yield the optimum logistic structure.

The major problem in the management subsystem is distribution of decision responsibilities among the several management levels. When conditions are steady-state, the criterion is to place the responsibility at a level at which all of the important conflicting variables are clearly visible and can be balanced. Thus, for example, pricing decisions would be made at the level above manufacturing, marketing, and R & D managers, because each of the former makes an important contribution to the overall decision. If applied to the extreme, this criterion would result in an overload in top management or would produce top-heavy management structure. There is therefore a need to decentralize the decision process [13].

Under steady-state there is a relatively low premium on speed of response to external or internal conditions. It is possible, therefore, to keep the management lean with just enough capacity to handle the decision load.

The second major criterion is *operating responsiveness* which measures the abilities of an organization to make quick and efficient changes in the levels of throughput. This may be necessitated by changes in the level of demand or competitive actions, such as, for example, a price reduction by competition, a drop in the firm's market share, or an unanticipated success of a new product.

Table I

	Steady-State Efficiency	*Operating Responsiveness*
Logistic system	—Economies of scale	—Short transfer times among logistic activities
	—Economies of skills and overheads (Synergy)	—Communication among logistic functions
	—Capacity matched to demand	—Standby logistic capacity
	—Minimum logistic transportation costs	—Standby information processing capacity
	—Logistic activities located in low cost labor and material areas	—Availability of product at market locations
	—Logistic activities are located where source resources are available	—Balanced inventory
Management system	—Decisions located at levels where all important tradeoffs are visible	—Internal management information system
	—Decisions centralized at levels which permit coordination of related lower level activities	—Competitive information system
	—Decisions decentralized to levels at which local optimization leads to global optimization	—Decisions decentralized to action level
	—Management capacity— minimum needed to meet demand (Minimum indirect to direct ratio of personnel)	—Decisions centralized to level required for introducing effective change in logistic throughput
	—Explicit (quantitative whenever possible) performance yardstick	—Clear decision assignment
	—Management by exception	—Clear decision priorities
		—Rapid decision response times
		—Standby decision capacity
		—Contingency plans for changes in throughput level

As Table I indicates, the desired characteristics of the logistic system tend to be antithetical to conditions of steady-state efficiency. For example, they put a premium on local facilities in distinction to consolidated ones, on standby as opposed to minimal capacity, etc. The management system needs to be similarly responsive. This requires continuous up to date information about the firm and the competition, and clear, rapid decision making. In contrast to steady-state, there is a preference for localizing decisions to "where the action is" in order to assure fast response.

The third major criterion is *strategic responsiveness* which measures the firm's ability to respond to changes in the *nature* (rather than volume) of its throughput, such as, obsolescence of products, changes in product technology, emergence of international markets, opportunities to enter new lines of business, changes in legal and social constraints under which the organization is forced to operate. Firms typically respond to these by changing composition of their products and markets, acquisition of other firms, or divestment from parts of existing operations.

Strategic responsiveness imposes difficult demands on an organizational structure. First, it must have a well-developed mechanism for surveillance of the firm's external environment. Strategic changes are often difficult to anticipate as, for example, in the case of a technological breakthrough or a sudden change in government in a politically unstable country. Mere availability of environmental information is not by any means a guarantee of organizational response. There is much evidence of failure of organizations to respond in time to visible "writing on the wall." Thus, a second requirement of the firm's structure is to provide for a decision center (or centers) which will be responsive to the intelligence inputs.

Thirdly, mere recognition of threats and opportunities does not usually indicate the specific response for the firm. Specific strategic moves must be generated. This is a very difficult task, first, because it involves creative activity and, secondly, because generation of strategic moves is not localized anywhere in the firm. It takes place in the logistic systems, particularly in the R & D and marketing departments. It also takes place at all management levels, particularly among managers in close contact with the firm's environment. As a result, the structure must provide stimuli for generation of ideas throughout the firm, for effective communication between the management and the logistic subsystems and for timely and unprejudiced evaluation of suggested alternatives.

Finally, the process of physical introduction of change within the logistic system runs contrary to steady-state efficiency. New products seldom become immediate replacements for the existing product line. The work of developing and introducing them is additional to the previous logistic activity. It is, further, disruptive to this activity. As a result, the logistic structure must provide for harmonious, simultaneous operation of both innovative and steady-state activities.

Criteria for assessing the adequacy of strategic responsiveness of the structure are summarized in Table II.

Structural responsiveness, the fourth criterion, measures the capabilities of an organization to change itself. When a firm is deficient in any of the three types of functional response, the solution is to adjust the structure. If the ability to adjust is inherent in the very nature of the structure, adjustment will be quick and without undue loss of efficiency. If structural flexibility is lacking, costly and slow transition is indicated.

An additional stimulus to structural response comes from changes in the technology of both the management and logistic processes. For example, introduction of computerized decision analysis makes it possible to restructure

Table II

	Strategic Responsiveness	*Structural Responsiveness*
Logistic system	—Perception of product-market threats and opportunities —Internal generation of strategic moves (Product-market R & D) —External search for strategic moves —Effective communication of threats, opportunities, and new moves to management —Minimal conflict between steady-state and innovative activities within each function —Transfer of new products from function to function —Capacity adequate for innovation —Transferability of assets to new products and markets —Transferability of skills and capacities to new products and markets —Work environment conducive to innovation —Reward system for strategic innovation	—Monitoring of process technology —Generation of changes in process technology (R & D on process technology) —R & D on management technology —Expandable/contractable structure —Transformability of assets into new configurations —Work environment conducive to innovation —Flexible promotion system —Reward system for structural innovation —Formal personnel and management training and development system
Management system	—Strategic information system —Clear statement of objectives and priorities —Strategy formulation —Communication of strategy to logistic function —Evaluation of strategic moves —System for transfer of innovation from function to function —Clear strategy decision assignment —Management capacity for strategic change —Compensation system encouraging strategic innovation	—Monitoring of management technology —Open multi-channel management information system —Anticipation of need for change —Evaluation of proposed changes —Participative decision making in structural changes —Participation of logistic personnel in decisions to change logistic system —Decentralized decisions —Management capacity for structural change —Compensation system conducive to structural innovation —Flexible promotion system

the management system into a more efficient form or automation of a manufacturing process makes possible a more economic grouping of the logistic activities. Thus, structural responsiveness must provide for quick reaction to changes in strategy and operations, as well as conditions for a continuing process of self-renewal.

As Table II indicates, this requires logistic system capacity for monitoring process technology of the firm, a basic structure which can be easily expanded, contracted, or changed, and assets which can be changed from one configuration to another. Thus, for example, general purpose buildings and machinery give the firm a greater structural responsiveness than specialized ones.

Since, in recent years, the management process has also become technologically intensive, it increasingly requires appropriate environmental monitoring. Provision of capabilities for structural change (for example in manufacturing research, process R & D, operations research, organization planning) is needed to enhance generation of new ideas and their evaluation. Generation of ideas may be enhanced in an organization in which structural decision making is decentralized, assuming general agreement on the goal: people are allowed to "organize themselves" to achieve it.

The four categories of organizational performance (steady-state efficiency, operating responsiveness, strategic responsiveness, structural responsiveness) generate distinctive design criteria which frequently are in conflict with one another. Therefore, their relevance is dependent on the particular objectives of the organization at a given time. In addition, there are design criteria which contribute importantly to organizational success independent of the particular objectives. These are decision and information quality criteria.

With the advent of electronic computers, information has become potentially the most responsive resource in the logistic process. Its role in the logistic process should, therefore, be to aid (economically) in minimizing delays to the orderly progress of the process. This basic characteristic is elaborated in Table III. Horizontal interfunctional exchange of information, both by formal and informal means, is a process of special importance, since it affects the effectiveness of transfer of resources between functions. Ineffective transfer has a two-fold undesirable consequence: it slows down operating responsivenss of the firm, and it generates management problems; and thus adds to the decision workload.

The first seven criteria in the management subsystem are concerned with several aspects of defining the decision responsibilties of an individual manager in a way which produces the most effective result. This has been of concern to organizational designers for many years.

The second group of criteria in Table III deals with the process for making decisions, rather than assignment of responsibilities. As the individual criteria indicate, the concern is with quality and timeliness of information inputs, timely recognition of decision needs, quality of decision analysis,

131

Table III

	Decision and Information Quality
Logistic subsystem	—Interfunctional communications $\begin{cases} \text{formal} \\ \text{informal} \end{cases}$
	—Timeliness of information
	—Availability of relevant information
	—Absence of irrelevant information
	—Economies of scale in data generation, processing, distribution
Management subsystem (a) Specification of decision responsibilities	—Match between decision level and relevant information
	—Time delay in decision making
	—Compatibility of authority and accountability
	—Decisions located at points where all relevant tradeoffs are visible
	—Clarity of assignment of authority, responsibility, and accountability
(b) Quality of decision making system	—Visibility of key decisions
	—Forecasting and environmental surveillance
	—Measurement of performance and capabilities
	—Communication to decision makers (timeliness, relevance)
	—Timeliness of recognition of decision needs
	—Quality of decision analysis $\begin{cases} \text{formal} \\ \text{informal} \end{cases}$
	—Match of intensity of analysis to importance of decisions
	—Communication to logistic process
	—Lateral communication among cooperating managers $\begin{cases} \text{formal} \\ \text{informal} \end{cases}$
	—Exercise of leadership in acceptance of decisions
	—Exercise of leadership in implementation

effectiveness of communication, and effectiveness of leadership in gaining decision acceptance.

Feasibility criteria

When the preceding five groups of criteria are fully met by an organizational configuration, the potential efficiency of the firm will be near optimum. However, except indirectly, the criteria do not make a provision for the human element. The underlying assumption in Tables I, II, and III is that the necessary talent is available, that individuals will accept organizational positions assigned to them, that they will do so to the best of their ability. Another underlying assumption is that the necessary financial and physical resources are available to build the preferred organization structure.

If any of these assumptions are not valid, the organizational design will not be feasible and must be modified to accommodate the limitations. To this end, additional feasibility criteria are needed:

1. *Economic feasibility* is measured by the availability of money, men, and physical resources necessary to build and maintain the organization. In the long run, feasibility could be reduced to availability of enough money. However, in order to be effective, many organizational changes have to be carried out within a relatively short time span. Under such conditions, availability of skills, particularly managerial and technical ones, frequently becomes the limiting factor in structural change.

Table IV presents a set of typical economic feasibility criteria. In an ongoing firm, economic feasibility is checked annually through the budgeting process. If new organizational structure can be specified in sufficient detail, the operating cost component of its feasibility can be checked by pro forma budgeting. However, this usually does not include start-up costs which are more difficult to estimate. Among these, costs of new facilities and personnel and estimation of borrowing power usually can be well approximated. The difficult and important component is the learning cost incurred in organizational start-up.

2. *Human resource feasibility* is measured by the match between available human resources and the requirements of the structure. As seen from Table IV, this should measure not only availability of the needed numbers of people but also acceptability of specified jobs to individuals, as well as incentives in these jobs [14].

In logistic design we are concerned with production workers. Since we are dealing with this design only down to the level of functional grouping, a number of important criteria are omitted from the table, such as participation in decision making, opportunities for personal self-realization on the job, individual incentives to innovate, effectiveness of interpersonal communication, etc. Therefore, the criteria presented in Table IV deal largely with aggregate availability of human resources and the compatibility of pay and incentive systems to labor markets.

On the management system side, availability of qualified managers, as well as their individual aspirations, are frequently a major constraint on organizational feasibility. This is expressed in the saying that "organizations are built around people." During a reorganization, managers of the firm have a deciding influence on the choice of the structure. In making this choice, they seek to perpetuate and increase their own prestige, power, and rewards and to minimize threates to themelves. This limitation on feasibility of a structure is reflected in the first four management system-human resource feasibility criteria in Table IV. Application of these criteria will

Table IV

	Economic Feasibility	*Human Resource Feasibility*
Logistic	—Availability of raw materials —Working capital acquisitions —Technology acquisition costs —Physical asset costs —Operating costs $\begin{cases} \text{direct} \\ \text{overhead} \end{cases}$ —Personnel recruiting costs —Training and organizational development costs —Timing of organizational buildup	—Availability of manpower in the firm —External market for manpower —Availability of required skills —Match of pay scales and benefits to market demands —Match of industrial relation policies to characteristics of labor market
Management	—Availability of financing —Management acquisition costs —Management system setup costs —Management training costs —Physical assets (offices, computers) —Management operating costs —Staff support costs	—Availability of management talent for new managerial roles —External market for managers —Match of prestige and power between present and new roles —Match of pay and incentives to position demands —Absence of behavioral conflict in position specifications —Areas of discretion for managers to exercise initiative and entrepreneurial talents

frequently require large enough modifications in an "ideal" structure to produce substantial loss of organizational efficiency.

A frequently observed approach to this problem is to program a gradual development of the organization to the "ideal" form. The "ideal" organization emerges as key individuals move or retire, as new positions are created, or as the firm expands and creates new managerial opportunities.

Conclusion

In this paper, we have developed a set of criteria for organizational design. One way to proceed about organizational design is through synthesis. Having identified general criteria, we could identify a particular sublist applicable to a given firm. Next, we could identify basic dimension of the organization, and then use the criteria to select and combine the dimensions into a desired organizational structure.

Another way to proceed is to identify several typical and basic organizational forms which are observed in practice. From these, we can construct a longer list of observable special variations. The particular criteria can then be applied to this "library" of forms to identify the structure which most closely fits the needs of the firm. This form can then be further tailored to the unique needs of a firm with particular emphasis on economic and human resources feasibility.

In the forthcoming Part II of this paper, we shall use the second approach because it is simpler and because it is possible to identify a number of what we shall call *basic forms* which have developed over the years in response to business requirements. With modification of terminology, the same process can be shown to apply to other purposive organizations.

In Part II, we will examine the historical evolution of business organizational forms including some new and emerging configurations. We will assess their effectiveness with respect to the criteria presented above. In addition, we will present a heuristic approach to the process of organization design.

Notes

This paper, and subsequent Part II, are based on: Ansoff, H. I. and Brandenburg, R. G., "A Language for Organization Design," in *Perspectives of Planning*, Jantsch, E. (ed.), Proceedings of OECD Working Symposium on Long Range Forecasting and Planning, Bellagio, Italy, October 27–November 2, 1968, pp. 349–393.

1 For a discussion of the historical development and detailed characteristics of these subroutines, see [3] and [5].

References

1 ACKOFF, R. L., "Rounding Out the Management Sciences," *Columbia Journal of World Business* (Winter 1966), pp. 33–36.
2 ANSOFF, H. IGOR, *Corporate Strategy*, McGraw-Hill, New York, 1965.
3 ——, "The Evolution of Corporate Planning," Stanford Research Institute Long Range Planning Service Report No. 329, Menlo Park, California, September 1967.
4 ——, "Vers une Théorie Strategique des Enterprises," *Economies et Sociétés*, Tome II, No. 3 (Mars 1968).
5 —— AND BRANDENBURG, R. G., "The General Manager of the Future," *California Management Review* (Spring 1969).
6 CARZO, R. AND YANOUZAS, J. N., *Formal Organizations: A Systems Approach*, Irwin-Dorsey, Homewood, Illinois, pp. 261–468.
7 CHANDLER, A. D., JR., *Stralegy and Structure*, The M. I. T. Press, Cambridge, Massachusetts, 1962.
8 CHARNES, A., COOPER, W. W. AND STEDRY, A., "Multidimensional and Dynamic Assignment Models with Some Remarks on Organization Design," Management Sciences Research Report No. 124, Graduate School of Industrial Administration, Carnegie-Mellon University, Pittsburgh, Penna., March 1968.
9 CYERT, R. M. AND MARCH, J. G., "Organization Design," in *New Perspectives in Organizational Research*, Cooper, Leavitt, Shelly (eds.) Wiley, 1964, pp. 557–566.
10 GALBRAITH, JOHN KENNETH, *The New Industrial State*, Houghton Mifflin Company, Boston, Massachusetts, 1967.

11 HABERSTROH, C. J., "Organizational Design and Systems Analysis," *Handbook of Organization*, March, J. G. (ed.), Rand McNally, 1967, pp. 1171–1211.

12 RUFFO, JOHN J., "Making Corporate Innovation Inevitable," presented to the Association for Corporate Growth, Inc., New York, September 13, 1967.

13 SENGUPTA, S. S. AND ACKOFF, R. L., "Systems Theory from an Operations Research Point of View," *IEEE Transactions on Systems Science and Cybernetics*, Volume SSC-1, No. 1 (November 1965), pp. 9–13.

14 SIMON, H. A., "On the Concept of Organizational Goals," *Administrative Science Quarterly*, Volume 9 (June 1964), pp. 1–22.

15 SLOAN, ALFRED P., JR., *My Years With General Motors*, Doubleday and Company, Inc., Garden City, New York, 1964.

16 Stanford Research Institute Long Range Planning Report #310, "Government Planning and Budgeting."

17 STIEGLITZ, H., *Organization Planning*, National Industrial Conference Board, New York, 1962.

8

A LANGUAGE FOR ORGANIZATION DESIGN: PART II

H. I. Ansoff and R. G. Brandenburg

Source: *Management Science* 17(12), Application series (1971): B717–B731.

This paper develops a language for designing the structure of a purposive organization so as to maximize organizational performance potential for achieving given objectives. Four categories of performance attributes are specified, each contributing to the particular objectives an organization pursues in seeking maximum return from the resources it employs:

> steady-state efficiency,
> operating responsiveness,
> strategic responsiveness,
> structural responsiveness.

A fifth category, decision and information quality criteria, further contributes to organizational success. These five types of criteria, combined with tests of economic and human resource feasibility, are used to select and tailor one of several basic organizational forms to meet the particular needs of a firm.

Basic organizational forms, observable in business practice, analyzed with respect to the above performance attributes, include:

> centralized functional form,
> decentralized divisional form,
> project management form,
> innovative form.

Several variations on these forms, which have been used in business, are listed along with conditions for the applicability of each, reflecting the need for individual firms to adapt basic structures to suit their distinctive requirements.

Major steps in the logic of the overall design process are specified.

In Part I of this paper, logistic activities and management activities of purposive organizations were defined as working concepts for organization design. Organizational performance was characterized in terms of four "process-oriented" attributes:

> steady-state efficiency,
> operating responsiveness,
> strategic responsiveness,
> structural responsiveness.

For each of these attributes, specific criteria were spelled out, enabling the analysis of performance of particular organizations. The four attributes and their associated criteria will take on different relative importance in individual cases. However, two other classes of criteria were detailed which contribute to organizational success, independent of the particular importance placed on the above categories of performance. These were:

> decision and information quality criteria,
> economic and human resource feasibility criteria.

At the first stage in the development, we shall construct a history of structures in terms of the following variables:

1. Levels of management responsibility and their relationship.
2. Types of decision assigned at each level: strategic, administrative, and operating. On occasion, we shall need to use the following subdivisions:

Strategic: S_a—expansion of present product-market position,

S_d—diversification to new product-market positions.

Administrative: A_s—structure of the firm,

A_r—acquisition and development of resources and capabilities.

3. On occasion, we shall need to subdivide responsibility for a particular type of decision into its respective components of planning, control, and implementation. We shall denote this by parentheses:

e.g. $S(P)$—strategic planning,

$A(I)$—implementation of administrative decisions.

4. Types of logistic function:

financing, purchasing, manufacturing, R & D, etc. On occasion we shall use a subscript to distinguish among logistic activities devoted to: throughput of current products; e.g., $(mfg)_c$, maintenance and improvement of present capabilities; e.g., $(R \& D)_i$, development of new capabilities; e.g., $(Mkt)_n$.

5. Grouping of both management and logistic functions by

—capabilities of the function,

—products,

—markets,

—geographic location.

These dimensions will be adequate for description of gross authority-responsibility and work flow relations, or *L-L forms* (Line Responsibility-Logistic organization structures) developed in this paper.

The centralized functional form

The first modern form evolved around the turn of this century in response to rapid growth in size and complexity of the business firm. It became known as the *centralized functional* (or *multi*-functional) organization and found widespread acceptance throughout American industry of the 1920's. It is still used widely both in this country and abroad.

The basic organizing principle is to group similar logistic activities under major functional managers who, in turn, report to a central headquarters.[1]

The functional form is shown structurally in Figure 2 below, and its salient characteristics are summarized in Table V.

The principal advantage of the functional form is steady-state efficiency attained from economies of scale, overheads, and skills (we shall call the latter two *synergy*). (For a full discussion of the concept of synergy, see [2, Chapter 5].) Economies of scale are generally proportional to the volumes of throughput for a particular product. On the other hand, economies of synergy will exist only if the skills, facilities process technologies, or managerial competence require similarity.[2]

The functional form is also operationally responsive, thanks to a relatively simple communication and decision network. However, the responsiveness begins to drop off when either the size of the firm or the number of product-markets in the product line becomes large. Under either condition, both the management and logistic processes begin to encounter a conflict of priorities, decisions and products begin to queue up, communication lines get longer, and time responsiveness to external conditions is degraded.

Strategic as well as structural responsiveness is inherently poor in the functional form. Since the same top management is responsible for operating, administrative, and strategic decisions, priorities have to be set-up and attention allocated among the three. In the process, operating decisions tend to preempt the other two because of their large volume, ease of recognition,

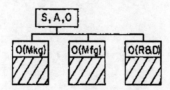

Figure 2 Functional Form. Note: Shaded boxes denote logistic activities; clear boxes are identified by decision responsibilities assigned to them.

Table V Basic Organizational Forms.

TYPE	Organizing Principle		Acceptability		
	Management	Logistics	Efficiency	Conditions	Shortcomings
Functional	1. S+A+O concentrated at corporate office	1. Like activities grouped	1. Steady-state economies of scale 2. Operationally responsive for limited product-market area	1. Stable environment 2. Small size 3. Single product-market firm	1. Slow strategy structure response 2. Top management overload in large firms 3. Top management priority conflict in multi-product firms 4. Loss of operational response in multi-product firms 5. Slow logistic response to innovation
Divisional	1. Group by product-market areas 2. Divisional P & L (S, A, O) responsibility by product-market area 3. Corporate responsibility for overall S, A, O 4. Corporate responsibility for common logistic functions	1. Duplicate most functions for each product-market area 2. Group some common functions	1. Operationally responsive for broad product-market area 2. Economies of scale in common functions 3. Strategically responsive for product improvement and market expansion	1. Operationally responsive in dynamic environment 2. Distributes top management load in large size 3. Resolves priority problem in multi-product-market firm 4. Geographically diversified divisions	1. Slow structural response 2. Poor response for product-market diversification by divisions 3. Acquires shortcomings of functional form as each division gets large 4. As number of divisions gets large, corporate office becomes overloaded—tends to holding firm 5. Loss of efficiency in firms with widely separated markets for respective product lines 6. Suboptimal efficiency by logistic function due to conflict of innovative and steady, state actions

and immediately of their needs. [2, Chapter 1]. Strategic responsiveness is further impeded *within* the logistic functions by a conflict between steady-state and innovative activities. Since the functional form usually focuses on steady-state efficiency, innovative activities receive second priority.[3] The problem is aggravated at points of transfer *between* two functions (for example, from R & D to manufacturing). Since for innovative activities transfer conditions are difficult to define, and since corresponding functions frequently have conflicting interests, the transfer process is slow and requires considerable management attention.

Structural responsiveness is impeded by lack of special organizational resources devoted to concern with generation and introduction of structural change.

However, with all of its shortcomings, the functional form is both a historical milestone and still an effective organizational form for certain firms. These are firms in operationally and strategically stable environments, a limited number of similar products in the product line.

The decentralized divisional form

Development of the second basic organizational form was pioneered by DuPont and General Motors Corporation in the 1920's. The form received relatively slow acceptance prior to World War II, but spread rapidly after the war to become the standard form used by a majority of the free world's large and medium sized corporations.[4] It is known as *decentralized divisional* (or multi-divisional) organization. Its characteristics are summarized in Table V and the structure shown in Figure 3.

The decentralized divisional form evolved as a response to the short-comings of the functional form discussed above. Both General Motors and

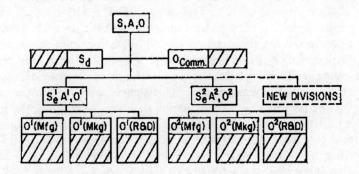

Figure 3 Decentralized Divisional Form. Note:
1. S_d denotes diversification strategy,
2. S_e denotes expansion strategy,
3. Superscripts (as in A^1) denote groupings of related product–markets,
4. O_{Comm} denotes activities common to divisions.

Dupont had grown to large size, and both multiplied their products to a point where operational responsiveness was not adequate to the demands of their markets. In the case of DuPont, diversification had created a heterogeneous product family which put limits on realizable advantages of scale and, at times, produced *negative* synergy: managers were making production, manufacturing, and development decisions over a range of distinctive products, many of which lay outside the manager's competence; standard logistic procedures which were optimal for some products were suboptimal for others.

The basic principle of the decentralized divisional form is to group activities by related product-markets and not by related logistic activities as is done in the functional form. Each group of product-markets (a division) is assigned to a manager who has complete responsibility for strategic, administrative, and operating decisions in the area assigned to him.

In terms of strategy, this usually limits the divisional manager's scope to strategic expansion (S_e) of the present position. The responsibility for diversification (S_d) is reserved for the corporation. The corporation may assign implementation of diversification to a division, or it may establish the required logistic activity at the corporate level as shown in Figure 3 by the shaded rectangle. In a majority of cases, this activity is focused on acquisition of other firms. However, in some firms, which are both technologically and diversification intensive, the corporate strategic activity develops a full range of logistic capabilities (again DuPont was one of the early pioneers in this area).

On the whole, the assignment of both management and logistic responsibilities for strategy is difficult and complex in a multi-divisional firm. In practice, this frequently results in lack of clarity of responsibilities and, consequently, poor management of strategic change.

In addition to diversification, it is common in multi-divisional firms to attach to the corporate office certain other logistic functions, such as purchasing, legal, financing, management training, and basic research. To qualify for this position, a logistic function should: (a) be common to more than one division, (b) offer advantages of scale on a multi-divisional basis, and (c) not degrade the efficiency of the respective divisions. In practice, criterion (c) is very difficult to measure, particularly since divisions find themselves competing for the services of the common function. As a result, the proper assignment of the common logistic functions becomes a bone of continued contention between divisional and corporate management. (The difficulty of resolving this contention for the purchasing function in the early days at DuPont has been clearly illustrated by Chandler. See [7, Chapter 2].)

The major purpose of the divisional form was to preserve operating responsiveness of firms which had grown large and complex. To the extent that this could be accomplished by subdividing the firm into divisions which had no common capabilities, an increase in operating responsiveness could be gained without loss of synergy or economies of scale. However, when a homogeneous product-market group had to be subdivided, economies of scale and synergies had to be sacrificed.[5]

One important variant of such subdivision occurred in firms (such as petroleum companies) whose operations were widely dispersed geographically and whose operating responsiveness was dependent on delegation of responsibility to local managers (who could respond quickly and who were attuned to special local conditions). In such firms, divisions were grouped by geographical regions, and all divisions had similar, if not identical, products.

Strategic and structural responsiveness of the divisional structure is, on the whole, superior to the functionally organized firm of comparable size. The smaller individual area of responsibility of each divisional manager permits him relatively greater attention to strategic questions than is possible at the headquarters of the functionally structured firm. On the other hand, the probable centralization of basic research forces him to compete with other divisions for research effort.

At the corporate level, the management workload is somewhat lighter than in a comparable functional firm. Strategic expansion decisions are delegated, and operating decisions are limited to monitoring divisional performance and approval of divisional plans. Thus, in principle, there is greater opportunity to consider diversification, overall strategy, and overall structure. In practice, corporate managements frequently fail to take advantage of these opportunities. They either continue to be overly responsive to operating problems or reduce the size of the corporate office to a minimum level at which no capacity exists for strategic and structural decision making.

Unless the firm establishes a large corporate logistic activity for innovation of new products and markets, the logistic capability for innovation of the divisional firm is subject to much the same problems as the functional form.

On the whole, the multi-divisional form was an important step in development of efficient structures. Its superiority over the functional form is that it combines steady-state efficiency with organizational responsiveness. However, it represents only a limited improvement in strategic and structural responsiveness.

Adaptive (project management) form

The next basic form received recognition in the post-World War II period. It evolved in response to need for structural responsiveness in firms whose product mix changed frequently, whose products were relatively short-lived, and which had to be both strategically and operationally responsive. Major users of this form have been technologically intensive defense firms in the

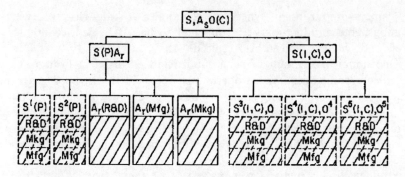

Figure 4 Adaptive Form. Legend: Superscript denotes distinctive product-market. Solid lines enclose permanent activities. Dotted lines enclose temporary activities. $S(P)$—strategic planning responsibility. $S(I, C)$—strategic implementation and control. A_s, —structural decision responsibility. A_r—resource and skills decision responsibility.

United States. It is illustrated in Figure 4 and described in Table VI. It is frequently called the Project Management Form, sometimes the Matrix Form. We shall name it the *Adaptive Form*.

In the adaptive form, the firm's activities are arranged into two groups: (1) a *development* group (left part of Figure 4) which is responsible for strategic planning, as well as for development and maintenance of the resources and skills of the firm, and (2) a *project* group which is responsible for implementing strategic plans, as well as for operating the resulting product-market positions.

The structure is fluid and flexible. The permanent parts are the corporate office and offices of the manager of development, the manager of projects, and the functional managers. The managers of projects are appointed as new markets are entered; they return to the functional areas of their specialties when the projects are terminated. The logistic resources and personnel are similarly rotated in and out of the functional competence groups.

Within the development group, temporary project planning teams may be formed drawing on management and logistic competences in the functional groups. Projects are initiated and planned within the competence group either by the ad-hoc teams or intrafunctionally. Upon corporate approval, implementation of strategy and operations are transferred to the project group.

The functional managers in the development group recruit personnel, develop organizational capabilities, and concern themselves with innovating in process and management technology of the firm.

The corporate body concerns itself with corporate overall strategic planning (as opposed to specific project planning in the competence group),

Table VI Basic Organizational Forms.

TYPE	Organizing Principle			Acceptability		
	Management	Logistic	Efficiency	Conditions		Shortcomings

TYPE	Management	Logistic	Efficiency	Conditions	Shortcomings
Adaptive	1. Competence group responsibility for A, resource acquisition and capability maintenance 2. Competence group responsible for strategic project planning $S^i(P)$ 3. Project group responsible for implementation and control of projects $S^i(I, C)$ 4. Projects group responsible for O^i operation of projects 5. Overall strategy S and A_s (Structure) at corporate level	1. Group by functions in competence group 2. Group by product-market in project group 3. Project duration limited by lifecycle 4. Free transfer of logistic resources between competence and project groups	1. Strategically responsive 2. Structurally responsive 3. Operationally responsive	1. Strategically dynamic environment 2. Limited duration of projects 3. Advantages of scale not important 4. Technologically intensive business 5. Marketing intensive business 6. Operationally dynamic environment 7. Structurally dynamic environment 8. Number of distinct projects limited	1. Minimal economies of scale 2. Degraded strategic response in multiproject firms-top management overloaded 3. Concept does not apply when assets are either: (i) nontransferable from project to project or (ii) nonseparable into project packages

Table VI (cont'd)

TYPE	Organizing Principle		Efficiency	Acceptability		Shortcomings
	Management	Logistic		Conditions		
Innovative	1. Innovation group (S, A, O) Profit & Loss responsibility until time of transfer 2. Innovation group structured as Profit and Loss responsible projects 3. Current business group has divisional or functional structure	1. Transfer of products from innovation to current group at end of "red ink phase"	1. Strategically responsive 2. Structurally responsive in innovative activities 3. Economies of scale and synergy in current business group 4. Operational responsiveness depends on current group's structure	1. Strategically dynamic environment 2. Large percentage of firm's budget in innovation 3. Technologically or marketing intensive business 4. Operationally dynamic environment 5. Advantages of scale important in current business		1. Loss of economies of scale between innovation and current groups 2. Costs and barriers in transfer to current group 3. Economies of scale minimal in innovative group (Synergy is a function of the product-market)

development of the organizational structure, approval and control of administrative plans of the development group, strategic plans of the development group, and operating plans of the project group.

The advantage of the adaptive form is its all-around responsiveness: strategic, structural, and operating. It is structurally responsive because the organization is open ended and can quickly change form and shape. Acceptance of change is enhanced by the nonpermanent assignments of both key managerial and logistic personnel coupled with job security and promise of new challenging assignments.

Operating responsiveness and rapid and effective implementation of strategy are assured by the focused concern of project managers on specific product-markets, as well as by exclusive dedication of logistic activities. Effective planning of strategy is made possible by: (1) limited load of responsibility at the corporate office, (2) dedication of the development group to planning and innovation, and (3) flexibility of project teams. Limited life-time of projects serves as a general incentive for concern with strategy and a deterrent to a preoccupation with operations.

The adaptive form also has two major limitations:

(1) It produces minimal economies of scale and only limited synergy in the competence group. Since much duplication of capacities and capabilities results, steady-state efficiency is poor.

(2) Successful application of the form depends on transferability of logistic resources among projects, and between projects and the competence group. The form clearly would not work for asset intensive industry, such as chemicals, aluminum, automotive, etc; nor would it be made to work whenever there is a serious difficulty in separating and assigning assets into separately controlled project packages.

In its pure form, use of the adaptive form is limited to firms where business is R & D intensive, whose production runs are limited, which has low asset intensity or flexible assets or assets fully amortizable over the lifetime of individual project.

The innovative form

This is the latest basic form to emerge from the continuing search by business firms which combines the virtues of all four major performance criteria: steady-state efficiency, operational response, strategic response, and structural response. Before describing it, we need to make a distinction between creativity and innovation. The former is the activity of generating ideas of promising new strategic moves for the organization. The latter includes creativity but also encompasses the process of translation of the idea to a full marketable and potentially profitable product. A successful competence group in the adaptive form would be called creative in this sense of the two words. But, if there is no mechanism for taking project ideas to

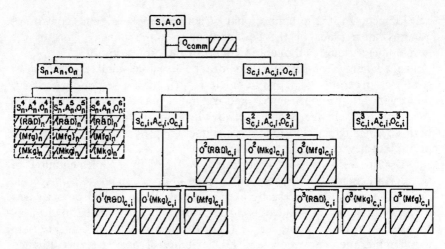

Figure 5 Innovative Form.

the market place, such a firm would probably have a very poor record as an innovator.

We could expect a competently run complete adaptive structure to be a successful innovator. However, as the preceding remarks indicate, the structure is not applicable in a large majority of manufacturing firms in which economies of scale are important, assets and competences are relatively inflexible, and products have long lives. It is important for such firms to meet the conditions of steady-state efficiency. The *innovative form*, which is shown in Figure 5 and described in Table V, is designed to meet this requirement. (For description of one application, see [12].)

The underlying principle is to gather currently profitable, established product-markets into a *current business group* and to place development of new product-market positions into an innovation group. The latter may include both diversification and expansion activities. (For a detailed description of the difference between strategic diversification and strategic expansion, see [4].) In this case, the strategic activity of the current group would be limited to exploitation of current position (such as increased market penetration) or incremental improvements in current products. Another possibility is to limit the innovation group to diversification activities, and assign full strategic expansion responsibilities to the current business group. This allocation of strategic action responsibilities is a matter of considerable importance and difficulty. On one hand, exclusive allocation of strategy to the innovation group would tend to get it out of touch with the current market opportunities but would offer synergies in performance of R & D. On the other hand, allocation of a large measure of strategic responsibility to the current business group defeats the very purpose of the innovative form which is to provide strategic and structural responsiveness.

The innovative form operates as follows. New product-market entries are conceived, planned, and implemented by the innovation group on a project basis. The group remains responsible for the project until its commercial feasibility has been established. This means, for example, that pilot production facilities have been constructed and market tests undertaken. At the point of feasibility, the project is transferred into the current business group where it may become a part of an existing division or (if the product-market is distinctive and its potential high enough) form the nucleus of a new division. The transfer may include all of the personnel and facilities or just the product and the technology. The former mode has considerable merit, because it exposes managers to operations in both the innovative and "steady-state" environment and provides a valuable exchange of information and experience. In some firms, such transfer is only temporary and the innovation oriented people return to the innovative group after a tour of duty.

The current business group in the innovative form can be structured either divisionally or functionally depending on which of the two forms of organization is more appropriate to the established product-markets.

The innovative form potentially offers high responsiveness on all four of the major organizational performance criteria. However, some economies of scale are sacrificed both because of duplication of resources in the two groups and because of the project structure of the innovative group. The separation of innovation from current operations poses problems of communication of the new needs, opportunities, and trends perceived by salesmen in the current business group to the new project generators in the innovation group. Unless this communication is well developed, there is a danger that the innovators will tend to neglect expansion opportunities in favor of diversification.

Modifications to basic form

None of the four basic forms is fully and equally responsive to the major organizational behavior criteria; each is a compromise designed to fit a distinctive set of conditions. In Part I of this paper, particular measures of steady state efficiency, operating responsiveness, strategic responsiveness, and structural responsiveness, as summarized in Tables I and II, suggest the difficulty of incorporating all such measures in any one organization without running into conflicts. Tables V and VI in Part II further indicate differing conflicts and tradeoffs among the four major criteria encountered when the basic functional, divisional, adaptive, and innovative organizational forms are compared. Therefore, in approaching the task of organizational design, each firm needs to select the set of design criteria (from the generic lists provided earlier in the paper) applicable to its particular business and environment. It can then apply these to the basic forms using the tables provided in this paper) to select the form which most closely approximates its

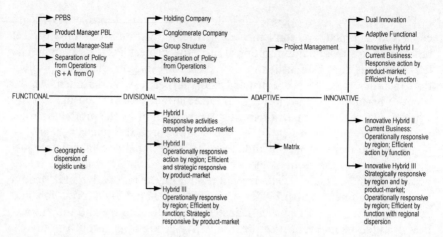

Figure 6 Tree of Organizational Development.

needs. In most cases, the basic form will fail to meet some special requirements unique to the firm. Therefore, further refinement of structure is necessary. This refinement is basically of two kinds: one is to combine more than one basic form in the same organization; the other is to subdivide the decision making responsibilities to assure appropriate decision priorities, or to distribute the workload, or to focus attention on a problem of particular importance to the firm.

Figure 6, titled "Tree of Organizational Development," shows the chronological sequence of the basic forms, together with a number of significant variations which have been observed in practice. Each is briefly described below together with conditions for its applicability.

Variations in the functional form

1. *Planning Programming Budgeting System* (PPBS). It was developed at the RAND Corporation, and applied by Hitch and McNamara to the Department of Defense. It is currently being applied in a number of business firms.

Basically PPBS is a planning system which provides visibility to the firm's product-market potential, its strategy, and its performance in respective product-market environments (McNamara called them "missions") in which the firm operates. [16] In a functionally organized firm, PPBS provides top management with information about the nature and direction of the firm's business which cannot be directly inferrred from analyzing the respective functions. Such visibility is useful if the firm's product-markets are, in fact, addressed to several distinctive demand environments, if the environments are strongly competitive and, particularly, if they are subject to rapid strategic change. Under these conditions, PPBS can improve both operational and strategic responsiveness of the firm; *but only at the planning level in the*

150

management subsystem, since the functional logistic subsystem remains unchanged.

Structurally, introduction of PPBS requires addition of a staff planning activity at the corporate level.

2. *Product manager organization*. The product manager structure is aimed at providing both operating and strategic responsiveness to individual products in a functional organization. It differs from PPBS, first, in its more narrow perspective on products of the firm and, second, in adding responsibility for various degrees of implementation and control in addition to planning. The two concepts are not contradictory and, in fact, complement each other.

In one extreme version of the concept, an individual manager is made accountable for the performance of a particular product. Accountability here means following implementation of plans, assessing the performance, and spotting and anticipating problems. The project manager is given no authority nor direct responsibility for the success or failure of the product. He is primarily responsible for generating and communicating information on the particular product.

At the other extreme, a product manager can be made fully profit and loss responsible for a product. This gives him responsibility for all decisions pertaining to the product, but in a functional structure he has to "buy" his logistic resources to carry out the decisions. His mechanism for this may vary from an internal market mechanism in which he purchases services from others in the firm, or it may be a mechanism of persuasion by implied authority: failing to get satisfaction from functional managers, he can take his case to a higher level of authority who is superior both to him and the functional managers.

Another variant of product management structure is to assign some logistic functions to the product manager (such as marketing) leaving him to obtain other logistic outputs from functional areas. The underlying rationale is that this arrangement makes it possible to combine operational responsiveness with steady-state efficiency.

3. *Separation of policy from operating responsibilities*. This modification, which applies equally to the divisional form, is intended to reduce the work-load of individuals in the corporate office, and also to provide a priority setting mechanism for attention to "policy" which in our language are the strategic and the administrative decisions. The titles of the president and executive vice-president are commonly used to designate the respective positions.

4. *Geographic dispersion of logistic units* which may be made necessary by transportation costs, or location of raw materials, or cultural and political barriers does not basically change the structure of the functional form, but places severe communication burdens on the organization. When operational and/or strategic responsiveness are important to success, wide geographic dispersion may make advisable a shift to the divisional structure, even at the expense of economies of scale.

Variations in the divisional form

1. *Works management* structure resembles the functional structure in that managers in control of logistic facilities are given only the authority for operating decisions, all of the strategic and administrative decisions being reserved for the headquarters. Thus, while the works manager (in this structure) may have several functional areas reporting to him, he must refer all nonoperating decisions to higher levels.

2. *Holding company* lies at the other extreme from works management. Under this concept, the central management delegates all decision responsibilities to the divisions (or subsidiaries) retaining only financial control and certain common logistic functions, usually corporate financing, legal, and real estate.

3. *Conglomerate company*. This is a closely related and currently very popular variant of the holding company. While performing the holding company functions, the corporate office places a major emphasis on diversification through acquisition of other firms and occasional divestment of divisions which do not meet the financial performance standards of the firm.

4. *Hybrid forms*. The lower part of Figure 6 shows several derivatives of the divisional form which group parts of the firm according to different principles in order to make them most responsive to a particular organizational performance criterion. For example, hybrid in a mass production competitive consumer industry would be represented by a firm which organizes its R & D and marketing on the divisional principle, and its manufacturing and distribution on the functional principle. In Hybrid II, marketing might be organized on a regional basis for all products of the firm, but R & D and manufacturing grouped by distinctive product lines. Hybrid III is a triple one; marketing might be regional; manufacturing, functional; and R & D, by major product line.

While hybrids provide a desired mix of organizational characteristics, they tend to create serious problems of internal communications, planning, and control. A solution frequently used is to create an internal market place with various parts of the firm buying and selling from one another. Since the market is usually too small for a fully competitive behavior, a difficult problem of setting transfer prices is created at top management levels.

Variations on the adaptive form

1. *Matrix* organization is a name which has been used to describe a variant of the adaptive form in which the administrative part of the competence group is organized not according to normal logistic functions, but rather to distinctive skills and competences of the firm.

2. The *project management* structure resembles the divisional form with project manager being equivalent to divisional manager. The distinction lies

in the fact that the projects have finite life times and the project portfolio changes as completed projects are phased out and new ones are started.

Variations on the innovative form

1. *Dual innovation* is a form under which both the innovative group and the current business group are made responsible for strategic change. The former is assigned diversification, and the latter, expansion.

2. *Adaptive-functional* form organizes the current business group on a functional basis. This would be appropriate to an industry which is technologically intensive, but in which requirement for operational respons-iveness is low, as compared to importance of steady-state efficiency. A technological leader (such as DuPont was in the '30's through the '50's) with strong patent protection on its inventions could successfully operate in this mode.

3. *Hybrid forms*. Since the innovative form is the richest in structural pos-sibilities, possible variations are correspondingly numerous. As mentioned above, each hybrid, while endowing a part of organization with particularly desirable characteristics, creates problems of internal interaction which are still very poorly understood. Hybrid I splits the current business group into functional and divisional-type activities. Hybrid II mixes regional and func-tional orientation. Hybrid III extends Hybrid II, first, by dispersing innovative activities geographically; and, then, assigning specific (world-wide) product-market responsibilities to each. This closely resembles the structure which is emerging in technologically intensive, multi-national firms such as I.B.M.

The process of organizational design

The purpose of this paper is to develop a language for organizational design useful in selecting that form which leads to efficient attainment of organiza-tional purpose. The design process employing this language is a heuristic method of matching the firm's organizational design criteria against com-monly used organizational forms and progressively refining the selected form until a satisfactory closure is attained between criteria and characteristics of the organization. The overall process is summarized in Figure 7. Execution of many of the steps requires complex data gathering and analysis activities. However, since our major concern here is with language specification, we will outline the design process only in broadest terms rather than elaborate each step in detail.

Using the master list of design criteria, the strategy of the firm, and the characteristics of its environment, we can generate a list of specific design criteria for the firm in the order of their priority.

An application of this list to the characteristics of the basic forms (shown in Tables I, II, and III) can help narrow the choice to the most suitable

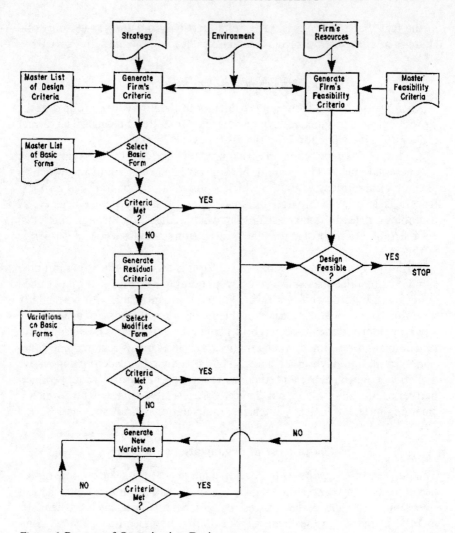

Figure 6 Process of Organization Design.

form. A check is then made for the gaps between characteristics of the form and the needs of the firm. If the differences are judged not large enough to warrant further search, the selected design can be tested for feasibility. If the decision is to proceed, a list of criteria which still remain to be met is compiled and applied to the modified forms list (shown on Figure 6).

If the selected modified form is still inadequate, a creative process of generation of new interesting variations is called for. This process continues until a judgement is made either that criteria are now met or that it is not worthwhile to proceed further (which, in fact, amounts to lowering the criteria of organizational performance).

154

The feasibility check proceeds similarly through iteration until a form is found whose resource costs are within the means of the firm.

Summary

In this paper, we have attempted to develop a practical language and an approach to selecting the organizational structure which best suits a particular efficiency seeking organization. In this effort, we have taken a task oriented view of the firm, approaching that used by organizational designers in business firms. Behavioral considerations are treated as constraining rather than primary variables. Our basic aim has been to develop a process for designing two closely coupled but different activities of the firm: its goods producing logistic process and the decision producing management process. Our language consisted of primary logistic activities of the firm, the primary types of decisions, and principal processes by which the decisions are made and carried out. This language has enabled us to enrich the descriptions usually found in organizational charts and to sharpen both the content and the relationships among management roles.

Our focus has been on what we have called L-L (Line Responsibility-Logistic) language. We have recognized but not elaborated a much richer L-S-L (Line-Staff-Logistic) language which is needed to describe fully the many new and growing uses of formal information processing assistance in support of both management decision making and the logistic flow of goods. Such description will be the subject of a later companion paper.

Notes

This paper is based on: Ansoff, H. I. and Brandenburg, R. G., "A Language for Organization Design," in *Perspectives of Planning*, Jantsch, E. (ed.), Proceedings of OECD Working Symposium on Long Range Forecasting and Planning, Bellagio, Italy, October 27–November 2, 1968, pp. 349–393.

1 In 1919, an internal DuPont strategy stated the principle as follows:
   "The most efficient results are obtained when we coordinate related effort and synegate to un-related effort. For example, purchase of materials is unrelated to the size of a finished product in a much greater degree than manufacture and sales, or manufacturing and purchasing; and legal work is still more unrelated to either of those mentioned."[7,p.69]
2 The economies of scale can be measured by reductions in unit cost of the product as the volume is increased, economies of synergy are measured by the difference between total cost of a combined product line and the sum of the costs of the same products produced by independent facilities.
3 For example, pay and incentive systems are typically designed to reward current profitability rather than risk taking for future profits.
4 However, as we shall see later, there are a number of significant variations on this basic form.
5 Such subdivision was made in General Motors and, subsequently, throughout the automotive industry. The loss of economies of scale between models has been

sought through enforced interchangeability of parts among divisions, and loss of synergy was remedied by creating large common logistic organizations (such as styling) at the corporate level. The negative effect of this was loss of important elements of control over the product by divisional managers.

References

1 ACKOFF, R. L., "Rounding Out the Management Sciences," *Columbia Journal of World Business* (Winter 1966), pp. 33–36.

2 ANSOFF, H. IGOR, *Corporate Strategy*, McGraw–Hill, New York, 1965.

3 ——, "The Evolution of Corporate Planning," Stanford Research Institute Long Range Planning Service Report No. 329, Menlo Park, California, September 1967.

4 ——, "Vers une Théorie Strategique des Entreprises," *Economies et Sociétés*, Tome II, No. 3 (Mars 1968).

5 ——AND BRANDENBURG, R. G., "The General Manager of the Future," *California Management Review* (Spring 1969).

6 CARZO, R. AND YANOUZAS, J. N., *Formal Organizations: A Systems Approach*, Irwin-Dorsey, Homewood, Illinois, pp. 261–468.

7 CHANDLER, A. D., JR., *Strategy and Structure*, The M.I.T. Press, Cambridge, Massachusetts, 1962.

8 CHARNES, A., COOPER, W. W. AND STEDRY, A., "Multidimensional and Dynamic Assignment Models with Some Remarks on Organization Design," Management Sciences Research Report No. 124, Graduate School of Industrial Administration, Carnegie–Mellon University Pittsburgh, Penna., March 1968.

9 CYERT, R. M. AND MARCH, J. G., "Organization Design," in *New Perspectives in Organizational Research*, Cooper, Leavitt, Shelly (eds.) Wiley, 1964, pp. 557–566.

10 GALBRAITH, JOHN KENNETH, *The New Industrial State*, Houghton Mifflin Company, Boston, Massachusetts, 1967.

11 HABERSTROH, C. J., "Organizational Design and Systems Analysis," *Handbook of Organization*, March, J. G. (ed.), Rand McNally, 1967, pp. 1171–1211.

12 RUFFO, JOHN J., "Making Corporate Innovation Inevitable," presented to the Association for Corporate Growth, Inc., New York, September 13, 1967.

13 SENGUPTA, S. S. AND ACKOFF, R. L., "Systems Theory from an Operations Research Point of View," *IEEE Transactions on Systems Science and Cybernetics*, Volume SSC–1, No. 1 (November 1965), pp. 9–13.

14 SIMON, H. A., "On the Concept of Organizational Goals," *Administrative Science Quarterly*, Volume 9 (June 1964), pp. 1–22.

15 SLOAN, ALFRED P., JR., *My Years With General Motors*, Doubleday and Company, Inc. Garden City, New York, 1964.

16 Stanford Research Institute Long Range Planning Report #310, "Government Planning and Budgeting."

17 STIEGLITZ, H., *Organization Planning*, National Industrial Conference Board, New York, 1962.

9

ON CONCEPTS OF ORGANIZATIONAL LANGUAGE

W. M. A. Brooker

Source: *Management Science* 19(4), Application series, part I (1972): 464–6.

The paper, "A Language for Organization Design" by Ansoff and Brandenburg, *Management Science*, Vol. 17, No. 12 (August 1971), raises a host of questions which are properly aired in *Management Science*. Briefly, I wish to make—argue—two points:

(1) The title does not reflect the contents.
(2) To outline the concepts raised by the title.

(1) The title does not reflect the contents

Editors of popular magazines, even those of the stature of the *Harvard Business Review*, are notorious for their predilection for changing their authors' titles to something which tends to attract readers. They do not, I suppose, intend to be deliberately misleading; but, given the choice between accuracy and appeal, one often gets the impression that they settle for the latter. However, scholarly journals—and I would include *Management Science* here— do not intentionally alter titles to create appeal. Furthermore, the first footnote to their paper indicates that the authors have already used the identical title.

What is wrong with the title? It does not reflect the contents. Language has attracted the scholarly attention of not only linguists as such but hyphenated anthropologists, psychologists and sociologists who have developed a vast store of knowledge and propositions about language. None of these are used by Ansoff and Brandenburg. Their paper is about organization design and not about language at all. The first reason is that the promise of the title is not borne out by the paper, and many readers, as I did, are going to read it and re-read it looking carefully for the linguistic connotations but finding none.

The second reason is that the management reader might assume that there is nothing to be gleaned from the language disciplines, and this would be as unfortunate as it is untrue. In order to provide data for this statement brings me to my second point:

(2) To outline the concepts raised by the title

Language studies in recent years have attracted a considerable amount of attention because of the ability of some of the new concepts to explain data which were hitherto unexplainable and to open new fields for scientific explanation. An example of new explanations for the hitherto unexplainable would be in the field of children learning their mother tongue. How do children learn and experiment with new words and sentences? Do they just repeat what is said to them parrot fashion? Previous explanations relied on the behaviourist stimulus-response model (S-R). This would not explain how some children will skip the stage of combining nouns like "Daddy car", "Mummy dress", and come out with complete sentences. Recent research by Chomsky and others suggests that language structure is a reflection of mind structure, and this notion therefore would open up entirely new sorts of questions and answers. One does not, for instance, express surprise that an infant reared on tender loving sounds should bark—if it has four hairy feet and a wet nose!

Other recent linguistic research is more germane to organizational matters. These are the studies which suggest a relationship between systems of kinship terminology and systems of language. This is particularly relevant because the organizational equivalents of kinship terminology are the job titles we use in the contemporary enterprise. If it is true that there is a relationship between language and kinship, then there will probably be one between language and organizational nomenclature. The relationship of nomenclature to organizational structure is the subject of my *Structure, Process and Nomenclature* (in press). I presented a case study which showed that, where a massive departure from conventional design was required, the organization designers and operators found it necessary to devise new terms to describe new elements in the organization. Thus "resources environment" became a job title no one had had before. But new names were also required for positions analogous to the conventional form. Thus "works manager" became "chairman, system operating council"; "personnel" became "human resources", and "secretary" became "secretarial services". Of course, the changes in name are inconsequential in themselves. What is important is how they fit into the overall scheme of things. Hall, in *The Silent Language* (1959), proposed a scheme of Sets, Isolates and Patterns. In a language, sets correspond to words, isolates to phonemes (or letters in written language) and patterns to sentences. Generally, we beg, borrow or learn sets first, later we learn how to break them down into isolates and link them into patterns.

For an innovation to succeed there must be an appropriate integration of isolates, sets and patterns. The relevance of this to *A Language for Organization Design* is simply this: do the terms proposed by the authors fit into any given overall pattern?

Hall and his collaborator George L. Trager developed a further way to apply the concepts of language to culture (and therefore potentially to organizations as a part of culture). This schema, which they call the major triad, is made up of formal, informal and technical. Things are formal when we do not consider any alternative. Formal organizational terms would include president and vice-president—we do not think about them. Technical terms are those where we have full freedom to consider alternatives. Ansoff and Brandenburg's article is full of technical terms, that is, terms about which we are fully aware. Informal terms are ones where we have some leeway. The boss may be called Mr. Jones or the manager, or John.

The relevance of the formal-informal-technical triad is that the acceptance of proposals for change depends on how the local organizational culture classifies the things the changes are about. If one is proposing a rational evaluation of organizational effectiveness which is implied by Ansoff and Brandenburg's article, then ideally the constituents of the proposal are classified as technical. If, however, these constituents are defined as formal then the proposals would never be considered. If, as is more likely, they are defined as informal then some consideration of them would be given. But at the point where the proposals begin to challenge the formal as feats their acceptance would waver.

All I am trying to argue in this note is:

(i) that there is a lot more to "language" than the word, and to use such a word in a scientific magazine is, however unintentional it may be, misleading;

(ii) to give some indication of the possibilities of true organizational language studies.

References

BROOKER, W. M. A., "Structure, Process and Nomenclature," *Studies in Linguistics* (in press).

CHOMSKY, N., *Cartesian Linguistics*, Harper & Row, New York, 1966.

HALL, E. T., *The Silent Language*, New York, 1959.

KROEBER, A. L., "Classification Systems of Relationships," *Journal of the Royal Anthropological Institute*, Vol. 39 (1909), pp. 77–84.

10

MANAGEMENT IN TRANSITION

H. Igor Ansoff

Source: T. C. Board (ed.) *Challenge to Leadership: Managing in a Changing World*, New York: The Free Press, 1973, pp. 22–63.

The dogmas of the quiet past are inadequate to the stormy present. The occasion is piled high with difficulty, and we must rise with the occasion. As our case is new, so we must think anew and act anew.

—Abraham Lincoln
Second Annual Message,
December 1, 1862

In the next thirty years most organizations will be confronted by drastically new and unprecedented challenges, and there are management gaps that must be filled if we are to meet these challenges. The focus of this paper is on these gaps.

Has our management system, once so successful,
become inadequate now?

At the outset we have to resolve an apparent paradox. During the first fifty years of this century, the challenges and problems that had to be met and overcome were formidable indeed, yet American industry did meet them, did elaborate and perfect a system of management that has been fabulously successful in creating national wealth. Why is it, then, that modern American management may not be adequate for coping with the new challenges?

The answer is twofold: (1) we are moving into a period marked by social challenges so distinct and different that it can be called a new era—the "Post-Industrial Era"; (2) modern management developed only over a long period of time—first it was learning by trial and error; then it accumulated enough know-how to become a practicioner's art; and finally it evolved, if not into a full-blown science, at least into a systematic technology. And we can expect a similar lag between the upsurge of a whole new set of forces and problems and the emergence of managerial techniques to handle them.

That is, unless we anticipate today the directions in which management technology must develop to be ready for tomorrow.

But before we do that, we must gain a clearer idea of where we stand today and how we got there. Only then can we look at management critically and constructively—management, first and primarily, in the business firm and, secondly but with less detail, in the institution of higher learning and in other purposive (nonprofit) organizations.

Management in the business firm

The rise of the business firm

The history of the business firm in the United States can be roughly divided into three distinct periods: the Industrial Revolution, the Mass-Production Era, and the Post-Industrial Era (see Figure 1).

Swift, Firestone, Carnegie, Ford—the great entrepreneurs
laid the groundwork

The Industrial Revolution, having commenced in the 1820's with construction of canals and railroads, was vastly accelerated by a series of major technological inventions that eventually gave birth to the modern firm and the modern market-place. At the outset, however, the social mechanisms for

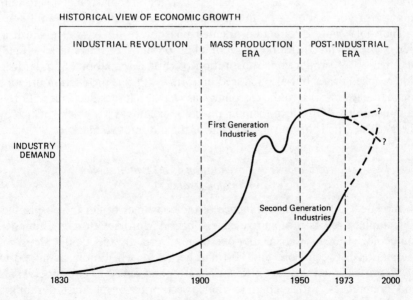

Figure 1

161

matching the technology to the marketplace did not exist. Most of the great inventions were brainchildren of talented individuals who, having given birth to new ideas, had no ready mechanism for converting them into reality.

This role was performed by the great entrepreneurs—like Swift, Firestone, Carnegie, Ford. On one hand, they identified the match between market and product and, on the other, marshalled human, physical, and monetary resources necessary to convert a potential match into commercial reality. These were entrepreneurial managers who focused on harnessing the vast strategic opportunities, rather than devote their efforts to elaborating structures or directing daily operations. They laid the groundwork for the profit and efficiency-seeking social organization known today as the business firm.

In the following Mass-Production Era, attention shifted from strategy to commercial exploitation, to development of organizational capabilities, and to use of these capabilities to make profits. The period was characterized by several overlapping phases from production orientation.

From production orientation
(Ford's "any color as long as it's black") . . .

The first, the *production-oriented* phase (in which Henry Ford I was the legendary pioneer), focused on elaboration of the productive mechanisms: purchasing, inventory control, manufacturing, distribution. The goal was to maximize economies of scale and to minimize the unit cost (and hence the price). The price was seen as the primary attraction to customers, who were hungry for goods, but not affluent enough to satisfy all of their wants.

The tools of the production-oriented phase were three: (1) standardization of the product, (2) subdivision of labor into most effective tasks, and (3) automation of production (substitution of capital for labor). Standardization reduced prices but also induced uniformity. In this production-oriented phase, the lower price to the customer was worth that sacrifice. Hence Ford's famous motto, "Give it to them in any color as long as it's black," which by the 1920's earned for him 65 per cent of the automotive market.

. . . to marketing orientation (GM's multimodel,
multicolor strategy)

In the late 1920's growing affluence of the consumer began to rob production emphasis of its competitive edge. General Motors with its multimodel, multicolor strategy was steadily overtaking Ford. By the 1930's, shares of the market between Ford and GM had been reversed. Emphasis shifted to *market* rather than product orientation. Responsiveness to consumer wants and preferences, rather than to the lowest price or greatest durability, became the determinant of the success of the firm. Not long thereafter, the two viewpoints were integrated into a "total marketing concept," which sought balanced attention to both production and marketing.

The effectiveness of the total marketing concept began to reach its limits as consumer demand became saturated. Industry's answer was twofold:

(1) *Stimulate demand:* The consumer was now affluent enough to be able to replace his still usable car, refrigerator, vacuum cleaner, or clothes with new ones which offered convenience features, greater esthetic appeal, or enhanced social prestige. The introduction of annual model changes by General Motors in 1932 symbolized and triggered the era of artificial obsolescence;

(2) *Create new demand through technology:* Seeds of diversification were sown earlier in the century when firms based on technologically complex products began to build research and development laboratories. By contrast with the Industrial Revolution, when inventions were made by outsiders, the laboratories internalized the inventive process. Their early focus, however, was on the improvement of efficiency, quality, and durability of the firm's traditional products. (Substitutions of artificial fibers for cotton and wool, synthetic rubber for natural, and plastics for steel are but a few examples of this trend).

The important departure came when R&D laboratories began, at the same time, to develop substitute technologies for traditional products and, also, to create new products and industries. (The birth of the electronics industry, and of computer industry, radio, and television, exemplifies this later trend.)

Shift of focus: from managing the firm to expanding its scope

Throughout industrial history, acquisition of other firms has been used as an alternative form of growth. The pattern, however, has changed over time. During the Industrial Revolution, the purpose of acquisitions was either to increase market share through acquisition of competitors or to control production costs through acquisition of sources of raw materials. Around the break of the century, a relatively brief but violent period of financial manipulation and empire building through acquisitions and mergers evolved. This development led to a public outcry against "smash-grab imperialism" and resulted in the enactment of the original antitrust laws.

In the late stages of the Mass-Production Era, acquisitions became a tool of growth through horizontal integration—rounding out of the firm's product line. This direction was followed by a shift to concentric diversification: diversification into new industries which were related to the parent business either through common technology, marketing, or production capability. The philosophy of these largely *synergistic* acquisition phases was in contrast with the *conglomerate* phase that arrived in the late 1960's. Under the latter phase, relationship among parts of the conglomerate was almost exclusively financial. Synergy was held to be an irrelevant and unrealistic concept. The emphasis was on "creative financing," an attitude reminiscent of the trust-building days of the 1890's.

Some of the concentric acquisition activity and almost all of the conglomerates resulted in a major shift in the focus of top management. Whereas before the main emphasis was on growth from within, with acquisition being a secondary balancing or remedial activity, the new emphasis was just the reverse. Top management began to shift its attention from managing the existing firm to creating new horizons and expanding the firm's scope.

The mass-production industries give way to technology-driven newcomers

The Great Depression undermined confidence in the self-regulatory mechanisms of the economy and broke the upward trend of the Mass-Production genius of the business firm. Then came World War II; a four-year hiatus in consumer goods production accumulated a demand which could not be satisfied out of existing capacities. For a period, the ability to buy a car of any color so long as one could get it shifted emphasis from marketing to expansion of capacity and enhancement of internal productivity (shades of the 1920's!).

By the early 1950's, however, signs of saturation again began to appear. The total marketing concept did less and less to revive demand. Accelerated product substitution through R&D became more and more the key competitive tool; so did expansion to foreign markets. (For an increasing number of traditional industries, though, not even these tools could stem a strong trend of saturation.)

At the same time, new R&D-based industries hungry for investment began to emerge, with rapid growth rates. It became increasingly apparent that a "changing of the guard" was in progress. Industries which were the chief engines of the Mass-Production Era were being replaced as growth leaders by the technology-driven newcomers. This shift alone would have been enough to cause a funda-mental change in the problems and concerns of management. Sixty years of concentration on gaining the customers' favor through competition, of struggle for growth, and of increased market shares were yielding progressively poorer results and promised, at best, modest growth and profitability prospects.

Economic demand shifts were not the only signs of drastic change. The firm progressively had to confront a different world: expansions of the marketplace from nation-state to virtually global dimensions, accelerated rates of change, the threat of sudden technological obsolescence, different attitudes of consumers, the changing nature of the labor force, pressures of consumerism, and growing governmental regulations. The Mass-Production Era was drawing to a close and a new era was in the making. We shall look at the shape of this new era in another section. In the meanwhile, we need to appraise the managerial capabilities that developed in response to the challenges of the Mass-Production Era.

Achievement of managerial competence

When, after World War II, U.S. industry began a massive invasion of the European market, the ability of American firms to outperform local industries had caused much local concern and puzzlement. An initial explanation, offered by both European and American observers, gave credit to the superior American industrial technology. Yet American firms seemed to succeed against competitors across a range of industries, only some of which were heavily technologically based. In seeking to explain this, the French journalist Servan-Schreiber argued that American superiority lay not so much in its technology but in a superior managerial competence.[1]

Individuals who have been exposed to management in the United States and abroad agree that the managerial capabilities of American firms on the average tend to be superior to those of European firms, and yet the average American manager does not appear to be a more intelligent or capable person than his counterpart. If anything, he is more likely to be narrower in outlook, less socially, politically, and culturally sensitive, than many of his counterparts. The explanation for the difference appears to lie less in inherent qualities of the individual and more in the culture which surrounds him.

A favorable social climate fed the growth of management efficiency

Throughout the first half of the twentieth century a central characteristic of the American scene was society's commitment to the accumulation of physical wealth. The doctrine of political populism on which the Republic was founded found a congenial philosophical companion in the doctrine of economic populism. Formulated by an Englishman, Adam Smith, the laissez-faire doctrine, which asserts that social welfare is maximized when business is encouraged to maximize its profits under a minimum of external constraints, found a fuller acceptance in the United States than in its country of origin, or in other European countries. When a senior industrial executive said, "What's good for General Motors is good for the country," his remarks may have been perceived as indelicate, but they were not far from the popular consensus of the times.

This centrality of the firm greatly simplified the environmental perspective of the manager. His unique focus was to be on the markets and the customers of the firm, his attitude toward government attempts to regulate the firm's behavior was justifiably negative, and any concern with issues other than single-minded pursuit of profit was an unwarranted diversion.

The benevolent social climate made the managerial profession the most respected and aspired-to in American society—a situation unmatched elsewhere in the world. The best of national brainpower was attracted by the profession's prestige, its challenges, and its promise of high economic rewards within the prevailing social ethic. To be rich was both prestigious and righteous.

While social contrality of the firm and homogeneity of its environment encouraged a single-minded commitment to the "business of business," the prevailing growth ethic suplied a universal yardstick for success. To grow was both necessary and good; not to grow was to stagnate and die. Rationalizations for growth were many: economies of scale and hence enhanced productivity, control of market behavior through dominant market share, managerial motivation and growth potential in an expanding organization, and "critical mass" for research, development, and other investments made available through size.

Personal prestige, centrality of the firm, social endorsement of profitability, commitment to growth, and ethnocentric market perspective—all provided an environment highly conducive to development of efficient management practices in American industry.

Changes in the economy bred changes in managerial practices

At the same time, the environment presented a number of absorbing challenges: the new directions needed when, as we saw in the preceding section, the focus shifted from developing mass-production technology through better use of workers and of capital, to developing goods and services in response to consumers' wishes, and stimulating their desire to buy, and then to creating new demands through artificial obsolescence and new product development.

The major achievements of management during the Mass-Production Era were the development of know-how and techniques for structuring, planning, supervising, motivating, and controlling the productive processes of the firm. The crowning success was "the Miracle of Mass Production" in World War II. Management was seen as "the art of getting things done through others," the "others" being mostly workers and not fellow managers. As firms grew and became complex, however, difficult and pressing problems began to arise in managing managers: structuring, planning, and controlling managerial work.

The separation of ownership and management was successfully made

One of the early trouble spots was the differentiation between managers and owners of the firm. In the early days of industry, owners of assets were also the key managers. As firms grew large and went public, ownership became widely distributed among outsiders who bought stock as an investment and had neither the expertise nor the interest in management, Management increasingly passed into the hands of professionals. A twofold problem arose: (1) how to motivate the managers to give their best effort to the firm, and at the same time (2) how to ensure that these efforts are unselfishly devoted to the owners' interests.

The first problem was solved through development of a cultural norm which may be called "surrogate ownership," which coalesced the managerial class, and which effectively set it apart from the workers. When a new manager, after a trial period, was given the symbolic "key to the executive washroom," and was admitted to the "in" group, he was henceforth expected to treat the firm as his own and devote all of his energies to the pursuit of its goals. In return, he was rewarded with prestige, power, stock options, and bonuses—all of which were tied in with continued success of the firm and hence reinforced his allegiance. In the United States, this norm became so ingrained that it survived many years of increasing managerial mobility among firms. In most Western European countries and in Japan it has remained even stronger, since the manager still typically spends his entire career in a single firm, as Drucker has noted (see p. 246).

Solution to the second problem of ensuring that managers acted in the interest of the owners was sought through a legal requirement for an elected board of directors empowered and required to guard the owners' interests. Wide distribution of ownership in a majority of firms, the lack of communication between directors and owners, management's control of information to outside directors, the practice of packing the board with "inside" directors —all these factors increasingly mitigated against this solution. Throughout the Mass-Production Era, management increasingly came to exercise virtual control over selection of the firm's growth thrusts as well as the conduct of operations. So long as the firm operated profitably, the board and the owners had a minimal influence on the course of the firm. The board of directors stepped in and took control only when substantial and chronic losses were incurred.

Interestingly enough, this benign neglect of responsibility seldom incurred social or public censure against the board for allowing the situation to get out of control. It was not until the late 1960's and early 1970's, well into the succeeding Post-Industrial Era, that the liability of the directors was reasserted through a proliferation of stockholder suits.

The problem of large, heterogeneous, dispersed
organizations was solved

As firms grew in size and diversified geographically, management changed from a small, closely-knit group to a large, heterogeneous, dispersed organization. Three related problems arose: (1) ensuring uniform adherence to a common goal, (2) motivating managers through a far-flung organization, and (3) responding expeditiously to local problems and opportunities.[2]

A dual solution evolved through trial and error early in the twentieth century and became widely adopted. First, each manager was not only made responsible for the performance of his unit but also given sufficient authority and control to exact that performance. Secondly, this authority and responsibility was decentralized to levels at which the best information was available for proper and expeditious response to local challenges. The principle of authority commensurate with responsibility and the principle of decentralization of authority both became important and distinctive cornerstones of American management culture. (This principle does not have similar importance in either European or Japanese managerial cultures, which place strong emphasis on collegiality—a sharing of authority among several persons.)

Decision making was decentralized—even passed to staff experts

The growth in the size of management was accompanied by growth and change in role of quasi-management commonly called "staff." The early function of this group was to collect, arrange, and transmit information on behalf of management, but not to participate in or to make decisions. Growth in complexity of operations and in specialized technical knowledge forced managers increasingly to involve staff and technical experts (legal, financial, engineering, public relations, etc.) in the process of decision making.

In distinction from the days of the Industrial Revolution, when a manager could justifiably consider himself expert on all important aspects of a decision, he was increasingly forced to use the expertise of others. Some observers have pointed out that this trend, together with decentralization, deprives top management of control not only over operational decisions but even over the fundamental strategic thrusts of the firm.[3] When this occurs, a coalition of technocrats takes over the decisions and leaves top management to "rubber stamp" their consensus.

(In fact, many firms have now reached the point of "management by technocracy." As we look at the scene today, we see that the role of top management in large firms has become increasingly ambiguous and less powerful; corporate staff have become the symbol of "lean" efficient corporate management; and goal setting for major strategic thrusts has been progressively delegated to lower management levels. Top management limits its scope to budgeting review, public relations, and management development.)

During the Mass-Production Era, abdication of strategic control by top management did not often spell disaster for the firm, but it did represent a further step in the loss of owners' control over the direction of the firm's fortunes. To the question, "In whose interests is the firm managed?" the answer became increasingly "In the interests of those who work in it," and less "In the interests of the owners."

Systematic arrangements were made for managerial work

The decentralization of managerial control, together with the size, complexity, and geographic dispersion of firms, increasingly emphasized the need for systematic arrangements of managerial work.

Early progress was made in the elaboration of structural management through more explicit assignment of authority, responsibility, and accountability. The fuctional organizational structure, which first emerged in response to demand for internal efficiency of the production-oriented phase, was not adequate to the later demands of market responsiveness. So this structure was gradually replaced by the more responsive divisional form. As firms diversified abroad and as the environment became more dynamic, the divisional forms, in turn, were found to be increasingly inadequate. Various hybrid forms emerged, and as the firm entered the Post-Industrial Era, the appropriate and effective organizational structure was yet to be discovered.[4]

Systematic control of operations was augmented by budgeting and profit planning. After World War II, long-range planning and control and its simpler version, management by objectives, found increasing acceptance. By the mid 1950's, however, it became increasingly clear that long-range planning, which is based on an assumption of a great deal of environmental stability, would have to be replaced by more advanced forms of planning.[5]

As for the manager himself (as an individual), the dynamics of the Mass-Production Era offered a favorable environment for his training. Amid rapid change there was continuity. In a smoothly growing world, past experience was a reliable guide to the future. It was possible to train a manager by moving him upward through an organization. The problems encountered at any managerial level were likely to be a repetition on a larger scale of problems experienced earlier.[6] The over-all character of the manager's problem world remained stable for the length of his managerial career. His world was built on a stable technological base, known customers, a familial internal organizational structure, and a familiar, if dynamic, competition. The problems and surprises, the risks and the opportunities that challenge him, came from changes in familiar variables (sales, inventory, costs, competition) and not from structural changes such as a major influx of foreign competition or drastic obsolescence of technology.

Thus, in response to the challenges, American industry has been very successful in developing an effective manager capable of dealing with challenges of the Mass-Production Era. His profile can be described by the following characteristics:

1. He is profit-minded, relates all of his decisions and actions to the over-all profitability of the enterprise.
2. He equates his personal success with the success of the enterprise.

3. He is experienced and familiar with the traditional business of the firm and has developed a feel for the critical variables which affect the success of the enterprise.

4. His problem-solving perspective is primarily a technological and economic one. He has had little exposure to the political, societal, and cultural influences which affect business decisions.

5. Within his perspective, he is an incisive *convergent* problem-solver. He is quick to relate a problem to a previous precedent, to isolate the critical variable, to devise an appropriate solution.

6. He is preconditioned to prefer the familiar solution to a novel one, an incremental change to a large one, a familiar risk to a gambler's plunge.

7. He is a skillful communicator and leader of men. In exercising leadership, he is preconditioned to exploit the historical dynamics of the organization. He is skillful in timing the introduction of a needed change in the organization. He is a skillful crisis manager so long as the options available to him include familiar solutions.

8. He has only limited skills in solving novel problems which have no precedent in his previous experience. Nor is he skilled in leading the organization on major departures from historical organizational development.

Of course not every firm had all the attributes described above, or had the right kind of managers, or achieved dynamic growth. Some led the way; some trailed, oriented more toward comfortable survival than toward vigorous competition.

Now, as society moves into the Post-Industrial Era, these two classes of firms face different problems. The leaders will need to adapt, not because of past imperfections, but because of drastic changes in challenges; while laggards, if they are not to go down completely, will have to leapfrog the whole way from a conservative past into a turbulent future.

Challenge of the Post-Industrial Era

During the Mass-Production Era, an outside observer of the firm would perceive the manager's world as relatively simple. His almost undivided attention was on "the business of business." He had a willing pool of labor (so long as the wage was right), and he catered to a receptive consumer. He was only secondarily troubled by such esoteric problems as tariffs, monetary exchange rates, differential inflation rates, cultural differences, and political barriers between markets. Research and development was a controllable tool for increased productivity and product improvement. Society and government, though increasingly on guard against monopolistic tendencies and competitive collusion, were essentially friendly partners in promoting economic progress.

170

From the insider's viewpoint, however, the manager found his life very complex, challenging, and demanding. Outside the firm, he had to fight constantly for market share, anticipate customers' needs, provide timely delivery of superior products priced below competitors, and ensure the retention of customer loyalty. Internally, he had to struggle constantly for increased productivity through better planning, more efficient organization of work, and automation of production. Continually, he had to contend with demands from labor unions for an increasing share of profits. He had to meet these demands and still maintain the level of productivity, retain his competitive position on the market, pay confidence-inspiring dividends to stockholders, and generate sufficient retained earnings to meet the company's growth needs.

Thus, it was natural for busy management to treat environmental changes, such as periodic economic recessions, inflation, growing governmental constraints, dissatisfaction of consumers, and changing work attitudes, as *distractions* from "the business of business," to be weathered and overcome within a basically sound framework of relationships with the environment. It took almost twenty years to bring about an awareness that such distractions signaled a fundamental transformation of society—the emergence of a new social era, which posed unfamiliar problems to the firm and thrust management into new roles.

The population is assured of economic wealth to meet its needs

The most significant element is a level of economic wealth adequate to meet the basic physiological and survival needs of the population. The Mass-Production Era was uniquely focused on a *search* for this level of affluence. The Post-Industrial Era *is* an age of affluence. Here are some of its parameters:

1. The arrival of affluence casts doubt on economic growth as the critical instrument of social progress. Social aspirations shift away from "quantity" to "quality" of life. Industrial bigness increasingly appears as a threat both to economic efficiency through monopolistic practices, and to society through "government-industrial" complexes. Large enterprises are challenged on their change-resisting bureaucratic tendencies, their lack of creativity, their failure to produce increased efficiency while increasing size. Acquisition of other firms is challenged on the grounds of bigness per se and not on the traditional antitrust rationale. Studies are prepared for dismemberment of giant firms. The growth ethic, which had provided a clear guiding light to social behavior, begins to decline. "Zero growth" alternatives are advanced, but without a clear understanding of how social vitality is to be retained when growth stops.

2. Realignment of social priorities focuses attention on the negative side-effects of profit-seeking behavior: environmental pollution, fluctuations

in economic activity, inflation, monopolistic practices, "manipulation" of the consumer through artficial obsolescence, blatant advertising, incomplete disclosure, low-quality after-sale service. All these effects begin to appear to be too high a price to pay for the laissez-faire conditions of "uncontrolled competition." The firm is now assumed to be able not only to maintain affluence under stringent constraints (which only 20 years ago would have been considered fundamentally subversive and socially destructive) but also to undertake "social responsibility." Thus, one of the consequences of affluence is the loss of social centrality for the institution that created it.

3. Having "filled their bellies," individuals begin to aspire to higher levels of personal satisfaction both in their buying and in their working behavior. They become increasingly discriminating—increasingly demanding "full disclosure" about their purchases, demanding "post-sales" responsibility from the manufacturer, unwilling to put up with ecological pollution as a by-product. They begin to lose faith in the wisdom of management and its knowledge of "what is good for the country." They challenge the firm directly through "consumerism" and put pressure on government for increased controls.

Managers begin to reject the role of "surrogate owners" of the enterprise expected to work for the "good of the firm." Workers begin to refuse technology-defined roles (no matter what the economic rewards) which are boring and monotonous, and which are not congruent with their new higher-level value systems.[7]

4. Satisfaction of survival needs, on the one hand, and an increase in discretionary buying power, on the other, produce fundamental changes in demand patterns. Buying attitudes change. Possession of material goods loses social prestige. The great American love affair with the automobile comes to an end. An increasing proportion of spenders are nonearners—the young and the old.

On the aggregate demand level, many industries that fueled progress in the Mass-Production Era reach saturation. These industries do not necessarily decline, but their growth slows down and their accumulated resources exceed their opportunities for reinvestment. New industries emerge that cater to the affluent consumer—luxury goods, recreation, travel, services, etc.

5. As a result of its affluence, the nation feels that it can afford to turn its attention to social problems that remained unsolved, or were even caused by profit-seeking activity: social justice, proverty, housing, education, public transportation, environmental pollution, ecological imbalance. The private sector is now called upon to perform a twofold role: (a) to restrain and remove its problem-causing activities (such as pollution), and (b) to take responsibility for positive social progress. New demands for social services create potential new markets, but they are not easy to serve because the government replaces the consumer as an intermediate buyer. Nor is it easy

to make a profit in them, because they have remained previously unattended precisely because they could not attract profit-seeking capital.

6. Technology fundamentally affects both supply and demand. Triggered by wartime demand and made possible by postwar affluence, massive investment in research and development spawns new technology-based industries on the one hand, and brings about obsolescence in others.

(As an offshoot of the growth ethic, the Mass-Production Era spawned an "R&D" ethic: i.e., to develop and change products is to remain competitive, to restrain new product introduction is to stagnate. As a result, from the firm's internal perspective, technology becomes an "R&D monster," with a dynamic of its own, which determines a firm's growth thrusts independently of, and sometimes in spite of, the aspiration of management.)[8]

7. Aided by vast improvements in communication and transportation, the marketplace loses its national identity and becomes global. In addition to the pains of saturation, many of the mature industries in the United States (e.g., steel, consumer electronics, consumer durables, automobiles) find themselves confronted with a foreign invasion of their traditional markets. The pressure becomes strong to expand to foreign markets that have not yet reached saturation.

Initially (1960–1970), U.S. technologically intensive industries held a commanding competitive advantage and were presented with lucrative growth opportunities abroad. But in the 1970's some U.S. industries will be increasingly confronted with a disadvantageous competitive gap in Europe and Japan.

The manager faces a very different world full of vexing problems

Thus, a manager who has been brought up in the Mass-Production Era, peering uneasily outward through the windows of the corporate office at the world of the 1970's, perceives a very different world full of vexing things.

It is a world which lost little of the original competitive complexity and acquired many others; a world of discontinuity in which it is dangerous to predict the future through reliance on history; a world full of novel problems and challenges for which past experience is a poor guide. In this world, the business firm has lost its Ptolemaic centrality. It is no longer the social sun around which revolve other less important planets. It has become a part of a Keplerian system of many interacting and independent planets.

To understand the world, new terminology and concepts are needed. The predominant emphasis during the Mass-Production Era was on *competitive behavior* and the profitable exploitation of the current markets of the firm. Externally to the firm, this behavior called for advertising, selling, distributing, purchasing; internally, for managing production, controlling various

173

inventories, maintaining motivation and morale of the organization, developing organizational and human capabilities, maintaining, expanding, and improving facilities.

In the background, another distinctive mode of behavior has been concerned, not with exploitation of the current business posture, but with developing and maintaining viable and potentially profitable relationships with the environment.

Externally to the firm, this behavior calls for setting the organizational objectives, determining the major growth and expansion thrusts of the firm, securing financial and human resources—internally, for developing new products, acquiring new physical, human, and financial capabilities; and, externally, test marketing and introducing new products/services to the customers. This interface maintenance and development behavior—we shall call it *entrepreneurial behavior*—received relatively minor attention in the Mass-Production Era. The major emphasis then was on competitive behavior.

New priority: not competitive behavior, but entrepreneurial behavior

In the Post-Industrial Era, the relative importance of the two modes shifts. Vigorous competitive behavior remains essential and becomes more challenging and complex. Externally to the firm, new problems include coping with a disaffected and increasingly recalcitrant consumer, competing against foreign competition at home, penetrating foreign cultures and markets abroad, coping with complexities of international monetary, economic, and political barriers. Internally, it requires accommodation to the new values and aspirations of both the management and the labor force, changing the basis of managerial authority (and still retaining control of operations), redesigning work roles to make them fulfilling and satisfying, and retaining productive efficiency.

These changes alone would have been enough to strain and challenge managerial capabilities of the Mass-Production Era. But the priority shifts to the previously secondary entrepreneurial behavior. Saturation in many industries, birth of new ones, product proliferation, shortening of product life-cycles, expanding opportunities abroad—all make vigorous entrepreneurial behavior a precondition for success and a prerequisite for survival.

Growing noneconomic interactions between the firm and society require broadening the decision horizon to include not only economic (competitive), but also technological, sociological, political, demographic trends and variables. Within this horizon, the environment calls for an ability to discern discontinuities which pose threats and opportunties to the firm and to translate these into growth thrusts and skills to develop new financial and other resources. The accelerating rate of death and birth of both industries and products moves entrepreneurial behavior to the forefront of continuous managerial attention.

174

The primary focus is no longer on exploiting the firm's business, it is on *changing* the business, including products-markets-industries-technologies which no longer offer the best potential.

The manager must have a new set of organizational capabilities

As one scans the list of the managerial capabilities of the Mass-Production Era presented earlier, it becomes apparent that major changes are needed to meet the new requirements of entrepreneurial behavior. The differences are in every element—individual skills, organizational capabilities, and value systems. A summary of the distinctive attributes for the respective modes of behavior is presented in Table 1. It suggests very strongly that the Post-Industrial Era requires development of a new set of organizational capabilities.

Capability for entrepreneurial behavior

The entrepreneurial manager is distinctive from his Mass-Production counterpart in the following respects:

1. He is globally profit-minded both in time and in space. His concern is both with immediate and with long-term profitability. He has no emotional attachment to the traditional business of the firm. All opportunities are to be weighed against the over-all profitability of the enterprise. He applies Alfred P. Sloan's creed: "The strategic aim of the enterprise is to produce a satisfactory return on the resources invested in it and if the return is not satisfactory, either the deficiency must be corrected *or resources allocated elsewhere*" (italics mine).[9]

2. He tempers his devotion to profitability with social awareness. He is a responsible citizen who does not believe that what is good for business is good for the country. On the other hand, he is clear-minded about protecting the primary wealth-generation purpose of the firm from erosion by unacceptable constraints or by diversionary or depressing activities.

3. He finds his satisfaction, not only in the extrinsic rewards of money and power, but also in the intrinsic satisfaction of creative managerial work.

4. His familiarity with his business firm is less on terms of what it has done and more in terms of what it can do: based upon its resources, strengths, and weaknesses, and the constraints on its behavior. He has a continuing interest in, and broad knowledge of, opportunities outside the traditional business of the firm.

5. His problem-solving perspective is broad: technological, competitive, economic, political, cultural, sociological. In the words of another paper, he is a man of many archetypal talents—entrepreneur, planner, administrator, system architect, politician, and statesman. (The difficulties of breeding this paragon of all virtues are formidable; perhaps group management is the only possible way to bring all these talents together.)[10]

Table 1 Comparison of Organizational Modes.

ATTRIBUTE	MODE	
	Competitive	Entrepreneurial
Objective	Optimize profitability	Optimize profitability potential
Goals	Extrapolation of past goals modulated by performance	Determined through interaction of opportunities and capabilities
Reward & Penalty System	(1) Rewards for stability, efficiency (2) Rewards for past performance (3) Penalties for deviance	(1) Rewards for creativity and initiative (2) Penalties for lack of initiative
Information Space	(1) Internal: performance; External: historical opportunity space	(1) Internal: capabilities (2) Global opportunity space
Problem Space	Repetitive, familiar	Nonrepetitive, novel
Leadership Style	(1) Popularity (2) Skill to develop consensus	(1) Charisma (2) Skill to inspire people to accept change
Organizational Structure	(1) Stable or expanding (2) Activities grouped according to resource conversion process (3) Search for economics of scale (4) Activities loosely coupled	(1) Fluid, structurally changing (2) Activities grouped according to problems (3) Activities closely coupled
Management Problem Solving		
(a) Recognition of action need	(1) Reactive in response to problems (2) Time lagged behind occurrence of problems	(1) Active search for opportunities (2) Anticipatory
(b) Search for alternatives	(1) Reliance on experience (2) Incremental departures from status quo (3) Single alternative generated	(1) Creative search (2) Wide ranging from status quo (3) Multiple alternative generated
(c) Evaluation of alternatives	(1) Satisficing-first satisfactory accepted	(1) Optimizing-best of a set of alternatives is selected
(d) Risk attitude	(1) Minimize risk (2) Consistency with past	(1) Risk propensive (2) Risk portfolio

6. He is a divergent creative problem solver. He continually searches for new alternatives; he is a habitual learner, quick to assimilate new information and isolate the controlling variables and devise novel solution procedures.

7. He is a skillful leader of group and organizational problem solving. Where he lacks personal expertise, he is skilled in the art of using experts.

8. His risk propensities are not biased in favor of the familiar, nor is he a habitual gambler on the unknown. He attempts to develop a balanced portfolio of risks commensurate with possible gain.

9. His leadership skills lie in inducing the organization to take bold departures from the past tradition.

The manager can only operate within
a new organizational environment

Just like the skilled competitive manager, the entrepreneurial manager can only operate within a conducive organizational environment. In entrepreneurial behavior, the design of this environment is focused not only on efficiency but also on over-all long-term effectiveness—not so much on strategic steady-state as on utilizing the best fields of opportunity open to the firm.

Some of the features of this environment are:

1. Authority based not on power but on knowledge, in which work is designed to the dual criteria of task effectiveness and intrinsic motivation of the individual.

2. An organizational structure which accommodates both stability of competitive behavior and fluidity of entrepreneurial behavior—a combination of efficiency-seeking bureaucracy and innovative "adhocracy." (The multidivisional, multinational structure prevalent today does not accommodate these demands; hence the search is on for new organizational forms.)

3. A decentralized substructure of "strategic business units" (a term used in the General Electric Company to describe such substructure) matched to the distinctive segments (demand-technology life cycles) of the firm's environment, with maximum entrepreneurial freedom for managers of each segment.

4. A top level corporate substructure devoted to balancing the firm's strategic portfolio of distinctive segments and to integrating entrepreneurial and competitive activities.

5. A surveillance system which scans the environment beyond limits of current business for major trends, projects these into the future, translates them into threats and opportunities to the firm, and injects this information into appropriate action points—a forecasting system, which does not assume the future to be an extrapolation of the past, but explores structural changes underlying current trends.

6. An information system which is rich beyond current operating data, which communicates up, down, as well as sideways, to link people according to common tasks.

7. A reward and motivation system which rewards both current profitability and imaginative investment in future profitability, which is tolerant of meaningful failure and risk-taking behavior, which builds rewards into

177

the content of jobs, and which recognizes the changed personal values of both workers and managers.

8. A control system which is future-oriented, based on "remaining cost to complete and remaining performance to accomplish" rather than on historical performance.

9. A closely coupled entrepreneurial management system (similar to an extension of PPBS) to be based on entrepreneurial analysis of multiple novel alternatives, which matches planning, programming, budgeting, implementation, and control into a coherent whole.

10. A career-long management development system which combines career planning, job rotation, and education, which is married neither to promotion from within nor hiring from without, and which develops managers through exposure both to the current operations and to the opportunities and challenges of the unfolding socio-political-cultural environment.

We have just looked at an aggregate description of entrepreneurial management. A more detailed analysis is presented in Table 2, where the profile of entrepreneurial management is compared with the profile of competitive management developed during the Mass-Production Era.

The comparison suggests that the two profiles are indeed very different, and that a major capability-building task is ahead for firms entering the Post-Industrial Era where the emphasis is on enterpreneurial behavior.

Management must grow, expand—must manage management

But beyond the problem of building the capability, lie equally different problems of accommodation and integration. Successful managements of the Mass-Production Era were built on the minimal-management principle, with managerial capacity just adequate to accommodate demands of competitive behavior. The addition of entrepreneurial problems requires a reevaluation of the minimal management concept. Experience shows that minimally managed organizations cannot anticipate discontinuities, cannot span them except through painful and lengthy trial and error. Entrepreneurial responsiveness requires much greater managerial capacity than competitive behavior, as well as new skills, both in line and staff. Thus, as new entrepreneurial skills are developed, management will have to grow and expand.

As this growth occurs, the two managerial processes—competitive and entrepreneurial—will come in conflict. In fact, the conflict occurs not only in management but also within the firm's logistic process. This conflict is familiar to everyone who has tried to introduce a major new product line to replace a previously successful one. It is a conflict of values, skills, work habits, risk attitudes, reward systems. Thus, a major managerial challenge will be to accommodate what has been called "bimodal behavior" within the firm.[11] The current emergence of innovative forms of organizational structure is one sign of search for such accommodation.[12]

Table 2 Comparison of Managers in the Mass-Production and Post-Industrial Eras.

MANAGER IN THE MASS-PRODUCTION ERA	MANAGER IN THE POST-INDUSTRIAL ERA
Values and Attitudes	*Values and Attitudes*
Surrogate Owner	Professional
Committed to laissez faire	Committed to social value of free enterprise
Profit optimizer	Social-value-optimizer
Seeks economic rewards and power	Seeks job satisfaction
Seeks stability	Seeks change
Prefers incremental change	Prefers entrepreneurial change
Skills	*Skills*
Experientially acquired	Acquired through career-long education
Familiar problem solver	Novel problem solver
Intuitive problem solver	Analytic problem solver
Conservative risk taker	Entrepreurial risk taker
Convergent diagnostician	Divergent diagnostician
Lag controller	Lead controller
Extrapolative planner	Entrepreneurial planner
Change control leadership	Change generation leadership
Action Perspective	*Action Perspective*
Intrafirm	Environmental
Intraindustry	Multiindustry
Intranational (regional)	Multinational
Intracultural	Cross-cultural
Economic	Economic
Technological	Technological
	Social
	Political
ORGANIZATIONAL ENVIRONMENT	ORGANIZATIONAL ENVIRONMENT
Basis of Managerial Authority	*Basis of Managerial Authority*
Surrogate asset ownership	Knowledge ownership
Power to hire and fire	Expertise
Power to reward and punish	Ability to challenge
	Ability to persuade
Organizational Rewards	*Organizational Rewards*
Rewards: Past contribution to profitability	Rewards: Creativity
"Total profit awareness"	Innovation
Cooperation	Novelty
Loyalty	Meaningful failure
Penalties: Failure	Penalties: Lack of initiative
Deviance	

Table 2 (cont'd)

Structure	*Structure*
Activities: Aggregation by function for economies of scale Aggregation by product for competitive response Entrepreneurial activity embedded in structure	Activities: Aggregated by task for entrepreneurial response Entrepreneurial activities segregated from competitive activities
Power: Unity of authority-responsibility Structured authority Decentralization for competitive response Centralization for decision optimality	Power: Decentralization for entrepreneurial response Strategic authority Decentralization for job enrichment Centralization for strategic portfolio control
Roles designed for task effectiveness	Roles designed for task effectiveness and job satisfaction

Information Environment	*Information Environment*
External surveillance: traditional environment	External surveillance: global environment
External information from competitive results	Dedicated surveillance system
Internal information generated by incurred costs	Internal information generated by activities capabilities and skills
Management information derived from logistic information	Management information directly generated
Communication: along authority structure results and problems upward instructions downward	Communication: problem lines opportunities and threats expertise upward guidelines downward

Management Decision-Making	*Management Decision-Making*
Change absorbing	Change generating
Risk minimizing	Risk propensive
Triggered by problems	Triggered by opportunities
Serial diagnosis	Parallel diagnosis
Convergent	Divergent
Consistent with experience	Novel
Incremental	Global
Sequential attention to goals	Simultaneous attention to goals
Satisficing	Optimizing

Systems	*Systems*
Financial accounting	Human resource accounting
Capital budgeting	Capability accounting
Expense budgeting	Capability budgeting
Historical control	Action budgeting
Long-range (extrapolative) planning	Strategic entrepreneurial planning Forward control

Another sign is the observable reversal of the trend toward "rubber stamp" top management. The reversal signifies a newly recognized need for *integrative management*, which can only take place at the top, which balances, accommodates, and guides the coexistence of the competitive and the entrepreneurial modes. Even in the early stages of the Post-Industrial Era one can observe top management in leading firms turning from operational-type concerns, such as budgeting, toward new nonoperational concerns. Some of these concerns are balancing resource allocation between competitive and entrepreneurial investments, the selection of the optimal strategic portfolio of demand-technology life cycles, the development of managers, and new structures and systems for successful coexistence and cooperation of the two modes.

During the Industrial Revolution, top managers were lonely entrepreneurial trail-blazers; in the Mass-Production Era, they became coordinators of complex organizations; in the Post-Industrial Era, they are reemerging as influential entrepreneurs.

Thus, the greatly increased complexity of choices and the recent rapid strides in technology of management make nonsense of the minimal-management principle. In the Post-Industrial world, to skimp on management will be to invite disaster through loss of the firm's relevance to its environment. Maximal management, however, can invite equal disaster through sluggishness, inefficiency, and unresponsiveness. A major focus of the early stages of the Post-Industrial Era has already become the *management of management*, the development and application of techniques or practices for efficient handling of the enlarged and expanded responsibility of management.

The question is: What is the ability of management technology to meet this challenge?

Can we meet the challenge?

Having progressed from a practitioner's art to an experientially based technology, management now needs to become a science-based technology. The trial-and-error method of art has the richness of reality, but it is slow and does not lend itself to teaching. The system of abstracting from experience is faster and more teachable, but it is not applicable when the problems to be met are quite new, and planning cannot be extrapolated from the past. The new science-based mode, with its breadth of vision *and* its danger of over-simplification, offers the only hope for success. Let us look at it more closely.

Science-based management technology combines
statistical decision making . . .

The 20-year period following World War II witnessed a flowering of management technology. There were two primary stimuli. One came from the wartime development of a technology of complex decision-making called

181

"operations research." Powerful analytic techniques developed for the planning of military operations supported a cadre of technologists who sought to apply their new skills to peacetime uses. The second stimulus came from a pressure from within business firms for better efficiency in meeting the economic needs of the times.

The resulting techniques were given the somewhat misleading name of management "science." It was not a science because it produced very few general theoretic insights either into behavior of firms or into management. For its so-called "scientific" foundation, management science used the basic hypotheses of profit-maximizing behavior advanced by Adam Smith back in 1776. To this, modern mathematics was added, particularly the new linear programming theory, probability statistics, and (to a much lesser extent) another new branch of mathematics known as game theory.[13]

This combination of disciplines was applied to a set of managerial problems which appeared accurately defined by these techniques. By and large this turned out to be a group of middle-management problems concerned with the movement and transformation of physical resources: inventory control, production scheduling, machine loading, goods distribution, and the selection of capital investment projects.

Toward the end of the 1960's, a welcome convergence began to take place between management scientists in academia and managers in industry. In its early development, the power of the scientific method to solve all managerial problems appeared unchallengeable. Management scientists felt that, given access to data and real operations, they could not only eventually solve all important problems, but also replace the manager-decision-maker in the process.[14] Naturally enough, this led to a conflict between managers and management scientists, the former being distrustful and apprehensive of the excessive claims, the latter perceiving the manager as myopic, unsophisticated, and unprepared to move with the times. Years of shared experience now appear to have led to a mutual appreciation of the role of management science in complex top management problem-solving as an important but auxiliary addition to the still important art of the manager.

... and application of behavioral science to complex organizational problems

A second major postwar trend was in the application of psychology and sociology to the problems of complex organizations. More diffuse than management science, these applications have been somewhat vaguely titled "behavioral science." This trend is a curious combination of a search for broad scientific understanding and experience-based technology.

While management science continued to rely on the profit maximization hypotheses of Adam Smith, behavioral science has sought to build a new theoretical understanding of organizational behavior. While management science dealt with the effective performance of physical profit-producing tasks, behavioral science has focused on human behavior, usually to the exclusion of concerns with task-effectiveness.

At the individual level, theorists have dealt with such issues as personality, change, learning, motivation, attitudes, and leadership; at the group level with norms, interaction patterns, group conflict, problem solving, and leadership; at the organizational level with communication between groups, intergroup conflict, organization structure, and the effects of participation on performance.[15]

An early and unique contribution to an understanding of organizational behavior was made by Chester Barnard. In *The Functions of the Executive*, published in 1938,[16] he laid much of the groundwork for the modern-day sociology of organizations as well as for the emerging general systems theory. He described the organization as "a system of consciously coordinated activities," and dealt with the relationship between the individual and the organization, the limits of decision-making, acceptance of authority, the overlapping of work groups, and the role of the informal organization.

Barnard's work has been followed by many distinguished researchers. To date, however, few of the results have been redefined for science-based technology. Most of them are couched in a specialized language of sociology (and not of management), on levels of abstraction which make it difficult to translate them into practical prescriptive models of behavior.

Much more influential has been a branch of behavioral science, called humanistic psychology, which takes the view that an individual's effectiveness within an organization is highly dependent on his self-awareness of his potentialities and limitations and on his ability to understand and relate to other humans. A large number of experiential behavior-modification techniques have been developed, the best known of which are T-groups (for individual self-actualization) and organizational development (for group building). The trouble is that humanistic psychology lacks both explanatory and predictive powers, and it offers no consistent theoretical explanations.

Nonetheless, the behavior-modification technology found easier acceptance in American industry than did management science. With its emphasis on "practical outcomes" through relatively simple and readily understood steps, the technology was congenial to the pragmatic tradition of American management. It appealed to the gregarious character of American social culture. Nor did it pose a threat of management obsolescence. On the contrary, it promised full development of the individual's potential and enhancement of his work and decision-making effectiveness. (The American experience is distinctive from the European, where for historical and cultural reasons behavior-modification technology was viewed with distrust and suspicion.)

Behavior modification is modified—and married to problem solving

Very recently, however, the popularity of the behavior-modification idea is beginning to decline. One reason stems from the fact that behavior-modification techniques have been focused on enhancing human attitudes and skills for what we have earlier called the competitive behavior of organizations—on cooperation, popular leadership, and compliance with prevailing social norms. As the demand for an entrepreneurial manager develops, it becomes increasingly apparent that an individual with a different behavioral profile is needed: an innovator, willing risk-taker, charismatic leader, self-actualizer, a loner who has the psychological strength to promote unpopular causes and live without social acceptance and approval.

A more immediate reason is simply that while this kind of "organizational development," as it is called, improves communications and organizational atmosphere, it usually fails to produce significant improvements in task-performance effectiveness.

The answer is just beginning to emerge. It appears to lie in a marriage of the behavior-modification technology with the branch of management science technology which concerned itself with techniques for rational (cognitive) problem solving.[17] The combination of the two holds the promise of a new behavior-modification technology that sets for its goal the development of integrated social-cognitive skills which will greatly enhance the decision making and problem-solving behavior of managers.[18]

Prospects for the future

As discussed in earlier sections, the advent of the Post-Industrial Era is characterized by the increasing interdependence of economic, psychological, social, cultural, and political variables. If management technology is to be responsive, a strong thrust toward a multidisciplinary approach is essential.

In the perspective of the preceding pages, it is apparent that both experiential and science-based management technology have lagged, rather than led, the priorities of management. They have helped managers solve their old problems better and more efficiently, but have not helped them to anticipate and prepare for new ones.

Such a lag is implicit in the nature of experientially-based technology, but is not necessary for the science-based. The lag of the latter has largely been due to the misplaced priorities of technologists, who, by and large, have sought a match between their scientific tools and existing problems, rather than seek out the important problems and develop appropriate tools. Put in somewhat exaggerated form, science-based technologists have been offering "solutions in search of problems."

The accelerating pace of change makes one fact quite clear: instead of lagging managers in the perception of problems, technologists must take the lead in anticipating them far enough in advance to develop solutions while the problems are still there to be solved.

Unfortunately, the economic success of the Mass-Production Era has produced self-satisfaction and euphoria among managers. The brilliant, if local, accomplishments of management technology have reinforced the scientist's conviction in the ultimate power of his method and have set up a powerful tendency to continue applying well-tested technologies, instead of seeking new ones. The bulk of the educational system today is focused on producing technology and training managers in the Mass-Production mold. There are stirrings of change, but how long it will take to move into the anticipatory and highly revelant mode of the Post-Industrial Era remains a major question.

Management in higher education

Peter Drucker has predicted that the Post-Industrial Era will cause the emergence of a society of knowledge workers. Daniel Bell contends that the university has replaced the business firm by becoming "the primary institution of the new society." Fritz Machlup reports that the production, distribution, and consumption of knowledge in America accounts for 30 per cent of the GNP. In addition, the production of knowledge alone is growing at twice the rate of the rest of the economy. The "industry" of higher education consists of 2,200 institutions with an annual revenue of $10 billion.

Faced with this new centrality, the institution of higher learning (IHL) is being forced to redefine its traditional role in society. For the past 200 years, universities and colleges have operated as closed systems, preserving a high degree of internal stability and deliberate *irrelevance* to the current problems of the environment. Frederick Rudolph, in his detailed history of American colleges and universities, referred to this policy as one of "drift, reluctant accommodation, belated recognition that while no one was looking, change had, in fact, taken place."

The recent tremendous growth and expansion in resource commitments to higher education, however, has created intense pressures for responsiveness to social problems. IHL's are being asked to perform their traditional functions more efficiently than before, to perform them for unprecedented numbers, and to accept new functions for which they have never been responsible (see Boyer, p. 150).

Yet traditional academic organizations have discovered that their capacities to respond to these environmental demands are inadequate. Years of incremental response have built up what sometimes appears as insurmountable inertia. Traditional decentralization of strategic decision-making authority has left chief administrators with little scope of influence for restructuring the institution and making it capable of effective response to change. This section will explore the reasons for this situation and discuss the managerial challenges which it poses for IHL's.

Management in IHL's has traditionally lagged
both business and government

In the past, both internal and external stability generated little survival pressure on the IHL. The need for management was minimal. As a result, there evolved a decentralized decision-making structure that was slow-moving and economically inefficient.

In the early organizational form, there was no separation of administrative functions from teaching functions. Whatever managing needed to be done was performed by members of the faculty. (When today many high-level administrators still teach.)

This organizational form was viable because of the simplicity of internal structure and low environmental survival pressure. The costs of maintaining academic organizations was a small proportion of GNP, and the sources of income were easily accessible. Great fortunes were being amassed, and universities and colleges became the recipients of large philanthropic donations. The value of higher education was unquestioned by society, so there was little or no attempt to subject the expenditure of funds to a market test. Within the organization, uncomplicated course schedules and small student bodies imposed minimal demands on management to be responsive to the needs.

In the final quarter of the nineteenth century, specialized administrative roles developed to handle increasing enrollments and the complexities of expanding curricula. Student personnel officers became responsible for the form and quality of student life; registrars began to cope with the massive paperwork which the adoption of the elective system imposed on the organization; and bursars became increasingly concerned with matching the organization's resources with its financial obligations. The attitude that the administration's role was to perform secondary service activity, rather than to give primary intellectual guidance, remained a basic characteristic of IHL's until the second half of this decade. Bureaucratic structure continued to expand in order to deal with nonacademic, administrative routine, but neither the nature of the adaptive response nor the role and the quality of management changed. Today, however, IHL's are being subjected to increasing societal and market pressures, which demand not only great improvements in economic efficiency but also major strategic adaptations as preconditions to survival.

Student disorders are symptoms of institutional failure to
keep up with the times

The Free Speech movement at the University of California Berkeley campus in 1964 was the first indication that the cumulative pressures of external environment, coupled with the inability of the internal mechanisms to manage change, had produced a systems failure. Administrators began to ask difficult questions which they had long avoided. And the answers revealed that the students were not the cause of institutional disorder, but only a symptom of institutional malaise which had accumulated over many years. Academic organizations which had grown into widely decentralized, multi-constituency settings left little scope for the managerial influence that could lead them in adapting and responding to the pressures of the changing times.

It is ironic that some of the most prophetic insights into the problems of the university were offered by an administrator who would bear the brunt of the first student disorder. Clark Kerr, then Chancellor of the University of California, delivered a series of lectures in 1963 that was later published under the title, *The Uses of the University*. In these lectures he discussed some of the threats that could confront IHL's in the near future. Others followed, and so the early 1960's became a time of self-analysis and reflection, and the latter half of that decade became the period of trial and experimentation.

What did the administrators discover during this period of self-analysis? Basically they realized that IHL's had been overtaken by changes in the environments which they had neither perceived nor adapted to. Enrollments had skyrocketed. In the last decade, the number of students attending IHL's doubled, going from 3.5 million to over 7 million.

The IHL—a huge knowledge factory without appropriate
management technology

The university was no longer chiefly responsible for providing knowledge in bucolic surroundings, but became huge knowledge factories with staggering budgets and monumental managerial inefficiencies (see Boyer's comments, p. 152).

Private universities encountered a widening gap between costs and available funds, and state universities were confronted with increasing budgetary pressures from legislatures. Available Federal support began to fall behind the demand for "soft-money" research programs, which had expanded rapidly in response to the needs of national priorities (defense, health, community needs), thus compounding the cost squeeze. Advanced management methods, such as program budgeting, seemed to be more useful for explaining causes of the ills than for finding cures. The complexity and inefficiency of growing operations, coupled with pressures for money-raising, increasingly absorbed the administrator's time. He ceased teaching and active research, thus becoming cut off from the faculty community.

His power for strategic decisions had also become severely limited. By their personal contacts in Washington, individual faculty members were able to attract hundreds of thousands of Federal dollars and thus commit the university to major strategic thrusts. Tenure protected the individual faculty member from administrative influence on the direction of his research and teaching. Thus, the power for determining the strategic thrusts of the university passed largely into faculty hands. A typical faculty's conception of its relationship to administration is that of a power conflict between bureaucracy and academic freedom. Attempts by the administration to influence academic affairs are regarded as an infringement on the prerogatives of the faculty.

Because of his primarily nonacademic pursuits, the administrator no longer had the time to spend with students and was, therefore, surprised and stunned when their discontent boiled over into confrontation. He had little power to respond on basic issues. Even if he had the power, he did not have the training. He was an "instant dean" or "instant president" or "instant department manager," often plucked from nonmanagerial, academic pursuits and plunged into complexities of administration that would frustrate the most highly trained manager.

ILH response to crisis: train the manager, use management technology

One important response is the growing concern with the training of educational administrators—in effect, management training. For example, both the University of California at Berkeley and the University of Michigan have centers for administrative research in IHL. Other universities have begun to sponsor workshops and seminars for college administrators. The American Council of Education has developed an internship program in which administrators with less than five years of experience spend nine months as participant-observers under the tutelage of a chief administrator on a campus other than his own. Most of the programs, developed with funds from the major foundations, have directed themselves to the present problems of in-service administrators. There is a parallel and equally urgent need to establish training programs for pre-service administrators before they are subjected to increasingly severe pressure which they will encounter on-line.

Within IHL's there is also a trend toward adoption of management technology from business and government. The increasing demand for accountability from state legislatures, the Federal Government, and the tax-paying public have necessitated more accurate record keeping. The program-planning-budgeting system (PPBS), instead of traditional line-item budgeting, is increasingly being used to satisfy both the public's need to know and the administrator's need for facts and figures for short-and long-term policy decisions. Computer simulation models have been an important development in planning for IHL's. An example of these models in CAMPUS (Comprehensive Analytical Methods for the Planning in University Systems), designed at the University of Toronto. The system simulates the interrelationship of major activities, considers a large number of variables, and then projects resource requirements based on the decision input of the programmer.

The proliferation of computers, EDP, systems analysis, PPBS, etc., have produced differing reactions. Many administrators suffer from "overkill" because of the towering amounts of data that these techniques are able to produce, and have questioned the need for such techniques. Very little attempt has been made to utilize these techniques for more than the clerical duties which they perform on most campuses. The trend is to accept them more for their vogue than for an insightful understanding of the sophisticated potential they have for providing relevant, vital information to high-level decision makers. Some administrators, like some of their counterparts in business management, are wary of allowing computers to do more than clerical bookkeeping and accounting for fear of the depersonalization of management.

Missing: entrepreneurial concern with
the thrusts and nature of the IHL ...

A survey of these responses leaves a strong impression that the predominant concern is with internal problems: accountability, cost controls, increase in operating efficiency, better resource allocation among existing programs, even divestment of some marginal academic and research programs. The management of these problems is within the power of IHL administrators, and the mass-production management technology offers many of the necessary tools.

What is missing is an address to the entrepreneurial questions about the thrust and nature of the university. Concern with the changed society and the university's role in that change is submerged in the reassertion of time-tested generalities—i.e., that the role of the university is to provide an environment in which each individual can satisfy his learning needs and find self-awareness, or that the role is to generate new knowledge. The crunching strategic questions that have caused riot and bloodshed on many campuses are avoided: *what* needs, *what* kind of self-awareness, *what* knowledge— knowledge to destroy the universe, to get to the moon, or to restore ecological balance? It has yet to be shown that the typical multi-constituency university of today has the abilities to overcome its collective inertia in coping with these questions.

... with one exception: the new and growing,
the democratic, community college

Significantly, the new strategies are being developed, not in established four-year institutions, but in community colleges. Community colleges are extensions of the junior colleges which underwent an identity crisis in the late 1950's. Until that time, junior colleges tried to prepare those whose academic credentials were not sufficient for entry into a four-year institution with two years of college level experience. After 1955, however, community colleges began to look at what they could do best which four-year institutions couldn't do, and they began to concentrate on these areas.

Personal counseling and vocational courses became their main concern. The community college looked toward the community in which it was located and away from the four-year institutions which it had been trying to emulate. Courses for senior citizens, for secretaries on lunch break, and for high school drop-outs were organized. By widely enlarging entrance requirements and tailoring the curriculum to the needs of the community residents, the community college has become the most truly democratic of institutions of higher learning in America. As a result these colleges have been able to attract more and more qualified teachers and to upgrade the academic level of their traditional curriculum offerings.

Still bigger challenges face the beleaguered IHL in the future

Beyond today's strategic challenges lie new ones in the future. The most obvious will be growth in enrollment, which will continue to increase at the same phenomenal rate of the past decade. University campuses will double and triple in size until they are forced to decentralize their facilities and give rise to Clark Kerr's "multiversity."

Rapid growth accentuates the already pressing problem of financing. Where will the dollars come from to support expanding facilities, new programs, and scientific installations? A report funded by the Carnegie Commission on Higher Education has observed that philanthropic and individual giving has decreased in the past decade. Larger foundations are allocating a higher proportion of their grants to social-need programs and cutting back on their gifts to IHL's. In addition, public reaction to campus disturbances has reflected itself in a legislative reluctance to increase educational budgets. Even without the reaction, the sheer growth and size of IHL's demands create pressures to contain them. While growth has been rapid, productivity increases in the education sector have been less than in any other sector of the economy. This fact, combined with a period of rising costs, means that the products of the educational system are becoming increasingly more expensive relative to other economic goods and services.

One possible answer lies in the capital-labor substitution made possible by advances in educational technology. The widespread use of educational television networks, the increased use of programmed teaching devices, and greater inter-institutional sharing of costly facilities should make higher education more capital-intensive.

However, IHL's still rely heavily on governmental support. The crucial question is the nature of the relationship between the IHL and the Federal Government. It is obvious that the Federal Government is the only institution available which has the necessary resources to maintain the current rate of expansion. An increased reliance on Federal funds has potential dangers for recipient academic establishments. To what degree can the national government heavily contribute without beginning to influence administrative decisions and thus subtly violating the cherished—and no doubt valuable—independence of IHL's?

Accompanying growth will be radically new products in education. Another Carnegie Commission report on higher education concluded that an increase in post-high school institutions below the college and university level will better serve educational needs than immediate accession to the university or four-year college. It should be made easy for an individual to drop out of the traditional four-year bachelor degree, as well as to return to it. Fast-paced technological society requires a shift of emphasis to continuing education from the present bachelor-master degrees. The latter should not be regarded as terminal points in individual personal learning careers, but only as milestones.

Will the present type of IHL fade gracefully—
or ungracefully—into obsolescence?

As noted, the administrative practice of colleges and universities has lagged far behind its business counterpart.

A benign environment, a peculiar institutional framework, and the nature of its technology, all combined to make the university a multi-constituency institution with widely decentralized strategic decisions and weak central administrations. The nature of the administrator's function was not conducive to the development of competent professional administrative cadres, similar to those in business management. The university evolved into what was, perhaps most successfully, an *un*managed cohesive and productive social organization. In this, it gained maximum freedom for the participating professional, at the cost of financial inefficiency and the inability for entrepreneurial response to social needs.

Much of management technology now available in the business sector can, and is, being applied to the university. It is, nevertheless, largely what we called mass-production technology, capable (within the peculiar institutional limits of the university) of improving efficiency and visibility of resource utilization, but inadequate to enable entrepreneurial response. Since the inefficiencies are so great and financial crises so pressing, there is a serious danger that preoccupation with financial efficiency will obscure the basic survival challenges which confront the university.

191

To address these challenges, the university needs to develop managerial capabilities that are not yet available in anyone's inventory of managerial technology. The central problem is not in educating entrepreneurial efficiency-minded managers, although these are needed. The problem is an restructuring the internal social fabric in ways that will enable the university to respond in nonincremental fashion to the discontinuities in the environment. It is not clear whether the solution will be found early enough to prevent the university as we know it today from being destroyed by violent confrontations, or whether the university will gracefully fade into obsolescence to be replaced by new and vital institutions.

Business vs. nonprofit organizations

Whenever an organization becomes so large and complex that voluntary co-operation and coordination among its members can no longer produce coherent and socially useful action, a need arises for an internal group devoted to the guidance and control of common behavior. In the business firm, this group is called management; in nonprofit organizations, administration. Over the years, each has created its separate art, technology, jargon, professional societies, and professional schools.

For reasons which have been explored in earlier sections, management has developed an image of the more professional, successful, sophisticated, and adventurous activity. Administration, on the other hand, has frequently been associated with routine, waste, inefficiency, and lack of responsiveness to its clients. Managers have had the status of respected, socially valuable entrepreneurs; administrators, that of wasteful unavoidable bureaucrats. Even as management is losing its "social centrality," there is an increasing demand for the application of "sound business principles" to straighten out "the mess in Washington," or in the ghetto, or in the city.

Business-management techniques have been advocated as the cure for the troubles of the government, hospitals, universities, and, more recently, the church. In some instances, such as in the application of PPBS to universities, the results are marginal; in application of the same technique to NASA's "race to the moon," the outcome has been spectacular, if not necessarily cost-effective. It is, therefore, not clear that indiscriminate transplantation of business management to other institutions will resolve or even address their important problems. An understanding is needed of the limits of its applicability.

In recent years, this understanding has become increasingly imperative. As society asks the nonprofit sector to address social problems in new and novel ways, nonprofit organizations increasingly need to exhibit entrepreneurial behavior not commonly found in administered bureaucracies. As an increasing fraction of social resources is diverted to "administered" institutions, effective application and efficient utilization of these resources become critical to national welfare. The peacetime cost-effectiveness of George Washington's army had minimal impact on the state of the Union. But today's $70-billion-a-year military-industrial establishment competes for resources with attempts to eradicate poverty, educational development, and improvement in the quality of the environment.

Is business management technology applicable
to other social institutions?

The purpose of the remainder of this chapter is to comment on the applicability of business management practice and technology to other social institutions. We shall look first at the comparative behavior of different organizations, and then at the commonalities and the differences of their managerial problems.

The business firm can be thought of as a member of a class of *purposive* social organizations, all of whom share these characteristics:

1. They deliver to society identifiable goods and/or services. They are rewarded for these in the form of sale price, university tuition, hospital charges, municipal water bill payment, and so on.
2. The goods and services are the result of an internal resource conversion process: "raw materials" are taken in (untutored student, sick patient); "value is added" to them by internal activities; and the final product is returned to society.
3. Because of their continuing need to replenish consumed resources, all purposive organizations need a consistently positive difference (called "profit" in the business firm) between costs incurred and the rewards received from the environment. If the difference remains negative for an appreciable period of time, the organization withers and dies.

The very fact that all members of a purposive organization (whether business or nonprofit) engage in activities directed toward a common output suggests that they pursue common objectives. The differences among organizations, however, are very significant.

In the *business firm*, the objectives are readily identifiable because they form the core of a common performance discipline. The focus is on the *outcome* of the activities, whether it be growth, profit, or market share. The performance against these objectives is measurable in quantitative terms and is usually measured through periodic reviews. New proposals for products, markets, or organizational changes, though not as easily measurable, are weighed in terms of their potential contribution to the objectives. A series of objective-setting techniques such as budgeting, management by objectives, and long-range planning is used in many firms. There are, of course, differences among firms in the extent to which they use the quantitative discipline of outcomes to run the business. Generally, firms that use it extensively are the more aggressive and successful ones.

The *nonprofit organization* resembles a less-aggressive business firm in its failure to use objectives as a management tool. The common agreement of the participants is not on common objectives but on the common *process* (e.g., curing patients, educating students, pursuing research excellence). Because nonprofit organizations are process-oriented, and because they lack quantitative measurements and techniques for evaluating outcomes, the performance discipline is usually lax and much less rigorous than in the business firm. This provides latitude for individuals to pursue their individual objectives simultaneously (though not always in accord) with those of the organization.

A case in point: the difficulty of applying advanced budgeting techniques

Enhancement of the effectiveness of resource allocation, as well as of performance efficiency through the quantitative discipline of objectives, has been the principal aim of PPBS (see Carey on use of PPBS, p. 78). It is not necessary to resolve the parentage of PPBS (whether it was brought by Mr. McNamara from Ford Motor Company or by Mr. Hitch from the RAND Corporation) to recognize that the application of PPBS tries to put nonprofit organizations on a "business-like basis." The failures and frustrations of PPBS in the government has been used to suggest that the nature of governmental activity does not lend itself to performance discipline. The extraordinarily disciplined performance of NASA in its rush to the moon, as well as a number of other special projects, suggests, on the other hand, that at least some parts of governmental activity do lend themselves to effective goal-focused management.

Perhaps, also, the the failures should not be charged to PPBS but to the fact that the technique was planted into unprepared ground, which lacked quantitative information, skilled analysis, necessary authority structure, appropriate motivation systems—all of which made PPBS akin to a foreign transplant which was bound to be resisted by the recipient body.[19]

Particularly revealing is the recent, hardly successful, rush to apply advanced budgeting techniques to university management. It isn't that the university doesn't badly need fiscal discipline; but putting expenditures in order, when the income sources are threatened and the product is becoming obsolete, will neither remove the threat nor rejuvenate the product. It will merely slow down progress on the road to bankruptcy. In a firm whose product line is obsolete, if a choice has to be made (and it usually doesn't have to be) between controlling expenses and devoting energies to development of new products and markets, the decision would be clearly in favor of the latter. By contrast, universities today are spending much more energy on endowment management and budget cutting than they are on revitalizing their role in society.

This is not an altogether deliberate misplacement of priorities. Good and tested budgetary management techniques are still scarce and poorly understood. Furthermore, entrepreneurial behavior implies major and discontinuous change in the over-all direction of an organization. This behavior is difficult enough in strongly purposive organizations where management can exercise strong guiding authority. It becomes very difficult in settings such as the university where entrepreneurial decision authority on major academic thrusts is widely decentralized throughout the faculty.

Rather than interpret the emphasis on budgets as a deliberate misplacement of priorities by university management, the explanation may lie in the lack of skills and of techniques for leading a multi-constituency organization through a major strategic realignment with the environment. To preserve sanity, lacking the power to initiate the most essential action, individuals tend to turn to the next most feasible task.

One can visualize a spectrum of purposiveness, with the business firm and highly monolithic governmental organizations (such as the armed forces and NASA) at one end, and with multi-objective, "multi-constituency" organizations (such as churches and universities) at the other. In principle, the performance discipline of quantified management by objectives is applicable across the spectrum, but one would expect application to be easier at the "uni-constituency" end.

*The business firm and the nonprofit organization must
learn from each other*

One can also visualize another spectrum along which purposive organizations can be arranged—a scale of environmental pressure. The business firm would tend toward one extreme, subjected to maximum pressure because of its primary dependence on market linkage and the higher intensity of pressure which that transmits, while nonprofit organizations would typically be under lower pressure to behave efficiently and to respond to environmental changes (with some notable exceptions, namely, NASA and the Post Office, which today are under greater societal pressure than many business firms).

Also, the question of cross-applicability of managerial capabilities is related to the organization's position on the spectrum. For example, a nonprofit organization that finds itself at the high-pressure end can use a high degree of business-like competence in both competitive and entrepreneurial management; but such competence would represent "overkill" in an organization whose environment permits steady unturbulent growth. The possibility of "underkill" is more real and potentially dangerous.

One danger is that well-developed and proven mass-production technology for handling marketing linkages may be inapplicable in an organization which needs to cope with its societal linkages. Thus, for example, techniques for influencing consumers through mass media have limited applicability in influencing budgetary decisions of the U.S. Government. Another danger is that, even when market linkages are at stake, competitive management may be applied in place of appropriate entrepreneurial techniques.

As we turn to the future, there is, on the one hand, a strong trend toward "publicness of private decision," as a result of increasing pressures on the firm through its societal linkages, and, on the other hand, a trend toward increased "privateness of public decision," as a result of pressures for entrepreneurial responses and for efficiency. As private organizations increasingly have to meet the societal test, public organizations will have to learn to meet the market test. The firm will increasingly have to cope with societal linkages; and nonprofit organizations, with market linkages. Thus, both will increasingly need to share the emerging Post-Industrial management abilities we described in earlier sections.

Management: the counterinertial force

Counterposed to the environmental pressure is an inertial tendency within the organization. It expresses itself in a resistance to change, a tendency to minimize response to the environmental pressures. Inertia is observable in all complex organizations, both profit and nonprofit. It is minimal in the birth stages when an organization is striving to establish and secure its linkages with the environment; it increases with age and maturity. It is more commonly observed in large organizations, but also appears in small mature organizations.

Its chief manifestations are a tendency toward routine, stable, or predictable behavior and the relaxation of internal performance discipline. A consequence is a low level of resource-conversion efficiency, such as is found in a business monopoly, a government department, or a university. There is also a tendency to stabilize interactions with the environment, to reduce environmental uncertainty, and to turn inward the focus of organizational attention. When this phenomenon occurs, individuals typically turn to the pursuit of personal goals, which often results in internal struggles and maneuvers for possession of critical resources, power, and prestige. Thus, a bureaucracy, which appears apathetic and change-resistant to its outside customers, may be a seething political cauldron within.

Because the business firm is under greater pressure and is forced to remain more active, its inertial tendency is less evident than in nonprofit organizations. One has only to observe mature entrenched monopolies, or firms in stable, slow-growing industries, however, to be convinced that nonprofit organizations do not have a monopoly on inertia. In fact, organizations show such a spread of differences in the degree of inertia and response to environment, both in the business sector and in the nonprofit sector, that there must be a very strong variable factor.

This variable is an internal *counter*inertial force called management (or administration). Management can affect organizational behavior in several different ways. At a minimum level, by increasing organizational awareness of the environment, it can control the "crisis gap" and enhance the probability of survival. Beyond that, it can increase the efficiency of internal operations, improve competitive behavior in the marketplace, and enhance the growth potential through new linkages with the marketplace. This role is accomplished through easily identifiable activities: setting of goals, anticipating changes in the environment, determining directions for organizational action, providing leadership, coordination, and assessment of action in pursuit of goals.

Key factors: (1) the applicability of managers' skills to
the particular culture . . .

There is a widely held view that the over-all quality of management is determined primarily by the quality of the managers. This view was valid in the days when firms were small and simple. Today in large and complex organizations, good managers are still critical but are only one of the factors determining the over-all quality. Of equal importance are the structure and process within which managers work. The total organizational capability is a complex vector of a number of different components, any one of which may be the weak link in the chain. Thus, for example, outstandingly qualified managers would produce bad decisions if given incorrect information by the system; they would produce uninspired decisions if the reward system failed to motivate them.

Another view which is widely held, "a manager, is a manager, is a manager," shows that his skills are generic and applicable across industries and institutions. A good business manager should be a brilliant success as a university president, a hospital administrator, or a head of a government department. In Table 1 (p. 36), we saw that the requirements for managers' skills, as well as the total managerial capability, change drastically from the environment of the Mass-Production Era to the Post-Industrial Era. Dramatic failures of attempts to transpose, without modification, American managerial culture to other lands, support this point. So do case studies of mergers and acquisitions where the managerial capability of the parent could not be applied successfully to the acquired firm.

Thus, in addition to quality, the success of a managerial capability depends on its applicability to the particular culture, technology, and problems and challenges confronting an organization.

*... and (2) match between managers' motivations and the
organization's reward system*

Within the over-all managerial capabilities, a critical contributor to success
is the match between personal motivation of the managers and the organizational reward system. Since the economists have constructed the model
of the profit-maximizing manager, the perception by outside observers has
largely been that managers seek primarily money, prestige and power. The
formal reward systems of the Mass-Production Era were largely focused on
these managerial aspirations.

Practicing managers, however, have long understood, and academic ones
have recently discovered, that additional and sometimes more powerful
motivators are a creative urge, a desire to make a difference, an excitement
of risk-taking, and the satisfaction of freedom to make choices and to act.
As pointed out earlier, the primary economic drives of managers are becoming saturated in the age of affluence. New reward systems are becoming
increasingly responsive to "higher" human aspirations. These freedoms have
been greater in private than in many public organizations because of the
traditionally larger degree of entrepreneurial freedom and turbulent environmental activity experienced by the firm.

A majority of governmental managers, on the other hand, have found
themselves in strategically stable environments and in institutions with
degrees of entrepreneurial freedom severely circumscribed by higher-level
policy makers. The policy makers, while enjoying the power of decision,
were frequently frustrated by remoteness from the "doing level" and an
inability to control performance and take credit for results. Thus, both the
doers and the policy makers have been denied the creative satisfaction of
being "one's own boss."

It is only in rare project-oriented activities, such as NASA or the Manhattan
Project, that entrepreneurial freedom and performance control have been
combined in one organization. More typically, nonprofit sector managers
enjoy this freedom only during the startup phases of new organizations.[20]
Once the organization reaches maturity, opportunities for the satisfaction
of creative drive become severely limited.

*Paradox: increasing need for change, but increasing difficulty in
effecting change*

As discussed previously, one of the characteristics of the multi-constituency
organization is a relatively great importance of the internally granted
authority, as compared with that which is externally conferred. In this
lies one of the major paradoxes of the Post-Industrial Era. As the firm
confronts new challenges, it must intensify its entrepreneurial involvement
with the environment. This involvement requires a major counteraction of

organizational inertia. But the basis of managerial authority is shifting from delegation from without to the internal "consent of the managed," thus increasing the inertia. The paradox, then, is that as the firm develops increasing needs for major changes, it will face increasing difficulties in overcoming resistance to these changes. The same paradox is already present in many bureaucratic nonprofit organizations confronted with new environmental entrepreneurial challenges.

In this connection, the convergence of problems and challenges among private, public, and voluntary organizations that we have observed throughout this discussion of purposive organizations may turn out to be a very favorable development—the convergence toward emphasis on entrepreneurial cost-effective behavior, on the one hand, and to more participative organizations, on the other. The hope is that all these types of organization will become increasingly alike, and will therefore be able to share and mutually reinforce emerging Post-Industrial managerial capabilities.

Management in the future

We have been looking at the effects of society's transition to a new era. Such transitions seem to occur when familiar value systems lose their validity and different new ones emerge in their place. Typically, the social infrastructure that evolved and adapted in response to the old challenges is not able to respond to new ones, short of drastic structural changes and dislocations. Thus, the transition is an "age of discontinuity" during which the environmental stimuli and the social infrastructure are realigned.[21] The realignment is never peaceful, always turbulent, sometimes violent. Traditional organizations decline, or are destroyed, and new ones emerge in their place.

A managerial perspective on the current age of discontinuity shows three major stimulus-respoose conflicts which define the work of managers in the coming years:

1. *Conflict between the rate of environmental change and the speed of organizational response.* While the rate of change is increasing, size, complexity, and geographic dispersion have been reducing the responsiveness.
2. *Conflict between the discontinuity of change and increasing organizational inertia.* While the environment increasingly poses discontinuous challenges, the new basis of participation and reduction of managerial authority are increasing inertia and reducing the capability for drastic realignment of organizational dynamics.
3. *Conflict between innovation and strategic steady-state.* Successful exploitation of environment requites a pattern of organizational capabilities and a managerial culture which is significantly different from the needs of entrepreneurial innovative behavior. The Mass-Production Era

perfected management of exploitative behavior. The Post-Industrial Era requires, not only a shift of focus to entrepreneurial behavior, but also a successful accommodation of both within a single organization.

In the business firm, in the institutions of higher learning, and in purposive organizations generally, the quality of management has been related to the quality of individuals that the respective institutions were able to attract. The business firm the United States has been in a fortunate position as the central and most prestigious social institution. As a result, it has benefited from managerial talent that made the firm of the Mass-Production Era into an outstanding success. The sister purposive institutions offered neither the challenge not the prestige of business. As a result, with brilliant exceptions, they had not had the benefit of outstanding managerial leadership.

The decline of social centrality of the firm in the Post-Industrial Era has started a "new ball game." We can increasingly expert the best young talent of the nation to turn its attention to managerial challenges of nonprofit institutions. The ability of the talented managers to influence their chosen organizations, however, will be limited by the freedoms for managerial action. These freedoms will be circumscribed, in part, by the historical development of the organizations, and, in part, by the environmental demands on them.

Historically, management of the firm enjoyed great freedoms of choice of the manner in which it related to the environment. The price of freedom was an almost total dependence for survival on the market forces. The sister institutions were both less free and less pressed by the environment, and, therefore, offered more limited opportunities for managerial leadership.

We must not let past successes blind us to future problems

As the Post-Industrial Era progresses, past managerial successes in conquering challenges of the Mass-Production Era become a deterrent rather than a stimulus to progress. Developed nations, other than the United States, not having the benefit of our success (the French, the Russians, the Japanese), have lets inertia born of past successes to contend with. If they are clear-minded enough to correlate our managerial hegemony to a past era, the chances will be good that they will focus their development on the new priorities and surge ahead of the United States. Perhaps the best act of self-serving chauvinism for the United States would be to initiate a massive managerial Marshall Plan—to inundate our friends and foes alike with boatloads of our mass-production managerial know-how while we focus development on management for the Post-Industrial Era.

If we were to do so, however, one major barrier, a major discontinuity in managerial know-how, would have to be crossed. Everything we said in this chapter about past managerial successes applies to *purposive* organizations.

These are organizations which are *single-constituent* in nature: their participants subscribe (by volition, coercion, or seduction) to a common set of organisational goals. But our analysis has repeatedly suggested that society's trend is toward *multi-constituency* organizations in which the common intersection of individual and group objectives is diminishing. While multi-constituency organizations are well recognized in descriptive theories, practical approaches to managing them are almost totally lacking.

The most common approach is to reduce a multi-constituency situation to a single-constituency equivalent—i.e., to require diverse factions to agree on a common set of goals. But the experience of many community-action programs shows that this aproach leads to conservative, inccemental, non-imaginative solutions that are unresponsive to demands of society. Hence, if social progress is not to be arrested and delayed by common denominator solutions, management art and technology will have to break out of its current uni-constituency perspective and move toward the much more difficult and challenging multi-constituency framework.

As society moves into the Post-Industrial Era, it brings with if the very impressive and successful management technology of the earlier era. Much of this will remain applicable as we carry our problems from one era into the next. But the past successes can obscure our vision of new problems, can invite us to rest on our laurels and make us blind to the urgent needs for new technology. The major practical and conceptual problems of management in the Post-Industrial society—little understood, much less formulated—must be the target of our efforts in the future.

Contributors

Helpful comments and inputs from the following members of the author's panel are gratefully acknowledged (the author, however, assumes full responsibility for choice of content and interpretation):

GENERAL A. J. GOODPASTER, Supreme Commander Europe, SHAPE
ULRIC HAYNES, JR., Senior Vice President, Spencer Stuart & Associates
SAADIA M. SCHORR, Manager International Planning, General Electric Co.

The author wishes to acknowledge important contributions by James Lowenthal, who aided in planning the paper and coauthored the portion on higher education; by Robert Schmid, who collaborated on material relating to management technology; and by Larry Kugelman.

Notes

1 Servan-Schreiber, *The American Challenge* (New York: Atheneum, 1968).
2 A. D. Chandler, Jr., *Strategy and Structure* (Cambridge: MIT Press, 1962).

3 John K. Galbraith, *The New Industrial State* (Boston: Houghton Mifflin, 1971).
4 H. I. Ansoff and R. G. Brandenburg, "A Language for Organizational Design," in E. Jantsch, ed., *Perspectives of Planning*, Proceedings of OECD Working Symposium on Long Range Planning, Bellagio, Italy, October–November 1968.
5 H. I. Ansoff, "The Evolution of Corporate Planning," SRI Long Range Planning Service, September 1967.
6 H. I. Ansoff, "Managerial Problem Solving," in John Blood, Jr., ed., *Management Science in Planning and Control*, Technical Association of Pulp and Paper Industry. Special Association Publication No. 5 (1969).
7 See *Business Week* articles on General Motors Fordtown Plant, March 4, 1972, pp. 69–70; March 25, 1972, pp. 46–49; also Judson Gooding, "The Accelerated Generation Moves into Management," *Fortune*, March 1971, pp. 101–104.
8 Hubert Kay, "Harnessing the R & D Monster," *Fortune*, January 1965, p. 160.
9 Alfred P. Sloan, Jr., *My Years with General Motors* (New York: Doubleday, 1963).
10 H. I. Ansoff and R. G. Brandenburg, "The General Manager of the Future," *California Management Reviews*, Spring 1969.
11 H. I. Ansoff, "The Innovative Firm," *Enterprise: Journal of the PE Consulting Group* (London), July 1967.
12 Ansoff and Brandenburg, "General Manager of the Future," op. cit.
13 *Ibid.*
14 Stafford Beer, *Decision and Control* (New York: John Wiley, 1966).
15 H. J. Leavitt, *Managerial Psychology* (Chicago: University of Chicago Press, 1964).
16 Chester I. Barnard, *The Functions of the Executive* (Cambridge: Harvard University Press, 1938).
17 See Ansoff, "Managerial Problem Solving," op. cit., and H. A. Simon, *The New Science of Management Decision* (New York: Harper & Row, 1960).
18 Andre Delbecq, "Management of Decision-Making within the Firm," *Academy of Management Journal*, December 1967.
19 Allen Schick, "Systems Politics and Systems Budgeting," *Public Administration Review*, March/April 1969.
20 J. G. March and H. A. Simon, *Organizations* (New York: John Wiley, 1958).
21 Peter F. Drucker, *The Age of Discontinuity* (New York: Harper & Row, 1969).

11

MANAGING STRATEGIC SURPRISE BY RESPONSE TO WEAK SIGNALS

H. Igor Ansoff

Source: *California Management Review* 18(2) (1975): 21–33.

If we could first know where we are and whither we are tending, we could better judge what to do and how to do it.

Abraham Lincoln, 1858

Everything (before the Arab oil embargo) is history . . . The future is a whole new game.

Irving Shapiro, Du Pont Company, 1975

Neither past experience nor academic training has prepared many younger managers for such reversal in the approach to business planning and operation.

John T. Hackett, Cummings Engine Company, 1975

The paradox of strategic military surprise has been a familiar phenomenon throughout recorded human history. From the Trojan Horse to Pearl Harbor to the Yom Kippur war, nations and armies have been confronted with sudden crises, in spite of ample information about enemy intentions.

The problem

The recent "petroleum crisis" was a comparable event in the industrial world: large and important firms were suddenly confronted with a major discontinuity, although advance forecasts of Arab action were not only publicly available, but on the day of the surprise, were to be found on the desks of some of the surprised managers. Because of its pervasive scope, the petroleum crisis highlighted the danger of strategic business surprises. But such surprises had overtaken numerous firms, one by one, from the early 1950s–enough of them to provide material for a *Fortune* book titled *Corporations in Crisis.*

In the aftermath, it was argued that these corporations were caught unaware because they lacked modern forecasting and planning systems. But in the 1970s a majority of the firms caught by the petroleum crisis had such systems. In the mid-1960s, the management of one of the world's largest conglomerates proudly displayed its planning and control. A week after the public display, the same management made a red-faced admission of two multimillion-dollar surprises: a major overrun in its office furniture division and another in its shipbuilding division.

The American automotive industry, a leader in modern planning and control, was certainly unprepared for the forceful congressional position on automotive safety. And a bare four years later it was again "surprised" by the success of the small car. Such events need little support from the voluminous literature on futurology to predict that discontinuities and surprises will occur with increasing frequency. If, as experience suggests, modern planning technology does not insure against surprises, the technology needs to be extended to provide such insurance. An exploration of such extension is the purpose of this article.

The nature of strategic surprise

Figure 1 plots, against time, the growth of a firm which can be measured by any one of the common yardsticks, such as sales, profits, or rate of interest (ROI). The middle line shows smooth extrapolation of past experience into the future. The two branching curves, a threat and an opportunity, show a significant departure, a *strategic discontinuity* from the past. In principle, such discontinuities can be anticipated by available forecasting techniques.

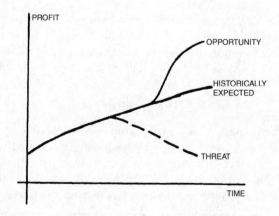

Figure 1 Impact of Threat/Opportunity.

Given enough warning, the firm should be able to avert the threat or seize the opportunity.

In fact, firms often fail to anticipate and suddenly discover that a fleeting opportunity has been missed or that survival of a product line is threatened. Typically, at the "moment of truth," neither the causes nor the possible responses are clear; the firm confronts an unfamiliar and often threatening event. Such events are *strategic surprises*: sudden, urgent, unfamiliar changes in the firm's perspective which threaten either a major profit reversal or loss of a major opportunity.

A firm that wishes to prepare for strategic surprises has two options. The first is to develop a capability for effective *crisis management*–fast and efficient, *after-the-fact* responsiveness to sudden discontinuities. A useful prototype is a firefighting company; unable to predict or control occurrence of fires, it prepares itself, through repeated practice, to respond quickly and effectively to a whole range of different alarms. The second approach is to treat the problem *before the fact* and thereby minimize the probability of strategic surprises–to prepare in such a way that a strategic discontinuity loses its suddenness, urgency, and unfamiliarity.

Both approaches deserve management attention: before-the-fact strategic preparedness because it is the more efficient approach, crisis preparedness because even the best advance efforts do not assume immunity from surprises. Each approach deserves full treatment; in this article, however, we shall limit our attention to before-the-fact strategic preparedness.

Limitations of environmental information

There is now a well-developed technology, called *strategic planning*, for converting environmental information about strategic discontinuities into concrete action plans, programs, and budgets. But to date strategic planning has had little success in dealing with surprises. One major reason is that strategic planning is overly demanding for input information. To be useful in strategic planning, information must satisfy two conditions. First, it must be available early enough to permit time for preparation of plans and programs. For example, a firm that takes five years to develop a new product needs a forecasting horizon of seven to ten years. Second, if strategic plans and programs are to be made, the content of the forecast must be adequate to permit the planners to estimate the impact on the firm, to identify specific responses, and to estimate the potential profit impact of these responses.

In both strategic planning literature and practice, an assumption is usually made that both timeliness and content conditions can be satisfied, that the forecaster can meet the needs of the planner. This expectation is not unreasonable when planning is concerned with "logical," incremental development of historical trends. Curves fitted to past experience can be smoothly extrapolated into a relatively distant future.

205

But when a potential surprise originates in an alien technology, with a previously unknown competitor, with a new political coalition, or with a new economic phenomenon, simple extrapolation will not suffice. In such cases these will be either discontinuous departures from past growth trends or, at least, sharp changes in the curvature of past growth curves. The firm planners can have longer range forecasts from the forecasters, but they must be willing to put up with content that becomes increasingly vague as the time horizon is extended. Or they can wait for originally vague information to become specific.

Thus, the recent phenomenon of stagflation is still imperfectly understood. The workings of the economy appear to have undergone a structural change which the economists have so far failed to explain. The simple question of when and how the current recession will come to an end has become difficult to answer except in very general and contradictory terms. In responding, firms have a choice of either basing their plans and actions on these generalities or waiting until the mechanism of recovery becomes clearer. Acting now implies taking risks on imperfect knowledge; waiting courts the danger of being late in important decisions that have long lead times, such as diversification, geographic expansion, and capital investment.

The timeliness of the firm's response depends on two variables: the rapidity with which the threat/opportunity, such as stagflation, affects the firm's growth and profits, and the amount of time needed by the firm to plan and effect the response. Since the 1950s these two variables have been on a collision course. The rate of environmental change has accelerated, and the firm's response has been made slower by growing size, complexity, and geographic diversification.

Thus, there is an apparent paradox: if the firm waits until information is adequate for strategic planning, it will be increasingly surprised by crises; if it accepts vague information, the content will not be specific enough for thorough strategic planning. A solution to this paradox is to change the approach to the use of strategic information. Instead of letting the strategic planning technology determine the information needs, a firm should determine what planning and action are *feasible* as strategic information becomes available in the course of the threat/ opportunity. Early in the life of a threat, when the information is vague and its future course unclear, the responses will be correspondingly unfocused, aimed at increasing the strategic flexibility of the firm. As the information becomes more precise, so will the firm's response, eventually terminating in a direct attack on the threat or an opportunity. But the prior buildup of flexibility will make this attack or opportunity occur earlier, and the attack will be better planned and executed.

We might call this *graduated response through amplification and response to weak signals*,[1] in contrast to conventional strategic planning that depends on strong signals. Such a practical method for planning a graduated response can be developed. The first task is to explore the range of weak signals that can be typically expected from a strategic discontinuity.

States of knowledge

The threat information typically required in strategic planning for evaluating the impact of threats/opportunities (TO's) gives the impression of being imperfect because of the uncertainties in both the occurrence and the probable course of the threat. A closer look shows that while uncertain, this is very *content-rich* information: the threat has to be well enough understood to compute the possible profit consequences, the responses well enough developed to estimate both their costs and their countereffects on the threat.

It is reasonable to expect this much knowledge from a threat/opportunity which arises from a familiar prior experience. This will be the case when a competitor introduces a new marketing approach, a new product, or a new pricing strategy. But when the T/O is discontinuous (such as the impact of laser technology on land surveying or of large-scale integration on electronic components), then in the early stages, the nature, impact, and possible responses are unclear. Frequently it is not even clear whether the discontinuity will develop into a threat or an opportunity.

Thus, when a threat/opportunity first appears on the horizon, we must be prepared for very vague information, which will progressively develop and improve with time. This progression may be characterized by successive *states of knowledge*. These are illustrated in Table 1, where level five, the highest state of knowledge, contains exactly the information required for strategic planning. Enough is known to compute both the probable profit impact of the discontinuity and the profit impact of the response.

At the other extreme, level one is the highest state of ignorance that can be of use to management. As the "No's" show, all that is known is that some threats and opportunities will undoubtedly arise, but their shape and nature and source are not yet known. In today's "political and economic fog of uncertainty"[2] many firms find themselves in exactly such a state of ignorance. Having experienced shocks of change in the recent past, managers are convinced that new ones are coming, but they cannot identify the source.

States of knowledge on level two improve matters somewhat. For example, in the early 1940s, it was generally recognized by physicists that solid-state physics had great potential for the electronics industry. But the invention of the specific discontinuity, the transistor, was still several years off. The source of the threat was clear, but not the threat itself. When the transistor was invented by Shockley and his team, the knowledge was raised to state three, but at the outset, the ramifications of the inventions were unclear, as were the defensive and aggressive responses that different firms were eventually to make.

Table 1 States of Ignorance Under Discontinuity.

States of Knowledge / Info Content	(1) Sense of threat/ opportunity	(2) Source of threat/ opportunity	(3) T/O Concrete	(4) Response Concrete	(5) Outcome Concrete
Conviction that discontinuities are impending	YES	YES	YES	YES	YES
Source of discontinuity identified	NO	YES	YES	YES	YES
Characteristics, nature, gravity, and timing of impact understand	NO	NO	YES	YES	YES
Response identified timing, action, programs, budgets can be identified	NO	NO	NO	YES	YES
Profit impact and consequences of response are compatable	NO	NO	NO	NO	YES

For those who wish to relate this to the terminology of statistical decision theory, we should note that the information in each state of knowledge may be certain, uncertain, or risky on the sense of definitions commonly used in the theory. The focus in the table is on illustrating the variability of content and not in the state of uncertainty. The dimension of uncertainty can by easily added of right to the table, thus creating a cube of possible states of information. In this cube, the states of information, treated in statistical decision theory, would be included in slice number 5.

When the firms developed and made the initial responses and knowledge was raised to level four, the eventual investments and profits were not yet visible. Pioneering firms were investing boldly into the new technology with little experience to guide them, in high hopes that their entrepreneurial risks would pay off. State five was not reached until knowledge of crystal yields and manufacturing process costs was sufficient to make reasonable predictions of the ultimate technology and its profitability. But by then the leaders were entrenched and those who originally held back had to pay a high cost of entry into the industry.

Practical threat/opportunity analysis

As indicated by the growing number of "Yes's" in Table 1, ignorance is reduced and information is enriched as a threat/opportunity evolves from state one to state five. As this evolution takes place, and as the management is trying to decide when and how to respond, the question of crucial importance is the time remaining before the impact on the firm passes a critical profit benchmark. For a threat this benchmark may be the level of loss beyond which the firm's survival is threatened; for an opportunity the point beyond which the cost of "climbing on the bandwagon" can no longer be recovered through profits.

Each threat and opportunity will pass through the respective stages of Table 1, some more quickly than others. Furthermore, each T/O will impact on different parts of the firm with varying strength. Therefore, we need a process for a systematic examination of T/O's and their impacts on the firm. The process described here is an extension of a well-known technique called *impact analysis*.

The first step is to compile a list of *strategic issues:* major environmental trends and possible events that may have a major and discontinuous impact on the firm. Today, most firms would list such issues as petroleum politics, stagflation, technology of energy generation, changing consumer attitudes, changing attitudes toward work, government regulation of business, and a growing demand for worker participation in decisions. Many of the strategic issues are shared by all firms, but each firm would find important issues which are specific to its industrial setting. Thus, firms in the automotive business would certainly add automotive safety legislation as a major strategic issue.

The second step is to estimate the impact of each issue on the firm. In the early days of strategic planning this was done by examining the impact on each self-contained organizational unit, division, or subsidiary. After a time it became apparent that unit-by-unit analysis gives a confusing picture of the future, particularly when a division has a number of product lines and operates in many markets.

Recently, an alternative approach has emerged which, instead of using an "inside out" organizational perspective on the firm's world, takes an "outside in" view. This is done by subdividing the environment into relatively independent *strategic business areas* (SBA's), each of which has distinctive trends, threats, and opportunities. (Recent strategic resource shortages, as well as sociopolitical pressures on the firm, focus attention on strategic resource areas and strategic influence areas. Thus, a complete analysis of threats and opportunities would include these two in addition to strategic business areas. However, we can illustrate the method of analysis by confirming our attention to the latter.)

For firms operating in a single homogeneous geographic area the SBA's will be synonymous with major product lines. But for geographically diversified firms, a geographic subdivision may be necessary. Thus, for example, a firm selling color television sets in North America, Europe, and South America would recognize three distinctive SBA's because of differences in the maturity of the markets, the political and competitive environments.

For firms whose product line is based on different technologies, a technological subdivision may be further necessary. If television manufacturers make both tube and integrated circuit sets, the respective products will have different growth prospects, stages of maturity, and strategic vulnerabilities in each of the geographic areas. Thus, to understand the future of the color television product line it may be necessary to construct as many as six significantly different SBA's.

Once the SBA's are identified, estimates are made of the impact of the strategic issues on each SBA. Four dimensions are: identification of the impact as a threat, or opportunity, or both; magnitude of the impact (measured by the probable range of loss or gain in the profit currently derived from the SBA); timing of the critical profit benchmark (using the range from the earliest to the latest possible moment); and identification of the present state of knowledge about the threat.

The precision and range of these estimates will depend on the state of knowledge. They will be more vague for emerging threats/opportunities and more precise for well-developed ones. Similarly, the methodology usable for estimation will vary. In lower levels of knowledge, simple judgment or expert opinion techniques such as Delphi will have to be used. In later stages, a variety of quantitative modeling and forecasting techniques become usable.

Table 2 shows the results of impact estimation through a simple example of a firm with one major threat/opportunity for each of its four SBA's.

Table 2 Threat/Opportunity Analysis.

Strategic Business Area	Profit Contribution	State of Knowledge				
		Sense Threat/ Opportunity	Source of Threat/ Opportunity	T/O Concrete	Response Concrete	Outcome Concrete
SBA$_1$	50%		Type of impact: Timing: Profit impact:	• T • 3.5 yrs. • 0.2–0.5		
SBA$_2$	30%	T/O 10–15 yrs. 0.0–0.2				
SBA$_3$	15%					Opportunity • O$_F$ generated • 1.2 yrs by the firm: • 2.5–3.0
SBA$_4$	5%	O 4–8 yrs. 2.0–5.0				
Status Environmental Awareness						

210

Immediately adjacent to the SBA column is the percentage of the firm's profit that it contributes.

As seen in the table, the range of the timing and profit impact estimates becomes wider as ignorance increases. Thus, the impact on SBA_2, which is ten to fifteen years off, may turn into either a threat or an opportunity, but it is clear that the impact is likely to be very serious. Clearly this discontinuity needs close watching. On the other hand, the profit estimates for the opportunity in SBA_3 can be estimated within a narrow range of both occurrence and impact.

Alternative response strategies

Just as we have expanded the states of information to include poorer knowledge, we need to enlarge the repertoire of responses to permit weaker responses. This is shown in Table 3, where management options are subdivided into two groups: responses that change the firm's relationship with the *environment* and responses that change the *internal dynamics and structure* of the firm. For each group there are three progressively stronger strategies: one that enhances the firm's awareness and understanding; one that increases the firm's flexibility; and one that directly attacks the threat/opportunity. Thus, the table provides a total of six response strategies.

The strongest *external action* strategy, as its name implies, mounts a direct counteraction against identified threats of opportunities. It proceeds through selection of the type of counteraction, preparation of programs and budgets, and implementation of the latter. The end result is a threat averted or an opportunity captured in the form of an enhanced potential for future profits. Selection of the best counteraction is the object of strategic planning.[3]

Table 3 Alternative Response Strategies.

Response Strategies / Domain of Response	Direct Response	Flexibility	Awareness
Relationship to Environment	External action (strategic planning & implementation)	External flexibility	Environmental awareness
Internal Configuration	Internal awareness (contingency planning)	Internal flexibility	Self-awareness

Internal readiness strategy matches the skills, structure, and resources of the firm to the demands of specific counteraction, creating a state of preparedness for external action. In strategic planning internal readiness is commonly referred to as strategy implementation, implying that preparedness must await selection of the course of action that it will support. The prescribed sequence is: strategic planning to internal preparation to action in the environment. But many of the preparedness measures can be successfully carried out in state three, as soon as the shape of the impending T/O becomes concrete and before strategic planning and external action become possible. Thus, the firm's response can be accelerated by reversing the sequence to internal preparedness to strategic planning to action in the environment.

The earliest possible response to an opportunity/threat is offered by the pair of *awareness strategies*, shown in the right column of Table 3. In most firms a degree of environmental awareness is provided through economic forecasting, sales forecasting, and analysis of competitive behavior. But all of these measures are extrapolative, based on a smooth extension of the past into the future, and do not provide information about strategic discontinuities. To broaden the awareness to include discontinuities, the firm must add special types of environmental analysis, such as environmental monitoring, technological forecasting, sociopolitical forecasting, and threat/opportunity analysis. Starting all of these activities in the firm requires no concrete information about threats/opportunities. Thus, the highest state of ignorance, a sense of threat, is adequate to justify a program for enhancing the firm's environmental awareness. A sense of threat is also adequate for starting many of the self-awareness measures, such as capacity audits, strength/weakness analysis, and financial modeling of the firm.

The *flexibility strategy* shown in the middle column of Table 3 differs from the direct action strategies in that its end product is an enhanced *potential* for the firm's future, rather than tangible changes in profits and growth. The *external flexibility* substrategy is concerned with positioning the firm in the environment in a way that satisfies two criteria: satisfactory *average potential* for profitability over the long term and adequate diversification of the firm's position to assure *coping with deviations* from the expected average-capture of attractive major opportunities and minimization of catastrophic reversals.

Formulation of the external flexibility strategy (commonly known as position strategy) is part of the strategic planning process, where it is usually assumed to require level-five information input. But measures such as balance of technological, business, and political-geographical risks can be substantially planned *and implemented* if the state of knowledge is no better than level two, long before the nature of the threat becomes concrete.

Logistic flexibility is concerned with configuring the resources and capabilities of the firm to permit quick and efficient repositioning to new products and new markets, whenever the need arises. One important element is the flexibility of the managers, including awareness of the environment, psychological readiness to face unpleasant and unfamiliar events, ability to solve unfamiliar problems, and creativity. Another element is the flexibility of the managerial systems and structure to permit expeditions and flexible response to change. A third element is the flexibility of logistic resources and systems–resource liquidity, diversification of work skills, modular capacities, and so forth.

Unlike external flexibility, *internal flexibility* received relatively little attention from strategic planners. But recent history shows it to be a crucial ingredient in strategic preparedness. In the area of managerial flexibility, the preparation of managers for strategic thinking and action is now recognized as essential and vital if the firm is to anticipate and deal with the growing turbulence of the environment. Without it, efforts to introduce strategic planning typically encounter strong resistance to planning.

Flexibility of the logistic resources has received even less attention than managerial flexibility. A major reason is the fact that the idea of flexibility runs contrary to the fundamental principle of the Industrial Age, which holds that maximum profitability is to be gained through the maximum possible specialization of facilities and machinery and through largest possible capacity, maximum capital-labor substitution, and longest possible production runs.

Application of this principle invariably leads to special-purpose, capital-intensive investments. In the recent past principle-maximum specialization has been repeatedly compromised when expensive specialized factories were made prematurely obsolete by unexpected technological changes or when the length of production runs was cut short by shrinking product life cycles. In the coming years, as strategic change accelerates, logistic flexibility will become increasingly important. As with external flexibility, the mere knowledge of the sources of threats/opportunities is sufficient to start a rigorous program of logistic preparedness.[4]

The preceding discussion shows that if management is receptive to weak signals, much can be done long before the threat becomes tangible and concrete. The possibilities are summarized in Figure 2, in which the shaded portions represent the areas of feasible response. As seen in the figure, all of environmental awareness measures, all of internal flexibility, and a substantial portion of external flexibility can be put in place before the threat becomes clear and definite. In our earlier example, this means that electronic component manufacturers could have attained a high state of readiness for coping with the transistor before the transistor was invented!

As Figure 2 shows, for direct response strategy it is necessary to have a good idea of the threats that one is proposing to attack. But even here, a sufficiently clear idea of the origin and shape of a threat is sufficient to launch a substantial percentage of internal readiness measures, including

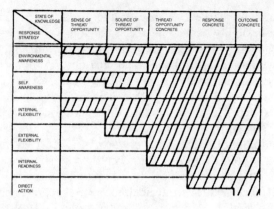

Figure 2 Feasible Ranges of Response Strategies.

acquisition of necessary technological, production, and marketing skills, new product development, and development of sources of supply.

Even direct external action need not, and *in practice frequently does not*, await information that makes possible reliable cash-and profit-flow calculations. This is where entrepreneurial risk takers become differentiated from cautious followers. Adventurous firms will typically launch their entry into a new industry at level four, before the technology, market, and competition are well enough defined to permit such calculations. More conservative firms will prefer to wait on the sidelines until the "ball game" is better defined.

Dynamics of response

Each of the six response strategies makes a complementary contribution to the firm's ability to handle strategic discontinuities. Each requires a different length of time for implementation. The total length of time for mastering a particular threat/opportunity depends on the prior preparedness of the firm, the vigor with which the firm responds, and the sequence in which the respective strategies are put in place.

As mentioned previously, conventional strategic planning proceeds from direct response, to flexibility, to awareness. Figure 2 and preceding discussion suggest that the reverse sequence–awareness to flexibility to direct response–enables the firm to start response much earlier, and finish earlier, utilizing weak signals. Figure 3 illustrates the dynamics of the firm's response, using this latter sequence. The vertical scale shows the time needed by the firm to complete the response, that is, to eliminate or stabilize operating losses or to make viable a new opportunity. The horizontal scale lists the states from which it may start. The curves show the obvious advantage of prior readiness: the better prepared the firm when it starts, the less time it will need to complete the response.

214

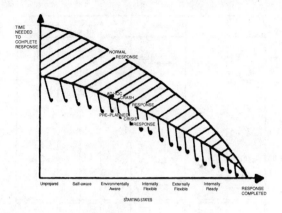

Figure 3 Dynamics of Internal Response.

The upper curve of Figure 3 traces the *normal response* in which the threat/opportunity is treated routinely by existing processes, structure, systems, and procedures. The lower solid curve, the *ad hoc crash response*, shows the time savings that can be effected when everything possible is done to speed up the response–normal rules and procedures are suspended, other priorities are pushed into the background, organizational lines are crossed, activities are duplicated, overtime is incurred, and so forth.

The mere "pulling out of the stops," implying an ad hoc improvisation when a crisis looms, is not the only emergency procedure open to the firm. If, in spite of best efforts to anticipate threats/opportunities, the firm still expects to be confronted with sudden, fast-developing threats, investment in a program of training in *crisis management* is worthwhile in much the same way that a firefighting company invests in a capability to fight unexpected types of fires. The result will be to lower the response time required to the level labeled *preplanned crisis response*, thus increasing the capability for handling strategic surprises.

The envelope of response times defined by the three curves in Figure 3 will of course differ among firms and from one discontinuity to another. Size, complexity, and rigidity of structure will lengthen the response times, and the nature of the threat/opportunity will be equally influential. Important factors will be the size of the discontinuity as well as its degree of unfamiliarity, both of which determine the magnitude of the response effort. Thus, again, a procedure is needed that will translate the theoretical curves of Figure 3 into practical application.

Practical preparedness diagnosis

Reference to Figure 2 shows that the respective states of knowledge will differ from SBA to SBA. Consequently, the range of possible responses

	Feasibility	STATUS	Relative import	Crash		Normal	
				Time	Cost	Time	Cost
Self-awareness	F	0% ___ 100%	VH	3		6	
Environmental awareness	F		H	1		2	
Internal Flexibility	F		M	2		4	
External Flexibility	F		L	4		8	
Action Readiness	F		M	2		4	
Action	1		VH	2		4	
Completed Response		0% ___ 100%		4 Yes	4.0	8 Yes	1.0

Figure 4 Preparedness Diagnosis: SBA_1.

will also differ. Thus, the first step is to determine the feasible responses for each SBA-threat/opportunity combination.

Continuing with the example of Table 2, we have chosen SBA_1, which had a single, clearly visible threat (T/O concrete stage). A reference to the feasibility table of Figure 2 shows that five of the six response strategies are feasible in this advanced stage of information. This is recorded as "F" or "I" (infeasible) in the second column of Figure 4.

The next step is to diagnose the firm's current state of readiness in each of the feasible strategies; the result is shown in column three of Figure 4. Letting 100 percent represent the maximum that can be done to respond to the T/O in the current state of ignorance, the entry is an estimate of the current readiness in each of the categories.

The roughly 15-percent entry for self-awareness suggests that, while the threat is concrete enough, the firm has done relatively little to determine the usefulness of its own capability for dealing with the threat. This might have been the case in the example of a vacuum tube firm which, having learned about the existence of the transistor, has not made the effort to analyze that applicability of its technology and organization to the emerging transistor industry. On the other hand, that firm appears to be well advanced in understanding the market, the potential competition, and the future of the transistor.

To continue with the example, the low rating on the internal flexibility shows that the firm's resources and facilities are highly specialized, and external flexibility shows that the firm's profits are largely dependent on its vacuum tube business and that it is therefore threatened by new technology.

The next and critical step is to estimate the time the firm will need to carry the state of readiness to 100-percent level for each of the preparedness

216

categories. The estimate is made category by category for both normal and crash responses. In the last line of Table 2 a summary estimate is made of four to eight years for completed responses. In our example this might have meant divesting from the vacuum tube SBA, narrowing to a market in which the tube will continue to be competitive, or making a successful entry into the transistor business.

The final step in readiness diagnosis is to estimate the cost-effectiveness of the total response. The cost of the response is shown in the last line of the table as a fraction of the percentage of current profits contributed by the SBA (see Table 2). If, as shown in Figure 4, a crash program will cost four times the current contributed profits, and if the response will prevent a loss of 0.2 to 0.5 of this profit, the investment will amortize itself in eight to twenty years. The cost-effectiveness is low, which suggests that the threat be written off and allowed to run its course. On the other hand, the normal response (if it turns out to be timely enough), costing 1.0, will be cost-effective, because the amortization period will be only two to five years.

Opportunity-vulnerability profile

The preceding discussion suggests two conclusions. First, the decision to respond should not be based on response costs alone, nor on the amount of profit loss or gain that is at stake. Rather, it should be based on the return on the costs incurred. We used the simple but useful payback measure of this return. With better data (particularly in the advanced states of knowledge), other measures can be employed. By doing this, "throwing of good money after bad" is avoided, especially when the threat looms large and the temptation is to attack it, no matter what the costs.

Second, the selection of the counteraction, in the range between normal and crash response, cannot be made independently of the timing of the threat. A comparison of the timing is provided by the opportunity-vulnerability profile, shown in Figure 5, which combines the results of the threat/opportunity analysis and the readiness diagnosis. The respective shaded rectangles enclose the "regions of probable impact" on the respective SBA's. Rectangles below the horizontal axis spell potential losses in profitability due to threats; those above indicate gains offered by opportunity. The height of the rectangle spans the probable range of loss/gain, the base spans the probable times when the discontinuity will reach the critical benchmark level of the firm. Both dimensions are obtained from the threat/opportunity analysis in Table 2.

The horizontal dotted lines in Figure 5, obtained from the readiness diagnosis (Figure 4), span the time of probable completion of successful response. Thus, the normal response for SBA_3 would be late, but the firm can assure itself of capturing the opportunity through a crash program. SBA_2 is "safe"; normal response will capture it, provided the firm continues

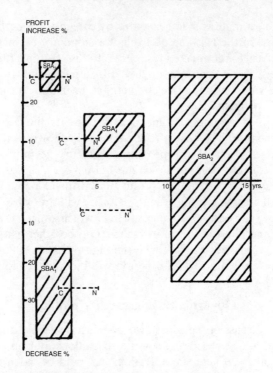

Figure 5 Opportunity-Vulnerability Profile.

to monitor the development of the contingency. SBA$_1$ is in trouble because even a crash response may be late; it looks like a "surprise" in the making.

These examples show that timing of the threat does not by itself determine the priority of the respective responses. The priorities are determined in part by the *urgency* derived from comparing the timing of the threat with the time needed for response. Thus, in our example, both SBA$_1$ and SBA$_3$ are expected to reach critical impact at about the same time. But, because of the longer response time needed, SBA$_1$ must be handled on an all-out crisis-response basis, while a moderately urgent response will suffice for SBA$_4$. The priorities also are determined in part by the potential *cost-effectiveness* of the responses determined in the manner discussed in the preceding section.

The opportunity profile also provides an overall perspective of significant strategic changes in the firm's future. The firm needs to check the impact of SBA$_1$, because if unchecked, a minimum of 15 percent and a maximum of 40 percent of the profit will be lost. Since, at best, timely arresting of this threat will be difficult, the crash response must be used. The firm also must make an effort to capture the opportunity in SBA$_3$, as an offsetting insurance. Further, if the firm wishes to capture the attractive opportunity in SBA$_4$, it needs to start right away to avoid a crash response later. Only SBA$_2$ seems to call for no immediate aggressive action. But its potential impact is so great that a vigorous monitoring program should be spotlighted on the strategic issues that give rise to this T/O.

A system for managing strategic issues

Selection of one response cannot be made independently of others, because they all lay claim on the time, managerial energy, and financial, human, and physical resources of the firm. The totality of the T/O's must be considered, in light of the continual changes in the environmental challenges, threats, and opportunities. And, given the evolving state of knowledge in each of them, the totality must be considered in a dynamic, changing perspective. Consideration of this totality should be made a part of a flexible and responsive management system. Such a system, which we shall call a *strategic issue management system* (SIM), is shown in the somewhat complicated Figure 6.

The upper part of each box identifies the involvement by four groups of actors: the planning staff, general management, task forces (drawn, as necessary, from all parts of the firm), and operating units. The lower part of the box describes the function performed in the successive stages of the process: the planning staff detects, tracks, and analyzes strategic issues; general management keeps up to date the list of important strategic issues, assigns specific issues for planning, approves the plans, and monitors the execution; and task forces and/or operating units plan and execute specific projects.

One distinctive feature of strategic issue management is its organizational flexibility. The general management groups involved may be the top management in small or medium-sized firms or several groups scattered through a large corporation. Both the planning and implementation of strategic issues are determined not by the organizational structure but by the nature of the problem involved. Whenever a problem cuts across organizational units or requires special attention, ad hoc ask forces are set up. The same task force may plan and execute, or the executive may be assigned, in part or in whole, to the permanent organizational units.

Another distinctive feature, not readily evident from the figure, is the *reul time* character of the process. It follows no fixed planning calendar; rather, the surveillance is continuous, strategic issue list updating is both periodic and triggered by appearance of major T/O's, and planning execution is ongoing throughout the year, with completed projects being succeeded by new ones.

A third distinctive feature, because the system responds to weak signals, is the special attention to the two different types of feedback shown in Figure 6–operating and strategic. The results obtained from executing the project are interpreted in two ways: first, to judge whether the programs and

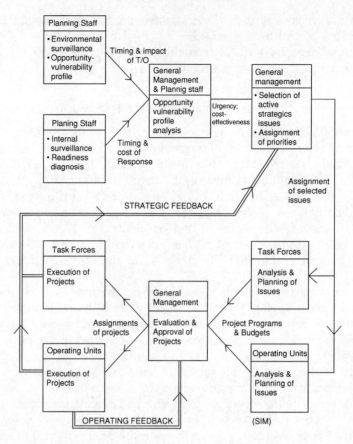

Figure 6 Strategic Issue Management System.

budgets are being followed (the operating feedback); and second, to determine whether the strategic issue has been well identified, whether it deserves the priority assigned to it, and whether the action strategy has been well chosen (strategic feedback).

When the issues arise from vague incipient trends, strategic feedback dominates and guides progressive redefinition of the response. In later stages of T/O, the focus naturally shifts to operating feedback. Thus, the *gradual response permits gradual commitment on the part of the management.*

Finally, strategic issue management is an action, and not a purely planning, system. The results of implementation feed directly back to management groups that originally selected and authorized the issues. Planning and implementation are not separated. An issue is not "resolved" until it is dropped from the list or concrete changes are produced in the profitability and growth of the firm.

Strategic issues and strategic planning

Strategic issue management is an expansion and extension of a planning technique of strategic issue analysis, which has emerged in practice in the past few years. Our expansion has been to admit weak signals as a basis of decision making, and the extension was from a purely planning to a total action system.

Strategic issue management overcomes a basic shortcoming of the strategic planning technology which has become increasingly evident in practice–the inability of strategic planning to handle quickly and efficiently individual fast-developing threats and opportunities. The reasons for this are several: the dependence of strategic planning on strong signals, which delays the recognition of a strategic issue; the rigidity of the planning calendar, including six- to nine-month delays between initiation and completion of the planning cycle; and organizational inflexibility of the strategic planning system, which cannot effectively handle strategic issues that simultaneously affect more than planning units. When an issue fails to fit into the perspective of a single unit, both its planning and implementation tend to "fall between the chairs."

In summary, preoccupation with system and organizational dynamics of the planning process leads to an inability to cope with the dynamics of rapidly developing threats and opportunities. In computer terminology, strategic planning is an off line process as compared to the real time character of strategic issue management. But in return for the real time responsiveness, strategic issue management incurs the penalty of lack of comprehensiveness. It is essentially an opportunistic approach that fails to capture the totality of the firm's future perspective. An examination of the strategic issue list reveals the potential threats and opportunities, but it offers little information about where the firm as a whole is headed.

If, for example, all of the firm's SBA's are in the state of maturity or decline, it is dangerous to use strategic issue management without adjoining strategic planning to it. SIM will focus attention on dealing with contingencies, whereas the need is for a fundamental realignment of the firm's strategic thrust. Thus, strategic issue management is a complement, rather than a replacement for strategic planning. The salient features of each are summarized in Table 4, which shows that the choice of one or the other, or both, depends on the strategic environment of the firm.

1. A firm that is in a relatively surprise-free environment, but whose basic business prospects are unsatisfactory because of market saturation, technological obsolescence, or change in the structure of demand, needs to engage in comprehensive strategic planning. A firm that seeks large-scale diversification from a position of strength would do likewise; so would a firm that needs a fundamental rebalance of its strategic business areas.

2. A firm whose growth prospects appear satisfactory, but whose environment is strategically turbulent, may confine itself to strategic issue

Table 4 Comparison of Strategic Planning and Strategic Analysis.

Strategic Planning	Strategic Issue Analysis
Deals with firm's total strategy	Deals with probable discontinuities
Focused on products-market-technology	Embraces discontinuities from all sources
Applicable when major strategic reorientation is desired	Applicable when insurance against surprises is desired
Responds to strong signals	Responds to weak signals
Strategic information needs dervied from decisions	Feasible decisions determined by available information
Prepared periodically	A continuous process
Organization-focused	Problem-focused

management. Today this would apply, for example, to the ball bearing industry, where Japanese competition is changing the market structure, the computer industry, where technology is changing rapidly, or the pharmaceutical industry, where both technology and societal relations are turbulent.

3. Firms that face both a fundamental realignment of the strategic thrusts and a turbulent, surpriseful environment would benefit from combining both strategic planning and strategic issue analysis into a comprehensive strategic management system.[5]

Anticipating resistance to planning

In the preceding pages we have developed a conceptual framework and a practical procedure by which a firm in a turbulent environment can cope with weak signals, thus minimizing the chances of surprise. The result is a new planning approach, which must be accepted and used by practicing managers to become effective. However persuasive and practical the approach, neither its acceptance nor its use can be taken for granted. To do so would be to disregard the numerous instances when similarly logical approaches encountered resistance to planning and were either rejected or emasculated by the using organizations.

To gain acceptance for this particular approach, it is necessary to assure within the firm a climate of openness to strategic risk and preparedness to face unfamiliar and threatening prospects. The creation of such a climate of strategic decisiveness is as complex and difficult a problem as the one discussed here. Therefore, we have explored decisiveness in two separate articles.[6,7]

These articles argue that management in most firms lacks the necessary strategic decisiveness to accept a system such as strategic issue management or genuine strategic planning. An attempt to introduce such a system is highly likely to encounter resistance and possible rejection. In a strategic crisis, strategic thinking and action will be the last resort, after historically successful operating remedies have been exhausted.

Enhancing strategic decisiveness involves making changes in decision-making technology, systems, information, distribution of power, and above all, in the risk attitudes and values of managers who are key to the strategic response. Thus, strategic decisiveness is an organizational state of mind–a culture–as well as a distinctive competence. The process of cultural change is difficult and requires special understanding and skills. But technology for inducing organizational change exists, has been described in voluminous literature, and has been successfully tested in practice.[8]

In the application of this technology, a typical "chicken and egg" problem arises: should strategic decisiveness be built up first, or should the new system be introduced? In most cases it is possible to join the two change processes in a single program of organizational transformation in which the new system and the new problem-solving skills are used as a vehicle for bringing about behavioral changes.[9]

References

1 W. W. Bryant (Manager, TEO Central, Phillips, Eindhoven, Holland), personal communication.

2 Leslie Smith (Chairman of the BOC Limited, London), personal communication.

3 For each of the six response strategies, a series of alternative types of counter-actions can be enumerated. See H. Igor Ansoff, "Managing Surprise and Discontinuity: Strategic Response to Weak Signals," Working Paper 75–21 (April 1975), European Institute for Advanced Studies in Management.

4 A detailed listing of possible measures for external and internal awareness, as for external and internal flexibility, can be found in Ansoff, op. cit.

5 One of the potential byproducts of such combination is an acceleration of strategic planning processes; see Ansoff, op. cit.

6 H. Igor Ansoff, J. Eppink, and H. Gomer, "Management of Surprise and Discontinuity: Problems of Management Decisiveness," Working Paper 75–29 (July 1975), European Institute for Advanced Studies in Management.

7 H. Igor Ansoff, "Enhancing Managerial Decisiveness in the Face of Strategic Turbulence," forthcoming.

8 H. Igor Ansoff, R. Hayes, and R. Declerck, "From Strategic Planning to Strategic Management," in *From Strategic Planning to Strategic Management* (London: John Wiley & Sons, 1976).

9 Pierre Davous and James Deas, "Design of a Consulting Intervention for Strategic Management," in *From Strategic Planning to Strategic Management*, op. cit.

12

H. IGOR ANSOFF

J. I. Moore

Source: J. I. Moore, *Writers on Strategy and Strategic Management: The Theory of Strategy and the Practice of Strategic Management at Enterprise, Corporate, Business and Functional Levels*, Harmondsworth: Penguin, 1992, pp. 15–33.

Igor Ansoff is one of the most influential figures to have appeared in business education in the last quarter of a century. His career has been characterized by a variety of academic posts on both sides of the Atlantic, a stream of papers and books – many written in co-operation with others, and a steady widening of the range of issues he has addressed, to the point where it might be thought he was attempting to develop a general theory of management. As this extension of his interests has taken place, he has not hesitated to press into service techniques, concepts and terminologies from a gallimaufry of disciplines – sometimes to curious effect. And his prolific output is unusual not just for the originality of some of his ideas, but also because of an engaging candour about those which have proved to be either flawed or impractical.

More than most of his fellows, Ansoff has an acute historical sense which he frequently reveals when giving perspective to his work. In looking at the US business scene, for example, he has divided the period from 1820 to the present day into three eras: mass-production, mass-marketing, and post-industrial – a term he adopts, after Daniel Bell, and prefers to P. F. Drucker's 'Age of Discontinuity'. This type of classification has enabled him to explain the changing, though largely internalized, preoccupations of business managers and their academic conternporaries up until the mid 1950s, when he believes the last era began. And it has additionally served to justify, almost as a matter of historical inevitability, the existence of our fascination with 'strategy' and everything 'strategic' – for which, to no small degree, he is responsible.

But what do these terms denote, in Ansoff's scheme of things?

In what is still his most popular book, *Corporate Strategy* – published in 1965 – he distinguishes four basic types of decision: strategy, policy,

Condition	Alternatives	Probabilities
Risk	Known	Known
Uncertainty	Known	Not known
Partial ignorance	Not known	Not known

Figure 1

programme and standard operating procedure. All but the first address recurring contingencies, such as the needs to organize overtime working, or prepare for bad weather. Once formulated, they obviate the requirement for an original decision every time additional work is called for, or it snows – for example. They thus assure consistency of action, realize what Ansoff calls 'economies of management', and, because of their characteristics, can be safely delegated to subordinate managers for execution.

Since these three types of decision deal with events which recur, much is known about the latter. It is, therefore, possible to identify all the alternatives and assign probabilities to the occurrence of each one. This approach, which Ansoff derives from the 'mathematical decision theorists', furnishes him with the typology given in Fig. 1.

It also enables him to rank his decision-types in the order of an increasing level of ignorance. At the bottom is the standard operating procedure, which addresses the most often occurring – and therefore the best known – events. This is closely followed by the programme, which is 'a time-phased action sequence . . . to guide and co-ordinate operations'. Ansoff associates both with 'conditions of certainty or partial risk'. Next are policy decisions. These are made in conditions of risk or uncertainty. And finally we have strategies, which are 'forced under conditions of partial ignorance'.

As can now be seen, a strategy is quite different to the other three types of decision. Because it is subject to the conditions of partial ignorance (where 'alternatives cannot be arranged and examined in advance'), it is not a contingent decision. Indeed, it is a decision rule: that is, it is 'a rule for making decisions'. And as such its implementation cannot be delegated downward, 'since last-minute executive judgement will be required'.

Having defined the noun (strategy), there should – one would think – be no trouble over its related adjective (strategic). But unfortunately, as Ansoff acknowledges, there is. One of Ansoff's most singular contributions to the subject has been his notion of decision classes – which we shall come to in a moment. The first of these he has called 'strategic': where this means 'relating to [the] firm's match to its environment'. Since strategies (along with standard operating procedures, programmes and policies) find a place in each of the decision classes – after all, partial ignorance can prevail anywhere – he cannot use 'strategic' in the other two decision classes where there is a condition of partial ignorance *but no firm/environment match issue*.

He resolves his linguistic dilemma by telling us that, since conditions of partial ignorance are dominant in the strategic decision class area (though not in the other two), 'the use of similar terminology is not entirely inappropriate'. But it is a resolution he, himself, is not entirely satisfied with: because, in a footnote to the same page, he adds, 'Perhaps a better term [for strategic] would have been *entrepreneurial*.' It is a thought which has a profound effect on his later work – as we shall see.

In describing how Ansoff initially construed 'strategy' and 'strategic', we have introduced – in passing – his decision class concept, and some of his ideas about what is conventionally covered by the umbrella term, risk.

Unlike financial theorists, who think of risk as being related to the variability of return on investment,[1] Ansoff – as we have observed – sees risk as being related to the quantity and quality of knowledge at the disposal of the manager; and, specifically, that means knowledge of the factors bearing on any decision, and the causal connections among those factors. This general position has been adopted by many, if not most, of those who followed after. But his particular typology has had few intellectual consequences. By contrast, that of decision classes has proved highly influential: demonstrating his abilities at their best – eclectic,[2] yet original. Derived from A. D. Chandler Jr's[3] distinction between strategy and structure – like so much in this field – Ansoff's model redefined both concepts and added a third.

His starting point is that 'from a decision viewpoint' the firm can be conceived of as a 'resource-conversion process'. (Resources being its human, physical and monetary components.) His key question is, then: how can one configure and direct this process so 'as to optimize the attainment of the firm's objectives'? To which question Ansoff begins his answer by dividing what he terms 'the total decision space' into three 'classes': (the now-familiar) strategic; administrative, encompassing Chandler's 'structure'; and his own contribution, operating.

Strategic decisions address the selection of product-market opportunities. Operating decisions have to do with the budgeting, scheduling, supervision and control of resources: and, as such, realize the potential of strategic decisions. While administrative decisions, being concerned with the 'organization, acquisition and development of resources', are triggered and modified by the nature and outcomes, respectively, of decisions in the other two classes.

Fig. 2 is a reduced version of Ansoff's 'principal decision class' diagram.

Ansoff's precise definitions of each kind of decision class have largely been ignored. But his broad distinctions have been accepted, becoming familiar as *strategy, structure* and *process*.

By contrast, his detailed work on what he called 'growth vectors' has found much favour. His basic matrix, showing their components, is shown in Fig. 3. In interpreting it, the reader should know that Ansoff uses 'mission' in an idiosyncratic manner. He wishes it to mean 'an existing product need'

	Strategic	Administrative	Operating
Problem	To select product-market mix which optimizes firm's ROI* potential.	To structure firm's resources for optimum performance.	To optimize realization of ROI potential.
Nature of problem	Allocation of total resources among product-market opportunities.	Organization, acquisition and development of resources.	Budgeting of resources among principal functional areas. Scheduling resource application and conversion. Supervision and control.
Key characteristics	Partial ignorance. Decisions: centralized; non-repetitive; not self-regenerative.	Decisions triggered by strategic and/or operating problems.	Risk and uncertainty. Decisions: decentralized; repetitive; self-regenerative.

Figure 2.2
Key *ROI = Return on investment

Mission	Product	
	Present	New
Present	Market penetration	Product development
New	Market development	Diversification

Figure 2.3

– so that he can distinguish between that need and the customer (whether firm or individual) who possesses it.

Since strategy difficulties are at their most extreme when a firm diversifies (that is – employing his definition – when it moves into new product-missions), Ansoff has devoted considerable attention to it. The matrix shown in Fig. 4 (which is an expansion of the bottom right quadrant of Fig. 3) constitutes a landmark in strategic scholarship, and has proved invaluable to practitioners as well. Arguably, it was the first construct to demonstrate coherently how horizontal, concentric, conglomerate, and vertical integration moves can be distinguished from one another.

Before passing on to his later work, two of Ansoff's other insights should be commented upon: his distinction between objectives and strategy, and what he termed 'the components of strategy'.

Customers	Products	
New missions	New products	
	Related technology	Unrelated technology
Same type	Horizontal diversification	Horizontal diversification
Firm its own customer	Vertical integration	Vertical integration
Similar type	Marketing and technology related*	Marketing related*
New type	Technology related*	Conglomerate diversification

Figure 4
* types of concentric diversification

His approach to strategy formulation in *Corporate Strategy* is avowedly normative.[4] In one of the best essays on objectives to be found in the literature of the period, he disagrees with R. M. Cyert and J. G. March's famous dictum by asserting that the firm can be said to have objectives which are distinct and different from those of its participants. He pronounces the firm's central purpose to be the maximization of 'the long-term return on [the] resources employed within the firm'. Once this has been precisely formulated as an objective, it will help guide the firm into the future, while it should be used retrospectively to measure what progress the firm has made along its chosen path. As such, an objective is seen as an end, while strategy is seen as a means to that end.

By separating objectives from strategy in this way Ansoff distanced himself from the position adopted by Chandler and his Harvard contemporaries, E. P. Learned, C. P. Christensen and K. R. Andrews.[5] He also began a debate, which is undecided to this day, as to the 'correct' relationship between objectives and strategy.[6]

For Ansoff, the separation is not a matter of convention. He perceives objectives and strategy as acting upon each other so that, together, they constitute a screening device when evaluating options. For example: having fixed upon a target ROI for some new product-market venture, the firm might discover that, regardless of what strategy it adopted, the target could not be reached; consequently, it could either lower its sights or reject the proposal entirely. Conversely, having calculated that a strategy promised more than the target return, the firm could raise its sights (with interesting effects on the way that it viewed its existing businesses) or, once again, reject the proposal. This means-ends concept of the relationship meant that the process of strategic decision-making became an iterative one, in which each cycle of the debate added refinement and realism to what had gone before.

Ansoff's 'components of strategy' approach was innovational at the time, and has been much imitated since. He devised it in an attempt to provide the firm with a rigorously definable 'common thread'. The notion of common thread (that is, a recognizable coherence of activities which identifies the firm to the outsider, and guides its management when thinking of the future deployment of its greatest strengths), exercised academics considerably in the 1960s. It was held to be important that strategists, especially, should have the correct 'concept of the firm's business'. Was the firm, for example, in the energy business, the transportation business, or the 'growth' business? If the answer was 'yes' to any of these, then the firm could – and perhaps should – tackle anything which, respectively, had to do with energy, transportation, or looked like growing.

Now, useful as this type of concept may be for managers who have become too restricted in their capacity to speculate, Ansoff argued that it was so broad that it might, arguably, seduce undoubted 'energy business' firms, such as oil producers, into thinking they could – out of their own resources – successfully diversify into, say, electricity generation.

To overcome this particular difficulty, and provide a practicable method of establishing a common thread between past and future activities, Ansoff proposed four strategy components:

1. Product-market scope – an industrial listing so delimited as to confine strategic search to the similar and familiar.
2. Growth vector – describing how the firm could expand, within and beyond its present field.
3. Competitive advantage – specifying what the firm had, or needed, to compete effectively.
4. Synergy – a desirable condition of complementarity between new and existing product-market activities.

Ansoff's next major work, *From Strategic Planning to Strategic Management* (1976), which was essentially a symposium of contributions from sympathetically-minded colleagues, celebrated a failure. Though he confirms his confidence in the salient points of his earlier scholarship, he has to confess that, while strategic planning[7] has been well known for some fifteen years, it has hardly been widely adopted. This is partly because translating its precepts into practice has proved difficult. But it is also because 'attempts to install rigorous strategic discipline typically run into . . . an organizational inertia which reject[s] planning efforts as a "foreign antibody"'.

But the way ahead is clear: external change, determined in conformity with the ideas laid down in *Corporate Strategy*, calls for major adjustments within the organization. Indeed, the 'entire pattern of internal capability[8] must . . . be changed'.

Returning to his earlier categorization of decision-classes, Ansoff identifies what he now terms 'modes'. Strategic decisions equate with the 'entrepreneurial mode', and operating decisions approximate to the 'competitive mode'. In the entrepreneurial mode, the firm 'seeks effectiveness (profitability potential) through new [product-market] linkages'; while 'the competitive mode is focused on efficient (profitable) exploitation of existing linkages'. It is a formulation that owes much to C. Barnard and P. F. Drucker.[9]

So distinct are these two modes that 'when a firm transforms itself from a focus on competitive behaviour to an emphasis on the entrepreneurial, a fundamental transformation takes place in each of its major characteristics: its objectives, its value systems, its managers, its processes, its structures'. In other words, when a firm diversifies nothing less than a revolution occurs!

At this point, Ansoff sees strategic planning as merely 'a rational approach to assessing and redefining the linkages of the firm with both its business and societal environments,'[10] while 'strategic management' (which includes strategic planning) is seen as the activity that will *both* discern the external possibilities, *and* bring about the appropriate capability changes.

If the distinction between the entrepreneurial and competitive modes is conceptually clear, in practice it may be blurred by differing 'intensities of behaviour' in either mode. Each type of trading environment will call for a certain intensity. However, firms will vary in their responses to the demands made upon them; and that responsiveness will be a function of, among other things, each firm's internal capability. For example, success relative to competitive (i.e. existing) linkages may be inhibited where, say, aggressive marketing is necessary, but where complacent management refuses to innovate, invest sufficiently in promotion, or develop a strong selling operation. Equally, entrepreneurial (i.e. novel) linkages will require an appropriate, but perhaps quite different, intensity of behaviour which should be matched by an equivalent, internal intensity. And, remembering that each mode has a different focus (efficiency in the competitive, and effectiveness in the entrepreneurial), any attempt to create a homogeneous culture within the firm may introduce the conditions for conflict.

Ansoff's resolution of this dilemma is to suggest that, increasingly, firms will have to learn to live with a number of cultures – each of which is attuned to its own trading environment; and that 'integrative management', a new kind of activity directed at ensuring peaceful co-existence, will have to evolve.

In examining how cultural transformation could be managed, he contrasts what he calls 'adaptive learning' (that is, incremental change brought about by trial and error) with 'planned change': by which he means the process of imposing a clinical rationality on the shaping of an organization. Both types of change have defects: the first because it can be unrealistically protracted, and may culminate in a structure which is incoherent, and the second because it only seems to succeed when it yields an organizational form which is essentially an extension of what existed beforehand.

In his latest (and perhaps last) *major* work, *Implanting Strategic Management* (1984), Ansoff brings together many of the strands of thought which had preoccupied him for the previous thirty years – modifying, refining and developing them.

More than ever convinced that the world is changing faster and becoming less easy to predict, he is also more sensitive to the increasing complexity of organizations and of the people who inhabit them. His redefinition of 'strategic management' reflects this sensitivity, for it has now become: 'a systematic approach for managing strategic change which consists of:

1.   positioning of the firm through strategy and capability planning;
2.   real time strategic response through issue management;
3.   systematic management of resistance during strategic implementation.'

The first is, of course, where he began when he invented the term. The second was added, principally, as a consequence of his experiences in the mid 1970s when, he concluded that the ordinary strategic planning cycle was too slow and cumbersome to accommodate what he called 'mid-year surprises', emanating from government, foreign competitors, or R & D developments. To deal with these sudden challenges, he describes and proposes 'strategic issue management'; a system which responds on a 'real time' (i.e. a near-immediate) basis. This is buttressed by two other proposals: a mechanism to detect 'weak signals' – and thus be in a better state of preparedness; and a 'strategic surprise system' which brings into play a 'strategic task force network', created in advance and rehearsed in readiness.

With the third element of his redefinition, Ansoff deals constructively with a phenomenon that has dogged him in the past (1976): the human and organizational inertias which have to be overcome when strategic change becomes necessary. His proposal is based upon a comparison of Western and Japanese methods of problem-solving. The former, he argues, are serial in character – largely because of our intellectual traditions, and most notably those originating with Descartes. The Japanese, by contrast, engage in what Ansoff calls 'a parallel planning-implementation process'. This not only leads to optimal decisions, but also – through the involvement of everyone concerned – ensures their 'cultural and political acceptance'. He then goes on to design a method which will, he believes, enable the process to be adopted in the West.

In 1987, Ansoff published a revised version of *Corporate Strategy*.[11] Not having re-read the original in some twenty years – in the belief that it was obsolete – he was surprised to find that a substantial part remained relevant. The new version 'is intended as an introduction to strategic management'. So, not unnaturally, that is the perspective from which he judges, and modifies, his earlier insights – in the first, and greater, part of the book. The manager-student is thus presented with an unusual, if not a unique, experience: a legitimate rewriting of the past which renders a complete body of work internally coherent. Our interest, at this point, is therefore to see what major modifications he has seen fit to make to his first book.

In comparing the two, one is immediately struck by how much of the first five chapters has been retained. Predictably, the examples he gave have, for the most part, been brought up to date. But on page after page, the original words have been reproduced. His excellent essay on objectives, referred to above, and the subsequent one modelling 'a practical system' for them, are barely changed. The same appears to be true for the chapter on synergy – until one notices two detailed alterations in a table showing functional synergy relationships among industries; and then reads that, 'the past twenty years of experience have shown that management synergy quickly becomes negative [instead of being "moderate"] when a firm diversifies into an industry whose . . . turbulence is significantly different' from what it has been used to.

This degree of textual fidelity means, of course, that the content remains essentially the same. The firm is still viewed as a resource-converter; the decision class concept is retained in every detail; synergy is what synergy was; and strategic decisions persist in being 'not self-regenerative'. (See Fig. 2, page 229.)

But why has so little changed in these early chapters?

In 1965, Ansoff was concerned to repair an intellectual omission. Cyert and March had produced (in 1963) a behavioural theory of the firm, and thus had 'made an important contribution to the study' of the operating class of decisions. In 1962, Chandler had shed 'important light' on the administrative class. Ansoff's purpose was 'to construct a practical framework' for the remaining class: strategic decisions. In the absence of 'adequate theory', he begins by 'constructing our own model of the firm': that is, in a typically normative or prescriptive fashion. A pertinent question about such modelling is: what is its basis? If it were systematically factual, then the approach would surely be descriptive – and not prescriptive at all. Does it stem from first principles? In which case it would be reasonable to ask where these came from. Or does it proceed from what might be called 'defensible assumptions' – defensible, perhaps, on the grounds of commonsense argument, or generally accepted propositions? Ansoff's model appears to be based on this last approach. (See page 20, note 4.)

The 1987 version, however, clears away all doubts. It is founded on 'practical prescriptions, invented largely within business firms'. 'Ideally,' as he tells us, 'theory is developed ahead of practical prescriptions.' But in the world of management, 'it has worked the other way round'. Problems beget solutions, which give rise to theories. And so it has proved to be in the case of the 1965 original – most of the material for which was based on prescriptions which have been validated by later theorizing and experience!

So, what in these early chapters has changed?

There is an addition – characteristic of the later Ansoff, as we have noted – of some seven pages of US business history. This concludes with the assertion that 'in the second half of the twentieth century, strategic and operating decisions require equal attention'; and that, consequently, the administrative decision class is brought into play by the need to provide a separate structure for each: that is, two structures which 'are not only different but inimical' to one another. We have, therefore, a timely connection – and not the only one – between the 1965 preoccupation with strategic decision-making and 1987 strategic management.

The main differences between the two versions become apparent with Chapter 6, in the middle of which we read: 'In summary, strategy is an elusive and somewhat abstract concept.' It is a view Ansoff compels us towards; for most of what seemed so straightforward then has now become highly sophisticated.

Certainly, there are familiar terms, usages and arguments. For example, risk, uncertainty, and partial ignorance continue as before. Objectives are still to strategy, as ends are to means; and, when employed together, 'filter projects'. But now *both* are decision rules – with primacy being given to the former; and they are interchangeable – according to timing, and organizational level.

Three of the original strategy components survive: growth vector (now known as geographical growth vector); competitive advantage; and synergy. Bringing the number, once again, to four is strategic flexibility. The first and the last of these are expressed in terms of three 'dimensions': market need, e.g. personal transportation; product/service technology, e.g. integrated circuitry; and market geography – which specifies the country, or some part of it, where the firm intends to do business.

These three replace Ansoff's original two, product and mission, which were used to describe his four basic growth directions. The matrix representing them – see Fig. 3, page 229 – has, therefore, been replaced by the one shown in Fig. 5. (In interpreting it, the reader will want to know that the most extreme move possible is from A to B. That is, from the present market need-geographical market-product/service technology combination, to a strategic position where each dimensional requirement is different. Plainly, there are many combinations of the three between A and B).

The four components form part of strategic portfolio strategy, which is one of two related types of strategy that 'in modern practice . . . are used to characterize the thrust of the firm's strategic development'; the other being competitive strategy. Portfolio strategy sets out to deal with the questions of what business(es)[12] the company is, and could be, in; and establishes, coincidentally, how these will relate to each other.

Competitive strategy, on the other hand, 'specifies the distinctive approach which the firm intends to use in order to succeed in each of the strategic business areas'. During the last twenty years – because markets could not be

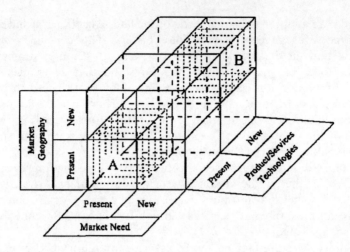

Figure 5

relied on to grow automatically, as they had in the past – new strategies have emerged to complement the familiar ones of 'market share maximization' (or 'cost/price minimization') and growth. Ansoff identifies these as: (1) market differentiation (market niche) – 'creating a distinctive image in the minds of potential customers for the firm's products/services'; and (2) product/service differentiation (product niche) – 'which differentiates the performance of the product/service' from those of the firm's competitors.

Whether talking of portfolio or competitive strategy, Ansoff distinguishes between incremental[13] and discontinuous changes. The first occurs when the firm 'makes a logical[14] and relatively small' strategic departure: e.g. an improvement in 'historical technology', or sales expansion to some part of another country.

By contrast, a discontinuous (or novel) change 'is a significant departure from the historical growth vector' of the firm. Two identifying tests can be applied:

1. The extent of the firm's departure from the market needs it knows how to satisfy, the technology its products are based upon, or 'the geographical, cultural, social, or political settings' it knows how to do business in.
2. The revisions in the firm's 'culture, power structure, systems, organizational structure and reward/incentives' called for by the change.

Having discussed what has occasioned discontinuous changes in the immediate past (e.g. external 'triggers' such as obsolescent technology, demand saturation, alterations in socio-political conditions; and internal

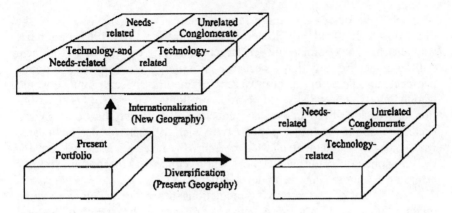

Figure 6

drives such as entrepreneurship), Ansoff tells us that 'the path to new horizons took two distinctive forms': internationalization and diversification.

In 1965, internationalization hardly merited a mention – being subsumed under diversification. Its separate treatment – if nothing else does – calls for the additional illustration set out below. Replacing his original matrix (see Fig. 4, page 230), it marks a substantial break with the past.

As Ansoff explains, this diagram divides the cube of Fig. 5 'into two major types of growth vector, illustrated by the upper and lower slices of the cube'.

A needs-related departure occurs when a technology new to the firm is acquired so as to go on serving historical markets. When a historical technology is applied to new needs (e.g. 'the current flood of solid state electronics into the automotive industry'), the type of diversification is called technology-related. Finally, we have conglomerate diversification: that is, where the new businesses are related neither by market nor technology needs to the firm's present ones.

Diversification, of course, can be by acquisition or through internal development. Aside from noting that the last type is usually brought about by acquisition, Ansoff asserts that the 'internal acquisition of a discontinuously different technology is a very difficult process'; which implies that the safer route is via takeover or merger.

Internationalization, in his view, can be extremely hazardous, because it may involve a two-step discontinuity: 'penetrating a new country *and* offering a novel technology to its markets'. Seeing them as alternative ways of portfolio expansion, he prefers diversification to internationalization – unless the firm's objectives cannot be met that way – because the latter 'involves much more drastic departures from the firm's past experience and competence than similar intranational diversification alternatives'.

In 1987, he once again discusses the relative merits of synergistic (the old 'concentric') and conglomerate diversification. His 1965 preference was unclear – he confined himself largely to setting out the cases for each. Although he did say that – because of synergy – when the economic prospects and flexibility of both were the same, the concentric move would usually involve fewer risks and be more profitable. Here also, his contribution to this long-lived debate is inconclusive. However, he does make a prediction about the future popularity of each. 'Wheeler dealer' managers, who enjoy the excitement of what he calls 'the merger game', will opt for the conglomerate route, while those whose concern is the optimization of returns will choose synergistic development.

Ansoff is not averse to making predictions: a practice which the layman might think entirely appropriate for a strategist with a sense of history; but which marks him out, in one more way, from his scholarly colleagues. Towards the end of *Implanting Strategic Management* he makes a number. They fall into two groups: those connected with the 'technology' of strategic management; and, more daringly, those to do with future strategic challenges. Among the latter, he includes a prophecy that commercial competition, on a world scale, will be characterized more by co-operation between industrial giants (in order to attain 'critical mass') than it will be by the currently fashionable free trade ideology which ostensibly owes so much to Adam Smith. The world waits.

Notes

1 See Malcolm S. Salter and Wolf A. Weinhold, pages 155–172.
2 As he says in the preface to *Corporate Strategy*, his purpose is 'to synthesize and unify' others' '*partial* analytical insights into strategic business problems'.
3 See Alfred D. Chandler Jr, pages 34–41.
4 Nevertheless, he contends that it is practical in two senses: its 'framework is an outgrowth of several concrete problems' he has helped solve; and it has 'proved useful' in teaching business policy on graduate and executive courses.
5 See Kenneth R. Andrews, pages 5–14.
6 See Charles W. Hofer and Dan Schendel, pages 216–229.
7 It will be noted that 'corporate strategy' has become 'strategic planning'.
8 By capability Ansoff means 'values, systems, structure, skills, power and technology'. 'Capability-pattern' *appears* to be synonymous with 'culture'.
9 See also Charles W. Hofer and Dan Schendel, pages 216–229.
10 Here we have a major development in Ansoff's thinking.
11 With the assistance of E. J. McDonnell.
12 Ansoff calls these strategic business areas (SBAs).
13 He associates this distinction with J. B. Quinn's 'logical incrementalism', apparently believing that the latter's theorizing advocated the *implementation* of small strategic steps; though, in fact, he was arguing for the *formulation* of strategy incrementally. See James Brian Quinn, pages 253–262.
14 He seems to be using 'logical' as though it meant 'coherent with past practice'.

Bibliography

H. Igor Ansoff, *Corporate Strategy*, McGraw-Hill Inc., 1965, revised 1987.

H. Igor Ansoff, Roger P. Declerck and Robert L. Hayes, *From Strategic Planning to Strategic Management*, John Wiley, 1976.

H. Igor Ansoff, *Implanting Strategic Management*, Prentice-Hall International Inc., 1984.

13

ANSOFF'S MATRIX, PAIN AND GAIN

Growth strategies and adaptive learning among small food producers

Gerald Watts, Jason Cope and Michael Hulme

Source: *International Journal of Entrepreneurial Behaviour & Research* 4(2) (1998): 101–11.

Introduction

This paper arises from a programme of research among food sector SMEs in the North West of England. The research project included both qualitative and qualitative phases and its primary focus was on the growth and development needs of the sample firms.

The first part of the title derives from the focus on growth and, more specifically, strategies for growth relative to the four quadrants of Ansoff's matrix (Ansoff, 1965): market penetration, market development, product development and diversification (Figure 1). In the analysis, we used this framework to categorise growth strategies and then attempted to relate them to other variables such as growth history and expectations.

The second part of the title is a reference to the inter-relationship between the "personal" and the "business", in that all of the sample were owner-managed businesses. It is well understood that owner-management has significant implications at the qualitative level (Bolton, 1971) and that many aspects of the business, including objectives and strategy are closely related to the personal characteristics and goals of the owner-manager. (Carson *et al.*, 1995).

As a specific focus, we wanted to explore the usefulness of the Greiner lifecycle model (Greiner, 1972) in interpreting the relationship between personal and business experience and learning in a small firm. Greiner's model depicts growth as occurring through phases of relatively stable expansion

	Current Products	New
Current Markets	Market Penetration	Product Development
New Markets	Market Development	Diversification

Figure 1 Anshoff's product/market growth.
Source: Igor Ansoff. "Corporate Strategy", McGraw-Hill. 1987

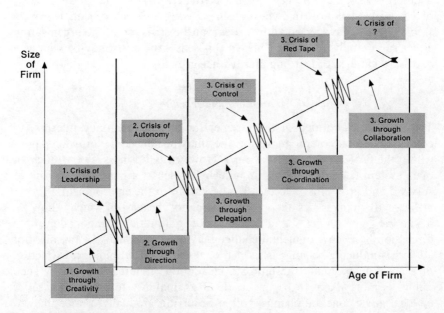

Figure 2 Greiner's life-cycle.

interspersed with periods of "crisis" which may result in successful adaptation and learning, facilitating a further phase of growth (Figure 2).

At a broader level, we have set out to refine our understanding of the complex relationship between the owner-manager and his or her business, in terms of such factors as growth, horizons, aspirations, limitations and learning.

Theoretical overview

Enterprise growth

A basic problem exists in understanding growth, in that larger, developed firms are so different from small firms "that in many ways it is hard to see that they are of the same genus" (Penrose, 1959); the same author likens this growth to the transformation from caterpillar to butterfly. To explain this metamorphosis in more gradual terms, patterns of enterprise growth are frequently conceptualised in the form of a business life cycle, comprising a number of phases or stages (Churchill and Lewis, 1983; Miller and Friesen, 1984; Scott and Bruce, 1987). These stages are then associated with generic management problems and organisational characteristics.

There is an intuitive descriptive reasonableness in such stage models and some longitudinal studies, such as that of Miller and Friesen (1984), have managed to substantiate these general patterns of transformation, albeit in a descriptive sense. Greiner's model (Greiner, 1972) includes an element of causal explanation in hypothesising growth as occurring in relatively stable phases, interspersed with "crises"; at the crisis point, the organisation either successfully adapts or fails. In this sense, the crisis may be seen as a necessary catalyst of learning and further growth.

Adaptation and learning

The "crises" elaborated in the Greiner model are essentially internal; to continue the lepidopteral metaphor, they may be likened to "growing pains" within the protective case of the pupa. However, a business is very much an open system (Bertalannfy, 1950) and, in this sense, a basic prerequisite of survival and growth is "successful" adaptation to the environment.

There are many issues of conjecture here, not the least of which is how we define the "environment" and to what is the adaptation being made. In the discussion here, environmental change may occur gradually or rapidly; not all "crisis-inducing" change is sudden or unexpected. In biology, extinction of a species represents the ultimate in adaptive failure. Biologically such failure is more likely to be the result of an inability to adapt to a series of local environmental changes, often occurring gradually, rather than to single moments of crisis – a macro-level parallel to Handy's "boiled frog" (Handy, 1989).

What do we really mean by "successful adaptation" in the business context? Not all adaptation is directional. In particular, the concept of learning implies directionality or purpose: "the creature that learns is not the mythical amphisbaena of the ancients, with a head at each end and no concern where it is going. It moves ahead from a known past into an unknown future and this future is not interchangeable with that past" (Wiener, 1950, p. 45).

The concept of purpose, intentionality of life span or the "survival instinct" is closely related to notions of strategy and planning. It is at such a fundamental level that concepts of strategy and learning might usefully be discussed in relation to SMEs. Dawkins (1988) has suggested that "complicated things have some quality, specifiable in advance, that is highly unlikely to have been acquired by random chance alone" (Dawkins, 1988, p. 9), a quality of adaptive ability.

One central concept relevant to this discussion is the notion of system boundary – where does the "environment" start and end? Adaptive ability can be linked to the idea of horizon or "range of vision"; Simon (1956) observed that "we see that the organism's modest capacity to perform purposive acts over a short planning horizon permits it to survive easily in an environment where random behaviour would lead to rapid extinction" (Simon, 1956, p. 134).

What becomes increasingly important is the notion of the interactive relationship between the enterprise and its many micro environments. In systems terms, the "environment and system do not just co-exist side by side. They interact to the point of mutual inter-penetration. Some aspects of the environment become "internalised by the system and some aspects of the system become externalised to become features of the environment" (Emery and Trist, 1975, p. 43). A central concept here is the extension of the environment in relation to the enterprise. Behind this lie notions of degrees of environmental knowledge, degrees of specialised adaptation and limits placed on knowledge of extended environments. Such limits may be completely explicit, having a basis in knowledge of the extended environment and therefore constituting a "knowledge strategy", or may be implicit or even "instinctual" with significant knowledge localised. However we conceptualise this, we should be aware that we are talking here in terms of relative degrees, rather than in any absolute sense.

Growth strategies

In the context discussed above, marketing strategy is a form of purposive adaptation, in most circumstances (but not necessarily) informed by learning. It might typically be proactive in nature, but the degree of proactivity is a relative concept; SME strategy is often characterised as primarily "reactive" (Fuller, 1994).

Carson (1990) combines the concepts of limited proactivity and personal management in the concept of an "involved" marketing style, describing how small firm marketing is often characterised by a high level of direct involvement on the part of the owner-manager and how it "relies heavily on intuitive ideas and decisions and probably most importantly on common sense" (Carson, 1990).

Addressing the problem of strategic choice, Cravens *et al.* (1994) hypothesise that "choice of marketing growth strategy (in an SME) is a function of strategic situation, organisational characteristics, and entrepreneur motivations" (Cravens *et al.*, 1994, p. 247). Many authors have commented on the typical limitations of strategic alternatives available to the small firm by virtue of such factors as small market share and limitations of resources and skills (e.g. Carson, 1985).

Because of these limitations, it has been suggested that certain strategic alternatives are typically more appropriate for a small firm, namely those that avoid direct competition with larger firms and that involve the development of close customer relationships and product adaptation (Storey and Sykes, 1996). In the specific language of Ansoff's Matrix, it has been suggested by Perry (1987) that for SMEs the most appropriate growth strategies are therefore product development and market development.

Primary research and findings

Methodology

The primary research included three phases: a number of exploratory interviews, a quantitative survey by means of a postal questionnaire supported by telephone introductions and prompts, and a series of 25 face-to-face interviews with a selected sub-sample of the respondents.

Sample profile

As defined by the sponsors, the sample frame included non-primary food producers in rural areas of Cumbria, Lancashire and Cheshire. A sample of 256 firms was selected as the respondents of the mail questionnaire and 79 completed questionnaires were returned. The profile of the sample was as follows:

- *Age of firm.* As shown in Table I, compared with the SME population as a whole, the sample was older than average, with a flatter age distribution than might be expected. This reflects the origin of many of the sample businesses in the agriculture sector.
- *Origins.* A total of 68 per cent were founder-owners, while a further 16 per cent were continuing a family firm.
- *Turnover.* The distribution of annual sales is shown in Table II.
- *Employment size.* Employment ranged from self-employed to a maximum of 395, with median employment at four full time and two part time. As might be expected in this industry, employment reflected seasonality of sales, with 51 per cent of respondents reporting fluctuation in employment throughout the year.

242

Table I Age of firm.

Age (years)	<5	5–10	10–20	20–40	>40
Per cent	19	23	23	12	20

Table II Distribution of annual sales.

T/O (£m)	<0.25	0.25–0.5	0.5–0.75	0.75–1.0	1.0–1.5	>1.5
Per cent	53	19	4	6	4	13

Table III Percentage growth patterns (over past two years).

Decrease	Stable	>10	10–25	25–50	>50
8	14	41	19	5	12

Growth patterns and aspirations

Recent historical growth (last two years). As shown in Table III, most of the sample (77 per cent) had experienced some sales growth over the last two years, with 36 per cent reporting growth of over 10 per cent and 12 per cent reporting growth of over 50 per cent.

Short-term growth expectations (next two years). Respondents were somewhat more optimistic about future growth, with 47 per cent expecting to grow by more than 10 per cent over the next two years, as shown in Table IV.

Of those forecasting growth, 76 per cent expected to create new jobs (full time or part time).

Objectives and growth strategies

Business objectives. Respondents were asked to rank their objectives for the business. The results are shown in Table V.

Sales growth took precedence, with 68 per cent of respondents naming growth as the primary objective. Surprisingly few respondents appeared to want to increase their personal (i.e. discretionary) time.

Growth strategy. Respondents were asked to rank their priority growth strategies, according to the categories of Ansoff's Matrix (the alternatives being specified in familiar business language). Results are shown in Table VI.

Respondents placed a high priority on finding new customers for their existing product range (penetration and market development), whereas they

Table IV Percentage short-term growth expectations.

Decrease	Stable	>10	10–25	25–50	>50
1	17	36	36	3	8

Table V Objectives and growth strategies.

Objective (rank)	1 (%)	2 (%)	3 (%)	4 (%)	5 (%)
Grow substantially	14	12	5	2	0
Grow moderately	54	6	6	0	1
Stay about the same size	3	0	2	3	1
Increase profit margins	22	31	11	1	0
Obtain more finance	5	13	18	11	5
Increase personal time	2	7	18	9	6

Table VI Priority growth strategies.

Growth strategy (rank)	1 (%)	2 (%)	3 (%)	4 (%)
Market penetration	22	15	7	11
Market development	55	21	5	3
Product development	12	25	24	2
Diversification	121	7	15	22

Table VII

Growth strategy	Sales growth expectations (%)					
	Negative	0	0–10	10–25	25–50	>50
Market penetration	0	30	35	25	0	10
Market development	2	15	33	42	4	4
Product development	0	36	36	18	0	10
Diversification	0	20	40	20	0	20

gave a lower priority to the offering of new products to existing customers (product development). On balance, there is limited support for Perry's (1987) hypothesis that product and market development would be favoured strategies. Priority growth strategies were then cross-tabulated with growth expectations, as shown in Table VII. This table therefore depicts the relationship between favoured growth strategy and growth expectations, i.e. the outcome of these strategies.

In exploring this relationship, one might expect to see an association between high growth expectations and the more radical or higher-risk strategies and vice versa, i.e. a strategy of market penetration being associated with lower growth expectations. On the basis of these findings, however, there does not seem to be much evidence of a clear relationship between strategy and growth expectations. One interpretation of this could be confusion about the language used to describe strategic alternatives; although a number of pre-tests were carried out in developing the questionnaire, this may have been a factor. Another explanation is that the adopted strategies were equally well developed; there is no reason why a strategy of market penetration should not yield significant growth. A further explanation is that at least some of the sample did not have an elaborated business strategy in the conventional sense. This issue was one object of exploration in the qualitative phase of this research.

Qualitative evidence

Interview focus

The interview objective was to review the historical development of the sample businesses through the personal account of the owner-manager, exploring the concept of "crisis" and attempting to understand the basis and meaning of "strategy" in each context.

The overall picture was one of immense diversity: of evolutionary pattern of the business and of personal background, values and aspirations of the owner-managers. What became strikingly apparent were the frequently occurring accounts of "chance" incidents causing changes in business direction, not all of which could be reasonably described as "crises". On the other hand, there was clear evidence among some businesses of a consistent strategy with relatively long-term horizons. A full analysis of the interviews is beyond the scope of this paper but the following vignettes will serve to illustrate a number of relevant issues.

Case 1: personal and business crisis

One interviewee ran a catering business but developed a small "traybake" operation as a secondary venture. She was visited by someone who, by chance, was the father of a major competitor. A few weeks after this incident, the son (i.e. the competitor) visited the main customer and took away the business. At the same time her mother died; the outcome of these two incidents was a period of depression. However, the interviewee recounted how she came out of this experience thinking "I've got lots to live for" and resolved, with later success, to develop the tray-bake venture as an alternative main business.

Case 2: reframing of personal motivation and aspirations

Another interviewee had become bored with his current business – a delicatessen. He was buying an important ingredient from a local company and found that the business was about to be sold. He bought the business and operated it in parallel with the original venture but soon found that he enjoyed it much more, in terms of the challenge and the pattern of working life. He decided to concentrate on this venture and successfully developed it to become the premier regional supplier; in retrospect, he observed that this incident "changed his life".

Case 3: an operational crisis leading to critical learning

Another respondent recounted a critical incident in which his freezer broke down, effectively bringing his business to a halt. He felt obliged to go round all of his customers and apologise for the disruption. This incident taught him both the importance of maintaining vital equipment and the value of customer relationships. More generally, he learned "not to take things for granted" and that he "should do it properly if he's going to do it at all".

Case 4: unplanned acquisition forcing adaptive learning

Another interviewee was a farmer, one of whose customers, a specialist fish and game retailer, got into financial difficulties and defaulted on payment. The farmer acquired the business in lieu of debts and, although he had no experience of a retail business, operated it in parallel with the farm. He made it work after an uphill struggle: "it was a shock not to have a guaranteed customer . . . I was stung a few times – a very expensive learning curve."

Case 5: long-term market development strategy

Another farmer was a producer of very high quality lamb, which, as is practice, was sold at auction; however, he always wanted to market his own product. He could also see subsidies coming to an end, which increased his resolve. He experimented with direct sales from his house, gained experience and confidence and now sells through three channels: direct, mail order and specialist dealer.

Case 6: successful opportunistic diversification

The proprietors of an historic water mill generated revenue by offering tours and producing specialist flour. Soon after acquiring the business, they realised that large numbers of people passed the door on the local train and on the bridleway, representing an attractive potential market, although walkers were not previously made welcome on the site. They built a tea-room and have successfully expanded the business.

Case 7: financially driven diversification

A producer of cakes found that competition had increased to the point that, although he had increased output tenfold, profits had barely doubled. Seeking a route to higher margin products, he started designing new product ranges from the customers' perspective and is now successfully exporting to Canada.

Conclusions

Strategy and adaptation

All of the cases discussed here are examples of successful "adaptation"; most resulted in what could be described as a new "strategy". They represent diversity in many dimensions: timescale, motivation, degree of proactivity and impact, both positive and negative, on the owner-manager and on the business.

Some of these are clear examples of "strategy that happened" or "emergent strategy" (Mintzberg, 1994) rather than the deliberate, logically planned or "intended" notion of strategy often espoused within the planning literature.

What has earlier been described as the "instinctual" combines concepts of learning and action as strategy in one node within the enterprise's environmental network. Such a strategy may not be explicit but rather tacit and localised. Importantly, at this level of discussion there is little or no distinction between tactics and strategy: "we find that the optimal strategy is just the simple tactic of attempting to do one's best on a purely local basis" (Schutzenberger, 1954, p. 98). Ashby (1960) takes this argument further to suggest that within such micro environments "the best tactic in the circumstances can be learnt only on a trial and error basis and only for a particular class of local environmental variances" (Schutzenberger, 1954, p. 197).

The business life cycle and "progress"

Scott and Bruce (1987) describe the birth phase of the business life cycle as being characterised by "owner-run firms trying to establish a niche for themselves through much product innovation". In this sense, many of the firms studied might be described as permanently in the birth phase.

This serves to illustrate one fundamental problem inherent in the very concept of the life cycle. Key words in this discussion have been environment and growth; an underlying but unspoken concept is that of unilinear

development or "progress". A consistent theme in our discussion, illum-
inated by our research, is that "growth" should more usefully be placed
within an environmental context and should not be confused with progress,
if the latter is seen as an imposition upon environmental change. Indeed,
growth here can be characterised as symbiotic within environments,
i.e. growth is not an "imposition" but rather an adaptation.

We have earlier used the term "instinctual" to characterise enterprises
operating in a purely local environment. Learning and strategy is task
based and the level of local adaptation is high. However we must avoid
the common mistake of regarding such enterprises as in "non-progressive"
stasis and lesser "successes" when compared to enterprises actively seeking to extend their environment. The act of survival in this view is itself
an active notion – indeed to maintain the Emery and Trist line one may
go further and relate extinction to a failure of the enterprise to act
symbiotically over time. Therefore the sole measure of "success" may well
be nothing more than temporal survival related to the enterprise's intended
life span.

Boundaries, learning and intervention

So often it seems that the owners' boundaries of vision, in both lateral and
longitudinal senses, were simply too narrowly defined and that substantial
benefits might derive from their expansion. Uexküll (1920) wrote that "every
organism cuts out a special part of the environment which part then
becomes its reality. The rest of the environment simply does not exist for the
organism". In this sense, the bakery in Cumbria supplying within a 30-mile
radius has a more limited environment than the national producer.

However, the local enterprise is embedded within many networks within
this environment and indeed "the firm's effectiveness will be a function of
how well it integrates the various types of network relationships" (Gibb,
1996). While these networks "attach" to wider environments, it is their
specific localised manifestation which forms the immediate topography of
the local environment.

Based on the environmental adaptation model it is reasonable to
argue that a key role of training in small firms becomes one of extending
environmental awareness such as to stimulate generative learning beyond
its naturally occurring level.

The owner-manager and the business

Clearly, the frequently-acknowledged "overlap" of the "personal" and the
"business" is much more than this; instead, it is a super-complex system
of evolving experience and learning that is informing horizons, goals and
strategies, sometimes subtly, sometimes radically.

Rather than a unidirectional influence of the owner-manager over the business, we find it useful to characterise the relationship as mutual and interactive: owners share learning with their businesses and there is mutual cross-influence in this process. Similarly, the development process can more usefully be conceived as multilinear or multi-directional, therefore also complicating the idea of growth itself.

In this context, the concept of "crisis" is clearly problematic, in that the causality of learning and growth is much more complex than that suggested by the Greiner model. This was borne out by our research, in that most interviewees found it difficult to recount specific crises of this nature.

Instead, we recommend that the "systems" view of the firm that we have developed throughout this discussion provides a richer and more useful framework for understanding these complex processes.

References

Ansoff, I. (1965), *Corporate Strategy*, McGraw-Hill, New York, NY.

Ashby, W. R. (1960), *Design for a Brain*, Chapman and Hall, London.

Bolton, J. E. (1971), *Report of the Committee of Enquiry on Small Firms*, Cmnd. 4811, HMSO, London.

Carson, D. J. (1985), "The evolution of marketing in small firms", *European Journal of Marketing*, Vol. 19 No. 5.

Carson, D. J. (1990), "Some exploratory models for assessing small firms' marketing performance (a qualitative approach)", *European Journal of Marketing*, Vol. 24 No. 11, pp. 5–51.

Carson, D., Cromie, S., McGowan, P. and Hill, J. (1995), *Marketing and Entrepreneurship in SMEs*, Prentice-Hall, London.

Churchill, N. C. and Lewis, V. L. (1983), "The five stages of small business growth", *Harvard Business Review*, May/June.

Cravens, D. W., Lunsford, D. A., Hills, G. E. and Laforge, R. W. (1994), "An agenda for integrating entrepreneurship and marketing strategy research", in Hills, G. (Ed.), *Marketing and Entrepreneurship: Research Ideas and Opportunities*, Greenwood, Westport, CT, pp. 235–53.

Dawkins, R. (1988), *The Blind Watchmaker*, Penguin, London.

Emery, F. E. and Trist, E. L. (1975), *Towards a Social Ecology*, Plenum, London.

Fuller, P. B. (1994), "Assessing marketing in small and medium sized enterprises", *European Journal of Marketing*, Vol. 28 No. 12, pp. 34–49.

Gibb, A. A. (1996), "Small firms' training and competitiveness. Building upon the small businesss as a learning organisation", *International Small Business Journal*, Vol. 15 No. 3, pp. 13–29.

Greiner, L. E. (1972), "Evolution and revolution as organisations grow", *Harvard Business Review*, July/August.

Handy, C. (1989), *The Age of Unreason*, Random House, London.

Miller, A. and Friesen, P. (1984), "A longitudinal study of the corporate life cycle", *Management Science*, Vol. 30, October, pp. 1161–83.

Mintzberg (1994), *The Rise and Fall of Strategic Planning*, Prentice-Hall, Maidenhead.

Penrose, E. T. (1959), *The Theory of the Growth of the Firm*, Blackwell, Oxford.

Perry, C. (1987), "Growth strategies: principles and case studies", *International Small Business Journal*, Vol. 5, pp. 17–25.

Scott, M. and Bruce, R. (1987), "Five stages of growth in small business", *Long Range Planning*, Vol. 20 No. 3, pp. 45–52.

Schutzenberger, M. P. (1954), "A tentative classification of goal-seeking behaviour", *Journal of Management Science*, Vol. 100, pp. 97–102.

Simon, H. A. (1956), "Rational choice and the structure of the environment", *Psychological Review*, Vol. 63, pp. 129–38.

Storey, D. J. and Sykes, N. (1996), "Uncertainty, innovation and management", in Burns and Dewhurst (Eds), *Small Business and Entrepreneurship*, Macmillan, Basingstoke, pp. 73–93.

Uexküll, J. V. (1920), *Umwelt und Innenwelt der Tiere*, Berlin.

Von Bertalanffy, L. (1950), "The theory of open systems in physics and biology", *Science*, Vol. 3.

Wiener, N. (1950), *The Human Uses of Human Beings*, Houghton Mifflin, New York, NY.

14

PROJECT MANAGEMENT
BY EARLY WARNINGS

Ilmari O. Nikander and Eero Eloranta

Source: *International Journal of Project Management* 19(7) (2001): 385–99.

Abstract

The increasing turbulence found in the corporate environments
today and concurrent engineering as applied to project-related
activities, there is growing demands on the flexibility of project management and the ability to anticipate the future. The
conventional methods of project control are not really capable
of rising to these challenges. The early warnings observed
in project-related activities or the weak signals as described in
Igor Ansoff's theory enable project managers to better anticipate and manage otherwise unforeseeable project problems.
This article explains the character of the phenomenon and some
other related factors. It shows how early warnings relate to
project problems and their causes, and develops a preliminary
model for the utilisation of early warnings. The article is a
continuation of an article published in the International Journal
of Project Management Vol. 15, No. 6 in 1997.

1. Background and a possible solution

Corporate management today is adamant about not yielding to changes
in project plans. Due to the economical pressures and turbulence in the
corporate environment, industrial construction projects have to be implemented in less and less time, often using the principles of concurrent
engineering. Project managers must be able to adapt to great changes
when market-related forces lead to such demands in the middle of a project.
These forces set more and more growing demands on the project leader's
ability to react to "unforeseeable" events. He/she should be increasingly
capable of anticipating the future progress of a given project. Conventional
methods of project management cannot properly address to challenges
of this nature.

In 1975, business economist Ansoff [1] claimed that sudden changes in a company's environment, affecting the activities within the company are at first identified as very vague "weak signals" which usually become stronger and more specific in time. He has also presented his ideas for utilising weak signals in corporate strategic management. Using various names, the idea of weak signals has been applied quite extensively in business economics, especially in the field of strategic planning and management, by developing various management models for the business environment. The research carried out in the fields of communication [2], military intelligence [3,4] and business economics (anticipation of bankruptcies) [5] encounters the idea of weak signals and early warnings. Project-related literature includes only allusions to similar weak signals, by the names early warnings, symptom, early indicator, presignals etc. However, the meanings of all of the above are essentially the same.

This article presents one possible answer to complete the methods of project management in use today. The idea and the model presented is not intended to replace any proven conventional methods. Instead, it aims to add to management and leadership an element of anticipatory action, which could speed up reaction to problems threatening a project.

2. Conventional methods of project control

The conventional methods of project control are based on what has already taken place, i.e. so-called historical information. They use trends to predict future events. Using trends, it is difficult to perceive unforeseeable changes or situations that are surprising or develop outside the scope of project plans. All such conventional methods adhere to the principle of so-called deviation management. The situation becomes even worse if the project manager is willing to take action only after observing large deviations, such as delays of several weeks in a time management report. Also, the methods do not address the problems relating to actual leadership (human and culture) at all.

Cost reporting gives the project manager an idea about the cost situation at the time of reporting. It addresses only to cost-related matters and forecasts the end result of the project. Conventional methods of time management include: bar chart schedule with break-line, schedule (time) performance, work performance, the earned value method and the cost/schedule control systems criteria (C/SCSC) guidelines. They all concern themselves with project events; on leading projects on the basis of facts. The methods are informative in nature, unless they are used in conjunction with rescheduling based on the critical path method (CPM) principle. The event forecasters, that work the best in a practical working environment, are forecast schedules implemented using the CPM or program evaluation and review technique (PERT) principles [6,7].

252

3. Project risk management (PRM)

Risk analysis and risk management have been popular subjects for research, articles, specialised literature and conferences during the 1990s [8–11]. Today's project risk management aims at proactive project management, which is also an objective of this study. PRM is a very important task during project planning and project control. The most popular computer programs used for project risk management are still somewhat primitive. They have not yet been developed into commonplace tools of project management in the same way as time management programs have, for example [12]. Essentially, almost all methods of risk management, presented in the literature on project management and commercial risk management computer programs appear to favour one-time identification, evaluation and analysis of risks. These methods do not seem to favour simple, quick risk analyses and demand a great deal of work. Commercially distributed programs mostly deal with the probable project outcomes. Commercial PRM computer programs fall into two primary categories, which are (1) risk analysis oriented programs such as @RISK, OPERA and CRYSTAL BALL; and (2) programs supporting PRM processes such as FUTURA and TEMPER SYSLA. Risk analysis does not necessarily reveal whether a risk is really becoming a reality but states the risk's level of seriousness, its effect on the project and the probability of its realisation. Also, risk analysis often remains a one-time procedure at the beginning of the project with very little true risk management being carried out during the course of the project.

4. Research at the Helsinki University of Technology (HUT)

In the HUT's Department of Industrial Engineering and Management, a study [13] was conducted on early warnings occurring in industrial construction projects and how to take advantage of this phenomenon. First, 17 project professionals were interviewed (basic material, 1993). Further research examined project problems observed in four case projects (case material, 1995) and sought to find early warnings which pointed to the problems by interviewing representatives of parties participating in the projects. The study was conducted according to the qualitative research principle, utilising the so-called thematic interviewing method [14]. The study includes an analysis of 68 basic types of early warnings and out of them, 11 main type groups. It also lays out the typology of the phenomenon and seeks to isolate the project problems they point to and the possible basic causes of the problems. Table 1 presents the basic groups of early warnings found in the study and their main groups (bold), including short descriptions of the early warnings [13].

The study found that observations conforming to the idea of early warnings can be made frequently in project activity environments. The warnings are

Table 1 Early warnings groups analysed from the material, with short descriptions [13,18].

Early warnings	Percent share basic (%)	Percent share case (%)	Description
Gut feelings	4.7	2.6	Anticipatory feelings are the signals the least easy to detect, identify and interpret. intuitive feeling
Personnel, project group	38.2	21.7	
Non-verbal information	3.8	1.4	Various non-verbal messages observed in meetings are the most important signals of reference for the negotiators in meetings
Personnel behavior	15.7	14.2	A large group of various behaviors
Personnel behavior in general	2.3	4.0	'Abnormal' or inconsistent behavior of the contractor/supplier almost always means trouble for the project
Mood, attitude	1.7	4.7	A mood of non-satisfaction in the Personnel
Conflicts	2.6	3.5	Conflictive situations
Talking behind the back			Talking behind the back (unnecessary criticism)
Indecision			The organization is stalling the progress of the project
Frank talks			Lack of trust expressed in no uncertain terms
Commitment	1.7		Weak commitment to the project expressing itself in many ways
Cliques			
Authority disputes			Typical to consultants, but not rare for contractors either
Making excuses			A phenomenon specific to each project
Lack of contact with the client			When it becomes obvious that Planning cannot meet all the requirements
Unrealistic Planning			A lack of working staff noticed
Lack of resources		3.1	A "phenomenon" especially common to consultants; changes in project Personnel
Changes in Personnel			The professional and project-related skills of Personnel
Professional skills			

Project manager, management	1.2	8.3	The personal qualities of the project manager
Project manager as a person			
Management style		6.1	
Project planning	4.5	13.0	
Preliminary plans		3.8	The level and quality of preliminary plans
Project plans			Inadequacies in project plans
Tender material			Deficiencies and insufficiencies in tender material
Contract	5.7		A contract drawn up unprofessionally or unambiguously
Contract with issues			A contract consciously drawn up to have little room for changes
Budgeting, budget contents			The budget has been poorly drawn up, the basis is insufficient and the budget is undersized
Advance material			Reference material
Project control and reporting	6.8	5.0	
Progress control	3.1	3.5	Classical schedule-based monitoring of progress
Monitoring	2.8	1.4	Classical methods of project activity
Monitoring in general			
Availability of materials			The contractor's (or the supplier's) ability to acquire materials
Working level, quality and speed			Speed and quality of work at the site
Budget corrections			Tendencies to change the budget without proper reason
Working within the project	7.7	10.4	
Work initiation	3.5	0.7	The efficiency of initiating work, its sluggishness is often revealing
Mobilization			Mobilization at the work site, slow initiation of work, and/or poor turnout at the site
Initial information/lack of information	3.0	6.9	Lack of initial information for Planning, their being late is very typical in projects
Same things repeatedly			If the same things come up again and again in meetings etc
Organization type		2.4	

Table 1 (cont'd)

Early warnings	Percent share basic (%)	Percent share case (%)	Description
Communication			
Communication	7.8	5.2	Messages lost along the way
General miscommunication	4.9	2.6	The tone of messages, especially when it changes, suggests that
Tone of messages			something has happened
Letters			Writing letters
Conflicting knowledge	3.0	2.6	Conflictive information
Insinuation			Many problems detected due to insinuation. People are not willing to say things straight out
Expressed by parties			
Typical to client	8.9	9.2	Delayed decisions, especially those caused by the client, is one
No decisions	7.1	9.2	of the worst factors causing problems in projects
Trust disappears	2.6	4.0	A third party notices the problem
End users		2.4	Late recruitment of production Personnel (staff)
Freezings			The "no decisions" group also includes not being able to "freeze" the design principles
CEO			No support from the company CEO for the project
Additional research			Very typical during a brand tendering phase
Procurement			Matters relating to procurement, delays etc
Supplier/Contractor			
Advance billing	1.7		Willingness for advance billing may be manifest already as Planning factors in negotiations or as a request for change

Documents	11.0		
Reporting	2.6	9.9	Quality, tone and lateness of reports are revealing factors
Schedules: level/quality/receiving	5.4	4.3	The level of the schedules can be estimated on the basis of the "symmetry" and readability
Symmetry Being logical			
Receiving/Level			How quickly a contractor will deliver schedules after reaching an agreement
Technical plans		4.3	Changes in plans, especially when there are lots of them, become warning signals
Incorrect revisions			Old drawings turning up at the site is a sign of communications problems
Responsibilities unclear			This situation relates to organizational problems
Differences and deficiencies in project culture	4.0	9.2	
First contact (to client)			First impression and the observations in first contact between parties are a good source for signals in the opinion of the interviewees
First impression			Observations made during meetings with the client
Project terminology			Differences in project terminology or low proficiency in the terminology reveal inexperience with projects
Lack of experience		3.8	Inexperience is revealed quickly and in many ways
American culture		2.6	A phenomenon specific to each project
External source	2.4	1.2	External sources; insinuation, may include unambiguous numerical data
No early warnings obtained	2.8	0.5	It is difficult to observe early warnings
Small groups and scattered signals		3.8	
Total	100	100	

in part information input (signals and stimuli) phenomena in accordance with Wiio's [15] "A System Model of Information and the Information Process" and in part clear communicative messages. Communicative warnings are surprising, contain a change in relation to the earlier situation and are always tied to the interpretation made by the receiver [16]. The warnings typology developed during the research indicates that the warnings were observed to occur in all project phases (planning, procurement, delivery and site activity), deliver information on all parties of the project, and are manifested in many ways (verbally, non-verbally, in writing, as events), with the sources being humans, groups of humans, companies, documents and situations. Concerning the (in)exactness of the information, the warnings brought up by the interviewees can, by and large, be located on the state of knowledge scale presented by Ansoff [1]. According to Wiio, the accuracy of the information obtained is very subjective [16]. It was found that the observer is unable to interpret obtained information in a meaningful way if there is an attempt to remove the signal from the environment in which it was observed. Project conditions are part of the informative content of the signal (see [17]).

5. The nature of the phenomenon

Fig. 1 illustrates the nature of the early warnings phenomenon and its relation to project events. The picture illustrates the factors relating to the phenomenon. In the picture, a project is depicted as a chronological flow of

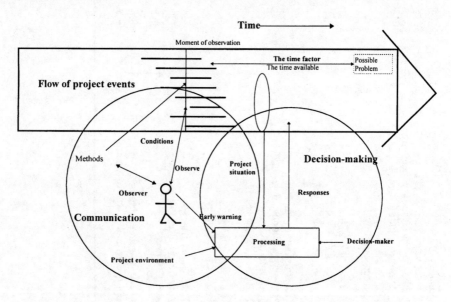

Figure 1 The early warnings phenomenon in a project environment [13,18].

events, from which an observer obtains information. The human observer makes observations, receives communication and messages. He/she may use various methods to obtain the desired information. The observer accepts and interprets the information obtained. This is the phenomenon's communicational phase which is tied to the human observer.

The second phase of the phenomenon can be considered to be the analysis of the information obtained and decisions made on the basis of the information obtained. The process also often involves a decision-maker. Activities in projects always have to do with upcoming events, the future. The nature of the phenomenon proposed by Ansoff in his theory of weak signals is different in the project environment. Ansoff requires companies to gain most of their information from their corporate environment. In projects, most of the information seems to come from within the project, with only a smaller part of it coming from the outside.

6. Project problems, their causes and responses

To make effective use of the phenomenon is most fundamental to relate an early warning to appropriate project problems and their causes. One must also identify the countermeasures to be undertaken in each case. It is important to know the interdependencies of these concepts. Fig. 2 presents the hypothetical dependencies between early warnings, project problems, causes of problems and responses (decisions to result in correction).

Tables 2 and 3 [13,18] present the project problems that came up in the study, their causes, and their percentage distribution in the material. According to the material, four project problems account for 54% of the observations in the material derived from the basic interviews and for roughly 84% in the case material: "schedule-related problems", "problems relating to delivery of equipment" "total management problems" and "problems related to technical design". Three causes for problems stand out from the basic material. They are: "differences in project culture", "personnel skill and talent", and "multiple (more than three) reasons". They account for roughly 57% of the observations. The dominant causes for problems in the case material are: "management methods" and "differences in project culture". They account for about 52% of the observations. Because the

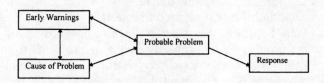

Figure 2 The hypothetical dependencies between early warnings, project problems, causes of problems and responses.

Table 2 Project problems, main groups [13,18].

Project problems, main groups	Basic material (%)	Case material (%)
Schedule problem, delay, time	19.0	9.5
Cost-related problem	5.3	5.0
Delivery problem, performance	8.8	24.8
Project environment, consultant	1.7	2.9
Goals unclear	1.9	
Client with, no CEO support	0.8	
Total management problems	18.8	22.2
Project manager as a person	3.5	3.3
Organization/Staff	2.1	0.6
Total staff problems	7.1	2.1
Total project planning	5.7	
Communication	5.0	0.8
Design, technology Planning	7.4	27.9
Financial matters	6.1	0.6
Differences in project culture	4.3	0.2
Non-definable	2.8	0.2
Total	100	100

Table 3 Causes of project problems [13,18].

Causes of problems	Basic material (%)	Case material (%)
Attitude-related	5.4	8.1
Management methodology	9.4	15.2
Project manager as a person	4.2	5.4
Differences in project culture	13.4	36.7
Organizational reasons	8.2	6.5
Personnel skill and talent	14.1	4.4
Lack of resources	8.7	9.6
Financial matters	5.7	9.4
Multiple reasons, more than 3	29.9	4.6
Non-definable	1	0.2
Total	100	100

questions used in the interviews were drawn up with problems in mind, one should not use this to make any conclusions on how common different project problems and their causes are in projects.

Tables 4 and 5 present the most frequent combinations of warning signals–project problems and problems–causes of problems found in the material [13,18]. The total material suggests that "the warning signals expressed by personnel" are obtained from within all of the problem groups. Also, it is significant that the interviewees have observed "gut feeling" in the context of very many problem groups. Left out of these tables are

Table 4 Early warnings, main groups-project problem, main groups [13,18].

Early warnings, main group	Project problems, main group (%)			
	Schedule problems	Delivery problems	Planning problems	Management style problems
Personnel, project group	2.31	3.09	4.02	6.38
Project parties	1.84	1.72	2.43	2.76
Documents	2.58	2.08	1.03	1.32
Working within the project	2.29	0.91	3.40	1.46
Project planning	0.94	3.10	1.55	0.76
Communication	0.44	1.14	0.58	2.23
Differences and deficiencies in project culture	0.17	1.19	1.29	2.64
Project control and reporting	2.76	1.36	0.81	0.54
Project manager, management	0.10	0.77	1.03	0.91

Table 5 Project problems-causes of project problems [13,18].

Project problems, main group	Causes of problems (%)						
	Management	Project culture differences	Many reasons	Organization	Personnel skills	Resource shortage	Attitude
Time, Schedule problems	1.68	3.25	4.75	1.06	1.09	1.43	0.88
Performance, Delivery problems	1.88	4.15	2.02	0.96	1.97	1.63	0.93
Problems in management, total	3.23	4.61	3.25	1.85	1.10	1.53	2.20
Planning, tech	2.76	6.59	1.35	2.35	0.57	2.67	1.29

many significant combinations, all of which account for at least 1% of the observations. In the material, the Pareto principle [26] (the 20/80 principle) is found to be at work. Table 4 contains combinations with an observation count of over 1% out of the total number of observations account for 16% of the number of combinations. They account for roughly 69% of the observations.

Table 5 appears to stress the same problem groups as Table 4, and the causes of problem stressed are: "management", "project culture", "multiple reasons", "organization", "Personnel skill and talent", "lack of resources" and "attitudes". These problems and their causes all affect one another. Combinations of over 1% account for 20% of the total table [13,18] and they account for roughly 71% of the percentage observations from the materials (Pareto principle).

6.1. Responses

As we detect early warnings of problems or start to suspect a project problem might be there to threaten the project, it is important that we do not stay content with this knowledge or suspicion, but actively start carrying out measures to lessen the threat. According to the study, the situations vary so greatly that no simple, general model for deciding what measures to undertake is easy to prepare on the basis of such a limited investigation. However, this knowledge can be supplemented by knowledge derived from the literature. Several books on project management have been written to find out what kinds of responses should be applied in different situations relating to project problems. Table 6 presents responses that came up in the study and also those that came up in the literature [13,18]. Among those that came up in the study were: "more effective monitoring", "communication with management" and in some cases, "adapting to the situation". Also evident were various people's ways of reacting, depending on their respective experience and methods of management: either a quick reaction or cautiousness. As for the effects of the procedures, it should be borne in mind that the so-called Hartney Effect has been observed quite unambiguously in project work. When the client expresses 'interest' in the activities of the other party, this has an improving influence on the quality of activity.

6.2. Dependency net

The material can be used for drawing up a "dependency" net (Fig. 3) between early warnings, causes of problems, problems and responses. It has early warnings on the left (rectangles), followed by the causes of problems (rectangles in bold type), then by the problems (rectangles with rounded corners) and the responses that came up in the study (rectangles with rounded corners in bold type). The figure includes the "dependencies" that occurred in at least 2% of the observation material. However, according to the qualitative research method, all observations are significant.

As a consequence, the complete observation material must be used (it can be found in the original research paper [13,18]). This becomes important when one is to examine the material on a basic classification level of early warnings and find out the problems the signals refer to and the prevalent reasons for them. At this stage, it becomes evident that the main classification and the picture derived using it may provide information that is "misleading", too generalising and coarse. Fig. 4 [13,18] depicts how large and diverse the net of early warnings related project problems and the causes of the problems can be in some cases.

This picture has the early warnings on the left, with the problems (scheduling problems) in the middle in halftone, and the causes of problems on the right. The arrows depict the dependencies. The problems and

Table 6 Responses to consider on the basis of the signals. [6,7,13,18–22,31].

Problems	Response recommendation
1. Project environment management	Problem external to the project Stakesholder Management [31]
2. Objective/Scope	Preparing the project plan
Technical Performance	Problem analysis methods
Delivery problem	Prequalification of suppliers
	Exerting Pressure as problem surface
	Delivery control (inspections)
	Schedule correction (adaptation)
	Hiring expertise from outside
	Preparing exact contracts
Cost overruns	Problem analysis methods
	Budget adaptation
	Strictly disciplined budgeting
Schedules	Problem analysis methods
	Schedule correction (adaptation)
	Increasing resources
	Negotiations
	Exerting pressure as problem surface
3. Client	Problem external to the project management
	Stakeholder Management [31]
	Client perspective [30]
	Being cautious
4. Project manager	Problem external to the project
5. Management and Leadership	The literature; the chapter on Mgn. and Ls
Mgn. and Ls. problems	Hiring expertise from outside
	Organization changes fake organization, unofficial channels
Differences in project culture	Negotiations
	Adapting to the situation
6. Project group/organization	The literature; Team management
Lack of resources	Acquiring additional resources
	Adapting schedules
7. Personnel/motivation	The literature; the chapters on leadership
8. Project Planning	The literature; making a project plan
	Making plans by ourselves
	No accepting of incomplete plans
9. Monitoring/Control	The literature; project control
10. Communication	The literature; communication

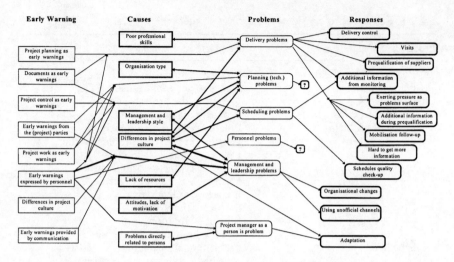

Figure 3 A net of early warnings–project problems–causes of problems–responses [13,18].

their causes may influence each other. The early warnings refer to problems only. Through the halftone field, there are broken lines to point out the early warning from which the cause of each problem was found in the study.

6.3. Methods

Methods is the group of procedures (responses) for obtaining more information on the situation. Thus, they are part of the model presented farther on, when the information available on the possibly impending problem is very inexact but it is estimated that there is enough time for countermeasures. Several other methods for finding early warnings also came up in the study conducted at HUT. They can be used to obtain more information on impending problems. Table 7 presents a summary of the methods identified.

The experience of the observers and their keenness to observe and identify preliminary signals can be considered the most important approach or method. A number of methods typical to project work also came up during research, e.g. "monitoring mobilisation at the site", "asking provocative questions in tender negotiations". According to the study documents, written material is one of the most common sources for early warnings. Thus, analysing them is a very fruitful method for gaining more information. Such analysis would include for example reading between the lines of contracts, observing the reports tone and regularity of publication, careful searching for loopholes in contracts etc. However, one should not forget the conventional methods used in project work for obtaining information, such as reporting in general, monitoring and control, setting goals and comparing

264

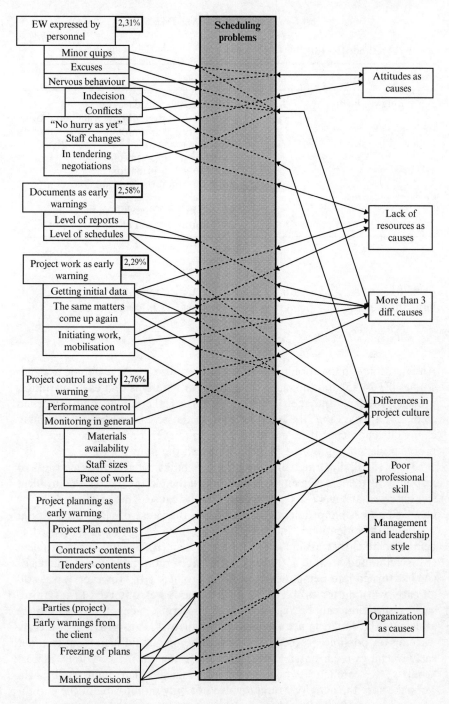

Figure 4 Dependencies between early warnings relating to scheduling problems and the causes of problems [13,18].

265

Table 7 Methods [13,18].

Project problems	Method
Scheduling problems	Advence schedule checkup
	More information obtain while monitoring
Cost-related problems	More information obtain while monitoring
Financial problems	Advance research
	Hard to get information
	Hard to get information
	More information in prequalification
Delivery problems	Visiting the supplier
	More information while monitoring
	Monitoring site mobilization

them to results, and regularly held project meetings. Still, these methods have the weakness of being based on "historical" information.

6.4. Chains

An interesting observation made from the literature [10,20,21], some research studies [23,24,25] and the material used for this study is that early warnings, project problems and their causes may form rather long, multi-branched chains. It appears that the interpretation of the observed phenomenon may change its character, from early warning up to even becoming a cause for a problem, depending on the point in time and the point of view.

Fig. 5 [13,18] illustrates the formation of chains, cited with some types of responses as the last element (not included in the picture). First, the problem (A) observed at time $T-n$ ("yesterday") has its cause. This problem (A) may be causing possible problem (B). Thus, it is the cause of (B). If this causal relationship is identified "immediately", problem (A) can be interpreted as being also an early warning for possible problem (B). Second, when problem (B) is actualised at time T ("today"), the interpretation of the character of (A) has turned into being the cause of the problem (B). However, it was still an early warning for problem (B) at the time it was observed ($T-n$). third, such a situation can be repeated at T ("today"), when the observations anticipate the situation at time $T + m$ "tomorrow", thus providing an early warning on possible problem (C). Naturally, one could also identify other early warnings for a possible problem. The chain can be very long, almost "endless". Research in risk management also indicates that chains can branch. To make sure the activity would involve not only monitoring of the current situation but to facilitate actual project management, many more things are needed (not included in the picture): countermeasures for the problems, follow-up, analysing, and observation regarding the early warnings.

266

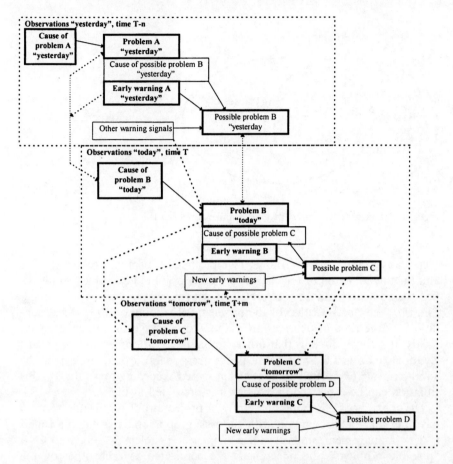

Figure 5 A chain of problem causes–problems–early warnings–responses [13,18].

7. Set theory and early warnings

This study [13,18] examined project problems found in the literature and their causes from various points of view. The problems and their causes were found to be so similar that they were combined in the same table. Fig. 5 examined how the interpretation of the phenomena observed in projects — early warnings, problems and their causes — may vary during the various stages of a project. The material found in literature and in the study would seem to indicate three things. First of all, it is possible during projects to observe and identify phenomena that can be interpreted "purely" to be warnings on future problems, signals expressing existing problems or actual causes of problems. However, in no circumstances could they be interpreted in more than one way. Second, the research study [13,18] found a significant similarity among project problems observed in project-related literature,

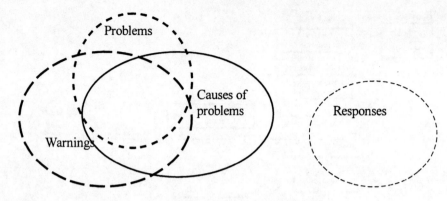

Figure 6 Groups of warnings, problems and causes [13,18].

their causes and early warnings (symptoms) of project problems. This and the phenomenon of the chains formed (Fig. 5) indicates that an identified phenomenon can be interpreted in various ways, such as a warning, as a problem or as a cause of the problem, depending on the project conditions at the time of observation in the various stages of project activity. Lastly, it is fairly obvious that other factors likely belonging to two groups could also occur. Corrective measures (responses) would appear to be another group completely separate from these. According to set theory, this situation can be expressed in the way it is presented in Fig. 6.

The contents of this common "group of project problems" would seem to have quite a lot in common with the risk groups and risk factors found in risk management studies. When a project problem is perceived as a "possible problem", the phenomena are connected to each other on the basis of the definition of risk.

8. Concepts relating to the phenomenon and the character of risks

According to the definition of risk, any possible problem is a risk. Because early warnings refer to a problem that might emerge in the future, the relation of the early warnings phenomenon to risk management is rather obvious. This is evident in both the literature [10] and in the empirical section of the study [13,18]. Fig. 7 presents the main concepts, their parallel concepts and how they influence each other.

9. Possibilities for utilisation

The observations made regarding the methods and the attitudes of the interviewees serve to indicate the possibility of utilising early warnings as a

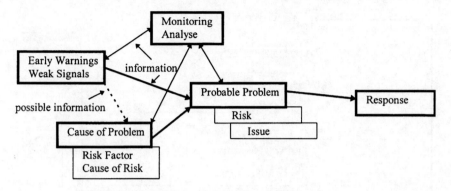

Figure 7 Concepts relating to the early warnings phenomenon and their relation to risk management [13,18].

tool in project management. Some models for utilising weak signals can be found in the literature. Ansoff [11] presents a strategic issue management system (SIMS) model in the area of strategic planning and management. He has later transformed this model into a model for weak signals strategic issue management (WSSIM) [11]. Several other writers have also presented their own SIMS models differing from that of Ansoff's mostly in detail. In his book Åberg [2] (written in Finnish) explains the external and internal scanning that is part of company communications. The model is based on the principles of the IPRA Mexico declaration [25]. Core questions posed by Åberg applicable also to project work are:

"Is the change observed a symptom of a larger, essential change or is it merely random variation."
"How is it possible to observe weak signals as soon as possible, so that there would be as much time as possible to respond to them".

[2, p. 250]

As part of his "managerial breakthrough" management model, Juran [26] states that sensors are required for activity based on "sensing before the fact". In this case, we would be looking at indicators of the early warning type.

None of the models presented in the literature is applicable in project work without modification. One could always try to apply the problem analysis model developed by Kepner–Tregoe Inc. [27]; however, this one is thorough but works slowly. The basic principles of the models presented are applicable to project work, but the procedures used must be very flexible, quick and simple.

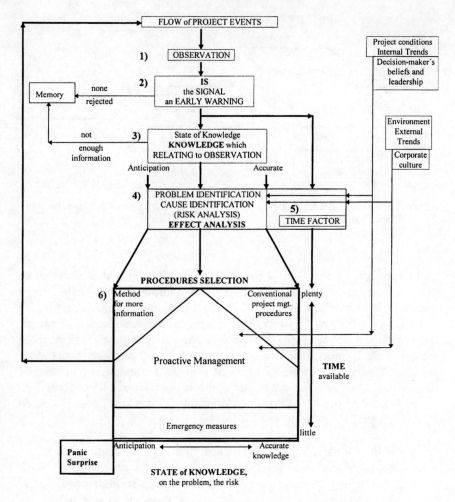

Figure 8 A model for utilising early warnings [13,18].

10. A model for the utilisation of the theory

Fig. 8 presents the model for utilising early warnings, developed during the research work reported herein. In addition to Ansoff's WSIM model, it was influenced by ideas presented by Åberg [2] and the structural model of the functional unit of social activity by Heiskala [28] and conversations about the phenomenon with a number of people.

In a warnings based situation depicted by Fig. 8, the first (1) phase is the identification of a warning (signal), almost always by a person, from the flow of project events. In the second phase (2), the observer accepts the finding and starts to react, i.e. considers it an "early warning" or considers it useless and rejects it. Now, we can use the typical groups of early warning types established by the research, including their descriptions and examples of the kinds of warnings there can be (Table 1). In the third (3) phase, the observer will try to determine the state of knowledge gained from the early warning, and the meaning of the information to the project. The scale of evaluation need not be absolute or generally applicable as long as it can somehow be specified in the situation. If the information obtained appears unnecessary or too scarce, it should still be recorded, because further information on the matter could come up later. In the fourth phase (4), the emerged problem (risk) and its possible causes (risk factors, the sources of risk) must be identified. In addition to all the information (typology) provided by the warning, this evaluation is also influenced at least by project conditions (internal trends), external trends and the "beliefs" of the interpreter regarding the signal. If not earlier, the possible utilisation of various methods of project risk management (risk analysis, etc.) will come up at this stage. One could also use a database such as the one developed in the course of the study [13,18], a database on the relation of early warnings to project problems (risks) and the knowledge on the dependencies between project problems and their causes (risk factors). Fig. 3 expresses this in a simplified manner. The time factor (5) is being considered along with the identification of risks. An answer to the following question should be sought: how much time is needed for countermeasures (responses) required by the problem (the risk)? In other words, what is the urgency of the situation? This is also strongly influenced by the project situation, project conditions (internal trends) and external trends, and the interpreter of the signals.

One of the problems in project work is that the person who identifies/interprets the early warnings is often not the same as the one who is making the decisions. Especially regarding the client, the final decision-maker is often rather inexperienced in the special matters relating to project work. The greatest difficulty in phases (4) and (5) likely is convincing the decision-maker that there is a problem, that it has an effect on the project and that corrective measures (responses) are necessary. Here, one could talk of a believability problem. It came up in the interviews and is strongly present in research concerning military intelligence, international security and risks [3,4]. The observer must convince the decision-maker that the impending problem has personal significance to the decision-maker. This can hardly be achieved with the help of any particular method; sensitivity toward early warnings (weak signals) must be instead cultivated. One must trust the information derived from the signals and make others believe in it as well.

Finally (6), one should try to decide which responses to focus on in any given situation. This is depicted by the lower part of the matrix in Fig. 8, which includes these aids for decision-making: (a) the information available on the problem (the risk) and its graded effect on the project, and (b) the urgency of countermeasures (the amount of time available). At least the following factors also directly influence the selection of responses: (c) project conditions (internal trends), (d) the environment (external trends), (e) the decision-maker's position within the project and/or his/her "beliefs", (f) corporate culture, and (g) the effects the response is hoped and believed to have on the project.

Extreme situations in the decision matrix are as follows:

(a) If there is plenty of time, but the quality of the information available is not so good (a feeling), one may settle for choosing "methods" for gaining more information. (Table 7) This is the upper left part of the matrix.
(b) When there is plenty of time and the information on the problem (the risk) is exact, conventional project management methods may be used. This is the upper right part of the matrix.
(c) If there is little time and the exactness of the information is anything between a feeling and exact information, various "emergency responses" may have to be used. This is the lower part of the matrix.
(d) When "outside" of the matrix, if there is no advance information on the risk and thus it materialises by surprise, some kind of a "panic situation" will probably emerge as the risk actualises.
(e) When in the "middle" of the matrix, one could think of applying proactive management. This study cannot be used to develop this idea any further.

It is also significant to note that many of the problems (risks) may be outside the authority of the person making the decisions. This becomes evident in the material when analysed.

No advance information should be entirely abandoned. Even insignificant information should be recorded somewhere for comparison with other older data and later with some new data. This is difficult to achieve manually, but technically possible using database programs.

11. Leadership

The application of the phenomenon of early warnings seemingly makes it possible to expand to greater portion of project management, especially in the domain of (human) leadership. The type groups of early warnings are related to the human factor in 47.5% of the observations in the basic material and in 49.6% of the case material. Of all the examples of early warnings that came up in the literature review, those that relate to humans account for roughly 66%. In all observations regarding early warnings, human activity has been kept in the background to say the least. For instance, documents are always drawn up by humans. Humans are the direct source of warnings in roughly 62% of the observations. In the empirical material, human-related problems account for 35.8% of the observation cells in the basic material and for 28.4% in the case material. As for the causes of problems, the observation is that the greater part of the causes are directly due to humans. Human action is the basis of all of the cause groups.

All of the view points presented here show how strongly the phenomenon of early warnings is connected to people and human behaviour. As a result, the signals could help in leadership issues. However, in doing this we would be going into the area of leadership and behavioural sciences, which were not considered by this study.

12. The effect of the study on theories

This study shows that it appears to be possible to observe, in project-related activity, early warnings that fulfil the criteria set by Ansoff's theory for the existence of such signals. The study appears to show that the different warnings observable in the project activity have a varying informative content. This is consistent with Ansoff's theory. No unambiguous scale exists in this study for measuring this informative content. The scale remains very imprecise. The same applies to the time factor with early warnings. The time factor appears to exist, but it cannot be measured from the material researched. The study enlarges the area of application for Ansoff's theory into project-related activity.

This investigation finds that many project professionals are already familiar with the existence and they make use of these indicators in some unstructured and often unconscious way. A similar observation can also be made of literature on project management. The study hopefully adds an element to project management theories that was previously known but little researched. This element is project control using imprecise information. We have attempted to explain the characteristics of this phenomenon in the study. The intent is to increase knowledge of the theories of project management.

This analysis states that the project problems to be forecast, using early warnings, are risks (the definition of risk). In this sense, the early warnings phenomenon can be said to be primarily a project risk management theory. Theories regarding project risk management acknowledge the existence of early warnings only as a reference (risk symptoms) [29], although Niwa [10] includes the idea of risk alarm in project risk management requirements. Despite the limitations of the study, it can be said that it confirms the risk symptoms element of the project risk management theories. This element may be used to increase the predictability of the actualisation of risks, however, further research is required.

13. Conclusions

There is less and less time to react to emerging challenges, problems and opportunities in projects in the changing, turbulent environment of companies and hence of projects as well. Companies cannot afford to have projects fail in any way, particularly with reference to time, finances or technology. The conventional methods of project management are based mainly on the "history" of project events and hence cannot really anticipate emerging or unforeseeable problems.

In the flow of project events, countless signals (early warnings) have been observed to occur, the precision and imprecision of the content of the information they provide varies greatly. At their most imprecise, they are mere "gut feelings", while at their most precise they can be given a numerical value and what can be done about the situation is known precisely. The precision of the signals improves in time but the time available for counter-measures decreases, because the problem's moment of manifestation is not likely to be moved farther.

Project managers may observe such signals and interpret them according to their experience and observation conditions, provided they have become sensitive to observe such signals. The management will gain information on emerging problems (opportunities). Management will be able to take appropriate action as the project situation, project environment and the time available allow. The sooner the better. In the least dangerous case, it would be possible use some method to collect more information on an emerging problem and at its worst, a problem will come as a complete surprise and panic-driven activity ensues. The biggest challenge is to get the actual decision-makers to believe in the possibility of problems and the necessity of counter-measures, because these people generally have little experience with the clients in projects.

In part, the model presented in this article may help resolve this problem.

Acknowledgements

The writers wish to thank all interviewees. Many thanks particularly to Emeritus Professor Tauno Olkkonen, Professor Karlos Artto (HUT) and Emeritus Professor Eino Tunkelo for their very decisive advice during the research. Thanks also to Kalle Kähkönen, PhD, for his valuable advice on the paper. Thanks to Mr A Jaskari, M.Sc.(Eng), Mr P Vesanto, M.Sc. (Eng), Mr V Ohlsson, M.Sc.(Eng), for evaluation of the materials of the research. Thanks to Mr Juho Tunkelo for translating the paper into English and to Dr Villard Griffin, Seneca, SC, USA for editing the paper.

References

[1] Ansoff Igor H. Managing strategic surprise by response to weak signals. California Management Review 1975;18(2):21–33.
[2] Åberg L. Viestintä-Tuloksen tekijä. 3rd ed. Helsinki, Finland: Tietopaketti Oy, 1989.

[3] Herman M. Intelligence power in peace and war. Cambridge, UK: Cambridge University Press, 1996.

[4] Betts KR. Surprise attack, lessons for defense planning. Washington, DC, USA: The Brookings Institution, 1982.

[5] Morris R. Early warning indicators of corporate failure, a critical review of previous research and further empirical evidence. UK: Ashgate Publishing, 1997.

[6] Kerzner H. Project management: a systems approach to planning, scheduling and controlling. 5th ed. Princeton, NJ, USA: Van Nostrand Reinhold, 1994.

[7] Harrison FL. Advance project management, a structure approach. 3rd ed. USA: Gower Publishing, 1993.

[8] International Journal of Project Management, 1994;Feb/May:12(1/2).

[9] The State-of the Art in Project Risk Management. International Project Management Association, Proceedings 1989, UK.

[10] Niwa K. Knowledge-based risk management in engineering. New York, USA: Wiley, 1989.

[11] Ansoff IH. Implanting strategic management. USA: Prentice-Hall, 1980.

[12] Ashley DB. Project risk identification using inference subjective expert assessement and historical data. In: The State-of-the-Art in Project Risk Management. International Project Management Association, Proceedings, 1989. p. 9–28.

[13] Nikander IO. Ennakkovaroitusmerkit teollisuusinvestointiprojekteissa, ja niiden hyväksikäytöstä projektinohjauksessa (Early warnings in industrial investment projects and how to use them as tools of project management). Licentiate's dissertation, Helsinki University of Technology, Department of Industrial Engineering and Management, Espoo, Finland, 1998.

[14] Hirsijärvi S, Hurme H. Teemahaastattelu. Helsinki, Finland: Yliopistopaino, 1993.

[15] Wiio OA. System models of information and communication. The Finnish Journal of Business Economics 1974;23(1):3–24.

[16] Wiio O. Viestinnän perusteet. 5th ed. Finland: Weilin-Göös, 1989.

[17] Nikander IO, Eloranta E. Preliminary signals and early warnings in industry investment project. International Journal of Project Management 1997;15(6): 371–9.

[18] Nikander IO. Application of theory of weak signals and early warnings in managing projects. Unpublished manuscript, copyright IO. Nikander, Lappohia, Finland, 1999.

[19] Lewis JP. The project manager's desk reference. USA: Probus Publishing, 1993.

[20] Kezsbom DS, Schilling DL, Edward KA. Dynamic project management. A practical guide for managers & engineers. New York, USA: Wiley, 1989.

[21] Lientz BL, Rea KP. Project management fot the 21st century. New York, USA: Academic Press, 1967.

[22] Whitten N. Managing software development projects, formula for success. 2nd ed. New York, USA: Wiley, 1967.

[23] Bufaied AS. Risks in the construction industry: their causes and their effects at the project level. Doctoral thesis, University of Manchester, Institute of Science and Technology, UK, 1987.

[24] Lim B, Ting C. Causal modeling construction project performance, (Volumes I and II). Ph.D. theses, Heriot-Watt University, UK, 1987.

[25] International Public Relations Association (IPRA). Mexican Statement, Mexico City, Mexico, 1979.
[26] Juran JM. In: Managerial breakthrough: the classic book on improving management performance (revised edition). New York, USA: McGraw-Hill, 1967. p. 284.
[27] Kepner-Tregoe Inc. Ongelmanratkaisu-ja päätöksentekoseminaari. Rastor Oy, Copyright 1983 by Kepner-Tregoe Inc., Helsinki, Finland, 1983.
[28] Heiskala R. Sosiologinen kulttuuritutkimus. In: Mäkelä K., editor. Kvalitatiivisen aineiston analyysi ja tulkinta. Helsinki, Finland: Gaudeamus, 1990. p. 9–29.
[29] Project Management Institute. Guide to the project management body of knowledge. USA: PMI, 1995.
[30] Kleim RL, Ludin IS. The PEOPLE SIDE of project management. UK: Gower Publishing, 1994.
[31] Cleland DI. Project management, strategic design and implementation. 2nd ed. New York, USA: McGraw-Hill, 1967.

15

THE DESIGN SCHOOL

Reconsidering the basic premises of strategic management

Henry Mintzberg

Source: *Strategic Management Journal* 11(3) (1990): 171–95.

Among the schools of thought on strategy formation, one in particular underlies almost all prescription in the field. Referred to as the 'design school', it proposes a simple model that views the process as one of design to achieve an essential fit between external threat and opportunity and internal distinctive competence. A number of premises underlie this model: that the process should be one of consciously controlled thought, specifically by the chief executive; that the model must be kept simple and informal; that the strategies produced should be unique, explicit, and simple; and that these strategies should appear fully formulated before they are implemented. This paper discusses and then critiques this model, focusing in particular on the problems of the conscious assessment of strengths and weaknesses, of the need to make strategies explicit, and of the separation between formulation and implementation. In so doing, it calls into question some of the most deep-seated beliefs in the field of strategic management, including its favorite method of pedagogy.

The literature that can be subsumed under 'strategy formation' is vast, diverse and, since 1980, has been growing at an astonishing rate. There has been a general tendency to date it back to the mid-1960s, although some important publications precede that date, such as Newman's initial piece 'to show the nature and importance of strategy' (p. iii) in the 1951 edition of his textbook *Administrative Action* (1951: 110–118). Of course the literature on military strategy goes back much further, in the case of Sun Tzu probably to the fourth century B.C. (Griffith, in Sun Tzu, 1971: ix).

277

A good deal of this literature naturally divides itself into distinct schools of thought. In another publication (Mintzberg, 1989), this author has identified ten of these. Three are prescriptive in orientation, treating strategy formation as a process of conceptual design, of formal planning, and of analytical positioning (the latter including much of the research on the content of competitive strategies). Six other schools deal with specific aspects of the process in a descriptive way, and are labeled the entrepreneurial school (concerned with strategy formation as a visionary process), the cognitive school (a mental process), the learning school (an emergent process), and the environmental school (a passive process). A final school, also descriptive, but integrative and labeled configurational, by seeking to delineate the stages and sequences of the process, helps to place the findings of these other schools in context.

This paper addresses itself to the first of these schools, in some ways the most entrenched of the ten. Its basic framework underlies almost all prescription in this field and, accordingly, has had enormous impact on how strategy and the strategy-making process are conceived in practice as well as in education and research. Hence our discussion, and especially critique, of this school can in some ways be taken as a commentary on the currently popular beliefs in the field of strategic management in general. Our intention, however, is not to dismiss so important a school of thought, but rather to understand it better and so place it into its natural context, and thereby open up thinking in the field in general.

This paper probes first into the basic model of the design school, then into the basic premises that underlie it. That leads to a critique of this school, which gives rise to an attempt to place it into its own viable context—the types of organizations and of situations most suited to it. In conducting this investigation we draw widely on the literature of this school, but use one text in particular—almost certainly this school's best known. In this sense this paper can also be viewed as a rather extensive review of a book that has had a major impact on the field of strategic management.

Origins of the design school

Ostensibly the simplest and most fundamental view of strategy formation is as a process of informal conception—the use of a few essential concepts to design 'grand strategy.' Of these concepts the most essential is that of congruence or match. In the words of the design school's best-known proponents: 'Economic strategy will be seen as the match between qualification and opportunity that positions a firm in its environment' (Christensen, Andrews, Bower, Hamermesh, and Porter, 1982: 164)[1] 'Capture success' seems to be the motto of the design school; 'find out what you are good at and match it with what the world wants and needs.' These capabilities or qualifications have been variously referred to as 'distinctive competence,' 'differential,' 'competitive,' or 'comparative advantage' (the latter more commonly used in the context of public policy), or more simply (and broadly) an organization's 'strengths and weaknesses.'

The design school has generally been associated with the Business Policy group at the Harvard Business School. That group has pursued its own strategy for, as we shall see later, there is a clear congruence between the view of strategy formation that it has promoted for several decades and its own pedagogical requirements in using the case study method.

The Christensen *et al.* book quoted from above, entitled *Business Policy: Text and Cases*, first appeared in 1965 (by Learned, Christensen, Andrews, and Guth) and quickly became the dominant textbook in the field, as well as the dominant voice for this school of thought.[2] Certainly its text portion, attributed in the various editions to co-author Kenneth Andrews (who also published this material separately (Andrews, 1971, 1980a, 1987)) stands as the most outspoken and one of the clearest statements of this school, although claims that this school, or even the concept of business strategy itself, originated with this group at Harvard (e.g. Bower, 1986: vii) do not stand up to scrutiny.

Some of the basic concepts that underlie the design school, at least as published, would (as we shall see) appear to have been first stated in the academic world by a Berkeley sociologist named Philip Selznick, in his book *Leadership in Administration*, published in 1957. Even earlier, though less specific, is a 1955 article by Reilley, possible the first reflection of this approach. Another key publication in 1962, *Strategy and Structure*, by historian Alfred Chandler (then at MIT), really established this school's concept of business strategy and its relationship to structure, although mention also has been made of the sophisticated discussion of 'Managerial Strategies' in David G. Moore's paper of that title in 1959. There followed an article by Seymour Tilles in 1963 (then a Harvard Business School lecturer) entitled 'How to evaluate corporate strategy', and a textbook chapter by William Newman of the Columbia University Business School in the same year (see especially 1963: 95–98; the passage noted earlier in the 1951 edition of the Newman textbook might make him the real father of the concept of business strategy in academe, although in private correspondence with this author, Newman has expressed the belief that the overall ideas may have originated in the McKinsey consulting practice, as reflected in the Reilley piece of 1955 (see also McKinsey, 1932, for early suggestions of this thinking)). The Andrews text followed in 1965, the same year that Igor Ansoff published his highly successful book *Corporate Strategy*, based on many of the same concepts (but more in the spirit of the planning school).[3]

Subsequently these ideas embedded themselves in the management literature. Indeed, by the 1980s the Christensen *et al.* textbook was one of the few left that represented them in their pure form, most others favoring the more elaborated renditions of the planning or positioning schools.[4] Accordingly, and given the impact that this rendition of the design school has had over the years—as well as its clarity and forcefulness of expression—we shall use it as a primary source in the discussion that follows, referring to it as the 'Andrews' text'. We shall draw primarily on the 1982 edition of this textbook, but shall also reference relevant variations in its earlier editions as well as the latest one, published in 1987, although the changes from 1965 to 1987 were relatively minor.

The basic design school model

In his 1957 book, Selznick wrote that:

> Leadership sets goals, but in doing so takes account of the conditions that have already determined what the organization can do and to some extent what it must do . . .

> In defining the mission of the organization, leaders must take account of (1) *the internal state of the policy*: the strivings, inhibitions, and competences that exist within the organization, and (2) *the external expectations* that determine what must be sought or achieved if the institution is to survive.
>
> (pp. 62, 67–68)

Selznick also coined the term 'distinctive competence' (pp. 43ff.) and noted that 'the task of leadership is not only to make policy but to build it into the organization's social structure' (pp. 62–63), an aspect of the process that came to be called *implementation*.

Andrews summarizes the essence of his model[5] as

> the intellectual processes of ascertaining what a company *might do* in terms of environmental opportunity, of deciding what it *can do* in terms of ability and power, and of bringing these two considerations together in optimal equilibrium. . . . what the executives of a company *want to do* must also be brought into the strategic decision [as must] what a company *should do*.

Finally, there is 'the implementation of strategy . . . comprised of a series of subactivities which are primarily administrative' (p. 98). The Andrews' text of 1982 splits into two 'books,' the first on 'determining', the second on 'implementing corporate strategy.'

Our depiction of the basic design school model (similar to Andrews' own figure of the development of 'economic strategy' (p. 187), but with other elements of his discussion added (see also his figure on p. 99)), is shown here in Figure 1. Consistent with the attention accorded in the text, the model

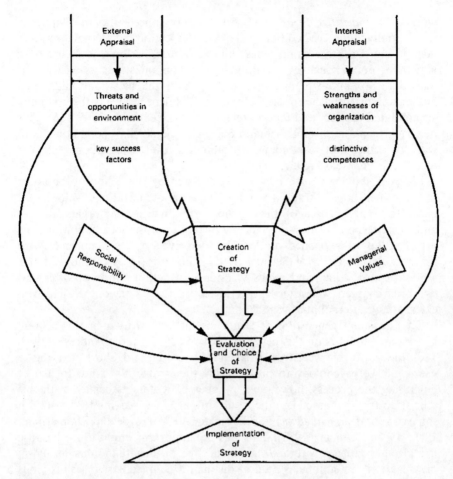

Figure 1 Basic design school model.

places primary emphasis on the appraisals of the external and internal situations, the former uncovering threats and opportunities in the environment, the latter revealing strengths and weaknesses of the organization. Secondary emphasis is placed on understanding the values of the management, as well as its social responsibilities. The match between these elements leads to the creation of strategies, which are then evaluated, with the chosen one subsequently implemented. Andrews does not provide extensive discussion of any of these issues (the whole text portion of the 1982 book numbers 114 pages, the rest of the 838-page book being cases), although others have developed some of these themes more extensively.

On external appraisal, Andrews' section on 'The nature of the company's environment' totals 20 pages, but 12 of these come from Michael Porter's work on *Competitive Strategy* (1980), literally spliced into the Andrews' text, initially in the 1982 edition.[6] Likewise, the section on internal appraisal, 'identifying corporate competences and resources,' is brief, touching on a variety of points, such as the difficulty 'for organizations as well as for individuals to know themselves' (p. 183) and the idea that 'individual and unsupported flashes of strength are not as dependable as the gradually accumulated product-and market-related fruits of experience' (p. 185). This ties back to an important theme in Selznick's book, that 'commitments to ways of acting and responding are built into the organization,' intrinsic to its very 'character' (1957: 67).

Figure 1 shows two other factors considered by this school to be taken into consideration in strategy-making. These are organizational values—the beliefs and preferences of those who formally lead the organization— and social responsibilities—specifically the ethics of the society in which the organization is embedded, at least as perceived by its managers. With the notable exception of Selznick (1957), however, most authors in this school accord values and ethics secondary attention. Andrews offers his two brief chapters well after he has developed the framework dealing with external and internal appraisals.

On the actual generation of strategies, little is written in this school, besides an emphasis on this being a 'creative act,' to quote Andrews (1982: 186). Indeed, if this were true, what more could be said, short of trying to use cognitive psychology to probe inside the strategist's mind. In lieu of describing the process, however, a number of writers associated with this school do try to characterize the result, in particular seeking to distinguish some core or *dominant element* of the strategy (e.g. Tregoe and Zimmerman, 1980: 43 and Ohmae, 1982). This has an important implication, because it replaces strategies within *strategy*. In effect, rather than considering an organization's intentions as a set of distinct, if coupled, strategies (as tends to be done in the planning and even the positioning schools), it treats them as an integrated concept.

Once strategies are created, the next step in the model is to evaluate them and choose the best one. The assumption, in other words—usually implicit— is that several alternative strategies have been produced, and one is to be selected. There is an ambiguity here, however, because even writers such as Andrews, who clearly view strategy formation as a custom-made process of design (for which there is evidence that organizations tend to produce only a single solution; Mintzberg, Raisinghani and Theoret, 1976), assume that alternate strategies (in other words, alternate conceptions of the business) will be evaluated to select a single one (Andrews' text, pp. 105, 109).

Tilles published first on this subject in an article entitled 'How to evaluate corporate strategy' (1963). Andrews (pp. 105–108) followed by combining Tilles's list of six criteria with other elements of the model, while Rumelt, a graduate of the Harvard doctoral program in policy, elaborated these ideas in a most succinct (1980) and sophisticated (1979) way, nevertheless retaining the spirit of the design school.

Finally, virtually all of the literature of this school makes clear that, once strategy is designed and agreed upon, it is then implemented. We show implementation on the diagram as flaring out from formulation, as if the process draws on a variety of data to narrow down to convergent choice before it diverges again to ensure implementation across the entire organization. Andrews, for example, is clear on the subordinate role of these elements (e.g. p. 543). Interestingly, here also is the one place where he becomes rather specific. He lists 12 steps in the implementation process (backed up by a fair amount of text), a list that seems to encompass any aspect of the strategy process not considered in formulation.[7] The same tends to be true of other design school publications as well.

Premises underlying the design school

Running through all of the literature that we identified with this school are a number of fundamental premises about the process of strategy formation. Some of these tend to be explicit, others implicit, but they are always evident. This is especially so in the Andrews' text, although all are at one time or another qualified in his discussion. But it is the central themes of a work that form the impression left with the reader, not the secondary qualifications. Below we discuss seven basic premises that underlie this school.

Premise 1: Strategy formation should be a controlled, conscious process of thought

It is not action that receives the greatest attention from the design school so much as reason—strategies formed through a tightly controlled process of conscious human thought. Action follows, once the strategies have been fully formulated. This theme runs through all of Andrews' writings, for example in the comment that managers 'know what they are really doing' only it they make strategy as 'deliberate as possible' (1981: 24), or more simply, in reference to his 'thesis' about 'conscious strategy' that should be 'consciously implemented' (Andrews' text, p. 543). But this is perhaps made most clear in his comments that, while the model may be simple, it is not necessarily natural (p. 185)—it must be learned, formally (e.g. Andrews' text p. 6).

Andrews is careful to position his view of this process clear of intuition on one side (non-conscious thought) and emergent strategy on the other (where action drives reflection). On intuition, for example, Andrews comments that 'if [strategy] is implicit in the intuition of a strong leader, the organization is likely to be weak and the demands the strategy makes upon it are likely to remain unmet' (pp. 105–106). Likewise, he writes of the need to change 'intuitive skill' into 'conscious skill' (p. 6). And as for his view of emergent strategy, which means pattern in action over time that is not driven by central intention (Mintzberg, 1978; Mintzberg and Waters, 1985), while Andrews presents a definition of strategy in his 1982 text that makes reference to pattern (p. 93), in a new passage in his 1987 text, he makes clear that he means pattern among and across 'goals and policies,' not over time (p. 15; see also Premise 5).

In this edition, as in all the others, Andrews clearly means to associate strategy with intentionality. Corporate strategy, for example, 'defines products and markets—and determines the company's course into the almost indefinite future' (1987: xi). In fact, in his 1982 text, Andrews equates emergent strategy with 'erosion:'

> Strategy will evolve over time, no matter what. It will be affected
> by the consequences of its implementation. But the elucidation of
> goals can transcend incrementalism to make it a series of forays
> and experiments evaluated continuously against stated goals to result
> in the deliberate amendment of strategy or in the curtailment of
> strategic erosion.
>
> (pp. 553–554)

Likewise, Andrews contrasts 'purpose' with 'improvisation,' 'planned progress' with 'drifting' (p. 20). At the end of his text he claims that 'a strategy may suddenly be rationalized to mean something very different from what was originally intended because of the opportunism which at the beginning of this book we declared the conceptual enemy of strategy' (pp. 828–829).[8]

Premise 2: Responsibility for that control and consciousness must rest with the chief executive officer: that person is THE strategist

To the design school, ultimately there is only one strategist, and that is the manager who sits at the apex of the organizational hierarchy. In Hayes' terms, 'this "command-and-control" mentality allocates all major decisions to top management, which imposes them on the organization and monitors them through elaborate planning, budgeting, and control systems' (1985: 117).

Again, the origins of this can be found in Selznick: 'it is the function of the leader-statesman—whether of a nation or a private association—to define the ends of group existence, to design an enterprise distinctively adapted to these ends, and to see that that design becomes a living reality' (1957: 37). Once more Andrews reiterates the point most clearly. On page 3 of his text, he associates the whole field with the 'point of view' of the 'chief executive or general manager'; on page 19, he entitles a section 'the president as architect of organizational purpose' (hence Zand (1981: 125) refers to this school as the 'rational architect' model); and on page 545 he writes that 'the general manager is principally concerned with determining and monitoring the adequacy of strategy, with adapting the firm to changes in its environment, and with securing and developing the people needed to carry out the strategy or to help with its constructive revision or evolution.' As we shall soon discuss, in the 1987 text Andrews widens the participation of others in the strategy formulation process, especially in the 'innovative' corporation, but not at the expense of the chief executive's central role.

It might be noted that this premise not only relegates other members of the organization to subordinate roles in strategy formation, but it also precludes external actors from the process altogether (except for the directors, who Andrews believes must review strategy (1980b, 1981)). This is most clearly reflected in Andrews' discussion of the ethics discussion in terms of the social responsibility of the managers rather than the sheer power of outsiders. This, in fact, is just one aspect of a larger problem associated with the design school—the relegation of the environment to a minor role, input to strategy formation but not an intrinsic part of the process, to be accounted for and then navigated through but not interacted with.

Premise 3: The model of strategy formation must be kept simple and informal

The Preface to the Harvard textbook contains a quotation by Andrews that 'the idea of corporate strategy constitutes a simple practitioner's theory, a kind of Everyman's conceptual scheme' (p. 14). Later, he adds in the text that this 'is not a "theory" attended in the rigorous sense by elegance and vigor', nor is it 'really a "model," for the relationships designated by the concept are not quantifiable;' rather it serves as an 'informing idea' (p. 12), or, as Rumelt puts it, 'a set of constructs' (1984: 558).

Fundamental to (what we nonetheless prefer to call) the model is the belief that elaboration and formalization will sap it of its essence. This premise in fact goes with the last: one way to ensure that strategy can be controlled in one mind is to keep the process simple. As Andrews writes: 'When the variety of what must be known cannot be reduced by a sharply focused strategy to the capacity of a single mind and when the range of a company's activities spans many industries and technologies, the problems of formulating a coherent strategy begin to get out of hand' (p. 182).

This premise, together with the first, forces Andrews to tread a fine line throughout his text, between nonconscious intuition on one side and formal analysis on the other, a position he seems to characterize as 'an act of judgment' (p. 108). This also seems to differentiate clearly the design school from the entrepreneurial school on one side and the other prescriptive schools of planning and positioning on the other (one emphasizing elaboration of the same basic model, with a vengeance, the other, formal analysis of certain of its components).

We have already noted Andrews' stand on intuition; on planning he writes that 'this book ... virtually ignores the mechanisms of planning on the grounds that, detached from strategy, they miss their mark' (p. 10).[9]

Of course, if elaboration is the problem, then even theory and research can pose a threat. Thus, Andrews adopts a position in the text that is not just atheoretical but decidedly anti-theory. For example, all of the research on organization structure is dismissed with the comment that 'the literature of organization theory is by itself ... of very little use in managing a live organization' (p. 554).

The introduction to the first edition of the textbook contained the following comment:

> A considerable body of literature purporting to make general statements about policy-making is in existence. It generally reflects either the unsystematically reported experience of individuals or the logical projection to general management of concepts taken from engineering, economics, psychology, sociology, or mathematics. Neither suffices.
>
> (Learned et al., 1965: 6)

On the latter Andrews added: 'The disciplines cited have much to do with business, but their purposes are not ours. Knowledge generated for one set of ends is not readily applicable to another' (p. 6). The text went on to note that 'research has been for some time under way, but is not yet advanced enough to make more than a modest claim on our attention ... the most valid literature for our purpose is not that of general statements but case studies' (p. 6). These comments survived virtually intact to the 1982 edition, the most significant change being that research now 'begins to make a claim on our attention' (p. 6). Moreover, added is the statement that 'the books referred to [in the footnotes] comprise a relevant but incidental source of knowledge'. (It is, in fact, instructive to consider these references. In all, there are 39 of them to theoretical works in the footnotes of the 1982 edition of the text, of which 31 are by faculty members or doctoral students at the Harvard Business School.)[10]

It might be noted that this treatment of theory extends even to the work of a co-author whose ideas are contained in the same book. As noted earlier, Michael Porter's views (centrally located in the positioning school) were literally spliced into that portion of the text on assessing the environment. The text on either side of it, however, questions assumptions fundamental to Porter's work (1980, 1985). To take just one obvious example:

> The choice of objectives and the formulation of policy to guide action in the attainment of objectives depend upon many variables unique to a given organization and situation. It is not possible to make useful generalizations about the nature of these variables or to classify their possible combinations in all situations.
>
> (Andrews' text, p. 5)

Thus the Porter graft does not take, and, more importantly, other theory has not been allowed to infiltrate the model.

Premise 4: Strategies should be unique: the best ones result from a process of creative design

As suggested above, it is the specific situation that matters, not any system of general variables. It therefore follows that strategies have to be tailored to the individual case: 'In each company, the way in which distinctive competence, organizational resources, and organizational values are combined is or should be unique' (Andrews' text, p. 187). Stronger words are offered on page 109: 'sometimes the companies of an industry run like sheep all in one direction' although imitation 'does not constitute the assurance of soundness.'

As a result of this premise, the design school says little about the content of strategies themselves, but instead concentrates on the process by which they should be developed. And that process above all should be a 'creative act' (Andrews' text, p. 186), to build on *distinctive* competence. Writing in support of the positioning school, Hofer and Schendel refer to what we are calling the design school as the 'situational philosophy' (1978: 203), at one extreme of the field, in contrast with the 'principles of management' approach at the other.

Premise 5: Strategies emerge from this design process fully formulated

As noted in passages cited above, this school offers little room to incrementalist views or emergent strategies. It is the big picture that results from the process—the grand strategy, an overall concept of the business. This is no Darwinian view of strategy formation but the Biblical version, with strategy the final conception! There is, in other words, a strong implication that strategy as perspective appears at a point in time, fully formulated, ready to be implemented. How else could Andrews have assumed that the process reduces to 'choice,' a word he uses often, referring also in the Preface to the 1987 edition to '*this* decision,' '*the* strategic decision,' 'the entrepreneurial decision . . . [once] identified' (p. xiv, italics added). In other words, the assumption is that the strategist is able to line

287

up alternative strategies before him to be evaluated so that one can be definitively chosen.

Premise 6: These strategies should be explicit and, if possible, articulated, which also favors their being kept simple

While Andrews accepts various reasons for not articulating strategy (such as confidentiality or difficulty of updating (see pp. 96–97)), he clearly views these as necessary evils. In common with virtually all the writers of this school, he believes that strategies should at least be explicit to those who make them and, if at all possible, articulated so that others in the organization can understand them: 'The unstated strategy cannot be tested or contested and is likely therefore to be weak. . . .

A strategy must be explicit to be effective and specific enough to require some action and exclude others' (pp. 105–106).

If strategies are to be so articulated, it also follows that they have to be kept rather simple: to the point, easily stated to be easily understood. 'Simplicity is the essence of good art,' writes Andrews, 'a conception of strategy brings simplicity to complex organizations' (p. 554). To him, strategy helps organizations make better decisions 'by reducing the world of detail to be considered to those central aspects of external environment and internal resources that affect the company and bear on the definition of its business' (p. 835).

Of particular interest to Andrews is the role of outside directors in strategy formation: he believes that they must be actively involved at least in the evaluation and review processes. But this can only happen if strategies are explicit, so that they can be articulated to the directors, and simple, so that they can be understood by people who have only brief time to devote to the organization: 'The power of strategy as a simplifying concept enabling independent directors to *know* the business (in a sense) without being *in* the business will one day be more widely tested at board level' (p. 834).

Premise 7: Finally, only after these unique, full-blown, explicit, and simple strategies are fully formulated can they then be implemented

We have already noted the sharp distinction this school makes between the formulation of strategies on one hand and their implementation on the other. Consistent with classical notions or rationality—diagnosis, prescription, then action—the design school clearly separates thinking from acting (see Bourgeois and Brodwin on their 'change model.' 1984: 246). (It is of interest that the word used is 'implement,' not 'achieve,' the assumption being that given proper implementation, achievement is a foregone conclusion.)

288

Central to this distinction is the associated premise that structure must follow strategy. As Andrews puts it: 'Corporate strategy must dominate the design of organizational structure and processes' (p. 543). The assumption seems to be that each time a new strategy is formulated, the state of structure and everything else organizational is to be considered anew: 'Until we know the strategy we cannot begin to specify the appropriate structure,' writes Andrews (p. 551), as if the existing structure does not bear on the new strategy.

Andrews' qualifications

While these seven premises are clearly evident in Andrews' text, as noted earlier he does qualify virtually all of them, tucking into his text here and there either nuances that soften their character or else comments that acknowledge the unfortunate reality, as compared with the preferred ideal. A number of them have also been added to the 1987 text, for example:

> False hope, oversimplification, and naivete, as well as zest for power, have often led . . . to the assumption that the chief executive officer conceives strategy single-mindedly, talks the board of directors into *pro forma* approval, announces it as fixed policy, and expects it to be promptly executed by subordinates under conventional command and control procedures.
>
> (p. 82)

Andrews rejects this view for all but 'the entrepreneurial startup stage,' while we see it as a not unreasonable caricature of his own text!

In his 1982 text Andrews wrote that 'strategy formulation is itself a process of organization, rather than the masterly conception of a single mind' (p. 827), in other words, at least in 'technically or otherwise complex organizations,' 'an activity widely shared in the hierarchy of management' (p. 828). In 1987 he even contrasted 'constructive engagement' with 'archaic notions of authority, responsibility, hierarchy, status, and centralized decision making' (p. 86). Yet his major justification for this seemed to be the generation of commitment to the strategy emanating from the apex of the organization's hierarchy. 'Commitment . . . is a simple reason for the involvement of whatever number of people is required to make a success of whatever is intended' (p. 120; see also pp. 55–56, 59).

Andrews also accepted that 'in real life the processes of formulation and implementation are intertwined' (exist in a 'reciprocal relationship' (1987: 853)), that 'the formulation of strategy is not finished when implementation begins' even though the cases in the book have been arranged around these two topics 'for the sake of orderly presentation' (1982 text, p. 541). He also acknowledges that 'we should look first at the logical proposition that structure should follow strategy in order to cope with the organizational reality that strategy also follows structure' (p. 99), in other words, that 'the structure and processes in place will in fact affect the strategy' (p. 552).

In the 1982 text Andrews acknowledges emergent strategy as well (e.g. p. 553), going further in the 1987 text to discuss 'a balance between focus and flexibility, between a sense of direction and responsiveness to changing opportunities. . . . Corporate strategy need not be a straitjacket. Room for variation, extension, and innovation must be provided' (p. 84). Yet he is careful to avoid association with what he calls extreme incrementalism, understood as reactive improvisation, muddling through, or following one's nose' (p. 83). And elsewhere in the 1987 edition, new sections also make clear the continuing commitment to deliberateness: 'It is not only possible but also essential to plot a course into a future that cannot be foretold . . .' (p. xiii, see also the comments on Japanese management on pp. vi–vii).

Adding all these qualifications together, one can easily come up with quite a different model of strategy formation. But of course, no reader can doubt for which model Andrews stands, and not just 'for the sake of orderly presentation'![11]

One obvious question that arises from a number of these qualifications is why practice seems to differ from the prescribed model, at least some of the time. Andrews does not address the question—research of course does, but he precludes the results of research from his text. Nor does he pursue these qualifications at any length. Most are presented as asides or afterthoughts, while his real commitment remains to the premises themselves as, of course, is natural if he is not to undermine his own position.

The fact is that the premises of the design school combine to form their own tightly integrated strategy—the whole thing really is a 'model' after all. By ultimately remaining true to its premises, Andrews positions the design school in its own niche, distinguishing it particularly from the planning and positioning schools on one side, which by elaborating the model shift it from the realm of judgement to that of analysis, and the entrepreneurial school on the other, which by mystifying the whole process locks it into the inaccessible (and unteachable) realm of intuition. The outstanding question is how large is that niche: how much of the viable strategic behavior of organizations, whether for purposes of description *or* prescription, is it reasonably able to encompass?

Critique of the design school

The writings of the design school can be critiqued on a number of levels. In perhaps the most general sense, the school has denied itself the chance to adapt. Research results that have put parts of it under suspicion were not considered; indeed, there was no reason to, if the model could not be elaborated upon. This problem is well illustrated by the book by Norman Berg (1984), also of Harvard, who provided, two decades after the original Andrews' text, almost the same chapter headings (save an application at the end to the divisionalized firm), with the same points made in the same ways, including even the same qualifications (see for example, pp. 28–33).

As Andrews so keenly argued, the source of data and inspiration for the model was to be the concrete case—the description of one firm in one situation. Ironically, however, his beliefs about theory kept him from using even this rich data base to build better theory. Certainly after 1965, if not before, if there was a relationship, then the model had to drive the writing of cases (for example, if you want to find out how strategy is made, go interview *the* strategist), not vice-versa, since the model has barely changed since then.

Of course, its supporters might contend that the model was good enough in 1965 and remains so today. We shall not promote this contention, however, its contribution has been profound, as we shall point out later, but it has never been good enough, indeed no one model can be. It describes but one approach to strategy formation, and even that one sometimes exhibits a level of generality and a tone of inevitability that seems overly simple in places and, at times, dogmatic. Indeed one sometimes wonders whether, like the testament of a religious prophet, it comprises a set of profound truths subtly buried in simple prescriptions, or else if 'the whole idea is just one big fat platitude' (as the Harvard authors, to their credit, quote a critical company executive in the final case of their 1982 edition (p. 821)).

In the Preface to this 1982 edition the authors wrote that 'our teaching focus then [when the core idea of the book was developed in the early 1960s], as today, emphasizes the determination of corporate strategy (Book One) and the implementation of corporate strategy (Book Two). This format has stood the test of time' (p. viii). But it has not, even in their own school, as attested to by recent difficulties and changes in the Harvard MBA Policy course. That course still splits into two on these lines, but formulation has been moved into the first year of the program, and refashioned in the spirit of the positioning school as Porter articulates it, while the second half on implementation remains (at the time of this writing) in a state of flux after several years of searching for a new formula.

Strategy can locate a system in a niche, but in so doing narrow its perspective. This is what seems to have happened to the design school itself with respect to strategy formation. As noted, the premises of the model deny certain important aspects of strategy formation, including incrementalism and emergent strategy, the influence of existing structure on strategy, and the full participation of actors other than the chief executive. We wish to elaborate on these short-comings in this critique, to indicate how they narrow its perspectives to certain contexts (as indeed, do the premises of most of the other schools).

One point should be made before we probe into the details. Andrews might well argue that we are interpreting his writings too literally, that it is unfair to take apart a *model*—a specified sequence of prescriptive steps—when all he meant to propose was a *framework*. Leaving aside the ambiguities in Andrews' own writings on this point,[12] even leaving aside the fact that an author must be interpreted by his central thrust rather than his secondary qualifications, in the most fundamental sense the two interpretations are not really different. Both are underlaid by some powerful assumptions, a critique of which will underlie our own argument. These concern the central role of conscious thought in strategy formation, that such thought must not only take precedence over action but must precede it in time, and correspondingly that the organization must separate the work of thinkers from that of doers. In our view, these assumptions often prove false, both descriptively and prescriptively. In other words, often not only don't organizations do these things, but by all accounts, they *should not*. This suggests that while the design school framework, if not the model, may never go out of *date*, it can easily go out of *context*.

We develop our critique by considering specific aspects of the model—first, the belief about the need for a conscious assessment of strengths and weaknesses, then the assumed sequence of strategy followed by structure, after that the premise that all strategies should be made explicit, and finally the assumed dichotomy between formulation and implementation. We shall conclude the critique by considering the relationship between the design school model and case study teaching, before closing the paper with a delineation of the contexts we believe to be most appropriate for this school. The reader is asked to bear in mind that although the other prescriptive schools of planning and positioning have broken with certain of the premises of the design school (notably in keeping the process simple and strategies unique, to a lesser extent also in introducing the planner and analyst into the introducing the planner and analyst into the process alongside the chief executive), the fact that they have accepted the most basic ones renders most of the following a critique of those schools as well.

Assessment of strengths and weaknesses: thinking vs. learning

Our critique of the design school revolves around one central theme: its promotion of thought independent of action, strategy formation above all as a process of *conception*, rather than as one of *learning*. We can see this most clearly in a fundamental step in the formulation process, the assessment of strengths and weaknesses.

How does an organization *know* its strengths and weaknesses? On this, the design school is quite clear—by consideration, assessment, judgement supported by analysis, in other words, by conscious thought. One gets the image of executives sitting around a table discussing the strengths, weaknesses, and distinctive competences of an organization, much as do students in a case study class. Having decided what these are, they are then ready to design strategies.

Some writers offer specific lists of potential strengths and weaknesses for all organizations, while others, though not offering such lists, do assume that types of strengths and weaknesses exist *in general*. Andrews, on the other hand, would only associate strengths and weaknesses with a particular organization—its competences are *distinctive* to itself. But does even that specify them precisely enough?

In his article on 'strategic capability', Lenz (1980) critiques the use of an 'organizational frame of reference'—usually based on some abstract ideal or a comparison with the situation of the past—with an external frame of reference. In other words, internal capability has to be assessed with respect to external context. But as we have already mentioned, there is a tendency in the design school to slight the environment in favor of a focus on the organization itself (which may manifest itself in a tendency to overstate strengths and under emphasize weaknesses (e.g. Katz, 1970: 350; see also Dimma, 1985: 251). But the problem of assessing strengths and weaknesses may go deeper still. Might competences not also be distinctive to time, even distinctive to application (Radosevich, 1974: 360; see also Hofer and Schendel, 1978: 148–150)? And can any organization really be sure of its strengths before it tests them, empirically?

The point we wish to make came out most clearly, if inadvertently, in a study carried out at Harvard by Howard Stevenson (1976), published under the title 'Defining corporate strengths and weaknesses'. Starting out with a conventional design school view of these (see p. 53), Stevenson asked managers to assess their companies' strengths and weaknesses *in general*. Overall, 'the results of the study brought into serious question the value of formal assessment approaches.' In general, 'few members of management agreed precisely on the strengths and weaknesses exhibited by their companies' (p. 55). The overall impression left by this study is that the detached assessment of strengths and weaknesses may be unreliable, all bound up with aspirations, biases, and hopes. In fact, Stevenson's managers seemed to understand the problem, their 'most common single complaint' being that strengths and weaknesses have 'to be defined in the context of a problem,' or to quote one of his subjects, 'As I see it, the only real value in making an appraisal of the organization's capabilities comes in the light of a specific deal—the rest of the time it is just an academic exercise' (p. 65).

Every strategic change involves some new experience, a step into the unknown, the taking of some kind of risk. Therefore, no organization can ever be sure in advance whether an established competence will prove to be a strength or a weakness. In its retail diversification efforts, a supermarket chain we studied (Mintzberg and Waters, 1982) was surprised to learn that discount stores, which seemed so compatible with its food store operations, did not work out well, while fast-food restaurants, ostensibly so different, did. The similarities of the discount store business—how products were displayed, moved about by customers, and checked out, etc.—were apparently overwhelmed by the subtle but different characteristics of merchandising—styling, obsolescence, etc. On the other hand, the restaurants may have looked very different, but they moved simple, basic, perishable, commodity-like products through an efficient chain of distribution much like the supermarket business did. The point we wish to emphasize is: how could the firm have known ahead of time? The discovery of what business it was to be in could not be undertaken on paper, but had to benefit from the results of testing and experience. (And the conclusion suggested from such experiences is that strengths generally turn out to be far narrower than expected and weaknesses, consequently, far broader (see Mintzberg and McHugh, 1985)).

Nowhere does this come through more clearly in practice than in attempts at related diversification by acquisition. Obviously no organization can undertake such activity without a prior assessment of its strengths and weaknesses. Yet the vast majority of experiences reported in the popular press and published research suggests that related diversification is above all a learning process, in which the acquiring firm has to make a number of mistakes until it gradually learns what works for it, if it ever does (see Miles, 1982; also Quinn, 1980: 28). And in the writings of academe, the problem is perhaps best illustrated by Levitt's (1960) popular 'marketing myopia' conception, that firms should define themselves by broad mission rather than narrow product or technology (e.g. transportation instead of railroad). The idea was enticing, but in many applications too easy, a cerebral exercise that could detach managers from the realities of the businesses they managed. What, in a few words on a piece of paper, would enable railroads to fly airplanes? Levitt, a marketing professor but here arguing in the spirit of the design school, wrote that 'once it genuinely *thinks* of its business as taking care of people's transportation needs, nothing can stop it from creating its own extravagantly profitable growth' (p. 33; our italics). Nothing except the limitations of its own distinctive competences!

Structure follows strategy . . . as the left foot follows the right

While the design school tends to promote the dictum, first articulated by Chandler (1962), that structure should follow strategy and be determined by it, in fact its model also accepts the opposite. Since the assessment of organizational strengths and weaknesses is an intrinsic part of the model, a basic *input* to strategy formulation, and since structure is a key component of this, housing the organization's capabilities, then structure must play a major role in determining strategy too, by constraining and conditioning it as well as guiding it.

While this may be an obvious point, hardly disputed even within the design school, it does have a broader implication, an important one in our critique of this school's model of strategy formation. No ongoing organization ever wipes the slate clean when it changes its strategy. The past counts, just as does the environment, and the structure is a significant part of that past. Claiming that strategy must take precedence over structure amounts to claiming that strategy must take precedence over the established capabilities of the organization, clearly an untenable proposition. By overemphasizing strategy, and the ability of the stategist to act rather freely, the design school slights, not just the environment, but also the organization itself. Structure may be malleable, but it cannot be altered at will just because a leader has conceived a new strategy. Many organizations have come to grief over just such a belief.

We conclude, therefore, that structure follows strategy as the left foot follows the right in walking. In effect, strategy and structure both support the organization. None takes precedence; each always precedes the other, and follows it, except when they move together, as the organization jumps to a new position. Strategy formation is an integrated system, not an arbitrary sequence.

Making strategy explicit: promoting inflexibility

Once strategies have been created, via the conscious assessment of strengths and weaknesses among other things, then the model calls for their articulation. While recognizing some reasons for not making strategy explicit, this school generally considers an unwillingness to articulate strategy as evidence of fuzzy thinking, or else of political motive. But there are other, often more important, reasons not to articulate strategy, which strike at the basic assumptions of the design school.

The reasons generally given for the need to articulate strategy are, first, that only an explicit strategy can be discussed, investigated, and debated (e.g. Andrews, 1981: 24); second, that only by making strategy explicit can it serve its prime function of knitting people together to 'provide coherence to organizational action' (Rumelt, 1980: 380); and third, that an articulated strategy can generate support—can rally the troops, so to speak, and reassure outside influencers. These all sound like excellent reasons for articulating strategy. And they are—so long as all the conditions are right. The most important of these is that the strategist is sure—knows where he or she wants to go, and has few serious doubts about the viability of that direction. In other words, the design school implicitly assumes conditions of stability or predictability. But organizations have to cope with conditions of uncertainty too. How can Andrews' company come 'to grips with a changing environment' when its 'strategy is [already] known' (1981: 24)? And how can its managers promote the necessary changes when its own board of

directors uses that articulated strategy 'to prevent the company from stray-
ing off its strategic course' (1980b: 32)?

Our point is that organizations must function not only *with* strategy, but
also *during* periods of the formulation and reformulation of strategy, which
cannot happen instantaneously. 'It is virtually impossible for a manager to
orchestrate all internal decisions, external environmental events, behavioral
and power relationships, technical and informational needs, and actions of
intelligent opponents so that they come together at a precise moment' (Quinn,
1978: 17). Indeed sometimes organizations also need to function during
periods of unpredictability, when they cannot possibly hope to articulate
any viable strategy. The danger during such periods is not the lack of explicit strategy but exactly the opposite—'premature closure,' the reification
of speculative tendencies into firm commitments. When strategists are not
sure, they had better not articulate strategies, for all the reasons given above.

Moreover, even when it makes sense to articulate strategies, because they
appear to be viable well into the future, the dangers of doing so must still
be recognized. Explicit strategies, as implied in the reasons for wanting
them, are blinders designed to focus direction and so to block out peripheral
vision. Thus, they can impede strategic change when it does become necessary: to put this another way, a danger in articulating strategy is that while
strategists may be sure for now, they can never be sure forever. The more
clearly articulated the strategy, the more deeply imbedded it becomes in
the habits of the organization as well as the minds of its strategists. There
is, in fact, evidence from the laboratories of cognitive psychology that the
explication of a strategy—even having someone articulate what he or
she is about to do anyway—locks it in, breeding a resistance to later change
(Kiesler, 1971).

Another reason not to articulate strategy is that pronouncements of it,
often necessarily superficial, can engender a false sense of understanding.
Andrews argues that 'a conception of strategy brings simplicity to complex
organizations' (p. 554). True enough. But at what price?

The potential danger of a little knowledge needs to be recognized: the
possible trivialization and distortion of the subtle needs of a complex
organization. As Wrapp has noted, sometimes it is impossible to articulate
direction 'clearly enough so that everyone in the organization understands
what they mean' (1967: 95). And the problems can magnify when outsiders
are involved in the process, even board members. Perhaps that is why
Andrews finds such strong managerial resistance to the inclusion of outside
board members in strategy-making.

To summarize, the problems of making strategy explicit essentially bring
us back to the need to view strategy formation as a learning process, at least
in some contexts. Sure strategies must often be made explicit, for purposes
of investigation, coordination, and support. The questions are: when? and
how? and when not? There is undoubtedly a need for closure at certain

points in an organization's history, moments when the process of strategy formation must be suspended temporarily to articulate clear strategies. But this need should not lead us to believe that it is natural for strategies to appear fully developed all of a sudden, nor should it allow us to ignore the periods during which strategies must evolve.

Separation of formulation from implementation: detaching thinking from acting

The formulation-implementation dichotomy is central to the design school—whether taken as a tight model or a loose framework. But is the distinction a valid one for conceptual and analytical, even pedagogical, purposes? In other words, should people concerned with strategy (including students learning about it) *think*, let alone behave, in terms of formulation and implementation?

How can anyone really question this distinction, or even the assumption that formulation must precede implementation? After all, this is just another version of the basic form of rationality that underlies western thinking—in its simplest form, that to act you must first know what you want to accomplish. Think first, then do.

The organizational form that corresponds to this dichotomy is the classical hierarchy, what we prefer to call 'machine bureaucracy' (Mintzberg, 1979). It above all emphasizes the distinction between the few people on top who are allowed to think and the many below who are supposed to act. Machine bureaucracy is common in mass production and the mass provision of services. It dominates thinking in the consulting profession (most of whose techniques promote this form of structure), in big business (outside of high technology), and in government, including the military.

In his article on the dysfunctions of traditional military organization, Feld (1959), noted the sharp distinction that is made between the officers in the rear, who have the power to formulate plans and direct their execution, and the troops on the front, who, despite their first-hand experience, can only implement the plans given them. These 'organizations place a higher value on the exercise of reason than on the acquisition of experience, and endow officers engaged in the first activity with authority over those occupied by the second' (p. 15). This 'is based on the assumption that their position serves to keep them informed about what is happening to the army as a whole ... [which] is supported by the hierarchical structure of military organization which establishes in specific detail the stages and the direction of the flow of information' (p. 22).

This, in fact, is the assumption fundamental to the formulation-implementation dichotomy: that data can be aggregated and transmitted up the hierarchy without significant loss or distortion. It is an assumption that fails often, destroying carefully formulated strategies in the process.

To use a quotation Feld (p. 15) meant for the military, in how many contemporary organizations do 'the conditions most favorable to rational activity, calm and detachment, stand in direct antithesis to the confusion and involvement' of the factory floor, the salesman's call, the government clerk's service? In how many does detached formulation render the organization ineffective? In how many is critical information ignored because it is deemed 'tactical'? Speaking from Japan, Ohmae goes so far as to suggest that 'separation of muscle from brain may well be a root cause of the vicious cycle of the decline in productivity and loss of international competitiveness in which U.S. industry seems to be caught' (1982: 226).

In recent years there has been a spate of books and articles on implementation (such as Hrebiniak and Joyce, 1984). Noting that few intended strategies are successfully realized—the figure cited by *Fortune* writer Walter Kiechel (1984: 8) that 'fewer than 10 percent of American corporations' implement their intended strategies, was deemed 'wildly inflated' by Tom Peters!—they they call for more attention to the implementation process. 'Manage culture,' executives are advised, or 'pay more attention to your control systems.' If one side of the formulation-implementation dichotomy does not work, then effort must be invested in the other.

Majone and Wildavsky point out that to study implementation is to raise 'the most basic question about the relation between thought and action: How can ideas manifest themselves in a world of behavior?' (1978: 103). As they characterize the 'planning-and-control model of implementation,' which sounds to us like the design school model in the public sector, 'good implementation is the irresistible unfolding of a tautology,' or to translate their terms into ours, the transformation of intended strategy into realized strategy through a 'suitable . . ."production function"', meaning goals, plans and controls, 'and—to take care of the human side of the equation—incentives and indoctrination' (p. 106); 'the perfectly pre-formed policy idea . . . only requires execution, and the only problems it raises are ones of control' (p. 114).

All that would be fine were only the world cooperative. Unfortunately, often it is not, in many cases for good reason, whether the resistance to the intended strategy comes from the environment in which it is to be implemented, the organization that is supposed to do the implementing, or even from the strategy itself.

Sometimes the 'implementors' who make up the rest of the organization are perfectly willing to proceed as directed from the center, but the environment simply renders the strategy a failure. It may change unpredictably, so that the intended strategy becomes useless, or it may remain so unstable that no specific strategy can be useful. Despite implications to the contrary, the external environment is not some kind of pear to be plucked from the tree of external appraisal, but a major and sometimes unpredictable force to be reckoned with.

In other cases it is not the environment but the implementors within the organization who resist. They may, of course, be narrow-minded bureaucrats too wedded to their traditional ways to know a good new strategy when they see one, or small-minded ones who do not understand the new strategy, or bloody-minded ones who prefer to go their own way (e.g. Thoenig and Friedberg, 1976 and Scheff, 1961). But sometimes they are right-minded people who do what they do to serve the organization despite its leadership. They may resist implementation because they know the intended strategies to be unfeasible—that the organization will not be capable of realizing them or, once realized, they will fail in an unsuitable external environment.

Implementational failure can also occur without inhospitable environments and resistant organizations. The problem can lie in the strategy itself; indeed, in part at least, it almost always does. For one thing, no intended strategy can ever be so precisely defined that it covers every eventuality. Moreover, while the formulators may be few, the implementors are typically many, functioning at different levels and in different units and places (Rein and Rabinovitz, 1979: 327–328), each with their own values and interpretations. They are not robots, nor are the systems that control them airtight. The inevitable result is some slipping between formulation and implementation.

'Slippage' is a term used in the public sector to mean that strategic intentions get distorted on their way to implementation; 'drift' is another term used there for realized strategies that differ from intended ones, but within their context (Majone and Wildavsky, 1978: 105; Kress, Koehler and Springer, 1980; Lipsky, 1978). Here, however, we would like to take a position beyond both concepts.

Certainly much formulation is ill-conceived, just as much implementation is badly executed. But often the fundamental difficulty lies not in either side, but in conceiving a distinction between formulation and implementation in the first place.

Behind the premise of the formulation-implementation dichotomy lies a set of very ambitious assumptions: that environments can always be known, currently and for a period well into the future, in one central place, at least by the capable strategists there. To state this more formally, by distinguishing formulation from implementation, the design school draws itself into two questionable assumptions in particular: first, that the formulator can be fully, or at least sufficiently, informed to formulate viable strategies, and second that the environment is sufficiently stable, or at least predictable, to ensure that the strategies formulated will remain viable after implementation. Under some conditions at least, one or the other of these assumptions proves false.

In an unstable environment, or one too complex to be comprehended in a single brain, the dichotomy has to be collapsed, in one of two ways. If the necessary information can be comprehended in one brain, but the environment is unpredictable—or perhaps more commonly, takes time to figure out after an unexpected shift—then the 'formulator' may have to 'implement' him or herself. In other words, thinking and action must proceed in tandem, closely associated: the thinker exercises close control over the actions. The leader—here Andrews' *one* strategist (or a small group)—develops some preliminary ideas, tries them out tentatively, modifies them, tries again, and continues until a viable strategy emerges, much as Quinn (1980) described the process, or continues to act even if one does not.

Such close control of a leader over both formulation and implementation is characteristic of the entrepreneurial mode of strategy-making, where power is highly centralized in a flexible organization (Mintzberg, 1973). But, as noted earlier, that mode, because it is rooted in the vagaries of intuition, tends to be dismissed by the design school. True, it may sometimes be 'opportunistic,' as Andrews claims, but such opportunism can be necessary, perhaps in and of itself or more productively perhaps, as a means to experiment and learn. Pascale (1984) provides a marvelous example of the latter in his description of how the Honda Motor Company executives in the United States backed their way into their highly successful motorcycle strategy of the 1960s, in contrast to the Boston Consulting Group's (1975) inference of that strategy as brilliantly deliberate. (In the 1987 textbook (p. vi), Andrews comments that 'Japanese management appears to be more truly strategic than improvisatory.' Perhaps for him, as for the Boston Consulting Group, believing is seeing.)

Where there is too much information to be comprehended in one brain— for example, in organizations dependent on a great deal of sophisticated expertise, as in high-technology firms, hospitals, and universities—then the strategy may have to be worked out on a collective basis. Here, then, the dichotomy collapses in the other direction: the 'implementors' become the 'formulators' (Hardy *et al.*, 1984; Mintzberg and McHugh, 1985). As Lipsky puts it, implementation is 'turned on [its] head' (1978: 397), and actions in good part determine thoughts, so that strategies also emerge.

Both situations—'formulators' implementing and 'implementors' formulating—amount to the same thing in one important respect: the organizations are *learning*. Andrews' great mistake was dismissing organizational learning by considering it opportunism. Even though he recognized the intertwining of formulation and implementation in practice, his making of the distinction *conceptually* led him to underestimate the important role of such learning, individually and especially collectively, over time, in strategy formation. More generally, the design school, by implicitly assuming that strategic learning somehow takes place in one head for a limited period of time and then stops, so that strategies can be articulated and implementation can begin, denied processes that have often proved critical to the creation of novel and effective strategies.

Out of all this discussion comes a whole range of possible relationships between thought and action. There are times when thought does, and should, precede action and guide it primarily, so that, despite some inevitable slippage, the dichotomy between formulation and implementation does hold up, more or less. In other words, while it may be true that 'literal implementation is literally impossible' (Majone and Wildavsky, 1978: 116), sometimes what is achieved is close enough. And here is where we might expect viable application of the design school model.

Other times, however, especially during or immediately after a major unexpected shift in the environment, thought must be so bound up with action in an interactive and continuous process that 'learning' becomes a better label, and concept, for what happens then is 'formulation-implementation'. The organization may be groping its way toward a new strategy, or may simply be coping until things settle down so that it can then do so. (For models of strategy-making making as a learning process, see Quinn (1980) on 'logical incrementalism,' Burgelman (1983) on 'corporate entrepreneurship,' Mintzberg and McHugh (1985) on a 'grass roots model,' and Mintzberg (1987) on 'crafting strategy.')

And then, perhaps most common, are a whole range of possibilities in between—'implementation as evolution,' as Majone and Wildavsky (1978) put it—where there is thought, then there is action, this produces learning which alters thought, followed by adjustments to action, and so on. Intended strategies exist, but realized strategies have emergent as well as deliberate characteristics. Here words like 'formulation' and 'implementation' should be used only with caution, as should be design school model of strategy formation.

To conclude this critique, this seemingly innocent model—for Andrews, just an 'informing idea'—in fact contains some ambitious assumptions about the capabilities of organizations and their leaders, assumptions that break down in whole or in good part under many common circumstances.

The design school and the case study method

We believe that the relationship between the design school model of strategy formation and the traditional method of case study teaching may help to explain why there has been so much reluctance in certain quarters to adapt the model to other views of strategy-making. The design school model matches perfectly the pedagogical requirements of the case study method, as Andrews and his colleagues note repeatedly. The students are handed a document of 20 or so pages that contains all the available information on the organization in question. They study it the evening before class (alongside the other cases they must prepare for that day), and then appear all ready to argue what it is that General Motors or the John F. Kennedy High School should do.

Bear in mind that time is short: the external environment must be assessed, distinctive competences identified, alternate strategies proposed, and these evaluated, all before class is dismissed in 80 minutes. Two days later it's on to Xerox or Texas Instruments. Here is how the process is described by the senior author of the Harvard textbook:

> how do those of us interested in management education strive to contribute to the development of future general managers? We do this first by disciplined classroom drill with the concept of strategy. Drill in the formal and analytic—what is the current strategy of the firm? What are its strengths and weaknesses? Where, in the firm's perceived industry, are profit and service opportunity? And, how can those corporate capacities and industry opportunities be effectively related? . . .
>
> Moreover, this analytic classroom process focuses attention on a key administration skill—the process of selecting and ordering data so that management asks the critical questions appropriate to a particular situation.
>
> (Christensen, in Christensen *et al.*, 1982: ix–x)

But how can a student who has read a short resumé of a company possibly know these things? How can words and numbers on paper possibly substitute for the intimate knowledge of a complex organization? Can the 'critical questions' really be asked through the process of 'selecting and ordering' *this* kind of data? And what effect does this 'drill in the formal and analytic' have on the students when they finally do enter the executive suite?

Given the requirements of case study teaching, how else can the faculty proceed but to keep the model simple, especially to presume that organizations can be quickly and easily understood, and to assume the necessity for fully developed and explicit but nonetheless simple strategies. And even if it is accepted that formulation and implementation are intertwined in practice, what good is that in the classroom where formulation (thinking) is possible while implementation (acting) is not?[13]

Of course, proponents of this school might argue that this is a small price to pay for bringing reality into the classroom, enabling the students to gain exposure to many different organizations. True enough. But need the reality—even the 'reality' of the 20-page case—be dealt with in only this way? Is there not another option, which is to open up the students' perspective beyond the design school model, indeed even to use cases themselves to do so, but written and taught from a broader point of view?

What effect has such case study teaching had on practice, on the generations of managers who have graduated from schools that rely on this pedagogy? If that has left managers with the impression that, to make strategy, they can remain in their offices with documents summarizing the situation and think—formulate so that others can implement—then it may well have done them and their organizations a terrible disservice, encouraging superficial strategies that violate the distinctive competences of their organizations. To quote Livingston (1971), a Harvard professor at the time himself, in his classic article 'The myth of the well-educated manager,' the problem of management education is its 'secondhandedness:' 'Managerial aspirants are required only to explain and defend their reasoning, not to carry out their decisions or even to plan realistically for their implementation;' they 'are rarely exposed to "real" people or to "live" cases,' but rather to 'problems or opportunities discovered by someone else, which they discuss, but do nothing about.' Thus, many 'are not able to learn from their own firsthand experience. . . . Since they have not learned how to observe their environment firsthand or to assess feedback from their actions, they are poorly prepared to learn and grow as they gain experience' (pp. 79, 83, 84, 89).

The fact is that the design school model dominates not only the world of pedagogy, either in its pure form, or as the foundation of the thinking behind the planning and positioning schools; it dominates beliefs in practice too. In other words, 'one best way' thinking is alive and well in the practice of strategic management, and it dictates that formulation must precede implementation, that this formulation must be conscious and controlled, by the chief executive as the architect of strategy, and that the resulting strategies must be deliberate and explicit. Here is how Robert McNamara, also formerly of the Harvard Business School, spelled out his approach to military strategy as Secretary of Defense: 'We must first determine what our foreign policy is to be, formulate a military strategy to carry out that policy, then build the military forces to successfully conduct this strategy' (quoted in Smalter and Ruggles, 1966: 70). He did just this in Vietnam, distant from the realities of the rice paddies and for too long deaf to the calls to learn from the devastating results. Or consider the comment of one manager about an earlier chief executive of the General Electric Company: 'Borch had a sense that he wasn't looking for lots of data on each business unit, but really wanted 15 terribly important and significant pages of data and analysis' (quoted in Hamermesh, 1986: 191). As noted earlier, the problem may be most acute in diversification by acquisition, which often appear to have been undertaken by detached executives sitting up in executive suites designing strategies quite independently of any intimate understanding of the organization's real strengths and weaknesses.

This 'one best way' thinking applies also to many of the consulting firms that specialize in this field—the so-called 'strategy boutiques.' Called in with limited knowledge of the industry in question, and limited time to find out, the design school provides a most convenient model. To quote from a popular book by two consultants: 'Four or five working days over a two-month period are required to set strategy. Two or three working days are required for the review and one-year update of strategy' (Tregoe and Zimmerman, 1980: 120). There is not a lot of money to be made in saying: 'It's too complicated for us; go back and do your own homework; learn about your industry and your own distinctive competences by immersing yourself in the details and trying things; get many people involved; maybe over a few years you'll be able to develop an effective strategy. It's your responsibility; no one can do it for you.'[14]

As for Andrews' proposals about directors, his claim about 'the power of strategy as a simplifying concept enabling independent directors to *know* the business (in a sense) without being *in* the business' (p. 834) might be more of a problem than a solution. Can anyone, director or student, even manager, really *know* an organization without being *in* it? The time of directors is limited; they must be briefed through short documents and snappy presentations that articulate strategies clearly and simply, so that they can be evaluated on the spot. Case study discussions in the boardroom. But at what cost in strategic thinking? And strategic action?

Andrews claims that 'graduates of a demanding Policy course feel at home in any management situation and know at once how to begin to understand it' (p. 6). But that may be the very essence of the problem. Mary Cunningham is a graduate of the course Andrews had in mind. She may not be typical, but her experience does reveal the problem in its extreme. With a great deal of publicity, Cunningham leaped from the Harvard MBA program to the personal assistantship of William Agee, chief executive of the Bendix Corporation, himself a Harvard MBA. Later she wrote a book on those experiences, entitled *Powerplay* (Cunningham and Schumer, 1984). Kinsley published a scathing review of it in *Fortune* magazine, at one point hitting precisely on the issue under discussion here:

There is nothing in *Powerplay* to support Cunningham's contention that she is a business genius. Her chapter about learning curves and other B-school buzzwords seems infantile. What little discussion there is of actual business consists mainly of genuflecting in front of a deity called *The Strategy*. The Strategy is what Mary and Bill were up to when nasty-minded people thought they were up to something else. Near as I can tell, it consisted of getting Bendix out of a lot of fuddy-duddy old-fashioned products and into glitzy high tech. What makes this a terribly ingenious idea, let alone a good one, she does not say. But she became very attached to it. 'How's The Strategy going?' she asked Agee the first time they met after her departure from Bendix. And at the book's emotional climax, as Agee realizes he's going to lose control of Bendix to Allied Corp., he says: '"Of course, you know what this means? . . . The Strategy that we've worked on so hard"—and here he nodded at me—"won't be in our hands."' And they cry.

(1984: 142)

If the case study method, based on the design school model, has encouraged leaders to oversimplify strategy, if it has given them the impression that 'you give me a synopsis and I'll give you a strategy,' if it has denied strategy formation as a long, subtle, and difficult process of learning, if it has encouraged managers to detach thinking from acting, remaining in their offices instead of getting into factories and meeting customers where the real information may have to be dug out, then it may be a major cause of the problems faced by contemporary organizations.

This critique may sound extreme. We do not believe it is; as we shall discuss below, there is much in the design school to recommend it, at least under certain circumstances (indeed much in using cases as pedagogical devices too). But not when it is applied without a depth of understanding of what a particular organization is, and how it must sometimes learn.

The design school: context and contribution

Our critique has not been intended to dismiss the design school model, but rather the assumption of its universality, that it somehow represents the 'one best way' to make strategy. In particular, we reject the model where we believe strategy formation must above all emphasize learning, notably in circumstances of considerable uncertainty and unpredictability, or ones of complexity in which much power over strategy-making has to be granted to a variety of actors deep inside the organization. We also reject the model where it tends to be applied with superficial understanding of the issues in question.

Andrews thought it sufficient to delineate one model and then add qualifications to it. The impression left was that this was the way to make strategy, although with nuance, sometimes more, sometimes less. But that had the effect of associating strategy-making with deliberate, centralized behavior and of slighting the equally important needs for emergent behavior and organizational learning. Another extreme—what we have elsewhere presented under the label of the 'grass roots model' (Mintzberg and McHugh, 1985) —makes no more sense, since it overstates equally. But by positioning these two at ends of a continuum, we can begin to consider real-world needs along it. In other words it is not Andrews' qualifications that will hold the model in check so much as an alternate depiction of the process. That is why the field of strategic management has need for these different schools of thought, so long as each is considered carefully in its own appropriate context.

Accordingly, we can begin to delineate the conditions that should encourage an organization to tilt toward the design school model end of the continuum. We see a set of four in particular.

1. *One brain can, in principle, handle all of the information relevant for strategy formation.* The assumption of the single strategist sometimes

does hold up: a chief executive (perhaps teamed up with other top managers), albeit one who is rather clever and especially adept at synthesis, can take full charge of the process for creating strategy. Here the situation must be relatively simple, involving a base of knowledge that can be comprehended in one brain.

2. *That brain has full, detailed, intimate knowledge of the situation in question.* The potential for centralizing knowledge must be backed up by sufficient access to, and experience of, the organization and its situation to enable the strategist to understand *in a deep sense* what is going on. We might add that he or she can only *know* the organization by truly being *in* the organization. This precludes the image of the case study classroom, the detached CEO with a pithy report, the 'quick-fix' consulting contract, the quarterly directors' meeting, even the weekend retreat of executives (although this may culminate the process). Rather it describes the strategist who has developed a rich, intimate knowledge base over a substantial period of time.

3. *The relevant knowledge is established and set before a new intended strategy has to be implemented—in other words, the situation is relatively stable or at least predictable.* Not only must the strategist have access to the relevant knowledge base, but there must also be some sense of closure on that base: at some point in time, the strategist must know what needs to be known to conceive an intended strategy that will have relevance well beyond the period of implementation. The world must, in other words, hold still, or—what amounts to a much more demanding assumption—the strategist must have the capability to predict the changes that will come about. What this means is that individual learning must come to an end before organizational action taking can begin. And that can happen effectively only when the future can, in fact, be known.

4. *The organization in question is prepared to cope with a centrally articulated strategy.* For one thing, others in the organization must be willing to defer to a central strategist. For another, they must have the time, the energy, and the resources to implement a centrally determined strategy. And, of course, there has to be the will to do that implementation.

These conditions suggest some clear contexts in which the design school model would seem to apply best—its own particular niche, so to speak, related to time as well as situation. In other words, this is a model to be applied only in certain kinds of organizations, and even there only in certain circumstances. Above all is the organization that needs a major reorientation, a new conception of its strategy. Newman recognized this early, referring to the 'quick reversal,' the 'sharp break' (1967: 117). Or, as Rumelt has put it, 'a good strategy does not need constant reformulation. It is a framework for continual problem solving, not the problem solving itself' (1980: 365; see also Henderson, 1979: 38).

Two conditions would seem to characterize what we call this *period of reconception*. First, there was a major change in the situation that previously supported the existing strategy, so that it has been seriously undermined. And second, there has developed the beginnings of a new stability, one that will support a new conception of strategy. In other words, the *design school model would seem to apply best at the junction of major shift for an organization, coming out of a period of changing circumstances and into one of operating stability.*

We would normally expect the provoking change to be one of a crisis or problem in the external condition of the organization, for example a major realignment of competition, a key shift in market demand, a technological breakthrough. Yavitz and Newman also suggest that what they refer to as 'total reassessment' can be proactive too, triggered, for example, by 'milestones in major programs,' periods when 'large commitments of resources must be made' or 'key uncertainties are resolved,' or simply 'a maximum period since the last full review' (1982: 215–216). Such strategic reassessments may also result from the introduction to the organization of fresh strategic thinking on the part of new leaders.

There is another context where the design school model might apply, and that is the new organization, since it must have a clear sense of direction in order to compete with its more established rivals (or position itself in a niche free of their direct influence). This *period of initial conception* of strategy is, of course, often the product of an entrepreneur with a vision who created the organization in the first place.

Context describes structure as well as time and situation. In the context described above, the structure tends to be simple—flexible, non-elaborated, very responsive to the dictates of a single leader (Mintzberg, 1979: chapter 17). Once under way, however, even simple structures with entrepreneurial leaders may not follow the design school model, even in times of reconception, because the leader's considerable personal discretion (including personal control of 'implementation') allows him or her to change strategy gradually, even continuously, without any need to articulate it. In a way, Andrews recognized this when he sought to distance his model from the entrepreneurial context and its reliance on intuition and 'opportunism.' But in so doing he also distanced it from some of the most creative strategy-making behavior found in organizations.

The structural context Andrews seemed to favor for his model (although he would hardly use the label we are about to apply to it), and the one that appears to be most appropriate for the period of reconception of strategy in an existing organization, is what we call 'machine bureaucracy' (Mintzberg, 1979: chapter 18). This is structure characterized by a centralization of authority and a relatively stable context of operations, typically used in mass production and the mass delivery of services. Machine bureaucracies commonly pursue highly articulated and stable strategies. They therefore require in periods of reconception much of what the design school has to offer: a process whereby someone in central command somehow pulls the new conception together—defines it if not actually creates it—and then articulates it fully at a point in time so that everyone else can implement it and then pursue it.

But there is an interesting anomaly here. The call from the design school for a personalized and creative form of strategic management (one strategist, strategies as novel conceptions) is not really compatible with machine bureaucracy, which tends to rely on standardized procedures and detached forms of control. In other words, machine bureaucracies are not mobiles to effect strategic change but stabiles for the continued pursuit of given strategies. For example, our own research on strategy formation (Mintzberg, 1978; Mintzberg *et al.*, 1986) suggests that chief executives of machine bureaucracies tend to be caretakers of existing strategies—fine-tuners of set directions rather than champions of radically new ones—in part because of the constraints imposed by their own standardized procedures. These organizations are, after all, machines dedicated to the pursuit of efficiency in very specific domains. Indeed, the whole array of mechanisms proposed in the design school's own model of implementation—performance measures, incentive systems, various other control procedures, not to mention the articulation of strategy itself, as noted earlier—once in place act not to promote change in strategy but to resist it. Formal implementation, ironically, impedes reformulation.

Our own evidence (Mintzberg, 1978), as well as that of Miller and Friesen (1984), suggests that major reformulation in machine bureaucracy typically occurs through a form of revolution; power is centralized around a single leader who acts personally and decisively to unfreeze existing practices and impose a new vision. In other words, in such 'turnarounds,' the organization tends to revert to the more flexible simple structure, and to its more entrepreneurial mode of strategy-making, at least until it has developed a new realized strategy, after which it tends to settle back down to its old machine bureaucratic way of functioning.

The implication of this is that while the machine bureaucracy may occasionally require a period of reconception as provided for by the design school model, its own procedures impede the faithful use of that model. In a sense, implementation fits, formulation does not. Indeed, initial use of the model itself discourages later use of it: by articulating strategy and implementing it, as prescribed, the machine bureaucracy finds it difficult to change its strategy later, to reformulate. Thus, the design school model tends here to get 'caught in the middle,' to use Porter's phrase, tilts toward the personalized intuition of entrepreneurship for major reformulation and toward the analysis of planning for the more routine pursuit of strategy. Can we conclude, therefore, that by trying to position the design school model free of intuition on one side and planning on the other, Andrews left it little room for real application, perhaps mainly marginal strategic change in the machine bureaucratic type of organization where leaders can exercise 'judgement' but not rely on intuition or analysis?[15]

As for more complex types of organizations, which depend on expertise for their functioning, as we have argued elsewhere, 'professional bureaucracies' and 'adhocracies' cannot rely on the conventional prescriptive approaches to strategy-making, whether design, planning, or positioning school oriented, but must instead tilt toward the learning end of the continuum, developing strategies that are more emergent in nature through processes that have more of a grass roots orientation (Hardy et al., 1984; Mintzberg and McHugh, 1985).[16]

To conclude, should we take the design school model literally? In assessing the real contribution of this school, perhaps we should not. For while the model (even the framework) may have restricted application and often be overly simplified, this school's contribution as an 'informing idea' has been profound. The design school has provided important basic vocabulary by which we discuss grand strategy, and it has provided the central notion that underlies all prescription in this field, namely that strategy represents a fundamental congruence between external opportunity and internal capability. These important contributions will stand no matter how many of this school's specific premises may fall away.

Acknowledgements

My thanks to one very thorough and considerate reviewer, also to Bill Newman for his comments on some of the early history of the use of the strategy concept in business.

Notes

1 Thus Lindgren and Spangberg (1981: 26) refer to this as the 'fit school.'
2 Undoubtedly encouraged by the fact that in the early years this group trained by far the largest number of doctoral students in business policy.
3 Porter (1981: 610; 1983: 173), a co-author in the 1982 and 1987 editions of the Harvard textbook, writes of how the ideas in the original text (the 'LCAG para-digm,' after the names of the four original authors) were 'subsequent[ly]' translated and extended by others, citing in particular Ansoff's book Corporate Strategy. In fact, Ansoff went to press with his similar ideas in the same year (1965) as Porter's co-authors' originally did, and neither book references any work by authors of the other (although Edmund Learned, the senior author of the first edition of the Harvard textbook, did himself note the similarities in a book published with Sproat one year later: 'Significantly, [Ansoff's] work offers numerous parallels with Harvard thinking that should not be obscured by differences in terminology, definitions, emphasis, and coverage' [1966: 94]). In the Preface to the first edition of the Harvard book, the authors write that the content of the book 'is the outcome of about ten years of case and course development' (Learned et al., 1965: vii), although in the 1982 version they refer to the core idea having

developed in the early 1960s (Christensen, Andrews, and Bower, 1982: viii; co-author Bower is more precise in a 1986 publication: 'The problem of corporate strategy was first phrased as a research question in 1959 when Kenneth Andrews reported his study of the Swiss watch industry in a note and a series of cases' (p. vi).) Ansoff published a rough version of his approach in article form two years earlier (Ansoff, 1964), although he referred there to an initial unpublished paper of 1958. Note should also be made of comments by Chester Barnard in a 1948 book (p. 169) which seem to be in the spirit of the design school, of the discussion of 'administrative strategy' (pp. 10–18) in the Hardwick and Landuyt textbook by that title in 1961, and of an article by Gilmore and Brandenburg in 1962 entitled 'Anatomy of corporate planning'. Although its detail and elaborated steps place this last paper clearly in the planning school, underlying these steps is the same model as that of the design school. (Gilmore and Brandenburg note in a footnote that 'we are indebted to Dr. H. Igor Ansoff for introducing the concept of synergy to us and for his assistance in clarifying a number of steps in our planning framework' (1962: 61).)

4 To this could be added Tregoe and Zimmerman's book *Top Management Strategy* (1980), although not a textbook. The latest Newman text (Newman, Warren, and McGill, 1987) remains largely in the spirit of this school (in chapter 4 at least), although it also reflects increased attention to the planning school.

5 We should point out that Andrews himself rejects the word 'model' (p. 12), a point we shall return to later.

6 The sentences immediately preceding and following this new material (pp. 167 and 179) are identical to those that appeared next to each other in the previous edition of the book (Christensen *et al.*, 1978: 251).

7 In their book *Implementing Strategy*, Hrebiniak and Joyce indeed refer to implementation as 'all the remaining components' (1984: 29).

8 Andrews' words are reminiscent of those of Selznick: 'When institutional leadership fails, it is perhaps more often by default than by positive error or sin. Leadership is lacking when it is needed; and the institution drifts, exposed to vagrant pressures, readily influenced by short-run opportunistic trends' (1957: 25).

9 Interestingly, in so dismissing planning at this point, Andrews resurrects intuition: 'All the knowledge, professional attitudes and analytical and administrative skills in the world cannot fully replace the intuitive genius of some of the natural entrepreneurs you will encounter in this book' (p. 10).

10 For the record, these are all the references found in the text portion of the book, as well as the Preface. References to cases, or references within the cases themselves, were not included. References were counted rather than sources, so that in a few cases the same source was referenced more than once. A source was considered to emanate from Harvard if at least one author was on the staff or was a doctoral student there. Lest this criticism be extended unfairly to all of the co-authors, or even the claims about the literature itself, it should be noted that Edward P. Learned, the senior author of the original edition of the textbook, in his book published together with Sproat in 1966, and entitled *Organization Theory and Policy*, contained perhaps half the amount of text, yet twice the number of references, only a small proportion of those emanating from the Harvard Business School. The 1987 edition of the Andrews' book contains 24 such references, 18 from Harvard.

11 Or 'temporary conceptual convenience', as Andrews put it in a memo to his colleagues in response to comments this author made in a talk given at the Harvard Business School in 1976:

whatever our preferences, let us avoid the allegation that the central conceptualization of Business Policy as a field separates formulation from implementation for anything except temporary conceptual convenience. The inter-relationships of a complex interdependency cannot be intelligently discussed all at once. What is being related can usefully be stopped and examined before reinstalling it conceptually in a dynamic process.

(Andrews, 1976: 4)

In a personal reply to Andrews, I concluded that with respect to this dichotomy, 'Aside from headings, we may be doing the same thing. The question is: do headings matter?!' We shall return to this later in our discussion.

12 Or even his support for the specific model: for example, 'the text is dispersed throughout the book so as to permit a *step-by-step* consideration of what is involved in corporate strategy and in the subactivities required for its formulation and implementation' (p. 11; italics added).

13 In his 1987 book, Andrews acknowledges that 'How to get results is harder to teach and to learn in a classroom than on the scene. This difficulty may explain the neglect in business education of the art of implementation in favor of the analysis of potentially ideal strategies' (p. ix).

14 In the early 1980s, frustration with the planning school and technique in particular, seems to have driven a number of practitioners and consultants back to the simpler design school model. Typical is the article by Walker Lewis (1984), founder of Strategic Planning Associates, and entitled 'The CEO and corporate strategy in the 1980s: back to basics.' It rediscovers all the elements of that model; for example, 'the CEO must be an informed generalist;' 'he must foster the building of comparative advantage;' 'good strategic management requires taking the *wide* view . . . it means setting a corporate direction based on . . . a comprehensively developed strategy;' 'In the end, it is the CEO who must serve as the force behind a return to basic integrated strategies in the 1980s;' and 'he must prod the corporation along the path to implementation' (pp. 1, 2, 6). Ironically, Lewis concludes his article with the claim that 'coming to terms with these changes requires more than the old answers' (p. 6), although that is precisely what he offers.

15 A study of the cases favored by the design school may be instrumental in this regard. Our own suspicion is that there is probably a predisposition toward mass production or mass service organizations, typically machine bureaucratic in nature, although the role of the intuitive leader in trying to effect turnaround in them in a personalized way may be more evident in the cases than in the theory (e.g. in the J. I. Case case, in Learned *et al.*, 1965: 82–102).

16 Note that, in describing the strategy-making process favored in different types of organizations, we are further making the case for the impact of structure on strategy (see also Normann, 1977: 9, 19 and Bower, 1970: 286–287).

References

Andrews, K. R. Memorandum: 'The formulation—implementation dichotomy' in the Concept of Corporate Strategy. Harvard Business School, 21 October 1976.

Andrews, K. R. *The Concept of Corporate Strategy*, Irwin, Homewood, IL, 1971; second edition, 1980a; Third edition, 1987.

Andrews, K. R. 'Directors' responsibility for corporate strategy' *Harvard Business Review*, November–December 1980b, pp. 30–44.

311

Andrews, K. R. 'Replaying the board's role in formulating strategy', *Harvard Business Review*, May–June 1981, pp. 18–28).

Ansoff, H. I. 'A quasi-analytical approach to the business strategy problem', *Management Technology*, June 1964, pp. 67–77.

Ansoff, H. I. *Corporate Strategy*, McGraw-Hill, New York, 1965.

Barnard, C. I. *Organization and Management: Selected Papers*, Harvard University Press, Cambridge, MA, 1948.

Berg, N. *General Management: An Analytical Approach*, Irwin, Homewood, IL., 1984.

Boston Consulting Group Inc. *Strategy Alternatives for the British Motorcycle Industry* (A report prepared for the Secretary of State for Industry, Government of Great Britain, 1975).

Bourgeois, L. J. III and D. R. Brodwin. 'Strategic implementation: Five approaches to an elusive phenomenon', *Strategic Management Journal*, 5, 1984, pp. 241–264.

Bower, J. L. *Managing the Resource Allocation Process: A Study of Corporate Planning and Investment*. Harvard Business School, 1970; revised edition, 1986.

Burgelman, R. A. 'A process model of internal corporate venturing in the diversified major firm', *Administrative Science Quarterly, XXVIII*, 1983, pp. 223–244.

Chandler, A. D. Jr. *Strategy and Structure: Chapter in the History of the Industrial Enterprise*, Massachusetts Institute of Technology Press, Cambridge, MA, 1962.

Christensen, C. R., K. R. Andrews and J. L. Bower. *Business Policy: Text and Cases*, fourth edition, Irwin, Homewood, IL, 1978.

Christensen, C. R., K. R. Andrews, J. L. Bower, R. G. Hamermesh and M. E. Porter. *Business Policy: Text and Cases*, fifth and sixth editions, Irwin, Homewood, IL, 1982 and 1987.

Cunningham, M. and F. Schumer. *Powerplay: What Really Happened at Bendix*, Simon & Schuster, New York, 1984.

Dimma, W. A. 'Competitive strategic planning', *Business Quarterly*, Spring 1985, pp. 22–28.

Feld, M. D. 'Information and authority: The structure of military organization', *American Sociological Review*, **XXIV**, 1959, pp. 15–22.

Gilmore, F. F. and R. G. Brandenburg. 'Anatomy of corporate planning', *Harvard Business Review*, November–December 1962, pp. 61–69.

Hamermesh, R. G. *Making Strategy Work*, Wiley, New York, 1986.

Hardwick, C. T. and B. F. Landuyt. *Administrative Strategy*, Simmons-Boardman, New York, 1961.

Hardy, C., A. Langley, H. Mintzberg and J. Rose. 'Strategy formation in the university setting.' In J. Bess (ed.), *College and University Organization: Insights for the Behavioral Sciences*, New York University Press, New York, 1984.

Hayes, R. H. 'Strategic planning—forward in reverse?', *Harvard Business Review*, November–December 1985, pp. 111–119.

Henderson, B. D. *On Corporate Strategy*, Abt Books, Cambridge, MA, 1979.

Hofer, C. W. and D. Schendel. *Strategy Formulation: Analytical Concepts*, West, St. Paul, MN, 1978.

Hrebiniak, L. G. and W. F. Joyce. *Implementing Strategy*, Macmillan, New York, 1984.

Katz, R. L. *Cases and Concepts in Corporate Strategy*, Prentice Hall, Englewood Cliffs, NJ, 1970.

Kiechel, W. III 'Sniping at strategic planning' (Interview with himself), *Planning Review*, May 1984, pp. 8–11.

Kiesler, C. A. *The Psychology of Commitment: Experiments Linking Behavior to Belief*, Academic Press, New York, 1971.

Kinsley, M. 'A business soap opera', *Fortune*, June 1984, pp. 141–144.

Kress, G., G. Koehler and J. F. Springer. 'Policy drift: An evaluation of the California Business Enterprise Program', *Policy Studies Journal*, Special Issue no. 3, 1980, pp. 1101–1108.

Learned, E. P., C. R. Christensen, K. R. Andrews and W. D. Guth. *Business Policy: Text and Cases*, Irwin, Homewood, IL, 1965.

Learned, E. P. and A. T. Sproat. *Organization Theory and Policy: Notes for Analysis*, Irwin, Homewood, IL, 1966.

Lenz, R. T. 'Strategic capability: A concept and framework for analysis', *Academy of Management Review*, 5, 1980, pp. 225–234.

Levitt, T. 'Marketing myopia', *Harvard Business Review*, July–August 1960, pp. 45–56.

Lewis, W. W. 'The CEO and corporate strategy: Back to basics'. In A. C. Hax (ed.), *Readings on Strategic Management*, Ballinger, New York, 1984.

Lindgren, U. and K. Spangberg. 'Corporate acquisitions and divestments: The strategic decision-making process', *International Studies of Management and Organization*, **XI**, 1981, pp. 24–47.

Lipsky, M. 'Standing the study of public policy implementation on its head'. In W. D. Burnham and M. W. Weinberg (eds), *American Politics and Public Policy*, MIT Press, Cambridge, MA, 1978.

Livingston, J. S. 'The myth of the well-educated manager', *Harvard Business Review*, January–February 1971, pp. 79–89.

Majone, G. and A. Wildavsky. 'Implementation as evolution', *Policy Studies Review Annual*, **II**, 1978, pp. 103–117.

McKinsey, J. O. *Adjusting Policies to Meet Changing Conditions*. American Management Association General Management Series, AM116, New York, 1932.

Miles, R. H. *Coffin Nails and Corporate Strategies*, Prentice-Hall, Englewood Cliffs, NJ, 1982.

Miller, D. and P. H. Friesen. *Organizations: A Quantum View*, Prentice-Hall, Englewood Cliffs, NJ, 1984.

Mintzberg, H. *The Nature of Managerial Work*, Harper & Row, New York, 1973.

Mintzberg, H. 'Patterns in strategy formation', *Management Science*, **XXIV**, 1978, pp. 934–948.

Mintzberg, H. *The Structuring of Organizations*, Prentice-Hall, Englewood Cliffs, NJ, 1979.

Mintzberg, H. 'Crafting strategy', *Harvard Business Review*, July–August 1987, pp. 66–75.

Mintzberg, H. 'Strategy formation: Ten schools of thought', in J. Fredrickson (ed.), *Perspectus on Strategic Management*, Ballinger, New York, forth-coming.

Mintzberg, H. and A. McHugh. 'Strategy formation in an adhocracy', *Administrative Science Quarterly*, **XXX**, 1985, pp. 160–197.

Mintzberg, H. and J. A. Waters. 'Tracking strategy in an entrepreneurial firm', *Academy of Management Journal*, **XXV**, 1982, pp. 465–499.

Mintzberg, H. and J. A. Waters. 'Of strategies, deliberate and emergent', *Strategic Management Journal*, 6, 1985, pp. 257–272.

Mintzberg, H., J. P. Brunet and J. A. Waters. 'Does planning impede strategic thinking?', *Advances in Strategic Management*, vol. 4, JAI Press, Greenwich, CT, 1986, pp. 3–41.

Mintzberg, H., D. Raisinghani and A. Theoret. 'The structure of "unstructured" decision processes', *Administrative Science Quarterly*, XXI, 1976, pp. 246–275.

Moore, D. G. 'Managerial strategies'. In W. L. Warner and N. H. Martin (eds), *Industrial Man*, Harper & Row, New York, 1959, pp. 219–226.

Newman, W. H. *Administrative Action: The Techniques of Organization and Management*, Prentice-Hall, Englewood Cliffs, NJ, 1951; second edition, 1963.

Newman, W. H., C. E. Summer and E. K. Warren. *The Process of Management Concepts, Behavior, and Practice*, Prentice-Hall, Englewood Cliffs, NJ, 1951; second edition, 1967.

Newman, W. H., E. K. Warren and A. R. McGill. *The Process of Management: Strategy, Action, Results*, Prentice-Hall, Englewood Cliffs, NJ, sixth edition, 1987.

Normann, R. *Management for Growth*, Wiley, New York, 1977.

Ohmae, K. *The Mind of the Strategist*, McGraw-Hill, New York, 1982.

Pascale, R. T. 'Perspectives on strategy: The real story behind Honda's success', *California Management Review*, Spring 1984, pp. 47–72.

Porter, M. E. *Competitive Strategy: Techniques for Analyzing Industries and Competitors*, Free Press, New York, 1980.

Porter, M. E. 'The contributions of industrial organization to strategic management', *Academy of Management Review*, VI, 1981, pp. 609–620.

Porter, M. E. 'Industrial organization and the evolution of concept for strategic planning: The new learning'. *Managerial and Decision Economics*, IV, 3, 1983, pp. 172–180.

Porter, M. E. *Competitive Advantage: Creating and Sustaining Superior Performance*, Free Press, New York, 1985.

Quinn, J. B. 'Strategic change: "Logical incrementalism"', *Sloan Management Review*, Fall 1978, pp. 7–21.

Quinn, J. B. *Strategies for Change: Logical Incrementalism*, Irwin, Englewood Cliffs, NJ, 1980.

Radosevich, R. 'A critique of "comprehensive managerial planning"'. In J. W. McLuin (ed.), *Contemporary Management*, Prentice-Hall, Englewood Cliffs, NJ, 1974.

Reilley, E. W. 'Planning the strategy of the business', *Advanced Management*, December 1955, pp. 8–12.

Rein, M. and F. F. Rabinovitz. 'Implementation: A theoretical perspective'. In W. D. Burnham and M. W. Weinberg (eds), *American Politics and Public Policy*, MIT Press, Cambridge, MA, 1979.

Rumelt, R. P. 'Evaluation of strategies: Theory and models'. In D. E. Schendel and C. W. Hofer (eds), *Strategic Management*, Little, Brown, Boston, MA, 1979.

Rumelt, R. P. 'The evaluation of business strategy'. In W. F. Glueck (ed.), *Business Policy and Strategic Management*, McGraw-Hill, New York, third edition, 1980.

Rumelt, R. P. 'Towards a strategic theory of the firm'. In R. B. Lamb (ed.), *Competitive Strategic Management*, Prentice-Hall, Englewood Cliffs, NJ, 1984.

Scheff, T. J. 'Control over policy by attendants in a mental hospital', *Journal of Health and Human Behavior*, 1961, pp. 93–105.

Selznick, P. *Leadership in Administration: A Sociological Interpretation*, Harper & Row, New York, 1957.

Smalter, D. J. and R. L. Ruggles. Jr 'Six business lessons from the Pentagon', *Harvard Business Review*, March–April 1966, pp. 64–75.

Stevenson, H. H. 'Defining corporate strengths and weaknesses', *Sloan Management Review*, Spring 1976, pp. 51–68.

Sun Tzu. *The Art of War* (S. B. Confitt, translator), Oxford University Press, New York, 1971.

Thoenig, J. C. and E. Friedberg. 'The power of the field staff: The case of the Ministry of Public Works and Urban Affairs and Housing in France'. In A. F. Leemans (ed.), *The Management of Change in Government*, Martinus Nijoff, The Hague, 1976.

Tilles, S. 'How to evaluate corporate strategy', *Harvard Business Review*, July–August 1963, pp. 111–120.

Tregoe, B. B. and J. W. Zimmerman. *Top Management Strategy*, Simon & Schuster, New York, 1980.

Wrapp, H. E. 'Good managers don't make policy decisions', *Harvard Business Review*, September–October 1967, pp. 91–99.

Yavitz, B. and W. H. Newman. *Strategy in Action: The Execution, Politics, and Payoff of Business Planning*, Free Press, New York, 1982.

Zand, D. E. *Information, Organization, and Power*, McGraw-Hill, New York, 1981.

16

CRITIQUE OF HENRY MINTZBERG'S 'THE DESIGN SCHOOL: RECONSIDERING THE BASIC PREMISES OF STRATEGIC MANAGEMENT'

H. Igor Ansoff

Source: *Strategic Management Journal* 12(6) (1991): 449–61.

Mintzberg's (1990) critique of the 'design school' of strategic management is evaluated on two criteria: methodological soundness and factual veracity. The critique is found to be deficient on both criteria. Mintzberg's own proposal for the basic principles of strategic management is critiqued using the same criteria. It is found that the exposition is deficient methodologically and that Mintzberg's descriptive and prescriptive assertions are at variance with facts observable in the current practice of strategic management. The variance is found to be due to several factors: lack of coherence in Mintzberg's presentation; his use of a definition of strategy which is at variance with the current practice of management, his failure to differentiate between prescriptive and descriptive statements; and his failure to define the context for his prescriptions. Using recent empirical research results on strategic success behaviors, Mintzberg's model is placed in a limited but important context in which it is a valid prescription for successful strategic behavior.

Introduction

The key conclusions of Mintzberg's (1990) paper are the following:

1. The 'Design School' at The Harvard Business School, having enunciated in the 1960s a set of prescriptive concepts for strategy formulation, 'denied itself' the opportunity to adapt these concepts ever since.

2. The 'other' prescriptive schools of strategy formulation (which are vaguely named, but not described by Mintzberg) shared the basic concepts of The Harvard Business School (HBS).
3. Like the Design School, the other prescriptive schools remained frozen in time.
4. The design principles shared by the design schools were, and still are, generally invalid except in a narrow specific context.
5. Interspersed with the critique of The Design School, are Mintzberg's own descriptions of the nature of strategy formation and prescriptions for the use of the 'emerging strategy' formation process, based on 'trial and experience'. Mintzberg argues that in unpredictable environments it is impossible to formulate an explicit strategy before the trial and experience process has run its course; and that it is not necessary to make strategy explicit in predictable environments.

Thus, according to Mintzberg, for all intents and purposes, all of the prescriptive schools for strategy formulation should be committed to the garbage heap of history, leaving the field to the 'emerging strategy' school which he represents.

Many readers will recognize that the author of this paper is a 40-year-long card-carrying member of one of the schools which Henry confines to obscurity. These readers are also likely to know that my entire professional career has been focused on helping organizations manage their strategic behavior in unpredictable environments.

Thus, if I am to accept Henry's verdict, I have spent 40 years contributing solutions which are not useful in the practice of strategic management.

Therefore, it should not be surprising that I rise in defense of at least one prescriptive school (the one to which I belong) in an effort to set the record straight and thus salvage a lifetime of work which has received a modicum of acceptance by practicing managers.

In situations like the present, it is easy to fall prey to a game of polemic charge-countercharge in the hope that the louder voice will carry the day. I will attempt to avoid this trap in two ways. First, I will show that the methodology by which Mintzberg disposes of the prescriptive school will hardly stand its day in the court of logic, and persuasiveness. Second, I will offer evidence of repeated instances in which Mintzberg's key assertions are factually wrong. Thirdly, I will fault Henry on the fact that, having confined the prescriptive schools to a narrow context, he does not place his own in an appropriate context.

Finally, I will identify the context which is appropriate for Henry's prescriptions. It is ironic that this context will appear very similar to the context to which he confines the prescriptive schools, but is somewhat larger in scope. Thus, to borrow a phrase which Henry uses in his critique of Professor Kenneth Andrews, his paper emerges as 'a caricature of his own model.'

Mintzberg's proof that the Design School denied itself the chance to adapt

Generalization from a sample of one

The writings of Professor Kenneth Andrews (1971) are the only source used in construction of this proof, and the Harvard Business School is made to appear to be solidly united behind him as the School's idealogue and spokesman.

Any reader who spent time in the halls of academe would automatically suspect this assumption of absence of differences in viewpoints and of conflicts which are typical of academic life. Therefore, Henry's generalization from a sample of one requires factual support.

Such support is not offered. Instead, Mintzberg attempts to minimize evidence to the contrary. Since world-wide visibility of Michael Porter cannot be left unnoticed, Mintzberg tries to minimize his influence on The Design School on the grounds that the HBS classic text on policy devotes only one chapter to Porter. Thus the reader is asked to believe that Porter's influence in the Harvard Business School has been confined to one chapter in a book!

Proof by implied intent

Having chosen Andrews as the 'mouthpiece' of the Design School, Mintzberg uses Andrews' own writings to prove that the school 'refused itself the chance to adapt' over time.

This is done by challenging Andrews' statements which suggest that the School's original design principles should be enlarged and modified.

The methodology is simple. First, having quoted a paragraph from Andrews, which suggests to an intelligent reader that the Design School did indeed continue to elaborate the original principles, Henry asserts (without any further evidence) that Andrews did not really mean what he said!

An example of one of several such 'proofs' should suffice to illustrate this 'methodology'. According to Mintzberg the second design principle advanced by the Design School (1990: 176) is as follows:

> Responsibility for (strategy formulation) must rest with the chief executive officer (CEO): that person is THE strategist.

In discussing Andrews' qualifications of this premise, Mintzberg quotes the following paragraph from Andrews' writings:

> False hope, oversimplification, and naiveté, as well as zest for power, have often led. . . . to the assumption that the chief executive officer

conceives strategy single-mindedly, talks the board of directors into *pro forma* approval, announces it as a fixed policy, and expects it to be promptly executed by subordinates under conventional command and control procedure.

(Andrews, 1987: 82)

Admittedly, the paragraph is turgid and elliptical, but a careful reading makes clear the author's intent: 'It is an improper assumption that the CEO should be THE only strategist.'

Mintzberg arrives at the same interpretation and then summarily and flippantly dismisses it in a half sentence.

. . . . . . we see it (the quotation), as a not unreasonable caricature of his own text.

(Mintzberg, 1990: 179)

A reader will find in Mintzberg's paper several other such 'proofs' by assertion that, whenever Andrews tries to enlarge the original principle, he really does not mean what he says.

Proof that other prescriptive schools have also remained 'frozen in time'

'Proof' by sweeping assertion

As mentioned before. Mintzberg offers no description nor discussion of 'the other' prescriptive schools. However, this does not prevent him from making the following sweeping assertion:

The reader is asked to bear in mind that although the other prescriptive schools of planning and positioning have broken with certain of the premises of the design school . . . . *the fact that they have accepted the most basic ones renders most of the following a critique of those schools as well.*

(Mintzberg, 1990: 181).
(italics added for emphasis)

In scientific practice, sweeping assertions, such as the preceding one, are not accepted as proofs and must remain suspect until proven to be true or false. I will use two generally accepted proofs to show that the above assertion is false.

The first is an epistemological proof suggested by Alfred North Whitehead (1962), who states that sweeping assertions should be tested for credibility against common experience.

Here is what Mintzberg expects his readers to accept as credible:

That a sizeable group of idiosyncratic individuals who derive a substantial part of their living by selling their intellectual capital to practicing managers, would forego their idiosyncracy and their competitive advantage, for the privilege of following intellectual leadership of The Harvard Business School.

To this author the above picture of academia is just as ludicrous as the earlier picture painted by Mintzberg of monolithic ideological unity within the HBS.

Contradictory factual evidence

The credibility test is subjective. A more persussive proof is a factual one. In such proof a single fact which contradicts the assertion is sufficient to falsify it. In mathematics this is known as the *Gegenbeispiel* principle of testing theoretical propositions.

Presented below are two facts which contradict Mintzberg's assertion that in the 1960s all prescriptive schools were basically alike.

The first fact may not have been available to Mintzberg. It is derived from a three-way meeting which took place at the Harvard Business School in 1962. The participants were two senior faculty members from each of the following major business schools: Sloan School of Management at MIT, Harvard Business School, and Graduate School of Industrial Administration at Carnegie-Mellon University. This writer was one of the participants.

During an intensive 2 days of discussion the participants explored two basic questions about strategy formation. The first was whether strategy has a distinctive content of its own or whether it was simply on integration of functional inputs, such as marketing, R&D, etc.

The second question was: if one assumed that strategy was a distinctive subject, is it possible to describe it in a structured manner, or must it of necessity remain an ephemeral concept which defies structuring and must, therefore, be studied by the verbal case method 'without writing anything down' (as was advocated in an early version of Harvard's classic case book on policy formation).

For the purpose of the present concern, suffice it to say that, at the end of 2 days, the three participant schools enunciated fundamentally different views which led to different 'design principles,' thus denying Mintzberg's assertion that all prescriptive schools were alike.

The second fact which contradicts Mintzberg's assertion should have been known to him, because it is discussed at length in a book published in 1965 (Ansoff, 1965), which he references in his paper.

This fact is that the concept of strengths and weaknesses, ascribed by Mintzberg to the Design School, was conceptually criticized in this book, and a detailed alternative method was proposed for identifying future strengths and weaknesses of an organization. Incidentally, this method met (in 1965) many of the objections which Mintzberg makes in 1990 to the strengths/weaknesses concept of The Design School.

Factual contradiction of assertion that all of the prescriptive schools denied themselves a chance to adopt with times

One factual counterexample will suffice to prove this assertion false. In this example, I will briefly trace the evolution of one of the prescriptive schools, which through the years, has stayed in close touch with the changing practice of strategic management, adopted many prescriptions which have emerged in practice, and in recent years made several original contributions to the practice of management.

I will refer to this School as the School of Holistic Strategic Management. (Because of his off-handed dismissal of 'the other' prescriptive schools, it is not possible to tell whether Mintzberg is aware of the existence of this school.) However, as shown below, its origins and its progress are well documented.

The extent of progress of The School of Strategic Management between 1965 and 1990 can be assessed by comparing two books by this author: *Corporate Strategy*, first published in 1965 (Ansoff, 1965) and *Implanting Strategic Management*, which first appeared in 1984 (Ansoff, 1984).

Following are the milestones of the School's Evolution:

1. As already discussed in a book published in 1965 (Ansoff, 1965), this School enunciated a concept of strengths and weaknesses which was drastically different from that of the Design School.
2. The same book presented a structured method for analytic strategy formulation (which was a codification of its author's practical experience), a procedure which at the time was being used in practice but was considered impossible at The Harvard Business School (Ansoff, 1965).
3. In 1978, the concept of strengths and weaknesses was replaced by a comprehensive concept of *Organizational Capability*, (Ansoff, 1978).
4. The original concept that strategy formulation should be centralized in the hands of the CEO was replaced by the concept *strategic bi-centralization* (Ansoff, 1984).
5. The concept of *Strategic Myopia* of key strategic managers and of *resistance to strategic change* were formulated and a practical procedure developed for overcoming both of them during strategy formulation and implementation (Ansoff, 1984).
6. A *diagnostic procedure* was developed *for sequencing strategyl-structure development*, according to the degree of urgency of strategic response being experienced by a firm. (Ansoff, Declerck and Hayes, 1974).

7. In 1972 the overall perspective of the subject was broadened from strategy formulation to the overall process by which organizations adapt and succeed in turbulent environments, and the concept of Strategic Management was introduced (Ansoff, 1972).

8. The concept of *real time response* was developed, as an alternative to periodic strategy planning, and three practical real time response procedures were proposed: (i) *Strong Signal Issue Management*; (ii) *Weak Signal Issue Management*; and (iii) *Surprise Management* (Ansoff, 1984; Ansoff, Kirsch and Roventa, 1980).

9. In 1979 an *applied theory* of strategic behavior was developed and published (Ansoff, 1979).

10. A *Strategic Success Hypothesis*, which is a keystone of this theory, was repeatedly tested and validated in a variety of organizational types and several countries. (Hatziantoniou, 1986; Salameh, 1987; Sullivan, 1987; Chabane, 1987; Lewis, 1989; Jaja, 1990; Ansoff and McDonnell, 1990; Ansoff, Sullivan *et al.*, 1990.)

11. Based on the findings of this research a practical *Strategic Diagnosis* procedure was developed for determining the strategy and capability changes which an organization will have to make in order to succeed in the future (Ansoff, 1984; Ansoff and McDonnell, 1990).

12. *Interactive Computer Software* for strategy formulation in turbulent environment was developed (Ansoff, 1986) and marketed.

In summary, at least one prescriptive school cannot be accused of having been a carbon copy of The Design School, either at its inception, nor during its subsequent evolution. Thus Mintzberg's assertion that *all* prescriptive Schools 'have accepted the premises' of The Design School and that they 'denied themselves the chance to adapt' is demonstrated to be false.

Many additional counterexamples can be found in the bibliography attached to Mintzberg's paper. One of these deserves particular attention because it occurred within the Harvard Business School. It is found in the work of Michael Porter. Having banished Porter from the design school, Mintzberg totally ignores his massive and distinctive contribution to the literature on strategy formulation which certainly does not qualify for inclusion among the original design school principles at the Harvard Business School.

Items 10 and 11 above show that The Holistic Strategic Management School, not only contributed new prescriptive principles, but also empirically identified the types of strategic behavior and their appropriate contexts which lead to organizational success. These findings will be used later in this paper for defining the appropriate context for Mintzberg's Model.

Mintzberg's model of strategy formation

Mintzberg leaves the reader in no doubt about his central theme:

322

> Our critique of the Design School revolves around one central theme: its promotion of thought independent of action, strategy formation above all as a process of *conception*, rather than as one of *learning*.
>
> (Mintzberg, 1990: 182)

The critique is not confined to proving that The Design School's and other prescriptive Schools' principles are wrong. Interwoven with the critique are Mintzberg's own descriptive assertions about the real world, which he proceeds to convert into prescriptions for the manner in which strategy formation should take place in organizations. These prescriptions are sprinkled throughout the text and they are not summarized, nor logically connected.

   Therefore, the summary given below is this writer's attempt at a faithful summary of Henry's proposals.

1.   The central prescription is that, with minor exceptions, all organizations should use what Mintzberg calls the 'emergent strategy' approach to strategy formation, using trial and experience process.
2.   The output of this process is an observable strategy which is the logic pattern underlying the historical sequence of successful trials.
3.   Except for minor exceptions, this strategy should not be made explicit:

> Explicit Strategies . . . . . are blinders designed to focus direction and so to block out peripheral vision.
>
> (1990: 184)

4.   It is not possible to formulate strategy in unpredictable environments:

> . . . during periods of unpredictability. . . . (organizations) cannot possibly hope to articulate any viable strategy.
>
> (1990: 184)

5.   Nor is it possible to formulate a viable strategy in predictable environments:

> The point we wish to emphasize is: how could the firm have known ahead of time? The discovery of what business it (firm) was to be in could not be undertaken on paper, but had to benefit from the results of testing and experience.
>
> (1990: 182)

The same quotation logically gives rise to the following conclusion, which is not articulated by Mintzberg:

6.   It is not possible to forecast the future with complete confidence.

Mintzberg's concern with managers' need 'to be sure,' and his assertion that they 'cannot' act before they are 'sure,' permeates the paper and is used as a basis for several descriptions and prescriptions, including the following:

7. Managers should not make statements about the future if they are not totally sure of what they are saying.
8. Managers should not evaluate their organization's strengths and weaknesses until they become evident from the trial and error experience.
9. In complex organizations it is not possible to plan and coordinate an organization-wide process of strategy formulation. This assertion is contained in the following quotation from Brian Quinn, used and approved by Mintzberg:

> It is virtually impossible for a manager to orchestrate all internal decisions, external environmental events, behavioral and power relationships, technical and informational needs, and actions of intelligent opponents so that they come together at a precise moment.
>
> (Quinn, 1978: 184)

Mintzberg makes no direct reference to the context in which his prescriptive principles should be used. But in his concern with what to do with The Design School, after he has demolished it, he does identify two contexts in which the explicit strategy formulation championed by the prescriptive schools may be applicable.

One of these contexts is:

> a new organization .... (during) .... the period of initial conception of strategy. ...
>
> (1990: 191)

(In this case Mintzberg implicitly suspends his earlier claim that in unpredictable environments strategy cannot be formulated and allows the founding entrepreneur to have a 'vision'.)

The other context is one in which:

> the design school model would seem to apply best ... (is when) an organization (is) coming out of a period of changing circumstances and into one of operating stability.
>
> (1990: 191)

With these two exceptions recognized, we can infer the following prescription implied by Mintzberg:

10. The 'emerging strategy approach' should be used in all situations with the exception of the two specified above.

In summary, Henry's prescription can be named as one of *implicit strategy formation*, under which strategy need not be a part of manager's concern, except under special circumstances. Managers should allow strategy and capabilities to evolve organically, through trial and experience, and focus their attention on the operating efficiency of the organization.

Thus, Mintzberg prescribes a world free of explicit strategy formulation and free of strategic managers.

Critique of Mintzberg's model

While reading the first part of the paper, one wonders why Mintzberg went to such length to prove that the prescriptive schools were identical and have jointly 'denied themselves' the opportunity to adapt to the changing times.

The reason becomes clear in the second part: Mintzberg is now free to criticize all of the prescriptive schools as if they were still adhering to their original design principles of 1965.

In the light of the methodological and factual deficiencies pointed out earlier in this paper, it is hardly worthwhile to challenge Mintzberg's criticisms of the original design principles, since they have been outstripped by developments, both in the practice of strategic management and in the writings of the prescriptive schools of thought. But Henry's own model of reality summarized in the preceding pages cries out for a critical appraisal. It is to this task that we now turn our attention.

As a person who has spent over 40 years of his life as manager, consultant, educator, and a close observer of the business scene, I have difficulty accepting Henry's model as description of strategic management reality.

And yet, Henry is an intellectually outstanding person, globally respected, and recognized as one of the leading contributors to the literature on strategic management.

As I studied his paper several explanations of this apparent paradox became clear. In the following pages I will present these explanations. As before, I will base my critique on methodological deficiencies and on factual contradictions between Henry's claims and the real world of strategic management.

Self-denial of a chance to study business environment

It is strange how in his paper Mintzberg repeatedly commits sins of which he accuses the Design and the other prescriptive schools. One of these is the accusation directed at the Design School that it 'slight(s) the environment in favor of a focus on the organization' (1990: 182).

Henry's paper shows that he commits the same sin. Below is the sum total of his references to the environment.

One learns that managers:

> cannot be sure of the future. Sometimes organizations need to function during periods of unpredictability. Sometimes organizations come out of a period of changing circumstances into a period of operating stability.

Nothing is said about how often is 'sometime', what is meant by 'unpredictability', by 'changing circumstances' or how long and how prevalent are the 'periods of operating stability.'

The only complete sentence devoted to the environment does not help very much:

> . . . . environment is not some kind of pear to be plucked from the tree of external appraisal, but a major and sometimes unpredictable force. . . .

> (1990: 185)

This cryptic statement begs all kinds of questions: whose environment is being discussed, what kind of influence does the force exert on organizations; under what circumstances is it exerted; what impact does it have on strategic behavior, etc?

This slight of the environment is unfortunate. If Henry had taken the minimum trouble to peruse the cover pages of *Business Week* for the past 4–5 years, he would have easily found answers to most of the above questions. In brief, he would have found the following information.

1.   In today's world, different types of organizations have different environments. Thus, since the 1940s the environment of many business firms has progressively become more and more turbulent, unpredictable, and surpriseful. On the other hand, the not-for-profit organization had enjoyed a relatively placid environment until the 1970s (Ansoff, 1984).
2.   Within the two classes of organizations, the environments of different industries became differentiated. At one extreme, some organizations continue to enjoy a relatively placid existence and at the other extreme are organizations which are experiencing very high turbulence (Ansoff, 1984).
3.   The level of environmental turbulence has become a driving force which dictates strategic responses necessary for success (Ansoff and Sullivan, 1990).
4.   In high turbulence environments success comes to firms which use strategies which are discontinuous from their historical strategies (Ansoff and Sullivan, 1990; Ansoff *et al.*, 1990).

5. In low turbulent environments success comes to firms which use strategies of incremental development of their historically successful product-development, (op cit.).
6. The final characteristic of the environment neglected by Mintzberg is the acceleration of the speed of change in the environment which has occurred during the past 30 years (Drucker, 1980).

The latter aspect of the environment puts in doubt the major prescription which Mintzberg offers in his paper. In turbulent environments, the speed with which changes develop is such that firms which use the 'emerging strategy formation' advocated by Mintzberg endanger their own survival. The reason is that when they arrive on a market with a new product/service, such firms find the market pre-empted by more foresightful competitors, who had planned their strategic moves in advance.

Thus, the first reason for the contradictions between Mintzberg's picture of reality and the observable real world is his failure to observe the current business environment.

Failure to meet validity tests for prescriptive and descriptive observations

To be valid, a descriptive observation must meet a single test: it must be an accurate observation of reality. A prescription must pass a much more rigorous test: it must offer evidence that use of the prescription will enable an organization to meet the objective by which it judges its success.

Mintzberg seems to be oblivious to the need for evidence to support his descriptive statements, and he converts descriptions into prescriptions without any offering evidence that they will bring success to organizations using them.

An example of such conversion is offered by Mintzberg's treatment of experience with related diversifications. He starts with a descriptive statement about the 'vast majority of experiences reported in the popular press' which shows that firms make a number of mistakes in their diversification programs and, without batting an eyelash, converts it into a prescriptive statement: 'acquiring firm *has to make* a number of mistakes until it gradually learns what works for it, if it ever does' (1990: 183) (italics added for emphasis). Thus a described pattern of successive failures is automatically transformed into a prescription for success.

I am not sure that Henry appreciates the consequences of advocating use of trial and error in diversification programs. Having been in charge of a diversification department of a major American firm, I can testify to the fact that trial and error diversification is enormously expensive. The successive acquisitions require major investments by the acquirer, and disinvestment from mistakes multiplies the costs, because an acquisition cannot be sold-off overnight as one would sell a portfolio of poorly performing shares.

327

But, even more importantly, the mere fact that 'the vast majority' of experiences has led to repeated mistakes is not a valid basis for recommending that others should follow the same path. What is being reported by Mintzberg are cases of failure and the fact that there are many of them does not mean that success seeking firms should follow their example.

In fact, a major research study of mergers and acquisitions has shown that it is the planned approach to diversification, and not the trial and error approach, that produces better financial results (Ansoff *et al.*, 1971).

A second example is of critical importance to Mintzberg's model of strategic management. Without any prior evidence Henry offers the following description:

> .... sometimes organizations. . . . need to function during periods of unpredictability, when they *cannot possibly hope to articulate any viable strategy*.
>
> (1990: 184) (italics added for emphasis)

Having stated the description, Henry offers the following prescription, again without any supporting evidence:

> When strategists are not sure, they had better not articulate strategies, *for all the reasons given above*.
>
> (1990: 184) (italics added for emphasis)

However, a careful and multiple rereading of the proceeding text fails to reveal any 'reasons' unless it is the unarticulated conviction of Mintzberg's, which permeates the paper, that strategy formulation is impossible unless the environment is 'stable and predictable.'

We must now deal with the origin of this conviction.

Descriptive definition of strategy

If Henry had taken the trouble to acquaint himself with the history and current practice of strategic management, he would have found widespread use of explicit *a priori* strategy formulation. Furthermore he would have found that explicit strategy formulation is typically used in environments in which managers are not 'sure' about the future (Steiner and Schollhammer, 1975).

Thus, once more, Henry's assertion is contradicted by facts. In this case the explanation is twofold.

The first is the black and white picture of the environment painted by Mintzberg: managers are either 'sure' or totally 'unsure' about the future. In the real world of management these two extremes are rarely observable

(Schwartz, 1990). In practice managers are typically partially 'unsure' (see concept of partial ignorance in Ansoff, 1965). And they formulate strategy precisely because being 'unsure' makes it dangerous to assume that the firm's future will be an extrapolation of the past.

The second explanation is found in the difference between Henry's definition of the concept of strategy and the definition used in practice. His definition is descriptive since, in order to identify the strategy, it is necessary to wait until a series of strategic moves has been completed.

But the concept used in practice is prescriptive and it stipulates that strategy should be formulated in advance of the events which make it necessary.

Thus Henry's failure to differentiate between descriptive and prescriptive statements once again places him in the position of contradicting observable reality.

Use of existential model of learning

The model of organizational learning advocated by Mintzberg consists of a sequential trial and error process, neither preceded nor interrupted, nor followed by cognitive strategy formulation.

To be sure, under special circumstances, he allows the possibility of postexperience strategy diagnosis. But nowhere in the paper does he suggest that the diagnosed strategy should in any way affect the choice of subsequent strategic moves. In fact, as cited before, Mintzberg considers explicit strategies to be 'blinders designed to block out peripheral vision.'

This model of learning is the oldest one in human history. It was the model of the prehistoric man when he ventured from his cave in search for food. It was also the model of the master builders in The Middle Ages who created glorious cathedrals by repeating lessons learned from past successes, without understanding of what made the cathedrals stand or fall. This was also the model which was used to train new apprentices by putting them to work under direct guidance of experienced master builders. We shall refer to it as the *existential model* of learning.

Henry's insistence on exclusive use of this most rudimentary model of learning in formation of strategy is ironic because it is the model on which The Harvard Business School Case method, which he criticizes at length, was originally built.

The age of enlightenment ushered a new model which recognized importance of cognition in the affairs of man. In this model decision-making is the first stage, followed by implementation of the decision. It became the standard model of the natural sciences, and it was the model used in the early prescriptions for strategic planning. We shall call this model the *rational model* of learning.

The rational model has several advantages over the existential:

1. In cases in which decision-making is less time-consuming than trial and error, the rational model saves time by selecting action alternatives which are most likely to produce success. This time saving is of great importance in organizations which find themselves in rapidly changing environments.
2. It permits additional savings of time through starting strategic response in anticipation of need to act—a process called strategic planning.
3. It reduces the number of strategic errors and reduces costs by eliminating the probable 'non-starters' from the list of possible strategic moves.

Thus, the rational model becomes particularly important when the cost of a failed trial is very high, as in the case of diversification by business firms.

Mintzberg makes no mention of the fact that the rational model is a legitimate alternative to the existential model. But he does devote a great deal of energy to proving that the existential model should be the only one used in strategic management. To support this claim, he makes a number of descriptive assertions which, as we have shown, are in conflict with factual evidence.

First, he declares that cognitive strategy formulation is not possible in unpredictable environments, a claim which is contradicted by the fact of habitual strategy formulation in business firms.

Second, he argues that, even in environments which are predictable, managers should not formulate a strategy unless they are sure of its consequences. He does this in the face of factual evidence that strategy formulation is typically found in firms whose managers are unsure about the future.

Thirdly, he claims that explicit strategy makes strategic action rigid and forecloses opportunities which were not anticipated by the strategy.

In making this claim, Henry neglects two facts which are readily available in the literature of the prescriptive schools (Ansoff, 1965).

The first is that the strategy concept used in practice does not specify alternatives. On the contrary, it sets guidelines for the *kinds of opportunities* the firm wants to develop through search and creativity.

The second fact is that successful practitioners of strategy typically use a *strategic control* mechanism which periodically reviews and, if necessary, revises the strategy in the light of experience.

Thus, use of explicit strategy in successful practice is not rigid and does not foreclose attention to new opportunities which are outside the scope of strategy. But use of explicit strategy does control erratic deviations from the strategy. This point was well made in a quotation from Andrews used and rejected by Mintzberg:

> Strategy will evolve over time, no matter what. . . . . But the elucidation of goals can transcend incrementalism (and) . . . result in the deliberate amendment of strategy or in curtailment of strategic erosion.
>
> (Christensen *et al.*, 1982: 553–554)

Use of strategic control converts the rational learning mode into a more sophisticated one. The model becomes a chain of cognition-trial-cognition-trial etc. We will refer to it as *strategic learning* model (See Chapters 2.6, 2.9, 5.3 in Ansoff and McDonnell, 1990).

Finally, Mintzberg attacks the rational model of learning by pointing out that it decouples strategy formulation from implementation, which causes organizational resistance and even failure of implementation.

This point underlines the irony of Mintzberg's insistence on criticizing outdated original principles of the Design School without acquainting himself with their subsequent evolution. As discussed earlier in this paper, the problem of resistance to change has been recognized and treated back in the 1980s without abandoning explicit strategy formulation (Ansoff, Part 6, 1984).

In summary, Mintzberg's 'proofs' that the rational model of learning does not apply to strategic management are contradicted by facts of management practice. And his insistence on universal use of the existential model invites managements to abdicate their role as strategic thinkers, and to confine their attention to optimizing the operating behavior of their organizations.

Failure to identify relevant context

The most curious and damaging aspect to Mintzberg's Model of strategy formation lies in his failure to identify the context in which his model is valid. It is curious because, as already discussed in this paper, Mintzberg does identify the context for the Design School Model. And in his other work he was one of the first researchers to call attention to the importance of contextual view of organizational structures (Mintzberg, 1979).

His failure to identify the context for his own work is damaging because it exposes his model to counterexamples from the entire field of 'organizationatives' and from the complete range of organizational settings. As a result, in the absence of contextual limits, Mintzberg inadvertently ventures to make comments on contexts to which he has had little exposure.

And yet, it is the opinion of this writer that, if streamlined and put into proper context, Mintzberg's model of strategy has demonstrable validity, both descriptively and prescriptively, and represents an insightful and important contribution to Strategic Management. In the remainder of this paper I will describe the appropriate descriptive and prescriptive contexts for Mintzberg's model.

Valid context for Mintzberg's prescriptive Model

Modification of Mintzberg's Model

A complete description of Mintzberg's Model was presented in this paper. From this model we abstract the following core concepts which can be shown to be valid in specified contexts.

1. To succeed, an organization should use the 'emergent strategy' trial and experience process of strategy formation.
2. No attempt should be made to formulate the firm's strategy in advance of the trial and experience process.
3. No formal organization-wide strategic planning should be used.
4. Except under special circumstances, the strategy which is implicit in the historical sequence of successful trials should not be made explicit.

Description of the relevant research

The relevant empirical research which makes it possible to identify the context within which the above Model is a valid prescription, was briefly referred to earlier in this paper. A somewhat more detailed description follows.

The research was addressed to testing the Strategic Success Hypothesis which was proposed by Ansoff in 1979. The Hypothesis states that an organization will optimize its success when the aggressiveness of its strategic behavior in the environment and its openness to the external environment are both aligned with the turbulence level of the organization's external environment.

The key contextual variable in this research was the concept of environmental turbulence which is an enlargement of the concepts of unpredictability and uncertainty used by Mintzberg.

In the research, five distinctive levels of observable environmental turbulence were identified, ranging from stable to creative. For the purpose of identification of context it is useful to aggregate turbulence levels into two categories: (1) *Incremental turbulence* in which environmental changes are a logical evolution of the historical change process, and the speed of the changes is slower than the response time of the organizations; and (2) *Discontinuous turbulence* in which successive changes are discontinuous from the preceding ones, and speed of change is greater than the speed of the organizations' response.

To date the Strategic Success Hypothesis has been empirically tested in six different settings:

1. A cross-section of U.S. firms (Hatziantoniou, 1986)
2. Banks in United Arab Emirates (Salameh, 1987)
3. Public Service Organizations in the U.S. (Sullivan, 1987)
4. Parastatal firms in Algeria (Chabane, 1987)
5. Banks in San Diego County (Lewis, 1989)
6. Major U.S. banks (Jaja, 1990)

In all six settings, the hypothesis was statistically sustained in all settings at 0.05 or better confidence level. And the levels of success in organizations which are aligned with the environment were substantially higher than in organizations which were out of alignment (Ansoff and Sullivan, 1990; Ansoff, Sullivan *et al.*, 1990).

The relevance of the research results to Mintzberg's model lies in the fact that Mintzberg's prescription for strategy formation is virtually identical with the type of strategic aggressiveness which was found to optimize firms' success in the extrapolative environment.

Thus, empirical research described above shows that *Mintzberg's Prescriptive Model is a valid prescription for organizations which seek to optimize their performance in environments in which strategic changes are incremental and the speed of the changes is slower than the speed of the organizational response.*

It should be noted that, except for difference in the language (academic vs. practical), Mintzberg's model is identical to the injunction to firms to 'stick to their strategic knitting' which was offered in a world famous book *The Search of Excellence* by Peters and Waterman (Peters and Waterman, 1982).

(It should further be noted that, while recommending conservative strategic behavior, Peters and Waterman recommend very aggressive competitive behavior by firms which aspire to succeed in extrapolative environments, a matter not mentioned by Mintzberg.)

The size of the domain of applicability of Mintzberg's model to the business sector can be determined from an extensive unpublished survey by this author (which was briefly described in the introduction of this paper). According to the survey, roughly 20 percent of the firms in developed economies will need to use the Mintzberg/Peters/Waterman model in order to succeed in the 1990s.

It must be mentioned that, in discontinuous environments, which constitute the remaining 80 percent of the sample, the research described above (and the aftermath of the Peters-Waterman research) both show that firms which persist in 'sticking to their strategic knitting' will not be among the successful performers and may jeopardize their own survival.

Finally it is necessary to recognize that the context of the *descriptive validity* of Mintzberg's is much larger than the prescriptive. This context includes firms which are successful in the extrapolative business environments (in the business jargon those are called market driven firms); firms in discontinuous environments which are suffering from loss of competitiveness; and, in 1990, it includes a majority of the not-for-profit organizations in the U.S.

Thus the paradox of a world-famous researcher opening himself to criticism could have been avoided if Henry had stuck to his own strategic knitting which is a deep knowledge of descriptive strategic behavior, particularly in not-for-profit organizations.

Conclusions

In this paper, the thrusts of critique of Mintzberg's proofs and concepts were two: methodological weakness of the arguments, and contradiction to factual evidence.

The conclusions of this critique are the following:

1. Mintzberg's proof that the Design School failed to adapt with times is methodologically unsound.
2. The assertion that other prescriptive schools shared their design principles with the Design School is factually inaccurate.
3. The assertion that the other prescriptive schools failed to adapt is factually inaccurate.
4. Because of the above conclusions, it is unproductive to address Mintzberg's specific criticisms of the Design School principles.
5. However, it is productive to critique the alternative to the Harvard Business School's design principles which is advanced by Mintzberg.
6. This critique finds that Mintzberg's proofs of his design principles are deficient on the following points:

   His 'self-denial' of knowledge of practice of strategic management in the business sector, which leads him to many assertions that are in direct contradiction to observable facts.

   Failure to meet validity tests for prescriptive and descriptive observations, which leads to unsupported claims for descriptions and arbitrary announcement of prescriptions.

   Use of a descriptive definition of strategy, which is different from the definition used in practice, which makes Mintzberg's conclusions appear contradictory to facts.

   Insistence on universal applicability of the existential learning model, which leads to assertions which contradict observable reality. Failure to specify the relevance context for his own model.

   By abstracting a set of coherent concepts from Mintzberg's model it is possible to show that the 'emerging strategy' model is a valid prescription for success in incremented environments, a valid description of poorly performing firms in discontinuous environments, and a valid description of the behavior of a majority of not-for-profit organizations.

References

Andrews, K. R. *The Concept of Corporate Strategy*, Irwin, Homewood, IL, 1971, 2nd edn, 1980; 3rd edn, 1987.

Ansoff, H. I. *Corporate Strategy*, McGraw-Hill, New York, 1965.

Ansoff, H. I., R. J. Brandenburg, F. E. Portner and H. R. Radosevich. *Acquisition: Behavior of US Manufacturing Firms 1946–65*, Vanderbilt University Press, Nashville, TN, 1971.

334

Ansoff, H. I. 'The concept of Strategic management', *Journal of Business Policy*, 2(4), 1972, pp. 3–9.

Ansoff, H. I., Roger P. Declerck and Robert L. Hayes. *From Strategic Planning to Strategic Management*, Wiley, New York, 1974.

Ansoff, H. I. 'Corporate capability for managing change', SRI Business Intelligence Program, Research Report, No. 610, 1978.

Ansoff, H. I. *Strategic Management*, MacMillan Press Ltd., London and Basingstoke, 1979.

Ansoff, H. I., W. Kirsch and P. Roventa. 'Dispersed positioning in strategic portfolio analysis', EIASM Working Paper, 1980.

Ansoff, H. I. *Implanting Strategic Management*, Prentice/Hall International, Englewood Cliffs, NJ, 1984.

Ansoff, H. I. 'Competitive strategy analysis on the personal computer', *Journal of Business Strategy*, 6, Winter 1986, pp. 28–36.

Ansoff, H. I. and P. Sullivan. 'Competitiveness through strategic response'. In Ralph Gilman (ed.), *Making Organizations More Competitive: Constantly Improving Everything Inside and Outside the Organization*, Jossey-Bass, San Francisco, CA, 1990.

Ansoff, H. I., P. Sullivan, P. Hatziantoniou, H. Chabane, R. Jaja, T. Salameh, A. Lewis, P. Wang and S. Djohar. 'Empirical validation of the strategic success hypothesis', paper in progress, 1990.

Ansoff, H. I. and E. McDonnell. *Implanting Strategic Management*, 2nd edn, Prentice Hall, New York, 1990.

Chabane, H. 'Restructuring and performance in Algerian state-owned enterprises: A strategic management study', Unpublished D.B.A. dissertation, United States International University, San Diego, 1987.

Christensen, C. R., K. R. Andrews, J. L. Bower, R. G. Hamermesh and M. E. Porter. *Business Policy: Text and Cases*, Irwin, Homewood, IL, 6th edn, 1987.

Drucker, P. F. *Managing In Turbulent Times*, Heinemann, London, 1990.

Hatziantoniou, P. 'The relationship of environmental turbulence, corporate strategic profile, and company performance, Unpublished D.B.A. dissertation. United States International University, San Diego, 1986.

Jaja, R. M. 'Technology and banking: The implications of technology myopia on banking financial performance, A strategic management analysis', Unpublished D.B.A. dissertation, United States International University, San Diego, 1990.

Lewis, A. 'Strategic posture and financial performance of the banking industry in California: A strategic management study', Unpublished D.B.A. dissertation, United States International University, San Diego, 1989.

Mintzberg, H. *The Structuring of Organizations*, Prentice Hall, Englewood Cliffs, NJ, 1979.

Mintzberg, H. 'Crafting strategy', *Harvard Business Review*, July–August 1987, pp. 66–75.

Mintzberg, H. 'The Design School: Reconsidering the basic premises of strategic management', *Strategic Management Journal*, 11(3), 1990, pp. 171–195.

Peters, T. and R. Waterman, *In Search of Excellence*. Harper and Row, New York, 1982.

Salameh, T. T. 'Analysis and financial performance of the banking industry in United Arab Emirates: A strategic management study', Unpublished D.B.A. dissertation, United States International University, San Diego, 1987.

Schwartz, P. 'Accepting the rise in forecasting', *The New York Times Forum*, September 2, 1990, p. 13.

Steiner, G. A. and H. Schòllhammer. 'Pitfalls in multi-national long range planning'. *Long Range Planning*, 8(2), 1975, pp. 2–12.

Sullivan, P. A. 'The relationship between proportion of income derived from subsidy and strategic performance of a federal agency under the Commercial Activities Program', Unpublished D.B.A. dissertation. United States International University, San Diego, 1987.

Whitehead, Alfred North. *The Function of Reason*, Beacon Press, Boston, MA, 1962.

17

LEARNING 1, PLANNING 0

Reply to Igor Ansoff

Henry Mintzberg

Source: *Strategic Management Journal* 12(6) (1991): 463–6.

In a way, it is unfortunate that Igor Ansoff has responded to my article on the design school. That is because in my pat world of schools of thought on strategy formation, his work slots into the planning school and not the design school *per se* (and so I shall address it in a forthcoming book on that school).

This may seem to be splitting hairs—in a sense it is—but to my mind there are two fundamental differences in the premises that underlie these two schools (both evident in Igor's work as well as that of Ken Andrews).

First, while one focuses (almost obsessively) on the CEO as "architect" of strategy, the other gives an awful lot of influence to the staff planners. And second, more importantly though closely associated with the first, while one school treats "SWOT" (strength and weaknesses, opportunities and trends) as a general framework, the other elaborates it into a detailed formal model, of an extensive sequence of clearly delineated steps supported by a host of analytical techniques (nowhere more evident than in Ansoff, 1965:202–203). To support the point that this formalization of the process, so characteristic of all of Igor's work, is hardly incidental, I need only quote Ken Andrews about his own writing on the design approach: "This book . . . virtually ignores the mechanisms of planning on the grounds that, detached from strategy, they miss their mark" (in Christensen, *et al.*, 1987:11). Thus, I doubt that the Harvard and other fans of the design school —and there remain many, either people who did not move on to other prescriptive schools that I call planning and positioning, or else moved back after the former took such a beating from the mid 1970s—would welcome Igor Ansoff as their spokesman.

But we vote in learned journals with our fingers and our stamps, and so that is who they get. Besides, while Igor may spend more time in his reply criticizing me and defending himself than supporting Andrews, his work does build on the other premises I associated with the design school. And Igor is certainly an eminent spokesman for the role of so-called "rationality" in strategic management.

I prefer not to enter into a elaborate rejoinder here. I will let my other writings stand on where I stand, including my original article on the design school, a long paper on all 10 schools (Mintzberg, 1990, which, I should add, sought to place *all* 10 schools into their limited contexts), and other empirical pieces on the processes of strategy formation (e.g., 1978, and with coauthors, 1982, 1984, 1985, 1986). There I hope the reader will agree with my claims that I do not commit the planning school "to the garbage heap of history" (only to the role of programing strategies already conceived, as, incidentally, does Andrews), that I do not bestow exclusive rights on either emergent strategy or the learning school, and that I do not deny the role of cognition in the learning process or argue that strategies should never be made explicit. To critique is not to dismiss, but sometimes only to try to push back into appropriate context.

What I do wish to address here is Igor's banner of science, which I see as the kettle trying to call the pot ever so awfully black. "Science" has always been the great smokescreen of the rationalists, worked to a fine art by many economists who have used all kinds of fancy methodologies to prove the details of their arguments while obscuring the fundamental premises on which they are based.

I am a great fan of Igor Ansoff's work. I say this sincerely, and believe that the comments in my planning book will bear this out. But he is hardly a noted empiricist. In fact, I read his work much as I used to read that of Marshall McLuhan—for his identification of important problems and creation of fascinating notions in the process of developing a questionable and often obscure line of argument. In fact, I believe Igor's real contribution to the literature, perhaps to his chagrin, is not prescriptive but descriptive, in the concepts he provided to us.

Claims of the scientific basis of his work and the unscientific basis of my article abound in Igor's reply. I am first of all accused of that most deadly sin of all, "the sample of one". Well, I happen to like samples of one. Piaget didn't apologize for studying his own children, and I doubt that the first physicist to split a single atom felt horror about his sample of one. Ken Andrews' text typifies a large body of literature I identify with the design school (a fair bit of which is referenced in my original article), not to mention the many Harvard MBAs and DBAs who carried his messages far and wide.

Perhaps the only words that appear more often than "turbulent" and "turbulence" in Igor's reply are "facts" and "factual evidence". In *fact*, not a single fact is ever supplied in the reply, only various references to such facts. One set comes from *Business Week*, which informs us, in Igor's words, that "since the 1940s the environment of many business firms has progressively become more and more turbulent, unpredictable, and surpriseful." I hope he means the late 1940s, because I wonder what has proved more surpriseful to American business than the early 1940s. Indeed, has any period during this century even remotely approached the pressures of the two world wars and the depression?

What in the world does "turbulence" mean anyway? And who has ever made a serious claim of measuring it? This is just a reflection of the groundless escalation of vocabulary in our held ("hyperturbulence" having followed, McCann and Selsky, 1984). When I look out my window, I see no turbulence. Nor when I visit all those companies who don't realize (alongside myself) that my expertise is supposed to be confined to the not-for-profit sector. These particular days I do see something akin to turbulence on my television screen, but that is in Northern Iraq, not corporate America. Pressured by some serious competition from abroad, due in my opinion, to the years so many American businesses spent with their collective heads buried in the sand of "rational" planning, everyone runs around like "Chicken Little" crying "The environment's turbulent! The environment's turbulent!"

Bear in mind when that term first entered the management literature: the same year Igor published *Corporate Strategy*, in an article by Emery and Trist in 1965. 1965! Some turbulence. What we face is not turbulence but overinflated egos.

More of those facts are claimed to come from a set of six dissertations carried out at Igor's university, presumably under his supervision. I cannot comment on these. I have not read them and await their assessment by peers in refereed journals. I do not mean to sound like a snotnosed academic. But there are facts and there are facts, and peer review helps to sort these out. I should add that, depending on how one judges the journals, none or almost none of the references Igor cites in his article about these various facts have been subjected to that scrutiny.

I have particular trouble with Igor's claims about the benefits of a rational approach to diversification. For one thing, I am gravely suspicious of anything having been proved in this regard. Certainly every particular story I have heard about the process—my own unsubstantiated facts— informs me that it often starts out as a rational, deliberate process, which almost inevitably fails, but when it does occasionally succeed, it ends up as an emergent one of painful learning. Just consider Michael Porter's (1987) "facts" on the incidence of failure in acquisition decisions. Maybe the rational models were *too* successful—in their incidence of adoption rather than the consequences of that adoption.

I would like to introduce just one fact here. In one sense, it is the only real fact I know in all of the literature of strategic management. While debates abound about rationality vs. incrementalism, or planning vs. learning, and great gobs of wonderfully scientific statistics have been collected on the

339

subject (not the best of which is that whole "does planning pay?" literature, which never proved anything), we do have one rather tangible data point. It is Richard Pascale's (1984) account by several Honda executives about how they developed on site the strategy that captured two-thirds of the American motorcycle market. What is especially fascinating about this messy account is that it stands in sharp contrast to the brilliantly rational strategy imputed to these executives by BCG (1975) consultants who apparently never bothered to ask.

Honda's success, if we are to believe those who did it and not those who figured it, was built precisely on what they initially believed to be one of Igor's "probable 'non-starters'"—namely the small motorcycle. Their own priors were that a market without small motorcycles would not buy small motorcycles. Had they a proper planning process in place, as Igor describes it in these pages, this non-starter would have been eliminated at the outset —plan "rationally" and be done with it. But Honda was badly managed in this regard, and so a few Japanese managers, riding around on those little things in Los Angeles, were pleasantly surprised. They learned. (General Motors was apparently well managed in this regard, because a product development manager there once told me that they had a mini-van on the drawing boards long before Chrysler ever did but that this "probable 'non-starter'" was scuttled in the planning process!)

We think we are so awfully smart. We can work it all out in advance, so cleverly, we "rational" human beings, products of the "age of enlightenment." We can predict the future, identify the non-starters, impose our minds on all that matter. And why not. After all, aren't we the ones who live in turbulent times? That makes us important, doesn't it?

Come on Igor. Of course we need to think. Of course we want to be rational. But it's a complicated world out there. We both know that we shall get nowhere without emergent learning alongside deliberate planning. If we have discovered anything at all these many years, it is, first, that the conception of a novel strategy is a creative process (of synthesis), for which there are no formal techniques (analysis), and second, that to program these strategies throughout complex organizations, and out to assenting environments, we often require a good deal of formal analysis. So the two processes can intertwine. I'll use your words: "cognition-trial-cognition-trial, etc." We may differ on where to begin, but once it has gone on for awhile, who cares? (Does it matter if the chicken or the egg came first?) You call it "strategic learning." I have no problem with that so long as you don't pretend it can be formalized. And in return I'll promise never to claim that planning shouldn't be formalized. (Sounds like a good deal to me!)

Winston Churchill is reported to have defined planning as "deciding to put one foot in front of the other." I like to say that strategy and structure proceed like two feet walking: strategy always precedes structure, and always follows it too. And so it is with planning and learning. BCG's mistake was not in what it *did* describe so much as in what it left out; the critical period of emergent learning that had to inform the deliberate planning process. In other words, strategy had to be conceived informally before it could be programed formally.

Our problem, in practice and academia, has always been one of imbalance, the assumption that planning (or learning) could do it all. As I see things, long ago we may have been weak on rational analysis, but today we have an excess of it. What you call "the age of enlightenment" has become blinding. Contrary to your criticism, I *am* well aware of the "widespread use of explicit *a priori* strategy formulation" in our organizations —that is exactly the problem. And it goes well beyond diversification decisions. For example, I have come to suspect that Harvard's great success may be business's great failure. In other words, the real danger of the design school may be in providing a seductive model whose superficial "rationality" in the classroom can so easily get promoted into the executive suite.

You claim, Igor, that rationality saves time. Maybe that is all too true: in formulating detached, easy strategies in case study discusions, later in executive meetings, which are not meant to be implemented, and later cannot be, and in giving all those "whiz kids" a head start down the "fast track." They can certainly tell a "probable 'non-starter'" from a "winner," at least *a priori*.

And let's not let ourselves be seduced by the "facts," or by "science." A score of 1–0 for informal learning over formal planning reflects not the wealth of management practice at all, but the poverty of the performance of all of us at the game of research. In any event, Igor, I look forward to doing this again in the next innings, at the planning school, where the fun may really begin.

References

Ansoff, H. I. *Corporate Strategy: An Analytic Approach to Business Policy for Growth and Expansion*, McGraw-Hill, New York, 1965.

Boston Consulting Group. *Strategy Alternatives for the British Motorcycle Industry*, Her Majesty's Stationery Office, 1975, London.

Christensen, C. R., K. R. Andrews, J. L. Bower, R. G. Hamermesh and M. E. Porter. *Business Policy: Text and Cases*, 6th Edn, Irwin, Homewood, IL, 1987.

Emery, F. E. and E. L. Trist. "The causal texture of organizational environments", *Human Relations*, February 1965, pp. 21–32.

McCann, J. E. and J. Selsky. "Hyperturbulence and the emergence of Type 5 environments", *Academy of Management Review*, 9(3), 1984, pp. 460–470.

Mintzberg, H. "Patterns in strategy formation", *Management Science*, May 1978, pp. 934–948.

Mintzberg, H. "Strategy formation: Schools of thought". In J. Frederickson (ed.), *Perspectives on Strategic Management*, Harper Business, New York, 1990, pp. 105–235.

Mintzberg, H. and A. McHugh. "Strategy formation in an adhocracy", *Administrative Science Quarterly*, June 1985, pp. 160–197.

Mintzberg, H. and J. Waters. "Tracking strategy in an entrepreneurial firm", *Academy of Management Journal*, 25(3), 1982, pp. 465–499.

Mintzberg, H. and J. Waters. "Researching the formation of strategies: The history of Canadian Lady, 1939–1976. In R. B. Lamb (ed.), *Competitive Strategic Management*, Prentice-Hall, Englewood Cliffs, NJ, 1984, pp. 62–93.

Mintzberg, H., P. Brunet and J. Waters. "Does planning impede strategic thinking? Tracking the strategies of Air Canada from 1937 to 1976". In R. B. Lamb and P. Shivastava (eds), *Advances in Strategic Management*, JAI Press, Greenwich, CT, 1986, pp. 3–41.

Pascale, R. T. "Perspectives on strategy: The real story behind Honda's suuccess". *California Management Review*, Spring 1984, pp. 47–72.

Porter, M. "From competitive advantage to corporate strategy", *Harvard Business Review*, May–June, 1987, pp. 43–59.

18

THE FUTURE OF QUALITY IN INDIANAPOLIS

Terence P. Osburn and Deborah L. Klimaszewski

Source: *Quality Progress* 38(10) (2005): 39–44.

Each of ASQ's geographical sections must submit an annual section management plan (SMP) to headquarters. The Indianapolis section's SMP has typically focused on deliverables that could be completed within the current annual cycle. These projects have been based on what the section has always done and have included the incoming chair's own set of priorities.

W. Edwards Deming noted the debilitating effects of short-range planning decades ago; indeed, the very first of his 14 points is to "create constancy of purpose toward improvement of product and service, with the aim to become competitive and to stay in business, and to provide jobs."[1] Strategic planning—with an emphasis on long-range planning and sustainability—is the second of the 2005 Malcolm Baldrige National Quality Award criteria—preceded only by leadership.[2]

Planning a long-range strategy is considered a good business practice for managing local volunteer organizations and enterprises trying to be responsive to the changing environment, either at a private or corporate level. A clearly stated strategy is needed to design and organize activities toward achieving predetermined goals, especially if they are different from what is currently being done.

The strategic plan provides the focus or reference point around which to align efforts and set boundaries that are essential to decision making. This can be especially helpful when an opportunity is presented unexpectedly; once leadership determines if it is consistent with the strategic plan, the ensuing discussion is much less complicated.

Investing in a formal strategic planning practice can have important internal and external ramifications. Often, knowing the plan and how everyone is contributing to the shared vision can re-energize workers, even volunteers, with renewed motivation to achieve results, improve operations and meas-ure progress toward a desired future state.

On a broader plane, planning for the future provides a means to share with stakeholders insights for the goals and objectives linked to what is considered of value to the customer. The resulting plan justifies the com-mitment of efforts beyond maintenance of current services.

The strategic planning process

Endeavoring to lead proactively, Indianapolis section leaders and directors authorized creation of a five-year strategic plan (2005–2009). The section's leaders followed a five-step process to prepare for, develop and begin to implement the plan. The first challenge was to identify the section's current situation—what are we already doing well, and where do we need to improve? The answers to these questions helped determine the objectives for which we needed to develop long-range strategies.

Step one: SWOT

Who best to tell us where we are now than our own members? The leaders decided to sponsor a section town hall in October 2004 during the pro-gram planning exercise for the 2004–2005 year. At the heart of the agenda was a brief review of ASQ's six national strategic themes[3] and the section's vision and mission (see sidebar "Vision and Mission Statements"), followed by a major group exercise to identify the section's strengths, weaknesses, opportunities and threats (SWOT).[4]

To encourage attendance, we charged half-price for the event and absorbed a small financial loss. The town hall attracted about 60 people. This was not an unusually high number for an event, but the mix of old and new faces led to some interesting perspectives.

To make best use of the hour, each table of six to eight people was assigned one of the four SWOT categories. Everyone received a paper with an explanation of a SWOT diagram on one side and the rules for the nominal group technique (NGT)[5] on the other (see Table 1). The NGT is a powerful version of brainstorming that gives everyone an equal oppor-tunity to participate and requires less time per stage than interactive or less structured methods. One section leader facilitated the NGT to minimize confusion.

After multivoting,[6] the volunteer scribe at each table announced the table's most important ideas to the town hall. At meeting's end, the section leaders collected the flipcharts, did a comprehensive tally and published the results on the section's website. An abbreviated example of the final SWOT is in Table 2, with factors listed in descending order of prioritization within each category.

Table 1 Nominal Group Technique.

Step one: preparation.
• Gather flipcharts, markers, index cards or sticky notes, pens, paper and masking tape.
• Develop open-ended question(s) and definitions about the strengths, weaknesses, opportunities and threats diagram.
• Designate a volunteer scribe at each table.

Step two: individual thinking.
• Ask each person to list as many phrases as possible in response to the question(s).
• Tell everyone to be creative.

Step three: collect responses.
• Ask the scribe to go around the table and get one short idea from each person.
• Someone may pass one round and get back in later.
• No discussion or criticism is allowed, but an individual can ask for or give clarification.
• An individual may use his or her turn to contribute a variation on an idea already recorded.

Step four: vote for priority.
• Tell everyone they have five votes (sticky notes) to use as they wish. For example, they can vote five times for one item or one time for each of five items.

Step five: open discussion.
• Tell the scribe to announce the top priorities to the whole town hall.

Table 2 Example SWOT Diagram.

Strengths:	Weaknesses:
• Networking.	• Lack of training courses; need more opportunities. Break down versions: Possibly offer Green Belt and shop floor/industry-oriented statistical process control training.
• Educational opportunities.	
• Strong section leadership and continuity.	
	• Low importance of ASQ to employers.
	• Considered as only a professional society.
Threats:	Opportunities:
• Narrow focus on a small set of items.	• Two or three joint meetings per year.
• Manufacturing focus—relatively little interest in sectors such as services and software.	• Create recognition of the ASQ brand.
	• More citywide or regional publicity.
• Compete with other organizations in quality or other fields.	

Step two: brainstorm possible strategies

After the town hall, several members came forward to help the section leaders develop the five-year strategic plan. To build a cohesive group atmosphere, one section leader facilitated the discussion of two icebreaker questions:

- What would you miss most if the Indianapolis section were gone?
- What would you like to see the section doing by 2010?

Scribes collected the responses on flipcharts (see Table 3, p. 42).

The volunteers then reviewed the town hall SWOT diagram and brainstormed possible strategies by making paired comparisons from the four categories of the SWOT:

- How can our strengths overcome our threats?
- How can we maximize our strengths by pursuing our opportunities?

Table 3 Results of the Icebreaker Exercises.

What would you miss most if the Indianapolis section were gone?
- Networking.
- The section's ability to expand my vision of quality beyond my field and beyond my own world.
- Monthly meetings.
- Convenience of local training and meetings.
- Opportunities to develop my leadership skills and experience.
- Information available for reasonable cost.
- Educational opportunities, including technical skills.
- Cross functional offerings.
- Leadership opportunities.

What would you like to see the section doing by 2010?
- Partnering with small and large businesses.
- Interacting with other organizations.
- Holding joint meetings with other organizations.
- Going on more plant tours and walk arounds.
- Sharing success stories at meetings.
- Getting business owners to recommend our offerings to other business people; creating a positive buzz about us.
- Encouraging outside suppliers to the big companies and representatives from the big companies themselves to attend the meetings.
- Creating a directory of members.
- Creating users' groups, working teams and specialty groups.
- Increasing the interaction among members at monthly meetings—more problem solving and trouble shooting.
- Offering other ways to participate, such as workshops or meetings on different nights.
- Discussing the other areas affected by "quality," which is becoming a fuzzy term.

- How can our opportunities compensate for our weaknesses?
- How can we defend against our weaknesses and threats?

After the two-hour brainstorming session, the weary volunteers reported the two icebreaker questions were most helpful in generating potential strategy ideas, but the SWOT exercise was unnecessarily rigid and, at times, confusing.

Step three: bucket and prioritize

Two weeks later, the volunteers gathered to finalize which strategies they would recommend to the section's executive committee.

Prior to the meeting, the facilitator transcribed all the ideas from the flipcharts onto individual sticky notes scattered randomly along the wall. The volunteers then did an informal affinity diagram[7] exercise by spontaneously arranging the ideas into natural groupings. They ended with four buckets of ideas sticking to the wall:

1. Infrastructure.
2. Current members.
3. Sharing knowledge.
4. Collaboration and networking.

During the next meeting, the volunteers prioritized the ideas within each bucket, considering the section's available resources over the next five years, which were limited by people's time. Because of the importance of this exercise, we did not use a formal tool when prioritizing the ideas. Through discussion, we were able to reach consensus on the order of strategies within each of the four buckets.

Step five: presentation and approval

The section's executive committee had been kept informed via e-mail about the strategy committee's progress since October and had little hesitation in approving the proposed plan at the February monthly meeting.

Table 4 illustrates the Indianapolis section's five-year strategic plan for 2005–2009. Each of the four buckets from the affinity diagram exercise developed into an objective. The highest priority strategies we believe we can resource adequately, by year, are listed next to each objective. However, the objectives and strategies are not isolated projects.

The entire effort for the next five years is depicted holistically in Figure 1 (p. 44). All our objectives begin and end with the goal of making the Indianapolis section the focal community for quality in the region. Our efforts to shore up our infrastructure will feed into that goal.

347

Table 4 The Five-Year Strategic Plan.
Section 903's mission is to promote the ultimate success of the quality profession through a participative environment built around networking opportunities, skill development, training and outreach to meet the current and future needs of our members, community, state and national association.

Objective*	2004–2005	2005–2006	2006–2007	2007–2009
1. Build an infrastructure and governance that model the quality philosophy and tools, develop new quality leaders and enable us to launch ambitious projects.	• Complete half of quality management system (QMS).	• Complete second half of QMS. • Recruit members for primary committees.	• Use QMS to strengthen committee collaboration and communication.	• Revise strategic plan.
2. Serve current members and better communicate our message. Goal is to re-energize members to be quality advocates in their communities and to attract new members who are in underrepresented categories, such as women, small business owners or those in a service industry or IT.	• Capture on videotape and extend meetings—test in April 2005. • During summer 2005, plan new ways to meet for next year. • May/June—do section management plan survey to ask members what they want. • Involve Indiana University-Purdue University Indianapolis (IUPUI) branch in one project this semester.	• Involve IUPUI branch in multiple projects. • Offer an introductory educational series to bosses and leaders on topics such as the cost of quality. Approach small businesses. • Act upon survey results.	• Continue to respond to survey feedback.	
3. Share quality knowledge via variety in media, topics, knowledge levels and audiences.	• Form future-looking committee. • Perform gap analysis.	• Establish a five-year education plan. • Establish planning group for Web content.	• Keep building the education program. • Form advisory board from target audiences. • Develop local marketing materials to create buzz. • Possibly offer audits to small companies.	• Continue to expand the education program. • Aim to have a major conference in Indianapolis in 2009. • Possibly have company coordinators.
4. Develop collaboration and networking to model the quality philosophy and tools for the community.		• Rethink/revitalize Koalaty Kid. • Begin some other service projects to model quality.		

* Each objective should include a Web tactic so www.indyasq.org becomes the most important local tool to link our members, interest groups, businesses and the Indianapolis community to each other, quality news, information and tools.

Figure 1 Holistic View of the Five-Year Strategic Plan.

As our quality community becomes more effective, we will be able to strengthen our educational programs and service projects. The better these programs become, the more quality will become a priority at local firms, which will complete the circle by further growing our focal community. The ultimate result of this virtuous circle will be a stronger regional economy with more jobs for everyone.

Now that the five-year strategic plan is complete, the section's executive committee will identify owners for each strategy, manage the development of detailed tactics and timelines and make wise investments of members' time for the next five years. As the Baldrige National Quality Program emphasizes, the execution of the long-range strategy is as important as the strategy itself.[8]

The five-year strategic plan has already begun to yield benefits. At our meetings, we have been able to make decisions more quickly about new opportunities, not just in terms of their individual merits and risks, but also in terms of which opportunities will best advance the objectives of our plan as a whole. We are also developing a feel for appropriate timing—if a project is worth doing, it may be better to tackle it at a later date when we can optimize the synergies with other initiatives.

Acknowledgements

We would like to thank the volunteers who developed the Indianapolis section's strategic plan: Jesse Berman, Lee Black, Dan Bridget, Carl Cummings, James Grimes, Jeffrey Lopez, Joe Lucas, Catherine Marriott, John Murphy, Matthew Rowe, Garth Smitman and Kier White.

References

1 Deming Electronic Network website, "Deming's 14 Points," http://deming.eng. clemson.edu/pub/den/deming_philosophy.htm#points.
2 Baldrige National Quality Program website, 2005 Criteria for Performance Excellence, category 2.1, www.quality.nist.gov/PDF_files/2005_Business_Criteria. pdf. (case sensitive)
3 ASQ website, www.asq.org/strategy/themes.
4 "SWOT Analysis," www.businessballs.com/swotanalysisfreetemplate.htm.
5 Department of Defense Quality Management Program website, "Decision Making Tools," http://quality.disa.mil/pdf/descntls.pdf.
6 Ibid.
7 ASQ website, "Idea Creation Tools," www.asq.org/learn-about-quality/idea-creation-tools/overview/affinity.html.
8 Baldrige National Quality Program website, category 2.2, see reference 2.

19

DIVERSIFICATION ENTRY

Internal development versus acquisition

George S. Yip

Source: *Strategic Management Journal* 3(4) (1982): 331–45.

Summary

The economic theory of barriers to entry is integrated with the corporate strategy concept of relatedness, to develop a model of the choice between internal development and acquisition in diversification entry into new markets. The model is tested on original data collected for this study from PIMS Program participants. These original data cover the parent company characteristics, entry strategy and entry outcome for 59 entrants into 31 markets. These entry-related data are merged with existing PIMS data on the structure of the entered markets and their incumbents. Results of binary regression analysis show that the choice between the two entry modes is well explained by measures of barriers and relatedness. Higher barriers are more likely to be associated with acquisition entry. Greater relatedness is more likely to be associated with direct entry.

Introduction

Internal development and acquisition are the two vehicles of corporate diversification.[1] The two pose radically different options, yet no model exists to integrate the factors influencing the choice between them. It has, of course, long been recognized that there is some linking mechanism to inform the choice: the synergy or relatedness between the diversifying firm and the new activity. Greater synergy or relatedness should favour internal development over acquisition (for example, as argued by Ansoff (1965) in his discussion of the 'make or buy' decision).[2] This paper develops a model that explicitly integrates the concepts of *relatedness* and *barriers to entry* to link the choice between the two diversification modes.

The model is limited:

351

(1) It deals only with the choice of entry mode given that a particular entrant has already selected a particular market into which to diversify.

(2) It is not complete in predicting the actual choice of mode. It deals only with the influence of barrier-related factors, separate from the traditional financial and managerial factors affecting this choice. The model's contribution is the hypothesis that barrier-related factors have their own predictable influence.

This paper also reports on empirical validation of the model, using original data collected for this study on entry into 31 markets, and the entry mode, strategies and characteristics of the entrants.

Barriers to (direct) entry

An extensive theory has been developed in industrial organization economics on how market structure can create 'barriers to entry'. These barriers pose disadvantages relative to market incumbents for those seeking to enter via internal development (direct entry). Incumbents can thereby enjoy higher profitability than in the absence of barriers. As first formulated by Bain (1956), and refined by subsequent writers, there are four classes of barriers: economies of scale, product differentiation, absolute costs, and the capital requirement.

Acquisition entry

The concept of barriers was formulated in regard to direct entry through internal development. Some forms of acquisition may, however, also qualify as entry—in the sense of the introduction of a 'new' competitor into a market (Hines, 1957).

Perhaps the classic example of 'acquisition entry' is that of Philip Morris into the beer industry in 1970 via the purchase of Miller Brewing. Heavy investment by Philip Morris propelled Miller Brewing from a seventh place 4% market share to a second place 22% market share in ten years. Philip Morris had the motivation, the means, and the management skills for expansion. Diversification from cigarettes was an obvious spur. Money from cigarettes allowed it to invest over $1 billion in the acquired company. Competitive skills from cigarettes turned out to be superior to those of incumbents, particularly Philip Morris highly transferable marketing expertise. The combination of financial cross-subsidization and transferable superior skills was disastrous for the prior incumbents—industry profitability was drastically reduced by the heightened level of competition which shifted eighteen market share points to Miller. The Miller experience is also an example of how acquisition breaches 'mobility barriers' (the barriers within markets as conceived by Caves and Porter, 1977), by transforming a minor competitor into a major one.

352

Clearly, not all diversifying acquisitions are entries (and horizontal acquisitions are not even diversification). A distinction can be made between acquisitions made for purely investment portfolio purposes and those made for entry purposes. Some features more characteristic of entry acquisitions than portfolio ones are:

(a) an intention to use the acquired business as a base for expansion in the new market;
(b) a desire to exploit relatedness/synergy between the acquired business and other parent businesses;
(c) an interest in the market, and not just in the acquired business, i.e., the acquiring company would have seriously considered entering directly.

A linkage of the direct and acquisition entry choice also has implications for public policy. The doctrine of 'potential competition' has been applied to prevent or reverse conglomerate (diversifying) acquisitions on the grounds that the acquirer would have entered directly. My model demonstrates that there are strong reasons why acquisition entrants would seldom have taken the direct entry route.

The choice between direct and acquisition entry

Analysis of the choice of entry mode has traditionally focused on financial, managerial and legal issues, and on the issue of whether acquisition candidates are available. The role of entry barriers has had limited or only implicit treatment.

Traditional considerations

Direct and acquisition entries differ in well-known ways in their *financial* implications for the entrant. These differences apply to both the balance sheet and the profit and loss statement, and such financial factors frequently seem to dominate managers evaluations of the choice of entry mode.

Direct and acquisition entries also differ in their *managerial* implications, presenting different risks and opportunities for the individual manager. Direct entry is typically more risky. It offers no guarantee of achieving an ongoing business of the required size or level of profitability. The usually lengthy initial period of start-up losses exacerbates the career risk. Biggadike (1976) found that his sample of 40 start-up (internal development) businesses required an average of eight years before reaching profitability—few managers stay so long with one business. Acquisition entry typically imposes different risks and demands on managers, such as to achieve rapid synergy or turnaround.

353

Direct and acquisition entries also differ in their *availability* as alternatives. The supply of acquisition candidates in a given market at a given
time is usually limited and volatile.

Finally, in addition to the doctrine of potential competition, there can
be other *legal* grounds for restricting acquisitions. The Clayton Act and
its amendments forbid acquisitions which result in the lessening of competition. Companies may also be individually constrained from certain types
of acquisitions by decrees from regulatory authorities (e.g., FTC consent
decrees in the U.S.).

Barrier considerations

Efficiency of capital markets implies that expected returns under the two
modes would be equal: the cost of direct breaching of entry barriers would
be included in the acquisition price of a business already behind those
barriers. The height of barriers would, therefore, have no systematic financial
influence on the choice of entry mode.

But this view of the neutrality of barriers can be rejected even without
questioning the efficiency of capital markets. First, career considerations
should discourage direct entry into higher barrier markets. Second, barriers
do indeed make a difference in expected returns under the two entry modes,
*because the relatedness which reduces barriers has an asymmetric impact
under the two modes*. Thus, the cost of direct entry should vary directly
with the degree of relatedness of the entering company to the new business
created in the entered market. In contrast, relatedness does not reduce the
price of an acquisition (and may even raise it), since the price is set by
the market for acquisitions. Other parties are involved: the seller with his
floor price, and other actual or potential bidders, and what they are, or
might be, willing to pay. The relatedness of other bidders to the market
should affect the price they are willing to pay, but that is a factor beyond
the control of the final buyer.

The nature and height of barriers, therefore, results in two direct influences on the choice of entry mode. First, higher barriers favour acquisition
entry. Second, greater relatedness favours direct entry. It is important,
however, to note that the combination of barriers and relatedness does
not *determine* the choice of entry mode. They are one set of factors to be
evaluated by managers along with others.

An overall model of the direct versus acquisiton choice

My arguments suggest that the choice between direct and acquisition entry
is a function of two distinct sets of considerations: (1) a target market's
barriers and the entrant's ability to breach those barriers; and (2) such other
considerations as finance, managerial motivation, legality and availability.

A model of the choice of entry mode should, therefore, include as explanatory variables measures of (a) the market's barriers, and (b) an entrant's ability to breach those barriers. Following Bain (1956), certain elements of market structure can represent the extent of barriers. These elements of market structure should include the resources of incumbents (as argued in Yip, 1982).

An entrant's ability to breach barriers depends primarily on relatedness, but should also be affected by parent company characteristics such as corporate size and diversity. In addition, the competitiveness of the entrant's initial position is a further indication of the ability to breach barriers. Its motivation for entry should also affect its choice of entry mode.

The market structure and entrant variables will also capture many of the managerial, availability and legal effects, where correlated with market structure. Financial factors, such as whether the entrant's balance sheet and P & L position favour one mode or the other, can be omitted from the model: they are unlikely to be correlated with sources of market barriers and entrant relatedness. The *managerial* factor of career risk is directly represented by the height of barriers and the entrant's ability to breach barriers. The likelihood of *legal* constraints on acquisition should also be captured by market structure and entrant characteristics since these are the criteria for antitrust action. The *availability* of acquisition candidates also depends on market structure: the number and health of competitors is a function of both market concentration and market growth rate. (A relevant factor exogenous to market structure is stock market conditions. The model will include a separate variable for this effect.) In discussing each independent variable I will show more specifically how market structure represents these managerial, legal and availability factors.

The dependent variable can be conveniently specified as Y_{da}, the probability of direct vs. acquisition entry. Thus the overall model can be represented as follows:

$$Y_{da} = f \text{(market structure and incumbent characteristics,}$$
$$\text{entrant parent characteristics,}$$
$$\text{entrant relatedness to entered markets,}$$
$$\text{entrant competitiveness,}$$
$$\text{entrant motivation.)}$$

The data base

To test the above model this study collected data on 59 entrants into 31 markets. Of the 59, 37 entered via internal development (direct entrants) and 22 via acquisition (acquisition entrants). The 31 markets were a subsample of the PIMS data base,[3] for which PIMS had already collected market structure and incumbent data. The additional entrant data were obtained by getting incumbents in those markets to report on the entry of new competitors: the number of entrants, their entry mode, their characteristics, strategy and performance.

Sample composition

The sample comprised six consumer non-durable product and twenty-five industrial product markets, all in the U.S. Twelve markets were in the *growth* state of the product life cycle, seventeen in the *maturity* stage, and two in the *decline* stage (none in the *introductory* stage). (Stages were estimated directly by managers of the reporting businesses.)

Definition of entry mode

The two types of entry were defined as follows:

> A *direct entry* occurs when a firm, whether newborn or already existing, begins selling on an ongoing basis in an existing market from which it was previously absent.

> An *acquisition entry* occurs when an existing competitor in an existing market is acquired by a firm not previously competing in that market. The acquirer should have the intention to use the acquired business as a base for expansion, and not merely hold it as a portfolio investment.

Incumbent businesses reported on up to three each direct or acquisition entries occurring into their markets within the previous seven years (1972 to 1978).

Explanatory variables

Market structure

Market structure variables which raise barriers should favour the choice of acquisition, and those which reduce barriers should favour direct entry. To save degrees of freedom, the model was tested on only five key structure variables in addition to the entrant characteristic and strategy variables.

These key structure variables together measure the strength of the standard set of conceptual barriers—differentiation, scale, capital requirements and incumbent reactions (omitting absolute cost, the least prevalent barrier)—and the degree of market disequilibrium weakening barriers.

356

Market growth rate

Rapid market growth should reduce the impact of barriers, by creating disequilibrium conditions, and therefore encourage direct entry.

Managerial motivations should also favour acquisition in slower growing markets—managers given a diversification charter usually face time pressures. Direct entry may allow an acceptable rate of expansion when made into a rapidly growing market, but not when into a low-growth market.

More acquisition candidates should be available in more mature, low-growth markets. Not only has there been a longer time for the number of companies to build up, but mature markets are likely to be consolidating by squeezing out weaker competitors. Such competitors may be suitable acquisition candidates.

Barrier, managerial and availability factors therefore all favour direct entry into high-growth, and acquisition entry into low-growth, markets.

Market growth rate is represented by MKT GRW, the four-year average annual change in market sales (constant dollars).[4]

Market concentration

This measures the extent of both reaction and scale barriers. The larger the share of market leaders the more likely they are to react against entrants, and the greater their market power to implement resistance. Concentration also indicates the presence of scale barriers. Higher levels of concentration should, therefore, favour acquisition entry to avoid both reaction and scale barriers.

Antitrust factors yield an opposite effect. The objection that acquisitions, even 'conglomerate' ones, can increase concentration is naturally salient in more concentrated markets. The latter markets should also, by definition, offer fewer acquisition candidates.

Thus the barrier effect of higher concentration favouring acquisition is offset by antitrust and availability factors. In empirical analysis, therefore, no direction of association can be predicted between market concentration and the choice of entry mode.

Market concentration is represented by CONC, the four-year average share of the reporting business and its three leading competitors in the common served markets as defined by the reporting business.[5]

Investment intensity

Along with concentration, investment intensity indicates the presence of scale barriers. Investment intensity is also a proxy for the need to commit large amounts of capital for entry. Greater capital requirements should be more problematic for direct entry, which typically uses internally generated funds. In contrast, acquisition entry often allows funding through exchange of equity. This latter mechanism imposes much less strain on both the balance sheet and the profit-and-loss statement. The investment intensity variable should, therefore, be negatively associated with the direct entry choice and positively with acquisition.

> *INVST is the average of each year's investment (net plant and equipment plus working capital) divided by revenues.*[6]

Advertising intensity

The advertising/sales ratio is generally accepted as the best single indicator of the height of the differentiation barrier. Previous studies have assumed that high levels of advertising intensity should create a strong barrier to entry. I propose that advertising intensity has more than just a barrier impact. High advertising intensity can also encourage direct entry because advertising campaigns can be mounted quickly regardless of scale. In contrast, R & D programmes or factory investments require longer lead times; the latter also increase with scale. Advertising is, therefore, a relatively fast strategic tool for entrants. Thus, high levels of advertising intensity provide attractions as well as deterrents to the direct entry mode. No hypothesis, in either direction, can therefore be made about the empirical association of advertising intensity and the choice of entry mode.

> *ADVT is the average of the reporting business's annual expenditures on media advertising expenses, divided by revenues.*

Incumbent parent size

The elements of market structure determining barriers to entry should include the resources of incumbents. Incumbents with greater resources should be able to mount stronger defences against entrants. This suggests that potential entrants particularly consider the absolute size of the parent companies of incumbent business. Entrants into markets with large incumbent parent companies should be more likely to choose acquisition in order to avoid competitive battles with incumbents backed by the resources of a large parent. In addition, the size of an entrant's parent company relative to those of incumbents should also be relevant. Greater relative size should favour the choice of direct entry.

> *INC PRN SZE is the absolute size, in dollars of revenue, of the reporting business's (the incumbent) parent company. REL PRN SZE*

is the ratio of the size of the entrant's parent company to that of the reporting business.

Entrant parent characteristics

Parent size

Having a larger parent should favour the direct entry mode in two ways:

> greater resources available to overcome direct entry barriers;
> more potential for antitrust objections to acquisition.

On the other hand, larger parents should be more capable of making an acquisition. It is, therefore, unclear what is the net effect of parent size. (As already argued, greater size *relative* to incumbents' parents should favour direct entry.)

> *ENT PRN SZE is the absolute size, in dollars of revenue, of the entrant business's parent company.*

Parent diversity

More diversified parent companies should be more likely to use acquisition entry because of their on-average greater previous experience in growth through acquisition. Entrants' parent companies were classified using Rumelt's (1974) categories, and dummy variables created to represent each category.

> *SNGL BUS, DOM BUS, REL BUS, and UNREL BUS are 0, 1 variables respectively representing Rumelt's single business, dominant business, related business and unrelated business/conglomerate categories.*[7]

Entrant relatedness

Two classes of entrant relatedness to the entered market should affect the choice of entry mode:

> type of diversification move;
> shared activities and customers.

Type of diversification move

The entries were classified by their overall relatedness to the existing business of the diversifier, as follows: geographic expansion, segment expansion,

359

related expansion, forward vertical integration, backward vertical integration, and unrelated diversification.[8]

Geographic expansion is included as entry because the expansion of an existing product into a new geographic area can face many of the standard barriers to entry. Segment expansion was defined as entry from one segment of a total market into another. Related expansion was defined as entry from a separate, but horizontally related, market. The other categories were defined in the usual ways. It is hypothesized that the more unrelated the entry move, the more likely it is that acquisition will be the entry mode.

Dummy variables were created to represent each classification separately: GEOG, SEGM, RELEXP, FWD VER, BCK VER, UNREL DIV.

Shared activities and customers

A more detailed measure of relatedness is the degree to which specific activities and customers are shared between parent and entrant. The degree of sharing also indicates actual synergy rather than just potential synergy. Greater sharing should, therefore, be associated with the direct entry mode.

Data were collected for several categories of shared activities and customers: manufacturing/production, R & D, distribution, sales, advertising and promotion, immediate customers, and end users. Entrants were classed on each type of activity/customer as sharing: (1) up to 10% of activities with parent, (2) 10% to 50%, (3) 50% to 90%, and (4) 90% to 100%.

To use in regression estimation, a composite variable, AVG SHR, average sharing, was created, weighting all seven categories equally, and treating the 1, 2, 3, 4 codings as a continuous scale.

Entrant competitiveness

Barriers and an entrant's ability to reduce them obviously affect the initial competitiveness of the entrant. Those who can achieve strong initial competitive positions relative to incumbents should be more likely to choose direct entry. An entrant who can achieve only a weak competitive position through direct entry should prefer acquisition entry. Although perhaps not entirely rational, *buying* a weak entry position seems more attractive than building a similarly weak one. The acquirer of a weak business can believe that its own skills and resources will transform the purchase—as was done, most notably, by Philip Morris with Miller Brewing, by Imperial Tobacco with Golden Wonder (see Bevan, 1974) and many others. Furthermore, available acquisition candidates are far more likely to have weaker than stronger competitive positions. Therefore, the direct entry mode should be more associated with stronger initial competitive positions, and acquisition with weaker.

Measures were obtained of eight overall aspects of competitiveness: product quality, prices, costs, production effectiveness, sales force effectiveness, distribution effectiveness, advertising and promotion expenditures, and reputation of company/strength of brand name. Entrant positions were rated on these dimensions relative to leading incumbents as being: (1) much lower, (2) somewhat lower, (3) about the same, (4) somewhat higher, and (5) much higher.

Variables were constructed for each dimension using the 1, 2, 3, 4, 5 codings as a continuous scale. For regression purposes, a composite variable, AVG POSN, was constructed averaging across six variables, excluding the price and cost variables. These latter variables REL PRC and REL COST were used individually in the regression analyses.

Motivation for entry

Separate from barrier considerations, an entrant's motivation for entry should affect its choice of entry mode. The direct mode should be more likely where entry is made into a new market to exploit advantages or competences developed in an existing market ('motivation—offence'). The same should hold when the entry is made to defend a position in an existing market ('motivation—defence'). In both cases there is a high degree of relatedness with the entered market.

Entrants motivated by a market's growth prospects ('motivation—market growth') should be more willing to use direct entry since it is the future growth from market participation which motivates them rather than the immediate growth provided by acquisition.

The complete set of motivations for which data were collected covered market profitability, market growth, share costs, offence, defence, access to suppliers, access to outlets, (achievement of) counter-cyclical sales, generate cash and use cash. Each motivation was rated as (1) 'little/no importance', (2) 'some importance', (3) 'major importance'.

Variables taking the values 1, 2 or 3 were constructed for each of the ten measures above, as follows: MOTV PROF, MOTV GRW, MOTV COSTS, MOTV ADVN, MOTV DEF, MOTV SUP, MOTV OUT, MOTV CYC, MOTV GEN, MOTV USE.

Active acquisition year

In addition to market structure and incumbent factors, stock market and other conditions affecting acquisitions in general may affect the choice of entry mode. To test for this effect a dummy variable for active acquisition years was included, DUM ACQ YR.[9]

Regression results

Methodology

Given the 0, 1 dependent variable, and the probabilistic specification of the model, binary regression seemed the most appropriate estimation method.[10] Since the dependent variable is coded 0 for direct entry and 1 for acquisition, the regressions estimated the probability that entry would be via acquisition rather than direct.

Given only 59 observations, and potentially a very large number of independent variables, it was necessary to select a small subset of explanatory variables in order to minimize correlation and to maximize the number of degrees of freedom. The five market structure/incumbent variables were selected from a larger set of variables regressed on the dependent variable. The selection was on the basis of the variables being theoretically important and having coefficients whose sign was stable in the absence and presence of correlated variables. This procedure was also followed for each set of entrant characteristics: type of parent, type of move, relatedness, motivation, sharing, relative position. The entire set within each category was regressed on the dependent variable, using, first, that set's variables only, and second, in conjunction with market structure/incumbent variables and other sets' variables. This procedure resulted in the selection of individual variables in each set (e.g., unrelated business parent within the set, type of parent) or composite variables representing the entire set (i.e., average sharing and average relative position). All the variables in the final equation presented here are, therefore, single variables or a single composite variable, and all showed stability in the signs of their coefficients in many different formulations of the equation. The end result was 14 independent variables. Table 1 presents the regression results, and Table 2 the correlation matrix. Figure 1 presents a visual summary of the impact of each independent variable on the probability of the acquisition mode.

Market structure and incumbent characteristics

Two of the five variables tested had significant coefficients of the predicted sign. Faster market growth (MKT GRW) was indeed more associated with direct entry, and larger incumbent parent companies (INC PRN SZE) were more associated with acquisition entry. Two variables, concentration (CONC) and advertising intensity (ADVT) for which no directional hypothesis could be drawn did, indeed, not have significant coefficients. The last structure variable, investment intensity (INVST) was predicted to be positively associated with acquisition. There was, instead a significant negative coefficient representing association with direct entry.

Table 1 Regression on direct vs. acquisition choice.

Variable	(1) P-standardized coefficient	(2) U-standardized coefficient	Probability of significance	Predicted sign	Significant* actual sign	Significant† association with
MKT GRW	-0.03	-0.35	0.96	-	-	direct
CONC	-0.01	-0.16	0.81	?		
INVST	-0.01	-0.35	0.96	+	-	direct
ADVT	-0.21	-0.23	0.84	?		
INC PRN SZE	0.00	0.51	0.98	+	+	acquisition
REL PRN SZE	-0.00	-0.16	0.71	-		
ENT PRN SZE	0.00	0.18	0.86	?		
UNREL BUS	0.66	0.31	0.97	+	+	acquisition
UNREL DIV	0.04	0.01	0.54	+		
MOTV GRW	-0.00	-0.64	0.99	-	-	direct
MOTV DEF	0.11	0.09	0.73	-		
AVG SHR	0.04	0.03	0.59	-		
AVG POSN	-0.79	-0.53	0.99	-	-	direct
DUM ACQ YR	0.11	0.05	0.63	+		

* At 90 per cent level or above.
† Negative sign represents association with direct entry ($Y = 0$), positive with acquisition entry ($Y = 1$).
(1) The P-standardized coefficient is the contribution to the estimated probability that $Y = 1$, for one unit change in the independent variable, at the point where $f(\text{Pr } Y = 1) = 0.5$. This latter restriction is a result of the non-linear-relationship between independent variables and the estimated Pr ($Y = 1$) inherent in binary regression.
(2) The U-standardized coefficient is as (1), for one standard deviation change in the independent variable. $R^2 = 0.62$; percentage of observations misclassified by model=8.5 per cent; mean of $Y = 1$ is 0.37; $n = 59$.

Table 2 Correlation matrix.

	(1)	(2)	(3)	(4)	(5)	(6)	(7)	(8)	(9)	(10)	(11)	(12)	(13)	(14)	(15)
Direct or acquisition (1)	1.00														
Real market growth (2)	-0.14	1.00													
Four firm share (3)	-0.15	-0.04	1.00												
Investment/revenues (4)	-0.19	0.49	-0.04	1.00											
Advertising/revenues (5)	-0.13	-0.00	0.34	0.34	1.00										
Incumbent parent size (6)	0.11	0.36	-0.28	-0.28	0.09	1.00									
Entrant size/incumbent size (7)	-0.13	-0.14	0.12	-0.20	-0.12	-0.18	1.00								
Entrant parent size (8)	0.02	0.25	-0.07	0.15	-0.13	0.23	0.16	1.00							
Unrelated business parent (9)	0.11	0.12	-0.01	0.13	-0.10	0.04	-0.13	0.04	1.00						
Unrelated diversification (10)	0.07	-0.00	-0.19	-0.14	0.03	-0.04	-0.05	0.19	0.23	1.00					
Motivation growth (11)	-0.52	0.12	0.10	0.19	-0.03	-0.12	0.06	-0.13	0.13	-0.12	1.00				
Motivation defence (12)	0.19	0.24	-0.38	0.18	-0.26	0.31	-0.28	0.18	0.13	-0.05	-0.23	1.00			
Average sharing (13)	-0.13	0.12	-0.00	0.20	-0.20	0.10	-0.23	0.01	-0.13	-0.27	0.24	0.31	1.00		
Average relative position (14)	-0.21	-0.00	-0.43	0.01	0.08	0.17	-0.13	0.25	-0.28	0.15	0.18	0.38	0.19	1.00	
Active acquisition year (15)	0.07	0.08	-0.01	0.12	0.01	0.13	-0.33	0.04	-0.14	-0.02	-0.24	0.24	0.21	-0.00	1.00

n = 59 entrants.
Correlations above [0.26] are statistically significant at 95 per cent level, two tail.

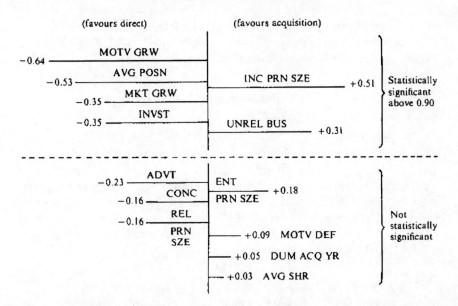

Figure 1 Visual summary of regression results. This chart depicts the contribution of one standard deviation. change in each independent variable to the probability that the entry mode will be acquisition. The base probability is 0.37. Coefficients are taken from column 2 of Table 1.

Entrant parent characteristics

Parent size

The conflicting effects of entrant parent size resulted in no definite hypothesis about the direction of association between this variable and the entry mode. The regression estimations do not contradict this conclusion—the coefficient for ENT PRN SZE was not significant.

It was, however, hypothesized that the size of an entrant's parent relative to that of an incumbent's parent would be negatively associated with the acquisition choice. The results were inconclusive as the coefficient for REL PRN SZE was not significant. The significance level did not increase in the absence of the two absolute measures of parent size, INC PRN SZE and ENT PRN SZE.

Parent diversity

The dummy variables representing all four of the parent diversity categories were tested. In support of the hypothesis that more diversified parents would favour acquisition, the dummy for unrelated business, UNREL BUS, had a positive and significant coefficient, both in the presence and absence of the dummy variables for dominant business and related business. UNREL BUS also had a very low correlation (0.04) with ENT PRN SZE. Thus the diversity effect was quite separate from that of parent size.

Entrant relatedness

Type of diversification move

This overall measure of relatedness did not discriminate between the two entry modes. None of the dummy variables representing each type of move [geographic expansion, segment expansion, related expansion, vertical integration (combining forward and backward) and unrelated diversification] had statistically significant variables. To save degrees of freedom, the final equation in Table 1 contains only the variable for unrelated diversification, UNREL DIV.

Shared activities and customers

These more specific measures of relatedness were also not statistically significant, either as individual variables or when combined into the composite measure, AVG SHR.

Entrant competitiveness

Three measures of entrant competitiveness relative to incumbents were tested in regression estimations: average prices, average costs and average relative position (the composite of the dimensions other than prices and costs). Neither the price nor the cost variables were significant and they were dropped from the final equation. The composite variable, AVG POSN, was, however, highly significant and of the expected sign. Thus even if the relatedness variables were not significant, the end result of relatedness—an entrant's competitive position—did show the predicted preference for direct entry. A further explanation of AVG POSN's significance could be that direct entry is the more effective way to exploit a competitive innovation. Why acquire a business already obsoleted by your own innovation?

It is also notable that acquisition seems to centre on the weaker members of the competitive structure. These frailer competitors are obviously more likely to be for sale. In addition they should offer more scope for improvement by a strong acquirer, or so acquirers seem to think!

Entrant motivation

The coefficients for market growth as a motivation, MOTV GRW, did indeed have a highly significant and positive association with the direct mode. This effect was separate from the actual past growth rate of the market—the MOTV GRW and MKT GRW variables had a very low correlation of 0.12, and the direction and significance of MKT GRW's coefficient were unchanged when MOTV GRW was dropped from the regression. The motivations to exploit an advantage, MOTV ADVN, and to defend a position, MOTV DEF, were not however statistically significant. This lack of significance might be attributed to the respondents' inability to judge such motivation.

Active acquisition year

The variable, DUM YR, did not have a significant coefficient.

Summary of results

The regression results are consistent with my model of how the choice between direct and acquisition entry is affected by market structure and entrant characteristics. The overall explanatory power is very high: the R^2 of 0.62 is high for a 0, 1 dependent variable, and the 8.5 per cent of observations misclassified by the model is very low.[11]

Only one variable had a significant sign opposite to that predicted: investment intensity. Five variables had significant signs of the predicted direction. Those negatively associated with the acquisition choice (and positively with direct) were market growth rate, investment intensity, market growth as an entrant motivation, and the average position of the entrant relative to incumbents. Those positively associated with the acquisition choice (and negatively with direct) were incumbent parent size, and entrants having diversified parents (unrelated business category).

Independent of the structure of the entered market and other variables, entrant parent characteristics appear, therefore, to be major determinants of the choice of entry mode. On the other hand, it seems that the degree of relatedness between entrant and parent is not important, contrary to what was expected. This unimportance of relatedness is offset by the result that the average competitive position relative to incumbents was highly important. A strong competitive position is largely the result of a high degree of relatedness. Entrants appear, therefore, to be, rightly, more influenced by what relatedness delivers in terms of a competitive position, than by the promise of relatedness *per se*.

Implications of this study

For managers

In choosing between the direct and acquisition entry modes, managers should take account of barriers as well as financial and other traditional considerations. A better guide of how much to pay for an acquisition should be provided by a better understanding of the barriers surrounding a market, and the cost of breaching them given the entrant's relatedness. Does the price demanded by the seller, or offered by other bidders, incorporate a higher barrier than would be faced by this entrant? Despite high apparent barriers the entrant's relatedness may allow a direct entry cost lower than an acquisition entry cost (or a better return for different-sized investments).

For public policy

The maintenance of easy direct entry conditions is a major goal of U.S. antitrust policy. One branch of this policy seeks to prevent acquisition entry, thereby forcing direct entry. This study questions whether potential entrants would enter directly if denied the acquisition route. Market structure and entrant characteristics appear to discriminate very clearly between the two entry modes. The current policy may merely preclude the enhanced market competitiveness sometimes caused by acquisition entry, without gaining new competitors via direct entry.

For researchers

This study has implications for both the specific issues of entry and diversification, and for the general issue of methodology in strategic research. For entry theory the study provides evidence that market-wide structure alone does not determine barriers. Entrants also take account of their own specific characteristics and of how these allow them to reduce the barriers they face. Acquisition should also be incorporated in the entry paradigm. High barriers do not a sanctuary make. Entrants do use acquisition to vault barriers, and do, on average, choose that mode on a systematic basis.

For diversification theory, the study addresses a high level strategic issue: not *what* businesses to be in, but *how* to get into them. It seems that market structure has far more impact on the choice of diversification vehicle than has been widely accepted. Decisions on diversification do not just depend on financial mechanics, executive preferences or corporate philosophy. Managers do recognize the constraints of competitive market forces.

For methodology in strategic research this study combines the perspectives of economics and corporate strategy, continuing the convergence of these two fields (Porter, 1981). More significant, this study provides a rare instance of combining market structure, business-level and corporate-level variables. This study may not have used the best variables in these three sets, but the latter undeniably constitute the tripod of competitive strategy.

Acknowledgements

The author thanks Dr. Sidney Schoeffler and Dr. Bradley Gale of the Strategic Planning Institute for providing the data base and support necessary for this project; and his dissertation committee. Michael E. Porter (Chairman), William E. Fruhan, Jr., and Hugo E. R. Uyterhoeven, for their guidance on the thesis on which this paper is based.

Notes

1 The term 'acquisition' is used here to include mergers—the financial and tax distinctions between these two forms are not relevant in this paper. Joint venture is a third vehicle for diversification. The joint venture mode seems sufficiently a compromise between the two primary modes that separate treatment here appears unnecessary.

2 There are many definitions of synergy and relatedness. Ansoff (1965) defined synergy as a joint effect measured between two product markets. Such effects occur if, by competing in both product markets, the combined costs are less than the sum of their parts, the combined required investment is less than its sum, or the combined sales are greater than their sum. Rumelt (1974) has provided perhaps the best expansion of the concept of synergy to the more general one of 'relatedness'. He defined the latter in terms of interdependency effects among businesses within one corporation. The definition is equally applicable for comparing an entrant's existing businesses with a new business in an entered market.

3 The PIMS Program collects extensive business strategy, market structure and business performance data. Its total data base covers 1500 business units, in primarily North American markets. The identities of the markets and companies are disguised—researchers know only the structural characteristics and basic industry types (e.g., consumer non-durable, industrial supplies). This study used the PIMS data base only, not the PIMS models. The data base and models have been extensively described in Schoeffler, Buzzell and Heany (1974); and Buzzell, Gale and Sultan (1975).

4 MKT GRW and several other variables are measured by PIMS for four-year periods only. To capture conditions existing at the time of entry, these periods are at the beginning (mainly 1972–1975) of the total seven-year period over which entries were reported.

5 The reporting business is among the largest four in almost all the PIMS markets used here, but when it is not CONC is less than the four-firm concentration ratio.

6 Investment intensity, advertising intensity and incumbent parent size were all measures for *one* incumbent only—the reporting business. It is necessary to assume that the reporting business is representative of all incumbents. The validity of this assumption is helped in that most PIMS reporting businesses are market leaders or near leaders in terms of share. It is the characteristics of market leaders which are most relevant in assessing barriers to entry.

7 Rumelt's four categories represent increasing degrees of diversification. Examples of each category are: single business, American Motors Corporation; dominant business, IBM; related business, General Electric; unrelated business, Textron.

8 'No pre-existing businesses' was a seventh category. Entrants whose parents had no pre-existing businesses were by definition 'new-born' firms. Such entrants

369

were excluded from the analyses reported in this paper because they would not have had the option of acquisition entry. New-born firms cannot begin life by acquiring another one.

9 The measure of acquisition activity was the total number of acquisitions reported for each year by the FTC Bureau of Economics. (Source: Salter and Weinhold, 1979, and latest editions of *Mergers and Acquisitions*.) For the observation period, 1972 to 1979, only 1972 and 1973 were coded 1 (highly active year). The other years were coded 0. Note that this is the only variable with a time dimension.

10 Maximum likelihood estimation and the logit transformation of the probability function were used. Binary regression was used rather than discriminant analysis because the dependent variable is a direct function of the values of the explanatory variables, not a prior classification from which the values of the independent variables derive (see Schlaifer, 1978, p. 229).

11 I.e., the coefficients generated by the regression model could be used to 'predict' whether each entry was direct or acquisition, and only 8.5 per cent or 5 of the 59 entries, were incorrectly predicted. Ideally, this measure of misclassification should have been obtained on a sample other than the one on which the model's parameters were estimated. The small sample available did not allow for the usual split sample approach. Nevertheless the downwardly biased 9 per cent error compares very favourably with the 37 per cent or 46 per cent errors of a naive model (37 per cent if the naive model classifies all observations as direct, given that 37 per cent was via acquisition; 46 per cent if the naive model assigns observations randomly between 63 per cent direct and 37 per cent acquisitions, as recommended by Morrison (1969).

References

Ansoff, H. Igor. *Corporate Strategy*, McGraw-Hill, New York, 1965.

Bain, Joe S. *Barriers to New Competition*, Harvard University Press, Cambridge, 1956.

Bevan, Alan. The U.K. potato crisp industry, 1960–72: a study of new entry competition, *Journal of Industrial Economics*, **XXII**, June 1974, pp. 281–297. See also Smith's Potato Crisps Ltd. IMEDE teaching case 1968 (distributed by HBS Case Services, Boston. No. 9–51 5–099).

Biggadike, E. Ralph. 'Entry, strategy and performance', DBA dissertation, Harvard Business School, 1976). Published as 'Corporate diversification: entry, strategy and performance', Division of Research, Harvard Business School, 1979.

Buzzell, Robert D., Bradley T. Gale, and Ralph G. M. Sultan, 'Market share—a key to profitability',
Harvard Business Review, **53**(1), January–February 1975. pp. 97–106.

Caves, Richard E. and Michael E. Porter. 'From entry barriers to mobility barriers: Conjectural decisions and continued deterrence to new competition', *Quarterly Journal of Economics*, May 1977. pp. 241–261.

Hines, Howard H. 'Effectiveness of "entry" by already established firms', *Quarterly Journal of Economics*, **LXXI**, February 1957, pp. 132–150.

Morrison, Donald G. 'On the interpretation of discriminant analysis', *Journal of Marketing Research*, May 1969, pp. 156–163.

Porter, Michael E. 'The contributions of industrial organization to strategic management', *Academy of Management Review*, **6**(4), 1981. pp. 609–620.

Rumelt, Richard P. *Strategy, Structure, and Economic Performance*. Division of Research. Harvard Business School, Boston, 1974.

Salter, Malcolm S., and Wolf A. Weinhold. *Diversification Through Acquisition: Strategies for Creating Economic Value*, The Free Press, New York, 1979.

Schlaifer. Robert. 'User's guide to the AQD collection', Harvard Business School, 7th edition, 1978.

Schoeffler, Sidney, Robert D. Buzzell, and Donald F. Heany. 'Impact of strategic planning on profit performance', *Harvard Business Review*, **52**(2), March–April 1974, pp. 137–145.

Yip, George S. *Barriers to Entry A Corporate Strategy Perspective*, D.C. Heath, Lexington, MA. forthcoming 1982.

20

STRATEGIC MANAGEMENT AND ECONOMICS

Richard P. Rumelt, Dan Schendel and David J. Teece

Source: *Strategic Management Journal* 12, Special Issue: Fundamental Research Issues in Strategy and Economics (1991): 5–29.

This essay examines the relationship between strategic management and economics. It introduces the special issue on this same topic by providing a guide to the eight papers contained in the special issue, and it offers the guest editors viewpoints on the contributions of each discipline to the other. The essay notes the major contribution from economics has been primarily from the industrial organization literature, with promises of important gains to be made from the 'new' economics as it breaks away from the neoclassical theory of the firm. Contributions from strategic management to economics are noted. Areas for further research utilizing the relationship between strategic management and economics are also indicated.

Introduction

The last decade has witnessed a minor revolution in strategic management research and writing. As never before, academics have adopted the language and logic of economics. This change is owed to the increased use of economics by strategy scholars and to the increased ability of economists, armed with new tools and richer theories, to attack problems of central interest to strategic management. Thus, during this past decade we have seen strategy scholars reaching out to use or reformulate economic theory, as in Porter's (1980) influential treatment of industry structure. In the other direction, we have seen some economists positioning their work as relevant to general managers, as in Jensen's (1989) views on corporate control and Williamson's (1975, 1985) analysis of the efficiency properties of the institutions of capitalism.

Although there can be little doubt that economic thinking is reshaping strategic management, opinion is divided as to the usefulness of this trend. Within strategic management, there is a growing group who cross over between the fields, but maintain an understanding of their distinct strengths and weaknesses. However, there are also some who see economics as the 'solution' to the strategy problem (or, perhaps, to the 'tenure' problem), rejecting the field's traditional preoccupation with situational complexity and managerial processes. Finally, there are some who strongly oppose the confluence, seeing economics as 'imperialistic,' as taking undue credit for formalizing that which was already known by others, and as insensitive to aspects of the human situation other than the rational pursuit of gain. Within economics, the situation is simpler: there are those who follow and appreciate the contributions of strategic management research, but there is a much larger group who are unaware of traditions outside of economics and apprehend business management only through their own constructs (and an occasional reading of the *Wall Street Journal*).

Our purpose for this special issue of the *Strategic Management Journal* is to examine the state of the current connection between strategic management and economics. This examination will be done in two ways. The first way will be in presenting papers from a larger collection of commissioned papers and commentaries that appear elsewhere[1] and which provide particularly salient examples of the intersection of the two fields. The second way is through this editorial essay which, in addition to providing our interpretations of the papers selected for this special issue, is extended to provide our own views about the connection between strategy and economics. These views are intended to challenge both economists and strategists to recognize each others' contributions, limitations, and the opportunities each faces in connecting theory and application. Along the way we hope that new directions and priorities for research will be surfaced for our readers, whether their primary interest is strategy or economics. Some comment will also be provided on the issue: What (and who) should guide the intellectual development of the strategic management field: strategic thinking and strategists, or economic theory and economists?

Our essay is organized in this way: the next section briefly reviews the evolution of the connection between economics and strategic management. The third section addresses important forces that have induced this connection. The fourth section examines the future of strategic management and economics, highlighting salient research issues. The fifth section provides a guide to the papers in this issue. Our summary comments close the essay.

A brief history of economics within strategic management

Strategic management, often called 'policy' or nowadays simply 'strategy,' is about the direction of organizations, and most often, business firms.[2] It includes those subjects which are of primary concern to senior management, or to anyone seeking reasons for the success and failure among organizations. Firms, if not all organizations, are in competition, competition for factor inputs, competition for customers, and ultimately, competition for revenues that cover the costs of their chosen manner of surviving. Firms have choices to make if they are to survive. Those which are *strategic* include: the selection of goals, the choice of products and services to offer; the design and configuration of policies determining how the firm positions itself to compete in product-markets (e.g. competitive strategy); the choice of an appropriate level of scope and diversity; and the design of organization structure, administrative systems and policies used to define and coordinate work. It is a basic proposition of the strategy field that these choices have critical influence on the success or failure of the enterprise, and, that they must be integrated. It is the integration (or reinforcing pattern) among these choices that makes the set a strategy.

Strategic management as a field of inquiry is firmly grounded in practice and exists because of the importance of its subject. The strategic direction of business organizations is at the heart of wealth creation in modern industrial society. The field has not, like political science, grown from ancient roots in philosophy, nor does it, like parts of economics, attract scholars because of the elegance of its theoretical underpinnings. Rather, like medicine or engineering, it exists because it is worthwhile to codify, teach, and expand what is known about the skilled performance of roles and tasks that are a necessary part of our civilization. While its origins lie in practice and condification, its advancement as a field increasingly depends upon building theory that helps explain and predict organizational success and failure. In the sense of expansion, codification, and teaching, theory is necessary, tested theory capable of prediction desirable, and the search and creation of both to better practice, absolutely at the heart of the field. Society is served by efficient, well-adapted organizations and strategic management is concerned with delivering them through the study of their creation, success, and survival, as well as with understanding their failure, its costs, and its lessons.

Strategic management has a rich tradition and long history as a teaching area in business schools, a history virtually as long as that of business schools themselves. Prior to the 1960s, the underlying metaphor of the (teaching) field was that of functional integration. Under this metaphor, the value-added by what was then called 'business policy' came from integration of specialized knowledge within broader perspectives. The perspectives were dual: that of the firm as a whole, including its performance, and that of the role of the general manager. Together with an intellectual style that stresses pragmatic realism over abstraction, these perspectives remain at the center of the field and distinguish it from other fields with different perspectives, but with similar interests in the same core issues.

A new metaphor was introduced in the 1960s, that of 'strategy.' Strategy was seen as more than just coordination or integration of functions—it embodied the joint selection of the product-market arenas in which the firm would compete, and the key policies defining how it would compete.

Strategy was not necessarily a single decision or a primal action, but was a collection of related, reinforcing, resource-allocating decisions and implementing actions. Depending upon whether one read Selznick's *Leadership in Administration* (1957), Chandler's *Strategy and Structure* (1962), Andrew's material in *Business Policy: Text and Cases* (1965), or Ansoff's *Corporate Strategy* (1965), a company's mission or strategy built upon 'distinctive competence,' constituted the firm's method of expansion, involved a balanced consideration of the firm's 'strengths and weakness,' and defined its use of 'synergy and competitive advantage' to develop new markets and new products. Ever since the sixties, the strategy metaphor has survived as a central construct of the field, even without the careful definition necessary for research purposes.

Where the sixties gave rise to basic concepts, the decade of the 1970s brought their development and application to practice, and in turn gave rise to research in the field as we now know it. The seventies were marked by the rapid expansion[3] of consulting firms specializing in strategy, the establishment of professional societies, and the advent of journals publishing material on strategy.[4] Three forces helped strategy flourish in the 1970s. First, the hostility and instability of the environment of the seventies led to a disenchantment with 'planning' and the search for methods of adapting to and taking advantage of the unexpected. The strategy doctrines of the seventies offered an alternative: building and protecting specialized strengths that weather change and expressing those strengths in new products and services as markets shift. The second important force was the continued expansion and further development of strategy consulting practices based on analytical tools and concepts. The Boston Consulting Group pioneered in this regard, creating the 'experience curve' and deriving the 'growth-share matrix.' The third key force at work was the maturation and predominance of the diversified firm. Top management began to see their corporations as portfolios of business units and their primary responsibility as capital allocation among business units. The new systems that evolved, dubbed 'strategic management,' forced business managers to define their plans and goals in competitive terms and generated a brisk demand for strategic tools and strategy analysis.

Until the seventies, academic strategy research consisted chiefly of clinical case studies of actual situations, with generalizations sought through induction. Although this style of research continues to play an important role, the seventies saw the rise of a new research style, one based in deductive methods, the falsification philosophy of Popper, and the multivariate statistical methods characteristic of econometrics. Almost simultaneously, three different streams of work were changing the face of the field. Two of these streams were conducted at Harvard, the third at Purdue University. At the Harvard Business School, students of Bruce Scott built on Chandler's (1962) pioneering work and inaugurated a stream of research on diversification and firm performance. At the Harvard Department of Economics, Richard Caves' students began to modify traditional Mason/ Bain studies of structure and performance to include differing positions of firms within industries, inaugurating the study of 'strategic groups' within industries. Meanwhile, at Purdue University, Dan Schendel, together with his and Arnold Cooper's students, began the so-called 'brewing' studies which explored the empirical links between organizational resource choices, interpreted as 'strategy,' and firm performance.[5] This work demonstrated for the first time the existence of structural heterogeneity within industries, and led to the first hard empirical evidence of the 'strategic groups' under discussion and development at Harvard. More important than the content of the Purdue and Harvard studies, however, was the different empirical nature of the work. In addition to cases used for induction, this new work used difficult data collection, and the rapidly growing power of the computer and multivariate statistical methods capable of handling large data bases, to test hypotheses in a deductive style of research.

This shift in research style ultimately led to questions that case research and simple hypothesis testing could not illuminate. Results were difficult to interpret, lacking any theory in which to embed them. Cumulation of questions occurred, but not of results that led to advice for practitioners, or to tests of theory useful for practice. Hence, the work of the seventies was instrumental in motivating the work of the eighties and its search for linkages to theory. As importantly, this work and style led to a new generation of researchers better equipped to handle the new style of research and its intellectual demands.

During the 1980s, owing to the changes noted, the pace of change accelerated; economic thinking moved closer to center stage in strategic management as disciplines were examined for theoretical motivation for the empirical work then building. The most influential contribution of the decade from economics was undoubtedly Porter's *Competitive Strategy* (1980). In a remarkably short time, Porter's applications of mobility barriers, industry analysis, and generic strategies became broadly accepted and used in teaching, consultation, and many research projects.

Whereas Porter's approach to strategy built on the structure-conduct-performance tradition, which studied market power, there was another tradition, associated with the University of Chicago, which saw industry structure as reflecting efficiency outcomes rather than market power. In this tradition differences in performance tend to signal differences in resource endowments. In addition, another new stream of thought began to emphasize the importance of unique, difficult-to-imitate resources in sustaining performance. Within strategic management, these approaches have flowed together and have been dubbed the *resource-based view* of the firm.[6]

In addition to these broad perspectives developed within the field, during the 1980s strategy scholars dramatically increased their use of economic theory and their sophistication in doing so as the examples that follow indicate. The event-study methods of financial economics were used to investigate strategic and organizational change as well as the strategic fit of acquisitions. New security-market performance measures were applied to old questions of diversification and performance, market share and performance, as well as new areas of inquiry. Transaction-cost viewpoints on scope and integration were adopted and new theories of the efficiency of social bonding advanced. Studies of innovation began to use the language and logic of rents and appropriability, and research in venture capital responded to the agency and adverse selection problems characteristic of that activity. Agency theory perspectives have been used in the study of firm size, diversification, top-management compensation, and growth. The new game-theoretic approach to industrial organization has informed studies of producer reputations, entry and exit, technological change, and the adoption of standards.

In looking backward over these three decades, what comes into focus is the search for theoretical explanations of very complex phenomena. A linking occurred for the first time between basic disciplines of the social sciences,[7] especially economics, and practical issues involved in managing the firm. What had begun in the sixties as rather simple concepts that gave insight into phenomena described in cases, ended in the eighties motivating a search for theory with causal and predictive power able to be used in practice.

Why economics in strategic management?

Why has the 'content' side of strategic management come to draw so heavily on economics? The trend cannot have been driven by practice; very few, if any, of the unregulated firms in the U.S. employ microeconomists to analyze strategies or help chart strategic direction. It cannot have been driven by teaching; most strategic management courses continue to rely on cases that are more integrative than analytic. We contend that the infusion of economic thinking has been driven by five forces or events, all connected with the research program of strategic management. They are: (1) the need to interpret performance data, (2) the experience curve, (3) the problem of persistent profit, (4) the changing nature of economics, and (5) the changing climate within business schools. Each of the forces or events has shaped the connection between economics and strategic management and each continues to pose practical and intellectual challenges that will shape future developments.

The need to interpret performance data

In the early 1970s strategy researchers began to look systematically at corporate performance data, particularly return on investment, in attempts to link results to managerial action. Fruhan's (1972) study of the airline industry, Rumelt's (1974) study of diversification strategy, Hatten, Schendel and Cooper's (1978) brewing industry study, Biggadike's (1979) study of entry and diversification, and the PIMS studies were the early examples of this new style of research. The problem implicit in each of these studies was that of interpreting the observed performance differentials. What meaning should be ascribed to performance differences between groups, or to variables that correlate with performance? The need to find an adequate answer to these questions was one of the forces engendering economic thinking among strategy researchers.

The story of the market-share effect provides a good illustration of this dynamic. The empirical association between market share and profitability was first discerned in IO economics research[8] where the relationship was intepreted as evidence of 'market power.' Why? Because using the structure-conduct-performance paradigm as the driver, market share represented 'structure' ('conduct' was implicit) and supernormal returns were interpreted as poor social 'performance.' Within the strategic management community, the market-share issue was raised by the Boston Consulting Group (BCG) and sharpened by the PIMS studies, carried out on the first business-level data base available for economic research. The leading role both BCG and PIMS gave to market share helped shape thought about strategic management in the late 1970s. The viewpoint they espoused saw market-share as an asset that could be 'bought' and 'sold' for strategic purposes.[9] BCG advised its clients to 'invest' in share in growing industries (where competitive reaction was either absent or dulled) and 'harvest' share in declining industries. PIMS researchers and consultants went further and told managers they could increase share, and thus profit, by redefining their markets (i.e. redefine their competitors and presumably their share position).

In 1979, Rumelt and Wensley (1981) began an empirical study using PIMS data that was designed to estimate the 'cost' of gaining market share. Their motivation was discomfort with the consultants' advice to gain share in growing markets (or new industries, etc.). The advice seemed to be too much of a 'free lunch.' Were there really simple rules of strategy that could always be expected to pay off? Expecting to find the cost of share-gains to be at least their worth in each context, they were quite surprised to find no cost to share-gains. Changes in share and changes in profitability were positively related in every context examined. *It was not possible to interpret this result without extensive forays into economic theory and advanced econometrics.* In the end, they adopted the assumption that share changes were properly 'priced' and interpreted their results as implying that the share-profit association was causally spurious. Instead, an unobserved stochastic process (i.e. luck, good management) was jointly driving both share and profitability. Subsequent empirical research has generally supported their view.[10] The market share issue also stimulated efforts to model competitive equilibria in which share and profitability are associated. Note that most of this work has been carried out within strategic management rather than by economists.[11]

The market share story exemplifies an argument over data analysis and equilibrium which continues in new forms today. Simply stated, equilibrium means that all actors have exploited the opportunities they face. Thus, competitive equilibrium rules out, (by assumption), the possibility that differences in firm wealth can be attributed to differences in freely variable strategy choices, or easily reversible decisions. Instead, observed differences in wealth must be attributed to phenomena that are uncontrollable or unpredictable, for example order of entry, nonimitable differences in quality or efficiency, and of course, luck. By making the assumption, the widely-used study of performance vs. some parameter or other loses much of its value. For example, if the world is in equilibrium, the fact that growing industries are more profitable does not mean that one should invest in growing industries. Instead, the assumption of equilibrium leads the researcher to presume that the observed profitability is balanced by the expectation of future losses, risk, or is sustained by impediments to entry, or is a reputation-based premium, or is otherwise balanced by unseen scarcity and cost.

Equilibrium assumptions are the cornerstone of most economic thinking and are the most straightforward way of modeling competition. Researchers who eschew equilibrium assumptions risk gross errors in the causal interpretation of data. On the other hand, the risk in adopting an equilibrium assumption is that it may be unwarranted. Observed differences in performance may actually reflect widespread ignorance about the phenomena being studied. Which risk is being undertaken is not just a matter of preference, but more likely one of conditions, especially in the presence of innovation and change. The general approach to making this judgement is to rule in favor of equilibrium when the underlying assets or positions are frequently traded or contested, when the level of aggregation and the type of data is familiar to actors in the industry, when the data is widely available and frequently reviewed, and when the connections between the data and profits are widely understood.

While equilibrium assumptions often drive out consideration of innovation, change, and heterogeneity, this does not need to be the case. In the neoclassical world, equilibrium meant that profits were everywhere zero, or more generally, that all opportunities bad been exploited. But more sophisticated views now permit more sophisticated equilibria. The basic idea of Nash equilibrium, wherein each actor does the best he or she can with what they individually know and control, especially when coupled with uncertainty, asymmetric information and unequal resource endowments, permits a broad range of intriguing outcomes. For example, one could model the gradual imitation of an innovation as a process in which competitors observe its operation and market results, and then gradually learn what the leader already knows. In such a model large profits would be earned, firms might enter and then exit, and competition would gradually increase. Although the product market would not be in neoclassical equilibrium, the behavior described is still equilibrium behavior in that no one has passed up any opportunities for profit that are *known to them*. Thus, it is possible to describe many aspects of innovation and the profit-creating transient responses they induce with 'equilibrium' models, although a plethora of nonneoclassical assumptions will be required.

An example of an equilibrium assumption of use in strategic management is that of 'no rule for riches'—that there can be no *general* rules for generating wealth. There is no substitute for judgement in deciding whether or not this exclusion should be applied to a particular context (that is, deciding how general is 'general'). Interestingly, this equilibrium assumption rationalizes traditional case-based situational analysis that has been the hallmark of strategic management instruction. If there are no general rules for riches, then a strategy based on generally available information and unspecialized resources should be rejected. Opportunities worth undertaking must be rooted in the particulars of the situation. They must flow from special information possessed by the firm or its managers, from the special resources, skills, and market positions that the firm possesses. Viewed in this light, traditional case analysis is a legitimate search for opportunity. What is worth recognizing is that the acceptance of this level of economic equilibrium does not nullify strategic management, nor does it imply that one should teach economic theorems rather than management. What it does imply is that professional educators are right in their focus on developing skills in the analysis of the particular rather than the general. In addition, it suggests a framework for where to look for opportunities and, once identified, a basis for judging their relative merits. Theory alone is insufficient absent intimate, unique knowledge of technical conditions and the ability to position assets and skills to create favorable competitive positions.

The experience curve

During the 1970s the experience curve doctrine, developed by the Boston Consulting Group,[12] was a powerful force within strategic management. Although the idea that some costs followed a learning-by-doing pattern had been around since the 1920s, it was largely ignored by economists because it was a theoretical nuisance; it destroyed the ability of standard models to reach equilibrium. BCG added four critical ingredients: (1) they argued that the pattern applied not just to direct labor, but to all deflated cost elements of value added; this expanded version of the learning curve was called the experience curve; (2) they provided convincing data showing experience effects in a broad variety of industries; (3) they argued that experience-based cost reduction was not restricted to the early stages of production, but

380

continued indefinitely;[13] and (4) they explored the competitive implications of the experience effect. An example of the latter is BCG's suggestion that '... there is no naturally stable relationship with competitors on any product until some one competitor has a commanding market share of the normal market for that product and until the product's growth slows. Furthermore, under stable conditions, the profitability of each competitor should be a function of his accumulated experience with that product.' (1970: 29)

The idea that cumulative production experience, not scale, could be a primary driver of unit costs implied a value in doing business apart from the immediate profits earned. In the second-half of the seventies, virtually every article, book, and presentation on strategy referred in some way to the experience curve. The idea's power was that it provided an explanation for the sustained dominance of leaders, and for heterogeneity, despite competition. There was also the simple fact that it supported many managers' tastes for pursuing dominance and growth at the expense of current profit.

The impact of the experience curve on the strategic management community extended beyond the overt content or correctness of the doctrine. The experience curve was the first wedge driven in the split that widened between the study of management process and the study of competitive action and market outcomes. In a field which had traditionally seen the firm as embedded within an 'environment,' the experience curve focused attention on the actions of alert rivals. Most importantly, the logic of the experience curve engendered a taste for a microeconomic style of explanation: For the first time there was a simple, parsimonious account of what competitive advantage was, how it was gained, and where it should be sought. Adding piquancy was the fact that the logic of experience-based competition was not imported from economics, but was instead developed within strategic management and then exported to economics. Finally, among those who sought more precision, there was the need to clarify assumptions about competitive behavior, to more exactly characterize the resulting equilibria,[14] and to empirically estimate the relative importance of scale, industry-experience, and firm-experience effects.[15] Thus, the very act of developing and grappling with the logic of experience-based competition encouraged economic thinking within strategic management.

The problem of persistent profit

One of the key empirical observations made by traditional strategy case research was that firms within the same industry differ from one another, and that there seems to be an inertia associated with these differences. Some firms simply do better than others, and they do so consistently. Indeed, it is the fact of these differences that was the origin of the strategy concept. In standard neoclassical economics, competition should erode the extra profits earned by successful firms, leaving each firm just enough to pay factor costs.

Yet empirical studies show that if you do well today, you tend to do well tomorrow; good results persist.

One of the factors in the 1970s that drove strategy researchers to search for theoretical explanations for persistent performance differences was the enormous success and legitimacy of the capital asset pricing model (CAPM). Developed by financial economists, the CAPM not only had practical usefulness, it gave great strength to the idea that markets were *efficient*. Consequently, an intellectual climate developed in the academy which tended to presume efficiency in all markets, even product-markets, and aggressively challenged assertions to the contrary. The experience curve doctrine provided a partial response to this challenge, but it clearly was not the whole story.

In searching for explanations for enduring success it was natural to reach for relevant economic theory. The most obvious theory was that of industrial organization economics and its various explanations for abnormal returns. Traditional entry-barrier theory yielded the concepts of scale economies and sunk costs; mobility barrier theory stressed the importance of learning and first-mover advantages in making specialized investments in positions within industries. The 'Chicago' tradition supported the notion that high profits were returns to specialized, high-quality resources. Game theory provided models of firms which use preemption, brand crowding, dynamic limit-pricing, signaling, and reputations for toughness to strategically protect market positions. The economics of innovation brought a focus on Schumpeterian competition, intellectual property, and the costs of technology transfer. And evolutionary economics yielded the idea that skills, embedded in organizational routines, resisted imitation and had to be developed anew by each firm.

Within strategic management there has been a great deal of work aimed at synthesizing these ideas into coherent frameworks. The most prominent effort is Porter's (1980, 1985). Taking the basic ideas of the Mason/Bain structure-conduct-performance paradigm, Porter changed the perspective from that of the industry to that of the firm, and formulated what had been learned from this perspective into a theory of competitive strategy. Porter catalogued, described, and discussed a wide range of phenomena which interfered with free competition, thus allowing abnormal returns, and suggested how their interaction and relative importance varied across contexts. Porter's (1985) later approach, delineated in *Competitive Advantage*, extended the earlier analysis of competitive strategy to encompass positioning within an industry (or strategic group) so as to achieve sustained competitive advantage. Positing two basic types of firm-specific advantage (cost-based or differentiation-based), Porter argued that advantage could be sustained from a product-market position and a configuration of internal activities that were mutually reinforcing (i.e. strong complementarities amongst activities and the conditions of demand).[16]

A second effort at synthesis is the resource-based view of strategy. This view shifts attention away from product-market barriers to competition, and towards factor-market impediments to resource flows. Identifying abnormal returns as rents to unique resource combinations, rather than market power, this perspective emphasizes the importance of specialized, difficult-to-imitate resources. The creation of such resources is seen as entrepreneurship: strategic management consists of properly identifying the existence and quality of resources, and in building product-market positions and contractual arrangements that most effectively utilize, maintain, and extend these resources. This perspective finds its greatest use in examining heterogeneity within industries, and in the discussion of 'relatedness' among diversified businesses. Nelson (this issue) discusses a recent version of this viewpoint, incorporating learning, that is called the 'dynamic capabilities' approach. Prahalad and Hamel's [1990] recent discussion of core competences is an expression of the resource-based view.

Ghemawat [1991] provides a new attempt at synthesis around the idea of *commitment*. His view is that the persistence of strategies and of performance both stem from mechanisms which link and bind actions over time. He identifies lock-in, lock-out, lags, and inertia as the key irreversibilities at work and reinterprets a great deal of strategic doctrine in terms of the selection and management of commitments.

In summary, the single most significant impact of economics in strategic management has been to radically alter explanations of success. Where the traditional frameworks had success follow leadership, clarity of purpose, and a general notion of 'fit' between the enterprise and its environment, the new framework focused on the impediments to the elimination of abnormal returns. Depending upon the framework employed, success is now seen as sustained by mobility barriers, entry barriers, market preemption, asset specificity, learning, ambiguity, tacit knowledge, nonimitable resources and skills, the sharing of core competences, and commitment. That 'fit' was correlated with success can be argued, that it is causal cannot be. The fit argument lies in the long line of work that Porter (this issue) describes as a continuing search for causal explanation. Teaching frameworks that suggest the importance of fit are correct so far as they go, but it is the new economic frameworks which establish the causal linkages. That has been learned from the pressure of asking questions from an economics perspective.

The changing nature of economics

The economist's neoclassical model of the firm, enshrined in textbooks, was a smoothly running machine in a world without secrets, without frictions or uncertainty, and without a temporal dimension. That such a theory, so obviously divorced from the most elementary conditions of real firms, should continue to be taught in most business schools as the 'theory of the firm' is a truly amazing victory of doctrine over reality. This era may, however, finally be coming to an end as the cumulative impact of new insights take their toll. During the past 30 years, and especially during the last 20 years, at least five substantial monkey wrenches have been thrown into what was a smoothly running machine. They are called *uncertainty, information asymmetry, bounded rationality, opportunism,* and *asset specificity.* Each of these phenomena, taken alone, violate crucial axioms in the neoclassical model. In various combinations they are the essential ingredients of new subfields within economics. Transaction cost economics rests primarily on the conjunction of bounded rationality, asset specificity, and opportunism. Agency theory rests on the combination of opportunism and information asymmetry. The new game-theoretic industrial organization dervies much of its punch from asymmetries in information and/or in the timing of irreversible expenditures (asset specificity). The evolutionary theory of the firm and of technological change rests chiefly on uncertainty and bounded rationality. Each of these new subfields has generated insights and research themes that are important to strategic management. Each is briefly treated in turn.

Transaction cost economics

Of all the new subfields of economics, the transactions cost branch of organizational economics has the greatest affinity with strategic management. The links derive, in part, from common interests in organizational form, including a shared concern with the Chandler–Williamson M-form hypothesis. They also derive from a common intellectual style which legitimizes inquiry into the reasons for specific institutional details. The clinical studies conducted by strategy researchers and business historians are grist for the transaction cost mill. A theory which seeks to explain why one particular clause appears in a contract is clearly of great interest to strategic management scholars, who have a definite taste for disaggregation.[17]

For many economists, the assumption of unlimitedly rational actors is the detining characteristic of their field. Consequently, transaction cost economics, which follows Simon in positing bounded rationality, has had a difficult uphill struggle for recognition and acceptance. The subfield got its start in the mid-1970s as some economists, building on Coase's (1937) seminal work, began to systematically probe questions of firm boundaries and internal organization. Williamson (1975) was the chief architect of a framework that explored the limits or boundaries of both markets and business firms as arrangements for conducting economic activity. His basic point was that transactions should take place in that regime which best economizes on the costs imposed by bounded rationality and opportunism. This framework was explicitly comparative (the relative efficiencies of markets and hierarchies were exposed) and enabled economists for the first time to say something about the *efficiency* properties of different organizational forms. (Previously economists had commonly sought and found monopoly explanations for complex forms of business organization; efficiency explanations were ignored or denigrated.) In addition to comparing markets and hierarchies, transaction cost researchers also began to look at questions of internal structure and the manner in which specific decisions and actions were taken. In particular, the Chandler–Williamson M-form hypothesis raised important issues relating to corporate control. These ideas began to achieve wider acceptance after being supported in a number of empirical studies.[18]

Within strategic management, transaction cost economics is the ground where economic thinking, strategy, and organizational theory meet. Because of its focus on institutional detail, rather than mathematical display, it has a broader audience among noneconomists than other branches of organizational economics. During the 1980s, a considerable amount of work was done in applying the transaction cost framework to issues in organizational structure. In particular, research has been carried out on vertical supply arrangements in a number of industries,[19] the structure of multinational firms (Buckley and Casson, 1976; Teece, 1981; Kogut, 1988), sales force organization (Anderson and Schmittlein, 1984), joint ventures (Hennart, 1988; Pisano, 1990), and franchising (Klein, 1980). Williamson [this issue] provides a useful review of additional applications of interest to strategic management.

Agency theory

Agency theory concerns the design of incentive agreements and the allocation of decision rights among individuals with conflicting preferences or interests. Although it deals with the employment transaction, agency theory is not compatible with transaction cost theory. Whereas transaction cost economics begins with the assertion that one cannot write enforceable contracts that cover all contingencies, agency theorists make no such presumption, and instead seek the optimal form of such a contract.

Agency theory has developed in two branches. The *principal-agent* literature is chiefly concerned with the design of optimal incentive contracts between principals and their employees or agents. Principal-agent economics is largely mathematical in form and relatively inaccessible to those who have not made investments in its special technology. The standard problem has the agent shirking unless rewards can be properly conditioned on informative signals about effort. The interesting aspect of the problem is that both parties suffer if good measures are not available. A version of the problem that links with strategic management concerns project selection and the design of incentives so that agents will not distort the capital budgeting process.

The second *corporate control* branch of the agency literature is less technical and is concerned with the design of the financial claims and overall

385

governance structure of the firm. It is this branch which is most significant to strategic management. The corporate control hypothesis most familiar to strategic management is Jensen's (1986) 'free cash flow' theory of leverage and takeovers. According to Jensen, in many firms, managers have inappropriately directed free cash flow towards wasteful investments or uses. Two cures to this problem have been proposed: use of high levels of debt to commit managements to payouts and hostile takeovers, which put new management teams in place. What should strike strategic management scholars is that BCG offered precisely this diagnosis for many diversified firms in the early 1970s. According to BCG, most firms mismanaged their portfolios, misusing the funds generated by mature cash-rich businesses ('cows'), usually by continuing to reinvest long after growth opportunities had evaporated.

The corporate control perspective provides a valuable framework for strategic management research. By recognizing the existence of 'bad' management, identifying remedial instruments, and emphasizing the importance of proper incentive arrangements, it takes a more normative stand than most other subfields of economics. However, scholars working in this area also have the tendency to see all managerial problems as due to incorrect incentives—a tautology for a perspective which assumes away any other sources of dysfunction (e.g. capital markets problems like those discussed by Shleifer and Vishny in this issue, managerial beliefs about cause and effect, management skills in coordination, and the presence or lack of character and self-control).

Game-theory and the new IO

Three of the papers in this special issue deal with implications of game theory for strategic management, so our remarks here will be brief. Mathematical game theory was invented by von Neumann and Morgenstern (1944) and Nash (1950). However, little progress was made in developing economic applications until the late 1970s. It was probably Spence's (1974) work on market signalling that sparked the modern interest of economists and it was Stanford's 'gang of four,' Kreps, Milgrom, Roberts and Wilson, (1982), who codified the treatment of sequential games with imperfect information.[20]

Modern game theory raises deep questions about the nature of rational behavior. The idea that a rational individual is one who maximizes utility in the face of available information is simply not sufficient to generate 'sensible' equilibria in many noncooperative games with asymmetric information. To obtain 'sensible' equilibria, actors must be assigned beliefs about what others' beliefs will be in the event of irrational acts. Research into the technical and philosophical foundations of game theory has, at present, little to do directly with strategic management, but much to do with the future of economics as the science of 'rational' behavior.

Game theory as applied to industrial organization has two basic themes of most interest to strategic management: commitment strategies and reputations. Commitment, as Ghemawat (1991) emphasizes, can be seen as central to strategy. Among the commitment games that have been analyzed are those involving investment in specific assets and excess capacity, research and development with and without spillovers, horizontal merger, and financial structure. Reputations arise in games where a firm or actor can have various 'types' and others must form beliefs about which type is the true one. Thus, for example, a customer's belief (probability) that a seller is of the 'honest' type constitutes the seller's reputation and that reputation can be lost if the seller behaves so as to change the customer's beliefs. Reputations can also describe relationships within the firm, and the collection of employee beliefs and reputations can be called its 'culture.' Given the competitive importance of external reputations, the efficiency properties of internal reputations, and the relative silence of game theorists about how various equilibria are actually achieved, there is clearly much room for contributions, including those from strategic management research.

Evolutionary economics

There has been a long-standing analogy drawn between biological competition (and resulting evolution) and economic competition, with both fields often pointing towards the other to ground ideas. Making the analogy concrete, however, has largely been the work of Nelson and Winter (1982), who married the concepts of tacit knowledge and routines to the dynamics of Schumpeterian competition. In their framework, firms compete primarily through a struggle to improve or innovate. In this struggle, firms grope towards better methods with only a partial understanding of the causal structure of their own capabilities and of the technological opportunity set. Key to their view is the idea that organizational capacities are based on routines which are not explicitly comprehended, but which are developed and bettered with repetition and practice. This micro-link to learning-by-doing means that the current capability of the firm is a function of history, making it impossible to simply copy best practice even when it is observed.

Because evolutionary economics posits a firm which cannot change its strategy or its structure easily or quickly, the field has a very close affinity to population ecology views in organization theory. Researchers interested in the evolution of populations tend to work in the sociology tradition, while those more interested in the evolution of firm capabilities and technical progress tend to work in the economics tradition. Both frameworks challenge the naive view that firms can change strategies easily, or that such changes will even matter when attempted and made.

The changing climate within business schools

Business schools have transformed themselves profoundly over the past 30 years. Business schools and their faculty have moved from collecting and transmitting best current practice to developing and communicating theoretical understandings of phenomena connected with management, principally, the management of complex business firms. This transformation, which occurred for larger reasons, has influenced the strategy field and its connection to economics in important ways. There are several reasons why that transformation has occurred: the impetus of the Ford Foundation and Carnegie Foundation; university hiring and promotion practices, the rise of consulting firms as repositories of best practice, and the relative proximity of economics departments. Without these changes collectively, the field as we know it would be different, and economics involvement in strategy would have been less.

In the late fifties, the so-called Gordon and Howell (1959), and the Pierson (1959) reports were published, both critiquing the business schools of their day. The criticisms were many and the changes they prompted were extensive, but one of the most far-reaching recommendations was that business schools needed to be infused with rigor, methods, and content of basic disciplines: mathematics, economics, sociology, and psychology. This recommendation was avidly followed, with the result that a good many economists, psychologists, and others trained solely in the basic social science disciplines found employment in business schools alongside traditional, professionally-oriented faculty members. The traditional faculty found its scholarship in studying business firms, identifying the best practice they could find, and transmitting what they learned in the classroom, typically through a case, and the occasional published article. Along the way such faculties were frequently cast in the role of consultants to practicing business managers and many found greater financial reward in such work than they did from their scholarship alone. The new, discipline-based faculty on the other hand found their scholarship inside the academy, in the writings of others similarly placed, and in advancing the theory of their field, often without resort to practice and application of what they learned. Their minds and rewards were concentrated on what they produced inside the academy. Set in motion was a process that retired practice-based scholars in favor of discipline-based ones.

In time, probably longer than anticipated, the discipline based preference in hiring and promotion led to a stronger and stronger presence of discipline based scholars, including economists. Indeed, some newer business schools and some older ones as well, were organized with the economics departments as part of their faculty. As business schools became more discipline based, their standards for hiring and promotion came into alignment with the social sciences. The primary measure of excellence became publication in discipline-based journals and acceptance by the community of discipline-based scholars, rather than relevance to practice or contributions to professional education. Discipline-based scholars not only earned internal rewards more easily, they also typically lacked the cushion of consultation that would otherwise allow a greater adaptation to the special circumstances of professional schools. This self reinforcing cycle is still present today.

Throughout most of this period very high growth rates characterized business schools, as they moved from granting about 12,000 to over 70,000 MBA degrees per year, and to many more schools offering the MBA. Well-trained faculties in specialty areas such as marketing, finance, accounting, and other functions were in short supply, especially in the earlier years of greatest growth. To fuel expansion it was a short step to hire disciplined based faculties directly, and worry about their adaptation to applications in business firms later. Some made the transition, some did not, but many who did retained an allegiance to their base disciplines that included seeking publication reputations, not in the field in which they were to profess, but in the basic discipline in which the faculty member had been trained.

In the world of business, more and more large firms began to create their own management development programs, aimed at filling the gap between the increasingly theoretical MBA education and the needs of practice. In addition, consulting firms grew in scope and sophistication. In many functional areas, including management and strategy, specialist consulting firms replaced business schools as repositories of best practice.

These factors led to an increased proportion of business school faculties either trained in economics directly, or importantly influenced by the standards common to discipline based scholars. Unforeseen by Gordon, Howell, and Pierson was the changing character of economics, and other social sciences. Less and less concerned with empiricism, economics became increasingly concerned with working out the internal logic of its theoretical structure and less and less concerned with describing real institutions. This trend continues today, with 'advanced' departments of economics offering Ph. D. programs in which price-theory is considered applied and not even covered during the first year of study.

These changes in business schools forced those interested in strategic management to 'take sides,' and adopt a discipline. Early on, the typical faculty member in strategic management (then called business policy) was recruited from those with experience and high rank in a functional area (e.g. marketing). The switch required was to that of the total enterprise and its general management function. The increased discipline base of business schools made this switch more difficult, and many schools began to hire young faculties and expect them to move up through the ranks on the merit of work done in strategy. To move through the system in this 'new' field was especially difficult, as it tended to lack the infrastructure peculiar to promotion needs: patrons, senior faculties who had been through the system; journals, venues for exchange of views. Additionally, it had a case-based tradition of research increasingly shunned by the academy. Consequently, groups interested in general management and strategy began to take either organization theory or economics as their base discipline.

Throughout the 1970s it appeared that organization theory was the discipline of choice for strategy groups. However, this balance was reversed in the 1980s, largely due to the success of Porter's approach to strategy. While some schools and their strategy faculty retained an essentially behaviorally focused group, many others moved to economics based views. Like economics itself, economic-based strategy groups now also differentiate themselves on their commitment to mathematical modeling vs. verbal reasoning and their interest in theory vs. empiricism. Within the behavioral groups, the split is chiefly between those following organization theory and those taking a managerial process view of strategic management.

Which group has the better idea? Who will dominate? That remains to be seen, but if what the top research-oriented (i.e. Stanford, Northwestern, Chicago, Berkeley, etc.) schools are doing now is any guide you have to bet on those emphasizing contribution of economics, if not total reliance on economists. If, on the other hand, the top European schools or practice is your guide, if what managers listen to makes a difference, those who combine a modicum of economics with a focus on managerial process are clear winners. No matter what you believe will be the outcome of this contest, economics has clearly infused and informed strategic management, not only by the power of its theory to yield insights, but by the transformation of the business school host, and the evolution of strategic management as a field.

However, from the viewpoint of strategic management we see a danger in these trends. We advocate a balanced view of the field, perhaps tipped slightly in favor of tests of theoretical constructs by practice and application. If the balance, as it has at some schools, goes too far toward theory or toward a single discipline base such as economics, there is no counterweight from practice and application likely in either research or teaching. Likewise, if the balance tips too far toward managerial process or even best practice, as it has at other schools, there are no theoretical constructions to accumulate and build for the good of the field. Either unbalanced outcome is bad. In our view, balance requires both theory and application, in their fullest and finest representations, in our research, in our teaching, and in our faculty. That such balanced views represented by portfolios of scholars, some at the discipline end, others at the practice end, do not exist, especially at our best schools, is a sad comment on the lack of administrative leadership and faculty understanding that exists about strategic management, its content, and its challenges. Simon's (1967) description of the problem of running a professional school has special relevance to strategic management:

390

Organizing a professional school . . . is very much like mixing oil with water . . . Left to themselves, oil and water will separate again [p. 16] . . . A professional school administration—the dean and senior faculty—have an unceasing task of fighting the natural increase of entropy, of preventing the system from moving toward the equilibrium it would otherwise seek. When the school is no longer able, by continual activity, to maintain the gradients that differentiate it from the environment, it reaches that equilibrium with the world which is death. In the professional school, 'death' means mediocrity and inability to fulfill its special functions.

[p. 12]

Unfortunately, strategic management is too often inhabited (inhibited?) by those who see no need for (fear?) the balance we advocate.

The future of the connection between economics and strategic management

We believe that strategic management has clearly profited from the infusion of economic thinking. There is no question that the presumption of equilibrium and the specification of alert rivals, rather than an amorphous 'environment,' has generated valuable new frameworks, new insights, and greatly sharpened thinking among strategy scholars. Nevertheless, it is vital also to recognize that this infusion has come only after the weakening of orthodoxy within economics. For decades economics impeded research into strategy by committing its intellectual capital and influence to static analysis, an almost exclusive focus on price competition, the suppression of entrepreneurship, a too stylized treatment of markets, hyper-rationality assumptions, and the cavalier treatment of know-how. Had orthodoxy weakened sooner, strategy would have had the benefits from useful economic thinking earlier. That orthodoxy weakened was perhaps partially a result of research in strategic management.

Economics has been chiefly concerned with the performance of markets in the allocation and coordination of resources. By contrast, strategic management is about coordination and resource allocation *inside the firm*. This distinction is crucial and explains why so much of economics is not readily applicable to the study of strategy, and why strategy can inform economics as much as economics can inform strategy. Twenty-five years ago economists, asked how a firm should be managed, would have (and did) argue that subunits should be measured on profit, they should transfer products, services, and capital to one another at marginal cost, and the more internal competition the better. Today, we know that this advice, to run a firm as if it were a set of markets, is ill-founded. Firms replace markets when *nonmarket* means of coordination and commitment are superior. Splendid progress has

391

been made in defining the efficient boundaries of firms—where markets fail and hierarchies are superior—but there are limits to building a theory of management and strategy around market failures. It is up to strategy scholars to flesh out the inverse approach, supplying a coherent theory of effective internal coordination and resource allocation, of entrepreneurship and technical progress, so that markets can be identified as beginning where organizations fail.

The most interesting issue regards the future of the competitive strategy portion of strategic management. It is this subfield which has turned most wholeheartedly towards the use of economic reasoning and models. If the trend continues, does the competitive strategy subject matter have an independent future, or will it become just a branch of applied economics? There are two reasons for concern about this. The first is parochial: The field's most elementary wisdom suggests that competing head on with economics departments in their own domain is a losing strategy. The second has to do with the internal integrity of the field. To split off part of a problem for separate inquiry is to presume its independence from other elements of the problem. Yet, the sources of success and failure in firms, and therefore the proper concerns of general management, remain an issue of debate (see, for example, Williamson's argument in this issue). It would be a great loss if the study of competitive strategy became divorced from the other elements of strategic management.

We believe that competitive strategy will remain an integral part of strategic management and that its connection with economics will evolve and take on new forms in the future. We believe that fears of 'absorption' will not be realized for these reasons: (1) strategy is not 'applied' economics; (2) economists will not learn about business; (3) microeconomics is a collage and apparently cannot provide a coherent integrated theory of the firm or of management; (4) that which is strategically critical changes over time; and (5) organizational capability, not market exchange, may increasingly assume center stage in strategic management research.

Strategy is not applied microeconomics

We assert this because it is patently clear that skilled practitioners do not develop or implement business or corporate strategies by 'applying' economics or any other discipline. There are economists who argue that this only proves that practitioners are not very skilled after all, but such a response is neither social science, which studies natural order, nor good professionalism, which seeks to solve, rather than ignore, the expressed problems of practitioners. We do not deny that economic analysis may be useful to a strategist, but so may demography, law, social psychology, and an understanding of political trends, as well as an appreciation for product design, process technology, and the physical sciences underlying the business. Part of any competitive strategy can be tested against known economic theory and models of competitive reaction; but most business strategies also contain implicit hypotheses concerning organizational behavior, political behavior, technological relationships and trends, and rely on judgements about the perceptions, feelings, and beliefs of customers, suppliers, employees, and competitors. Competitive strategy is integrative—not just because it integrates business functions and helps create patterns of consistent, reinforcing decisions, but also because creating and evaluating business strategies requires insights and judgements based on a broad variety of knowledge bases.

Economists will not learn about business

Economics has a strong doctrinal component that resists displacement. Strategic management, by its nature and audience, is pragmatic. If certain approaches do not shed light on business practices, or if practitioners deny their validity, the proclivity of the strategy field will be, and should be, to reject them. In addition, we believe that economics will not delve very deeply into business practices to generate new theory. This belief is based on judgements about long-term trends in academia. As Simon (1969: 56) commented on academic tastes, 'why would anyone in a university stoop to teach or learn about designing machines or planning market strategies when he could concern himself with solid-state physics? The answer has been clear: he usually wouldn't.' Having become as mathematical as physics, and more axiomatic, mainstream economics will not learn enough about business and management to challenge strategic management in its domain. Thus, for example, as industrial organization increasingly becomes infatuated with formal modeling (it didn't until the mid-1970s), it may lose the rich empirical base that made it possible for the Mason/Bain tradition to undergird Porter's work. Put differently, industrial organization may have already made its important contributions to strategy.

An example may help illustrate the very real gap between theory, economic or otherwise, and the need to internalize a vast amount of information pertaining to business practice. A case instructor used to ask 'What are this company's strengths?' Economic reasoning has now helped us understand that what we may mean to ask is 'What firm-specific, nonimitable resources or sustainable market positions are presently under-utilized?' The restatement helps: it is more precise, it provides a definition of 'strength,' and it defends against critics who insist on a discipline base behind university education. But are economists better equipped to answer the question? We suspect not. It is probably much easier to teach these economic concepts to a generalist than it is to teach economists about business.

393

Microeconomics is a collage

The upshot of all the ferment in economics is that with regard to issues of most concern to strategic management, the neoclassical theory of the firm is no longer a contender. However, there is no new 'theory of the firm' to replace it. Instead, there are areas of inquiry characterized by the assumptions that are acceptable in building models and by the phenomena to be explained. There is excitement and vitality in the new economics because the range of phenomena that can be explained has been dramatically enlarged. However, there is also confusion over the loss of the old determinism. With the old theory of the firm, everyone knew how to price— you just set marginal revenue equal to marginal cost. But now price can signal quality to customers and price may tell a potential entrant something about the profits to be made. With the old theory of the firm, a topic like 'corporate culture' was outside the realm of consideration, and classified with faith healing and voodoo. But now it is clear that there can be many types of social equilibria among the actors within a firm, with the equilibria depending upon sets of beliefs and history, and that these equilibria have radically different efficiency properties. More generally, it used to be that given a technology, the neoclassical theory delivered a prediction about the allocation of resources. But now one has to specify the technology, the information sets of the actors, including their beliefs, and the order of play and one still usually obtains many possible equilibria. The descriptive power of the new economics has been paid for by the loss of determinism.

The limitation of the new microeconomics is that it *explains* rather than *predicts*. That is, it tends to consist of a series of models, each of which has been purposefully engineered to capture and illustrate a particular phenomena. Models have been constructed to examine markets with consumer loyalty, experience effects, producer reputations, complex signaling games, the strategic use of debt, multimarket deterrence, and causal ambiguity. In addition, models have been used to explore joint ventures, venture capital, vertical integration, the appropriability of intellectual capital, governance structures, and many other phenomena. All of this has been informative and provides strategic management with a panoply of useful insights. However, these phenomena have not been *deduced* from these models or from some general theory. Rather, each of these many models has been carefully engineered to deliver the phenomena being studied. The contribution of a good modeler is in finding the least aggressive assumptions that enable the phenomena in question. Consequently, the new microeconomics is essentially a formal language for expressing knowledge elsewhere obtained. Camerer (this issue) calls this the 'collage problem.'

The 'collage problem' is simply that formal theorizing has collapsed to examples. Consequently, part of the intellectual structure of the new microeconomics is evolving to look more like strategic management. Any scholar working in strategic management must be aware of the traditional economist's normal reaction to most of the work in our field: 'The subject is interesting, but there is no tight theory—it looks like a bunch of lists.' But the new economics, taken as a whole, is a 'bunch of lists.' More precisely, it delivers a large number of tightly reasoned submodels, but no strong guidance as to which will be important in a particular situation.

The new microeconomics is still a developing field and in the future we will see further elaboration of existing frameworks. But we can also confidently expect to hear the clangs of new monkey wrenches being thrown. One already in the air is the strong evidence for persistent biases in human judgement and decision-making. Another which can be anticipated is the fact that managers not only have different information sets, they also differ in their beliefs[21] and in their understandings of the causal mechanisms they face. A third, emphasized by Nelson (this issue), is that firms do not apprehend complete sets of alternatives, but grope forward with but limited understanding of their own capabilities and the opportunities they face.

The implications of this research style for strategic management are several. First, it should be clear that knowledge about what phenomena need be studied is outside its scope. Hence, there remains a central and important role for scholars who identify phenomena worth studying. For example, it is up to strategy and management scholars to convince financial economists that most firms really do budget as if they were equity constrained—only then will useful models of this phenomena appear. Similarly, it is up to strategy researchers to reveal the patterns of global interdependence and competition—economic modeling will come after the fact. Second, the economist's approach to these phenomena is to show their existence; yet this is rarely sufficient to help in practical strategy work. Yes, it is useful to know that reputational equilibria are enabled when product quality cannot be determined by inspection and warranties are unavailable, but this is of little help to a firm that wants to know whether or not its reputation in the U.S. for workshirts will help it in Eastern Europe. It is up to strategy (or marketing, or other functional fields) to develop the measures, tools, and methods to help in specific situations. Third, each of the economist's models tends to be minimal and independent of the others—they do not integrate into any cohesive theory of the firm. For example, game theorists can model entry deterrence as based on reputations for toughness, as flowing from asset specificity, as responsive to uncertainty about post entry performance, and find that entry is encouraged by opportunities for learning, by the presence of technology options, and by economics of scope involving related products. However, these separate models provide little or no information about which of these phenomena, if any, will predominate in a specific situation, nor do they help much in determining even the rough magnitudes of the wealth impacts each of these phenomena can induce. This lack of specificity not only hinders empirical testing, it renders the professional utility of these concepts dramatically smaller than model builders imagine.

What is strategic changes over time

What is strategic changes as time and discovery alter the basis of competition. These changes arise, in part, because of technological, legal, social, and political changes. They also arise because education and research disseminate knowledge, reducing the degree to which a particular issue can be a source of advantage. The rise of Japanese competition, for example,has substantially altered the research agenda for strategy scholars. By contrast, little or no accommodation to such changes is seen in microeconomics. Business school deans like to argue that their research programs, though abstract, constitute the practices of tomorrow. The opposite is closer to the truth. Yesterday's business strategies are the subject of today's research in strategic management (e.g. takeovers and LBOs, Kaizen), and economics is just beginning to theorize about phenomena that developed half a century ago (e.g. separation of ownership and control, the diversified firm, national advantages). Today's strategic issues (e.g. the growth of new 'network' empires in Europe and Asia, time-based competition) are only dimly perceived by anyone within the academy.

Advantage may be internal

Both theoretical and empirical research into the sources of advantage has begun to point to organizational capabilities, rather than product-market positions or tactics, as the enduring sources of advantage. If this is so, our investigations will increasingly take us into domains where economics is presently at its weakest—inside the firm. There are bids by transaction cost economics and agency theory to become 'organization science,' and we can expect new and important insights from these fields. However, their comparative advantage is the analysis of individual responses to incentives. If behavior turns on interacting expections, beliefs and routines, and if diagnosis, problem solving, and the coordination of knowledge rather than effort are central, then economic views of organization will continue to be useful, but also will be only one part of the story.

For this set of reasons we believe the boundaries between strategic management and economics will remain distinct, but proximate and somtimes fuzzy, But the applied nature of strategic management and its extensive scope will require intersection with theory from other social science disciplines as well.

A guide to the papers

The eight papers in this special issue each raise or address issues which lie in the terrain between economics and strategic management. The authors are leaders in their fields: Colin Camerer in competitive strategy and the experimental economics of games, Alfred Chandler in business history as well as corporate strategy and structure, Richard Nelson in the economics of technological change, Michael Porter in competitive strategy, Garth Saloner in game-theoretic industrial organization economics, Andrei Shleifer and Robert Vishny in financial economics and corporate control, and Oliver Williamson in organizational economics. The commentator on Camerer's and Saloner's papers, Steven Postrel, is a contributor to both game-theory and competitive strategy.

It is worth emphasizing that each author was assigned the topic for his paper by the editors. The topics were selected to reveal the state-of-the-art in the connection between economics and strategic management. The happy consequence of having this uniquely talented group respond to our requests is that we obtain an unobstructed view of our subject. Because each author has been involved in the development of the concepts and theories they use and describe, there are no problems of misinterpretation, lack of comprehension, or misinformation.

The very heartening aspect of these papers, especially those written by discipline-based economists, is that no one questions the importance of the issues that are raised in strategic management. Twenty five years ago there would have been no such agreement. Furthermore, there is general agreement that neoclassical microeconomics is woefully inadequate to deal with important issues of strategy. The fracture lines begin to appear over which of the newer economic subfields supply the greatest insights into strategic advantage. Not surprisingly, game theorists tend to bet on game theory . . . and so on.

The alert reader will discern three basic frameworks in these papers (some papers use more than one). The first stresses the centrality of avoiding direct competition and has no great problem with fairly strong rationality and equilibrium assumptions (e.g. Saloner and Camerer, as well as Porter's treatment of the structure of advantage). The second framework stresses the importance of governance and of getting the match right between the technologies to be managed and the system of ownership, administration, planning, and control. The writers using this framework (Chandler, Shleifer and Vishny, and Williamson) mix a static model of efficient arrangement with the willingness to see real firms as making mistakes and learning from them. The third framework stresses the centrality of innovation, learning, and discovery in shaping advantage (e.g. Nelson, as well as Porter's treatment of the origin of advantage).

The papers

The development and proper scope and structure of the diversified firm is one of the central issues in our field. Alfred Chandler's original study of this subject was a key stimulus for the development of a scholarly research tradition in strategic management. In this paper he revisits the question, using the events of the last 25 years to inform a new view of the administrative limits of corporate headquarters units. In particular, he examines how continued growth forced the standard M-form organizations of the immediate post-WWII era to a three-tiered structure, and how prosperity (and hubris) led to diversification strategies that overtaxed these structures.

The basic conceptual scheme Chandler brings to this paper is that developed in *Scale and Scope*, (Chandler, 1990). Heavy and technologically complex industries are characterized by inexhaustible technical economies of scale and scope, but the ability of firms to exploit these economies is limited by their entrepreneurial skill in guiding complementary investments and their administrative skill in coordination of the resultant operations. Thus, it is the managerial capabilities of the corporate office that ultimately determines the size, scope, and success of the enterprise. In this paper, Chandler uses Goold and Campbell's [1987] topology of headquarters styles, identifying those using purely financial controls as essentially administrative and those using strategic planning or strategic control methods as performing some entrepreneurial functions. He analyzes the recent histories of British and U.S. firms and concludes that multibusiness companies employing financial controls have been successful only when they have restricted their ownership to firms in services and in simply mature industries. Where industries are mature, but complex and require substantial investments, headquarters units must engage in strategic control. And where complexity is combined with technological advance, headquarters offices must supply entrepreneurially oriented strategic planning.

As in Chandler's other works, many of his conclusions fit easily within an 'economizing' institutional economics framework. Thus, for example, the fact that advancing technology increases the need for headquarters strategic planning can be seen as induced by the costs of haggling and hold-up that would be borne were the divisions to plan on a decentralized basis. However, Chandler's essential contributions go far beyond this static picture. In reaching his conclusions, Chandler uses the methods he has perfected: the historical analysis of challenge and managerial response. In this paper we do not see firms 'applying' concepts or somehow driven to the efficient response by selection pressure. Instead, we see management getting it wrong, suffering consequences, struggling to understand the nature of their dilemmas, and then, perhaps, creating new structures, policies, and methods to cope with, and perhaps transcend, the problem. Chandler's real message is not that one must get the headquarters design just right, but that those firms which dominate their industries are those which have shown the most resilience and insight in responding to the challenges that their own growth and expansion have generated.

Andrei Shleifer and Robert Vishny investigate some of the same terrain as Chandler—the wave of unrelated diversification followed by a wave of restructuring and retrenchment. Shleifer and Vishny review the available evidence and conclude that unrelated diversification did not improve economic efficiency. Unrelated diversification was carried too far in the 1960s, they argue, because of antitrust enforcement as well as agency problems connected with multidivisional structures: 'The M-form begot the monster of the conglomerate.'

What makes Shleifer and Vishny's paper especially interesting is their treatment of the efficient market hypothesis. Since the stock market responded to conglomerate acquisitions in the 1960s, many researchers have concluded that they created value. This paper argues that the stock market was merely reflecting the *mistaken* beliefs of a majority of investors. Drawing on their research on arbitrage and market fads, Shleifer and Vishny contend that fads persist because it is too costly for the best-informed investors to bet against them.

The boom and bust of conglomerates is a convenient vehicle for this argument, but its implications extend well beyond the issue of conglomeration. Event studies, using stock market residuals, have become a standard way of investigating the 'value' of various policies and strategies. If these studies do not really measure value, but only what investors think is value, then this whole methodology may be significantly weakened.

Richard Nelson's paper addresses the question of how and why firms differ, an extremely deep question in strategic management. If different firms display different levels of performance or competitive advantage, despite competition, then the reasons for these persistent differences reveal the basis of competitive advantage. In this paper Nelson tackles the especially difficult version of this question: how *discretionary* considerations—such as the strategies and structures adopted by management—help underpin such differences. Although the existence of discretionary differences is comfortable for many students of strategy, it is at odds with neoclassical microeconomic theory, which Nelson sees as 'badly limited' and hence unhelpful to the field of strategy. It is badly limited because it is often too abstract and rarely deals with economic aggregates smaller than the industry, and because economists see the economic problem as basically about getting private incentives right, not about identifying the best things to do, and how to do them. In this regard, Nelson and Williamson see eye-to-eye. Neither has much time (nor do the editors of this special issue) for the long, but gradually eroding tradition in economics which treats firms as black boxes.

Nelson stresses that if economics is to inform fundamental questions in strategy, economists must break away from the assumption of clear and obvious choice sets and correct understanding of consequences of making various choices. He offers a Schumpeterian perspective, one which stresses the importance of fundamental uncertainty, perceptions about feasible paths, and trial and error learning, as a better way to come to grips with firms and firm behavior. More particularly, he argues that it is the differences among firms in their abilities to generate and profit from innovation, not differences in command over particular technologies, that are the basis of durable, difficult-to-imitate differences in firm performance. It is the issue of firms' *capabilities to innovate* which the strategy and competitiveness literature ought to be more forthright in tackling.

Oliver Williamson's paper is a call to arms. The war is against the idea that strategizing is a source of competitive advantage, and in favor of stressing the importance of economizing. It argues that whereas the field of strategy should be concerned with first-order economizing ('rectangles'), it has imported doctrines from industrial organization economics which are focused on second-order economizing ('triangles'). Williamson contends that if strategic management is to unlock the sources of long-run competitive advantage, and if it is going to rely on economic thinking to assist it, then it ought not to rely so uncritically on economic perspectives which appeal to market power (strategies that restrict product competition) as the source of advantage. Rather, the field should develop more of an efficiency perspective—that being good at what you do and avoiding waste is more important than exploiting switching costs or playing oligopoly games.

Note that Williamson's *economizing* firm is miles away from Porter's *low-cost producer*; the economizer is not necessarily efficient at production, but in the broad range of business functions. For example, the economizer may be very efficient at managing the transition from design to production, or at tailoring products to local tastes. Williamson's position on this issue is at variance with the traditional (economic) assumption that firms are 'on their cost curves.' If firms are assumed to be technically efficient, the problem is simply to determine the level of output. Williamson, by contrast, sees the fundamental challenge as organizing and governing activities so as to eliminate waste.

Because transaction cost economics, which Williamson pioneered, is concerned with first-order economizing, he suggests that it has much to offer the field of strategy. (Of course, there are other approaches which focus on economizing too.) His paper goes on to identify several important insights from transaction cost theory which are relevant to strategy. Transaction costs are the costs of organizing the economic system. Internal structures, managerial control systems, and the positioning of the boundaries of the firm all impact transaction costs. Williamson outlines a framework which helps explain why these costs differ across organization forms and then shows how the framework applies to several issues in strategic management.

Michael Porter has played the key role in shaping the currently dominant perspective on competitive strategy. That perspective attempts to explain how a particular configuration of activities, resources, and industry characteristics combine to shield a firm's profits from rapid competitive erosion. In this paper Porter makes the point that the dominant perspective explains competitive success at a given point in time, solving what he labels the *cross-sectional problem*, but that the dynamic process by which firms perceive or attain superior market position, what he labels the time series or *longitudinal problem*, is much less developed. His paper attempts to suggest what we know and what we need to know to develop a theory of firm performance linked to managerial choice, initial conditions, and environmental circumstance.

Porter begins with what he labels the chain of causality (Figure 2 in his paper). In his cross-sectional explanation, success flows from advantage inherent in industry structure and relative position. Advantage, in turn, is due to the configuration of activities. The activities provide support to the configuration, in turn, because of drivers (i.e. activity-level sources of advantage). Backing up longitudinally, activity configurations and drivers arise from 'initial conditions' and managerial choices. In the paper he then moves even further back, noting that initial conditions are the result of past managerial choices, luck, and the nature and quality of the local (business) environment. One can, of course, then step back again, seeing the character of the local environment as due to the policy choices made by a variety of institutional leaders and natural physical endowments. This chain of causality map not only helps unify Porter's own theorizing on competitive strategy, it also clarifies the different levels at which explanation can be attempted or equilibrium assumptions applied.

Why do some managements make the right choices in selecting products, industries, and activity configurations? Porter reviews the degree to which game theory, commitment views (Ghemawat, 1991), and the resource-based theory of strategy can provide answers. Not surprisingly, none does the job, but we obtain insights about each approach along the way. Where, then, to turn? Porter's (1990) own current answer is luck and local environment. Drawing on his research in *The Competitive Advantage of Nations*, he argues that managerial insight does not spring up randomly, but is concentrated, in each industry, in certain locales. In those locations, clusters of competing and supporting firms have grown up which collectively embody a great deal of specialized know-how. One of the most intriguing ideas advanced here, one drawn from *The Competitive Advantage of Nations*, is that strength is frequently the fruit of adversity.

What seems to keep us from making better progress on understanding managerial choice? Porter suggests that a key missing element is a theory of action that is not rooted in choice, but which deals with creating new options and discovering new approaches. In this sense, he joins forces with

Nelson who also calls for a model of search and discovery to help inform the discussion of innovation and change.

Three papers in this special issue address the connections between modern game theory and strategic management. Garth Saloner provides a viewpoint on the usefulness of game theoretic modeling in strategic management. His basically positive view is conditioned by two major cautions: there is no evidence of any real-world use of game theory by companies, and game theoretic approaches are 'too hard' to be applied to anything but very simple 'boiled down' models of reality. The second issue may, of course, be the reason for the first and it is interesting to speculate on what consequences would flow from the invention of a game theory 'engine' that quickly and clearly yielded the equilibria of very complex models.

Saloner's enthusiasm for game theoretic models survives these two considerations and is based on their necessity, the 'audit trail' they provide, their metaphorical value, and their growing importance in empirical research. Once you begin to consider the reactions of rivals to one another's moves, he argues, you are doing game analysis, and the current theory is simply the distilled wisdom about the most sensible way to do it. The great value of explicit modeling is the clear record of assumptions and logic—the audit trail—that permits others to verify and modify one's analysis. Saloner dismisses the use of game theory to calculate actual behavior, stressing instead the value of understanding why certain results obtain in certain situations and the possibility of novel insights. As work progresses, he argues, research will build up a mosaic of models, each providing insights about a particular aspect of strategic interaction. Game theory's contribution to strategic management will be the sum total of the insights this mosaic provides.

One of the most challenging questions Saloner tackles is the reasonableness of the rationality imputed to players in game theory. He points out that in many games, such as Cournot competition, the rationality required is not very great. However, in many modern game models, equilibria are based on quite complex considerations, straining the credulity of the rationality assumption. There is no escape, he suggests, from using judgement on this matter and notes that your own play in a game might be affected by whether your opponent was David Kreps, a fourth grader, an average undergraduate, or the CEO of a typical U.S. firm.

Colin Camerer also addresses the utility of game theory to strategic management. Like Saloner, Camerer is concerned with the sparseness of modern analysis, termed 'no fat' modeling, and with the fact that game analysis is hard. If neoclassical analysis is like eating with a fork, he analogizes, game theory is like using chopsticks. Game theory is not only hard, Camerer stresses, it is also too easy. That is, it is too easy to generate explanations for all sorts of behavior. This happens because behavior is not just determined by preferences, but also by the presence of hidden information.

The heart of Camerer's essay addresses the rationality assumption—is it too demanding to be reasonable? His own laboratory work on games shows that people do not arrive at strategies using the cognitive methods of the theorist. Consequently, theoretical equilibria are usually approached only after repeated play. Nonetheless, through processes of adaptation and/or evolution, theoretical equilibria are approached. Camerer also points out that the strict rationality assumptions of the theorist are sometimes only an analytical convenience; the same equilibria can often be justified with weaker assumptions, though the analysis is more difficult.

Despite these and other difficulties in living with game theory, Camerer favors welcoming it into the strategic management family. Like Saloner, he feels that it is the best way to look at interactions among alert rivals. In addition, Camerer sees opportunities to inform areas of interest to strategic management, such as the properties of collective resources (reputations and capabilities). Finally, he argues that the problem of too many explanations and too many equilibria provides opportunities for good empirical work to point the way.

Steven Postrel's paper is a comment on Saloner's and Camerer's discussions of game theory and strategy, especially the 'Pandora's Box' problem that the theory has too few constraints on generating explanations of behavior. Using a humorous setting, Postrel shows how a game-theorist could build a model to rationalize unreasonable behavior. His point is that game theory is not really a theory of strategy but is only a methodology for analyzing games. Other than rationality, the substantive theory present in a model is in the assumptions, not in the mechanics.

These then are the papers offered in the special issue. All offer informed and interesting views, and we hope will in their own right inform the reader on boundary conditions, future challenges, and research opportunities that lie in considering economic reasoning on strategic management issues.

Summary and conclusions

We have tried to show the relationship between economics and strategic management in this essay. It is more than some admit, and less than some would hope. We have tried to show that economics and strategic management are not the same thing, in research or in practice. We have tried to indicate that it is the new economics that offers the most promise, but it is old economics in the form of industrial organization that, thus far, has made the greatest contribution. There can be little question that the development of the strategic management field has benefited from the influence of economics, but the influence is not unidirectional either.

Where do we go from here? One trend that has recently emerged and deserves mention is the new attention to internal organization. Strategic management is increasingly concerned with understanding the administrative processes that select and coordinate the firm's activities. The capabilities of the firm, and the asset structures that accumulate, appear central to advantage and success. The assets that matter do not appear purely physical or separable. The conjunction of physical and intangible assets results from innovative managerial choice and action not easily duplicated. About such matters the new economics cited and discussed here, both in the papers, and this essay, are just beginning to have something to say. However, in this new and complex realm, economics will be only one of the logical systems in use. Where organizational relationships turn on exchange and on individual incentives, various economic approaches will have much to say. Where the coordination and accumulation of knowledge is key, and where patterns of belief and attitude are important, other disciplines will have more to say.

Along with the internal turn taken by research, comes increasing concern over dynamic explanation. Game-theory brings a fanatical attention to sequences of action and reaction, history provides stories of challenge and response, innovation is inherently dynamic, and so are the processes whereby skillful managers make sense of and respond to an evolving environment. In the more practice-oriented side of the field there is great interest in time-based competition and in the interplay between product-market strategy and the development of organizational capabilities.

More important than these trends in subject matter is the gradual enlargement of strategic management to include discipline-based scholars who share our interest in understanding the direction of enterprises. Caution in this regard is only reasonable. Strategic management scholars are small in number and struggle to maintain integration amongst frameworks and between theory and practice; most disciplines are populous and tend to compete, rather than cooperate, with other disciplines. Nonetheless, intellectual and social mechanisms must be found to make the very best of the discipline-based scholars welcome in strategic management. Their participation and *variety* are key to the long-run survival of our field.

Notes

1 The larger collection of papers appears in *Fundamental Issues in Strategy*, Richard P. Rumelt, Dan Schendel, and David J. Teece, (Eds.). Harvard Business School Press, 1992. This book contains the papers in this special issue, in some cases in extended form. This companion volume extends the discussion of strategic management and economics presented in this special issue, broadens the scope to include other social science disciplines, and provides a wider discussion of research issues facing the field.

2 We will use a variety of terms interchangeably and assume throughout the reader will interchange them easily as well. Such alternatives as firm/organization/enterprise; product/service; policy/strategy/strategic management; administrative structure/organization structure/management process are examples of terms and concepts we use more or less interchangeably for sake of variety and convenience, and we trust, with no loss of generality.

3 It should be noted that The Boston Consulting Group, the first of the firms specializing in strategy, and the firm that spun off many similar firms, was started by Bruce Henderson in the early sixties.

4 Technically, journals specializing in strategy such as this one, began publication in the eighties. However, the agreement to launch the SMJ was made in 1978. The Strategic Management Society started in 1981, but other groups such as the North American Society of Corporate Planners, Division of Business Policy and Planning of the Academy of Management. The Planning College of TIMS, and others can be traced to the seventies.

5 See Hatten and Schendel (1977), Hatten, Schendel, and Cooper (1978), and Schendel and Patton (1978).

6 This view was named and defined by Wernerfelt (1984a). Additional contributions were made by Teece (1982), Lippman and Rumelt (1982), Rumelt (1984, 1987), Barney (1986), and Teece, Pisano, and Shuen (1990). Grant (1991) reviews the subject and Conner (1991) provides a comprehensive evaluation.

7 It should be understood that this special issue of the SMJ focuses on economics and strategy, but theoretical contributions were also forthcoming from other basic disciplines such as psychology, sociology, political science, and anthropology. Indeed, the theoretical linkage search was conducted on a broad scale and was by no means limited to economics alone.

8 Imel and Helmberger (1971), Shepherd (1972), and Gale (1972) all address this phenomena. In the marketing literature there were also models proposed and studied that linked market share to profitability, but without much attention paid to the underlying theoretical issues involved.

9 Their views were also echoed by some economists. Shepherd [1979: 185] claimed that 'present market share . . . will yield a given profit rate . . . The firm can maintain that profit rate. Or it can raise it now, while yielding up some of its market share to other firms. Or it can 'invest' present profits in building up a higher future market share.'

10 See Jacobson (1990). For an intermediate view, see Boulding and Staelin (1990). Schendel and Patton (1978) as part of the Purdue brewing studies provided a simultaneous view of the search for market share, profitability, and growth.

11 Lippman and Rumelt's (1982) theory of uncertain imitability generates this sort of equilibrium as does the differentiated oligopoly modeled by Karnani (1985). Elegant models in which market share 'matters' have been developed by Wernerfelt (1984b, 1991).

12 See, *Perspectives on Experience*. The Boston Consulting Group, 1970.

13 This was a critical issue. Scherer's [1970: 74] contemporaneous industrial organization text dismissed the importance of learning-by-doing in mass production industries because 'the rate of cost reduction evidently declines as cumulative output rises beyond several thousand units. 'Interestingly, the second revised edition, published in 1980, abandoned the disclaimer and treated learning-by-doing as an important phenomena, citing BCG, among others.

14 Experience-based equilibria are analytically intractable. Spence's [1974] work remains the best analysis, accomplished by ignoring discounting.

15 Lieberman [1984], studying 37 chemical products, found learning effects much larger than scale economies and showed that they were associated with cumulative output rather than calendar time.

16 This argument can be couched in strict equilibrium terms by introducing strategy-specific assets or other sources of first-mover advantage.

17 See, for example, Joskow's [1988] treatment of price-adjustment clauses in long-term coal contracts.

18 Armour and Teece [1978] demonstrated returns to the adoption of the M-form as well as showing eventual dissipation of excess returns through imitation; Monteverde and Teece [1982] established that specific assets affected the vertical structure of organizations.
19 Early contributions were Monteverde and Teece's [1982] study of auto components and Masten's [1988] study of aerospace.
20 Much of the technical foundation they used had been laid by Selten [1965] and Harsanyi [1967].
21 A belief is a prior probability assignment to an unobservable variable. Interesting beliefs are those which affect decisions yet which are not significantly updated by events.

References

Anderson, E. and D. C. Schmittlein. 'Integration of the sales force: An empirical examination', *Rand Journal of Economics*, **15**, 1984, pp. 385–395.

Ansoff, H. I. *Corporate Strategy*, McGraw-Hill, New York, 1965.

Armour, H. O. and D. J. Teece. 'Organizational structure and economic performance: A test of the multidivisional hypothesis', *Bell Journal of Economics*, **9**, Spring 1978, pp. 106–122.

Barney, J. B. 'Strategic factor markets: Expectations, luck, and business strategy', *Management Science*, **32**, October 1986, pp. 1231–1241.

Biggadike, R. E. *Corporate Diversification: Entry, Strategy, and Performance*, Division of Research, Harvard Business School, 1979.

Boston Consulting Group. *Perspectives on Experience*, Boston Consulting Group, Boston, MA, 1968, 1970.

Boulding, W. and R. Staelin. 'Environment, market share, and market power', *Management Science*, **10**, 1990, pp. 1160–1177.

Buckley, P. J. and M. Casson. *The Future of the Multinational Enterprise*, Macmillan, New York, 1976.

Caves, R. E. and M. E. Porter. 'From entry barriers to mobility barriers: Conjectural decisions and contrived deterrence to new competition', *Quarterly Journal of Economics*, **91**, May 1977, pp. 241–261.

Chandler, A. D., Jr. *Strategy and Structure*, The MIT Press, Cambridge, MA, 1962.

Chandler, A. D., Jr. *Scale and Scope: The Dynamics of Industrial Capitalism*, Harvard University Press, Cambridge, MA, 1990.

Coase, R. H. 'The nature of the firm', *Economica*, **4**, 1937, pp. 386–406.

Conner, K. R. 'A historical comparison of resource-based theory and five schools of thought within industrial organization economics: Do we have a new theory of the firm?' *Journal of Management*, **17**, 1991, pp. 121–154.

Demsetz, H. 'Industry structure, market rivalry, and public policy', *Journal of Law and Economics*, **16**, April 1973, pp. 1–9.

Fruhan, W. E., Jr. *The Fight for Competitive Advantage*, Division of Research, Harvard Business School, 1972.

Gale, B. T. 'Market share and rate of return', *Review of Economics and Statistics*, **54**, (4), November 1972, pp. 412–423.

Ghemawat, P. *Commitment: The Dynamic of Strategy*, The Free Press, New York, 1991.

Goold, M. and A. Campbell, *Strategies and Styles: The Role of the Center in Diversified Corporations*, Basil Blackwell, Oxford, 1987.

Gordon, R. and J. Howell. *Higher Education for Business*, Columbia University Press, New York, 1959.

Grant, R. M. 'The resource-based theory of competitive advantage', *California Management Review*, **33**, 1991, pp. 114–135.

Hansen, G. S. and B. Wernerfelt. 'Determinants of firm performance: The relative importance of economic and organizational factors', *Strategic Management Journal*, **10**, September–October 1989, pp. 399–411.

Hatten, K. J. and D. E. Schendel. 'Heterogeneity within an industry', *Journal of Industrial Economics*, **26**, December 1977, pp. 97–113.

Hatten, K. J., D. E. Schendel and A. C. Cooper. 'A strategic model of the U. S. brewing industry: 1952–1971', *American Management Journal*, **21**, 1978, pp. 592–610.

Harsanyi, J. 'Games with incomplete information played by 'Bayesian' Players. I: The basic model'. *Management Science*, **14**, 1967, pp. 159–182.

Hennart, J. F. 'A transactions cost theory of equity joint ventures', *Strategic Management Journal*, **9**, 1988, pp. 361–374.

Imel, B. and P. Helmberger, 'Estimation of structure–profit relationships with application to the food processing sector'. *American Economic Review*, **62**, 1971, pp. 614–627.

Jacobson, R. 'What *really* determines business performance? Unobservable effects —The key to profitability'. *Management Science*, **9**, 1990, pp. 74–85.

Jensen, M. 'Agency costs of free cash flow, corporate finance, and takeovers'. *American Economic Review*, **76**, 1986, pp. 323–329.

Jensen, M. 'The eclipse of the public corporation'. *Harvard Business Review*, **67**, 1989, pp. 61–74.

Joskow, P. L. 'Price adjustment in long-term contracts: The case of coal'. *Journal of Law and Economics*, **31**, 1988, pp. 47–83.

Karnani, A. 'Generic competitive strategies', *Strategic Management Journal*, **5**, 1985, pp. 367–380.

Klein, B. 'Transaction cost determinants of 'unfair' contractual arrangements'. *American Economic Review*, **70**, 1980, pp. 356–362.

Kogut, B. 'Joint ventures: Theoretical and empirical perspectives', *Strategic Management Journal*, **9**, 1988, pp. 319–332.

Kreps, D., P. Milgrom, J. Roberts and R. Wilson. 'Rational cooperation in the finitely repeated prisoners' dilemma'. *Journal of Economic Theory*, **27**, 1982, pp. 245–252.

Learned, E. P., C. R. Christensen, K. R. Andrews and W. D. Guth. *Business Policy: Text and Cases*. Richard D. Irwin, Homewood, IL, 1965.

Lieberman, M. 'The learning curve and pricing in the chemical processing industries'. *Rand Journal of Economics*, **15**, 1984, pp. 213–228.

Lippman, S. A. and R. P. Rumelt. 'Uncertain imitability: An analysis of interfirm differences in efficiency under competition'. *Bell Journal of Economics*, **13**, 1982, pp. 418–438.

McGee, J. and H. Thomas. 'Strategic groups: Theory, research and taxonomy', *Strategic Management Journal*, **7**, March–April 1986, pp. 141–160.

Masten, S. E. 'The organization of production: Evidence from the aerospace industry'. *Journal of Law, Economics, and Organization*, **4**, 1988, pp. 403–418.

Monteverde, K. and D. J. Teece. 'Supplier switching costs and vertical integration. *Bell Journal of Economics*, **13**, 1982, pp. 206–213.

Nash, J. 'The bargaining problem'. *Econometrica*, **18**, 1950, pp. 155–162.

Nelson, R. R. and S. G. Winter. *An Evolutionary Theory of Economic Change*, Harvard University Press, Cambridge, MA, 1982.

Pierson, F. *The Education of American Businessmen: A Study of University-College Programs in Business Administration*, McGraw-Hill, New York, 1959.

Pisano, G. 'The R&D boundaries of the firm'. *Administrative Science Quarterly*, **34**, 1990, pp. 153–176.

Porter, M. E. *Competitive Strategy: Techniques for Analyzing Industries and Competitors*, The Free Press, New York, 1980.

Porter, M. E. *Competitive Advantage*. The Free Press, New York, 1985.

Porter, M. E. *The Competitive Advantage of Nations*, The Free Press, New York, 1990.

Prahalad, C. K. and G. Hamel. 'The core competence of the corporation', *Harvard Business Review*, May–June 1990, pp. 79–91.

Rumelt, R. P. *Strategy, Structure, and Economic Performance*. Division of Research, Harvard Business School, 1974.

Rumelt, R. P. 'Towards a strategic theory of the firm'. In R. B. Lamb (ed.), *Competitive Strategic Management*. Prentice-Hall, Englewood Cliffs, NJ, 1984, pp. 556–570.

Rumelt, R. P. 'Theory, strategy, and entrepreneurship'. In D. J. Teece (ed.) *The Competitive Challenge: Strategies for Industrial Innovation and Renewal*, Ballinger, Cambridge, MA, 1987, pp. 137–158.

Rumelt, R. P., D. Schendel and D. J. Teece. (eds) *Fundamental Issues in Strategy*, Boston, MA, Harvard Business School Press, forthcoming (1992).

Rumelt, R. P. and R. Wensley. 'In search of the market share effect', *Proceedings of the Academy of Management*, August 1981, pp. 1–5.

Schendel, D. and R. Patton. 'A simultaneous equation model of corporate strategy', *Management Science*, **24**, 1978, pp. 1611–1621.

Scherer, F. M. *Industrial Market Structure and Economic Performance*, Rand McNally, Boston, MA, 1970, (2nd edn), 1980.

Selten, R. 'Spieltheoretische behandlung eines oligopolmodells mit nachfrägetragheit', *Zeitschrift für die gesamte Staatswissenschaft*, **12**, 1965, pp. 301–324.

Selznick, P. *Leadership in Administration*, Harper & Row, New York, 1957.

Shepherd, W. G. 'The elements of market structure', *Review of Economics and Statistics*, **54**, 1972, pp. 25–37.

Shepherd, W. G. *The Economics of Industrial Organization*, Prentice-Hall, Englewood Cliffs, NJ, 1979.

Simon, H. A. 'The business school: A problem in organizational design', *Journal of Management Studies*, **4**, 1967, pp. 1–16.

Simon, H. A. *The Sciences of the Artificial*, The MIT Press, Cambridge, MA, 1969.

Spence, M. *Market Signaling*, Harvard University Press, Cambridge, MA, 1974.

Spence, A. M. 'Investment strategy and growth in a new market', *Bell Journal of Economics*, **10**, 1979, pp. 1–19.

Teece, D. J. 'The market for know-how and the efficient transfer of technology'. *The Annals of the Academy of Political and Social Science*, 1981, pp. 81–96.

Teece, D. J. 'Towards an economic theory of the multiproduct firm'. *Journal of Economic Behavior and Organization*, **3**, 1982, pp. 39–63.

Teece, D. J., G. Pisano and A. Shuen. 'Firm capabilities, resources, and the concept of strategy', Working Paper, University of California, Berkeley, 1990.

von Neumann, J. and O. Morgenstern. *The Theory of Games and Economic Behavior*, John Wiley and Sons, New York, 1944.

Wernerfelt, B. 'A resource-based view of the firm', *Strategic Management Journal*, **5**, 1984a, pp. 171–180.

Wernerfelt, B. 'Consumers with differing reaction speeds, scale advantages, and industry structure'. *European Economic Review*, **24**, 1984b, pp. 257–270.

Wernerfelt, B. 'Brand loyalty and market equilibrium'. *Marketing Science*, **10**, 1991, pp. 229–246.

Wernerfelt, B. and C. A. Montgomery, 'Tobin's q and the importance of focus in firm performance', *American Economic Review*, **78**, March 1988, pp. 246–251.

Williamson, O. E. *Markets and Hierarchies: Analysis and Antitrust Implications*, The Free Press, New York, 1975.

Williamson, O. E. *The Economic Institutions of Capitalism: Firms, Markets, Relational Contracting*, The Free Press, New York, 1985.

21

TOWARDS A DYNAMIC
THEORY OF STRATEGY

Michael E. Porter

Source: *Strategic Management Journal* 12, Special Issue: Fundamental Research Issues in Strategy and Economics (1991): 95–117.

This paper reviews the progress of the strategy field towards developing a truly dynamic theory of strategy. It separates the theory of strategy into the causes of superior performance at a given period in time (termed the cross-sectional problem) and the dynamic process by which competitive positions are created (termed the longitudinal problem). The cross-sectional problem is logically prior to a consideration of dynamics, and better understood. The paper then reviews three promising streams of research that address the longitudinal problem. These still fall short of exposing the true origins of competitive success. One important category of these origins, the local environment in which a firm is based, is described. Many questions remain unanswered, however, and the paper concludes with challenges for future research.

Introduction

The reason why firms succeed or fail is perhaps the central question in strategy. It has preoccupied the strategy field since its inception four decades ago. The causes of firm success or failure encompass all the other questions that have been raised in this collection of essays. It is inextricably bound up in questions such as why firms differ, how they behave, how they choose strategies, and how they are managed. While much of the work in the field has been implicitly domestic, it has become increasingly apparent that any search for the causes of firm success must confront the reality of international competition, and the striking differences in the performance of firms in a given industry based in different nations.

Yet, the question of why firms succeed or fail raises a still broader question. Any effort to understand success must rest on an underlying theory of the firm and an associated theory of strategy. While there has been

410

considerable progress in developing frameworks that explain differing competitive success at any given point in time, our understanding of the dynamic processes by which firms perceive and ultimately attain superior market positions is far less developed. Worse yet, some recent research has tended to fragment or dichotomize the important parts of the problem rather than integrate them, as I will discuss later.

My purpose in this essay is to sketch the outlines of a dynamic theory of strategy. Drawing on recent research, some parts of the outline can be filled in. Many unanswered questions remain, however, and I will try to highlight some of the most important of them.

As a starting point for building a dynamic theory of strategy, we must step back from specific hypotheses or models and look broadly at the literature in both strategy and economics. I will begin by describing the traditional rationale for company success that emerged in the early literature on strategy. This reflected an orientation of the strategy field that has differed in important respects from that which has characterized most research in economics, arguably the discipline with the most obvious connection to strategy. The strategy field's traditional answer to why firms succeed or fail was also based on a set of largely implicit, but crucial assumptions about the nature of firms and the environment in which they operate.

Although these assumptions grew out of a deep understanding of practice, they raise profound challenges for a theory of strategy. I will outline some of the most important challenges and the trade-offs they raise in both theory and empirical testing. Taking these challenges as a starting point, I will then describe my own answers to the causes of superior firm performance at a given point in time, which can be framed as a chain of causality. This problem, which I term the cross-sectional problem, is logically prior to a consideration of dynamics and better understood. A body of theory which links firm characteristics to market outcomes must provide the foundation for any fully dynamic theory of strategy. Otherwise, dynamic processes that result in superior performance cannot be discriminated from those that create market positions or company skills that are worthless.

I will then move to the dynamic process by which positions are created, which I term the longitudinal problem. To understand the dynamics of strategy, we must move further back in the causality chain. I will explore three recent streams of research that begin to address it: game theoretic models, models of commitment under uncertainty, and the so-called resource-based view of the firm. While illuminating important characteristics of the dynamic processes by which advantage is created and sustained, however, this research still falls short of exposing the true origins of advantage, and I will discuss the reasons why. One important category of these origins, that has emerged from my recent work, is the nature of the 'local' environment in which the firm is based. We observe striking concentrations of successful firms in a particular industry in particular locations, which suggests that something about these locations is fundamental to creating and sustaining advantage. I will summarize some of my findings about these issues. Many questions remain unanswered in our search for a dynamic theory of strategy, however, and this essay will conclude with some challenges for future research.

Determinants of firm success: The early answers

Any discussion of the determinants of firm success must begin with a clear definition of what success means. For purposes of this essay, I will assume that firm success is manifested in attaining a competitive position or series of competitive positions that lead to superior and sustainable financial performance. Competitive position is measured, in this context, relative to the world's best rivals. Financial success derived from government intervention or from the closing of markets is excluded. A successful firm may 'spend' some of the fruits of its competitive position on meeting social objectives or enjoying slack. Why a firm might do this, however, is treated as a separate question.

To explain firm success, the early literature on strategy defined three essential conditions.[1] The first is that a company develop and implement an internally consistent set of goals and functional policies that collectively defined its position in the market. Strategy is seen as a way of integrating the activities of the diverse functional departments within a firm, including marketing, production, research and development, procurement, finance, and the like. An explicit and mutually reinforcing set of goals and functional policies is needed to counter the centrifugal forces that lead functional departments in separate directions. Strategy, in modern language, is a solution to the agency problem that arises because senior management cannot participate in or monitor all decisions and directly ensure the consistency of the myriad of individual actions and choices that make up a firm's ongoing activities.[2] If an overarching strategy is well understood throughout the organization, many actions are obviously ruled out and individuals can devise their own ways to contribute to the strategy that management would be hard pressed to replicate.

The second condition for success is that this internally consistent set of goals and policies aligns the firm's strengths and weaknesses with the external (industry) opportunities and threats. Strategy is the act of aligning a company and its environment. That environment, as well as the firm's own capabilities, are subject to change. Thus, the task of strategy is to maintain a dynamic, not a static balance.

The third condition for success is that a firm's strategy be centrally concerned with the creation and exploitation of its so-called 'distinctive competences'.[3] These are the unique strengths a firm possesses, which are seen as central to competitive success. The recent interest in the notion of firm resources or competences is interesting in light of this heritage.[4] I will return to this stream of work later.

The early strategy literature contained only broad principles governing firm success. It is instructive to understand why these authors, coming as they did from a heritage that stressed the administrative point of view and the study of in-depth cases, chose to approach the question in this way. There were two principal reasons. The first was that their orientation, and that of many in the strategy field, was to inform business practice. A theory that sought to explain part of a phenomena, but which left out important elements that precluded the offering of credible guidance for individual companies, was seen as inadequate to the task.

A second reason for the early formulation was the recognition, indeed the preoccupation, with the fact that competition was complex and highly situation-specific. The early scholars in the strategy field, especially those at Harvard, recognized that firms were composed of numerous functions and subfunctions, and that many diverse aspects of a firm and its environment could be important to success in particular cases. Indeed, it was the act of achieving consistency of action in the many parts of the firm that was seen as crucial to competitive success. Scholars such as Andrews saw each company as unique, with its own history, personality, capabilities, and set of current policies. Every industry was also unique, with its own circumstances and critical success factors. Finally, every period of time was seen as unique, because both companies and their environment were in a state of constant change. Yet firms were seen as possessing considerable ability to build on their strengths and overcome their weaknesses, latitude in influencing or altering their environment, and the ability to influence change over time, not merely respond to it. Indeed, the recognition that industry structure and other exogenous conditions affect performance and constrain choices had to await further work.

The challenges for a theory of strategy

The view of the world that guided the early efforts to formulate a theory of strategy raises profound challenges for research. The complexity, situation specificity, and changing nature of the firm and its environment strains conventional approaches to theory building and hypothesis testing. Indeed, the early research offered no theory for examining the firm and its competitive environment at all; instead strategy formulation took place through applying the broad principles of consistency and fit to individual case studies.

Four principal issues emerge from the nature of actual economic competition as one contemplates a theory of strategy:

Figure 1 Approaches to theory building.

Approach to theory building

First, there is a fundamental question about the approach to theory building that will most advance both knowledge and practice. The broad alternatives are represented in Figure 1.

On the one hand, one might approach the task of developing a theory of strategy by creating a wide range of situation-specific but rigorous (read mathematical) models of limited complexity. Each model abstracts the complexity of competition to isolate a few key variables whose interactions are examined in depth. The normative significance of each model depends on the fit between its assumptions and reality. No one model embodies or even approaches embodying all the variables of interest, and hence the applicability of any model's findings are almost inevitably restricted to a small subgroup of firms or industries whose characteristics fit the model's assumptions.

This approach to theory building has been characteristic of economics in the last few decades.[5] It has spawned a wide array of interesting models in both industrial organization and trade theory. These models provide clear conclusions, but it is well known that they are highly sensitive to the assumptions underlying them and to the concept of equilibrium that is employed. Another problem with this approach is that it is hard to integrate the many models into a general framework for approaching any situation, or even to make the findings of the various models consistent. While few economists would assert that this body of research in and of itself provides detailed advice for companies, these models, at their best, provide insights into complex situations that are hard to understand without them, which can inform the analysis of a particular company's situation.

Given the goal of informing practice, the style of research in the strategy field, including my own, has involved a very different approach.[6] To make progress, it was necessary to go beyond the broad principles in the early work and provide more structured and precise tools for understanding a firm's competitive environment and its relative position. Instead of models, however, the approach was to build frameworks. A framework, such as the competitive forces approach to analyzing industry structure, encompasses many variables and seeks to capture much of the complexity of actual competition. Frameworks identify the relevant variables and the questions which the user must answer in order to develop conclusions tailored to a particular industry and company. In this sense, they can be seen as almost expert systems. The theory embodied in frameworks is contained in the choice of included variables, the way variables are organized, the inter-actions among the variables, and the way in which alternative patterns of variables and company choices affect outcomes.

In frameworks, the equilibrium concept is imprecise. My own frameworks embody the notion of optimization, but no equilibrium in the normal sense of the word. Instead there is a continually evolving environment in which a perpetual competitive interaction between rivals takes place. In addition, all the interactions among the many variables in the frameworks cannot be rigorously drawn.[7] The frameworks, however, seek to help the analyst to better think through the problem by understanding the firm and its environ-ment and defining and selecting among the strategic alternatives available, no matter what the industry and starting position.

These two approaches to theory building are not mutually exclusive. Indeed, they should create a constructive tension with each other. Models are particularly valuable in ensuring logical consistency and exploring the subtle interactions involving a limited number of variables. Models should challenge the variables included in frameworks and assertions about their link to outcomes. Frameworks, in turn, should challenge models by highlighting omitted variables, the diversity of competitive situations, the range of actual strategy choices, and the extent to which important para-meters are not fixed but continually in flux. The need to inform practice has demanded that strategy researchers such as myself pursue the building of frameworks rather than restrict research only to theories that can be formally modelled. As long as the building of frameworks is based on in-depth empirical research, it has the potential to not only inform practice but to push the development of more rigorous theory.

Chain of causality

A second fundamental issue in creating a theory of strategy is where to focus the chain of causality. A stylized example will illustrate. We might observe a successful firm and find that its profitability is due to a low relative cost position compared to its rivals. But the firm's cost position is an outcome and not a cause. The question becomes: Why was the firm able to attain this cost position? Some typical answers might be that it is reaping economies of scale, or has moved aggressively down the learning curve. But again, the question becomes why? Some possible answers might include entering the industry early, or the firm's ability to organize itself particularly well for cost reduction. Once again, however, the question becomes why? And we could continue moving along such a chain of causality even further.

Another way of framing the same set of issues is as the problem of drawing the boundary between exogenous and endogenous variables. Should the environment be taken as given or not? Is the firm's scale an outcome or

415

a cause? And so on. The literature in both strategy and economics addresses many different points in this chain of causality. Indeed, many differences are less conflicts than theory positioned at different points in the chain, as we will see later.

Any theory of strategy must grapple with how far back in the chain of causality to go. The answer may well be different for different purposes. A theory that aims very early in the chain may be intractable or lack operationality. Also, aspects of the firm that are variable in the long run may be fixed or sticky in the short run. Conversely, a theory oriented later in the chain may be overly limiting and miss important possibilities.

Time horizon

A third challenge for theory is the time period over which to measure and understand competitive success. Should we be building theories for explaining success over two or three years, over decades, or over centuries? Clearly, the likelihood of significant environmental change will differ, as will the exogenous and endogenous variables. A theory that aims at explaining success over 50 years will focus on very different variables, almost inevitably more internal ones, than a theory that addresses success over one or two decades. This is because industry and competitive conditions are likely to be wholly different over a half century, placing greater emphasis on a firm's ability to transform itself. Time period relates closely to position in the chain of causality. Over long periods, theories aimed earlier in the chain would seem more appropriate.

Empirical testing

A final important issue is how to test theories of strategy empirically. Empirical testing is vital both for frameworks and models. Testing of models is difficult given the need to match their assumptions. Given the myriad of relevant variables in frameworks and the complex interactions among them over time, rigorous statistical testing of frameworks is also difficult, to say the least. In my own research, I pursued cross-sectional econometric studies in the 1970s but ultimately gave up as the complexity of the frameworks I was developing ran ahead of the available cross-sectional data. I was forced to turn to large numbers of in-depth case studies to identify significant variables, explore the relationships among them, and cope with industry and firm specificity in strategy choices.

The need for more and better empirical testing will be a chronic issue in dealing with this subject. Academic journals have traditionally not accepted or encouraged the deep examination of case studies, but the nature of strategy requires it. The greater use of case studies in both books and articles will be necessary for real progress at this stage in the field's development.

416

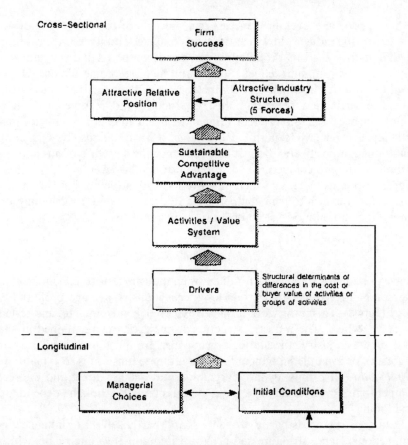

Figure 2 The determinants of success in distinct business.

Towards a theory of strategy

To explain the competitive success of firms, we need a theory of strategy which links environmental circumstances and firm behavior to market outcomes. My own research would suggest a chain of causality for doing so, outlined in Figure 2.

The basic unit of analysis in a theory of strategy must ultimately be a strategically distinct business or industry. While firms can redeploy or share resources, activities, and skills across different businesses, the competitive value of such actions can only be measured in terms of some set of rivals delivering a discrete product or service to some set of buyers. Meaningful approaches to corporate-level strategy for diversified firms must grow out of a deep understanding of how companies prosper in individual businesses, and the role of the corporate office and other sister business units in the process.

417

At the broadest level, firm success is a function of two areas: the attractiveness of the industry in which the firm competes and its relative position in that industry. Firm profitability can be decomposed into an industry effect and a positioning effect. Some firm successes come almost wholly from the industry in which they compete; most of their rivals are successful, too! The distinction between industry structure and relative position is important because, among other things, the firm can choose strategies that will improve one while harming the other. Firms' actions, by triggering imitation, can positively or negatively influence the structure of an industry without leading to competitive advantage. Ideally, however, a firm's actions trigger responses by rivals which improve industry structure but simultaneously allow the firm to gain competitive advantage because rivals' ability to imitate the chosen mode of competition is incomplete.

Industry structure

I have presented a framework for diagnosing industry structure, built around five competitive forces that erode long-term industry average profitability (see Figure 3). This framework has been explored, contributed to, and tested by many others. The industry structure framework can be applied at the level of the industry, the strategic group (or group of firms with similar strategies) or even the individual firm. Its ultimate function is to explain the *sustainability* of profits against bargaining and against direct and indirect competition. Profit differences *vis-à-vis* direct rivals, though, depend on positioning.

Industry structure is partly exogenous, and partly subject to influence by firm actions. Hence structure and firm position ultimately interrelate, which makes separating them a simplification though a useful one for analytical purposes. The firm's scope for influencing industry structure, and ways of modeling it, are a fruitful area for research. My focus here, however, is on relative position because this is where many of the most interesting questions for a dynamic theory of strategy lie.

Relative position

Holding industry structure constant, a successful firm is one with an attractive relative position. An attractive position is, of course, an outcome and not a cause. The question becomes why, or how did the attractive position arise? The answer must be that the firm possesses a sustainable competitive advantage *vis-à-vis* its rivals. To understand competitive advantage, however, we must decompose it. Competitive advantages can be divided into two basic types: lower cost than rivals, or the ability to differentiate and command a premium price that exceeds the extra cost of doing so. Any superior performing firm has achieved one type of advantage, the other,

418

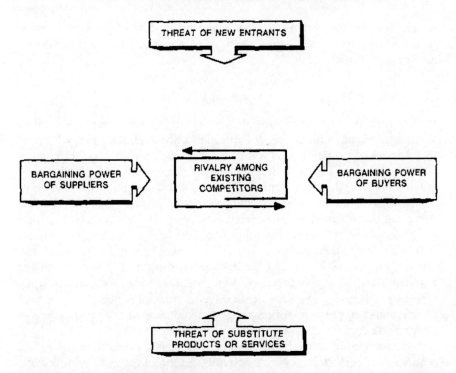

Figure 3 Five forces: Summary of key drivers.
'The five forces' (p. 4): From *Competitive strategy: Techniques for Analyzing Industries and Competitors* by Michael E. Porter. Copyright © 1980 by The Free Press, a Division of Macmillan, Inc. Reprinted by permission of the publisher.

or both. To say it another way, superior profitability can only logically arise from commanding a higher price than rivals or enjoying lower costs (including, at a lower level in the causality chain, asset costs).[8]

Competitive advantage cannot be examined independently of competitive scope. Scope encompasses a number of dimensions including the array of product and buyer segments served, the geographic locations in which the firm competes, its degree of vertical integration, and the extent of related businesses in which the firm has a coordinated strategy. Competitive advantage is attained within some scope, and the choice of scope is a central one in strategy. Scope choices can also influence industry structure.

These principles make it clear that the essence of strategy is choice. There is no one way to position within an industry, but many positions involving different choices of the type of advantage sought and the scope of the advantage. Several positions can be attractive in absolute terms, and a variety of positions may be relatively the most attractive depending on the firm's starting position. Choice is essential, however, because there are logical inconsistencies in pursuing several types of advantage or different scopes simultaneously. Also, the firm must stake out a distinct position from its rivals. Imitation almost ensures a lack of competitive advantage and hence mediocre performance.

Activities

If an attractive relative position results from possessing competitive advantage within some scope, the question once again becomes why does that happen? In order to address it, we must decompose cost, differentiation, and scope. This requires a theory which provides an elemental look at what firms do. My own approach to such a theory, and to the sources of competitive advantage, centers around *activities*. (Porter, 1985). A firm is a collection of discrete, but interrelated economic activities such as products being assembled, salespeople making sales visits, and orders being processed. A firm's strategy defines its configuration of activities and how they interrelate. Competitive advantage results from a firm's ability to perform the required activities at a collectively lower cost than rivals, or perform some activities in unique ways that create buyer value and hence allow the firm to command a premium price. The required mix and configuration of activities, in turn, is altered by competitive scope.

The basic unit of competitive advantage, then, is the discrete activity. The economics of performing discrete activities determines a firm's relative cost, not attributes of the firm as a whole. Similarly, it is discrete activities that create buyer value and hence differentiation.

The activities in a firm can be schematically arrayed in what I term the value chain and the value system (see Figure 4). The term value refers to customer value, from which the potential profit ultimately derives. A firm's strategy is manifested in the way in which it configures and links the many activities in its value chain relative to competitors. The value chain distinguishes centrally between activities that directly produce, market, and deliver the product and those that create or source inputs or factors (including planning and management) required to do so. Support activities, then, are integral to the process by which assets internal to the firm are acquired and accumulated.

Discrete activities are part of an interdependent system in which the cost or effectiveness of one activity can be affected by the way others are performed. I term these linkages. The cost of after-sale service, for example, is influenced by how product design, inspection, and installation are performed. Such linkages can extend outside the firm to encompass the activities of suppliers, channels, and buyers. The concept of linkages begins to operationalize the notion of internal consistency.

Activities involve human resources, purchased inputs, and a 'technology' for performing them, broadly defined to include organizational routines. Activities also use and create information.[9] Performing an activity requires

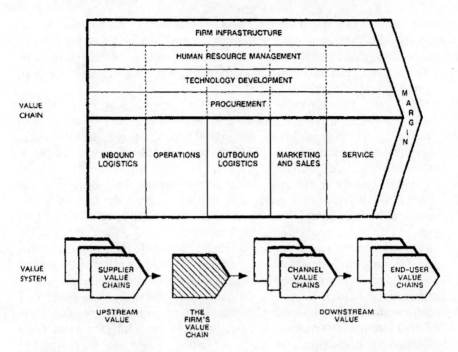

Figure 4 Value chain and value system.
'The Value Chain' (p. 37) and 'The Value System' (p. 35): From *Competitive Advantage: Creating and Sustaining Superior Performance* by Michael E. Porter. Copyright © 1985 by Michael E. Porter. Reprinted by permission of The Free Press, a Division of Macmillan, Inc.

tangible and intangible assets that are *internal* to the firm, such as physical and often financial assets (e.g. working capital) as well as intangible assets embodied in human resources and technology. Performing an activity, or a group of linked activities, also creates assets in the form of skills, organizational routines, and knowledge. While the tangible assets normally depreciate, the intangible assets involved in performing activities can cumulate over time (provided the environment remains relatively stable). These become an important part of corporate balance sheets, as many writers have stressed.[10]

Performing activities can also create assets *external* to the firm. Some are tangible assets such as contracts. Most, however, are intangible assets such as brand images, relationships, and networks. These external assets then feed back to influence the cost or effectiveness of performing activities on an ongoing basis. A strong brand reputation because of cumulative past advertising, for example, can lower the cost of current advertising or make a given rate of spending more effective. Without reinvestment, however, both the external and internal intangible assets attached to activities or groups of activities depreciate. Maintaining or enhancing these assets demands reinvestment through performing activities. Both the external and internal

421

assets are not valuable in and of themselves, however, but because they fit industry structure and a particular strategy. Activities performed poorly, or inconsistently with buyer needs, can create liabilities not assets. At the same time, technological and other industry changes can nullify assets or turn them into liabilities.

The value chain provides a template for understanding cost position, because activities are the elemental unit of cost behavior.[11] The move to activity-based costing is a manifestation of this perspective.[12] The value chain also provides a means to systematically understand the sources of buyer value and hence differentiation. Buyer value is created when a firm lowers its buyer's cost or enhances its buyer's performance. This, in turn, is the result of the ways a firm's product as well as its other activities affect the value chain of the buyer. Firms must not only create value, but 'signal' that they will do so, through their sales forces and other activities. Households and individual consumers have value chains, just as do industrial or institutional buyers. By understanding how households perform activities related to a product (e.g. procurement, storage, use, disposal, etc.), the sources of differentiation can be better understood. Finally, the value chain provides a tool for analyzing the added costs that differentiating may require. Only differentiation that results in a price premium exceeding the extra costs of delivering it results in superior performance.

Drivers

If competitive advantage grows out of discrete activities, however, we once again confront the question, 'why?' Why are some firms able to perform particular activities at lower cost or in ways that create superior value than others? My answer to this question is the concept of *drivers*. These are stuctural determinants of differences among competitors in the cost or buyer of activities or group of activities. The most important drivers of competitive advantage in an activity include its scale, cumulative learning in the activity, linkages between the activity and others, the ability to share the activity with other business units, the pattern of capacity utilization in the activity over the relevant cycle, the activity's location, the timing of investment choices in the activity, the extent of vertical integration in performing the activity, institutional factors affecting how the activity is performed such as government regulation, and the firm's policy choices about how to configure the activity independent of other drivers. The same set of drivers determines both relative cost and differentiation. The mix and significance of individual drivers varies by activity, by firm, and by industry.

Moving to the level of drivers also sheds light on the important question of sustainability. The sustainability of competitive advantage *vis-à-vis* rivals depends on the number of competitive advantages in the value chain and, especially, the particular drivers underlying each one. The durability of an advantage based on learning, for example, depends on the ability to keep the learning proprietary, while the sustainability of advantages due to timing of factor positions depends on factor market imperfections.

Drivers constitute the underlying sources of competitive advantage, and make competitive advantage operational. For example, brand reputation is a typical competitive advantage identified by managers. But brand reputation may be a source of cost advantage (less need for marketing) in some cases and a source of differentiation (and a premium price) in others. The substantive implications are very different depending on which it is. Yet, brand reputation is an outcome, not a cause. The real question is how and why brand reputation is an advantage. To understand this, one must move to the level of drivers. For example, timing may have allowed the firm to begin advertising early and hence to develop a reputation uncluttered by the competing claims of rivals. The reputation from cumulative advertising then allows the firm to spend less on current advertising or to spend at a comparable rate to rivals but command a premium price. Alternatively, greater current company sales volume may lead to efficiencies in advertising that allow the firm to enjoy a superior reputation while spending at a rate comparable to its rivals. Only by moving to the level of underlying drivers can the true sources of competitive advantage be identified. Tying advantage to specific activities/drivers is necessary to operationalize the notion in practice.

The value chain also provides the basic architecture for analyzing international strategy and diversification, both fundamentally questions of competitive scope. The central issue in international strategy involves the spread of activities to other countries (configuration) and the integration of dispersed activities (coordination) (Porter, 1986). In corporate-level strategy for diversified firms, the central issue is how firms can share activities across businesses, or share proprietary skills in how to perform particular activities though the value chains of business units are distinct (Porter, 1987).

The origins of competitive advantage

This set of frameworks aims to build a careful link between the underlying choices a firm makes in terms of its industry, positioning, and configuration of activities and market outcomes. The proper choices depend on a firm's existing position, which can be evaluated systematically via its value chain and drivers. The best strategy also depends on the capabilities and likely behavior of rivals, which can also be assessed through their value chains and drivers. Finally, strategy depends on a sophisticated understanding of industry structure.

Firms inherit positions that constrain and shape their choices, but do not determine them. They have considerable latitude in reconfiguring the value chain with which they compete, expanding or contracting their competitive scope, and influencing important dimensions of their industry environment. Strategy is not a race to occupy one desirable position, but a more textured problem in which many positions can be chosen or created. Success requires the choice of a relatively attractive position given industry structure, the firm's circumstances and the positions of competitors. It also requires bringing all the firm's activities into consistency with the chosen position.

While these frameworks have pushed a considerable distance backward along the chain of causality, the focus thus far has been on what might be termed the *cross-sectional* problem. What makes some industries, and some positions within them, more attractive than others? What makes particular competitors advantaged or disadvantaged? What specific activities and drivers underlie the superior positions?

But in answering these questions, we again confront the question of causality. Why were particular firms able to get into the advantaged positions and sustain/or fail to sustain them? This is what might be termed the longitudinal problem, which requires crossing the dotted line on Figure 2.[13]

The frameworks for addressing the cross-sectional problem are agnostic as to the process by which the superior positions were attained, and largely unaffected by it. Whether the strategy was consciously chosen, happenstance, the result of incremental steps, or driven by one major decision does not itself affect the attractiveness of the position independently of the activities and drivers on which it rests. Similarly, the past process by which firms accumulated their strengths and capabilities is not, in and of itself, decisive. The cross-sectional frameworks address the choice of strategy given whatever array of capabilities the firm and its rivals possess at a point in time and can feasibly develop in the future. The effort by some to dichotomize process and substance is simply incorrect.[14] Both are necessary and important to understand.

The cross-sectional problem is also logically prior. Without a rather specific understanding of what underpins a desirable position, it is virtually impossible to deal analytically with the process of getting there. Strategy becomes an aimless process in which luck determines the winners.

Assuming an understanding of the cross-sectional problem, however, the longitudinal problem takes on prime importance. Why do some firms achieve favorable positions *vis-à-vis* the drivers in the value chain? Why do some firms gain scale advantages? Why do some firms move early, or late, whichever leads to advantage? Why do some firms conceive of and implement superior configurations of activities or spot entirely new and desirable competitive positions?

Logically, there are two answers. The first is *initial conditions*. Firms may have pre-existing reputations, skills, and in-place activities as a result of their history. These initial conditions may reside within an individual firm or, as I will discuss later, in the environment in which the firm is based. Initial conditions clearly influence feasible choices as well as constrain them.[15]

The second reason that firms might achieve favorable positions is through pure *managerial choices*, or choices independent of initial conditions, putting aside for the moment the process by which the choices were made. These managerial choices, which are made under uncertainty about the future, define the firm's concept for competing (positioning), its configuration of activities, and the supporting investments in assets and skills. Pure managerial choices lead to the assembly or creation of the particular skills and resources required to carry out the new strategy.

Numerous case studies illustrate vividly that highly successful firms often arise out of creative acts where there were few initial strengths. Wal-Mart decided to locate in small- and medium-sized towns and configure its logistical system in a particular way because it had a better idea, not because of any compelling pre-existing strengths. If anything, its choices were shaped more by what it did not possess than what it did. The same could be said about Federal Express, Apple Computer, Crown Cork and Seal, and many other companies. American Airlines developed its MIS systems almost by accident. Its frequent flyer program was partly a function of the existence of its MIS system, but other airlines had these as well. American's management was simply more creative.

Many strategies clearly reflect some combination of initial conditions and creative choice. The balance between the influence of initial conditions and acts of pure managerial choice varies by company and industry. Yet there may well be a tendency, for a variety of reasons to be discussed later, to overstate the role of initial conditions.

Lying behind all initial conditions internal to the firm were earlier managerial choices. The skills and market position a firm has built today are the result of past choices about how to configure activities and what skills to create or acquire. Some of these choices, as Ghemawat's (1991) work among others had emphasized, involve hard-to-reverse commitments down certain paths (path dependency). Earlier choices, which have led to the current pool of internal skills and assets, are a reflection of the external environment surrounding the firm at the time. The earlier one pushes back in the chain of causality, the more it seems that successive managerial choices and initial conditions *external* to the firm govern outcomes.

The importance of managerial choice is also highlighted by the cross-sectional problem. Whatever configuration of activities and skills a firm has inherited may or may not be competitively valuable. Simply having pools of skills, knowledge, or other resources is not in and of itself a guarantee of success. They must be the right ones. If managers can understand their competitive environment and the sources of competitive advantages, they can better search creatively for favorable positions that are different from competitors', assemble the needed skills and assets, configure the value chain appropriately, and put in place supportive organizational routines and a culture which reinforces the required internal behavior. The most successful firms are notable in employing imagination to define a *new* position, or find *new* value in whatever starting position they have.

Towards a dynamic theory

How, then, do we make progress towards a truly dynamic theory of strategy? Scholars, in both strategy, organizational behavior, and economics, sensing this as the frontier question, have made some headway. There are three promising lines of enquiry that have been explored in recent years. Each addresses important questions, though focusing on a somewhat different aspect of the problem.

Game theoretical models

The first line of inquiry is the proliferation of game theoretic models of competitive interaction, referred to earlier, which seek to understand the equilibrium consequences of patterns of choices by competitors over a variety of strategic variables such as capacity and R&D. Since this literature is reviewed elsewhere in this volume,[16] the treatment here can be brief. The central concern of these models is to understand the conditions that lead to mutually consistent equilibria and the nature of these equilibria. Each model is restricted to one or a few variables, and the environment (technology, products, preferences, etc.) is assumed fixed except for the variables examined. Given this structure, timing plays a central role in determing outcomes. With a frame of reference in which these assumptions are plausible, Shapiro (1989) terms this literature a theory of business strategy.

These models have helped us understand better the logical consequences of choices over some important strategy variables. In particular, these models highlight the importance of information and beliefs about competitive reaction and the conditions required for a set of internally consistent choices among rivals.

Yet, this line of work stops short of a dynamic theory of strategy. By concentrating sequentially on small numbers of variables, the models fail to capture the simultaneous choices over many variables that characterize most industries. The models force a homogeneity of strategies. Yet it is the trade-offs and interactions involved in configuring the entire set of activities in the value chain that define distinct competitive positions. Finally, the models hold fixed many variables that we know are changing. Ironically, these models explore the dynamics of a largely static world. (The papers by Saloner, Camerer and Postrel in this volume raise additional useful questions.)

Commitment and uncertainty

Another body of work is beginning to emerge on the problem of making irreversible commitments under uncertainty. Ghemawat's recent book (1991) is a notable example. The notion here is that strategy is manifested in a relatively few investment decisions that are hard to reverse, and which tend to define choices in other areas of the firm. These commitments must be made under uncertainty. Ghemawat highlights the importance of such choices, and argues that they should consume much of the attention in strategy analyses. He posits that analysis of such decisions must begin with cross-sectional frameworks. In choosing among feasible positions, however. Ghemawat stresses the need to carefully examine their sustainability and the influence of uncertainty in choosing among them. He brings a broader perspective to bear on sustainability than is present in the game theory models.

Related to Ghemawat's research is work that seeks to define ways of understanding the uncertainties a firm faces, and the alternative ways it can be addressed in strategy choices. The scenario technique for organizing and bounding uncertainty has received much attention.[17] More recently, taxonomies have begun to emerge which atternpt to categorize the ways in which firms can respond to uncertainty.[18] In addition, Teisberg (1991b) begins to explore the biases and heuristics in decisionmaking in complex and uncertain circumstances that distort strategy choices, drawing on work in behavioral decision analysis and cognitive psychology.

This emerging stream of work emphasizes the lumpiness of strategy choices and the importance of uncertainty in making them. It sheds important light on how to approach discrete investment decisions from a rich strategic perspective. This comes at the price, however, of a focus on large, discrete, sequential investments rather than the simultaneous set of choices throughout the value chain that define a firm's competitive position. Like the game theoretic models, the environment is taken as relatively stable (though uncertain) so that commitments have long-lived consequences and the possibilities for reconfiguring the value chain are limited. This approach tends to stress the value of flexibility in dealing with change rather than the capacity to rapidly improve and innovate to nullify or overcome it. By focusing on discrete choices, the discretion a firm has to shape its environment, respond to environmental changes, or define entirely new positions is implicitly limited or not operationalized by most treatments.[19]

The resource-based view

A third body of research in search of the origins of competitive advantage is the so-called resource-based view of the firm.[20] Closely related to the resource-based view is the notion of 'core competences' and treatments that stress intangible assets. Since this literature is more prominent and more extensive than that on commitment/uncertainty, it deserves a more detailed treatment.

Of the three literatures, the resource-based view is the most introspective and centered on the firm itself. The argument is that the origins of competitive advantage are valuable resources (or competences) that firms possess, which are often intangible assets such as skills, reputation, and the like. These resources are seen as relatively immobile, and as strengths to be nurtured and which should guide the choice of strategy. The implicit focus of much of this literature is on the underpinnings of successful diversification. It is, of course, essential when diversifying to understand a firm's distinctive strengths (remember Andrews).

The resource-based view has been proposed as an alternative theory of strategy.[21] What is really unique about a firm, so the argument goes, is its bundle of resources. It is factor market impediments, then, rather than product market circumstances that define success. The role of internal resources is an important insight for economic modelers, though less novel a notion for strategy researchers.

The promise of the resource view for the strategy field is the effort to address the longitudinal problem, or the conditions that allow firms to achieve and sustain favorable competitive positions over time. As with the other literatures, however, more work remains to be done. At its worst, the resource-based view is circular. Successful firms are successful because they have unique resources. They should nurture these resources to be successful.[22] But what is a unique resource? What makes it valuable? Why was a firm able to create or acquire it? Why does the original owner or current holder of the resource not bid the value away? What allows a resource to retain its value in the future? There is once again a chain of causality, that this literature is just beginning to unravel.

Some authors have begun to deal with these questions by seeking to specify the conditions under which resources are valuable. Valuable resources are those that are superior in use, hard to imitate, difficult to substitute for, and more valuable within the firm than outside. Yet valuable resources, in order to yield profits to the firm, have been acquired for less than their intrinsic value due to imperfections in input markets, which Barney (1986) argues are usually due to informational asymmetries (read better managerial choices) or luck.

Yet, the resource-based view cannot be an alternative theory of strategy. It cannot be separated from the cross-sectional determinants of competitive advantage or, for that matter, from the conception of a firm as a collection of activities. Stress on resources must complement, not substitute for, stress on market positions.[23]

Resources are not valuable in and of themselves, but because they allow firms to perform activities that create advantages in particular markets. Resources are only meaningful in the context of performing certain activities to achieve certain competitive advantages. The competitive value of resources can be enhanced or eliminated by changes in technology, competitor behavior, or buyer needs which an inward focus on resources will overlook. More reliable Japanese products, for example, degraded the value of Xerox's copier service organization. The immobility of resources, then, is as likely to be a risk as a source of strength. For every firm with resources that convey advantage, there will be another (and perhaps many others) whose bundle resources impeded change or proved to be a liability in light of environmental changes.

Competitive advantage derives from more than just resources. Scale, sharing across activities, an optimal degree of integration, and other drivers have independent influences unless 'resources' are defined so broadly as to strain credibility. It is the collective advantage gained from all sources that determines relative performance.

The conditions which make a resource valuable bear a strong resemblance to industry structure. Bargaining power of suppliers refers to input markets, substitutability to the threat of substitution, and imitability to barriers to entry/mobility. The bargaining power of buyers, and the dissipation of resource rents through rivalry via price cutting or competition from alternative resource bundles, represent additional threats to the profitability of firms.

The connection between resources and activities is even more fundamental, however, because resources represent an inherently intermediate position in the chain of causality. Resources arise either from performing activities over time, acquiring them from outside, or some combination of the two. Both reflect prior managerial choices. Performing an activity or group of linked activities over time creates internal skills and routines which accumulate. It also can create external assets. A firm's reputation, for example, is a function of the history of its marketing and customer service activities among other things. Both internal and external assets depreciate, however, unless they are reinvigorated through continuing to perform activites. The rate of depreciation appears to vary widely across different types of assets, and can be rapid. Firms, then, have accumulated differing resources because of differing strategies and configuration of activities. Resources and activities are, in a sense, duals of each other.[24]

Resources, then, are intermediate between activities and advantage. An explicit link between resources and activities, along with the clear distinction between internal and external resources that was drawn earlier, is necessary to carefully define a resource in the first place. Some firm attributes termed resources are activities—such as sales forces or R&D organizations. A second and more appropriate category of resources is skills, organizational routines, or other assets attached to particular activities or groups of interrelated activities.

The concept of activity drivers allows more precision in defining how resources were created. Some skills and routines emerge because of learning over time. This learning is a reflection of past strategy choices which have defined how activities are configured. Other resources were obtained through well-timed factor purchases (timing). Still others are the result of the ability to share across units. In turn, the resource view adds an important dimension to the concepts of activities and drivers. Underlying the ability to link activities or share them across business units, for example, are organizational skills and routines that represent important assets.

A final category of resources is external assets such as reputation and relationships.[25] These are normally created through performing activities over time. Recognizing these assets, and their link to the ongoing cost or differentiation of activities, is another valuable contribution of the resource view. The existence of such assets is implicit in the concept of drivers but not well developed.

All this still leaves unanswered the question, however, of the origins of competitive advantage. Why can valuable resources be created and sustained? Interestingly, the requirement of imperfect factor markets points strongly in the direction of managerial choice, and goes against the primacy of prior resources (initial conditions) in determining competitive advantage.

Resources whose value is obvious are bid up in value. Hence the presence of resources/activities within the firm that are rent-yielding is likely to reflect past managerial choices to assemble resources in unique ways, combine particular resources in a consistent way with many others, pursue new undiscovered market positions, or create resources internally. This allows resources to be acquired cheaply and avoids the bargaining away of their value to employees. Few resources begin as inherently scarce. Their scarcity is created through choice. Current managerial choices, in turn, allow the innovative assembly of new resources and the rendering obsolete of prior ones.

The resource-based view will have the greatest significance in environments where change is incremental, the number of strategic variables and combinations is limited, so that a few scarce resources can govern outcomes, and the time period is short to intermediate term so that managerial choices can replicate or offset resource stocks. The greatest value of the resource view will be in assessing opportunities for diversification, provided the resource and activity views are integrated.[26] A resource-based view of diversification that defines resources broadly, however, runs the risk of justifying the sort of unrelated diversification that was so disastrous in the 1970s and 1980s.

The origins of the origins

We are left still short of a dynamic theory of strategy, though we are beginning to learn about the subprocesses involved. In order to understand why firms choose and successfully implement the right strategies, and why their internal activities and assets are what they are, at least four important issues must be addressed.

First, a theory must deal simultaneously with both the firm itself as well as the industry and broader environment in which it operates. The environment both constrains and influences outcomes, which the more introspective resource view neglects. Second, a theory must allow centrally for exogenous change, in areas such as buyer needs, technology, and input markets. If there is little exogenous change, the choice of strategy can be viewed as a once-and-for-all game and the initial stock of (properly defined) resources can be crucial. In a world where exogenous change is rapid or relatively continuous, however, the analytical problem becomes far more complicated. The value of past resources is continually depreciated or even rendered negative. The choice of strategy is a series of ever-changing games in which the position in one game can influence, but does not determine, the position in the next one. Case after case illustrates that the leaders in one generation of products often fail to lead in the next.

Third, a theory must provide latitude to the firm not only to choose among well-defined options but to create new ones. The firm cannot be seen only as optimizing within tight constraints, but as having the ability to shift the constraints through creative strategy choices, other innovative activity, and the assembly of skills and other needed capabilities. There are alternative strategies open. The extent to which the environment shapes initial conditions and choice, in contrast to idiosyncratic, creative decision-making process within the firm is a fundamental question.

A final issue that cuts across the others is the role of historical accident or chance. There is a growing belief that historical accidents influence competitive outcomes. Some of what economists term historical accidents may simply be good strategy choices, or reflect so far unmeasured aspects of the environment. There are often reasons why firms are 'lucky', as I will stress below. Be that as it may, the extent of randomness in competition, and the role of true luck, has an important influence on how one develops a theory of strategy.

Origins within the firm

How then, do we explain good strategic choices and the ability to carry them out? One view is that since the number of variables is substantial and environmental change is continuous and unpredictable, the problem is not selecting good strategies but creating a flexible organization that learns and is able to continually redefine its strategy. The resource view, taken to an unhealthy extreme, is sometimes argued as encompassing this position. The critical resources are the capacity for learning and adaptation.

The problem with this notion is its collision with empirical reality. Most successful organizations improve but do not change strategy very often.[27] They gain advantage from new insights into competition and from consistent refinement of their ability to implement a stable overall

431

strategy (e.g. differentiation) though its details are continually evolving and improving.

Another view of the origins of advantage is that it lies in the ability to make good strategy choices and implement them. While this can happen by chance, the odds are elevated by better information and careful analysis. Once a choice is made, the successful organization is one that can bring all its activities into consistency with the strategy and rapidly accumulate the necessary activities and resources. New choices are made as the environment changes or as accumulating activities and resources open up new options. But, it must be said, a prominent role for choice and capacity for implementation still begs the question of why some firms are better at it than others.

The environment as the origin of advantage

Instead of solely within the firm, the true origin of competitive advantage may be the proximate or local environment in which a firm is based. The proximate environment will define many of the input (factor) markets the firm has to draw on, the information that guides strategic choices, and the incentives and pressures on firms to both innovate and accumulate skills or resources over time. Competitive advantage, then, may reside as much in the environment as in an individual firm. The environment shapes how activities are configured, which resources can be assembled uniquely, and what commitments can be made successfully.

This richer view of the role of the environment has emerged from my study of the causes of international competitive success in a large sample of industries in 10 leading trading nations. This line of work emerged from a puzzle. After having written about global strategy, and the ability of firms to transcend national markets, I observed that competitive advantage in particular industries was often strongly concentrated in one or two countries, often with several if not many successful home-based competitors. These local rivals pursue different strategies and push each other to innovate and improve much more rapidly than foreign rivals, which allows them to penetrate and prosper in foreign markets. The concentration of successful competitors was particularly pronounced if one examined strategically distinct industry segments rather than broad aggregates, and if one excludes cases where firms were not truly successful but merely surviving or sheltered by government intervention. While the focus of the research was on the role of the national environment, it was also clear that successful firms were also geographically concentrated *within* nations. The same theoretical framework can be used to help explain the concentration of success in nations, regions within nations, or even cities. It also seems possible to extend it to help explain why one particular firm outperforms others.

The starting point for the theory is that environmental change is relentless and firms, through innovation, have considerable latitude in both influencing their environment and responding to it. Firms create and sustain competitive advantage because of the capacity to continuously improve, innovate, and upgrade their competitive advantages over time. Upgrading is the process of shifting advantages throughout the value chain to more sophisticated types, and employing higher levels of skill and technology. Successful firms are those that improve and innovate in ways that are valued not only at home but elsewhere. Competitive success is enhanced by moving early in each product or process generation, provided that movement is along a path that reflects evolving technology and buyer needs, and that early movers subsequently upgrade their positions rather than rest on them. In this view, firms have considerable discretion in relaxing external and internal constraints.

These imperatives of competitive advantage, however, collide with the organizational tendencies of firms. Firms value stability, and change is difficult and unsettling. Strong external or environmental influences are often essential in overcoming these tendencies.

Environmental determinants of innovation and upgrading

Four broad attributes of the proximate environment of a firm have the greatest influence on its ability to innovate and upgrade, illustrated in Figure 5. These attributes, which I collectively term the diamond, shape the information firms have available to perceive opportunities, the pool of inputs, skills and knowledge they can draw on, the goals that condition

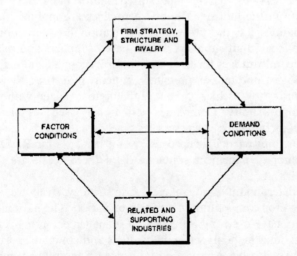

Figure 5 Determinants of national competitive advantage.
'Determinants of national competitive advantage' (p. 72): From *The Competitive Advantage of Nations* by Michael E. Porter. Copyright © 1990 by Michael E. Porter. Reprinted by permission of The Free Press, a Division of Macmillan, Inc.

investment, and the pressures on firms to act. The environment is important in providing the initial insight that underpins competitive advantage, the inputs needed to act on it, and to accumulate knowledge and skills over time, and the forces needed to keep progressing.

The most important factors of production are highly specialized factors tailored to the needs of particular industries. Generalized factor pools are either readily available or easy to source through global networks. Specialized local factor pools support the most rapid accumulation of skill and the greatest rate of innovation. Generic technology is readily sourced from distant suppliers, but transfer of know-how benefits from proximity. Specialized factors are almost always created through private and social investments. The presence of unique institutional mechanisms for creating them in particular industries is an important determinant of competitive success. Selective disadvantages in the more basic factors (e.g. unskilled labor, natural resources) are, paradoxically, often a source of advantage. They break dependence on factor costs and trigger innovation and upgrading.

Home demand is important more for its character than its size. Home demand plays a disproportionate role in influencing the perception of buyer needs and the capacity of firms to improve products and services over time. Sophisticated and/or especially demanding home customers often stimulate competitive success, as do home market needs that anticipate those elsewhere.

Competitive advantage is also strongly influenced by the presence of home-based suppliers and related industries in those products, components, machines, or services that are specialized and/or integral to the process of innovation in the industry. Inputs themselves are mobile, but there are local externalities for the process of innovation in interactions between the firm and local input suppliers. Home-based suppliers and related industries provide advantages in terms of information, signalling, access to new technologies, and market pressures. In many industries, the scarce technology is know-how, which can be difficult to transfer without cultural and physical proximity. Companies with home-based suppliers have the opportunity to influence their suppliers' technical efforts, help establish specifications to fit particular needs, serve for test sites for R&D work, and maintain senior management contact. All of these accelerate the pace of innovation.

The final determinant of advantage is firm strategy, structure, and rivalry, or the context for competition in a region or nation. The national and local environments have a strong influence on management practices, forms of organization, and the goals set by individuals and companies. The presence of local rivalry also has a profound influence on the rate of improvement, innovation, and ultimate success in an industry. Local rivals provide a greater stimulus to upgrading than foreign rivals. Proximity speeds information flow and improves incentives to compete. The presence of domestic competitors negates basic factor advantages and forces firms to develop higher order and more sustainable advantages. Actual rivalry provides a greater stimulus than potential rivalry. Intense local rivalry may hold down profits in the home market but spurs advantages that allow attractive profits (contingent on overall industry structure) in global markets.

Local rivalry also feeds back to improve other parts of the diamond. It overcomes monopsony-based impediments to the development of specialized suppliers, stimulates greater investments in specialized factors such as university programs and specialized infrastructure, helps to upgrade local demand, and so on.

There is a role for true chance events and historical accidents in the process by which competitive advantage is created, an issue which I raised earlier. However, historical accidents are less common than upon first impression. What appear to be accidents are really events driven by conditions in the diamond. Also, the role of accidents cannot be seen independently of more stable aspects of the local or national environment. True accidents rarely result in competitive industries unless other favorable conditions in the diamond are present. Similarly, accidents that simultaneously occur in different locations result in a competitive firm in that location with the most favorable diamond.

There are many cases where a company founded in one location, through an act of pure entrepreneurship, relocated its operations to another location or even to another country because that new location offered a better setting in which to nurture or reap the rewards of that innovation. The pilgrimage of aspiring actors and actresses to Hollywood is simply one example of how ideas and talent flow to the environment in which they can command the highest returns. The ability to command the highest returns depends on the simultaneous presence of unusual local demand, related industries, active rivals bidding, and other aspects of the diamond.

A final influence on the environment for competitive advantage is government. The role of government policy is best understood by looking at how it influences the diamond. Government at all levels can improve or impede national advantage through its investments in factor creation, through its influence on the goals of individuals and firms, through its role as a buyer or influencer of buyer needs, through its competition policies, and through its role in related and supporting industries, among other ways. Government plays an important part in shaping the pressures, incentives, and capabilities of the nation's firms.

Government's proper role is as a catalyst and challenger. It is to encourage, or even push, companies to raise their aspirations and move to higher levels of competitive performance, even though this process may be unpleasant and difficult. Government plays a role that is inherently partial, and that succeeds only when working in tandem with favorable underlying conditions in the diamond. Government policies that succeed are those that create an environment in which companies can gain competitive advantage rather than those that involve government directly in the process. (It is an indirect, rather than direct, role).

The diamond as a dynamic system

These aspects of the local environment constitute a dynamic system. This character of the environment bears centrally on the firm processes that give rise to advantage. The effect of one determinant depends on the state of others. The presence of sophisticated and demanding buyers, for example, will not result in advanced products or production processes unless the quality of human resources enables firms to respond to buyer needs. There must also be a climate that supports sustained investment to fund the development of these products and processes. Similarly, having selective disadvantages in basic factors (e.g. higher labor, energy, or raw material costs) will not spur innovation and upgrading unless there is an environment of vigorous competition among firms to trigger innovation in people, products, and processes. It is this contingent relationship that explains why, for example, a selective factor disadvantage stimulates innovation in one country while hastening decline in another.

The parts of the diamond are also mutually reinforcing. The development of specialized supporting industries, for example, tends to increase the supply of specialized factors. Vigorous domestic rivalry stimulates the development of unique pools of specialized factors. This is particularly likely if the rivals are all located in one city or region. The University of California at Davis, for example, has become the world's leading center for wine-making research, working closely with the California wine industry. Active local rivalry also upgrades home demand through educating buyers and providing choice, and promotes the formation of related and supported industries. Japan's world-leading group of semiconductor producers, for example, has spawned world-leading Japanese semiconductor equipment manufacturers.[28]

The effects can work in all directions, and causality can become blurred over time. Sometimes world-class suppliers become new entrants in the industry they have been supplying. Or highly sophisticated buyers may enter a supplier industry, particularly when they have relevant skills and view the upstream industry as strategic. In the case of the Japanese robotics industry, for example, Matsushita and Kawasaki originally designed robots for internal use before selling them to others.

The diamond also bears centrally on a nation's ability to *attract* factors of production, rather than merely serve as a location for them. This represents a final form of mutual reinforcement. Mobile factors, particularly ideas and highly skilled individuals, are becoming increasingly important to international competitiveness. Mobile factors tend to be drawn to the location where they can achieve the greatest productivity, because that is where they can obtain the highest returns. The theory outlined above, because it focuses on the determinants of productivity, also explains the attraction of mobile factors. The same features that make a nation an attractive home base also help it attract mobile factors.

The national and local environment for competing in a particular industry itself evolves in a dynamic process. The environment is created over time through the mutual reinforcement of the determinants. It begins with an inheritance drawn from other industries and history, and exists amid a set of local institutions, values, and attitudes. The mutual reinforcement of the determinants, which reflect in part the actions of firms themselves, build up the environment over time. As this process proceeds, causality becomes blurred.

In industries with modest levels of skill and technology, firms can gain advantage solely on the basis of factor advantages such as cheap labor or abundant raw materials. Such advantages are notoriously unstable, however, in a world of globalization, technological change, and rapid substitution. Competitive advantage in more sophisticated industries and industry segments, on the other hand, rarely results from strength in a single determinant. Sustained success in these industries and segments usually requires the interaction of favorable conditions in several of the determinants and at least parity in the others. This is because advantages in various parts of the diamond are self-reinforcing.

It is thus the juxtaposition of advantages throughout the diamond in one location that leads to competitive success, far more than the presence of any single advantage no matter how compelling. The firm's home base, which consists of that group of activities most centrally involved in the process of innovation and learning, must be located in the same place to allow the internal coordination and contact with the local environment that is necessary for rapid progress. The ability of a firm to progress rapidly and appropriately by integrating research and production spread widely among several locations, combining machines sourced from many disparate distant suppliers, and so on is limited. The firm that concentrates its core activities at a favorable home base, while competing nationally and globally, will normally progress more rapidly. Activities outside the home base are focused on sourcing low-cost basic factors and securing market access.

These same arguments explain why we observe *clusters* of competitive industries in one location. Clusters involve supplier industries, customer industries, and related industries that are all competitive. Such clusters are characteristic of every advanced economy—American entertainment, German chemicals, Japanese electronics, Danish foods. Clusters grow and transform themselves through spinoffs and diversification of firms into upstream, downstream, and related industries and activities. The fields where

437

several clusters overlap are often fertile grounds for new business formation. In Japan, for example, the interstices between electronics and new materials are spawning new competitive strengths in fields as diverse as robotics and displays.

Another implication of this theory is the importance of geographic concentration of successful firms and clusters within particular cities or regions. National clusters are often themselves geographically concentrated. Geographic concentration elevates and magnifies the interaction of the four determinants, improves information flow and signaling, makes innovation-enhancing interactions with customers and specialized suppliers less costly, and provides a check on opportunistic behavior, among other benefits.[29]

Firms lose competitive advantage either because of emerging weaknesses in their local environment or due to rigidities or other internal problems that external circumstances cannot overcome.[30] For example, a major shift in technology may require an entirely new set of specialized suppliers that are not present, or local demand characteristics may evolve in ways that distract from instead of foreshadow international needs. However, firms sometimes fail not because their environment is unfavorable but because of organizational or managerial rigidities that block improvement and change. The environment can provide important pressures to advance, but firms differ in their responsiveness to them.

Environmental influences on the dynamics of strategy

The environment, via the diamond, affects both a firm's initial conditions and its managerial choices. The diamond, through its influence on information and incentives, shapes the content of strategies. It influences the ability of firms to carry out particular types of strategies, hence limiting choice. Choices that may look accidental or internally driven are often partly or wholly derived from the local diamond. Over time, through its stress on markets for difficult-to-trade inputs, the state of the diamond conditions the rate of accumulation of resources. It also sets the pressures on firms to improve and upgrade. The diamond, then, begins to address a dynamic theory of strategy early in the chain of causality.

Yet firms retain a central role. Firms must understand and exploit their local environment in order to achieve competitive advantage. There are often sharp differences in the performance of firms based in the same region or nation. These differences are partly a function of managerial choices, differential rates of resource accumulation, or chance. The differences also appear, however, to be partly a function of the subenvironment of each particular firm—its particular early customers, supplier relationships, factor market access, etc.

An important role for the local environment in competitive success does not eliminate the role of strategy nor the need for competitive analysis.

Industry structure, positioning, activities, resources, and commitments remain important. Rather, the diamond highlights new issues for strategy that are normally ignored, such as the importance of developing and nurturing home-based suppliers, the importance of local specialized factor markets, and the balance between home-based activities and those dispersed to other locations as part of a national or global strategy.

The local environment creates potential for competitive success, but firms must sense and respond to it. Firms also have a considerable ability to influence their environment in ways that reinforce or detract from their capacity to accumulate skills and resources and to innovate—there is a feedback loop between firm actions and the local diamond. Many if not most firms, even in favorable environments, do *not* achieve competitive advantage. Firms based in an unattractive environment, however, face profound challenges in achieving competitive success. More and more firms are relocating their home bases accordingly.

Issues for further research

Recent research has begun to shed some light on the chain of causality that constitutes a dynamic theory of strategy, but many unanswered questions remain. I would highlight four that deserve special attention. First, we need to better understand the balance between environmental determinism and company/leader choice in shaping competitive outcomes. What is emerging is the beginnings of a more sophisticated way of understanding how the environment surrounding a firm influences both firm choices and outcomes, and of the internal processes of choice and of skill and asset (resource) accumulation that underpin competitive advantage. It is clear that company actions still matter, and that firms in a given environment achieve widely different levels of success. Can we, by looking across different firms in a given nation or city, isolate unique subenvironments that explain these differing levels of performance? Or, can we identify patterns of commitments to activities and resource accumulation that characterize superior performers?

Second, we need to better understand the degree of stickiness or inertia in competitive positions once a firm stops progressing, or, to put it another way, the durability of early mover advantages? How important is a burst of innovation vs. the capacity to improve and innovate continuously? How important are pure rents from scarce factors vs. advantage resulting from innovation or which raise the value of factors? My research suggests that the latter is characteristic of successful firms who have sustained their competitive positions, but much more investigation is necessary.

Third, we need to know how necessary or helpful it is to push even further back in the chain of causality. I have argued that resources are an intermediate step in the chain, from which we can learn. Yet an important theoretical issue is where in the chain of causality to best cut into the problem. An example will illustrate that even a focus on the local environment of the firm does not go to the ultimate origin of advantage. The presence of a specialized skill in a region or nation is often the result of skill pools inherited from other industries as well as human resources trained at pre-existing institutions. These institutions, however, often draw to some extent on the general education system which itself is affected by social values and history. Just how far back to the ultimate source does one need to go to best examine these questions? I chose in my own research to model the phenomena at the level of the diamond, while highlighting that each of its components is the result of history and other local conditions. The appropriateness of this choice is a subject for research. It should be said that understanding the ultimate origins of advantage may not always be necessary for thinking about how to improve future advantage.

Finally, there is the important challenge of crafting empirical research to make further progress in understanding these questions. Some argue that models that exceed a certain level of complexity can never be tested. Yet it is clear that there are many aspects of both firms and their environment which determine competitive success. How can we collect and analyze data to help us discriminate among explanations and weigh the various factors? I concluded in my most recent research that detailed longitudinal case studies, covering long periods of time, were necessary to study these phenomena. Moreover, these case studies had to encompass a large number and wide range of industries and national contexts in order to develop confidence about the appropriate variables and their influence on outcomes. This style of research nudges strategy research, and indeed industrial economics, into the world of the historian. It also involves enormous fixed costs. I am convinced that more research of this type will be needed to address the dynamics of strategy. It also raises the question of whether there are other approaches to empirical testing to address these issues, or whether we must wait until theories have been much better developed before we can highlight the relatively few variables which can be measured and rigorously examined statistically.

Acknowledgements

I am grateful to Pankaj Ghemawat, Cynthia Montgomery, and others in the Competition and Strategy group at Harvard for a long series of discussions that have immensely benefitted my thinking about these issues, and to Jay Barney, Richard Rumelt, and Garth Saloner for their insights while visiting. David Collis, Cynthia Montgomery, Richard Rumelt, Elizabeth Teisberg and Dan Schendel provided helpful comments on this manuscript.

Notes

1 See Learned *et al.* (1965). See also Andrews (1971).
2 In the absence of a strategy, the narrow motivations and logistics of each functional area will guide behavior.
3 This notion is due originally to Selznick (1957).
4 See, for example, Wernerfelt (1984) and Prahalad and Hamel (1990).
5 Interestingly, the earlier work in industrial economics, in the Mason/Bain tradition, was much closer to strategy research in its effort to capture complexity.
6 See examples such as Porter (1985) and Ghemawat (1991).
7 Frameworks can also be challenged because their complexity makes it difficult to falsify arguments. Yet ascribing this property to models is also problematic if they omit important variables.
8 A firm that can command higher volume at a given price takes its superior profitability in the form of lower cost provided costs are scale sensitive.
9 See Porter and Millar (1985).
10 See, for example, Itami (1987) and Baldwin and Clark (1991).
11 See Porter (1985, Chapter 3).
12 See Johnson and Kaplan (1987), Cooper and Kaplan (1988, 1991).
13 I avoid the terms static and dynamic intentionally, because both the cross-sectional and longitudinal problems have both static and dynamic components.
14 See, for example, Mintzberg (1990).
15 Initial conditions can also he set at different points in time. See below.
16 Editor's Note: See the articles by Garth Saloner, Colin Camerer, and Steven Postrel.
17 See Wack (1985a, b) and Schwartz (1991).
18 See Wernerfelt and Karnani (1987), Porter (1985, Chapter 13), Teisberg (1991a), and Collis (1991a).
19 Teisberg's (1991a) essay, by making the influencing of industry structure a way of dealing with uncertainty, is an exception.
20 Conversations with Cynthia Montgomery have stimulated and informed my interest in this literature. Perhaps the pioneer of this school is Penrose (1963). An early paper was Wernerfelt (1984). For other references, see the bibliographies in Peteraf (1990) and Collis (1991b). Recent papers include Barney (1991) and Grant (1991).
21 Some writers in the resource school draw stylized comparisons with industrial organization (IO)-based theories that confuse rather than clarify. For example, Peteraf's survey (1990) asserts that IO-based models focus only on the heterogeneity of markets while denying the heterogeneity of firms and the existence of differential competitive positions, to be based only on monopoly rents, to lead only to strategies of collusion, and to he restricted to formulating strategy at the business unit level. This view is puzzling unless one is talking about the IO-based models of the 1970s, before research aimed at bridging IO and firm strategy began.
22 In this respect, the paper by Prahalad and Hamel (1990) is perhaps the most inward looking and the most troubling.
23 Collis's (1991b) recent paper concludes on this point, which emerges from his detailed case study of ball bearings.
24 Since the great preponderance of resources are created either by past activities or managerial choices to assemble outside resources in new activity configurations, my own view is that activities are logically prior. Yet it is clear that causality becomes blurred as accumulated resources affect the cost or uniqueness of activities.

25 Defining a market position as a resource is inappropriate, because it confuses the longitudinal problem with the cross-sectional problem and obscures the mechanism by which advantage is created.

26 See Montgomery and Wernerfelt (1988) and Montgomery and Harihatan (1991).

27 See Porter (1990) and Ghemawat (1991).

28 The mutual reinforcement of the determinants suggests a particularly important role for local rivalry, healthy new business formation, and the responsiveness of local institutions to signals from industry. Local rivalry stimulates improvements in all the other determinants. New business formation, whether through start-up or internal development, is a *sine qua non* of developing related and supporting industries as well as healthy rivalry. Competitive advantage also depends on the capacity of the local education system, infrastructure providers, and government institutions to respond to the specialized needs of particular industries. Institutional responsiveness allows the proper types of skills, resources, and infrastructure to be created.

29 For a detailed treatment and empirical tests, see Enright (1990). See, also, Krugman (1991).

30 I discuss these issues more fully elsewhere. See Porter (1990).

References

Andrews, K. R. *The Concept of Corporate Strategy*, Dow Jones-Irwin, Homewood, IL, 1971.

Baldwin, C. Y. and K. B. Clark. 'Capabilities and capital investment: New perspectives on capital budgeting', Harvard Business School Working Paper #92–004, Rev. 7/15/1991.

Barney, J. B. 'Strategic factor markets: Expectations, luck and business strategy', *Management Science*, **32**, October 1986, pp. 1231–1241.

Barney, J. B. 'Firm resources and sustained competitive advantage. *Journal of Management*, **17**(1), 1991, pp. 99–120.

Collis, D. J. 'The strategic management of uncertainty', Harvard Business School Working Paper #89–019, Rev. 3/1991a.

Collis, D. J. 'A resource-based analysis of global competition: The case of the bearings industry', *Strategic Management Journal*, Special Issue, Summer 1991b, pp. 49–68.

Cooper, R. and R. S. Kaplan. 'Measure costs right: Make the right decisions', *Harvard Business Review*, September–October 1988, pp. 96–103.

Cooper, R. and R. S. Kaplan. *The Design of Cost Management Systems*. Prentice Hall, Englewood Cliffs, NJ, 1991.

Enright, M. J. 'Geographic concentration and industrial organization', unpublished doctoral dissertation, Business Economics Program, Harvard University, 1990.

Ghemawat, P. *Commitment: The Dynamic of Strategy*. Free Press, New York, 1991.

Grant, R. M. 'The resource-based theory of competitive advantage: Implications for strategy formulations', *California Management Review*, Spring 1991, pp. 119–135.

Itami, H. (with T. W. Roehl). *Mobilizing Invisible Assets*, Harvard University Press, Cambridge, MA and London, England, 1987.

Johnson, H. T. and R. S. Kaplan. *Relevance Lost: The Rise and Fall of Management Accounting*. Harvard Business School Press, Boston, MA, 1987.

Krugman, P. R. *Geography and Trade*, MIT Press, Cambridge, MA, 1991.

Learned, E. P., C. R. Christensen, K. R. Andrews and W. D. Guth. *Business Policy Text and Cases*, Richard D. Irwin, Homewood, IL, 1965.

Mintzberg, H. 'The Design School: Reconsidering the basic premises of strategic management', *Strategic Management Journal*, **11**(3), March–April 1990, pp. 171–195.

Montgomery, C. A. and B. Wernerfelt. 'Diversification, Ricardian Rents, and Tobin's q', *Rand Journal of Economics*, **19**(4), Winter 1988, pp. 623–632.

Montgomery, C. A. and S. Hariharan. 'Diversified expansion by large established firms', *Journal of Economic Behavior and Organization*, **15**, 1991, pp. 71–89.

Penrose, E. T. *The Theory of the Growth of the Firm*, Blackwell, Oxford, 1963.

Peteraf, M. A. 'The resource-based model: An emerging paradigm for strategic management', Discussion Paper 90–29, J. L. Kellogg Graduate School of Management, Northwestern University, August 1990.

Porter, M. E. *Competitive Strategy: Techniques for Analyzing Industries and Competitors*, Free Press, New York, 1980.

Porter, M. E. *Competitive Advantage: Creating and Sustaining Superior Performance*, Free Press, New York, 1985.

Porter, M. E. 'From competitive advantage to corporate strategy', *Harvard Business Review*, May–June, 1987, pp. 43–59.

Porter, M. E. *The Competitive Advantage of Nations*, Free Press, New York, 1990.

Porter, M. E., (ed.) *Competition in Global Industries*, Harvard Business School Press, Boston, MA, 1986.

Porter, M. E. and V. A. Millar, 'How information gives you competitive advantage', *Harvard Business Review*, July–August 1985, pp. 149–160.

Prahalad, C. K. and G. Hamel. 'The core competence of the corporation', *Harvard Business Review*, May–June 1990, pp. 71–91.

Schwartz, P. *The Art of the Long View*, Doubleday, New York, 1991.

Selznick, P. *Leadership in Administration: A Sociological Interpretation*, Harper & Row, New York, 1957.

Shapiro, C. 'The theory of business strategy', *Rand Journal of Economics*, **20**, Spring 1989, pp. 125–137.

Teisberg, E. O. 'Strategic response to uncertainty', Harvard Business School case, #N9–391–192, Rev. 4/11/1991a.

Teisberg, E. O. 'Why do good managers choose poor strategies?' Harvard Business School Case #N9–391–172, Rev. 3/5/1991b.

Wack, P. 'Scenarios: Uncharted waters ahead', *Harvard Business Review*, September–October 1985a, pp. 73–89.

Wack, P. 'Scenarios: Shooting the rapids', *Harvard Business Review*, November–December 1985b, pp. 139–150.

Wernerfelt, B. 'A resource-based view of the firm', *Strategic Management Journal*, **5**(2), April–June 1984, pp. 171–180.

Wernerfelt, B. and A. Karnani, 'Competitive strategy under uncertainty', *Strategic Management Journal*, **8**(2), 1987, pp. 197–194.

22

WHAT IS STRATEGY?

Michael E. Porter

Source: *Harvard Business Review* 74(6) (1996): 61–78.

I. Operational effectiveness is not strategy

For almost two decades, managers have been learning to play by a new set of rules. Companies must be flexible to respond rapidly to competitive and market changes. They must benchmark continuously to achieve best practice. They must outsource aggressively to gain efficiencies. And they must nurture a few core competencies in the race to stay ahead of rivals.

Positioning – once the heart of strategy – is rejected as too static for today's dynamic markets and changing technologies. According to the new dogma, rivals can quickly copy any market position, and competitive advantage is, at best, temporary.

But those beliefs are dangerous half-truths, and they are leading more and more companies down the path of mutually destructive competition. True, some barriers to competition are falling as regulation eases and markets become global. True, companies have properly invested energy in becoming leaner and more nimble. In many industries, however, what some call *hypercompetition* is a self-inflicted wound, not the inevitable outcome of a changing paradigm of competition.

The root of the problem is the failure to distinguish between operational effectiveness and strategy. The quest for productivity, quality, and speed has spawned a remarkable number of management tools and techniques: total quality management, benchmarking, time-based competition, outsourcing, partnering, reengineering, change management. Although the resulting operational improvements have often been dramatic, many companies have been frustrated by their inability to translate those gains into sustainable profitability. And bit by bit, almost imperceptibly, management tools have taken the place of strategy. As managers push to improve on all fronts, they move farther away from viable competitive positions.

Operational effectiveness: necessary but not sufficient

Operational effectiveness and strategy are both essential to superior performance, which, after all, is the primary goal of any enterprise. But they work in very different ways.

A company can outperform rivals only if it can establish a difference that it can preserve. It must deliver greater value to customers or create comparable value at a lower cost, or do both. The arithmetic of superior profitability then follows: delivering greater value allows a company to charge higher average unit prices; greater efficiency results in lower average unit costs.

Ultimately, all differences between companies in cost or price derive from the hundreds of activities required to create, produce, sell, and deliver their products or services, such as calling on customers, assembling final products, and training employees. Cost is generated by performing activities, and cost advantage arises from performing particular activities more efficiently than competitors. Similarly, differentiation arises from both the choice of activities and how they are performed. Activities, then, are the basic units of competitive advantage. Overall advantage or disadvantage results from all a company's activities, not only a few.[1]

Operational effectiveness (OE) means performing similar activities *better* than rivals perform them. Operational effectiveness includes but is not limited to efficiency. It refers to any number of practices that allow a

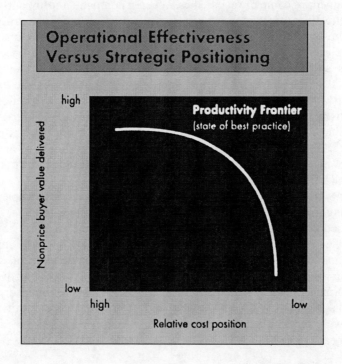

company to better utilize its inputs by, for example, reducing defects in products or developing better products faster. In contrast, strategic positioning means performing *different* activities from rivals' or performing similar activities in *different ways*.

Differences in operational effectiveness among companies are pervasive. Some companies are able to get more out of their inputs than others because they eliminate wasted effort, employ more advanced technology, motivate employees better, or have greater insight into managing particular activities or sets of activities. Such differences in operational effectiveness are an important source of differences in profitability among competitors because they directly affect relative cost positions and levels of differentiation.

Differences in operational effectiveness were at the heart of the Japanese challenge to Western companies in the 1980s. The Japanese were so far ahead of rivals in operational effectiveness that they could offer lower cost and superior quality at the same time. It is worth dwelling on this point, because so much recent thinking about competition depends on it. Imagine for a moment a *productivity frontier* that constitutes the sum of all existing best practices at any given time. Think of it as the maximum value that a company delivering a particular product or service can create at a given cost, using the best available technologies, skills, management techniques, and purchased inputs. The productivity frontier can apply to individual activities, to groups of linked activities such as order processing and manufacturing, and to an entire company's activities. When a company improves its operational effectiveness, it moves toward the frontier. Doing so may require capital investment, different personnel, or simply new ways of managing.

The productivity frontier is constantly shifting outward as new technologies and management approaches are developed and as new inputs become available. Laptop computers, mobile communications, the Internet, and software such as Lotus Notes, for example, have redefined the productivity frontier for sales-force operations and created rich possibilities for linking sales with such activities as order processing and after-sales support. Similarly, lean production, which involves a family of activities, has allowed substantial improvements in manufacturing productivity and asset utilization.

For at least the past decade, managers have been preoccupied with improving operational effectiveness. Through programs such as TQM, time-based competition, and benchmarking, they have changed how they perform activities in order to eliminate inefficiencies, improve customer satisfaction, and achieve best practice. Hoping to keep up with shifts in the productivity frontier, managers have embraced continuous improvement, empowerment, change management, and the so-called learning organization. The popularity of outsourcing and the virtual corporation reflect the growing recognition that it is difficult to perform all activities as productively as specialists.

As companies move to the frontier, they can often improve on multiple dimensions of performance at the same time. For example, manufacturers that adopted the Japanese practice of rapid changeovers in the 1980s were able to lower cost and improve differentiation simultaneously. What were once believed to be real trade-offs – between defects and costs, for example – turned out to be illusions created by poor operational effectiveness. Managers have learned to reject such false trade-offs.

Constant improvement in operational effectiveness is necessary to achieve superior profitability. However, it is not usually sufficient. Few companies have competed successfully on the basis of operational effectiveness over an extended period, and staying ahead of rivals gets harder every day. The most obvious reason for that is the rapid diffusion of best practices. Competitors can quickly imitate management techniques, new technologies, input improvements, and superior ways of meeting customers' needs. The most generic solutions – those that can be used in multiple settings – diffuse the fastest. Witness the proliferation of OE techniques accelerated by support from consultants.

OE competition shifts the productivity frontier outward, effectively raising the bar for everyone. But although such competition produces absolute improvement in operational effectiveness, it leads to relative improvement for no one. Consider the $5 billion-plus U.S. commercial-printing industry. The major players – R.R. Donnelley & Sons Company, Quebecor, World Color Press, and Big Flower Press–are competing head to head, serving all types of customers, offering the same array of printing technologies (gravure and web offset), investing heavily in the same new equipment, running their presses faster, and reducing crew sizes. But the resulting major productivity gains are being captured by customers and equipment suppliers, not retained in superior profitability. Even industry-leader Donnelley's profit margin, consistently higher than 7% in the 1980s, fell to less than 4.6% in 1995. This pattern is playing itself out in industry after industry. Even the Japanese, pioneers of the new competition, suffer from persistently low profits. (See the insert "Japanese Companies Rarely Have Strategies.")

The second reason that improved operational effectiveness is insufficient – competitive convergence – is more subtle and insidious. The more benchmarking companies do, the more they look alike. The more that rivals outsource activities to efficient third parties, often the same ones, the more generic those activities become. As rivals imitate one another's improvements in quality, cycle times, or supplier partnerships, strategies converge and competition becomes a series of races down identical paths that no one can win. Competition based on operational effectiveness alone is mutually destructive, leading to wars of attrition that can be arrested only by limiting competition.

The recent wave of industry consolidation through mergers makes sense in the context of OE competition. Driven by performance pressures but

447

Japanese Companies Rarely Have Strategies

The Japanese triggered a global revolution in operational effectiveness in the 1970s and 1980s, pioneering practices such as total quality management and continuous improvement. As a result, Japanese manufacturers enjoyed substantial cost and quality advantages for many years.

But Japanese companies rarely developed distinct strategic positions of the kind discussed in this article. Those that did – Sony, Canon, and Sega, for example – were the exception rather than the rule. Most Japanese companies imitate and emulate one another. All rivals offer most if not all product varieties, features, and services; they employ all channels and match one anothers' plant configurations.

The dangers of Japanese-style competition are now becoming easier to recognize. In the 1980s, with rivals operating far from the productivity frontier, it seemed possible to win on both cost and quality indefinitely. Japanese companies were all able to grow in an expanding domestic economy and by penetrating global markets. They appeared unstoppable. But as the gap in operational effectiveness narrows, Japanese companies are increasingly caught in a trap of their own making. If they are to escape the mutually destructive battles now ravaging their performance, Japanese companies will have to learn strategy.

To do so, they may have to overcome strong cultural barriers. Japan is notoriously consensus oriented, and companies have a strong tendency to mediate differences among individuals rather than accentuate them. Strategy, on the other hand, requires hard choices. The Japanese also have a deeply ingrained service tradition that predisposes them to go to great lengths to satisfy any need a customer expresses. Companies that compete in that way end up blurring their distinct positioning, becoming all things to all customers.

This discussion of Japan is drawn from the author's research with Hirotaka Takeuchi, with help from Mariko Sakakibara.

---

lacking strategic vision, company after company has had no better idea than to buy up its rivals. The competitors left standing are often those that outlasted others, not companies with real advantage.

After a decade of impressive gains in operational effectiveness, many companies are facing diminishing returns. Continuous improvement has been etched on managers' brains. But its tools unwittingly draw companies toward imitation and homogeneity. Gradually, managers have let operational effectiveness supplant strategy. The result is zero-sum competition, static or declining prices, and pressures on costs that compromise companies' ability to invest in the business for the long term.

II. Strategy rests on unique activities

Competitive strategy is about being different. It means deliberately choosing a different set of activities to deliver a unique mix of value.

Southwest Airlines Company, for example, offers short-haul, low-cost, point-to-point service between midsize cities and secondary airports in large cities. Southwest avoids large airports and does not fly great distances. Its customers include business travelers, families, and students. Southwest's frequent departures and low fares attract price-sensitive customers who otherwise would travel by bus or car, and convenience-oriented travelers who would choose a full-service airline on other routes.

Most managers describe strategic positioning in terms of their customers: "Southwest Airlines serves price- and convenience-sensitive travelers," for example. But the essence of strategy is in the activities – choosing to perform activities differently or to perform different activities than rivals. Otherwise, a strategy is nothing more than a marketing slogan that will not withstand competition.

A full-service airline is configured to get passengers from almost any point A to any point B. To reach a large number of destinations and serve passengers with connecting flights, full-service airlines employ a hub-and-spoke system centered on major airports. To attract passengers who desire more comfort, they offer first-class or business-class service. To accommodate passengers who must change planes, they coordinate schedules and check and transfer baggage. Because some passengers will be traveling for many hours, full-service airlines serve meals.

Southwest, in contrast, tailors all its activities to deliver low-cost, convenient service on its particular type of route. Through fast turnarounds at the gate of only 15 minutes, Southwest is able to keep planes flying longer hours than rivals and provide frequent departures with fewer aircraft. Southwest does not offer meals, assigned seats, interline baggage checking, or premium classes of service. Automated ticketing at the gate encourages customers to bypass travel agents, allowing Southwest to avoid their commissions. A standardized fleet of 737 aircraft boosts the efficiency of maintenance.

Southwest has staked out a unique and valuable strategic position based on a tailored set of activities. On the routes served by Southwest, a full-service airline could never be as convenient or as low cost.

Ikea, the global furniture retailer based in Sweden, also has a clear strategic positioning. Ikea targets young furniture buyers who want style at low cost. What turns this marketing concept into a strategic positioning is

449

the tailored set of activities that make it work. Like Southwest, Ikea has chosen to perform activities differently from its rivals.

Consider the typical furniture store. Showrooms display samples of the merchandise. One area might contain 25 sofas; another will display five dining tables. But those items represent only a fraction of the choices available to customers. Dozens of books displaying fabric swatches or wood samples or alternate styles offer customers thousands of product varieties to choose from. Salespeople often escort customers through the store, answering questions and helping them navigate this maze of choices. Once a customer makes a selection, the order is relayed to a third-party manufacturer. With luck, the furniture will be delivered to the customer's home within six to eight weeks. This is a value chain that maximizes customization and service but does so at high cost.

In contrast, Ikea serves customers who are happy to trade off service for cost. Instead of having a sales associate trail customers around the store, Ikea uses a self-service model based on clear, in-store displays. Rather than rely solely on third-party manufacturers, Ikea designs its own low-cost, modular, ready-to-assemble furniture to fit its positioning. In huge stores, Ikea displays every product it sells in room-like settings, so customers don't need a decorator to help them imagine how to put the pieces together. Adjacent to the furnished showrooms is a warehouse section with the products in boxes on pallets. Customers are expected to do their own pickup and delivery, and Ikea will even sell you a roof rack for your car that you can return for a refund on your next visit.

Although much of its low-cost position comes from having customers "do it themselves," Ikea offers a number of extra services that its competitors do not. In-store child care is one. Extended hours are another. Those services are uniquely aligned with the needs of its customers, who are young, not wealthy, likely to have children (but no nanny), and, because they work for a living, have a need to shop at odd hours.

The origins of strategic positions

Strategic positions emerge from three distinct sources, which are not mutually exclusive and often overlap. First, positioning can be based on producing a subset of an industry's products or services. I call this *variety-based positioning* because it is based on the choice of product or service varieties rather than customer segments. Variety-based positioning makes economic sense when a company can best produce particular products or services using distinctive sets of activities.

Jiffy Lube International, for instance, specializes in automotive lubricants and does not offer other car repair or maintenance services. Its value chain produces faster service at a lower cost than broader line repair shops, a combination so attractive that many customers subdivide their purchases,

Finding New Positions: The Entrepreneurial Edge

Strategic competition can be thought of as the process of perceiving new positions that woo customers from established positions or draw new customers into the market. For example, superstores offering depth of merchandise in a single product category take market share from broad-line department stores offering a more limited selection in many categories. Mail-order catalogs pick off customers who crave convenience. In principle, incumbents and entrepreneurs face the same challenges in finding new strategic positions. In practice, new entrants often have the edge.

Strategic positionings are often not obvious, and finding them requires creativity and insight. New entrants often discover unique positions that have been available but simply overlooked by established competitors. Ikea, for example, recognized a customer group that had been ignored or served poorly. Circuit City Stores' entry into used cars, CarMax, is based on a new way of performing activities – extensive refurbishing of cars, product guarantees, no-haggle pricing, sophisticated use of in-house customer financing – that has long been open to incumbents.

New entrants can prosper by occupying a position that a competitor once held but has ceded through years of imitation and straddling. And entrants coming from other industries can create new positions because of distinctive activities drawn from their other businesses. CarMax borrows heavily from Circuit City's expertise in inventory management, credit, and other activities in consumer electronics retailing.

Most commonly, however, new positions open up because of change. New customer groups or purchase occasions arise; new needs emerge as societies evolve; new distribution channels appear; new technologies are developed; new machinery or information systems become available. When such changes happen, new entrants, unencumbered by a long history in the industry, can often more easily perceive the potential for a new way of competing. Unlike incumbents, newcomers can be more flexible because they face no trade-offs with their existing activities.

buying oil changes from the focused competitor, Jiffy Lube, and going to rivals for other services.

The Vanguard Group, a leader in the mutual fund industry, is another example of variety-based positioning. Vanguard provides an array of common stock, bond, and money market funds that offer predictable performance and rock-bottom expenses. The company's investment approach deliberately sacrifices the possibility of extraordinary performance in any one year for good relative performance in every year. Vanguard is known, for example, for its index funds. It avoids making bets on interest rates and steers clear of narrow stock groups. Fund managers keep trading levels low, which holds expenses down; in addition, the company discourages customers from rapid buying and selling because doing so drives up costs and can force a fund manager to trade in order to deploy new capital and raise cash for redemptions. Vanguard also takes a consistent low-cost approach to managing distribution, customer service, and marketing. Many investors include one or more Vanguard funds in their portfolio, while buying aggressively managed or specialized funds from competitors.

The people who use Vanguard or Jiffy Lube are responding to a superior value chain for a particular type of service. A variety-based positioning can serve a wide array of customers, but for most it will meet only a subset of their needs.

A second basis for positioning is that of serving most or all the needs of a particular group of customers. I call this *needs-based positioning*, which comes closer to traditional thinking about targeting a segment of customers. It arises when there are groups of customers with differing needs, and when a tailored set of activities can serve those needs best. Some groups of customers are more price sensitive than others, demand different product features, and need varying amounts of information, support, and services. Ikea's customers are a good example of such a group. Ikea seeks to meet all the home furnishing needs of its target customers, not just a subset of them.

A variant of needs-based positioning arises when the same customer has different needs on different occasions or for different types of transactions. The same person, for example, may have different needs when traveling on business than when traveling for pleasure with the family. Buyers of cans – beverage companies, for example – will likely have different needs from their primary supplier than from their secondary source.

It is intuitive for most managers to conceive of their business in terms of the customers' needs-based positioning is not at all intuitive and is often overlooked. Differences in needs will not translate into meaningful positions unless the best set of activities to satisfy them *also* differs. If that were not the case, every competitor could meet those same needs, and there would be nothing unique or valuable about the positioning.

In private banking, for example, Bessemer Trust Company targets families with a minimum of $5 million in investable assets who want capital preservation combined with wealth accumulation. By assigning one sophisticated account officer for every 14 families, Bessemer has configured its activities for personalized service. Meetings, for example, are more likely to be held at a client's ranch or yacht than in the office. Bessemer offers a wide array of customized services, including investment management and estate administration, oversight of oil and gas investments, and accounting for racehorses and aircraft. Loans, a staple of most private banks, are rarely needed by Bessemer's clients and make up a tiny fraction of its client balances and income. Despite the most generous compensation of account officers and the highest personnel cost as a percentage of operating expenses, Bessemer's differentiation with its target families produces a return on equity estimated to be the highest of any private banking competitor.

Citibank's private bank, on the other hand, serves clients with minimum assets of about $250,000 who, in contrast to Bessemer's clients, want convenient access to loans-from jumbo mortgages to deal financing. Citibank's account managers are primarily lenders. When clients need other services, their account manager refers them to other Citibank specialists, each of whom handles prepackaged products. Citibank's system is less customized than Bessemer's and allows it to have a lower manager-to-client ratio of 1:125. Biannual office meetings are offered only for the largest clients. Both Bessemer and Citibank have tailored their activities to meet the needs of a different group of private banking customers. The same value chain cannot profitably meet the needs of both groups.

The third basis for positioning is that of segmenting customers who are accessible in different ways. Although their needs are similar to those of other customers, the best configuration of activities to reach them is different. I call this *access-based positioning*. Access can be a function of customer geography or customer scale-or of anything that requires a different set of activities to reach customers in the best way.

Segmenting by access is less common and less well understood than the other two bases. Carmike Cinemas, for example, operates movie theaters exclusively in cities and towns with populations under 200,000. How does Carmike make money in markets that are not only small but also won't support big-city ticket prices? It does so through a set of activities that result in a lean cost structure. Carmike's small-town customers can be served through standardized, low-cost theater complexes requiring fewer screens and less sophisticated projection technology than big-city theaters. The company's proprietary information system and management process eliminate the need for local administrative staff beyond a single theater manager. Carmike also reaps advantages from centralized purchasing, lower rent and payroll costs (because of its locations), and rock-bottom corporate overhead of 2% (the industry average is 5%). Operating in small communities also allows Carmike to practice a highly personal form of marketing in which the theater manager knows patrons and promotes attendance through personal contacts. By being the dominant if not the only theater in its markets – the main competition is often the high school football team – Carmike is also able to get its pick of films and negotiate better terms with distributors.

Rural versus urban-based customers are one example of access driving differences in activities. Serving small rather than large customers or densely rather than sparsely situated customers are other examples in which the best way to configure marketing, order processing, logistics, and after-sale service activities to meet the similar needs of distinct groups will often differ.

Positioning is not only about carving out a niche. A position emerging from any of the sources can be broad or narrow. A focused competitor, such as Ikea, targets the special needs of a subset of customers and designs its activities accordingly. Focused competitors thrive on groups of customers who are overserved (and hence overpriced) by more broadly targeted competitors, or underserved (and hence underpriced). A broadly targeted competitor–for example, Vanguard or Delta Air Lines – serves a wide array of customers, performing a set of activities designed to meet their common needs. It ignores or meets only partially the more idiosyncratic needs of particular customer groups.

Whatever the basis – variety, needs, access, or some combination of the three – positioning requires a tailored set of activities because it is always a function of differences on the supply side; that is, of differences in activities. However, positioning is not always a function of differences on the demand, or customer, side. Variety and access positionings, in particular, do not rely on *any* customer differences. In practice, however, variety or access differences often accompany needs differences. The tastes – that is, the needs

---

The Connection with Generic Strategies

In *Competitive Strategy* (The Free Press, 1985), I introduced the concept of generic strategies – cost leadership, differentiation, and focus – to represent the alternative strategic positions in an industry. The generic strategies remain useful to characterize strategic positions at the simplest and broadest level. Vanguard, for instance, is an example of a cost leadership strategy, whereas Ikea, with its narrow customer group, is an example of cost-based focus. Neutrogena is a focused differentiator. The bases for positioning – varieties, needs, and access – carry the understanding of those generic strategies to a greater level of specificity. Ikea and Southwest are both cost-based focusers, for example, but Ikea's focus is based on the needs of a customer group, and Southwest's is based on offering a particular service variety.

The generic strategies framework introduced the need to choose in order to avoid becoming caught between what I then described as the inherent contradictions of different strategies. Trade-offs between the activities of incompatible positions explain those contradictions. Witness Continental Lite, which tried and failed to compete in two ways at once.

454

– of Carmike's small-town customers, for instance, run more toward comedies, Westerns, action films, and family entertainment. Carmike does not run any films rated NC-17.

Having defined positioning, we can now begin to answer the question, "What is strategy?" Strategy is the creation of a unique and valuable position, involving a different set of activities. If there were only one ideal position, there would be no need for strategy. Companies would face a simple imperative – win the race to discover and preempt it. The essence of strategic positioning is to choose activities that are different from rivals'. If the same set of activities were best to produce all varieties, meet all needs, and access all customers, companies could easily shift among them and operational effectiveness would determine performance.

III. A sustainable strategic position requires trade-offs

Choosing a unique position, however, is not enough to guarantee a sustainable advantage. A valuable position will attract imitation by incumbents, who are likely to copy it in one of two ways.

First, a competitor can reposition itself to match the superior performer. J.C. Penney, for instance, has been repositioning itself from a Sears clone to a more upscale, fashion-oriented, soft-goods retailer. A second and far more common type of imitation is straddling. The straddler seeks to match the benefits of a successful position while maintaining its existing position. It grafts new features, services, or technologies onto the activities it already performs.

For those who argue that competitors can copy any market position, the airline industry is a perfect test case. It would seem that nearly any competitor could imitate any other airline's activities. Any airline can buy the same planes, lease the gates, and match the menus and ticketing and baggage handling services offered by other airlines.

Continental Airlines saw how well Southwest was doing and decided to straddle. While maintaining its position as a full-service airline, Continental also set out to match Southwest on a number of point-to-point routes. The airline dubbed the new service Continental Lite. It eliminated meals and first-class service, increased departure frequency, lowered fares, and shortened turnaround time at the gate. Because Continental remained a full-service airline on other routes, it continued to use travel agents and its mixed fleet of planes and to provide baggage checking and seat assignments.

But a strategic position is not sustainable unless there are trade-offs with other positions. Trade-offs occur when activities are incompatible. Simply put, a trade-off means that more of one thing necessitates less of another. An airline can choose to serve meals – adding cost and slowing turnaround time at the gate – or it can choose not to, but it cannot do both without bearing major inefficiencies.

Trade-offs create the need for choice and protect against repositioners and straddlers. Consider Neutrogena soap. Neutrogena Corporation's variety-based positioning is built on a "kind to the skin," residue-free soap formulated for pH balance. With a large detail force calling on dermatologists, Neutrogena's marketing strategy looks more like a drug company's than a soap maker's. It advertises in medical journals, sends direct mail to doctors, attends medical conferences, and performs research at its own Skincare Institute. To reinforce its positioning, Neutrogena originally focused its distribution on drugstores and avoided price promotions. Neutrogena uses a slow, more expensive manufacturing process to mold its fragile soap.

In choosing this position, Neutrogena said no to the deodorants and skin softeners that many customers desire in their soap. It gave up the large-volume potential of selling through supermarkets and using price promotions. It sacrificed manufacturing efficiencies to achieve the soap's desired attributes. In its original positioning, Neutrogena made a whole raft of trade-offs like those, trade-offs that protected the company from imitators.

Trade-offs arise for three reasons. The first is inconsistencies in image or reputation. A company known for delivering one kind of value may lack credibility and confuse customers – or even undermine its reputation – if it delivers another kind of value or attempts to deliver two inconsistent things at the same time. For example, Ivory soap, with its position as a basic, inexpensive everyday soap would have a hard time reshaping its image to match Neutrogena's premium "medical" reputation. Efforts to create a new image typically cost tens or even hundreds of millions of dollars in a major industry – a powerful barrier to imitation.

Second, and more important, trade-offs arise from activities themselves. Different positions (with their tailored activities) require different product configurations, different equipment, different employee behavior, different skills, and different management systems. Many trade-offs reflect inflexibilities in machinery, people, or systems. The more Ikea has configured its activities to lower costs by having its customers do their own assembly and delivery, the less able it is to satisfy customers who require higher levels of service.

However, trade-offs can be even more basic. In general, value is destroyed if an activity is overdesigned or underdesigned for its use. For example, even if a given salesperson were capable of providing a high level of assistance to one customer and none to another, the salesperson's talent (and some of his or her cost) would be wasted on the second customer. Moreover, productivity can improve when variation of an activity is limited. By providing a high level of assistance all the time, the salesperson and the entire sales activity can often achieve efficiencies of learning and scale.

Finally, trade-offs arise from limits on internal coordination and control. By clearly choosing to compete in one way and not another, senior management makes organizational priorities clear. Companies that try to be all things to all customers, in contrast, risk confusion in the trenches as employees attempt to make day-to-day operating decisions without a clear framework.

Positioning trade-offs are pervasive in competition and essential to strategy. They create the need for choice and purposefully limit what a company offers. They deter straddling or repositioning, because competitors that engage in those approaches undermine their strategies and degrade the value of their existing activities.

Trade-offs ultimately grounded Continental Lite. The airline lost hundreds of millions of dollars, and the CEO lost his job. Its planes were delayed leaving congested hub cities or slowed at the gate by baggage transfers. Late flights and cancellations generated a thousand complaints a day. Continental Lite could not afford to compete on price and still pay standard travel-agent commissions, but neither could it do without agents for its full-service business. The airline compromised by cutting commissions for all Continental flights across the board. Similarly, it could not afford to offer the same frequent-flier benefits to travelers paying the much lower ticket prices for Lite service. It compromised again by lowering the rewards of Continental's entire frequent-flier program. The results: angry travel agents and full-service customers.

Continental tried to compete in two ways at once. In trying to be low cost on some routes and full service on others, Continental paid an enormous straddling penalty. If there were no trade-offs between the two positions, Continental could have succeeded. But the absence of trade-offs is a dangerous half-truth that managers must unlearn. Quality is not always free. Southwest's convenience, one kind of high quality, happens to be consistent with low costs because its frequent departures are facilitated by a number of low-cost practices – fast gate turnarounds and automated ticketing, for example. However, other dimensions of airline quality – an assigned seat, a meal, or baggage transfer – require costs to provide.

In general, false trade-offs between cost and quality occur primarily when there is redundant or wasted effort, poor control or accuracy, or weak coordination. Simultaneous improvement of cost and differentiation is possible only when a company begins far behind the productivity frontier or when the frontier shifts outward. At the frontier, where companies have achieved current best practice, the trade-off between cost and differentiation is very real indeed.

After a decade of enjoying productivity advantages, Honda Motor Company and Toyota Motor Corporation recently bumped up against the frontier. In 1995, faced with increasing customer resistance to higher automobile prices, Honda found that the only way to produce a less-expensive car was to skimp on features. In the United States, it replaced the rear disk brakes on the Civic with lower-cost drum brakes and used cheaper fabric for the back seat, hoping customers would not notice. Toyota tried to sell a version of its best-selling Corolla in Japan with unpainted bumpers and cheaper seats. In Toyota's case, customers rebelled, and the company quickly dropped the new model.

For the past decade, as managers have improved operational effectiveness greatly, they have internalized the idea that eliminating trade-offs is a good thing. But if there are no trade-offs companies will never achieve a sustainable advantage. They will have to run faster and faster just to stay in place.

As we return to the question, What is strategy? we see that trade-offs add a new dimension to the answer. Strategy is making trade-offs in competing. The essence of strategy is choosing what *not* to do. Without trade-offs, there would be no need for choice and thus no need for strategy. Any good idea could and would be quickly imitated. Again, performance would once again depend wholly on operational effectiveness.

IV. Fit drives both competitive advantage and sustainability

Positioning choices determine not only which activities a company will perform and how it will configure individual activities but also how activities relate to one another. While operational effectiveness is about achieving excellence in individual activities, or functions, strategy is about *combining* activities.

Southwest's rapid gate turnaround, which allows frequent departures and greater use of aircraft, is essential to its high-convenience, low-cost positioning. But how does Southwest achieve it? Part of the answer lies in the company's well-paid gate and ground crews, whose productivity in turnarounds is enhanced by flexible union rules. But the bigger part of the answer lies in how Southwest performs other activities. With no meals, no seat assignment, and no interline baggage transfers, Southwest avoids having to perform activities that slow down other airlines. It selects airports and routes to avoid congestion that introduces delays. Southwest's strict limits on the type and length of routes make standardized aircraft possible: every aircraft Southwest turns is a Boeing 737.

What is Southwest's core competence? Its key success factors? The correct answer is that everything matters. Southwest's strategy involves a whole system of activities, not a collection of parts. Its competitive advantage comes from the way its activities fit and reinforce one another.

Fit locks out imitators by creating a chain that is as strong as its *strongest* link. As in most companies with good strategies, Southwest's activities complement one another in ways that create real economic value. One activity's cost, for example, is lowered because of the way other activities are performed. Similarly, one activity's value to customers can be enhanced by a company's other activities. That is the way strategic fit creates competitive advantage and superior profitability.

Types of fit

The importance of fit among functional policies is one of the oldest ideas in strategy. Gradually, however, it has been supplanted on the management agenda. Rather than seeing the company as a whole, managers have turned to "core" competencies, "critical" resources, and "key" success factors. In fact, fit is a far more central component of competitive advantage than most realize.

Fit is important because discrete activities often affect one another. A sophisticated sales force, for example, confers a greater advantage when the company's product embodies premium technology and its marketing approach emphasizes customer assistance and support. A production line with high levels of model variety is more valuable when combined with an inventory and order processing system that minimizes the need for stocking finished goods, a sales process equipped to explain and encourage customization, and an advertising theme that stresses the benefits of product variations that meet a customer's special needs. Such complementarities are pervasive in strategy. Although some fit among activities is generic and applies to many companies, the most valuable fit is strategy-specific because it enhances a position's uniqueness and amplifies trade-offs.[2]

There are three types of fit, although they are not mutually exclusive. First-order fit is *simple consistency* between each activity (function) and the overall strategy. Vanguard, for example, aligns all activities with its low-cost strategy. It minimizes portfolio turnover and does not need highly compensated money managers. The company distributes its funds directly, avoiding commissions to brokers. It also limits advertising, relying instead on public relations and word-of-mouth recommendations. Vanguard ties its employees' bonuses to cost savings.

Consistency ensures that the competitive advantages of activities cumulate and do not erode or cancel themselves out. It makes the strategy easier to communicate to customers, employees, and shareholders, and improves implementation through single-mindedness in the corporation.

Second-order fit occurs when *activities are reinforcing*. Neutrogena, for example, markets to upscale hotels eager to offer their guests a soap recommended by dermatologists. Hotels grant Neutrogena the privilege of using its customary packaging while requiring other soaps to feature the hotel's name. Once guests have tried Neutrogena in a luxury hotel, they are more likely to purchase it at the drugstore or ask their doctor about it. Thus Neutrogena's medical and hotel marketing activities reinforce one another, lowering total marketing costs.

In another example, Bic Corporation sells a narrow line of standard, low-priced pens to virtually all major customer markets (retail, commercial, promotional, and giveaway) through virtually all available channels. As with any variety-based positioning serving a broad group of customers, Bic

Mapping Activity Systems

Activity-system maps, such as this one for Ikea, show how a company's strategic position is contained in a set of tailored activities designed to deliver it. In companies with a clear strategic position, a number of higher-order strategic themes can be identified and implemented through clusters of tightly linked activities.

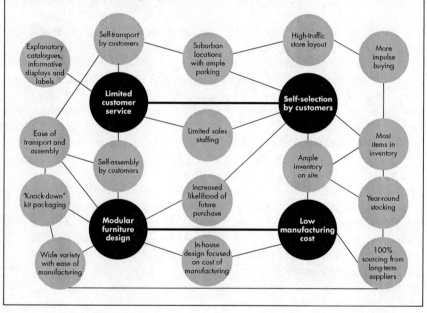

emphasizes a common need (low price for an acceptable pen) and uses marketing approaches with a broad reach (a large sales force and heavy television advertising). Bic gains the benefits of consistency across nearly all activities, including product design that emphasizes ease of manufacturing, plants configured for low cost, aggressive purchasing to minimize material costs, and in-house parts production whenever the economics dictate.

Yet Bic goes beyond simple consistency because its activities are reinforcing. For example, the company uses point-of-sale displays and frequent packaging changes to stimulate impulse buying. To handle point-of-sale tasks, a company needs a large sales force. Bic's is the largest in its industry, and it handles point-of-sale activities better than its rivals do. Moreover, the combination of point-of-sale activity, heavy television advertising, and packaging changes yields far more impulse buying than any activity in isolation could.

Vanguard's Activity System

Activity-system maps can be useful for examining and strengthening strategic fit. A set of basic questions should guide the process. First, is each activity consistent with the overall positioning – the varieties produced, the needs served, and the type of customers accessed? Ask those responsible for each activity to identify how other activities within the company improve or detract from their performance. Second, are there ways to strengthen how activities and groups of activities reinforce one another? Finally, could changes in one activity eliminate the need to perform others?

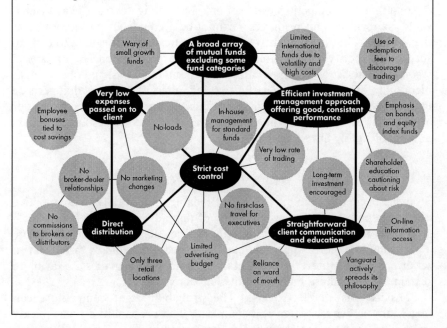

Third-order fit goes beyond activity reinforcement to what I call *optimization of effort*. The Gap, a retailer of casual clothes, considers product availability in its stores a critical element of its strategy. The Gap could keep products either by holding store inventory or by restocking from warehouses. The Gap has optimized its effort across these activities by restocking its selection of basic clothing almost daily out of three warehouses, thereby minimizing the need to carry large in-store inventories. The emphasis is on restocking because the Gap's merchandising strategy sticks to basic items in relatively few colors. While comparable retailers achieve turns of three to four times per year, the Gap turns its inventory seven and a half times per

461

year. Rapid restocking, moreover, reduces the cost of implementing the Gap's short model cycle, which is six to eight weeks long.[3]

Coordination and information exchange across activities to eliminate redundancy and minimize wasted effort are the most basic types of effort optimization. But there are higher levels as well. Product design choices, for example, can eliminate the need for after-sale service or make it possible for customers to perform service activities themselves. Similarly, coordination with suppliers or distribution channels can eliminate the need for some in-house activities, such as end-user training.

In all three types of fit, the whole matters more than any individual part. Competitive advantage grows out of the *entire system* of activities. The fit among activities substantially reduces cost or increases differentiation. Beyond that, the competitive value of individual activities – or the associated skills, competencies, or resources – cannot be decoupled from the system or the strategy. Thus in competitive companies it can be misleading to explain success by specifying individual strengths, core competencies, or critical resources. The list of strengths cuts across many functions, and one strength blends into others. It is more useful to think in terms of themes that pervade many activities, such as low cost, a particular notion of customer service, or a particular conception of the value delivered. These themes are embodied in nests of tightly linked activities.

Fit and sustainability

Strategic fit among many activities is fundamental not only to competitive advantage but also to the sustainability of that advantage. It is harder for a rival to match an array of interlocked activities than it is merely to imitate a particular sales-force approach, match a process technology, or replicate a set of product features. Positions built on systems of activities are far more sustainable than those built on individual activities.

Consider this simple exercise. The probability that competitors can match any activity is often less than one. The probabilities then quickly compound to make matching the entire system highly unlikely ($.9 \times .9 = .81$; $.9 \times .9 \times .9 \times .9 = .66$, and so on). Existing companies that try to reposition or straddle will be forced to reconfigure many activities.

And even new entrants, though they do not confront the trade-offs facing established rivals, still face formidable barriers to imitation.

The more a company's positioning rests on activity systems with second- and third-order fit, the more sustainable its advantage will be. Such systems, by their very nature, are usually difficult to untangle from outside the company and therefore hard to imitate. And even if rivals can identify the relevant interconnections, they will have difficulty replicating them. Achieving fit is difficult because it requires the integration of decisions and actions across many independent subunits.

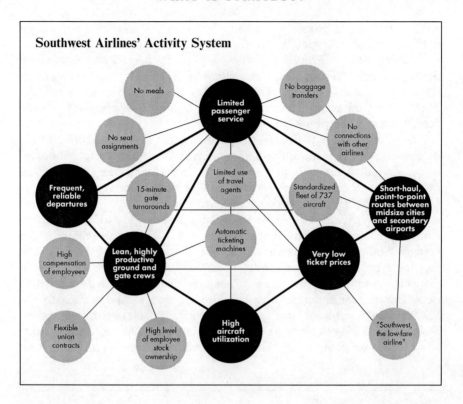

Southwest Airlines' Activity System

A competitor seeking to match an activity system gains little by imitating only some activities and not matching the whole. Performance does not improve; it can decline. Recall Continental Lite's disastrous attempt to imitate Southwest.

Finally, fit among a company's activities creates pressures and incentives to improve operational effectiveness, which makes imitation even harder. Fit means that poor performance in one activity will degrade the performance in others, so that weaknesses are exposed and more prone to get attention. Conversely, improvements in one activity will pay dividends in others. Compaines with strong fit among their activities are rarely inviting targets. Their superiority in strategy and in execution only compounds their advantages and raises the hurdle for imitators.

When activities complement one another, rivals will get little benefit from imitation unless they successfully match the whole system. Such situations tend to promote winner-take-all competition. The company that builds the best activity system – Toys R Us, for instance – wins, while rivals with similar strategies – Child World and Lionel Leisure – fall behind. Thus finding a new strategic position is often preferable to being the second or third imitator of an occupied position.

The most viable positions are those whose activity systems are incompatible because of tradeoffs. Strategic positioning sets the trade-off rules that define how individual activities will be configured and integrated. Seeing strategy in terms of activity systems only makes it clearer why organizational structure, systems, and processes need to be strategy-specific. Tailoring organization to strategy, in turn, makes complementarities more achievable and contributes to sustainability.

One implication is that strategic positions should have a horizon of a decade or more, not of a single planning cycle. Continuity fosters improvements in individual activities and the fit across activities, allowing an organization to build unique capabilities and skills tailored to its strategy. Continuity also reinforces a company's identity.

Conversely, frequent shifts in positioning are costly. Not only must a company reconfigure individual activities, but it must also realign entire systems. Some activities may never catch up to the vacillating strategy. The inevitable result of frequent shifts in strategy, or of failure to choose a distinct position in the first place, is "me-too" or hedged activity configurations, inconsistencies across functions, and organizational dissonance.

What is strategy? We can now complete the answer to this question. Strategy is creating fit among a company's activities. The success of a strategy depends on doing many things well – not just a few – and integrating

---

Alternative Views of Strategy

The Implicit Strategy Model of the Past Decade

- One ideal competitive position in the industry
- Benchmarking of all activities and achieving best practice
- Aggressive outsourcing and partnering to gain efficiencies
- Advantages rest on a few key success factors, critical resources, core competencies
- Flexibility and rapid responses to all competitive and market changes

Sustainable Competitive Advantage

- Unique competitive position for the company
- Activities tailored to strategy
- Clear trade-offs and choices vis-à-vis competitors
- Competitive advantage arises from fit across activities
- Sustainability comes from the activity system, not the parts
- Operational effectiveness a given

among them. If there is no fit among activities, there is no distinctive strategy and little sustainability. Management reverts to the simpler task of overseeing independent functions, and operational effectiveness determines an organization's relative performance.

V. Rediscovering strategy

The failure to choose

Why do so many companies fail to have a strategy? Why do managers avoid making strategic choices? Or, having made them in the past, why do managers so often let strategies decay and blur?

Commonly, the threats to strategy are seen to emanate from outside a company because of changes in technology or the behavior of competitors. Although external changes can be the problem, the greater threat to strategy often comes from within. A sound strategy is undermined by a misguided view of competition, by organizational failures, and, especially, by the desire to grow.

Managers have become confused about the necessity of making choices. When many companies operate far from the productivity frontier, trade-offs appear unnecessary. It can seem that a well-run company should be able to beat its ineffective rivals on all dimensions simultaneously. Taught by popular management thinkers that they do not have to make trade-offs, managers have acquired a macho sense that to do so is a sign of weakness.

Unnerved by forecasts of hypercompetition, managers increase its likelihood by imitating everything about their competitors. Exhorted to think in terms of revolution, managers chase every new technology for its own sake.

The pursuit of operational effectiveness is seductive because it is concrete and actionable. Over the past decade, managers have been under increasing pressure to deliver tangible, measurable performance improvements. Programs in operational effectiveness produce reassuring progress, although superior profitability may remain elusive. Business publications and consultants flood the market with information about what other companies are doing, reinforcing the best-practice mentality. Caught up in the race for operational effectiveness, many managers simply do not understand the need to have a strategy.

Companies avoid or blur strategic choices for other reasons as well. Conventional wisdom within an industry is often strong, homogenizing competition. Some managers mistake "customer focus" to mean they must serve all customer needs or respond to every request from distribution channels. Others cite the desire to preserve flexibility.

Organizational realities also work against strategy. Trade-offs are frightening, and making no choice is sometimes preferred to risking blame for a bad choice. Companies imitate one another in a type of herd behavior, each assuming rivals know something they do not. Newly empowered employees, who are urged to seek every possible source of improvement, often lack a vision of the whole and the perspective to recognize trade-offs. The failure to choose sometimes comes down to the reluctance to disappoint valued managers or employees.

The growth trap

Among all other influences, the desire to grow has perhaps the most perverse effect on strategy. Trade-offs and limits appear to constrain growth. Serving one group of customers and excluding others, for instance, places a real or imagined limit on revenue growth. Broadly targeted strategies emphasizing low price result in lost sales with customers sensitive to features or service. Differentiators lose sales to price-sensitive customers.

Managers are constantly tempted to take incremental steps that surpass those limits but blur a company's strategic position. Eventually, pressures to grow or apparent saturation of the target market lead managers to broaden the position by extending product lines, adding new features, imitating competitors' popular services, matching processes, and even making acquisitions. For years, Maytag Corporation's success was based on its focus on reliable, durable washers and dryers, later extended to include dishwashers. However, conventional wisdom emerging within the industry supported the notion of selling a full line of products. Concerned with slow industry growth and competition from broad-line appliance makers, Maytag was pressured by dealers and encouraged by customers to extend its line. Maytag expanded into refrigerators and cooking products under the Maytag brand and acquired other brands – Jenn-Air, Hardwick Stove, Hoover, Admiral, and Magic Chef – with disparate positions. Maytag has grown substantially from $684 million in 1985 to a peak of $3.4 billion in 1994, but return on sales has declined from 8% to 12% in the 1970s and 1980s to an average of less than 1% between 1989 and 1995. Cost cutting will improve this performance, but laundry and dishwasher products still anchor Maytag's profitability.

Neutrogena may have fallen into the same trap. In the early 1990s, its U.S. distribution broadened to include mass merchandisers such as Wal-Mart Stores. Under the Neutrogena name, the company expanded into a wide variety of products – eye-makeup remover and shampoo, for example – in which it was not unique and which diluted its image, and it began turning to price promotions.

Compromises and inconsistencies in the pursuit of growth will erode the competitive advantage a company had with its original varieties or target customers. Attempts to compete in several ways at once create confusion and undermine organizational motivation and focus. Profits fall, but more revenue is seen as the answer. Managers are unable to make choices, so the company embarks on a new round of broadening and compromises.

Reconnecting with Strategy

Most companies owe their initial success to a unique strategic position involving clear trade-offs. Activities once were aligned with that position. The passage of time and the pressures of growth, however, led to compromises that were, at first, almost imperceptible. Through a succession of incremental changes that each seemed sensible at the time, many established companies have compromised their way to homogeneity with their rivals.

The issue here is not with the companies whose historical position is no longer viable; their challenge is to start over, just as a new entrant would. At issue is a far more common phenomenon: the established company achieving mediocre returns and lacking a clear strategy. Through incremental additions of product varieties, incremental efforts to serve new customer groups, and emulation of rivals' activities, the existing company loses its clear competitive position. Typically, the company has matched many of its competitors' offerings and practices and attempts to sell to most customer groups.

A number of approaches can help a company reconnect with strategy. The first is a careful look at what it already does. Within most well-established companies is a core of uniqueness. It is identified by answering questions such as the following:

- Which of our product or service varieties are the most distinctive?
- Which of our product or service varieties are the most profitable?
- Which of our customers are the most satisfied?
- Which customers, channels, or purchase occasions are the most profitable?
- Which of the activities in our value chain are the most different and effective?

Around this core of uniqueness are encrustations added incrementally over time. Like barnacles, they must be removed to reveal the underlying strategic positioning. A small percentage of varieties or customers may well account for most of a company's sales and especially its profits. The challenge, then, is to refocus on the unique core and realign the company's activities with it. Customers and product varieties at the periphery can be sold or allowed through inattention or price increases to fade away.

A company's history can also be instructive. What was the vision of the founder? What were the products and customers that made the company? Looking backward, one can reexamine the original strategy to see if it is still valid. Can the historical positioning be implemented in a modern way, one consistent with today's technologies and practices? This sort of thinking may lead to a commitment to renew the strategy and may challenge the organization to recover its distinctiveness. Such a challenge can be galvanizing and can instill the confidence to make the needed trade-offs.

Often, rivals continue to match each other until desperation breaks the cycle, resulting in a merger or downsizing to the original positioning.

Profitable growth

Many companies, after a decade of restructuring and cost-cutting, are turning their attention to growth. Too often, efforts to grow blur uniqueness, create compromises, reduce fit, and ultimately undermine competitive advantage. In fact, the growth imperative is hazardous to strategy.

What approaches to growth preserve and reinforce strategy? Broadly, the prescription is to concentrate on deepening a strategic position rather than broadening and compromising it. One approach is to look for extensions of the strategy that leverage the existing activity system by offering features or services that rivals would find impossible or costly to match on a stand-alone basis. In other words, managers can ask themselves which activities, features, or forms of competition are feasible or less costly to them because of complementary activities that their company performs.

Deepening a position involves making the company's activities more distinctive, strengthening fit, and communicating the strategy better to those customers who should value it. But many companies succumb to the temptation to chase "easy" growth by adding hot features, products, or services without screening them or adapting them to their strategy. Or they target new customers or markets in which the company has little special to offer. A company can often grow faster – and far more profitably – by better penetrating needs and varieties where it is distinctive than by slugging it out in potentially higher growth arenas in which the company lacks uniqueness. Carmike, now the largest theater chain in the United States, owes its rapid growth to its disciplined concentration on small markets. The company quickly sells any big-city theaters that come to it as part of an acquisition.

Globalization often allows growth that is consistent with strategy, opening up larger markets for a focused strategy. Unlike broadening domestically, expanding globally is likely to leverage and reinforce a company's unique position and identity.

Companies seeking growth through broadening within their industry can best contain the risks to strategy by creating stand-alone units, each with its own brand name and tailored activities. Maytag has clearly struggled with this issue. On the one hand, it has organized its premium and value brands into separate units with different strategic positions. On the other, it has created an umbrella appliance company for all its brands to gain critical mass. With shared design, manufacturing, distribution, and customer service, it will be hard to avoid homogenization. If a given business unit attempts to compete with different positions for different products or customers, avoiding compromise is nearly impossible.

The role of leadership

The challenge of developing or reestablishing a clear strategy is often primarily an organizational one and depends on leadership. With so many forces at work against making choices and trade-offs in organizations, a clear intellectual framework to guide strategy is a necessary counterweight. Moreover, strong leaders willing to make choices are essential.

In many companies, leadership has degenerated into orchestrating operational improvements and making deals. But the leader's role is broader and far more important. General management is more than the stewardship of individual functions. Its core is strategy: defining and communicating the company's unique position, making trade-offs, and forging fit among activities. The leader must provide the discipline to decide which industry changes and customer needs the company will respond to, while avoiding organizational distractions and maintaining the company's distinctiveness. Managers at lower levels lack the perspective and the confidence to maintain a strategy. There will be constant pressures to compromise, relax trade-offs, and emulate rivals. One of the leader's jobs is to teach others in the organization about strategy – and to say no.

Strategy renders choices about what not to do as important as choices about what to do. Indeed, setting limits is another function of leadership. Deciding which target group of customers, varieties, and needs the company should serve is fundamental to developing a strategy. But so is deciding not to serve other customers or needs and not to offer certain features or services. Thus strategy requires constant discipline and clear communication. Indeed, one of the most important functions of an explicit, communicated strategy is to guide employees in making choices that arise because of trade-offs in their individual activities and in day-to-day decisions.

Improving operational effectiveness is a necessary part of management, but it is *not* strategy. In confusing the two, managers have unintentionally backed into a way of thinking about competition that is driving many industries toward competitive convergence, which is in no one's best interest and is not inevitable.

Managers must clearly distinguish operational effectiveness from strategy. Both are essential, but the two agendas are different.

The operational agenda involves continual improvement everywhere there are no trade-offs. Failure to do this creates vulnerability even for companies with a good strategy. The operational agenda is the proper place for constant change, flexibility, and relentless efforts to achieve best practice. In contrast, the strategic agenda is the right place for defining a unique position, making clear trade-offs, and tightening fit. It involves the continual search for ways to reinforce and extend the company's position. The strategic agenda demands discipline and continuity; its enemies are distraction and compromise.

Emerging Industries and Technologies

Developing a strategy in a newly emerging industry or in a business undergoing revolutionary technological changes is a daunting proposition. In such cases, managers face a high level of uncertainty about the needs of customers, the products and services that will prove to be the most desired, and the best configuration of activities and technologies to deliver them. Because of all this uncertainty, imitation and hedging are rampant: unable to risk being wrong or left behind, companies match all features, offer all new services, and explore all technologies.

During such periods in an industry's development, its basic productivity frontier is being established or reestablished. Explosive growth can make such times profitable for many companies, but profits will be temporary because imitation and strategic convergence will ultimately destroy industry profitability. The companies that are enduringly successful will be those that begin as early as possible to define and embody in their activities a unique competitive position. A period of imitation may be inevitable in emerging industries, but that period reflects the level of uncertainty rather than a desired state of affairs.

In high-tech industries, this imitation phase often continues much longer than it should. Enraptured by technological change itself, companies pack more features – most of which are never used – into their products while slashing prices across the board. Rarely are trade-offs even considered. The drive for growth to satisfy market pressures leads companies into every product area. Although a few companies with fundamental advantages prosper, the majority are doomed to a rat race no one can win.

Ironically, the popular business press, focused on hot, emerging industries, is prone to presenting these special cases as proof that we have entered a new era of competition in which none of the old rules are valid. In fact, the opposite is true.

Strategic continuity does not imply a static view of competition. A company must continually improve its operational effectiveness and actively try to shift the productivity frontier; at the same time, there needs to be ongoing effort to extend its uniqueness while strengthening the fit among its activities. Strategic continuity, in fact, should make an organization's continual improvement more effective.

A company may have to change its strategy if there are major structural changes in its industry. In fact, new strategic positions often arise because of industry changes, and new entrants unencumbered by history often can exploit them more easily. However, a company's choice of a new position must be driven by the ability to find new trade-offs and leverage a new system of complementary activities into a sustainable advantage.

Notes

This article has benefited greatly from the assistance of many individuals and companies. The author gives special thanks to Jan Rivkin, the coauthor of a related paper. Substantial research contributions have been made by Nicolaj Siggelkow, Dawn Sylvester, and Lucia Marshall. Tarun Khanna, Roger Martin, and Anita McGahan have provided especially extensive comments.

1 I first described the concept of activities and its use in understanding competitive advantage in *Competitive Advantage* (New York: The Free Press, 1985). The ideas in this article build on and extend that thinking.
2 Paul Milgrom and John Roberts have begun to explore the economics of systems of complementary functions, activities, and functions. Their focus is on the emergence of "modern manufacturing" as a new set of complementary activities, on the tendency of companies to react to external changes with coherent bundles of internal responses, and on the need for central coordination – a strategy – to align functional managers. In the latter case, they model what has long been a bedrock principle of strategy. See Paul Milgrom and John Roberts, "The Economics of Modern Manufacturing: Technology, Strategy, and Organization," *American Economic Review* 80 (1990): 511–528; Paul Milgrom, Yingyi Qian, and John Roberts, "Complementarities, Momentum, and Evolution of Modern Manufacturing," *American Economic Review* 81 (1991) 84–88; and Paul Milgrom and John Roberts, "Complementarities and Fit: Strategy, Structure, and Organizational Changes in Manufacturing," *Journal of Accounting and Economics*, vol. 19 (March–May 1995): 179–208.
3 Material on retail strategies is drawn in part from Jan Rivkin, "The Rise of Retail Category Killers," unpublished working paper, January 1995. Nicolaj Siggelkow prepared the case study on the Gap.